D1196697

THE GREAT WAR

THE GREAT WAR

A Combat History of the
First World War

PETER HART

OXFORD
UNIVERSITY PRESS

Oxford University Press

Oxford University Press is a department of the University of Oxford. It furthers the University's
objective of excellence in research, scholarship, and education by publishing worldwide.

Oxford   New York
Auckland   Cape Town   Dar es Salaam   Hong Kong   Karachi
Kuala Lumpur   Madrid   Melbourne   Mexico City   Nairobi
New Delhi   Shanghai   Taipei   Toronto
With offices in
Argentina   Austria   Brazil   Chile   Czech Republic   France   Greece
Guatemala   Hungary   Italy   Japan   Poland   Portugal   Singapore
South Korea   Switzerland   Thailand   Turkey   Ukraine   Vietnam

Oxford is a registered trade mark of Oxford University Press in the UK and certain other countries.

Published in the United States of America by
Oxford University Press
198 Madison Avenue, New York, NY 10016

Library of Congress Cataloging-in-Publication Data
Hart, Peter, 1955–
The Great War : a combat history of the First World War / Peter Hart.
pages cm
"First published in Great Britain in 2013 by Profile Books Ltd."—T.p. verso.
Includes bibliographical references and index.
ISBN 978-0-19-997627-0 (acid-free paper) 1. World War, 1914-1918—Campaigns. I. Title.
D521.H327 2013
940.4—dc23   2012049148

ISBN-13: 978-0-19-997627-0

1   3   5   7   9   8   6   4   2

Printed in the United States of America on acid-free paper

CONTENTS

MAPS

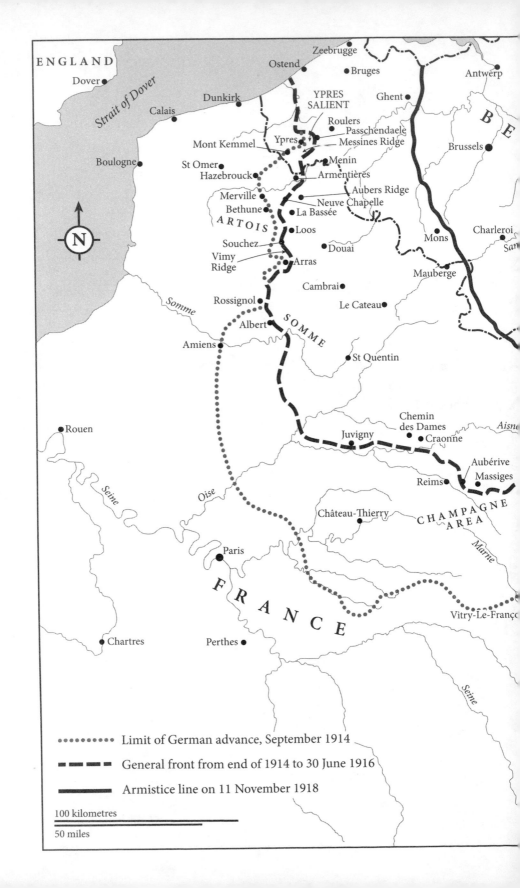

ENGLAND

Dover

Strait of Dover

Calais

Dunkirk

Boulogne

Zeebrugge

Ostend

Bruges

Antwerp

Ghent

YPRES
SALIENT

Roulers

Passchendaele

Mont Kemmel

Ypres

Messines Ridge

Brussels

BE

St Omer

Menin

Hazebrouck

Armentières

Merville

Aubers Ridge

Bethune

Neuve Chapelle

ARTOIS

La Bassée

Mons

Charleroi

Loos

Souchez

Douai

Mauberge

Vimy
Ridge

Arras

Somme

Rossignol

SOMME

Cambrai

Le Cateau

Albert

Amiens

St Quentin

Rouen

Chemin
des Dames

Aisne

Juvigny

Craonne

Seine

Oise

Aubérive

Massiges

Reims

Château-Thierry

CHAMPAGNE
AREA

Paris

Marne

FRANCE

Vitry-Le-Franço

Chartres

Perthes

Seine

• • • • • • • • Limit of German advance, September 1914

━ ━ ━ ━ General front from end of 1914 to 30 June 1916

━━━━ Armistice line on 11 November 1918

100 kilometres

50 miles

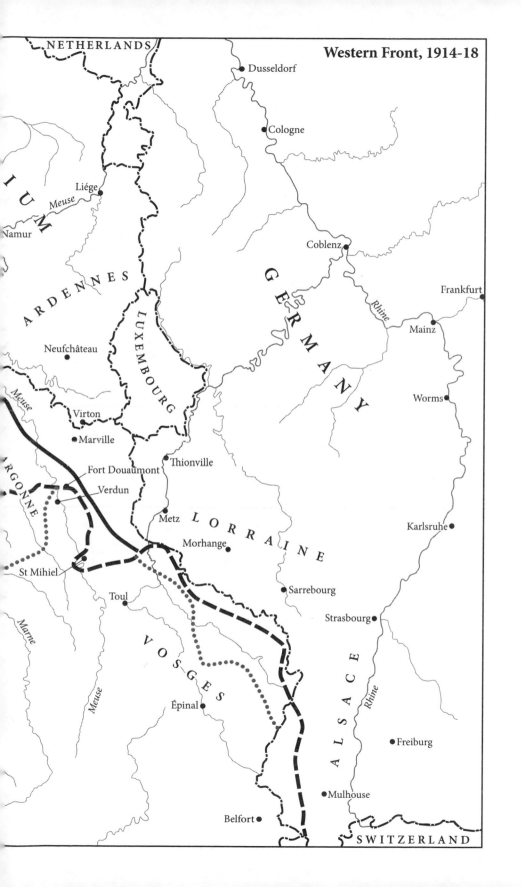

Western Front, 1914-18

NETHERLANDS

Dusseldorf

Cologne

Liége

Meuse

Namur

Coblenz

ARDENNES

G E R M A N Y

Frankfurt

Neufchâteau

L U X E M B O U R G

Rhine

Mainz

Meuse

Virton

Worms

Marville

Thionville

Fort Douaumont

Verdun

Metz

L O R R A I N E

Karlsruhe

ARGONNE

Morhange

St Mihiel

Toul

Sarrebourg

Marne

Strasbourg

V O S G E S

Meuse

Épinal

A L S A C E

Rhine

Freiburg

Mulhouse

Belfort

S W I T Z E R L A N D

Eastern Front, 1914-18

SWEDEN

Stockholm

Helsingfors

Gulf of Finland

Revel

Narva

Estonian
Islands

Pskov

Baltic Sea

Riga

Dvina

DENMARK

Memel

Königsberg

*Lake
Naroch*

Danzig

Gumbinnen

Vilnius

EAST
PRUSSIA

Angerburg

Berlin

Tannenberg

Augustow

Mins

BELARUS

Vistula

Osowiec Fortress

Posen

GERMAN EMPIRE

Narew

*Masurian
Lakes*

Lodz

Warsaw

Pinsk

Pripet

POLAND

Pilica

SILESIA

Prague

Vistula

GALICIA

San

Cracow

Dunajec

Tarnow
Gorlice

Rawa-Russka

Przemysl

Lemberg

Tarnopol

Vienna

Bratislava

Carpathian Mountains

Dniester

Danube

AUSTRIA - HUNGARY

Budapest

Trieste

Transylvanian Alps

ROMANIA

Belgrade

Jagodnja Mtns

Bucharest

Sarajevo

*Adriatic
Sea*

SERBIA

Danube

Limit of Russian advances,
1914-15

Limit of German advances,
1915-16

Extent of German penetration
into Russia by 3 March 1918,
Treaty of Brest-Litovsk

300 kilometres

200 miles

N

St Petersburg

Moscow

Smolensk

R U S S I A N   E M P I R E

Don

Volga

per

Kharkov

Tsaritsyn

Dnieper

ev

Don

Rostov

dessa

Sea of
Azov

Sevastopol

Black Sea

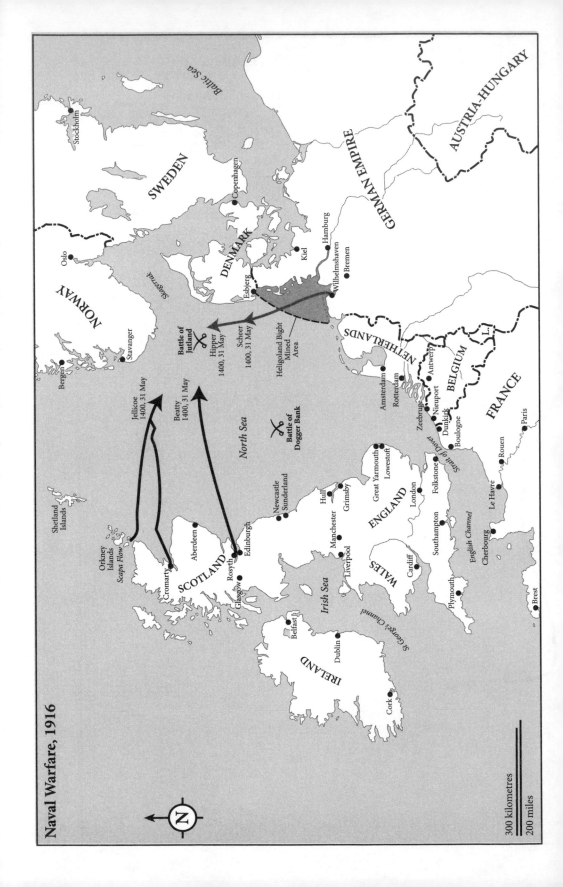

Naval Warfare, 1916

STOCKHOLM

Baltic Sea

SWEDEN

Copenhagen

NORWAY

Oslo

DENMARK

Kiel
Hamburg
Bremen
Esbjerg
Wilhelmshaven

GERMAN EMPIRE

AUSTRIA-HUNGARY

Bergen

Stavanger

Skagerrak

Battle of Jutland

Hipper
1400, 31 May

Scheer
1400, 31 May

Heligoland Bight
Mined
Area

NETHERLANDS

Amsterdam
Rotterdam
Antwerp
Zeebrugge
Nieuport
Dunkirk
Boulogne

BELGIUM

L.

FRANCE

Paris

Rouen

Jellicoe
1400, 31 May

Beatty
1400, 31 May

North Sea

Battle of
Dogger Bank

Strait of Dover

Le Havre

Shetland
Islands

Orkney
Islands
Scapa Flow

Cromarty

Aberdeen

SCOTLAND

Rosyth
Edinburgh
Glasgow

Newcastle
Sunderland

Hull
Grimsby

Great Yarmouth
Lowestoft

London

Folkstone

Southampton

English Channel

Cherbourg

Brest

Manchester
Liverpool

WALES

Cardiff

Plymouth

Irish Sea

St George's Channel

Belfast

Dublin

IRELAND

Cork

ENGLAND

N

300 kilometres
200 miles

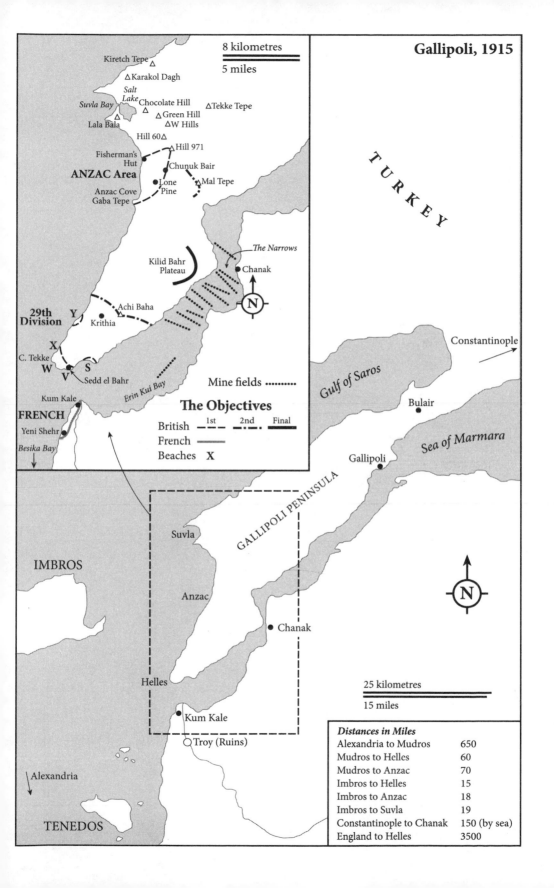

Gallipoli, 1915

8 kilometres
5 miles

Kiretch Tepe △

△ Karakol Dagh

Salt Lake
Suvla Bay △
Chocolate Hill △
△ Tekke Tepe
△ Green Hill
Lala Baba
△ W Hills

Hill 60 △
△ Hill 971

Fisherman's Hut

ANZAC Area
Chunuk Bair
Lone ● Pine
△ Mal Tepe

Anzac Cove
Gaba Tepe

The Narrows

Kilid Bahr
Plateau
● Chanak

29th Division
Y
△ Achi Baba
● Krithia

X
C. Tekke
W
V ● S
Sedd el Bahr

Erin Kui Bay

Mine fields ··········

Kum Kale ●

FRENCH
Yeni Shehr ●
Besika Bay

The Objectives

	1st	2nd	Final
British	—·—·—	— ·· — ··	——
French	————		
Beaches	**X**		

TURKEY

Constantinople →

Gulf of Saros

Bulair ●

Sea of Marmara

Gallipoli ●

GALLIPOLI PENINSULA

Suvla

Anzac

● Chanak

Helles

IMBROS

● Kum Kale

○ Troy (Ruins)

Alexandria ↓

TENEDOS

25 kilometres
15 miles

Distances in Miles

Alexandria to Mudros	650
Mudros to Helles	60
Mudros to Anzac	70
Imbros to Helles	15
Imbros to Anzac	18
Imbros to Suvla	19
Constantinople to Chanak	150 (by sea)
England to Helles	3500

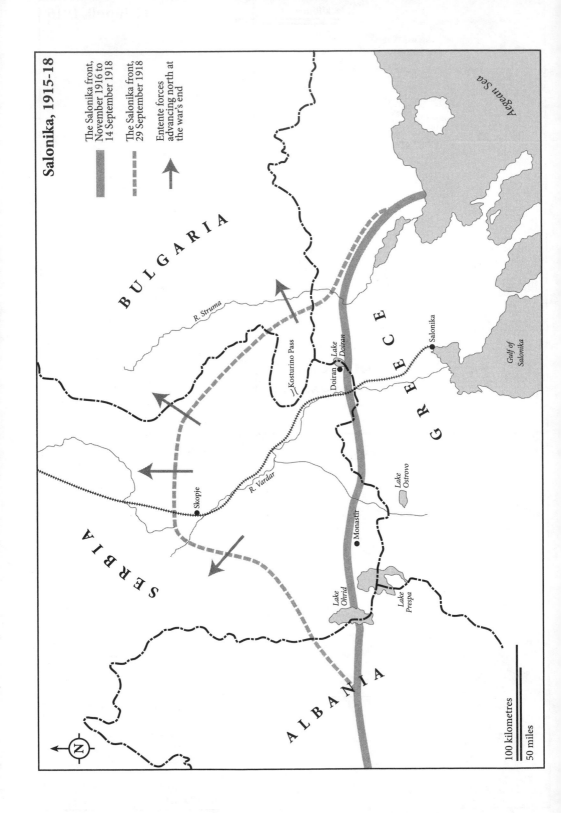

Salonika, 1915-18

The Salonika front,
November 1916 to
14 September 1918

The Salonika front,
29 September 1918

Entente forces
advancing north at
the war's end

BULGARIA

SERBIA

ALBANIA

GREECE

R. Struma

Kosturino Pass

Doiran
Lake
Doiran

Salonika

Skopje

R. Vardar

Lake
Ostrovo

Monastir

Lake
Ohrid

Lake
Prespa

Gulf of
Salonika

Aegean Sea

100 kilometres

50 miles

N

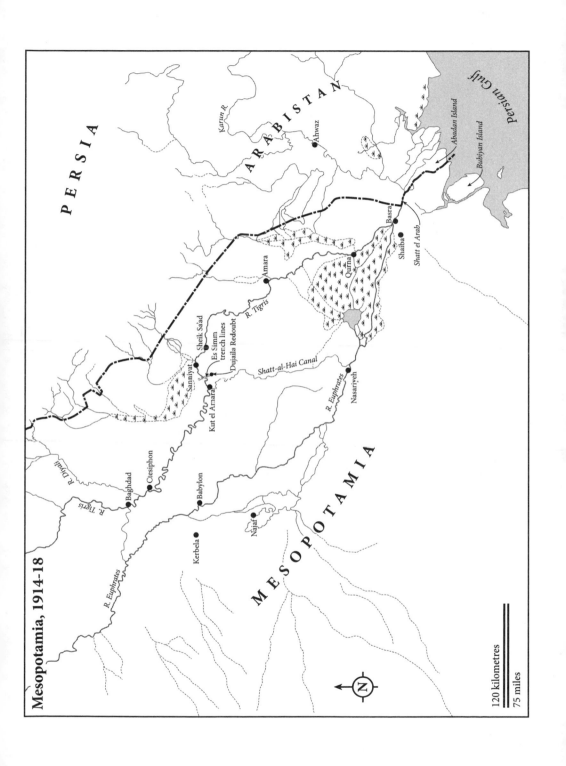

Mesopotamia, 1914-18

PERSIA

ARABISTAN

Persian Gulf

Karun R.

Ahwaz

Abadan Island

Bubiyan Island

Basra

Shatt el Arab

Shaiba

Qurna

Amara

R. Tigris

Sheik Saad

Es Sinn
trench lines
Dujaila Redoubt

Sanniyat

Kut el Amara

Shatt-al-Hai Canal

R. Euphrates

Nasariyeh

Ctesiphon

R. Diyala

Baghdad

Babylon

R. Tigris

Najaf

Kerbela

MESOPOTAMIA

R. Euphrates

N

120 kilometres
75 miles

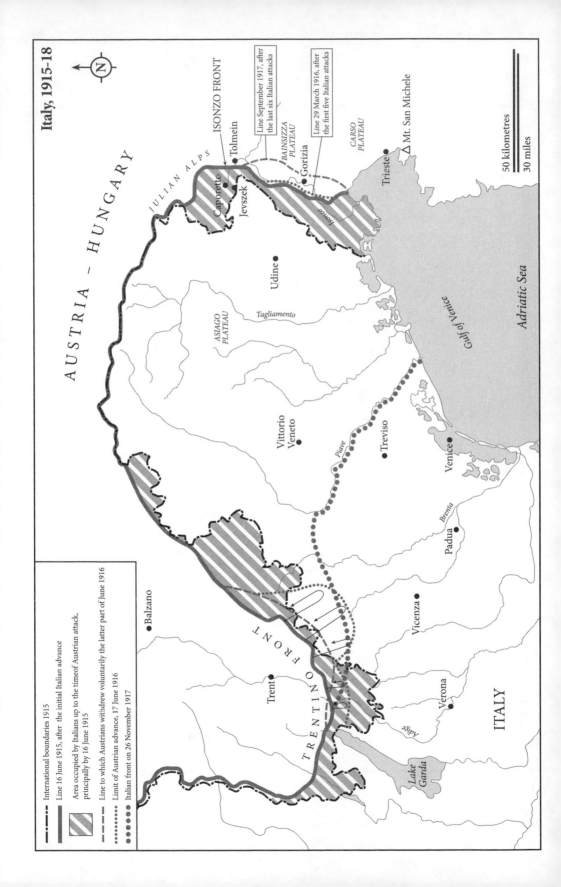

Italy, 1915-18

ISONZO FRONT

Line September 1917, after the last six Italian attacks

Line 29 March 1916, after the first five Italian attacks

A U S T R I A – H U N G A R Y

JULIAN ALPS

Tolmein

Caporetto

Jevszek

BAINSIZZA PLATEAU

Gorizia

CARSO PLATEAU

Trieste

△ Mt. San Michele

Udine

ASIAGO PLATEAU

Tagliamento

Isonzo

Vittorio Veneto

Treviso

Piave

Venice

Gulf of Venice

Adriatic Sea

Brenta

Padua

Vicenza

●Balzano

T R E N T I N O   F R O N T

Trent

Verona

Adige

Lake Garda

ITALY

50 kilometres

30 miles

International boundaries 1915

Line 16 June 1915, after the initial Italian advance

Area occupied by Italians up to the time of Austrian attack, principally by 16 June 1915

Line to which Austrians withdrew voluntarily the latter part of June 1916

Limit of Austrian advance, 17 June 1916

Italian front on 26 November 1917

N

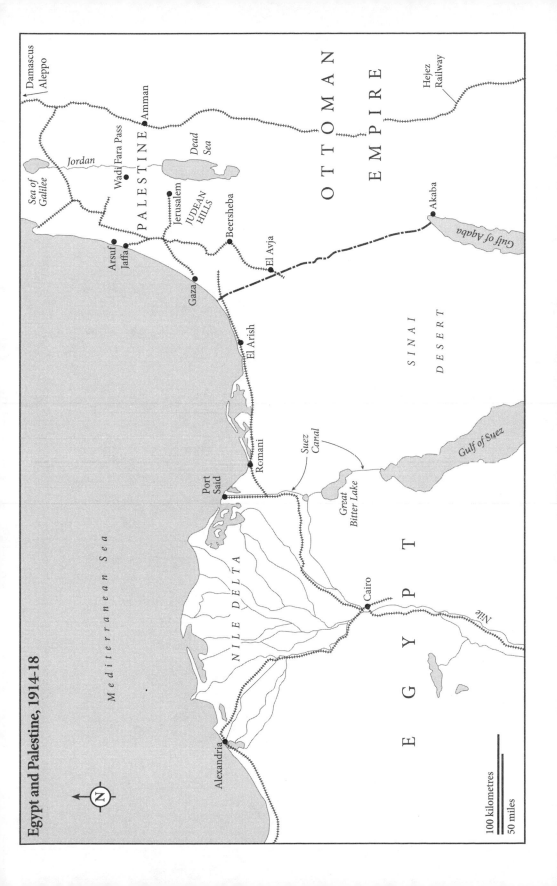

Egypt and Palestine, 1914–18

N

Mediterranean Sea

Alexandria

Port Said
Romani
Suez
Canal

NILE DELTA

Cairo

Nile

E G Y P T

Great
Bitter Lake

Gulf of Suez

S I N A I
D E S E R T

El Arish

Gaza

Arsuf
Jaffa

Beersheba
El Avja

Gulf of Aqaba

Akaba

Jerusalem
JUDEAN
HILLS

P A L E S T I N E

Wadi Fara Pass

Jordan

*Dead
Sea*

*Sea of
Galilee*

Amman

Damascus
Aleppo

O T T O M A N
E M P I R E

Hejez
Railway

100 kilometres
50 miles

PREFACE

THE GREAT WAR was the single most important event of the twentieth century, shaping the world that we live in today. Yet it is often regarded as a pointless war; a catastrophic mistake fought for little or no reason. Historians, politicians and economists may testify to its over-arching importance, but somehow the popular belief remains that it was all for nothing. Yet how could that be? Was everyone afflicted by a communal madness? Or were there really some very important issues at stake in this frontal collision between forces whose vision of Europe and the world could no longer co-exist peacefully? In 1914 there was an absence of any real attempts by statesmen on either side to resolve their difficulties through compromise and meaningful negotiation, making war all but inevitable given the aggressive posture adopted by the Austro-Hungarian and German Empires after the assassination of Archduke Ferdinand on 28 June. Once started the Great War had to be fought to the finish as none of the participants could countenance a defeat that would mark the end of their economic, political, military and imperial ambitions. This was not a 'war to end war' but rather an attempt to resolve the main issues of the day in one fell swoop. When industrial nation states resorted to armed conflict they generated a monstrous capacity for death and destruction, while at the same time the vastness of their populations meant that there were a lot of people to kill before victory could be proclaimed.

The men who fought in those epic battles may all be dead, but the direct consequences of their collective actions still surround us. The war subverted the rules by which men had hoped wars would be fought, unequivocally sucking in the civilian non-combatants that had been hitherto at least partially excluded from the mayhem. Of course this was not the first time that armed conflict had strayed from the path of civilised behaviour. But it was the sheer scale of the transgressions that distinguished the Great War. This was an all-embracing conflict reaching far and wide across the continents. It premiered devilish new weapons and created new methods of mass slaughter. Most awful of all, it gave birth to the twin concepts of 'a nation at arms' and 'total war'. Previously the Thirty Years War, Seven Years War, Napoleonic Wars and American Civil War had seemed the benchmarks for horror; but these were as nothing in comparison to the long years of frantic mayhem that stretched from August 1914 to November 1918. By the end of the Great War the old European order that had ruled the world had been swept away. Once mighty empires had fallen as the German, Russian, Austro-Hungarian and Ottoman hegemonies were all trampled into the dust. The French and British were left drained of energy, wealth and prestige even as they drank from the poisoned chalice of victory. New world powers would rise in the aftermath of the war. Most obviously, the United States converted her hitherto unrealised military potential into a reality, while her economy began to achieve worldwide pre-eminence. The Japanese too were stirring. They had been involved only on the periphery of the fighting, but they watched with interest the humiliating exposure of the traditional Western imperial powers. In the post-war years Japan would attempt to expand her role in the Far East, seeking to establish a new Empire of the Rising Sun. Powerful political forces were unleashed by the war. Communism had been lurking in the wings for a while, but the success of the Bolsheviks in Russia would spread its spectre, real and imagined, across the globe for the rest of the century. The ugly creed of fascism was created from the fall-out of the war: a pernicious amalgam of racism, nationalism and right-wing dogma all nurtured by the dreadful post-war social and economic conditions which left millions looking for easy answers to impossible questions. The war had even created a fertile breeding ground for a new plague, the influenza virus known as 'Spanish flu', which spread across the globe, causing a loss of life on a scale that would dwarf even the slaughter of war.

In this book we will look at the whys and wherefores of the military conduct of the Great War in an attempt to discern what was really going on, rather than attempt to reference every political, social or artistic movement. At heart, this is a history that will examine the nature of the immense problems encountered by the commanders who bore the ultimate responsibility in battle; the strategic imperatives that drove them into battle; and the tactics they devised to achieve success. Direct quotes from the generals and admirals will show that there was usually a rhyme and a reason to their decisions, while evocative accounts from the men they commanded will show the terrible consequences of those orders for the men who had to enact them. In this, the book will reflect what they knew, or thought they knew, at the time, rather than offer insights vouchsafed by hindsight. Sadly, there was no easy way to victory for either of the great power blocks. If there was a madness then it surely lay in the initial decision to go to war, not in the tactical decisions of the commanders in the field. Whatever they did the war would still have bitten deep, killing millions, as millions fought to the death. This was the modern industrial age and flesh and blood would have to face new weapons of war deployed in an ever-changing tactical clash between attack and defence, whoever was in charge. While it is only human to feel pity at the terrible suffering endured over the four years of war, the intention here is to explain the desperate nature of the fighting, not to create a false aura of victimhood for the soldiers who died as they tried to kill. The military history of the Great War is often misrepresented by academics from other disciplines, who settle for the easy clichés such as the 'butchers and bunglers' calumny, spouting as gospel the sort of unreferenced nonsense which would make them blanch within their own fields.

I have followed the course of battles primarily from a British perspective, but also taking into account what was really significant in this truly global conflict. In a single-volume history the main narrative line must follow the most dramatic battles and those that actually had the potential – in theory, at least – to end the war. As such, battles and campaigns against the German Army, the driving force of the Central Powers, have generally taken precedence. The Eastern Front is fully reviewed as it had a huge influence on our main narrative: in fact, you cannot understand what was happening on the Western Front without understanding events on the Eastern Front. Those with special interest in the more obscure campaigns, such as the capture of Tsingtao, the Russo-Turkish Caucasian Campaign, the Senussi Rebellion, naval actions in the Baltic and Black Sea, or the heroic German resistance in East Africa, will find them omitted in favour of more detail on the dramatic key campaigns that still shape our lives today. For British readers, used to their forces being presented as always at the centre of affairs, their occasional demotion to the sidelines may seem strange, especially during the first two years of the war, when the French and Russian forces were battering away at the Germans with only peripheral help from the British Army. With the Somme Offensive in 1916, the British began to play a far greater part, but it was only from mid-1917 that they began to take the lead role. The input of the Americans was crucial as, despite the lateness of their appearance on the Western Front, their expanding armies offered such a threat that it did much to undermine German resolve in 1918. All these immense contributions to Allied victory must be acknowledged and due tribute paid. But the Germans themselves knew who had beaten them. The determined enmity and resilience of France, their most serious military foe, was taken for granted, but it was the participation of the British in the war that had tipped the balance against Germany. The combination of the unyielding Royal Navy blockade, the key role of British troops in the dogged attritional battles of 1916–17, followed by the brutally effective campaign spearheaded by British troops during the 'Advance to Victory' on the Western Front – these were the nails that hammered down the lid on the German coffin.

The Second World War saw the British Empire cast very much as a supporting player. Of course, British forces in the early stages helped ensure that the Allies did not lose. But it is indisputable that the hard graft to destroy the armed might of Germany and Japan was carried out primarily by Russia and the United States respectively – the two great powers whose subsequent Cold War would dominate the remainder of the twentieth century. The era when Great Britain could be ranked as a first-rank global power had vanished and the origins of that decay lay in the Great War. The loss of nearly a million dead had fatally undermined British resolve to make military sacrifices, while the excruciating financial cost of the war had injured an economy that was already falling back from its nineteenth century primacy. The rise of concepts like nationalism and communism had further loosened Britain's grip on its polyglot empire. Within a few decades of the end of the Great War the British Empire had collapsed.

1

THE ROAD TO WAR

'Anyone who has ever looked into the glazed eyes of a soldier dying on the battlefield will think hard before starting a war.'[1]

Chancellor Otto von Bismarck

GERMANY WAS AT THE HEART of the Great War. Wherever you begin to examine the causes of that terrible conflagration, your eye will be unerringly drawn to the crucial role played by the German Empire. It was a creation of the late nineteenth century, a federation of German states, pulled together and then dominated by the Kingdom of Prussia. The guiding hand during the crucial period from 1862 had been Chancellor Otto von Bismarck, who had proved an exceptionally astute pilot through some remarkably choppy waters. Taking advantage of the temporarily fractured balance of power between Russia, France, Turkey and Britain in the aftermath of the Crimean War in 1854–6, Prussia had provoked, fought and won the Austro-Prussian War in 1866, thereby ending any chance of an Austrian-based unification of the German states. This was followed by the Franco-Prussian War of 1870–71, which resulted in a humiliating defeat for the French, leaving a unified Germany as the dominant power in Europe, a moment cruelly symbolised when Kaiser Wilhelm I was crowned German Emperor at Versailles in 1871. Bismarck then devoted himself to avoiding any further wars and trying to maintain the international isolation of France. This policy reached its apogee with the formation of the League of the Three Emperors between Austria-Hungary, Russia and Germany in 1873. This inherently unstable alliance soon collapsed as the Austro-Hungarian Empire and Russia fell out over Russian activities in the Balkans, which the Austrians considered within their sphere of interest. Although it was briefly reincarnated in 1881, the Balkan pressures were not resolved and the alliance finally ended in 1887. Meanwhile, Bismarck had secured the Dual Alliance with Austria-Hungary in 1879, a defensive arrangement which promised support should either be attacked by Russia, or a benevolent neutrality if one was attacked by another European power – which at that stage clearly meant France. This alliance was augmented by the newly unified Italy to form the Triple Alliance in 1882. As a further precaution Bismarck also signed the Reinsurance Treaty with Russia in 1887, guaranteeing neutrality unless Russia attacked Austria-Hungary. His motives in building this web of treaties were exemplified by a prescient speech made to the Reichstag in 1888 during yet another Balkans crisis:

> Bulgaria, that little country between the Danube and the Balkans, is far from being an object of adequate importance ... for which to plunge Europe from Moscow to the Pyrenees, and from the North Sea to Palermo, into a war whose issue no man can foresee. At the end of the conflict we should scarcely know why we had fought.[2]
>
> Chancellor Otto von Bismarck

But the accession of Kaiser Wilhelm II that same year led quickly to Bismarck's downfall. The new Kaiser had a very different vision for Germany, concerned with the possibilities of new territorial gains and becoming a leading voice on the world stage, whereas Bismarck concentrated on the more mundane business of securing what had already been achieved. Wilhelm II grew increasingly impatient with the cautious foreign policy and conservative social policies of his 75-year-old Chancellor, until he finally 'dropped the pilot' in 1890.

There was no doubt that Germany had several inherent strengths. Her unification had coincided with an impressive surge in industrialisation which, by the dawn of the twentieth century, had converted a predominantly agricultural economy into the pre-eminent industrial power in Europe. Production of coal, iron and steel had rocketed; these were the essential bedrock for any modern nation. But Germany also had an excellent education system which had resulted in almost universal literacy among the population at large. This created a constant stream of experts in every conceivable subject as well as an exceptionally lively scientific, literary and artistic community. Germany could also be regarded as one of the great centres of progressive thought. But lurking deep at the very heart of state was the Army. This remarkable construct had been swiftly welded together from the Prussian, Bavarian, Baden and Saxon state armies by highly trained staff officers who inculcated a common military doctrine into the units and ensured that they were trained to the highest standards. Underpinning it was a system of compulsory conscription by which some 60 per cent of young men were called up at twenty years old, whereupon they would be diligently trained for two years (three years in the artillery and cavalry) before being returned to civilian life. They then had a commitment to annual training with a reserve unit until they were twenty-seven, before joining a secondary reserve unit (the *Landwehr*) until they were thirty-nine, when they were finally transferred to the tertiary reserve (the *Landsturm*). Only at forty-five years old were they finally free of military commitments to the state. This created a reservoir of trained reserves which could be called up quickly in the event of war to allow a massive expansion in the size of the army. The German Army could not be regarded as a defensive expression of a nation's desire for security within its own borders. It posed a clear threat, which in turn forced most of the nation states of Europe to increase their military strength by dint of similar conscription schemes.

For all its strengths, Germany also had fundamental problems. Political modernisation had not kept pace with economic progress and an imperfect system of universal suffrage was undermined further by the opaque nature of the fragmented constitution which left a great deal of power in the hands of the Kaiser. The accession of Wilhelm II only exacerbated this situation. His personality tended towards self-important posturing, without the intellect or sense of purpose to allow the evolution of a mature and consistent policy. Unpredictability and the love of the dramatic gesture proved to be his defining characteristics. Yet he had direct control of the Army and of foreign policy. In addition, he was responsible for all major government appointments and had the right of unfettered direct access to all elected officials, which allowed him to exercise undue influence on multifarious affairs of state. Unfortunately for Germany, the image of the Kaiser, in all his blustering militaristic pomposity, came to symbolise the German state to the detriment of more sensible elements within his government. This created an exaggerated sense of threat to the not unreasonable attempts by Germany to have a greater voice and status in world affairs concomitant to its new power: *Weltpolitik*. Seeking to gain political and economic spheres of influence across the world, Germany was very active in the last scramble for colonies in Africa, while gazing eagerly at vast possibilities offered in China and jockeying for pole position when the Ottoman Empire finally disintegrated. But as the Kaiser and his ministers struggled to gain global recognition, their enemies stood ready to pounce on their perceived aggression.

France was the most committed adversary of Germany, still smarting from her defeat in the Franco-Prussian War and bitterly resenting the loss of the province of Alsace-Lorraine. Recently defeated countries are rarely content at their lot and internecine conflicts thrived in the Third Republic established after the fall of Napoleon III in 1870. There was a whole variety of divisive issues, including the possible re-establishment of the monarchy, the role of religion in society and the domination of left- or right-wing political viewpoints. Despite strong pressures a system of parliamentary democracy survived with a Chamber of Deputies, a Senate and a President acting as the head of state. Despite all the internal political turmoil, France still yearned to maintain her position as a strong imperial power. Unsurprisingly, the one area of near-total national consensus was over the necessity to rebuild the Army for the challenges ahead, although even there political or religious affiliations could make, or break, an officer's career.

The French's determination to exact revenge was demonstrated by their vigorous attempts to match German military strength. In 1870 France had faced the might of Prussia alone and had been found wanting. After this chastening experience she sought the active acquisition and military support of allies wherever they could be found. Germany's failure to renew the Reinsurance Treaty with Russia gave France a chance to move into the vacuum and the Franco-Russian Alliance was duly signed in 1892. Although this alliance was essentially defensive in its nature, guaranteeing mutual support in the event of an attack by Germany, the military negotiations that ensued emphasised the importance of securing an early concentration of forces with the express aim of committing Germany to a simultaneous war on two frontiers: east and west. This scenario would form the defining narrative of the first years of the Great War.

France did, however, have a second powerful motivating force in determining her foreign policy. This was an unwavering desire to maintain and expand her large global empire. The French had kept a few scattered dominions after 1815, but in the nineteenth century had begun a major thrust into North Africa with the acquisition or control established over Algeria and Tunisia, before expanding with considerable effect into northern, western, and central Africa, seeking a band of possessions right across the continent. France also had her beady eye on the longer-term future of both Syria and the Lebanon in the Middle East, and had been assiduously acquiring numerous territories in China and the Far East. It is worth reflecting, then, that France was still an aggressive colonial power; Germany was not the only country seeking its place in the sun.

Russia was the most enigmatic of the Great Powers. Possessed of staggering potential, she remained a fitfully dozing giant. Her land mass was enormous, reaching across great swathes of Europe and Asia, while her armies seemed inexhaustible, fuelled by a population of some 170 million. Yet Russia was a country only slowly feeling its way into the twentieth century. Although there had been some acceleration in her slow industrialisation, she was still by no means a modern state and was deeply reliant on the financial assistance offered by France to develop her infrastructure.

Yet Russia was by no means just a tool of the French and had her own distinct territorial and geo-political ambitions. Firstly, she had an interest in propagating the nebulous idea of Pan-Slavism, which propounded the cultural and political unity of all Slavs – a concept rendered problematic by the spirited objections and refusal to co-operate of several of the existing Slavic states and revolutionary movements. Such Slavs saw their future as independent countries, not as subservient elements in the Russian Empire. However, Russia had developed strong links with Serbia, which had emerged from the suzerainty of the Ottoman Empire to become internationally recognised at the Congress of Berlin in 1878; although at the same time the disputed area of Bosnia, where the population was also predominantly of Serbian Slav origin, was assigned to the control of the Austro-Hungarian Empire. There would be no formal alliance between Russia and Serbia, but Russia was determined – where possible – to protect the small Serbian state from her aggressive neighbours, whether they be Austria-Hungary, Bulgaria (a Slavic country less enamoured with Russia) or the fading Ottoman Empire. On the other hand,

Russia's own ambitions in the region precluded too great an expansion of Serbia. Such criss-crossing motivations were symptomatic of the murky world of Balkan politics.

A second enduring Russian foreign policy ambition, better described as an obsession, lay in securing control of the exit from the Black Sea, via the Bosphorus and the Dardanelles, to the Mediterranean; an aim that ultimately would require the conquest of Constantinople and the dissolution of the Ottoman Empire. Several wars had already been triggered by this aggressive intent, most notably the Crimean War of 1854–6 and the Russo-Turkish War of 1877–8. The Russian balance of trade, particularly the bulk export of grain, was dependent on its safe passage through the Dardanelles and government ministers were all too conscious that any closure of the Straits would cause severe economic damage. Russia was naturally extremely concerned at any threatened augmentation of Turkish naval strength in the Black Sea. But there was also a jealous determination to prevent any other country – whoever it might be – from securing control of the Straits. Although if it was not to be Russia herself, then better the Turks than some more virile challenger such as Bulgaria or Greece.

Finally, Russia had also sought to spread out to the east, expanding beyond Central Asia, pressing into Siberia and eventually seeking a port to provide access to the Pacific Ocean. These ambitions led Russia into conflict with Japan, a hitherto little considered nation which had successfully acquired many of the trappings of a modern nation state. In the Russo-Japanese War of 1904–5, the Russians had been badly beaten and forced into a humiliating climbdown. This, however, was only a temporary halt to the Russian programme of imperial expansion across borders not shared with a fellow Great Power. In a great swathe stretching from Manchuria, Mongolia and Turkestan, through Afghanistan to Persia and Anatolia, the Russians were pushing and probing, seeking undue influence and sending in settlers and political agents with the intent of destabilising the local regimes.

Yet while Russia was growing rapidly, there were severe internal pressures caused by her anachronistic system of government: an autocracy ruled over by Tsar Nicholas II since 1894. The tensions lay between reactionary conservatives who wanted to preserve the status quo, liberals who were working towards social reform presided over by a more restrained constitutional monarchy, and revolutionaries of all complexions who wanted to tear down the state and bring power to various factions of the people. The social unrest boiled over in a widespread revolution in 1905. Amidst a plethora of strikes and mutinies, workers' councils were established in major centres of population. In the end Nicholas II was forced to concede with a degree of political reform, creating a central legislative body in the Duma with some voting rights, thus taking the first tentative steps on the road to a constitutional monarchy. The various opposition factions were divided in their response between those who were satisfied for the moment and those for whom it was not enough. This disunity allowed the state to re-establish control, but there was no doubt as to the underlying threat to the established order.

Thus Russia was plagued by the spectre of revolution, dragged down by her systematic internal problems and in desperate need of modernisation. The Russo-Japanese War had demonstrated that quantity was not enough, there had to be quality too. The Russians needed a well-trained army equipped with modern weapons, a strong naval presence on every coast and a total reorganisation of the logistical sinews of war. Whether or not this required industrialisation of the economy and a further democratisation of the state would be a moot point. It was clear, however, that, given time, Russia would be a valuable ally to France.

The enmity of both France and Russia was a cross for Germany to bear. But worse was to come, as the Kaiser's global ambitions led to disagreements with the leading colonial power. The British Empire was huge and slightly ramshackle, but by no means a spent force. A colonial empire founded on conquest and naked commercial exploitation, it truly spanned the globe and ruled a quarter of the world's population. Britain was determined not only to maintain her global position but also to expand – particularly in Egypt, Mesopotamia and Persia. Colonial friction was exacerbated when Germany began to construct a fleet plainly intended to challenge the Royal Navy in its undisputed control of the oceans. The British had secured that domination by means of maintaining a fleet that was capable of defeating the next two strongest navies – the strategic benefits of which meant that the Empire could be defended by a relatively small professional army in sharp contrast to the massive conscript-centred armies required by continental powers. Sentimentalists will often aver that Britain was a country at peace with itself before the Great

War; in fact, it was a society under severe stress. In the colonies, nationalism was a potent threat, with issues of self-governance and independence stirring all over the Empire. Closer to home, Home Rule for Ireland dramatically polarised opinion, not just in Ireland but also in the Army required to enforce any punitive measures. The home of the Industrial Revolution was also suffering from a legacy of ageing factories, terrible working conditions, problematic labour relations and a declining industrial base. Britain's sharply delineated class system promoted resentment at the privileges exercised by the few to the manifold disadvantage of the majority, which was reflected in the rise of socialist parties and the trades union movement. Vigorous suffragette campaigns marked the desire of women for emancipation and equal political rights with men.

Plagued by her own problems, Britain would have preferred to remain on the sidelines of any European disputes. But this was not possible. Not only was the supremacy of the Royal Navy under threat from the German Navy, but there was no doubt that if Germany beat France and Russia then she would achieve total control of Europe. This was contrary to the prime maxim of British foreign policy: always to seek a balance between the Great Powers. France sensed the opportunity and assiduously courted her former enemy. In the absence of conciliatory moves from Germany and tormented by the naval threat, Britain was pushed towards France. There was still suspicion there – indeed, in the early stages neither side was a faithful suitor – but they had a common enemy in Germany. In April 1904 the Anglo-French Entente was signed, which cleared the decks of existing colonial disagreements and gradually mutated into the Entente Cordiale as the two countries began to co-ordinate their naval and military arrangements in a manner which, while not binding, clearly imposed a moral requirement on the British to intervene on the French's behalf in the event of war triggered by German aggression.

A rapprochement with Russia was not such an easy matter. Britain and Russia had been competing for power across Central Asia in the strategic rivalry famously depicted by Kipling as 'The Great Game', with the British long concerned over a latent Russian threat to India. Much of the tension emanated from the struggle to control Afghanistan, variously seen as a buffer zone or staging post, depending on perspective. There were also tensions over the mutual jockeying for position in China. But with the threat of Germany much more immediate and far closer to home, such differences had to be laid aside, with the result that the Anglo-Russian Convention was signed in 1907. This defined borders and areas of interest in a manner tolerable to both sides, but more importantly marked the *de facto* birth of the Triple Entente of France, Russia and Britain. This was a total disaster for Germany. It was evident that, since the departure of Bismarck, the German state had developed a disturbing knack of making powerful enemies.

Germany did, however, have one faithful ally: Austria-Hungary. Unfortunately, the Austro-Hungarian Empire was a rather ancient institution that had grown up over hundreds of years of strife and miscellaneous dynastic marriage settlements. The latest incarnation was the Dual Monarchy created by an 1867 agreement whereby the Austrian Empire and the neighbouring Hungarian Kingdom would share the same monarch – Emperor Franz Josef I, who had ruled the Austrian Empire since 1848 and who also became King of Hungary. More a historical curiosity than a vibrant modern nation state, the Empire was a mosaic of different nationalities in which indigenous Austrians and Hungarians were comfortably outnumbered by other ethnic groups swept up into the Empire over the years. The political system was complex, with separate Austrian and Hungarian parliaments and governments claiming a variety of powers, while Emperor Franz Josef and his ministers exercised control of foreign policy and the armed forces. Inefficiency was rife and the national parliaments were, not unnaturally, unwilling to finance anything but the bare minimum of military expenditure for an army which they did not themselves control. But the biggest problem was the spectre of Pan-Slav nationalism which so enthused the Russians. There was a widespread yearning among the Slavs within the Austro-Hungarian Empire for separatism and unification, although in truth few among them could agree as to what this was or how it was to be achieved. This craving was given a powerful external stimulus by Serbia, which both overtly and covertly supported Slavic groupings within the Empire. Serbia was increasingly symptomatic of everything that grated on Austro-Hungarian sensibilities.

Germany's other ally in the Central Powers was Italy, but this was a far more dubious relationship. Italy was made up of formerly independent states that had been only been lately unified during the nineteenth century from the springboard provided by the north-western province of

Piedmont. Blocked from further expansion by France and Austria-Hungary on the European mainland, Italy looked to North Africa to establish colonies, but had been considerably frustrated by competition with France in the same region, as evinced in the French annexation of Tunisia in 1881. Desperate for allies to guarantee safety in a dangerous world, Italy had joined the Triple Alliance in 1882. Yet they were always unlikely bed-fellows for Italy had fought several wars against the Austro-Hungarian Empire during her tortuous process of unification and there remained serious outstanding border disputes relating to the Austrian occupation of the Trentino, Istria and Trieste regions. It was clear that an alliance with Austria could never really be accepted by the Italian people and few believed that their government would honour the treaty, even if Germany or Austria-Hungary were the innocent victims of an unprovoked assault by France or Russia. In essence, this was a one-way alliance.

Stuck on the sidelines of Europe was Turkey, the remnants of the Ottoman Empire. The Turks shared many of the problems of their old adversaries of the Austro-Hungarian Empire. Only half the population was indigenous Turks and the rest were a conglomeration of many nationalities including Slavs, Greeks and Arabs, all further cross-cut with a variety of religious differences. Turkey had lost most of her European territories as Greece, Rumania, Serbia, Montenegro and Bulgaria had all gained their independence. There was also the long-standing threat from Russia to consider. Turkey seemed surrounded by enemies while the pressures of nationalism gnawed away at her vitals. The major European powers hovered in the wings, demanding ever-more concessions and 'areas of interest', which promised a comprehensive dismemberment in the near future. The Turks had to face all these threats hamstrung by an agricultural economy, minimal heavy industries, little or no exploitation of natural resources and crippled by a huge national debt. The country was ruled by the 'Young Turks', who had taken partial power in 1908. Their goal was modernisation, but they did not have the means to achieve it – outside assistance only came with strings attached that threatened a further spiral of decline. Although the British professed friendship to Turkey and had sent a Naval Mission, it was the Germans who seemed most willing to assist – or take advantage of – the Turks. Their Military Mission was deeply embedded in the Turkish Army, while the Berlin to Baghdad railway was an ambitious project with which they sought to secure and exploit new commercial spheres of influence for German industry. Turkey was in a dangerous position and it was difficult to see how war could benefit a country that was already near-bankrupt. Certainly Turkey could not afford to be on the losing side: that would surely mark the final dissolution of her tottering Empire

As Europe slowly evolved into two gigantic armed camps, the years leading up to war were marked by an upsurge in the arms race which came to dominate the economies of the Great Powers. Each had their own gigantic arms manufacturers churning out weapons of war at an unprecedented rate. Each step forward in the fields of small arms, machine guns or artillery was mimicked, countered, then trumped by the other powers. Constant experimentation was going on to develop the best, the most reliable, the most deadly weapons possible. Already they were looking to aircraft and airships as future weapons of war, while at sea there was steady progress in the development of submarines. Nobody could afford to be left behind; but it wasn't just about weapons. Huge conscript armies had to be raised, fed and clothed, armed, accommodated in barracks, trained and regularly exercised in field manoeuvres, None of this was cheap. The arms race threatened to consume national budgets at an unprecedented rate.

Planning for the unthinkable

As the Central Powers and Triple Alliance became more deeply established competing entities, so their respective military establishments constantly updated their plans for war. That, after all, was their function: they could not allow themselves to be taken by surprise by the vagaries of international politics. The incompetence of German diplomacy following the departure of Bismarck caused severe problems for the German Army. Several of its more far-sighted officers had already been deeply disturbed by its inability to finish off France after initial crushing victories over the French Army had culminated in the humiliating capture of Emperor Napoleon III in September 1870. Instead, a radical French provisional government had rejected German peace terms outright and launched a 'people's war' using mass conscription to raise a 'new' army that almost doubled the numerical strength of the French Army. Such a rapid expansion of an army was a fantastically difficult undertaking, as suitably trained officers and NCOs were in scarce supply and, while the new recruits may have exuded potential, they were not in any real sense soldiers. They also lacked the heavier weaponry and tools of their trade, in particular artillery. Yet the Germans had found this new conscript army very difficult to deal with and it had taken them several months to achieve a final victory, against a background of the pinpricks of swarms of francs-tireurs harassing their lines of communications.

The reaction of the German Chief of General Staff, General Helmuth von Moltke, to this unexpected French resurgence was interesting. He recognised it as a signpost to a fundamental change in the nature of warfare, marking a move away from wars fought between professional armies to a world in which whole nations took to arms. But his immediate reaction was fearsomely robust, in that he resolved to crush every scrap of resistance out of France, not just by beating her armies *per se*, but by eradicating the resources from which they could spring – in essence, he conceived of a war of extermination. When Paris fell, the French finally sued for peace but Moltke wanted to fight on, only to be over-ruled by Bismarck. Moltke would always regret what he saw as a missed opportunity to deal with the French threat once and for all. In the years that followed, as the French introduced conscription and rearmed, Moltke was all too aware that France would no longer fall easy victim.

> If war should break out no one can estimate its duration or see when it will end. The greatest powers of Europe, which are armed as never before, will fight each other. None can be annihilated so completely in one or two campaigns that it would declare itself vanquished and be compelled to accept hard conditions for peace without any chance, even after a year's time, to renew the fight. Gentlemen, it might be a seven, or even a thirty years' war – but woe to him who sets Europe alight and first throws the match into the powder-barrel![4]
>
> General Helmuth von Moltke, Chief of General Staff, Imperial German Army

Worse still, Moltke was well aware that Germany might have to fight France and Russia at the same time. It would clearly be difficult to defeat one before reserves had to be transferred to counter the offensive operations of the other. His war plans, with their emphasis on the strategic defensive, reflected this pessimistic approach, although he also planned for savage thrusts to weaken the early resolve of his opponents and bring them to the peace table.

When General Alfred von Schlieffen took over as Chief of General Staff in 1892, he returned to the drawing board and commissioned plans for every conceivable eventuality: war with France; war with Russia; or war with both – a situation rendered a probability, rather than a possibility, by the removal of Bismarck. His numerous staff worked through the problems using a plethora of war game scenarios, field exercises, staff rides and feasibility studies. As Schlieffen estimated that in a war with both France and Russia the German forces would be outnumbered by around five to three, he sought to avoid a lengthy war in which his opponents' big battalions would have the opportunity to press home their numerical advantage. This meant that, despite all the difficulties, Schlieffen was determined to seek a quick decision, or risk destroying Germany both militarily and economically.

The temptation was to strike first at the far weaker Russian Army, which was still in the process of modernising. But the difficulty of forcing victory against the Russian hordes who could simply withdraw deep into Russia was acutely worrying – as Napoleon's catastrophic retreat from Moscow in 1812 still cast its powerful shadow. Hence Schlieffen took the view that it was not possible to overwhelm Russia *quickly*. Gradually he was edging towards the idea of holding Russia to the east with a relatively small force while Germany launched a knock-out blow against France in the west. This in turn generated considerable military problems, for not only was the French Army a far more formidable opponent than the Russian Army, but the French had also established several modern fortresses behind the Franco-German border. These too seemed to militate against a quick German victory.

Schlieffen's solution was simple: he would go round the French fortress line. Violating the neutrality of Holland, Belgium and Luxembourg to drive into northern France and envelop the French armies, seeking a quick decisive battle to shatter the resistance of the French and allow Germany to dictate terms or to turn on Russia as required. At first this was a contingency plan, but as the German Army gained in strength so it was gradually adopted as the main war plan. The origins of the 'Schlieffen Plan' have been clouded by those who have rightly pointed out that it was trialled in many versions and constantly re-tweaked in the light of the latest intelligence and availability of troops. However, it was certainly never the static entity of popular imagination, but rather a mutating plan that had its origins in only one powerful strand of Schlieffen's overall planning activities. The much-vaunted 1905 and 1906 Schlieffen memoranda, once popularly supposed to contain the essence of the plan, proved a sad disappointment when they were revealed to contain little of real operational detail. Indeed, in his last war game before his retirement in 1906, Schlieffen himself stood on the defensive and eschewed the kind of offensive manoeuvres which have been attributed to him; it is apparent that even at that late stage of his career, Schlieffen was still thinking, still experimenting with solutions to the dilemma inflicted on the German Army by the failures of German foreign policy.

The Schlieffen Plan was above all of its time. In 1906, the Russians were still deep in the throes of despair after their defeat by the Japanese. Schlieffen believed that the Russian Army was in such poor condition that until it was fundamentally reformed it would not be capable of effective offensive operations. Yet the Russians would soon demonstrate a regenerative capacity that would utterly confound German hopes. Indeed, the 'Great Programme' of army reform commencing in 1913 promised to deliver a peacetime Russian Army some 2,200,000 strong by around 1918. This prospect of vastly augmented Russian military might would be at the heart of the conundrum bequeathed to Schlieffen's successor as Chief of General Staff, General Helmuth von Moltke (the Younger – he was the nephew of von Moltke the Elder). Germany would face not just war on two fronts, but ultimately the daunting prospect of a huge modern Russian army rapidly mobilised on to the Russo-German border by means of its railways, newly financed thanks to substantial French investment. Moltke reviewed the problem, but failed to develop a coherent strategy to match Germany's deteriorating position. It was apparent that Russia could not be attacked and beaten quickly, so the main thrust had to be against France. As it was unlikely that the French could be disposed of quickly by a direct attack across the Franco-German border, the Schlieffen Plan still offered some hope, which Moltke clung to in the absence of anything better. Whether the more resourceful Schlieffen would have been similarly constrained is a matter for conjecture.

A theoretical memorandum or position paper is not the same as a practicable plan, and it was Moltke and his staff who drew up all the operational war plans. Moltke also made some important adjustments to reflect some of the changes in the tactical and political situation. Firstly, he was forced to strengthen the German forces held on the Franco-German border to counter the near inevitable French invasion of Alsace-Lorraine. Secondly, unwilling to add to the roster of Germany's enemies, he decided to avoid invading Holland. Thirdly, he timetabled an early surprise attack on the strong Belgian Liège forts to ensure that they did not hold up the thrust through Belgium. Fourthly, he sought to make the alliance with Austria-Hungary more of a military reality. Just *one* of the eight mobilised German armies would be assigned to the Eastern Front, where it would need as much assistance from the Austro-Hungarian Army as possible if he was to hold that front while France was defeated. Moltke the Elder and Schlieffen had been very sceptical of the potential worth of the Austrian Army, but Moltke, who was more desperate, tried his best to incorporate it in his plans. He liaised with the Austrian Chief of General Staff, General Franz Conrad von Hötzendorf, to try to secure his full co-operation in holding back any early Russian attacks.

Moltke's other main concern was far more sinister. Fearful of the growing strength of Russia and France he wanted war as quickly as possible, before Germany's situation relative to her enemies could deteriorate further. In the end, Germany would go to war borne up by the hope of a quick victory utilising the superior operational efficiency of her army before her enemies could properly mobilise their resources. When the opportunity arose, Moltke grasped at the chance for war. The irony is that in his heart of hearts he always lacked faith in ultimate German victory.

THE EARLY FRENCH PLANS immediately following the debacle of 1871 were, as one might expect, essentially defensive in character. A formal system of conscription was introduced to create a truly national army, while to safeguard their borders the French constructed an expensive chain of modern fortresses inside the new Franco-German frontier. The French Army also at least partially embraced modernisation, with the introduction of much of the burgeoning paraphernalia of war to enable it to try to match the German advances. Behind the scenes there was a long-term improvement of the logistical infrastructure of war, with particular attention paid to the railways for use in deploying troops quickly to the German borders. A more professional system of staff officers and a unified high command also began the process of welding together a coherent military doctrine.

The alliance formed with Russia in 1892 opened up more offensive opportunities and French military strategy soon began to reflect the possibility of launching an offensive into the lost province of Alsace-Lorraine. The French staff officers worked through a wide selection of plans distinguished, with Gallic logic, by a sequence of Roman numerals. They were at least theoretically aware of the threat of a major German offensive swinging through northern France and Belgium – as had in fact been proposed by Schlieffen. Although many of the French high command could not readily countenance the concept of the Germans so brutally violating Belgian neutrality, their plans began to reflect that possibility; indeed, from 1906 they began to deploy more troops in the north. However, the French still did not have enough troops to be present in strength everywhere from Switzerland to the North Sea, so hard choices would have to be made. The man they chose to make them was General Joseph Joffre. Born into a rural background in 1852, Joffre had his first experience of active service while still an officer cadet at the siege of Paris during the Franco-Prussian War. Following this he served as an engineer officer in the French colonies of Indo-China and North Africa. Promotion followed and, in 1904, he was appointed as Director of Engineering, whereupon he demonstrated a mastery of administrative detail coupled with the drive to get things done – qualities that led to him being promoted rapidly to command a division, a corps and finally, in 1911, to Chief of General Staff with the associated role as Commander in Chief in the event of war. Untainted by specific political or religious affiliations he was relatively acceptable to all sides, while his reassuring stolidity of character meant he was regarded as a safe pair of hands.

Joffre immediately began a thoroughgoing re-evaluation of strategy, taking into account the prevailing view that Britain would join the French in war with Germany and expressing a firm resolve to crush Germany and regain the lost provinces. These ideas were further bolstered by promises from the Russians that they could deploy 700,000–800,000 men for an offensive into East Prussia about two weeks after mobilisation. In view of the relative slowness of the Russian mobilisation process, it might well seem that the best option for France was to stand on the defensive until the Russians were up to full strength on Germany's eastern borders. Unfortunately, by this time the French Army had been overwhelmed by a belief in the power of the offensive, as opposed to the defensive, approach.

Military theorists proclaimed the moral superiority of the attack and postulated that new weapons systems would allow such a concentration of firepower on the defending troops that their will to resist would be broken. Tactics were considered as of nothing compared to the inspirational effects of élan that flowed through the bloodstream of every French *poilu*; highly motivated and well-led troops, fearing nothing, could surmount any obstacles by the sheer boldness of their assaults, hitting enemy defences before they knew what was happening and pressing home their attacks at the point of the bayonet. Such ideas were reflected in doctrinal statements to the effect that 'Only the offensive yields positive results'. This was, however, a gross simplification of the complexities of modern warfare. While the offensive approach may indeed grant its initiator the ability to choose the place and time of attack, if due attention was not paid to the military situation it could also lead to crippling losses which would swiftly erode effective military capacity. Such misgivings were, however, not permissible in France's pre-war frenzy extolling the power of the '*offensive à l'outrance*'.

It was against this background that Joffre created of Plan XVII, the last revision of French strategy for what would be the Great War. This was not quite such a blind lunge for Alsace-Lorraine as has often been caricatured. Joffre had become convinced that the Germans would attack through Belgium, and indeed came to see it as a future battleground, but his civilian politician masters – mindful of the attitude of the British – wisely insisted on the proviso that Germany must have violated Belgian neutrality first. This uncertainty rather precluded the possibility of the main French offensive driving into Belgium and left Alsace-Lorraine as the main option. It was primarily a concentration plan which placed four armies along the German, Luxembourg and Belgian borders with another army held in reserve. Once in position they were expected to push into Alsace-Lorraine, but with the option of deploying two armies to counter German forces attacking through Belgium and northern France. As such it did not commit Joffre to any particular course of action. But the presumption was always that he would attack somewhere and that meanwhile the Russians would be attacking on the Eastern Front. Some of the extra men Joffre would need for his task were secured by the passing of the Three Year Law in 1913, which extended the service of every French conscript to three years. This meant that, although Germany had a population of approaching 60 million (some 20 million more than France), France's longer term of conscription would allow for an army of equal size to the German Army. The French, like the Germans, thought in terms of a short war, although there was some inkling that an initial decisive series of battles might not be the end of the matter. It was estimated that, even if successful, it would take them six long months even to reach the Rhine, where the Germans might still be expected to put up a great deal of resistance. And of course the reverse would apply should things go badly for France. Yet little or nothing practical was done to prepare for a long war: the extant supplies of munitions were presumed sufficient and there was no concept of harnessing industry to the common cause.

ONCE BRITAIN JOINED the Triple Entente the exigencies of alliance warfare meant that not only would she be required to shoulder most of its naval burdens, but she would also be expected to contribute a significant land force. The Royal Navy would secure the North Sea, English Channel and Atlantic, while the French Navy would take on the main role in the Mediterranean. But the French were also desperate for a British Expeditionary Force (BEF) to take its place in the line. The French hoped for six infantry divisions and a cavalry division within sixteen days of mobilisation, trivial forces in themselves in the huge armies massing for war, but a symbol of British involvement. Joffre planned to place them on the left of the French armies, therefore facing the right of the German armies, although its positioning was of no great significance. Early in a war the significance of the alliance with Britain lay in her naval contribution; nothing of consequence could be expected on land for more than a year and this was beyond the French strategic horizon. Of far greater importance to the French was the early Russian commitment of serious military forces to an assault on the Germans on the Eastern Front.

ON THE EASTERN FRONT the Russians were well aware that the Germans intended to attack the French first and so would be wishing merely to stand fast in East Prussia. The question was how best to deploy the massed Russian armies in the crucial first month of the war. The Russian High

Command had to bear in mind the configuration of the border between Russia and the Central Powers, which was in itself a problem. The last partition of Poland had left the huge salient of 'Russian' Poland thrusting some 230 miles deep into the Central Powers, wedged between the Austro-Hungarian Carpathian Mountains to the south and German East Prussia in the north. There were no naturally defensible borders; indeed, a logical military response would have been to evacuate the whole area. Such a withdrawal would of course not suit the French facing the main German offensives, who needed the Russians to exert the maximum pressure on their enemy. The Russians were aware of their obligations to the French, but their plans had to balance French needs with the requirement to face the forty divisions of the Austro-Hungarian Army, which had only the Serbian Army to contend with.

In 1910 the Russians produced Plan 19, which boldly envisaged deploying most of their mobilised forces – fifty-three divisions – against Germany with just nineteen divisions left to face the Austrians facilitated by the withdrawal from Russian Poland to a more defensible shorter border. Opponents to the plan within the Russian High Command pointed out the considerable risks of Austrian offensive operations overwhelming the forces facing them and pictured mass cavalry intervention harassing the flanks and communications of the Russian forces deployed against the Germans. There were also political considerations as to the wisdom of evacuating Poland, which it might prove difficult to regain, especially given the doubtful adherence to the Russian state of many Poles. The result was a compromise with the Plan 'A' and 'G' variants of Plan 19. While 'G' presented a slightly modified version of the original plan to concentrate against Germany (forty-three divisions against Germany and thirty-one against Austria), 'A' was far more focussed on Austria-Hungary, with the bulk of the mobilised forces – forty-five divisions in the Third, Fourth and Fifth Armies – to face the Austrians while what remained would do their best to assist the French. Thus the Russian First and Second Armies, totalling twenty-nine divisions, would be launched against the nine divisions of the German Eighth Army in East Prussia. In the event it was Plan 'A' that was chosen.

The Russians also had a wide variety of theoretical plans relating to their long-term ambitions to secure Constantinople. War games based on this theme were a perennial occupation of the Russian High Command, but these plans represented an aspiration, a goal to be achieved later in the war, rather than a realistic option now. Turkey, after all, was not at war in August 1914.

The plans of Austria-Hungary are of considerably less account, for although technically a great power, in reality she was incapable of affecting events outside the confines of the Balkan region. Although involved in discussions with Moltke to try to harness the Austrian divisions to the cause against Russia, there was still a strong intent to concentrate against Serbia evident in all of the Austrian plans. Two variants existed: Plan 'B' pictured three Austrian armies invading Serbia while three more guarded the Russian frontier – a disposition that would be almost useless to their German allies; while Plan 'R' sought to guard against a substantial Russian intervention to protect Serbia with four armies while just two invaded Serbia. In the end, the Austrians seem to have played it by ear, still prioritising the destruction of their Serbian arch-enemies over the greater good of the Central Powers.

Close to the edge

The years leading up to the outbreak of the Great War in 1914 had been riven by a series of diplomatic incidents and general sabre-rattling between the Great Powers as they tested the limits of what they could achieve without actually resorting to war. The tensions originating in German jealousy of French influence in North Africa were most evident in the First Moroccan Crisis of 1905–6. France was determined to acquire Morocco to complement her existing North African colonies. Bismarck, who regarded colonies with scepticism, would surely have stepped back to allow imperial rivalries to fester between France and Britain. But the Kaiser paid a visit to Tangier in March 1905 and gave an inflammatory speech in which he directly opposed the French moves, thus triggering a great deal of anxiety across Europe. An international conference resolved the situation with a compromise which left France in *de facto* control of Morocco.

Another serious crisis emerged in 1908 when Austria-Hungary formally annexed Bosnia and Herzegovina. Previously, under the Treaty of Berlin of 1878, the Austrians had ruled the provinces, replacing the former Turkish administration. But this seemingly insignificant change in status provoked much angst, with almost every major power in the region taking a spirited interest, as each tried to push forward their own agenda. In the end Serbian protests were ignored and the annexation was accepted, but a further layer of distrust had been created between the Austrians and the Russians. The annexation itself had been intended to draw a line under Slav nationalism, but it merely fuelled Bosnian demands for separatism. The Balkan powder keg seemed increasingly likely to explode at the slightest provocation.

A Second Moroccan Crisis would break out in April 1911, when the French sent a small military force to 'defend French citizens' in Morocco during a revolt by the indigenous population against the rule of the Sultan. Germany believed that this was merely a step on the road to French annexation, which would thwart forever the German colonial ambition to establish a naval base in Morocco with access to the Atlantic. Germany therefore despatched a gunboat, the *Agadir*. This action in turn exacerbated the anxiety of the British, who sought to deny Germany an Atlantic port. For a while the diplomatic temperature was dramatically raised, but gradually fell away as none of the protagonists took further provocative action. Eventually Germany was bought off with a worthless parcel of territory in the African Congo, while France finally made Morocco a protectorate in 1912. The whole imbroglio left Germany publicly humiliated, but there was little she could do.

The next big threat to the status quo came in September 1911, when the Italians declared war on Turkey and tried to seize Tripolitania and the Dodecanese Islands in a blatant attempt to take advantage of the fast-decaying Ottoman Empire. However, this action was in turn swallowed up by the outbreak of the First Balkan War, when Serbia, Greece, Bulgaria and Montenegro took advantage of the Italian distraction and banded together to attack Turkey in October 1912. The Turks fought a poor campaign and were soon overwhelmed. But then the alliance between her Balkan opponents spontaneously imploded over their competing territorial claims when Bulgaria attacked her erstwhile allies, Greece and Serbia, and so began the Second Balkan War in June 1913. Bulgaria was hopelessly isolated and by the time the war ended in August 1913 Turkey, all but unnoticed, had succeeded in regaining much of the Balkan territory she had initially lost. The overall weakness of Turkey was not lessened, but the crisis also exposed the uncertainty as to the correct response of both the Austrians and the Russians, either of whom might have been expected to intervene. The Austrians made some exploratory movements, but when it became apparent that the Germans were content to let events take their course, they did nothing even as their Serbian enemies prospered – Serbia almost doubled in size during the Balkan Wars. The Russians at one stage also seemed inclined to order a partial mobilisation, directed against Austria, but that idea was abandoned when the Russian leaders realised that such a radical gesture would provoke retaliatory mobilisations across Europe. No one was ready – or desperate enough – to risk triggering a full-scale war in 1912.

Another year; another crisis. Anything seemed to provoke uproar. In December 1913 the Germans were set to appoint Lieutenant General Otto Liman von Sanders as commander of the Turkish I Corps. There was a long-standing German Military Mission in Constantinople, but this move gave Liman actual command of the very unit responsible for the defence of the Straits. This jagged at exposed Russian nerves as they faced the prospect of a Turkish Army strengthened by ongoing close military co-operation with Germany. This was in addition to a significant Turkish naval rearmament with the co-operation of the British Naval Mission – much to the frustration of the Russians, who felt they might have expected more consideration from their Entente partners. A reinvigorated Turkey with a strong Black Sea Fleet played no part in Russia's long-term plans for Constantinople. There was much sabre-rattling before a compromise was reached whereby Liman was promoted to Inspector General of the Turkish Army and hence not actually in command of the Straits. This defused the immediate crisis but left Russian animosity and underlying fears unresolved. Resentments were building up on all sides.

Any of these convoluted problems could have triggered war in the years leading up to 1914. They symbolised the prevailing weaknesses of the Great Powers. But in every case a combination of old-fashioned diplomacy, statesmanlike restraint, natural trepidation and a lack of readiness for war at that particular moment in time prevented an outbreak of serious hostilities. Perhaps there was also a strong element of luck, but it surely could not last. Each of the Great Powers feared they were losing ground to their rivals, which in turn gradually fuelled a spiralling collective paranoia. Most of all, the German Empire was in an exceptionally difficult position, trapped as she was under the flawed world vision of Kaiser Wilhelm's regime: tied by necessity to Austria-Hungary and doomed to face war sooner or later with France, Russia and probably Great Britain. But the increasing power of Russia, meant that Germany's only feasible plans for victory could not be relied on for much longer – perhaps only until 1917, and certainly not beyond 1922. For Germany there was no point in delaying war; if it had to come, then let it be as soon as possible. By August 1914 the last remaining restraints had been frayed away and preparations for war were complete. The scene was set for Armageddon.

The assassination of Franz Ferdinand

The final trigger for war would be the pent-up pressure of nationalism within the polyglot Austro-Hungarian Empire. Various nationalist group-ings were plotting, of which the most significant would prove to be the Serbian *Narodna Odbrana* (National Defence), established in 1908, along with its rather intimidating secret terrorist wing, 'The Black Hand'. Their intention was to liberate all Serbs from their oppressors to create a Greater Serbia, and in particular to reverse the formal annexation of Bosnia by the Austrians in 1908. To this end they had recruited a formidable member-ship within an interlinked nest of organisations such as 'Young Bosnia'. Collectively, they were highly motivated conspirators and in June 1914 they were given their chance to change the world.

> A tiny clipping from a newspaper, mailed without comment from a secret band of terrorists in Zagreb, capital of Croatia, to their comrades in Belgrade, was the torch which set the world afire with war in 1914. That bit of paper wrecked old, proud empires. It gave birth to new, free nations. I was one of the members of the terrorist band in Belgrade which received it. The little clipping declared that the Austrian Archduke Franz Ferdinand would visit Sarajevo, the capital of Bosnia, June 28, to direct army manoeuvres in the neighbouring mountains. It reached our meeting place, the café called Zlatna Moruna, one night in the latter part of April 1914. At a small table in a very humble café, beneath a flickering gas jet we sat and read it. There was no advice nor admonition sent with it. Only four letters and two numerals were sufficient to make us unanimous, without discussion, as to what we should do about it.[4]
>
> Borijove Jevtic, The Black Hand

The culmination of months of plotting would be the assassination of the

Archduke in Sarajevo on 28 June 1914. In the intervening period Serbian intelligence officers covertly provided the conspirators with weapons and training, before facilitating their re-entry into Bosnia. On that fateful day the putative assassins were spread out in the waiting crowd on the streets of Sarajevo as the cars containing the Archduke and his entourage passed by. Their initial efforts were less than lethal: one lost his nerve, while a second hurled a hand grenade which wounded people in the car behind the Archduke's and the others missed their chance as the car accelerated away. But then in the confusion that followed, the Archduke's car got lost, stalled and by a dreadful coincidence rolled to a stop within a couple of yards of one of the hitherto frustrated assassins: a 19-year-old student called Gavrilo Princip. Whipping out his revolver, Princip fired twice at point blank range into the open-top car. He did not miss. The first bullet hit Franz Ferdinand in the neck, while the second tore open the stomach of his pregnant wife Sophie as she tried to protect her husband. On the running board Count Franz von Harrach was a horrified witness.

> As the car quickly reversed, a thin stream of blood spurted from His Highness's mouth on to my right check. As I was pulling out my handkerchief to wipe the blood away from his mouth, the Duchess cried out to him, 'For God's sake! What has happened to you?' At that she slid off the seat and lay on the floor of the car, with her face between his knees. I had no idea that she too was hit and thought she had simply fainted with fright. Then I heard His Imperial Highness say, 'Sophie, Sophie, don't die. Stay alive for the children!' At that, I seized the Archduke by the collar of his uniform, to stop his head dropping forward, and asked him if he was in great pain. He answered me quite distinctly, 'It is nothing!' His face began to twist somewhat but he went on repeating, six or seven times, ever more faintly as he gradually lost consciousness, 'It's nothing!' Then came a brief pause followed by a convulsive rattle in his throat, caused by a loss of blood. This ceased on arrival at the governor's residence. The two unconscious bodies were carried into the building where their death was soon established.[5]
>
> Count Franz von Harrach

Princip and his co-conspirators were swiftly arrested and interrogated. Although as Bosnians they were Austro-Hungarian citizens, it soon became manifest from confessions extracted by 2 July that the Serbian state was deeply implicated – even if at arm's length – in the assassination. The Serbian Prime Minister, Nicholas Pasic, was placed under intense pressure by the furious Austrians. Their annoyance was genuine but, riven as they were by internal problems, the crisis with Serbia also provided a convenient way out for them. If Germany could counterbalance the threat of intervention from Russia, then perhaps the upstart Serbians could be dealt with once and for all. A soundly trounced Serbia would quash the endless calls for Slavic autonomy for at least a generation. The rickety structure of the Austro-Hungarian Empire might even survive the death of the elderly Emperor Franz Josef I. War offered hope where before only disintegration had beckoned. Before reacting publicly, on 5 July Austria's Foreign Minister, Count Leopold von Berchtold, sent his emissary to Berlin asking for support in dealing with his country's now irreconcilable differences with Serbia.

What was Germany to do? She could of course abandon Austria-Hungary, her only real ally, but that would leave her more isolated in Europe than ever. On one level some German politicians seem to have believed that a quick war could be fought between Austria and Serbia which might lance their ally's most annoying carbuncle without triggering a general European conflagration. But, on the other hand, the powerful German military leaders were all too aware that if there was to be a European war then better before Germany's enemies had gained even greater strength. Then there were also the glittering prizes offered by victory. Their main enemy – France – could be emasculated once and for all, just as Moltke the Elder had wanted back in 1871, to prevent any future military revival. Germany could gain great swathes of territory in the east, pressing beyond Poland and deep into Russia. And with domination of Europe achieved, Germany, backed by her strong High Seas Fleet, could finally attain the status of a world power with the colonies to match those wider imperial ambitions. War was not an inconceivable measure to the German hierarchy: after all, within their own lifetimes they had witnessed their country emerge from the crucible of war. The crisis in the summer of 1914 left them little option but to support their Austro-Hungarian allies, yet let there be no doubt that the Germans had their own very aggressive agenda. This policy had been explicitly spelled out by the Chief of General Staff, General Helmuth von Moltke, on 1 June 1914, well before the assassination crisis: 'If only things would finally boil over – we are ready; the sooner the better for us.'⁷ Although he was prey to some wavering, this remained Moltke's default position throughout the crisis. The German military were prepared to take risks, to go the very brink of war and beyond to seize the moment should they be given any kind of legitimate pretext. And so it was that first the Kaiser and then the German Chancellor, Bethman Hollweg, offered their full support to the Austro-Hungarian Empire in whatever course they decided to pursue in bringing Serbia to heel – even if it meant provoking war with Russia and hence a general European war.

After considerable dithering, on 23 July the Austrians finally issued their ultimatum, which contained ten stringent demands of the Serbs requiring answers within just two days. At the same time, clearly antici-pating a rejection of those demands, they began to mobilise their forces. Serbia was required not only to desist but also publicly to condemn all forms of nationalist or separatist propaganda, while allowing Austro-Hun-garian officials to supervise the detention, interrogation and punishment of all Serbs implicated in the assassination of Franz Ferdinand. After order-ing the precautionary mobilisation of their relatively small army, the Serbs buckled, unwilling to face war without the explicit backing of Russia. Then, as the deadline loomed, significant news came through to Belgrade from Russia. In a moment the situation had changed: for the better, perhaps, for Serbia in the short term, but for the worse for the people of Europe.

On 25 July, Tsar Nicholas II proclaimed the 'Period Preparatory to Mobilisation' whereby among other measures the youngest reservists were called up to their units. Hitherto, for all the heightened interna-tional tension, it was still possible to see the crisis as a national dispute between Austria-Hungary and Serbia. But the Russian mobilisation was a key moment. Even partial mobilisation would cut down the time it would take the Russian armies to appear on Germany's Eastern Front and, given the delicately balanced nature of the German war plans, this was a real threat. The Germans were still in control of the situation, confident in their speed of mobilisation, and so they immediately sought to portray Russia as the aggressor in order to help get the backing of their own people as war loomed ever closer.

The Russian decision is puzzling in many respects. They were well aware that their programme of re-armament and improved railway links to the German Eastern Front had not yet really come to fruition. Although they had recovered their military strength after the debacle of the Russo-Japanese War, this represented a very bold step. Yet at the same time they clearly felt that they could not allow Serbia to be overwhelmed. As the Austro-Hungarians had brusquely rejected Russian requests for compromise, the Russians wished to add more bite to their diplomatic representations. Also, risks could be taken because, if the worst came to the worst, then although they would have to fight a war with Austria-Hungary and Germany, they would have the guaranteed support of the French, and perhaps even of the British. If the war went well, then perhaps they could finally dismember Turkey and at last secure Constantinople and that long-coveted route to the Mediterranean.

The Serbians naturally took some heart at this concrete evidence of Russian support. In their answer to the Austrian ultimatum, although they still accepted the broad thrust of the Austro-Hungarian demands, they had the temerity to attach conditions to various points and utterly rejected the concept of Austrian officials prosecuting the investigation of the assassination from within Serbian territory. This in turn was rejected out of hand by the Austrians, and a declaration of war with Serbia was obviously imminent.

The French government was determined to preserve the integrity of the Triple Entente, which meant not only not letting down Russia but also making sure that they did not invite any blame for their own actions that might lose them British support. Broadly passive as the crisis unfurled, they warned the Russians to be prudent, yet at the same time restated their commitment to join with Russia should war be forced upon them. The French may not have sought war in the summer of 1914, but equally they did little to avoid it, buoyed up by the opportunity finally to gain revenge on Germany, backed by both Russia and Britain.

The British were aghast as they observed these distressing developments. The Prime Minister, Sir Herbert Asquith, summed up his frustration in a private letter.

> Austria has sent a bullying and humiliating ultimatum to Serbia, who cannot possibly comply with it, and demanded an answer within 48 hours – failing which she will march. This means, almost inevitably, that Russia will come to the scene in defence of Serbia and in defiance of Austria, and if so, it is difficult for Germany and France to refrain from lending a hand to one side or the other. So that we are in

measurable, or imaginable, distance of a real Armageddon. Happily, there seems to be no reason why we should be anything more than spectators.[8]

Prime Minister Sir Herbert Asquith

The British attempted to calm the situation. On 26 July, their Foreign Secretary, Sir Edward Grey, proposed to convene a Four Power Conference (Britain, France, Germany and Italy) to defer the crisis, allow mediation and give Serbia, Austria-Hungary and Russia the chance to step back from the brink. This was traditional diplomacy in accordance with the loose arrangements whereby any serious crisis would prompt a Great Power conference and allow a compromise answer that, while it might not please everyone, would at least avert war. But by this time the Austrians were intent on a violent resolution and a minor clash on the border with Serbia provided an all-too-convenient excuse for them to declare war on 28 July. In Berlin the Kaiser was wavering, and indeed engaged in a sad little exchange of friendly telegrams with his blood relative Nicholas II, but by this time it was too late. The decisions that mattered had already been taken. At the same time, German diplomats were preoccupied with trying to ensure that the British did not come to the assistance of the French and Russians. Asquith was not impressed by their efforts as he pondered anew on the overall state of affairs on 30 July.

> The European situation is at least one degree worse than it was yesterday, and has not been improved by a rather shameless attempt on the part of Germany to buy our neutrality during the war by promises that she will not annex French territory (except colonies) or Holland or Belgium. There is something very crude and childlike about German diplomacy. Meanwhile the French are beginning to press in the opposite sense, as the Russians have been doing for some time. The City, which is in a terrible state of depression and paralysis, is for the time being all against English intervention. I think the prospect very black today.[9]
>
> Prime Minister Sir Herbert Asquith

At this stage, given the demonstrable aggressive intent of Germany and the Austro-Hungarian Empire, a general European war was inevitable, without a change of attitude or intent from all sides. So it was that on 31

July Germany ordered a preparatory level of mobilisation and issued two stern ultimatums: one to Russia demanding that she completely demobilise within twelve hours, the other to France requiring a declaration of neutrality within eighteen hours allowing the German occupation of frontier forts to demonstrate good faith. Such demands were, of course, impossible either to concede or implement.

On 1 August Germany mobilised and formally declared war on Russia while the French ordered a general mobilisation for 2 August. Even then the Kaiser was wavering, wrongly believing that there was some prospect of France and Britain remaining neutral if France was not attacked. Inspired by this belief, Wilhelm made a farcical attempt to jettison the whole of the German war plans, suggesting that they attack only Russia. Such proposals were abruptly rebutted by Moltke, who pointed out in no uncertain terms that German troops were already moving against France and that such a change at this late stage was simply impossible. Too many elements within the German military establishment were set on war – they could not conceive of backing down once the timetables were running. That night the first German troops began to invade Luxembourg border posts in preparation for the great sweep through Belgium. This would indeed be a Great European War, although, to no one's surprise, on 2 August Italy bailed out of her alliance with the Central Powers, announcing primly that popular pressure precluded Italian involvement in what she considered to be a war of aggression by her erstwhile German and Austro-Hungarian allies.

The British still had no real stomach for war, but as a signatory of the 1839 Treaty of London, Britain had long been a guarantor of Belgian neutrality, so if Germany invaded Belgium this would be a potent factor in overwhelming British reluctance to get involved. Slowly, Britain found herself sliding into war. On 2 August, she promised naval support to the French should Germany attack the coastline of northern France. The same day a German ultimatum demanded Belgium throw open her borders to allow the passage of the German Army through to France and on 3 August Germany formally declared war on France. When the Foreign Secretary spoke before the House of Commons on 3 August all realistic hope of keeping Britain out of the war had evaporated

> What other policy is there before the House? There is but one way in which the Government could make certain at the present moment of

keeping outside this War, and that would be that it should immediately
issue a proclamation of unconditional neutrality. We cannot do that.
We have made the commitment to France that I have read to the House
which prevents us from doing that. We have got the consideration of
Belgium, which prevents us also from any unconditional neutrality,
and, without those conditions absolutely satisfied and satisfactory, we
are bound not to shrink from proceeding to the use of all the forces
in our power. If we did take that line by saying, 'We will have nothing
whatever to do with this matter' under no conditions – the Belgian
Treaty obligations, the possible position in the Mediterranean, with
damage to British interests, and what may happen to France from
our failure to support France – if we were to say that all those things
mattered nothing, were as nothing, and to say we would stand aside, we
should, I believe, sacrifice our respect and good name and reputation
before the world and should not escape the most serious and grave
economic consequences.[10]

Secretary of State for Foreign Affairs Sir Edward Grey

Sentimentality over 'poor little Belgium' undoubtedly played well to the
gallery of the British public at large, but there was also a degree of hard-
nosed calculation that underpinned the British road to war: Germany was
already strong – perhaps too strong – and should she emerge victorious in
a war with France and Russia, then the balance of Europe would be shattered for generations. Nor had the German naval threat been forgotten
and the idea of German control of French and Belgian ports could not
be stomached. When Germany declared war on Belgium on 4 August,
the British reaction came the same day. At 19.00 an ultimatum demanding that the Germans commit to an immediate withdrawal from Belgium
was personally delivered by Sir Edward Goschen to the German Foreign
Minister, Gottlieb von Jagow, and Chancellor Theobald von Bethmann-
Hollweg. It was a fraught meeting.

I found the Chancellor very agitated. His Excellency at once began
a harangue, which lasted for about twenty minutes. He said that the
step taken by His Majesty's Government was terrible to a degree; just
for a word – 'neutrality', a word which in war time had so often been
disregarded – just for a scrap of paper Great Britain was going to make
war on a kindred nation who desired nothing better than to be friends
with her. All his efforts in that direction had been rendered useless by

this last terrible step, and the policy to which, as I knew, he had devoted himself since his accession to office had tumbled down like a house of cards. What we had done was unthinkable; it was like striking a man from behind while he was fighting for his life against two assailants. He held Great Britain responsible for all the terrible events that might happen. I protested strongly against that statement, and said that, in the same way as he and Herr von Jagow wished me to understand that for strategical reasons it was a matter of life and death to Germany to advance through Belgium and violate the latter's neutrality, so I would wish him to understand that it was, so to speak, a matter of 'life and death' for the honour of Great Britain that she should keep her solemn engagement to do her utmost to defend Belgium's neutrality if attacked. That solemn compact simply had to be kept, or what confidence could anyone have in engagements given by Great Britain in the future? The Chancellor said, 'But at what price will that compact have been kept. Has the British Government thought of that?' I hinted to His Excellency as plainly as I could that fear of consequences could hardly be regarded as an excuse for breaking solemn engagements, but His Excellency was so excited, so evidently overcome by the news of our action, and so little disposed to hear reason that I refrained from adding fuel to the flame by further argument.[11]

Sir Edward Goschen, British Ambassador to Germany

Of course Germany would not – indeed, could not comply – and so with the expiry of the ultimatum at midnight on 4 August 1914, Britain was at war with Germany. As Sir Edward Grey memorably expressed it: 'The lamps are going out all over Europe, we shall not see them lit again in our lifetime.'[12] At a stroke, the European hostilities had taken on a truly global complexion – this would be the first world war.

2

THE WESTERN FRONT, 1914

'No plan of operations extends with certainty beyond the first encounter with the enemy's main strength.'[1]

Field Marshal Helmuth von Moltke (the Elder)

THE BATTLE OF THE FRONTIERS was the gigantic clash that would make or break the hopes of both Germany and France. The two great competing visions of the war: the latest versions of the Schlieffen Plan and Plan XVII would be put to the ultimate test, moving at long last from theory to practice. They could not both be successful but, as Moltke the Elder's Clauswitzian aphorism indicates, there was the very distinct possibility of mutual failure in the fog of war, where the vagaries of chance melded with incompetence and the unforeseen activities of opposing forces could thwart the most enterprising of commanders. The German main thrust, which would ultimately set the agenda, was the advance of the First and Second Armies across the Belgian border and sweeping across the Belgian plains and plunging deep into northern France. The neighbouring Third Army would also pass through the Belgian Ardennes, while the Fourth and Fifth Armies would advance through Luxembourg and the French Ardennes. This meant that effectively all five armies would be performing a gargantuan wheeling manoeuvre to overwhelm the French left flank. Meanwhile, the German Sixth and Seventh Armies would stand fast in Alsace-Lorraine.

The tools for the German plans were yielded by mobilisation, which swelled the Army's peacetime strength from 754,000 to a rather more imposing 2,292,000, as the reservists – the Landwehr and Landsturm – were recalled to the colours to be organised into seventy-nine divisions, of which sixty-eight were to be deployed on the Western Front. As far as was humanly possible, the German Army was ready for war, superbly equipped and diligently trained over the years of peace. The infantry was armed with the 8 mm Mauser Gewehr 98, a magazine bolt-action rifle which was an accurate weapon capable of a reasonable speed of fire. The German soldier was drilled to be capable not only of individual accuracy but also of concentrating fire, in a squad or platoon, on to identified targets to maximise the impact. Each infantry regiment of three 1,000-man battalions also had a machine gun company of six Maxim machine guns which could be utilised together to lay down an intense concentration of fire both in defence and in support of an attack. The field artillery consisted of the excellent 77 mm field gun and the 105 mm howitzer, but they had also integrated much heavier 150 mm howitzers (the famous 5.9 inch of subsequent British nightmares) at corps level. These were superb multi-function weapons which offered the capacity, through their longer range, to overwhelm utterly the field artillery of their opponents. Even heavier artillery pieces were available at army level to deal with concrete fortifications. German attack tactics emphasised the importance of winning the fire fight before launching the attack in open order, with tightly controlled short bounds, the men dropping to the ground as required before finally over-running the enemy position and preparing for a possible counter-attack. All these functions were rehearsed on large training areas spread across Germany. These allowed for full-scale manoeuvres which attained a considerable degree of realism in operating across unknown terrain, with copious live firing elements, night attacks and often facing an 'enemy' force in detailed and physically exhausting scenarios that tested their limits in attack or defence. These were the kind of exercises that were impossible to implement in more densely populated France or more parsimonious Britain and Russia. The German Army was a professional body that took war very seriously indeed.

The French Army was also an extremely powerful continental army. Mobilisation expanded the existing army of 750,000 men to an intimidating total of 2,944,000. But the vast size of the French Army concealed some fundamental weaknesses. Although great strides had been made to modernise the army, they had been hampered by the poisonous military politics of the day, which had affected its preparations for modern war. The most obvious inadequacy became apparent every time a French soldier put on his uniform. A prevailing conservatism had stymied various attempts to introduce a modern camouflage uniform and the French *poilu* still stood proud in his bright red trousers and blue jacket which was almost indistinguishable from the uniform worn by his grandfather in the Franco-Prussian War of 1870. When the lessons of the Balkan Wars had finally hammered home the necessity of a less obvious plumage, trials began to select a replacement. By the summer of 1914 the military authorities had plumped for 'horizon blue' (a light blue) but it was far too late and the French Army would go to war dressed in nineteenth-century uniforms. The issue of new uniforms would only begin in earnest in 1915. In addition, the basic rifle issued to the French infantry was also not equal to the demands of modern warfare. The 8 mm Lebel rifle dated back to the 1880s and, although modifications had been made, it was still heavy, over-long and slow to load; there were also problems in maintaining accuracy during rapid fire. The 1886 bayonet, so much revered by the acolytes of the offensive, was 20 inches long and so thin that it was liable to snap in just the kind of close-quarter combat dreamed of by the more bloodthirsty commanders. The French's air-cooled 8 mm Hotchkiss machine guns were heavy but acceptable for the requirements of 1914.

There was, however, another unaddressed problem with the French Army. The mobilised field artillery numbered 4,076 superb 75 mm field guns which fired 16 lb shells at a rate of up to fifteen rounds a minute in extremis. When enemy troops were in the open these guns came into their own; but they could do little against well-constructed fortifications, while the flat trajectory of their shells prevented indirect fire across all but the lowest hills. Counter-battery fire was not really considered at all. The French had no modern howitzers, and pre-war efforts to address the problem had been thwarted by the High Command's inability to agree on what exactly was needed. Similarly, the influence of minds clouded by the necessity for mobility and a quick war meant that there were only 308 heavy artillery pieces. Although there were many other guns scattered about the country in various arsenals or forts, most were redundant through either obsolescence or location. They would be of little relevance to the imminent Battle of the Frontiers. A military culture based on the cult of the offensive and the short war had prevented more far-sighted provision for the future.

There was a final defect in the French Army, a failing that was probably the most serious of them all: a lack of proper tactical training. In contrast to the endless manoeuvres of the German Army, the French lacked the large training areas necessary for realistic field exercises and were further hamstrung by stringent financial controls. Every conscript served for three years, but the training programme running from brigade through to corps and army level took place on a four-year schedule with the inevitable consequence that no recruit ever experienced a complete cycle. Training was centred on building up the physical strength and aggressive qualities of the individual, with a heavy concentration on bayonet drills. The reservists were even less well catered for as, although they were called up for some forty days' service a year, they did hardly any field exercises, spending most of their time in barracks up and down the country. After eleven years in the Reserve the recruits were eligible for a final fourteen years in the Territorial Army and Territorial Army Reserve. None of the French reserve forces displayed the military competency of their German equivalents.

Schlieffen Plan: the capture of Liège

The necessity of quickly capturing the fortresses at Liège in Belgium had much exercised the minds of German military planners in the years running up to the war. Liège lay within twenty miles of the German frontier and was defended by a series of twelve forts on either side of the Meuse River, which bisected the city. Most of the defences had been constructed between 1888 and 1892 to house some 400 guns behind reinforced concrete capable of withstanding shells of up to 210 mm calibre. The garrison totalled some 40,000 troops under the command of Lieutenant General Gérard Leman. Any serious delay in overcoming this obstacle could be fatal to the German plans. Thus it was that the six infantry divisions and single cavalry division of the Belgian Army would have the dubious honour of being the first to face the Germans onslaught. The Belgians had decided not to occupy the naturally strong defensive line along the Meuse, stretching between Liège and the Namur fortress, as it seemed unwise to place their entire army within such easy reach of the Germans. In the end it was decided to concentrate further back, behind the Getter River, where the Belgians hoped to be sheltered by the Liège fortress until the French and British could arrive to solidify the line. The German advance troops flooded across the Belgian border sweeping aside the token Belgian frontier forces and driving on to Liège. Leman had got his men to entrench between the forts, so when the Germans launched their initial assault on the night of 5 August the defenders managed to stand firm, although the German 14th Brigade had some success in penetrating the Belgian lines. This action involved Major General Erich von Ludendorff of the Second Army, who was there as an observer when he was obliged to take control of the brigade on the death of the commander. After much hard fighting and a fair amount of good fortune the 14th Brigade managed to reach the centre of Liège. By this time Leman believed his situation to be hopeless. Aware of the greater strength of the German forces and further harassed by reports of cavalry feeling their way behind his lines, he resolved to evacuate his mobile troops of the 3rd Belgian Division while they could still escape on the afternoon of 6 August. Thus, when the 14th Brigade pushed further into the Belgian defences on the morning of 7 August, they became slowly aware that the resistance was weakening.

> As we entered, many Belgian soldiers who were standing about surrendered. Colonel von Oven was to occupy the Citadel. As a result of the reports he received, he decided not to do this, but to take the road toward Fort de Loncin, on the north-west side of the town, and take up a position at that exit from Liège. Thinking that Colonel von Oven was in possession of the Citadel, I went there with the brigade adjutant in a Belgian car which I had commandeered. When I arrived no German soldier was to be seen and the citadel was still in the hands of the enemy. I banged on the gates, which were locked. They were opened from inside. The few hundred Belgians who were there surrendered at my summons. The brigade now came up and took possession of the citadel, which I immediately put in a state of defence.[2]
>
> Major General Erich von Ludendorff, Headquarters, Second Army

The Germans were at this point in the strange position of having taken the city itself, but not the bulk of the surrounding fortifications. The forts were reduced in turn by a combination of 21 cm heavy mortars – which the fortifications had been designed to withstand – augmented from 12 August by the devastating power of the huge 42 cm mortars – which they emphatically had not. The huge mortar shells battered the forts one by one into submission. When the Fort de Pontisse, which commanded the crossings over the Meuse to the north of Liège, fell on 13 August, the gateway to Belgium swung ajar for the German First Army to begin its advance on 14 August. General Leman was trapped inside Fort de Loncin when at 05.00 on 15 August the Germans commenced a dreadful bombardment which was to continue for most of the day.

> A shell wrecked the arcade under which the general staff were sheltering. All light was extinguished by the force of the explosion, and the officers ran the risk of asphyxiation by the horrible gases emitted from the shell. When firing ceased, I ventured out on a tour of inspection on the external slopes, which I found had been reduced to a rubble heap. A few minutes later, the bombardment was resumed. It seemed as though all the German batteries were together firing salvoes. Nobody will ever be able to form any adequate idea of what the reality was like. I have only learned since that when the big siege mortars entered into action they hurled against us shells weighing 1,000 kilos, the explosive force of which surpasses anything known hitherto. Their approach was to be heard in an acute buzzing; and they burst with a thunderous roar, raising clouds of missiles, stones and dust. After some time passed amid these horrors, I wished to return to my observation tower; but I had hardly advanced a few feet into the gallery when a great blast passed by, and I was thrown violently to the ground. I managed to get up, and continued on my way, only to be stopped by a choking cloud of poisonous gas. It was a mixture of the gas from an explosion and the smoke of a fire in the troop quarters. We were driven back, half-suffocated. Looking out of a peephole, I saw to my horror that the fort had fallen, slopes and counter-slopes being a chaos of rubbish, while huge tongues of flame were shooting forth from the throat of the fortress. My first and last thought was to try and save the remnant of the garrison. I rushed out to give orders, and saw some soldiers, whom I mistook for Belgian gendarmes. I called them, then fell again. Poisonous gases seemed to grip my throat as in a vice. On recovering consciousness, I found my aide-de-camp, Captain Colland, standing over me, also a German officer, who offered me a glass of

water. They told me I had swooned, and that the soldiery I had taken for Belgian gendarmes were, in fact, the first band of German troops who had set foot inside the forts.[3]

Lieutenant General Gérard Leman, Liège Garrison

The final fort would surrender on 16 August. For all their courage, Leman and his garrison had little impact on the main advance of the German Army, which had only just completed its rail mobilisation. They may not have achieved much, but the determined resistance of the hitherto barely rated Belgian Army would act as an encouraging example to the Allies in the traumatic weeks that followed.

Plan XVII: the Alsace-Lorraine offensive

The French mobilisation had concentrated all five of their field armies in north-east France by 10 August. Plan XVII had hardly proscribed Joffre's options, for his armies were then well placed to counter-attack north-wards into Belgium, or thrust either side of the German Metz-Thionville fortress complex where Joffre believed the main strength of the German Army would be concentrated. In fact, his first operation had already been launched on the right flank, close to the Swiss border, when the First Army was ordered to send forward its VII Corps under the command of General Louis Bonneau. French troops had crossed the German border on 7 August in an effort to secure an early morale-enhancing victory on the sacred soil of Alsace. At first they met with very little resistance and pushed forwards to take the town of Altkirsch after a brief skirmish which was topped off as per the manual with a dramatic bayonet charge. They then pushed on to take Mulhouse on 8 August without further opposition. All seemed well, but this was far too weak a force to be pressing so deep into hostile territory. The German Seventh Army, commanded by General Josias von Heeringen, was preparing a counter-attack, hoping to cut off the presumptuous invaders. But then again, the French considered themselves anything but interlopers, as can be seen from Joffre's stirring proclamation to the people of Alsace.

> Children of Alsace! After forty-four years of sorrowful waiting, French soldiers once more tread the soil of your noble country. They are the pioneers in the great work of revenge. For them what emotions it

calls forth, and what pride! To complete the work they have made the sacrifice of their lives. The French nation unanimously urges them on, and in the folds of their flag are inscribed the magic words, 'Right and Liberty. Long live Alsace. Long live France'.[4]

General Joseph Joffre, General Headquarters, French Army

The French would not celebrate for long. On 9 August the German forces stormed back, unceremoniously ejecting the French from Mulhouse and, with no significant reserves available, Bonneau pulled swiftly back to Belfort on 10 August in order to avoid being cut off by the superior German forces massing against him. This chastening dénouement provided a somewhat cruel disillusionment to all those French Alsatians who had prematurely celebrated the relief of Mulhouse. Overall it had been a humiliating experience. Recriminations were swift and Joffre dismissed the hesitant Bonneau, who was somewhat unfairly blamed for this reverse.

Although irritated at this failure, Joffre still believed that the Germans had not committed their reserve divisions to the frontier battles. He was therefore confident that he would be facing just six, instead of the actual eight, corps in the Alsace-Lorraine area when he launched his main attack there on 14 August, timing it to coincide with the expected Russian offensive on East Prussia. He swiftly bolstered his forces on the right, creating a new Army of Alsace to be commanded by the distinctive figure of General Paul Pau, a one-armed veteran of 1870. This new army would again attack towards Mulhouse and secure the right flank. Alongside it the First Army under General Auguste Dubail would push through the Vosges Mountains and towards the Rhine, while the Second Army under General Édouard de Castelnau would advance on the left, driving towards Morhange. But this was just the first phase of Joffre's planned assault. Once he was clear as to the line of the German assault in Belgium, he planned an attack north of Metz-Thionville striking at the weak hinge of the main German attack. As for the British, it had been reported that they would not be ready for action until 26 August and that in the first instance they would have only four infantry divisions instead of the expected six. Joffre would not wait: why would he? The British forces would be useful, true enough, but they were hardly essential in the greater scheme of things.

As before, the Germans were willing to cede ground as the French advanced across the border into Lorraine. The German Sixth Army, led by Crown Prince Rupprecht, and the Seventh Army, led by General Josias von Heeringen, were acting in accordance with the overall strategy laid down by Moltke, which aimed to suck in the maximum number of French troops. The French armies advanced up to eighteen miles in the first three days of the offensive: Mulhouse fell to Pau, Dubail captured Sarrebourg and de Castelnau's men closed in on Morhange. Throughout, the Germans fought an excellent delaying battle, falling back, trying to avoid committing too many infantry units, while using artillery to inflict heavy casualties. In addition the French were beginning to experience a number of related problems that slowed and confused their advance. The armies were attacking on wide, and widening, fronts, the terrain was often difficult and, in such circumstances, it was all but inevitable that significant gaps would begin to open up between formations. There was also the failure by the French commanders to organise and maintain tactical reserves ready to counter-attack in the event of a reverse. Crown Prince Rupprecht was well aware of the opportunities that lay before him and pleaded to be allowed to go on the offensive. This was strictly contrary to the overall German strategic plan, but short-term tactical temptations overwhelmed long-term good intentions. In the end Moltke gave way and, on 20 August, a crushing counter-attack was launched against the overstretched French Second Army in the Battle of Morhange. The French artillery found themselves outranged by the heavier and better sited German guns and were generally doomed to lose any counter-battery duel. This then left their infantry prey to heavy bombardments prior to German attacks.

When the Second Army fell back in considerable confusion this uncovered the flank of the First Army and then the Army of Alsace. They, too, were forced to surrender their gains and, by 22 August, they had tumbled right back to their original start lines. By this time Rupprecht had lost sight of the overall German strategic vision and was entirely caught up in the excitement of prosecuting his own battles. He envisaged a breakthrough to capture Nancy which would thereby threaten the envelopment of the right flank of the main French forces, thus mirroring the threat to the French left flank posed by the main German advance through Belgium. Once again Moltke assented and Rupprecht launched a major offensive between Toul and Épinel. However, this time the French were in prepared defensive positions rather than straggled across the countryside – and put up a stiff resistance for four long days, thereby consuming huge numbers of German reserves with their dogged resistance. At the same time the French were able to send the equivalent of four army corps to join the battle against the main German assault through Belgium. For the Germans, this ill-considered addition to the main plan was proving very costly.

Plan XVII: the Ardennes offensive

Joffre planned a second great offensive by his Third, Fourth and Fifth Armies striking through the lower Ardennes north of Metz-Thionville to commence on 22 August. The growing awareness of the German presence marching through Belgium further north had already forced a major adjustment in the role of the Fifth Army under the command of General Charles Lanrezac. It was moved across to the north-west to take up a line along the River Sambre, ready to attack the German right wing when it appeared; that offensive intent makes it evident that Joffre still did not appreciate the extent of the threat to his own left flank. His mind was still firmly centred on the Ardennes offensive, intended to break through the German centre and threaten the flank of the German Second Army wheeling through Belgium. The Fourth Army, commanded by General Fernand de Langle de Cary, was to move on Neufchâteau in the central Ardennes, while the Third Army under General Pierre Ruffey would advance towards Virton and Metz. Here it would encounter head-on the German Fourth Army commanded by Duke Albrecht von Württemberg and the Fifth Army commanded by Crown Prince Friedrich Wilhelm, which had been pushing cautiously into the Ardennes, carefully entrenching at every pause. The series of encounter battles that ensued on 22 August were bloody affairs, complicated by the wooded hilly terrain and poor visibility caused by fog. When the French advanced they often found the Germans dug in on the forward edge of thick woods.

In a day of disasters for the French the worst calamity was that suffered by the 3rd Colonial Division at Rossignol some ten miles south of Neufchâteau. Six battalions launched successive attacks on entrenched German troops in the woods just north of the village. Much of the fighting was confused in the extreme.

We spotted some infantry in the bushes on our right; they soon fell back, running. A voice cried out from our Company, 'Don't shoot, they're French!' Lieutenant Colonel Vitart beckoned me towards him, shouting out loud, for the noise was deafening, 'Extend to the right and at them with the bayonet!' I return to my Company and give the command, 'Forward the Seventh: fix bayonets!' Followed by my four sections I entered the woods as ordered. We moved quickly, on the road near to us we can hear the bugles calling – it lifted the men – they were a superb sight. But the wood was thick and as the sections advanced at varying speeds, soon I could no longer see all of my company. We advanced 300 to 400 metres. The charge was hardly begun when it faltered under rapid fire at close range from the enemy sheltering behind earthworks. Several of the Germans wearing Silesian shakos, were standing to get a better sight of us. One of them took a deliberate aim at me – his shot struck the Sergeant at my side – but he himself fell almost simultaneously. The officers of colonial troops did not wear the kepi cover and their distinctive headdress made them obvious targets. The fighting became confused, my sections were dispersed – I could not see my No. 2 Section, I looked back and saw that the No. 3 and No. 4 Sections had not followed our advance, they were facing the road firing straight ahead. I could clearly hear the orders shouted – or rather bellowed – by the enemy commanders. I got the impression that my company was going to be split in two. A soldier came up and reported, 'Lieutenant Fichefeux is dead!' He was the leader of the No. 1 Section. I set off immediately to the leading section with the aim of moving them towards the No. 2 Section. But I barely had time to go a few steps before I got a bullet that hammered into the top of my left arm. The shoulder was shattered, my arm left hanging only by pieces of flesh. I fell half-fainting.[5]

Captain Ignard, 1st Colonial Infantry Regiment

The French *poilus* were obvious enough in their red and blue uniforms, but their officers stood out even more, adorned as they were with white kepis and gloves. Rossignol witnessed a terrible slaughter. Captain Ignard, although badly wounded, was in a sense lucky: the post-war monument for the 3rd Colonial Division commemorates 4,083 soldiers killed on 22 August. Their total losses are estimated at 10,500 killed, wounded and taken prisoner out of a total of some 15,000.

In these battles few people at any level of command had much idea of what was happening and for the troops on the ground it was all utterly baffling. Pre-war tactics seemed to have no impact. Bayonet charges led only to more slaughter, while calling up artillery support was often doomed to failure.

> How was I to get forward in these conditions? The answer to this question was quite instinctive: I must call on the support of the artillery. I sent a note to the colonel to let him know the situation and to ask for the assistance of the artillery. At that time no officer was attached to liaise between the battalion making an attack and the gun batteries charged with supporting the assault.[6]
>
> Lieutenant Colonel Pierre Lebaud, 1st Battalion, 101st Infantry Regiment

Lebaud appealed in vain as he did not get the help he needed so badly. Sometimes the gunners were too far behind, sometimes too close and caught under fire from the longer-range German guns. Whatever the reason, the infantry were often left in desperate straits.

> My Company was sustaining heavy losses. Evidently its action was hampering the enemy who concentrated the combined fire of his infantry, artillery and machine guns on us. We were surrounded by a heavy cloud which at times completely veiled the battlefield from our eyes. Little Bergeyre sprang up, shouted, 'Vive la France!' at the top of his voice and fell dead. Among the men lying on the ground one could no longer distinguish the living from the dead. The first were entirely absolved by their grim duty, the others lay motionless. The wounded offered a truly impressive sight. Sometimes they would stand up bloody and horrible looking, amidst bursts of gunfire. They ran aimlessly around arms stretched out before them, eyes staring at the ground, turning round and round until, hit by fresh bullets, they would stop and fall heavily. Heart-rending cries, agonising appeals and horrible groans were intermingled with the sinister howling of projectiles. Furious contortions told of strong and youthful bodies refusing to give up life. One man was trying to replace his bloody dangling hand to his shattered wrist. Another ran from the line holding the bowels falling out of his belly and through his tattered clothes. Before long a bullet struck him down. We had no support from our artillery! And yet there were guns in our division and in the army corps, besides those destroyed on the road. Where were they? Why didn't they arrive? We were alone![8]
>
> Captain Alphonse Grasset, 103rd Regiment

Lacking the experience of realistic peacetime manoeuvres the French artillery batteries were relatively ineffective in comparison to their well-drilled
German counterparts. Unsure of their targets and unable to open fire, the
French guns had often been caught out in the open fields as the morning
mists cleared away.

> Near the crest of the hill we took up our position on the edge of an
> oat field. The limbers went off to the rear to shelter somewhere in the
> direction of Latour, the steeple of which could be seen overtopping the
> trees in the valley on our left. Crouching behind the armoured doors
> of the ammunition wagons and behind the gun shields, we awaited
> the order to open fire. But the Captain, kneeling down among the oats
> in front of the battery, his field-glasses to his eyes, could discover no
> target, for yonder, over the spreading woods of Ethe and Etalle, now
> occupied by the enemy, a thick mist was still floating. All round us,
> behind our guns, over our heads, and without respite, high-explosive
> and shrapnel shells of every calibre kept bursting and strewing the
> position with bullets and splinters. Death seemed inevitable. Behind the
> gun was a small pit in which I took refuge while we waited for orders.
> A big bay saddle-horse with a gash in his chest from which a red stream
> flowed, stood motionless in the middle of the field. What with the
> hissing and whistling of the shells, the thunder of the enemy's guns,
> and the roar from a neighbouring 75 mm battery, it was impossible to
> distinguish the different noises in this shrieking inferno of fire, smoke,
> and flames. The battery became enveloped in black, nauseating smoke.
> Somebody was groaning, and I got up to see what had happened.
> Through the yellow fog I saw Sergeant Thierry stretched on the ground
> and the six members of the detachment crowding round him. The shell
> had burst under the chase of his gun, smashing the recoil-buffer, and
> effectually putting the piece out of action.[8]
>
> Gunner Paul Lintier, 11th Battery, 44th Artillery Regiment

Often the only positive thing the French could do was retreat before they
were over-run by the Germans.

> Over the crest of the hill came some infantry in retreat. The sound of
> the machine-guns approached and eventually became distinguishable
> from the roar of the artillery. The enemy was advancing and we were
> giving way before them. Shells continued to fly over us, and entire
> companies of infantry fell back. The officers consulted together. 'But

what are we to do? There are no orders, no orders!' the Major kept repeating. And still we waited. The Lieutenant had drawn his revolver and the gunners unslung their rifles. The German batteries, possibly afraid of hitting their own troops, ceased firing. At any moment now the enemy might set foot on the ridge. 'Limber up!' The order was quickly carried out. We had to carry Thierry, whose knee was broken, with us. He was suffering horribly and implored us not to touch him. In spite of his protests, however, three men lifted him on to the observation-ladder. He was very pale and looked ready to faint. 'Oh!' he murmured. 'You are hurting me! Can't you finish me?' The rest of the wounded, five or six in number, hoisted themselves without assistance on to the limbers and the battery swung down the Latour road at a quick trot. We had lost the battle.[9]

Gunner Paul Lintier, 11th Battery, 44th Artillery Regiment

At the end of that terrible day, up and down the battlefield the French fell back.

In the evening we gathered in a field at the entrance to Harnoncourt. Without doubt we were going to billet there overnight. But no! After having checked our arrangements my company went on – exhausted!! We marched for ages, climbing the hillsides, passing along narrow paths, shattered, we penetrated deep into a wood. A civilian guide was leading us. It was a very black night, walking in single file we were obliged to keep in physical touch to prevent us getting lost as we couldn't see each other. There was absolute silence. We marched for a long, long time. Tangled up in the bushes, we marched in the mud, the water, without a clue of where we were going. We fell down with fatigue, we wanted to sleep. Suddenly we heard a cry of bewilderment. One man has lost touch with the man in front of him. We are lost! Alone in this huge dark wood, traversed by Uhlan patrols. The officers weren't with us! What were we to do? We stood still. You listen out – nothing! You whistle – nothing! You shout out – still nothing! We are panicking! What about our officers left with only four or five men? What about ourselves? What was to become of us left stewing in our ignorance in the long black night? At last we retraced our steps to the edge of the forest and fell asleep awaiting the dawn.[10]

Private Alfred Joubaire, 1st Battalion, 124th Infantry Regiment

The battlefield was littered with French units retreating in various states of confusion and disarray, physically or metaphorically lost. It had been a day to remember for all the wrong reasons: it is shocking to record that some 27,000 Frenchmen died on 22 August alone. This was an almost unprecedented slaughter in the long history of warfare.

> All day I was fighting, I was slightly wounded by a bullet that went through my haversack, passed through my overcoat, scraped across my chest and hit me in the hand. I show the bullet to my friend, Marcel Loiseau, and put it in my wallet. I continue the fight, until Loiseau is hit in the leg and we see my lieutenant cut through by a bullet. The fight goes on, a lot of my friends lying dead or wounded all around me. About 3 o'clock in the afternoon, while shooting at the enemy occupying a trench 200 metres from me, I was hit by a bullet in the left side, I felt a terrible pain as if I'd broken a bone. The bullet passed through the whole of my body, through the pelvis and lodged above the knee. Immediately I was suffering greatly with a burning fever. The bullets continue to rain down all around me, I may be hit again, so I do my best to drag myself into a hole, I find it hard to gain any comfort. The fight is over: all my comrades have retreated, and we wounded are left without care, dying of thirst. What an awful night! Nothing but more shooting, every sound made by the wounded triggered a resumption of fire. Machine guns swept the ground, bullets flying over my head, but they can no longer touch me in my hole. Thirst tortures me more. As I suffer, I think about my parents, especially my mother, remembering when I was sick and very young. It wasn't only me thinking of their mothers, for I could hear the wounded and dying calling out for their 'Maman'.[11]
>
> Private Désiré Renault, 3rd Battalion, 77th Infantry Regiment

It was a terrible night not only for those, like Renault, who had been wounded and would ultimately be picked up and made prisoner by the Germans, but also for those who had been left unscathed but who could hear their comrades suffering with little hope of rescue.

> Night fell. The cold became intense. This is the time, when the battle is over, that the wounded that we haven't yet found, cry out loud in their pain and suffering. And these shouts, these plaintive cries, these moans torment all those who can hear them; an especially cruel punishment for soldiers who must stick to their post, when all they wanted to do was run to the gasping comrades, to tend to them, to comfort them.

But they cannot, they must remain static, weighed down by a heavy heart, raw nerves, actually trembling at the unceasing frantic calls in the night. 'Drink! Are we going to let me die here?' 'Stretcher-bearers!' 'Drink!' 'Stretcher-bearers!' 'I hear one my men say, 'Yes, what the bloody hell are they doing, the stretcher-bearers? They only know how to hide, those pigs! It's like the police; you never see one when you need one!' And before us the dark shadow seems to groan with all the wounds that bled and were not dressed. Faint voices, weary from crying out: 'What have I done to get killed in this war?' 'Mother, oh mother!' 'Jeanne, my little Jeanne! Oh, say that you can hear me, my Jeanne?' 'I'm thirsty! I'm thirsty! I'm thirsty! I'm thirsty!' The cries appal us, they cut us to the quick. 'I don't want to die here, oh God!' 'Stretcher-bearers! Stretcher-bearers!' 'Bastards! Is there no one with any pity?' A German (he can't have been more than 20 metres away) intones, *'Kamerad Franzose! Kamerad! Kamerad Franzose!'* And lower down, pleading: *'Hilfe! Hilfe!'* His voice bends, breaks and quavers like a crying child. Then his screeching grows and all night long he was like a dog howling to the moon. It was a dreadful night.[12]

Lieutenant Maurice Genevoix, 106th Infantry Regiment

The next day Joffre wanted to renew the offensive but was soon thwarted. It was simply impossible to reorganise the shattered units; more pertinently, the Germans were driving deep into the French, throwing the Third and Fourth Armies right back to their start lines. There was widespread chaos; no one knew what was happening and terrible mistakes were made which added to the massive casualty toll. Certainly it was typical that the senior officers of the 300th Infantry Regiment seemed to have no grasp whatsoever of the urgency of the situation as they began their retreat on 24 August.

The weather continued to be splendid. Colonel Colombier, commanding the Regiment, gave the order the evening before to dump in the nearest field to their primitive trenches, the sheaves of straw which the men had gathered to help spend the night in the wood. This task although hardly explicable in the circumstances, was nevertheless carried out punctually and without much complaint. At last when everything was ready to set out on the march, another order was issued for the officers and NCOs to inspect their men to ensure they were correct in their marching order. After a good half hour devoted to the execution of these various orders emanating from another era, the Battalion was finally on the road, the regimental transport at the head of the column, followed by Colonel Colombier on his horse, with each of the four Companies marching behind in columns of four but there was a failure to put into effect any of the precautionary measures necessary for any movement in the field – the vanguard, flankguard or rearguard detachments. We had hardly gone 100 metres when we spotted behind us an artillery battery galloping along at full speed in our direction in the middle of a veritable dust storm. Everyone was convinced that they could not be anything but French artillery and the battalion continued to march quietly onwards. When they got to within 400 or 500 metres of us the artillerymen dismounted and dropped their battery into action: in less time than it takes to write shells were raining down on our heads. At the centre and rear of our column a hail of 77 mm shells burst with great force in the ploughed fields and enveloped us all in a thick cloud. This surprise attack was all the more unexpected because everyone was convinced that other French units were staying behind to protect our backs. It had the effect of creating panic in the ranks and there was a terrible disorder as the men, deaf to the appeals of their NCOs, began dumping their equipment to allow them to run faster, dashing madly towards the Forêt du Banel, a distance of about 100 metres away. Some of them were shouting, 'Treason!' but it was all really the fault of our Colonel, who failed, through sheer short-sightedness, to take even the most elementary precautions.[13]

Lieutenant Jacques Cisterne, 4th Battalion, 300th Infantry Regiment

This was a reserve unit unexpectedly caught up in the action, but the colonel's attitude was symptomatic of an inability among a whole generation of French officers to realise the serious nature of war.

Yet it was not all one-way traffic. This was open warfare and the Germans, too, could be caught unawares. When they had the chance, the French 75 mm guns could provide formidable opposition. At Marville on 25 August Lintier's guns could at last open up with their own deadly staccato fire.

'Fire!' The gun reared like a frightened horse. I was shaken from head to foot, my skull throbbing and my ears tingling as though with the jangle of enormous bells which had been rung close to them. A long tongue of fire had darted out of the muzzle, and the wind caused

by the round raised a cloud of dust round us. The ground quaked. I
noticed an unpleasant taste in my mouth, musty at first and acrid after
a few seconds. That was the powder. I hardly knew whether I tasted
it or smelled it. We continued firing, rapidly, without stopping, the
movements of the men co-ordinated, precise and quick. There was no
talking, gestures sufficing to control the manoeuvre. The only words
audible were the range orders given by the Captain and repeated by the
Nos. 1. 'Two thousand five hundred!' 'Fire!' 'Two thousand five hundred
and twenty-five!' 'Fire!' After the first round the gun was firmly settled,
and the gun-layer and the firing number now installed themselves on
their seats behind the shield. On firing, the steel barrel of the 75 mm
gun recoils on the guides of the hydraulic buffer, and then quietly and
gently returns to battery, ready for the next round. Behind the gun
there was soon a heap of blackened cartridge cases, still smoking.[14]

Gunner Paul Lintier, 11th Battery, 44th Artillery Regiment

Somewhere those shells were streaming down from the skies, killing and
maiming Germans. This was what the famous 'soixante-quinze' had been
designed to do. But they were soon located by German aircraft, those
eyes in the skies that were something new to warfare. Once they spotted
the battery positions, they used flares to work a simple system of artillery
observation bringing shells down on their target.

Another aeroplane; the same black hawk silhouetted against the pale
blue sky which at every moment was getting brighter. The men swore
and shook their fists. What tyranny! It was marking us down! Suddenly
the enemy's heavy artillery opened fire on the hills we were occupying
as well as on a neighbouring wood. It was time to change position,
since for us the most perilous moment is when the teams come up to
join the guns. A battery is then extremely vulnerable. Before the enemy
could correct his range the Major gave an order and we moved off to
take up a fresh position.[15]

Gunner Paul Lintier, 11th Battery, 44th Artillery Regiment

Thus the French gunners were harassed incessantly as the retreat continued.

OVERALL IT WAS EVIDENT that the Germans were more tactically astute,
better equipped and far more skilled and drilled in the arts of war than

their opponents. It was not that the French did not fight hard: instances of sangfroid and heroism, grit and determination abound. But it was all for nothing. The 24-year-old Lieutenant Charles de Gaulle summed up the essence of the experience in a few short words.

> Suddenly the enemy's fire became precise and concentrated. Second by second the hail of bullets and the thunder of the shells grew stronger. Those who survived lay flat on the ground, amid the screaming wounded and the humble corpses. With affected calm, the officers let themselves be killed standing upright, some obstinate platoons stuck their bayonets in their rifles, bugles sounded the charge, isolated heroes made fantastic leaps, but all to no purpose. In an instant it had become clear that not all the courage in the world could withstand this fire.[16]
>
> Lieutenant Charles de Gaulle, 33rd Infantry Regiment

The tragic outcome was evident for all to see. French casualties during these failed offensives exceeded 200,000, of which over 75,000 were dead in just a few days of desperate fighting. They elicited little sympathy from their German opponents, as witnessed by a young German civilian, William Hermanns, in Koblenz.

> I saw French prisoners escorted over the Rhine bridge to the fortress Ehrenbreitstein. They wore red trousers, and the people were amused that France should send its soldiers as living targets against our troops that were so efficiently camouflaged in uniforms of earth grey. Women singing 'Deutschland Über Alles', accompanied these prisoners-of-war. I watched a well-dressed woman shout in French to one of the prisoners, who was wearing patent leather shoes, 'You thought you'd dance into Germany, didn't you?'[17]
>
> William Hermanns, Koblenz

The Battle of the Frontiers was not just a disaster for the French Army; it was a disaster for the whole French nation.

The Schlieffen Plan: advance through Belgium

The worst threat was yet to come. The Battle of the Frontiers had not gone well for France, but the main drive would be launched by the German First Army commanded by General Alexander von Kluck on the far right flank, alongside the Second Army under General Karl von Bülow and the Third Army commanded by General Max von Hausen – together a truly formidable force. The Germans advanced through Belgium, capturing Brussels and sweeping aside the Belgian Army, which fell back on Antwerp. The only real opposition facing them was the French Fifth Army commanded by General Charles Lanrezac, who, with just fifteen divisions, found himself confronted by the thirty-eight divisions of the German Second and Third Armies. Lanrezac had long been worried by the vulnerability of his left flank, where it was intended to station the four divisions of the British Expeditionary Force when they had completed their mobilisation and concentration at Maubeuge. But Joffre did not share Lanrezac's misgivings, not least because he underestimated the scale of the German onslaught. This led to a series of confrontations that soured relations between the two men without achieving anything concrete. By the time there was unequivocal evidence that Lanrezac was right it was almost too late, but Joffre grudgingly allowed the Fifth Army to move towards Namur in Belgium. By 20 August, Lanrezac had stationed I Corps as a flank guard on the right looking east across the River Meuse with his main strength of the X, III and XVIII Corps disposed along the River Sambre looking more to the north. Joffre had still not grasped the scale of the German threat and issued orders for the Fifth Army for an attack across the Sambre on 21 August. This offensive intent would be forestalled when von Bülow's Second Army launched its own offensive, crossing the Sambre between Namur and Charleroi. Over the next two days of severe fighting known as the Battle of Charleroi, the Fifth Army was attacked on both flanks and forced back, first from the Sambre, then from the Meuse. Lanrezac's position was dire and he had no chance of help from the neighbouring Fourth Army, which was busy fighting for its very existence in the Ardennes.

The Battle of Mons, 23 August 1914

Amidst all the mayhem of the Battle of the Frontiers, the BEF had been making its way to the front. The BEF was ridiculously small for a country with the imperial pretensions of Great Britain. Just four divisions and the equivalent of a cavalry division were sent to France under the command of General Sir John French. Born in 1852, French had had a glittering career culminating in considerable success as a cavalry leader in the Boer

War. This had been followed by further rapid promotion and he was Chief of Imperial General Staff from 1912 to 1914. His task was complicated by the necessity of falling in with the plans of Joffre, clearly the man in charge of the overall campaign, while Lanrezac, as the commander of the neighbouring Fifth Army, disposed a force that dwarfed the BEF. Hence Anglo-French relations would be crucial and in hindsight it is doubtful whether French's relatively slim staff experience qualified him for the diplomatic intricacies of alliance warfare. He did not speak French and he had a reputation for irascibility. In this at least he would meet his match in Joffre!

The BEF I Corps (1st and 2nd Divisions) was commanded by Lieutenant General Sir Douglas Haig. Born in 1861, he too was a cavalry officer with a distinguished record of service in both the Sudan and Boer Wars. Haig, however, had a sharper intelligence than French, combined with brilliant organisational skills and a mind more open to new ideas. He had excelled in a series of pre-war staff appointments and indeed, while Director of Military Training at the War Office, had been partially responsible for the creation of Britain's Territorial Army. Haig had already been marked down as a future Commander in Chief, but the war had come too early for him to ascend to that post. The II Corps (3rd and 5th Divisions) was commanded by General Sir Horace Smith-Dorrien, who had taken over at short notice following the untimely death of its original commander, Lieutenant General Sir James Grierson. Born in 1858, Smith-Dorrien was a career infantry officer who had managed to survive the massacre at the Battle of Isandlwana on 22 January 1879 during the Zulu War. He then had considerable success during widespread active service during the Egypt, Tirah, Sudan and Boer War campaigns, followed by stints at the Aldershot and Southern Command.

The BEF was a highly trained force made up entirely of volunteer soldiers. Men served seven years with the colours and were then liable to a further five years in the reserves. The British Army had learnt a great deal in the Boer War, but lacked any experience of modern warfare against a comparable European opponent. The individual soldiers were armed with the bolt-action Short Magazine Lee Enfield (SMLE) Mark III rifle. It had been introduced in 1907 and was very accurate up to about 600 yards, while the ten-round magazine allowed a trained rifleman to fire around fifteen aimed rounds a minute. Each battalion was equipped with two of the excellent Maxim or Vickers machine guns. The British gunners were equipped with the 18-pounders or 4.5 inch howitzers, both fine quick-firing field artillery pieces with a range of up to 6,500 yards. However, as with the French, there was little provision of heavy artillery. Furthermore, artillery tactics were primitive and pre-war field exercises had done little to prepare them for their role in a modern battlefield. Concepts such as indirect firing or prolonged barrages were simply not understood. But the defining characteristic of the BEF as a military force was its size: it was as the Kaiser memorably put it 'a contemptible little army', although this more reflects German frustration than any considered indictment.

The BEF had begun landing in France on 12 August and then moved up to its designated concentration area at Maubeuge. The deployment had been somewhat delayed and it was not until 21 August that it began to edge into Belgium. On the afternoon of 22 August the BEF reached the town of Mons. Despite reports of attacks on the neighbouring French Army, coupled with cavalry and aerial reconnaissances, there was still a great deal of confusion as to the exact nature of the threat facing the BEF.

> That night I was happy in my mind, for official news of the enemy given me indicated no great strength, and I fully expected that the Chief's expressed intention of moving forward again next day would be carried out. I had been given no information of the somewhat serious happenings in the French army on our right, which I learned years later, namely, that it had been forced back, and was already some 9 miles south of Mons with a gap of at least 9 miles between the right of our II Corps and the left of the XVIII French Corps, thus leaving us in a very vulnerable, indefensible and salient position. Had I known of this serious situation I doubt much if my night's rest would have been as enjoyable as it proved to be – for I should have been racking my brain as to what the object of our remaining so isolated was and why we did not retire. Mercifully, I was in blissful ignorance – nor was I disillusioned next morning when at about 6 am the Chief appeared at my headquarters, and, addressing his Corps and Cavalry Division commanders assembled there, told us that little more than one, or at most two, enemy Corps, with perhaps a Cavalry Division, were facing the BEF. So it was evident that he, too, was in blissful ignorance of the real situation. Sir John was in excellent form, and told us to be prepared to move forward, or to fight where we were, but to get ready for the

latter by strengthening our outposts and preparing the bridges over the canal for demolition.[18]

General Sir Horace Smith-Dorrien, Headquarters, II Corps

In the event, 23 August would find the II Corps in a defensive line stretching along the Mons–Condé Canal, while the I Corps was echeloned back towards the left of the French Fifth Army. This position had several weaknesses: in particular around Mons itself there was an extremely awkward salient, but elsewhere there were inadequate fields of fire, poor artillery positions and a lack of effective protection from shell fire.

When von Kluck's First Army crashed into Smith-Dorrien's II Corps from 06.00 on 23 August, the battle that ensued was to enter British military folklore. The myth is one of a heroic successful defence, with well-trained British 'Tommies' mowing down hordes of German repeatedly attacking in mass formations. Finally, the British would be forced to retreat only because the fickle French had given way on their right flank. This view of the battle is a great yarn but, like the 'Angels of Mons', at heart it is the product of wishful thinking.

The reality was very different. For one thing, the 'battle-hardened' British soldiers of legend were anything but. Some had had experience more than a decade before in the Boer War, but they were in the minority. Most had never seen action and their training exercises bore little resemblance to the reality of war. In particular they had no concept of battle inoculation. Tucked away in many of the accounts of the battles are clues that even the much-vaunted British musketry could waver under the supreme stress and excitement of battle.

> We got into a position on the embankment and as the enemy
> came through the wood about 200 yards in front, they presented
> a magnificent target, and we opened rapid fire. The men were very
> excited as this was their first 'shot in anger'. Despite the short range a
> number of them were firing high but I found it hard to control the fire
> as there was so much noise. Eventually I drew my sword and walked
> along the line beating the men on the backside and, as I got their
> attention, telling them to fire low. So much for all our beautiful fire
> orders taught in peacetime![19]

Lieutenant George Roupell, 1st East Surrey Regiment

The British were convinced that they were massively outnumbered and there are many accounts redolent of massed formations. One such is that of Private Tom Bradley, who was occupying a shallow scraped rifle pit close to the canal bridge at Obourg to the west of Mons. As he recalled, the Germans attacked in great close-order columns.

> They went down like ninepins until all we could see in front of us was a regular wall of dead and wounded. Above the noise of rifle fire, you could hear a strange wailing sound and they turned and ran for the cover of the fir trees.[20]
>
> Private Tom Bradley, 4th Middlesex Regiment

Unfortunately, there is little evidence to substantiate this somewhat fanciful version of events. It certainly bears no resemblance to most German accounts, which seem to indicate that their infantry advanced in open order, but only after having attempted to win the fire fight by bringing up both machine guns and artillery. British historians seek confirmation in their views through the account of the novelist Captain Walter Bloem of the German 12th Infantry Regiment. This single overblown account has become the holy grail for all who believe that the Germans were slaughtered in their thousands at Mons. But even Bloem makes clear reference to the Germans advancing in a series of controlled rushes.

> We had no sooner left the edge of the wood than a volley of bullets whistled past our noses and cracked into the trees behind. Five or six cries near me, five or six of my grey lads collapsed on the grass. Damn it! This was serious. The firing seemed at long range and half-left. 'Forward!' I shouted, taking my place with three of my 'staff' ten paces in front of the section leader, Holder-Egger, and the section in well-extended formation ten paces behind him again. Here we were, advancing as if on a parade ground. 'Huitt, huitt, srr, srr, srr!' about our ears, away in front a sharp, rapid hammering sound, then a pause, then more rapid hammering – machine guns. Over to our left the rifle and machine gun fire was even more intense, the roar of guns and bursting shells increasing. A real battle this time![21]
>
> Captain Walter Bloem, 2nd Battalion, 12th Infantry Regiment

There seems to have been a failure in the 12th Infantry Regiment sector to deploy the artillery sufficiently far forward to give the infantry the support it needed to win the firefight. Bloem claims that his beloved battalion, the Regiment even, was all but destroyed, though this was an exaggeration as the three battalions of the 12th Regiment between them suffered some 600 casualties – severe losses, no doubt, but nothing like as many as some have claimed. Furthermore, this was the exception and most of the German units involved seemed to have escaped such a serious drubbing.

As to the II Corps being undefeated and forced to fall back only to conform with the French on their right flank, this is pure nonsense. The reality is that on many occasions the Germans seemed to have been all too successful in forcing a retreat.

> We held the Germans all day, killing hundreds, when about 5 pm the order to retire was eventually given. It never reached us and we were left all alone. The Germans got right up to the canal on our right, hidden by the railway embankment and crossed the railway. Our people had blown up the bridge before their departure. We found ourselves alone and I realised we had about two thousand Germans and a canal between myself and friends. We decided to sell our lives dearly. I ordered my men to fix bayonets and charge, which the gallant fellows did splendidly, but we got shot down like ninepins. As I loaded my revolver I was hit in the right wrist. I dropped my revolver; my hand was too weak to draw my sword, this afterwards saved my life! I had not gone far when I got a bullet through the calf of my right leg, which brought me down. Those who could walk the Germans took away as prisoners. As regards myself, when I lay upon the ground I found my coat sleeve full of blood, so I knew an artery of some sort had been cut. The Germans had a shot at me when I was on the ground to finish me off, that shot hit my sword, which I wore on my side, and broke it in half, just below the hilt; this turned the bullet off and saved my life. We lay out there a night, for 24 hours. I had fainted from loss of blood and when I lost my senses I thought I should never see anything again.[22]
>
> Captain William Morritt, 1st East Surrey Regiment

Luckily for Morritt he had fallen across his wounded arm so that the weight of his body acted as a kind of tourniquet and staunched the flow of blood. He was picked up the next day along with eight other wounded men by local Belgian civilians and sheltered in a convent before being discovered and captured by the Germans.

It is undeniable that several of the British battalions fought well, but modern scholarship[23] has revealed that the Germans manoeuvred skilfully to secure a local superiority against the weak points in the British defences. Wherever possible they operated against the flanks, forcing the British to fall back or risk being cut off and totally destroyed. Throughout, the Germans seem to have handled their artillery and machine guns with a great tactical dexterity borne of long practice, operating them in tandem to dominate the British in the fire fight, effectively rendering rifle fire of secondary importance. The British were turned out of their defensive positions in a matter of a few hours and even failed to destroy several of the canal bridges. Both the immediate flanks were threatened and the Germans had broken through to seize Mons itself. The higher estimates of German casualties suffered at Mons – which can reach as high as 10,000 – are apparently extrapolated from the fate of the 12th Infantry Regiment and have no basis in fact. Germanophile historians[24] indicate that they may have been as low as about 2,000 killed or wounded, which is comparable to the 1,600 killed, wounded and missing suffered by the British. Although many German accounts mention the admirable skill of the British musketry it was probably the least important aspect of a battle resolved by tactical manoeuvres and the efficient utilisation of infantry, artillery and machine guns to attain specific tactical objectives. In particular, the British defence was static, with no use of reserves and a severe lack of co-ordination between neighbouring units.

When the great retreat from Mons began, the BEF soon found that von Kluck's First Army was in close pursuit. The I and II Corps were soon physically separated as they fell back on either side of the Forest of Mormal. Hard-pressed as he was and with his troops betraying signs of exhaustion, Smith-Dorrien decided that if the II Corps (by this time augmented by the belatedly arrived 4th Division) was to have any chance of properly disengaging from their pursuers then they must turn and fight to try to dissuade the Germans from following so closely. The II Corps took up positions near Le Cateau stretching some ten miles through to Beauvois. But the defensive positions selected were often poorly sited; there was no time to dig proper trenches; and the artillery was once again often placed too far forward, with many batteries consequently in plain view of the Germans. There was only a feeble tactical reserve held in hand to allow Smith-Dorrien the chance to intervene in the battle. The Battle of Le Cateau on 26 August that followed bore many similarities to Mons. The overblown British accounts claiming miracles cannot mask the fact that the Germans had rather the better of the clash. The truth might be indicated by the casualty figures: the British officially lost some 7,812 killed, wounded and missing (2,600 of them prisoners), while estimates of the total German losses come in at around 2,900. While some individual British battalions or batteries resisted with great courage, overall they had not fought well or cohesively as brigade, division, corps or even army. Communications, command and control were all poor or non-existent, and with good reason: the BEF was both new to the task at hand and had no practical experience of the sheer complexities of modern warfare. After the battle the French certainly thought the British had been beaten, and the Germans were convinced they had won. The German pursuit was complicated not so much by a 'bloody nose', as the British assumed, but more delayed by nightfall and von Kluck's failure to anticipate correctly the direction of Smith-Dorrien's retreat.

Following Le Cateau the whole of the BEF was in retreat. Often marching day and night, the troops paid scant attention to the needs of the swarms of Belgian refugees that clogged the roads.

> One of the saddest sights of that day, was the huge columns of refugees on the main road to Guise. Carts heaped with household treasures led by crying women and frightened children. These carts were ruthlessly swept off the road to make a passage for the troops. This was absolutely necessary, of course, in spite of its cruelty. None of these poor people could have crossed the river at Guise, as we had to blow up the bridge after crossing – and held back the fugitives to do it.[25]
>
> Captain Herbert Rees, 2nd Welsh Regiment

On and on they marched. Most officers and men had little idea of where they were, where they were going or what was happening around them. There was a constant underlying fear of some drastic intervention by the much-dreaded Uhlans. The ordinary soldiers were at the end of their tethers. After all, many were reservists who had been out of the Army for several years and were not in peak physical condition.

> All along the road we saw signs of a hurried retreat. Overturned motor and other wagons and dead horses were strewn by the roadside while

numbers of fed-up and exhausted men sat looking disconsolate and cross on the bank. The sight of those men had the effect on our men of making them wonder why they were footslogging along instead of sitting down on a nice bank, for they all of them seemed to become suddenly exhausted and unable to keep up, and from now onwards for a couple of days, my life became a burden to me as I was all the time urging, persuading and even kicking men on. It was no good to explain to them that there was no choice but going on or falling into the hands of the Germans, they simply did not believe me.[26]

Captain Beauchamp Tudor St John, 1st Northumberland Fusiliers

Officers like Tudor St John tried their best to goad their men on while trying to keep order in the swaying, exhausted ranks.

I had already several times gone to sleep while marching and had found myself in the ditch. I gave up trying to drive men back to the ranks. When they fell they knew what was in store for them by now as well as I did! And I knew the agony they must be suffering from their feet, many having raw heels and toes from the hard marching we had done. Not many gave in absolutely. Some would fall out but at the next halt they would come limping in again. The pace to begin with had been killing. We came to paved roadway along which we painfully hobbled. I can't call it anything else. I don't suppose we were doing 2 miles an hour. I myself was suffering from an abscess on my toe which felt like hot knives at every step.[27]

Captain Beauchamp Tudor St John, 1st Northumberland Fusiliers

The BEF fell back to beyond the River Marne in such a poor state that both Sir John French and the French High Command began to wonder whether they would ever be able to stand and fight again. They would have their answer soon enough.

Denouement: the Battle of the Marne

With disaster looming everywhere up and down the front, Allied attention now fell on the portly phlegmatic figure of General Joseph Joffre. The Germans were seeking absolute victory prior to turning their attentions to the Russian Army. Joffre knew that his armies were hurting, but he was also convinced that France was not yet beaten. The French Army was so huge that, just as Moltke the Elder had feared way back in the 1870s, a knock-out blow was extremely difficult for the Germans to deliver. An army of millions had an enormous capacity to absorb punishment. But the French needed sure leadership if they were not to fall apart at the seams. This, then, was Joffre's moment. He had based his General Head-quarters at Vitry-le-François, where early on he had established a routine that would continue through good times and bad. It may not have been exciting or dramatic but the decisions made at the regular meetings would at times decide the fate of nations.

> GHQ at that time consisted of some fifty officers, counting those be-longing to the Services (railways, subsistence, medical department, mail section, code section, motor-cars and headquarters commandant). The routine at GHQ, as established from the very start, continued unchanged throughout the war. There were two reports each day: the first called the Grand Report, was held in my office at 7 a.m; the second took place towards 8 pm. At the Grand Report there were normally present the Chief of Staff, the Assistant Chiefs of Staff, the Director of the Rear, the Chiefs of Bureaux and the officers of my cabinet. At both the morning and evening meetings I was informed as to the contents of reports sent in from the various armies relating the events of the preceding twelve hours, together with all information gathered during that time concerning the enemy. Naturally, if important reports or despatches arrived during the course of the day or night they were immediately presented to me; but the principal interest attaching to the two daily reports consisted in what might be called 'taking our bearings'. At the morning report the general situation was established. I frequently requested the officers present to express their personal opinions on the questions before us; after listening to what they had to say, I gave my decisions.[28]
>
> General Joseph Joffre, General Headquarters, French Army

In many ways Joffre could only progress from the moment he accepted that his original assessments of the situation had been utterly mistaken: the wrong tactics had been followed and, to some extent, the wrong men had been put in charge of operations. One understandable response might have been panic, but that was not Joffre's style. Slowly, methodically, he began working his way through the mass of problems that flowed across his desk.

It was apparent that the principles of the offensive which we had tried to inculcate in the army before the war had often been poorly understood and badly applied. From all points of the front came reports of mistakes made in handling troops, mistakes which had brought about heavy losses and sometimes reduced to nought the offensive and defensive qualities of the men. I was told that advanced guards, through a false comprehension of the offensive spirit, were nearly always sent into action without artillery support and occasionally got caught in close formation under the enemy's artillery fire. Sometimes it would be one of the larger units which, moving forward with its flanks unguarded, would suddenly become exposed to unexpected and costly fire. The infantry was almost always launched to the assault when at too great a distance from its objective. Conquered ground was never organised before starting off to the attack of a new position; in this way, if the latter failed, the troops were driven back without even reaping the fruits of their first effort. Far and beyond all, the co-operation of the infantry and the artillery was constantly neglected.[29]

General Joseph Joffre, General Headquarters, French Army

Joffre issued orders to correct these mistakes, but in the press of battle it was difficult to get a whole army to adjust its long-standing mentality and for new ideas to penetrate. However, there was something he could do about the generals he considered to have been found wanting in action.

When the test came, a large number of our generals had shown that they were not equal to their task. Amongst them were some who in time of peace had enjoyed the most brilliant reputation as professors; there were others who, during map exercises, had displayed a fine comprehension of manoeuvre; but now, in the presence of the enemy, these men appeared to be overwhelmed by the burden of their responsibility. In some of the larger units there had been a complete abdication of command.[30]

General Joseph Joffre, General Headquarters, French Army

Joffre was determined to get the right men in charge. Once people were identified – rightly or wrongly – as too timid, too slow, too stupid or too old, then they were simply replaced by younger, better men.

Joffre also began to consider his tactical options if he was to counter the onrushing march of the German right wing now wheeling through northern France. His staff reviewed the situation but in the end, it was Joffre who decided on the course to be followed.

> My own preference consisted in creating on the outer wing of the enemy a mass capable, in its turn, of enveloping his marching flank. If we were to have time to assemble in the region of Amiens a force large enough to produce a decisive effect against the marching flank of the enemy, it was necessary to accept a further retreat of our armies on the left. But we had reason to hope that by making good use of every obstacle by which the enemy's advance might be retarded, and by delivering frequent counter-attacks, these armies need not fall back farther than the general line of the Aisne, prolonged by the bluffs running from Craonne to Laon and La Fère. The Third Army would rest on the fortifications of Verdun, which would thus serve as a pivot for the general movement in retreat. The French Fourth and Fifth Armies, the British Army and the Amiens group, constituted with forces taken from our right wing, would furnish a mass capable of resuming the offensive at the moment the enemy, debouching from the wooded regions of the Ardennes, would have to fight with this difficult ground lying behind him. My conception was a battle stretching from Amiens to Rheims with the new army placed on the extreme left of our line, outside of the British and in a position to outflank the German right.[31]
>
> General Joseph Joffre, General Headquarters, French Army

To build up this powerful new army on the left of the line, Joffre had to act decisively, taking risks in stripping divisions or even corps from the armies already fully engaged in fighting the Germans right along the front. This meant taking up a decidedly defensive posture in most places, which, given the disaster of 22 August, was probably no bad thing. Nevertheless it would prove an amazing achievement in the midst of such a hectic campaign; more than that, it was a logistical marvel. But the end result was the creation of a new Sixth Army on the left flank of the fast retreating BEF. Victory has many fathers but Joffre certainly deserves much credit for his decisive role in setting in motion the course of events that others would drive to victory. In one particular matter, Joffre needed all his calm to maintain any semblance of Entente Cordial.

> French came in, accompanied by General Murray, his Chief of Staff. I expected to find the same calm officer whose acquaintance

I had made a few days before; but, to my great surprise, the British Commander in Chief started out immediately in a rather excited tone to explain that his army had been violently attacked, and that, the evening before, General Haig's corps had been obliged to fall back on Guise and the Cavalry Corps on Bohain (that is to say, into the zone assigned to the French Fifth Army); that his II Corps and General Snow's 4th Division were being pressed by the enemy in the direction of Le Catelet. He explained to me that since hostilities had begun his troops had been submitted to such hardships that he could not for the moment contemplate resuming the offensive. He considered the situation as being very delicate. More than once he made complaints concerning the manner in which the Fifth Army, his neighbour, had acted. He accused this army of having broken off the fight and left him completely isolated. In reply, I said to the Field Marshal that all the Allied troops without exception had been pushed hard by the enemy and that he must not suppose that the British Army was the only one which had suffered from the severe conditions of the campaign.[32]

General Joseph Joffre, General Headquarters, French Army

The British perception of the retreat was centred around their own concerns, while giving scant consideration to the situation of the French. But from the French perspective the BEF was failing to pull even its meagre weight, falling back faster than either the French Fifth Army on the right or the Sixth Army, still under creation, on the left. Indeed, Joffre was forced to order an unwilling Lanrezac to launch a counter-attack against the German Second Army on 29 August to relieve pressure on the faltering BEF. Throughout, the pace of the BEF retreat forced Joffre continually to adapt his plans over the next few days. He had originally hoped to stop the withdrawal on the Somme but this was doomed, so the Marne or even the Seine would be where he planned finally to hold. Joffre summed up his newly cautious demeanour.

In the presence of the enemy's wide encircling movement against our left, it was evident that we could not accept battle immediately. The engagement of one of our armies would bring on that of all our forces. The Fifth Army would find itself in a situation which the advance of the German First Army, aided by the incursion of the German Cavalry Corps, would render extremely perilous. The slightest check would run the risk of becoming transformed into an irremediable defeat. Besides this, our troops had been marching and fighting continuously; they were worn out and greatly needed to have their ranks filled up. Our situation in the coalition imposed upon us the duty of holding out as long as possible, while keeping the maximum number of German forces occupied in front of us and wearing them down by attacks undertaken upon every favourable occasion; but we had to avoid any decisive engagement as long as we did not hold enough trumps in our hand to give us a distinct chance of success.[33]

General Joseph Joffre, General Headquarters, French Army

This might be Joffre's last opportunity to avoid disaster. Timing would be all-important. In the meantime the Fifth Army and the BEF would continue to fall back, with the Third Army acting as the pivoting point, anchoring the two retreating armies to the rest of the French line. Joffre also dismissed the pessimistic Lanrezac, replacing him with the far more aggressive General Franchet d'Espèrey, who had already distinguished himself as a corps commander during the fighting on the Charleroi Front.

Yet by this time the Germans were also encountering ever-increasing difficulties. Their plans demanded a great deal of the troops on the right wing.

The First Army had now completed two-thirds of the wheel through Brussels on Paris. The requirements of the strategic situation made it impossible to give any rest days in the true sense of the word. Marches and fights, battles and marches, followed one another without interval.[34]

General Alexander von Kluck, Headquarters, First Army

The sheer distances covered were staggering, with the infantry marching between fifteen and twenty miles a day, a physically exhausting schedule even if they were not then required to fight as well. Even as the German right wing advanced it was decreasing in strength. The equivalent of three corps had already been left behind to counter Belgian forces at Antwerp, to occupy Brussels and to invest the remaining fortress towns. Worse still, the Russian offensive on the Eastern Front was beginning to take effect: Moltke believed that victory was in sight over France and he had detached two corps (one from the Second Army and one from the Third) and despatched them east. All told, this severely reduced the weight of the German right wing and gaps began to open between the Third, Second and First Armies. Moltke acted to counter this by foreshortening the original planned line of advance circling round Paris. Instead, the Second, Third and Fifth Armies were to turn south early; 'The intention is to drive the French in a south-easterly direction from Paris. The First Army will follow in echelon behind the Second Army and will be responsible for the flank protection of the armies.'[35] This did not sit well with von Kluck. He was proud of the achievements of his men and was determined to press onwards, eschewing the lesser role of flank guard to any French troops massing in the Paris region.

> The message of the Supreme Command, in accordance with which the First Army was to follow in echelon behind the Second, could not be carried out under the circumstances. The intention to force the enemy away from Paris in a south-easterly direction was only practicable by advancing the First Army.[36]
>
> General Alexander von Kluck, Headquarters, First Army

But as the German First Army wheeled round to push in a south-easterly direction, von Kluck was turning a naked flank to the newly created French Sixth Army.

By this time Joffre had managed to create a significant concentration of forces on his left flank, having judged the manifold risks to a nicety. All along a great stretch of the front from Switzerland to the Verdun fortress sector the situation had stabilised into a defensive stalemate. Now the French had gained superiority at the decisive point. When the German change in axis was finally confirmed on 4 September, Joffre, encouraged by Military Commander of Paris, General Joseph Gallieni, was ready to launch his Sixth Army into the badly exposed flank of von Kluck's First Army, while the BEF and the Fifth Army counter-attacked as vigorously as they could. Joffre also managed finally to overcome the innate caution of Field Marshal Sir John French. Joffre's amusing account of their meeting at the Château de Vaux-le-Pénil has the ring of truth.

> I put my whole soul into the effort to convince the Field Marshal. I told him that the decisive moment had arrived and that we must not let it escape – we must go to battle with every man both of us had and free from all reservations. 'So far as the French Army is concerned,' I continued, 'my orders are given and, whatever may happen, I intend

to throw my last Company into the balance to win a victory and
save France. It is in her name that I come to you to ask for British
assistance, and I urge it with all the power I have in me. I cannot
believe that the British Army will refuse to do its share in this supreme
crisis – history would severely judge your absence.' Then, as I finished,
carried away by my convictions and the gravity of the moment, I
remember bringing down my fist on a table which stood at my elbow,
and crying, 'Monsieur le Marshal, the honour of England is at stake!'
Up to this point French had listened imperturbably to the officer who
was translating what I said, but now his face suddenly reddened. There
ensued a short impressive silence; then, with visible emotion he murmured, 'I will do all I possibly can!' Not understanding English, I asked
Wilson what Sir John had said. He merely replied, 'The Field Marshal
says, "Yes!"' I had distinctly felt the emotion which seemed to grip the
British Commander in Chief; above all, I had remarked the tone of his
voice, and I felt, as did all the witnesses to the scene, that these simple
words were equivalent to an agreement signed and sworn to. Tea, which
was already prepared, was then served.[37]

General Joseph Joffre, General Headquarters, French Army

The tea is, surely, the conclusive touch. The scene was set: the Battle of
the Marne would commence on 6 September 1914. Joffre issued a chilling
order of the day.

We are about to engage in a battle on which the fate of our country
depends and it is important to remind all ranks that the moment
has passed for looking to the rear; all our efforts must be directed to
attacking and driving back the enemy. Troops that can advance no
farther must, at any price, hold on to the ground they have conquered
and die on the spot rather than give way. Under the circumstances
which face us, no act of weakness can be tolerated.[38]

General Joseph Joffre, General Headquarters, French Army

What followed was a complex battle that defies easy explanation. By this
time the German right wing was actually outnumbered by the French divisions rushing up from the south. As the German First Army tried to turn
to face the assault from the French Sixth Army along the line of the River
Ourcq, a huge chasm of some thirty miles opened up between von Kluck
and the Second Army on his left flank. Amidst the chaos, the men of the

BEF, having dutifully about-turned, found themselves advancing alongside the French Fifth Army into the gap between the German First and Second Armies. There was no great battle, no huge drama, but the penetration between their armies threatened utter disaster for the Germans and on 9 September Moltke ordered his right wing to retreat towards the River Aisne. The Battle of the Marne proved a stunning strategic triumph for the French. As might be expected there were many claimants for the laurels of victory, but there is no doubt who would have been blamed had it all gone wrong: Joffre. Therefore, the greatest credit should go to him.

Over the next few days, the German First and Second Armies fell back on the heights of the Chemin des Dames Ridge which rose up to 600 feet behind the Aisne. This was an obvious position for them to stand and fight, gaining time for a much-needed reorganisation. Joffre used all his considerable powers of persuasion to drive on his armies in close pursuit, but it was physically impossible for the exhausted troops. By the time they reached the Aisne on 12 September the Germans had dug a line of trenches along the heights and established their artillery on the rear slopes. The Battle of the Aisne is often presented as a British affair, but to their left and right were the French Sixth and Fifth Armies. Neither the BEF nor the French had the artillery, or tactical skills, required to turn the Germans out of such a strong natural defensive position, especially as the Germans began to move up reinforcements to plug any remaining gaps in their lines. The Allied response on 14 September was to dig in directly facing the German trenches. From Switzerland to the Aisne, the front was stabilising. The fighting had been hard. At times the Germans had seemed close to success, but the French armies had shown a resilience in defence that had thwarted any decisive breakthrough.

On the same day, 14 September, General Helmuth von Moltke was dismissed and replaced as Chief of General Staff by General Erich von Falkenhayn. Moltke had proved incapable of successfully prosecuting the war he had so much desired: the Schlieffen Plan as defined by Moltke had failed. Within two years he was dead – a broken man. Falkenhayn was born in 1861 and had experienced active service during the Boxer Rebellion in China in 1900. His evident abilities allowed him rapid promotion and in 1913 he had been made Prussian Minister of War. He was also noted for his cold-blooded detachment, which allowed him to assess a military situation on its merits, with the minimum of emotion.

The next phase of the fighting has often been described as the 'Race for the Sea', which accurately describes what it was not. In fact, it consisted of a series of outflanking manoeuvres, in which both sides sought, not to reach the sea, but to get round the northern flank of their opponent. Both sides still had hopes of victory, moving spare units out of the line in areas where the situation had settled and rushing them north. During the first stages, the BEF remained dug in on the Aisne sector, while the French and German forces engaged in a bloody series of encounter battles as they leapfrogged to the north. There was still a lot at stake. Although the war would clearly not be over in the near future, there were still the Channel ports of Boulogne, Dunkirk, Calais, Zeebrugge and Ostend, the industrial heartlands and coalfields of northern France, the vital rail junctions at Hazebrouck and Roulers, and the fate of the bulk of the Belgian Army still trapped in Antwerp – all these glittering prizes – to consider in addition to the chance of outflanking and thereby 'rolling up' the opponent's trench lines.

Like tiring heavyweights, the German and French forces exchanged blows, each finding it within them to thwart their opponent, but unable to go on to achieve a worthwhile victory. The logistical problems were phenomenal. Whole armies were consigned to overstretched railways and then pushed on from the railheads down crowded roads. Time was of the essence and both sides took incredible risks thrusting units into action well before they were ready. But when it mattered soldiers dug in and held out, gaining the time for reinforcements to be brought up. So the line solidified and attention turned to the next bound north. Clashes occurred across the Somme area in late September, then up around Arras in early October. Then came Lens, Armentières and finally Ypres. All these place names, then relatively unfamiliar, would become a litany of pain in the battles that followed over the next four years.

Meanwhile, Sir John French was becoming frustrated by his static positions on the Aisne Front. The old cavalryman sent a heartfelt plea to Joffre to allow him to move to take up station on the left flank of the French, which would greatly facilitate supply arrangements via the Channel ports. Thus the BEF would become involved in the final operations in northern France and around Ypres where it would try to exploit – or defend – the last possible gap before the North Sea stopped any opportunity for outflanking manoeuvres.

The BEF, alongside the French Second and Tenth Armies, would become part of the hastily assembled Northern Army Group, all under the control of the feisty figure of General Ferdinand Foch. Foch was a force of nature, endowed with incredible vigour, a considerable intellect and the ability to inspire those around him to greater things. Certainly Sir John French was swept away by Gallic passion.

> In appearance he is slight and small of stature, albeit with a most wiry and active frame. It is in his eyes and the expression of his face that one sees his extraordinary power. He appreciates a military situation like lightning, with marvellous accuracy, and evinces wonderful skill and versatility in dealing with it. Animated by a consuming energy his constant exclamation, 'Attaque! Attaque! Attaque!' reflected his state of mind, and there can be no doubt that he imbued his troops with much of his spirit.[39]
>
> General Sir John French, Headquarters, BEF

Born in 1851, Foch was a famed academic tactician who had served as Commandant at the École Supérieure de Guerre and was closely linked with the French pre-war cult of the offensive. His performance in the first weeks of the war had not inspired confidence but, like Joffre, he had the ability to adapt his views to meet the realities he faced rather than the theories he had once taught. He gained new priorities forged in adversity: 'Infantry was to be economised, artillery freely used and every foot of ground taken was to be organised for defence.'[40] Of course, morale *was* important, but most of all a successful attack needed numerical supremacy, backed up by overwhelming firepower. Even then, success was useless without consolidation to resist the inevitable German counter-attacks. Having gained his command of the Northern Army Group, Foch was determined to break through the gap he was convinced must exist between the German units that had captured Lille and those that were occupying Belgian Antwerp, which they had recently over-run.

The BEF had begun slowly to expand, with the creation of a III Corps (4th and 6th Divisions) under Major General Sir William Pulteney and the makeshift IV Corps (7th Division and 3rd Cavalry Division) under Lieutenant General Sir Henry Rawlinson. As the BEF moved into the line north of La Bassée Canal, near Béthune, it soon became involved in severe fighting. In the end, the main attention would fall on Ypres, a small market town in Belgium. Ypres had no particular value in itself, but it was the gateway to success for both sides. For the Germans it offered a way through to the Channel ports, and for the British the route to Menin, Roulers and the chance to cut German rail communications. German cavalry had briefly passed through the town on 7 October, but then it remained unoccupied until the IV Corps under Rawlinson arrived on 14 October, followed by Haig's I Corps on 19 October. At this point Sir John French, in accordance with Foch's orders, still had it in mind to push towards Roulers, but it was Falkenhayn who suddenly regained the initiative by moving up the Fourth Army under Albrecht, Duke of Württemberg. This was a massive, newly constituted formation containing the XXII, XXIII, XXVI and XXVII Reserve Corps, manned mainly by half-trained wartime volunteers and conscripts. The only experienced troops were the III Reserve Corps, which had been responsible for the capture of Antwerp.

Under Falkenhayn's plan, the new Fourth Army, assisted by the more northerly elements of the Sixth Army, were to smash through the thin trench lines scratched into the ground by British, French and Belgian units between Armentières and the sea. 'The Fourth Army is to advance, without regard for casualties, with its right wing resting on the coast, first on the fortresses of Dunkirk and Calais, then to swing south at St Omer.'[41] This was a risky endeavour as most of these German troops were nowhere near the quality of the original assaulting divisions of August 1914. The recruits were willing enough, motivated by raw enthusiasm, but they had not had the benefit of a methodical training in drill, musketry or field tactics. They were more like a militia, often poorly equipped and lacking in all but the simplest soldierly skills. They were used in action so early only because Falkenhayn and his staff could think of no alternative and they regarded this as probably their last real chance to finish the war that year.

From 17 October, the III Reserve Corps stationed on the right of the German Fourth Army tore into the Belgians and French, forcing them back towards the River Yser. The fighting was hard and at times they were harassed by heavy bombardments from naval units headed by the pre-dreadnought *Venerable* as they advanced towards the Belgian occupied town of Nieuwpoort. But, to their chagrin, the Germans were stymied when the Belgians opened the floodgates to systematically inundate the low-lying polders that protected the town, in effect forcing the Germans to retreat leaving a huge lake behind them. There was no way through here. It appeared that any decision would have to take place further inland on the low ridges rising from Ypres towards the village of Passchendaele.

The main German assault began on 20 October, with the initial pressure falling mainly on Smith-Dorrien's II Corps well to the south of Ypres who were caught somewhat unawares by the fury of the assault. The fighting was at times exceptionally severe and by 31 October, despite drafts, they had been reduced by the accumulated campaigns to a skeleton force of just 14,000 men. It was fortunate for the British that the Indian Corps had arrived just in time to replace them in the line, although they soon betrayed their inexperience and suffered many unnecessary casualties. For the British, the focus of attention then shifted on to the front held by the I and IV Corps digging in on the ridges in front of Ypres itself.

As the power of the assaults built up, there is no question that, for the most part, the British soldiers were making a better fist of the battle. As they gained the experience their pre-war training had not given them, their tactical dispositions slowly gained in subtlety, although there were still mistakes and instances of panic. Co-operation increased between neighbouring units, while the necessity of maintaining (if possible) a reserve at hand for plugging gaps or organised counter-attacks seemed to have been grasped. The artillery, too, was generally better handled, not left so exposed to the power of the German guns. There was also little doubt that the German troops lacked the skills of their predecessors. The concepts of 'fire and movement' – going to ground, co-ordinating rifle, machine guns and artillery to win the fire fight, before the final attack and careful consolidation of gains – were often conspicuous by their absence.

> We had imagined that our baptism of fire would be somewhat different. There can be nothing more depressing than the very public failure of an attack launched as though on exercise against an invisible enemy. Unthinking, section after section ran into the well directed fire of experienced troops. Every effort had been put into our training, but it was completely inadequate preparation for such a serious assault on battle-hardened, long-service colonial soldiers. We had just reached a meadow on a hillside, which was surrounded by trees and hedges, when the first British caps came into view. Forgotten for a moment was that little we had learned about modern battle drills, cover and

exploitation of ground. In two ranks and, in some places, three, kneeling or standing, we poured down fire with an abandon which can only be understood by the excitement of the first great moment of this day of assaults. After hours of demoralising hopelessness, here was a task which was visible and achievable. After two rounds fired standing unsupported, as if on the range, the inevitable happened. Just as I was taking the first pressure on the trigger, I was hit in the left buttock and I immediately felt the effects of the last strenuous days of marching – days for which we had not in the slightest been prepared – and the loss of blood from the wound weakened me far more than should have been the case. Everywhere there was confusion. Men were flooding back from the front, it was impossible to miss what was happening. Withdrawal? Enemy counter-attack? Would we be able to advance once more? Would we wounded not have to be cared for? Yet again we were back to the total hopelessness and paucity of thought which had marked our attacks from the very beginning. The gruesome reality was that I was no longer buoyed up by the elation of being close up to the enemy, but was inwardly extremely agitated by my first experience of being wounded, and externally by the total confusion of the events which surrounded me and which seemed to make no sense. How, in the circumstances, could an inexperienced wartime volunteer make clear decisions?[42]

Private Willi Kahl, 2nd Battalion, 236th Reserve Infantry Regiment

Their rawness led to scenarios that matched everything the British had claimed at Mons and Le Cateau, but there is no doubt that this time they really were slaughtering the German troops stumbling towards them. A typical British account is provided by Captain Harry Dillon of the 2nd Oxfordshire and Buckinghamshire Light Infantry, in a letter written on 22 October.

A great grey mass of humanity was charging, running for all God would let them, straight on to us not 50 yards off. Everybody's nerves were pretty well on edge as I had warned them what to expect, and as I fired my rifle the rest all went off almost simultaneously. One saw the great mass of Germans quiver. In reality some fell, some fell over them, and others came on. I have never shot so much in such a short time, could not have been more than a few seconds and they were down. Then the whole lot came on again and it was the most critical moment of my life. Twenty yards more and they would have been over

us in thousands, but our fire must have been fearful, and at the very
last moment they did the most foolish thing they possibly could have
done. Some of the leading people turned to the left for some reason,
and they all followed like a great flock of sheep. I don't think one could
have missed at the distance and just for one short minute or two we
poured the ammunition into them in boxfuls. My rifles were red hot at
the finish. The firing died down and out of the darkness a great moan
came. People with their arms and legs off trying to crawl away; others
who could not move gasping out their last moments with the cold
night wind biting into their broken bodies and the lurid red glare of
a farm house showing up clumps of grey devils killed by the men on
my left further down. A weird awful scene; some of them would raise
themselves on one arm or crawl a little distance, silhouetted as black as
ink against the red glow of the fire.[43]

Captain Harry Dillon, 2nd Oxford and Buckinghamshire Light Infantry

Both sides were reliant on artillery to soften up the enemy before an
assault. Private William Quinton of the 2nd Bedfordshires was stationed
in trenches in front of Gheluvelt on 24 October. It was not long before
they came under heavy fire and it was evident the Germans were about
to attack. Many men were experiencing concentrated shellfire for the first
time. It may have been a light shower compared to the artillery storms to
come, but for them it was torment.

Shrapnel shells were now bursting over our trench, the bullets
shooting downwards and burying themselves in the back wall of it
as we crouched under the parapet. The report as they burst, about 12
feet above our heads, was deafening, and made our ears sing, so that
conversation was practically impossible. The machine gun fire was now
more intense, and I could also distinguish rifle fire from the lines. We
knew that this outburst was the preliminary to an attack, but we also
knew that they would not come over whilst they were still shelling our
front line, as they would be running into their own fire. As soon as they
lifted their fire and concentrated it on our support and reserve lines,
that would be the moment of attack. Grey dawn was taking the place
of darkness. I was trembling. I looked at Bosely. His knuckles showed
white through the flesh, he was gripping his rifle so hard. His face was
white and set, and he looked at me as if he didn't recognise me.[44]

Private William Quinton, 2nd Bedfordshire Regiment

Suddenly the bombardment stopped and Quinton realised that the moment had come.

> The Company officer came dashing round to our gun position. 'Get ready boys!' he shouted, flourishing his service revolver, 'Give them a warm reception!' Rifle fire broke out along our line, we jumped to the parapet, head and shoulders above it. The sight that meet my gaze was one that I shall never forget. A horde of Germans were on their way towards our trenches, rifles with bayonets fixed held before them. Hundreds more were clambering out of their trenches and forming a second line, as they broke into a sharp trot towards us. They were so close together that their shoulders touched as they ran. As fire broke from our lines, they shouted hoarse cries and broke into a charge. I observed all this in one brief moment. I took aim with my rifle and fired: I blazed away into that oncoming mass of humanity that was out to annihilate us. At the same time our machine gun began to bark. The Germans immediately in front of us, the foremost being less than 100 yards away, began to fall like ninepins. I was firing my rifle as hard as 1 could, only pausing to reload the magazine with ten fresh rounds. A few of the enemy had got in advance of the rest, and were only about 50 yards away, when our gun stopped.[45]
>
> Private William Quinton, 2nd Bedfordshire Regiment

Quinton, who was part of the machine gun section, took over on their Maxim.

> What if our gun failed now? Even a temporary failure and they would be all over us. In fact, it flashed through my brain that, with the number of Germans coming over, it was just a matter of time before they swarmed into our trench to bayonet what was left of us. Suddenly Bosely winced, let go the gun, and grabbed his right shoulder. He slid down into the shelter of the trench, and I hastily took over. Grasping the firing handles and pressing my thumbs on the trigger lever, I fired without taking aim into the grey mass in front of us. Steam was now coming from the escape plug near the muzzle, as the water in the barrel casing began to reach boiling point. Belt after belt of cartridges went through her, till I began to think our ammunition supply must be getting low. Still those grey-clad figures came on. Hundreds of them, dead and wounded, lay out in No Man's Land. A fresh line leapt from their trenches and made a wild rush towards us, but were met with a

withering fire. They got about halfway across, their officers urging them on, then wavered and stopped, and finished up by throwing themselves flat and sheltering behind their own dead. They found effective shelter behind this gruesome barricade, for the dead were piled two and three high. I played the gun on them, just skimming the barricade, but they did not attempt to come forward again. They lay there, not risking to expose themselves and not daring to return to their own trenches. We had a little breathing space now, the attack having died away to nothing. Whereas before the attack I had been shivering, I was now wet with perspiration. Our trench presented a terrible sight. Of the twelve machine gunners, only five of us were left.[46]

Private William Quinton, 2nd Bedfordshire Regiment

This is typical of the British accounts of the fighting. Although they were indeed causing severe casualties, at the same time the British battalions were slowly being eroded away by the German attacks and the fierce artillery bombardments that preceded them. A salient was formed, with the British lines bending back on either side of the Menin Road as the Germans edged forward, village by village, ridge by ridge, copse by copse. Yet still they did not quite break through: in consequence the increasingly desperate German High Command resolved to move some more experienced units from the south to form an impromptu Army Group under the command of General Max von Fabeck, slotting in between the German Sixth and Fourth Armies.

The British were fortunate in the leadership provided by Haig, the commander of I Corps, which bore the brunt of the middle stages of the battle at Ypres. Haig kept his nerve and deployed his meagre reserves as best he could. The crisis came at the 'point' of the salient at Gheluvelt, where a see-saw battle raged for two days from 29 October. When Gheluvelt was lost on 31 October, it appeared for a while as if the Germans had broken through. Haig rode forward up the shell-bespattered Menin Road, where his insouciance under fire seems to have calmed the situation.

Haig moved the cavalry brigade, his last reserves, to the support of 1st Division. He traced across his map a line a little more than a mile from the walls of Ypres, to which the Corps should retire if it were driven back. 'And there,' he said, 'it must fight till the end!' Then, with his personal staff and escort, he rode slowly up the Menin Road, through the stragglers, back into the shelled area, his face immobile and inscrutable – saying no word, yet by his presence and his calm restoring hope to the disheartened and strength to his exhausted troops.[47]

Colonel John Charteris, Headquarters, I Corps

When informed of the difficulties facing I Corps, Foch responded in very similar fashion to Haig: 'It is absolutely imperative that no retreat is made, and to that end to dig in on the ground on which you happen to be.'[48] In the end, a successful counter-attack by the 2nd Worcesters at Gheluvelt Château briefly stabilised the situation and the ring around Ypres contracted a little – but held. Haig would always carry it in his mind that the Germans could have broken through at Ypres if they had just made one more concentrated assault. It would certainly influence his own conduct of battles later in the war.

In November 1914, the BEF was being eroded away. On 1 November, Captain Beauchamp Tudor St John was caught unawares as he approached the village of Wytschaete up on the Messines Ridge slightly to the southeast of Ypres.

> I walked quietly out from behind the cover of the cottage and proceeded towards the wood. I had not gone very far, however, when I became the centre of attraction of a hot fire which must, I think, have come from a machine gun. I started to run to the wood at once and the ground all round me was spattered up like the surface of a puddle in a rainstorm. I got another 30 or 40 yards when I felt as if I had suddenly hit my right arm against a hard obstacle in the dark. It was a very hard and very sharp blow and left a numb sort of tingling sensation in my arm quite different from the stinging of the blows of one or two pebbles which had been knocked into my legs by the shots on the ground which had hurt me quite as much. I still ran on but the wood looked a long way off and the shock of the wound had scared me a bit and I felt rather dizzy and out of breath. So I decided I would do a 'die' and selecting as comfortable a place as I could I wheeled round in the most approved fashion and fell on my face. This had the desired effect for a minute or two and the firing stopped.[49]

Captain Beauchamp Tudor St John, 1st Northumberland Fusiliers

Unfortunately, as he tried to get himself comfortable and to check the state of his wound, the Germans realised he was not dead and took action to correct their error.

I must have wriggled too much, however, for again a hot fire was opened on me. I lay for a few seconds wondering where it would get me, the bullets splashing mud all round me. Suddenly I felt as if someone had gently drawn something rather hot along my shoulder and round my throat. This could not have been the bullet as it appeared to me to take quite an appreciable time to get from my left shoulder to the right side of my throat. I think it must have been the blood flowing. Certainly as soon as it reached my throat I began to cough blood through my mouth and nose and felt as if I were choking and everything looked a sort of blue colour. I thought I was done for and wondered how my family would take the news and whether I would know how they took it. I felt aggrieved and angry at the thought of leaving this jolly old world for to me it had always been a jolly place and it seemed hard lines having to leave without seeing Roger and Madge again. However, I prayed to God to hurry the matter up as I was getting very uncomfortable.[50]

Captain Beauchamp Tudor St John, 1st Northumberland Fusiliers

The BEF fell back step by step, pushed off the Messines Ridge and thrown back from the Passchendaele Ridge. They just about clung on to the bulk of the Gheluvelt Plateau, although the village of Gheluvelt itself fell to the Germans. In the end Foch and the French performed as near-perfect allies, moving up their reserves and gradually taking over more and more of the salient as the BEF shrank. The successful defence of Ypres was to the equal credit of the French and the British. In the end the Germans were held back.

By the end of the First Battle of Ypres the trenches stretched from Switzerland to the North Sea. They had been tested repeatedly, but neither side could break through. It was clear that trench warfare was no temporary phenomenon. A young French marine, thrust into the line near Nieuwpoort, frustratingly close to his more natural element, reflected on the remarkable ability of even a crude trench to blunt the power of the guns.

The German artillery is quite remarkable. The fire of the heavy guns is admirably precise and well regulated. The other day I saw six shell craters in a 30 metre diameter circle; and these shells came from more than 7,000 metres away. But however accurate their fire, a trench gives shelter untouchable by artillery. Well dug-in infantry can only be dislodged by infantry, and properly by enemy bayonets.

Unfortunately we are little versed in trenches – being sailors – and lack any understanding of what is required! There is much talk of military engineering, but as far as the Naval Brigade is concerned, you don't see it. So our trenches are really just holes in the ground, sited at random where men get precarious rest on slippery clay, covered with a thin bed of straw.[51]

Lieutenant Pierre Dupouey, 3rd Battalion, 1st Naval Regiment

In December both sides tried exploratory attacks, often designed to straighten the line or to secure a tactically significant position, but to little real effect. It is symptomatic of the modern age that one curious anomaly has attained great renown: the Christmas Truce. In some sectors of the line the opposing forces momentarily decided to abandon fighting. This was the experience of Private William Quinton, who was in the trenches on 24 December.

All around us lay about 3 inches of snow, a typical picture-postcard Xmas. Things very quiet. That 'peace and goodwill to all men' feeling seemed to be in the air. We could hear the Germans still strafing up Ypres way, but the next night, Xmas Eve, even up there was much quieter. Something in the direction of the German lines caused us to rub our eyes and look again. Here and there showing just above their parapet we could see very faintly what looked like very small coloured lights. What was this? Was it some pre-arranged signal, and the forerunner of an attack, or was it to make us curious and thus expose ourselves to a sudden raking of machine gun fire? We were very suspicious, and were discussing this strange move of the enemy when something even stranger happened. The Germans were actually singing! Not very loud, but there was no mistaking it. We began to get interested. The enemy at least were going to enjoy themselves as much as the circumstances would permit. Suddenly, across the snow-clad No Man's Land, a strong clear voice rang out, singing the opening lines of 'Annie Laurie'. It was sung in perfect English and we were spellbound. No other sound but this unknown singer's voice. To us it seemed that the war had suddenly stopped! Stopped to listen to this song from one of the enemy. Not a sound from friend or foe and as the last notes died away a spontaneous outburst of clapping arose from our trenches. Encore! Good old Fritz![52]

Private William Quinton, 2nd Bedfordshire Regiment

Through the action of courageous individuals risking their lives to test the good intentions of their enemies, a truce was arranged and together the two sides began to bury the corpses littering No Man's Land.

> As daylight crept in, we were surprised to see the Germans waist-high out of their trenches, gazing across at us with impunity. Imagine the position: whereas yesterday the mere sight of a bit of field-grey uniform would have caused a dozen British rifles to crack, here was the enemy in full view of us, gazing serenely across No Man's Land at us, and we at him. To us in the front line the whole world had changed. We could take stock of our surroundings at our leisure. At 9 o'clock precisely, the German burying party climbed from their trenches, shovels and picks on their shoulders. They advanced about 10 yards in our direction and waited expectantly. A word from our company officer and our party were soon out. The officers looked on apparently conversing. The digging party soon lost interest in their task and before long were busy fraternising. Cigarettes were being exchanged and they seemed to be enjoying themselves immensely! Needless to say, before very long we in the trenches were soon out on top, sauntering about in the snow, but keeping this side of our wire entanglements. Likewise the Germans. For the whole of that day and for many days to come, friend and foe mixed freely out on No Man's Land. Except for the fact that a few of the enemy could speak a little English, we found the language difficulty a bar to conversation, but we made do with signs and gestures. I remember distinctly a German holding out an opened box of chocolates for me to take one! The Germans wanted to play us a football match on No Man's Land, but our officers would not allow it![53]
>
> Private William Quinton, 2nd Bedfordshire Regiment

The truce eventually ended when, so it was rumoured, a Scottish unit moved into neighbouring trenches and opened fire on a German working party, triggering the renewal of hostilities. This truce was wider than many have imagined. The French and Germans also ceased fighting in some sectors.

> Our four days in the trenches have been difficult because of the cold with a hard frost, but the Germans have left us alone. On Christmas Day, they made a sign that they wanted to talk to us. It was me that went to within 3 or 4 metres of their trench from which three of them emerged to talk. It was the Christmas Day holiday, a day of festivities

and they wanted no shooting from us during the day and night, saying they themselves wouldn't fire a single shot. They were tired of making war, they were married like me (they had seen my ring), did not want to fight the French but the English! They passed me a bundle of cigars, a box of gold tipped cigarettes, I gave them the *Petit Parisien* in exchange for a German newspaper. I returned to the French trench where I was soon robbed of my German tobacco! Our neighbours across the way kept their word better than we did! Not a shot. The next day, so they could see it was Christmas no longer, our artillery sent them a few well directed shells right into their trench.[54]

Adjutant Gustave Berthier, 256th Infantry Regiment

Although often represented as some kind of triumph of humanity, the truce can equally well be seen as an indictment of men all too willing to return to the killing despite seeing for themselves that their enemies were men just like themselves. The reality was that they were willing participants in the war, a war furthermore that at this time still satisfied popular opinion among all the combatant nations. There was no real desire for compromise or negotiation: the Christmas Truce was an exercise in sentimentality and nothing more.

BY THE END OF 1914 it was evident that General Alfred von Schlieffen had been both right and wrong. He was right that if the war continued for a substantial time Germany's enemies would use their sheer press of numbers to defeat her. But in seeking a swift victory the Germans had lost their best chance of maximising lesser tactical gains and then negotiating peace from a position of relative strength. In seeking outright victory in the summer of 1914 the Germans had in the end fallen short. The war was set on a grim path of attritional fighting, with all sides engaged in attempting to degrade the opposition forces to the level that they could no longer resist. With all sides able to draw on millions more men it was nigh on impossible to secure an easy victory. Far too many would die before the war would be resolved.

3

THE EASTERN FRONT, 1914

'To the training of our army in peacetime alone did we owe this feat.
The battle was a glorious triumph for the generals and their troops,
indeed, for every officer and man, and the whole country. Germany and
Austria-Hungary rejoiced – the world was silent. At my suggestion, the
battle was named the Battle of Tannenberg.'[1]

Major General Erich von Ludendorff, Headquarters, Eighth Army

THE RUSSIAN ARMY OF 1914 was a huge beast. Even though the reservoir for conscription was largely restricted to the Russian Christian population, and multifarious reasons were justification for exemption, the empire was so huge that the standing army of 1,400,000 would reach 5 million on mobilisation. Individual conscripts served three years in the infantry on call up, then seven years in the reserve, followed by eight years in the second-class reserve, before a final period in the militia until they reached the age of forty-three. In 1914, the mobilisation plans were greatly speeded up by a combination of preparatory measures and the French-financed improvements to the railway system, which allowed the Russians to place 2 million men ready for action on the Eastern Front within thirty days. Their training had been rudimentary, concentrating on basic soldierly skills, with little effort made to combine in the higher formations or to engage in realistic exercises; nor indeed was there much practice in co-operation between the infantry, artillery and cavalry. Yet in some areas, the Russian Army was surprisingly innovative, with a large Imperial Air Service and much experimentation ongoing into the possibilities of armoured cars. Yet many of these new weapons were not in an operational state and neither aeroplanes nor armoured cars had yet been fully integrated into basic tactical doctrine – indeed, Russian military doctrine generally was weak.

The Russian officer corps was also distinctly variable in quality. The top was riven by personal animosities, professional jealousies, factionalism and regional parochialism. Many officers had also been distracted by extensive counter-insurgency duties in the aftermath of the 1905 Revolution, while others were swamped by paperwork, or thwarted by the innate conservatism of many of their superiors. Another dragging factor on the efficiency of the Russian Army was the illiteracy of the vast majority of the lower ranks, a function of the poor Russian educational system.

Theoretically, the Russian Army was better equipped than is sometimes imagined, with the standard rifle the magazine bolt-action 7.62 mm Mosin-Nagant rifle, which was a reliable and accurate weapon. The infantry regiments of 4,000 men were further equipped with eight machine guns of the belt-fed water-cooled Maxim M1910 type, also firing 7.62 mm bullets, which proved to be both efficient and practical in action. Like the British and German infantry, the Russian soldier wore a camouflage uniform, a greenish-khaki which came in many different shades, especially after heavy wear.

The main field gun, the Pulitov 76.2 mm, was a fine weapon, while the heavier 122 mm and 152 mm Schneider guns were the main heavy artillery – although, as with most armies, there was a severe shortage. But other shortages would become apparent during mobilisation and even more so when the fighting began: rifle and machine gun ammunition, shells and, frustratingly, many basic items of equipment and uniform, including an inexplicable dearth of boots – surely an easily calculable essential. The problems of the Army were deep set within the state for Russia was still a backward, primitive society which could only ever harvest a small proportion of its huge assets even in the cause of war. This was just as well for the Central Powers, for Russia's population outnumbered those of Germany and Austria-Hungary put together.

Facing the Russians was the Austro-Hungarian Army. In peacetime it numbered some 440,000 men, but on mobilisation would expand to a more intimidating 3.35 million, deployed in forty divisions. Yet this was another state that had neither the internal cohesion nor the modernised infrastructure to capitalise on its huge size. With a population of around 50 million, it was the third most populous state in Europe in 1914, but it had no concept of nationhood; here was a country ready to be torn apart by nationalism. The infantry conscripts were called up at eighteen years old and served two years before passing on to ten years in the Landwehr reserve, followed by a further period with the inactive Landsturm until they were fifty-five years old. Overall their standard of training was basic. Dressed in a light blue uniform, they were armed with the 8 mm bolt-action magazine Mannlicher M1895 rifle, which was both reliable and capable of extremely high rates of fire – up to thirty-five rounds a minute! Austrian machine gun companies tended to have four sections, each armed with two water-cooled 8 mm Schwartzlose M.07/12, guns which had the advantage of being significantly lighter than their competitors', although at the cost of some loss of range and penetrating power. The artillery was functional with a high proportion of mountain guns of various calibres. Unlike most countries, Austria had developed some formidable heavy artillery typified by the Skoda 305 mm 1911 siege howitzer. This beast had a crew of at least fifteen and was towed by a 15 ton motorised tractor. When in place it fired either an armour-piercing delayed action fuse shell weighing 850 lb which could penetrate six feet of concrete, or a 630 lb shell which had incredible explosive power creating craters eight yards wide and threatening any exposed infantry within a quarter of a mile. Eight Skodas would be lent to the Germans to assist in the reduction of the Belgian forts on the Western Front in August 1914. The Austrians had a similar expertise in the manufacture of powerful – and deadly – mortars.

On 1 August 1914, Germany declared war on Russia following the Russian general mobilisation on 31 July. It is ironic that Austria-Hungary, which had declared war on Serbia on 28 July, only belatedly declared war on Russia, on 6 August. Rumania and Bulgaria had resolved to stay out of the war but the Eastern Front created was still immense, stretching some 1,000 miles. The distances involved in military operations were vast, forcing a dependence on railways as the only feasible means of moving the huge armies of men and the incalculable quantities of supplies and munitions they needed to live in the field. For the Germans and Austrians, blessed with superb railway networks, this was not a problem, but over the border in Russia the system was far more ramshackle. Russian railway lines were a sparse resource which linked only the main population centres, while there was an additional complication in the wider track system they employed. French investment had improved matters a little, but the paucity of their railways restricted the ability of the Russians to respond quickly to changing circumstances. The Russian Commander in Chief was Grand Duke Nicholas, the Tsar's brother. In the north, the Russian First and Second Armies faced the German Eighth Army. Deep behind the salient of Russian Poland, the Ninth and Tenth Armies, which had been belatedly added to the plans, were slowly forming up with the intention of eventually advancing right through Poland to threaten the lightly defended German Silesia. In the south, the Fourth, Fifth, Third and Eighth Armies faced the Austrian First, Fourth, Third and (eventually) Second Austrian Armies. Three great empires were fighting for their very existence in a titanic battle in which defeat was unthinkable: the scene was set for a murderous campaign that would match the Western Front in every respect.

The most dramatic early campaign took place in the north, in East Prussia. The Russian First and Second Armies were mobilising well behind the frontier, fearful of being caught by surprise while still vulnerable. The plan was simple: the First Army, commanded by General Paul von Rennenkampf, would advance into East Prussia north of the Masurian Lakes, while the Second Army, under General Alexander Samsonov, would advance south of the lakes. The whole offensive would be co-ordinated, at least in theory, by General Yakov Zhilinsky, although communications would prove dire, and problems with ciphers led to many occasions when orders were broadcast uncoded over the wireless – to the enormous benefit of the listening Germans. This confusion in command and control was exacerbated by a virulent personal feud between Samsonov and Rennenkampf dating back to disagreements during the Russo-Japanese War.

On 16 August Rennenkampf began his advance, pushing aside resistance from the German Eighth Army, commanded by Lieutenant General Max von Prittwitz, during heavy fighting at Gumbinnen on 20 August. Both sides lost around 17,000 casualties, but the Germans were forced to retreat by weight of numbers. Rennenkampf followed up tardily, first reorganising his units for a couple of days and then advancing far too slowly, thereby allowing the Germans to break contact with his forces. This might not have mattered much, as Prittwitz was already panicking, concerned as he was by the threat to his communications from Samsonov's Second Army which he knew was poised to begin crossing the Prussian border from Russian Poland on 21 August. A desperate Prittwitz resolved to retreat all the way back to the Vistula River, thereby abandoning the whole of East Prussia. This was far too much for Moltke, who immediately dismissed the hapless Prittwitz and replaced him with General Paul von Hindenburg, a traditional, stolid-looking officer, born in 1847, who had enjoyed a successful career, rising to general but then retiring in 1911 before being recalled to the colours. He was accompanied by his Chief of Staff, Major General Erich von Ludendorff, a far more mercurial character. Born in 1865, he was a piercingly intelligent and exceptionally hard-working staff officer who had been involved in some of the pre-war reworking of the Schlieffen Plan, and had already earned considerable renown for his conduct during the Battle of Liège on the Western Front. They would prove to be one of the great command teams of the Great War.

When Hindenburg took command on 23 August he was immediately proffered a plan of action by the Eighth Army staff officer Colonel Max Hoffmann. This plan fell in with Ludendorff's own early inclinations to take advantage of the failure of the Russian armies to co-ordinate their operations thus far. Hoffmann suggested leaving only screening forces in front of the slow-moving First Army and utilising the efficiency of the superb German railway system to switch the bulk of the Eighth Army to challenge Samsonov's Second Army head on as it marched north and north-west into East Prussia. The plan was to defeat the superior Russian forces in detail, switching the Eighth Army from front to front, allowing it to fight in turn first the Second Army and then the First Army. This was a risky scheme at least partially reliant for its success on the failure of Rennenkampf to advance, or react with any speed as events unfolded. Yet the new command team grasped that it was their best – if not only – opportunity for success and so the Eighth Army's retreat was stopped in its tracks and the complex redeployment begun. The German staff were much helped in their analysis of the situation by the regular interception of Russian orders transmitted without encryption over the wireless

– an astounding lack of basic security. Shortly afterwards Hindenburg was pleased to discover that Moltke, under heavy pressure from various civilian sources over the perceived threat to the East Prussian homelands, had detached two corps and a cavalry division from the forces currently wheeling through Belgium. Given the Germans' overall strategy of knocking France out of the war in the west before turning to the east, this represented a considerable change in tack.

Samsonov knew nothing of this, but he was already dogged by serious problems. Countless lakes and woods scattered the countryside, splitting up his corps and even divisions, while transport conditions were dreadful and his communications almost non-existent, leaving him operating in a vacuum – just as Hoffmann had predicted. Whatever Samsonov thought was happening, reality burst upon him only in stages: first his left wing was attacked, then his right. Before the Russians could react it was already too late: by 28 August the whole of the Second Army was cut off, at first only by a weak German force, but as the Germans pressed on the Russians found themselves effectively surrounded by a ring of steel, with no chance of escape. The various entrapped formations flailed away ineffectively, trying to punch their way out, but there was no co-ordinated effort and the Germans fended them off easily. Rennenkampf attempted to move his First Army south to rescue them, but by now it was far too late. Soon the Russians had no option but to surrender. By the end of August, over 90,000 would have trudged off into captivity. A further 78,000 were dead or wounded and just 10,000 escaped. Samsonov was not one of them. He is reputed to have committed suicide wandering alone in the dark, forbidding forests. The Battle of Tannenberg, as it would be known, was an unmitigated disaster for the Russian Army; the Germans suffered only 13,000 casualties.

Then it was time for the second stage: the Germans moved smoothly round from the north, leaving only token screens behind them, ready to take on Rennenkampf's First Army. By this time the Eighth Army had received the two corps of reinforcements whisked across Germany from the Western Front. Chastened by the destruction of the Second Army, Rennenkampf had suspended his advance and withdrawn to a more defensible line stretching from Königsberg in the north down to the Masurian Lakes to the south. The Germans concentrated on the left of his line and on 7 September managed to break through. The Tenth Army was still forming up in Poland and so was unable to lend any assistance. Rennen-kampf was forced into a humiliating retreat, falling back across the Prussian border he had crossed with so much hope less than a month before. The Russians finished the campaign in utter disarray: Samsonov was dead; Rennenkampf was rumoured to be panicking under the pressure; and Zhilinsky, the man who bore ultimate responsibility, was dismissed. The Germans had not only held East Prussia but now stood poised to attack. Only in November 1914, after weeks of fighting, with a German lunge into Russia followed by waves of Russian counter-attacks swaying drunkenly backwards and forwards, did the lines finally settle down not far from the original borders. Trench warfare and prepared defensive positions had gradually blocked all freedom of manoeuvre. In view of the requirements of the Schlieffen Plan merely to hold in the east, this represented a very considerable achievement by the Eighth Army.

Meanwhile, the first gigantic clashes were occurring in Austrian Galicia between the Russian Fourth, Fifth, Third and Eighth Armies (under the overall command of General Nikolai Ivanov), and the Austrian First, Fourth and Third Armies, commanded the Austrian Chief of Staff General Conrad von Hötzendorf. The Russian advance commenced on 18 August and the series of epic battles that ensued were redolent of an earlier age of warfare. Slow-moving, monolithic armies crashed into each other on the Galician plains, complete with cavalry skirmishing in the gaps between the armies and dramatic manoeuvring as both sides sought the flanks of their opponents while desperately fending off threats to their own. All this while severely hampered by minimal communications, and with a near total lack of accurate intelligence as to their opponents' movements. One thing was certain: both sides suffered shocking casualties as simplistic infantry tactics frequently exposed men *en masse* to the coruscating power of modern weaponry. But something else was also becoming apparent: for all their manifold problems the Russians had the edge over the Austrians in battle. On 3 September the Russian Third Army captured Lemberg, a key railway centre and the fourth largest city in the Austro-Hungarian Empire. This success can be seen as the first major Allied victory of the war. Further complex fighting followed until the Austrians were forced to withdraw back to the San River on 11 September. This left the important fortress town of Przemyśl besieged by the Russians from 22 September, although they lacked the super heavy artillery to make much of a dent on the ring of modern fortifications that defended it. Still the Austrians fell back to the south-west, finally finding a defensible line along the Dunajec River–Biala River line east of Cracow.

By this time the Russians had managed to position their units in roughly a north–south line and had two main options before them. The first was to reinforce Ivanov's success and carry on attacking the hapless Austrians in the south-west with the intention of capturing Cracow and bursting through into Hungary. Alternatively, they could launch the Ninth and Tenth Armies across Poland and into German Silesia. By now some of the urgency had been removed: the situation on the Western Front may not have been resolved, but the Battle of the Marne had been fought and won by the French early in September 1914. Nevertheless, in the end Grand Duke Nicholas and his headquarters, the Stavka, resolved to continue with the Silesia option, fearing that a vigorous campaign to the south-west could be taken in the flank by the Germans from the north.

The Germans had their own problems to contend with, namely that their Austrian allies had already suffered the loss of some 325,000 men, while having inflicted only around 225,000 losses on the Russians. Such an exchange rate was hardly a problem for the Russians, but it certainly was for the Austrians. Grudgingly, the Germans took action to bolster their faltering allies by swiftly creating a new Ninth Army in German Silesia to be commanded by the now much acclaimed Hindenburg–Ludendorff team. Already, the phlegmatic Hindenburg had proved to be the ideal foil for Ludendorff, who, though brilliant, was prone to panic under pressure. On several occasions during the tense build up to the Tannenberg encirclement, Hindenburg had exerted his calming influence on Ludendorff to prevent him from switching plans unnecessarily when faced by relatively trivial obstacles.

The Ninth Army linked up with its Austrian neighbours and from 29 September began to advance into Russian Poland, reaching as far as the line of the Vistula by early October. However, Grand Duke Nicholas and the Stavka utilised a rare intelligence coup in their favour to re-jig their plans and allow the Russian Fourth and Ninth Armies to attack the new German Ninth Army frontally across the Vistula, while the First Army would move on their right to strike at the German left flank. This promising plan was ruined by the continuingly lax Russian wireless security leaking orders and the capture of plans indicative of the existence of a trap. The Germans swiftly transferred across their XI Corps in time to protect the vulnerable left flank of the Ninth Army. But it had been a close run thing and, as the Russian forces built up around them, the Germans were eventually forced on 18 October to fall right back to their start lines from their furthest point of penetration just seven miles west of Warsaw.

Meanwhile, the Austrians had taken advantage of Russian distraction to advance once again to the San River line and were able to relieve Przemyśl on 9 October. However, it would soon be cut off again, once more to languish behind the Russian lines, hostage to the see-saw battles, as Conrad was once again forced to order a retreat to the Dunajec River–Biala River line.

At last the Russians were ready to implement their long-planned and, due to poor wireless secrecy, much-advertised lunge into German Silesia, intended to commence on 14 November. But the Germans were more than ready for them. By this time the German Chief of Staff, Erich von Falkenhayn, had been inveigled into appointing Hindenburg as Commander in Chief of the Eastern Armies, with Ludendorff as his Chief of Staff, while General August von Mackensen was promoted to command of the Ninth Army. Ludendorff used information provided by Russian intelligence gaffes to carry out a manoeuvre which would have been logistically unthinkable for his opponents. The German Ninth Army was spirited away as if by magic and moved by rail north from where it could attack the right flanks of the Russian invading armies; indeed, the Germans managed to attack first with devastating force on 11 November. Russian dreams of a Silesian offensive had to be put aside, as they fell back to the supply centre of Lodz, where their Second and Fifth Russian Armies concentrated to to block Mackensen's further advance. Again the fighting had a strange fluctuating quality as both sides attempted to encircle their opponents and the Germans pushed hard to capture Warsaw. Both sides came close to disaster, evading it by the narrowest of margins. To make matters worse the weather broke – hardly a surprise in late November – and it began to snow heavily. In the end the German Ninth Army fought its way out of trouble, successfully pulling back from Łódz. The Russians entrenched, hacking away at the rock-solid frozen ground to carve out a front line west of the Vistula.

While the Russians dug themselves in for the winter, the Germans pondered their next move at a conference in Posen attended on 1 December by Falkenhayn, the Kaiser, the recently promoted Field Marshal Hindenburg and Ludendorff. Falkenhayn found himself bombarded with demands for more reinforcements with the twin objectives of bolstering the faltering Austrians and knocking Russia out of the war. This was a philosophy utterly rejected by Falkenhayn, who firmly believed that the war could only be won in the west, not on the endless plains of the east facing the inexhaustible manpower of Russia. Furthermore, he believed that the strategic situation was such that the best option was to secure a significant victory and then to negotiate a political settlement, which in turn meant scaled down war aims. Neither side would concede the case and a grudging agreement to differ was hardly a positive step forwards. All that Hindenburg would get were the three corps that Falkenhayn had already grudgingly agreed to despatch from the Western Front. He might not have bothered had he known what Ludendorff was planning: a winter frontal assault, lacking even a pretence of subtlety, on the Russian lines in Poland.

The Ninth Army began its assault well, capturing Lodz on 6 December, only to crash into the Russian trench lines. The German guns raged and both sides attacked again and again, small tactical objectives taking on an importance that existed only in the minds of obsessed local commanders. The Russians proved doughty defensive fighters and the Germans could make little progress, unable to breach the river line. German casualties mounted wildly, totalling up to 100,000 in the last six weeks of the year. Finally Ludendorff had to give in. He was running out of troops and it was unlikely that Falkenhayn would countenance their replenishment for such an ill-conceived operation.

Throughout the Siege of Przemyśl was progressing with only occasional outbreaks of mild excitement. By this time there were some 127,000 Austrian troops trapped in the city. They were lucky, in that it had been a former storehouse for munitions, supplies and food, but even so they could not hold out for ever. Attempts were made to break out, but each had failed dismally. A localised Christmas Truce temporarily raised the spirits of the troops on all sides, but the underlying situation of the besieged Austrians did not change. The Russian armies under Ivanov were also making considerable progress in a drive on Cracow, the city widely held to be the gateway to both Silesia and Hungary. Sadly for Russian ambitions the Germans despatched reinforcements, which stiffened the Austrians' resistance and managed to force the Russians back to the Dunajec River–Biala River line by 17 December.

The see-saw nature of the fighting in the east – two steps forward, three steps back, one step forward – was becoming increasingly apparent all along the line. In the north, for all their efforts the Russians only managed to hold on to a token sliver of East Prussia. In contrast, they had lost much of Russian Poland to the German advance, but the strategic drawback of occupying this territory was such that this was not a particular disadvantage in the broader scheme of things. It was in the south, against the Austrians, that the Russians had made their biggest gains as they had over-run nearly all of Austrian Galicia. Just as on the Western Front, the scale of forces involved had been incredible: by the end of the year 143 Russian divisions faced fifty-three Austrian and thirty-eight German divisions. Losses on all sides had been simply breathtaking. By the end of 1914 up to 750,000 Russian soldiers, 500,000 Austro-Hungarians and 140,000 Germans had become casualties. All this in just five frantic months of mayhem.

THERE WAS, HOWEVER, ANOTHER EASTERN FRONT to consider: the Austro-Serbian War that had commenced with the Austro-Hungarian declaration of war on 28 July. The approximately 200,000-strong Serbian Army was commanded by the elderly figure of Field Marshal Radomir Putnik, who had to endure the embarrassment of being promptly interned by the Austrians in Budapest, where he had been undergoing an untimely medical treatment. Strangely, he was then released, presumably because the Austrians thought he would hardly be fit to exercise a competent wartime command. However, his offer to resign on the grounds of ill health having been rejected by King Peter I of Serbia, Putnik would go on to oversee the strategic direction of the Serbian Army, while his subordinates did all the work in the field. He would prove a formidable directing intelligence to Serbian military operations. The small Serbian First, Second and Third Armies faced the 270,000 men amassed in the Austrian Fifth and Sixth Armies with little immediate tactical ambitions other than to endure till their Russia allies had triumphed. The Serbian Army had recent experience in the Balkan Wars, but it was woefully equipped for a full-scale conflict with a major power.

Under orders from Conrad, the Austrian Fifth Army crossed the Drina River border on 12 August. The Austrians were determined to finish the matter quickly and saw no problems in defeating their weak opponents. In doing so they not only attacked with only half their available strength, but worse still they were advancing into the rough country of western Serbia rather than the northern plains. Putnik was initially taken aback by the attack, imagining it to be a feint, but recovered swiftly to rush in reinforcements. The resulting four-day battle forced the Austrians to fall back with the loss of some 23,000 casualties, the Serbs themselves losing 16,500. Small-scale Serbian offensives incurring on to Austro-Hungarian territory were markedly less successful, so the next major act occurred when, on 7 September, the Austrians launched a twin-pronged attack by the Fifth and Sixth Armies across the Drina to secure a firm bridgehead. The fighting was murderous, as Putnik marshalled his smaller forces as best he could, launching counter-attacks to disrupt the Austrian advance. The fighting climaxed in another four-day battle in the mountains, marked by a series of sanguinary frontal assaults by both sides. Eventually numbers told and the Serbs fell back and trench warfare took its iron grip. Here the Serbs had a crippling disadvantage: they had few guns and almost no ammunition, so the artillery exchanges were remarkably one-sided.

The Austrians attacked again on 5 November, when they used their artillery superiority to push back the Serbs. The Serbs withdrew slowly at first but pulled right back to shorten their front, although this meant that the capital, Belgrade, had to be abandoned, which the Austrians duly entered on 2 December. In the interim, supplies of artillery shells had arrived for the Serbs, despatched from the British and the French. This slightly rebalanced the equation, especially as the insightful Putnik divined that the Austrians were becoming overstretched as they pushed deep into Serbia. Putnik sensed a very real, although possibly brief, opportunity to defeat his opponents in detail. On 3 December he launched a counter-attack crashing first into the Austrian Sixth Army. The results were spectacular: the Sixth Army broke and fell back in complete disorder, at which point Putnik turned his forces on to the Fifth Army, which also crumbled under the pressure. Facing complete defeat, the Austrian armies retreated back to the borders and Belgrade was recaptured by the Serbs on

15 December. The campaign had been a fiasco for the Austrians: nothing had been achieved, thousands of men had died and the hated Serbs still preened themselves across the border, acting as beacons for all the disaffected minorities within their domains. Austria-Hungary had the war with Serbia she had craved in July 1914: distracted by the menace of the Russian armies, she did not have the strength to win it.

ON BOTH THE MAIN EASTERN FRONT and the Serbian sideshow the traditional break enforced in previous campaigns by the awesome power of 'General Winter' was simply ignored. The troops stayed out in the field, stoically manning their trenches: indeed not just in the fields, but deep in the dark forests, high in the mountains and on barricades winding across frozen lakes. As the temperature plummeted and the snow fell, living conditions became indescribably bad. Communication lines faltered and basic food rations were often scarce or non-existent in the front lines. Trees were hacked down by soldiers desperate for firewood to try and get a glimmer of warmth, but many men froze to death at their posts. Conditions were bad enough on the Western Front, but they were far worse in the depths of a continental winter on the Eastern Front which approached the limits of human endurance. Overall, the troops of both sides showed tremendous resilience: they knew there would be no going home for Christmas 1914.

4

THE SEA WAR, 1914–15

'It is not, in my opinion, wise to risk unduly the heavy ships of the Grand Fleet in an attempt to hasten the end of the High Seas Fleet, particularly if the risks come not from the High Seas Fleet itself, but from mines and submarines.'[1]

Admiral Sir John Jellicoe, HMS *Iron Duke*, Grand Fleet

NAVAL POWER WAS SOMETHING MUCH TO BE DESIRED at the end of the nineteenth century. The pre-eminent position of the Royal Navy and the manifest advantages this bestowed upon the British Empire were self-evident: the acquisition and maintenance of colonies; the safe passage for commercial traffic; and the ability to deploy troops rapidly at critical trouble spots across the globe. Without a significant degree of naval power overseas colonies would always be vulnerable to capture by stronger maritime forces in times of war. The British naval dominance was based on a navy grown organically from a thriving maritime commerce, which in turn was driven by the need to service and harvest the produce of overseas colonies. Indeed, there were enormous difficulties in creating a powerful navy without such a background, for a modern navy demanded a considerable investment, not only in the technical demands of constructing and manning state-of-the-art fighting ships, but also in the infrastructure of dockyards, ports and naval bases. The British were well aware of the origins of their power and the Royal Navy had adopted a simple but effective 'two-power standard', which sought to maintain its strength at a level equal to the next two strongest naval powers – usually France and Russia.

The rise of Germany in the late nineteenth century brought a third main challenger to Great Britain. The origins and effects of British naval domination had been spelled out by the American naval historian Alfred Mahan in his definitive work *The Influence of Sea Power Upon History: 1660–1783*, a masterpiece which had gained much currency with Kaiser Wilhelm II, who had become enamoured with the prospect of projecting German military strength overseas by means of a strong fleet. The German Navy had been gaining in strength, but it was proving a slow process. German naval deficiencies had been highlighted during the Franco-Prussian War, when the far superior French fleet had blockaded both the major German naval bases of Kiel and Wilhelmshaven. The Prussian iron-clads had remained quiescent in harbour, strictly forbidden to emerge. One young officer was beside himself with frustration.

> The army reproached us for not attacking the whole French fleet when it suddenly appeared off Wilhelmshaven on its way home. We youngsters were also indignant at not being let loose on the enemy, but this caution was correct. We were three armoured ships to their eight, and we could only do 10 knots; and even if Captain Werner had advertised the *König Wilhelm* as the strongest ship in the world, this was not sufficient to counterbalance a three-fold superiority. In view of the lack of any possibility of refitment we should have had to expect the loss of our whole fleet, without reaping any advantage thereby. It was also difficult for the lay mind to understand why we did not at least attempt a raid. An engagement begun at sea, however, cannot be broken off if the enemy has the greater speed. In any case the navy was blamed for its inactivity, and we were not even allowed to count these years as war service.[2]
>
> Sub Lieutenant Alfred Tirpitz, SMS *König Wilhelm*

After this humiliating debacle the German Navy stumbled on, unsure of its purpose: was it coastal defence, piratical commerce raiding, or was there really the commitment required to become a major naval power? This confusion continued until the advent of a new Secretary of State of the Imperial Naval Office, Admiral Alfred Tirpitz, who took over in 1897. By this time Tirpitz was a splendid figure: bald, extravagantly bearded, bad-tempered, yet at the same time capable of exerting great charm and persuasiveness. Throughout his career he was driven by the belief that Germany must create her own battle fleet within a strictly limited timescale.

> Two lines of thought were emerging at that time: the tactical necessity for a battle fleet, if we were striving for sea-power and wanted to build ships to some purpose; and the political necessity of establishing a protecting navy for Germany's maritime interests which were growing at such an irresistible pace. The navy never seemed to me to be an end in itself, but always a function of these maritime interests. Without sea-power Germany's position in the world resembled a mollusc without a shell. The flag had to follow trade, as other older states had realised long before it began to dawn upon us.[3]
>
> Admiral Alfred Tirpitz, Secretary of State of the Imperial Naval Office

These intense ambitions would be encapsulated within the Navy Act passed by the Reichstag in 1898. This envisaged a navy of nineteen battleships (two squadrons of eight battleships, a flagship and two spare ships), which was then doubled to thirty-eight in the subsequent Navy Act of 1900. The excuse for this was provided by the high-handed action of the British in stopping and searching three German mail boats for contraband intended for the Boers. The German fleet would embody two principles that would complicate the position of the Royal Navy in the early twentieth century. The first was the concept of the 'risk fleet'.

> To protect Germany's sea trade and colonies in the existing circumstances there is only one means – Germany must have a battle fleet so strong that even for the adversary with the greatest sea power a war against it would involve such dangers as to imperil his position in the world. For this purpose it is not necessary that the German battle fleet should be as strong as that of the greatest naval power, for a great naval power will not, as a rule, be in a position to concentrate all its striking forces against us. But even if it should succeed in meeting us with considerable superiority of strength, the defeat of a strong German fleet would so substantially weaken the enemy that, in spite of victory, he might have obtained, his own position in the world would no longer be secured by an adequate fleet.[4]
>
> Memorandum, Naval Act, 1900

Although the Royal Navy was never mentioned, there could be no confusion as to who this 'greatest naval power' was. Britain had substantial responsibilities and commitments around the globe and would find it difficult to concentrate a superior fleet for any moment of decision chosen by the German Navy. The British were well aware of the German threat. Their pace of battleship construction increased, more squadrons were recalled to home waters and, as we have seen, the era of 'splendid isolation' came to an end with the Entente Cordiale, in which the bulk of naval responsibility for the Mediterranean was handed over to the French and at the same time committing the British Expeditionary Force to fighting alongside the French on what would be the Western Front.

There were other challenges to the Royal Navy. Technology was on the march and the conventional pattern of battleship design was in danger of drifting into obsolescence due to cumulative advances in gunnery and propulsion. At the Admiralty the First Sea Lord, Sir John Fisher, had the responsibility of co-ordinating Britain's response to this threatening situation. If they were too slow in responding then the Royal Navy would fall behind her competitors, but take a wrong turning in the design of the new battleships and she could lose years. The British had to get it right first time. When the final designs for the prototype that would give its name to a generation of capital ships, the *Dreadnought*, emerged, they certainly represented a marked step forward. She was armed with ten 12-inch guns which allowed a broadside of eight 12-inch guns, with armour plate that fully matched conventional standards but was also capable of an impressive 21 knots powered by the very latest Parsons turbine engines. Once Fisher had made his decision, its execution was stunning: the *Dreadnought* was laid down on 2 October 1905, launched on 10 February 1906, went for her sea trials in October 1906 and was finally fitted out and completed by December 1906. The naval race had been rebooted from scratch, but the Royal Navy had managed to secure a huge advantage. While other nations pondered how to respond, British shipyards resounded with hammering and riveting as the new generation of dreadnoughts took shape on the stocks. The Germans began their own dreadnought programme in July 1907 but not only had the British secured a crucial lead, they had the determination to press home their advantage.

It was a similar story with the other great Fisher innovation, which indeed became his great passion: the battlecruiser. This was an entirely new class of ship with a strong main armament of eight 12-inch guns, but with only the relatively thin armour of a cruiser. It was intended to be used to clear the seas of any commerce-raiding cruisers which found themselves unable to fight or flee. For Fisher, the battlecruisers rather than the dreadnoughts would be the real future: he believed that speed would be their armour. This became his mantra and he constantly campaigned for bigger guns and more speed over the next few years as summed up in a letter to the First Lord of the Admiralty, Winston Churchill, in December 1911.

> The first desideratum of all is speed! Your fools don't see it – they are always running about to see where they can put on a little more armour! To make it safer! You don't go into battle to be safe! No, you go into battle to hit the other fellow in the eye first so that he can't see you! Yes! You hit him first, you hit him hard and you keep on hitting. That's your safety! You don't get hit back? Well that's the improved 13.5-inch gun! You don't care a damn then whether your bottom's dirty or a compartment bashed in with a torpedo making you draw water, because you have a big margin of speed over your Noah's Ark *Dreadnought* of 21 knots![5]
>
> First Sea Lord Sir John Fisher

But the introduction of German battlecruisers meant that the battlecruisers ended up fighting each other and their thin armour meant that both sides delivered blows that they themselves could not withstand. The additional problem was that their heavy-gun armament provided a temptation to include them in the battle line. The battlecruisers would prove to be the main protagonists in the engagements between the British and German fleets and as such the intended function of the class was compromised and they would prove distressingly vulnerable.

The naval race between 1906 and 1914 was of exceptional severity. In both Britain and Germany there were naval scares which caused extravagant spurts in construction. Proposals for 'naval holidays' during which both sides would suspend building for a period were sunk by mutual suspicions. For the British the situation was complicated by the proliferation of dreadnoughts under construction all around the world, but particularly in the Mediterranean where the French dreadnought fleet would soon be joined by a conglomeration of Italian, Austrian and Turkish dreadnoughts over the next few years. The permutations seemed endless and the costs ruinous, for these mighty ships were the very acme of modern technology. Each successive class of battleship brought incremental improvements that raised the stakes ever higher. Size may not have been everything, but it certainly allowed for heavier guns, improved armour protection and better engines. In just eight years the *Dreadnought*, went from being the mistress of all she surveyed to near obsolescence upon the advent of the super-dreadnoughts under construction in 1914.

In contrast to the British fixation on guns and speed, the Germans concentrated their efforts on making their ships as near possible to unsinkable. German armour was generally both thicker and covered far more of the vital areas. The German ships also had the advantage of being built only for service in the North Sea and North Atlantic, so for the brief periods that they were at sea their crews could put up with the discomfort caused by cramped mess decks and a high level of bulk-head subdivision below decks. This was impossible to countenance for British ships and crews operating in a global role. Tirpitz explained his philosophy:

> So long as a ship is afloat, it retains a certain fighting value and can
> afterwards be easily repaired. Thus the deadly injury of that part of a
> ship below the water line is the ultimate aim of the weapon of attack,
> and the increasing of the buoyancy of the vessel the main object of
> protective measures. As soon as the Navy Bill was settled I caused this
> question of buoyancy to be taken up with great thoroughness. We soon
> found out that we had to experiment with real explosions in order
> to gain sufficient experience. As we could not sacrifice modern ships,
> and could not learn enough from the older ones, we built a section
> of a modern ship by itself and carried out experimental explosions
> on it, with torpedo heads, carefully studying the result every time.
> We tested the possibility of weakening the force of the explosion by
> letting the explosive gases burst in empty compartments without
> meeting with any resistance. We ascertained the most suitable kind of
> steel for the different structural parts, and found further that the effect
> of the explosion was nullified if we compelled it to pulverise coal in
> any considerable quantity. This resulted in a special arrangement of a
> portion of the coal bunkers. We were then able to meet the force of the
> explosion, which had been weakened in this way, by a strong, carefully

constructed steel wall which finally secured the safety of the interior of the ship. This 'torpedo bulkhead' was carried without interruption the whole length of the vital parts of the ship. These experiments, which were continued through many years, and on which we did not hesitate to expend millions, yielded moreover information concerning the most suitable use of material and the construction of the adjoining parts of the ship. In addition to this, the whole of the underwater parts of the ship were designed for the event of failure to localize the effects of the explosion, or of several hits being made, and so forth; endless labour was expended upon details such as the pumping system or the possibility of speedily restoring a listing ship to a vertical position by flooding certain compartments. Finally, we completely abandoned the practice of connecting the compartments below the water line by doors. The buoyancy which was attained by our system stood the test. In contrast to the British ships, ours were well-nigh indestructible.[6]

Admiral Alfred von Tirpitz, Secretary of State of the Imperial Naval Office

The German construction work was watched carefully by the Admiralty, but it had little time to react and was also restricted by physical factors such as the size of available dry docks. There would be few better examples of the importance of careful research and preparation to the practical business of war at sea. The differences in characteristics of the opposing dreadnoughts and battlecruisers would define the nature of the encounters between the British and German fleets during the Great War. Time and time again British ships would be sunk and lost for ever, while far more severely damaged German ships would struggle home to fight again.

The dreadnought was not the only innovation that was changing the traditional face of naval warfare. The advent of the practical submarine was also crucial, although at this stage neither side truly appreciated its potential; indeed, some within the Royal Navy still regarded it as a somewhat underhand weapon of war. Nevertheless, they could not be ignored and far-sighted advocates were diligently developing a Royal Navy submarine service that was gradually improving its capabilities, especially after the advent of the long-range torpedo. This mirrored developments in Germany where their U-boats (*Unterseeboot*) were generally still considered defensive weapons for use against ships trying to impose a close blockade. Once submerged, the U-boat provided an undetectable menace against which no effective counter-measure had been developed. Another near-invisible weapon was the mine which was a potent weapon against all forms of shipping, whether employed to defend a specific port or to deny whole areas and sea lanes from passage. Minesweeping methods were soon developed, but they were both time-consuming and dangerous – especially in hostile waters. The freedom of the North Sea in particular was soon greatly restricted once war was declared.

Germany had also built up a formidable fleet of destroyers. These fast, lightly armed ships were originally described as torpedo boat destroyers, but were now themselves also armed with torpedoes and as such posed a potent threat to the mighty dreadnoughts. Fleets found they could not set out to sea without screens of destroyers to protect them from the depredations of their opposing numbers – and to threaten the torpedoing of enemy dreadnoughts should they be given half a chance. The necessity of maintaining a destroyer escort severely restricted the movement potential of the main fleets as destroyers had a far more limited range than the great battleships. Unlike the old fleets of sailing ships that could remain out at sea for months, modern fleets could only make short-lived two- or three-day sorties.

The combined menace posed by German submarines, mines and destroyers forced a secret decision by the Royal Navy in 1912 to abandon any idea of establishing a close blockade of German ports. Instead a distant blockade would be substituted, based at the vast natural harbour of Scapa Flow in the Orkneys. The intention was to use the geographical location of Germany to her disadvantage by blocking the 20-mile-wide English Channel and the 200-mile gap between the Orkneys and Norway. At a stroke Germany would be cut off from the oceans of the world. Only the Baltic and the North Sea would remain open to her unless the iron grip of the Royal Navy could be forcibly loosened.

On the outbreak of war the capital ships deployed in the British Grand Fleet numbered twenty dreadnoughts, eight pre-dreadnoughts and just four battlecruisers (three were stationed in the Mediterranean); while opposing them were the German High Seas Fleet of thirteen dreadnoughts, sixteen pre-dreadnoughts and three battlecruisers. Both fleets had numerous squadrons of cruisers, light cruisers and the ubiquitous destroyer flotillas. There were also nineteen British pre-dreadnoughts in the Channel Fleet at Medway. The British did have one very real advantage: they had mobilised their fleet early. A test mobilisation of the whole fleet had culminated in the Spithead Review on 20 July 1914. After the review, although the ships had then dispersed to their home ports, the First Sea Lord, Prince Louis of Battenberg, after consultation with the First Lord of the Admiralty Winston Churchill, decided to halt the dispersal of the reservists pending the resolution of the July crisis – or war. This greatly simplified matters when the Grand Fleet and all other naval units were required to take up their war stations.

The Commander in Chief of the German High Seas Fleet, tucked away in harbour at Wilhelmshaven, was Admiral Friedrich von Ingenohl, who had been given clear instructions as to his priorities in the coming war. These originated not from Admiral Tirpitz who as Secretary of State of the Imperial Naval Office found himself restricted to an administrative role with no influence on operational decisions. Instead they reflected the cautious policy of the Kaiser himself, who still took a great interest in the fleet he had created, and the Chancellor, Bethmann-Hollweg, who saw an intact fleet as a considerable bargaining tool in any peace negotiations. The Army seemed happy so long as the High Seas Fleet remained intact and protected the Baltic coast from any possible British or Russian landings. At the heart of this timid approach was the concept of a 'fleet in being', that is, a fleet powerful enough to threaten British naval supremacy but which did not put the matter to the test in a great battle. In this way the German fleet could continue to threaten maritime communications, challenging British command of the sea and hamstringing Britain in the exercise of her naval power. The Royal Navy would constantly have to be on its guard against the emergence of the German fleet from Wilhelmshaven. This superficially attractive position – it entailed doing nothing – had one very serious drawback that Tirpitz clearly identified.

> It was simply nonsense to pack the fleet in cotton wool. The 'fleet in being' had some meaning for England, for her fleet thus achieved its purpose of commanding the seas. But the principle was meaningless for Germany, whose object must be to keep the seas free for herself. Besides, we could not allow the war to develop into a war of exhaustion, but must attempt to shorten matters. The world prestige of the English rests in the main on the very belief in the invincibility of their armada. A German sea victory, or even a doubtful success for England, would

have worked the gravest injury to England's position. Any penetration of British naval power would awaken the Indian, Egyptian and other questions, deprive England of the further allies that she needed to encompass our defeat, and incline her to peace. England understood the danger, and appreciated our strength, better than we did at home. That was why she hesitated to enter the war, and that is why, when she had entered, she avoided battle. In the first year our prospects were good, and even later they were still tolerable. Even an unfavourable sea battle would not have made our prospects materially worse. It could be safely assumed that the losses of the enemy would be as great as ours. Nothing, indeed, that could happen to our fleet could be worse than its retention in idleness.[7]

Admiral Alfred von Tirpitz, Secretary of State of the Imperial Naval Office

For all his efforts, indeed for all the heavy financial and political sacrifices incurred since 1898, now that it had actually come to war the German Navy was once again a bystander – just as in 1870.

The British Commander in Chief of the Grand Fleet facing the Germans across the North Sea was Admiral Sir John Jellicoe. Born in 1859, Jellicoe had joined the Navy as a cadet at twelve years old. He became a gunnery specialist, earning both the approval of Fisher and rapid promotion. He had seen active service in the Boxer Rebellion and had been badly wounded in the left lung while trying to rescue the European embassy staff besieged in Peking. On recovery he served in a variety of senior sea and staff appointments, always demonstrating a remarkable capacity for hard work and a logical rigour in his approach to any problems placed before him. His evident abilities, combined with his success in naval exercises held in 1913, had earmarked him for future command of the Grand Fleet. On the outbreak of war, despite his anguished protests, he was immediately brought in to replace the incumbent Admiral Sir George Callaghan, who was considered too old for the stresses of wartime command.

At first the British were in a quandary, for although the Grand Fleet was theoretically based at Scapa, that base was without defences of any kind and hence wide open to deadly surprise submarine attack. In effect the fleet was safer at sea screened by destroyers than as sitting ducks in a harbour well within the operational range of the more modern German U-boats. Hence the Grand Fleet spent a fair amount of time sweeping down into the North Sea while at the same time fulfilling its other main role of covering the safe transport of the BEF across the Channel. This mission was achieved and indeed the BEF would be indebted to the Navy for successfully maintaining the cross-Channel links with very little drama throughout the whole war.

The first major action of the naval war came with the Battle of Heligoland Bight on 26 August 1914. This engagement had its origins in the desire of Commodore Reginald Tyrwhitt of the Harwich Force to launch a raid on German destroyer patrols off the islands of Heligoland in conjunction with a force of submarines commanded by Commodore Roger Keyes. Jellicoe was unenthusiastic at such an inherently risky operation, but the Admiralty approved the plans, only allowing the detachment of the 1st Battlecruiser Squadron under Vice Admiral Sir David Beatty to provide a degree of back-up. The situation was extremely chaotic as poor staff work meant that most of the British forces had no idea who exactly was at sea, leaving a huge potential for disaster. Confusion summed up the whole course of the fighting as Tyrwhitt aboard the light cruiser *Arethusa* led the Harwich Force into the Heligoland Bight.

> Our battlecruisers were scattered by, and made violent attempts to sink a squadron of our own submarines. Our light cruisers, sent into support, were in two cases supposed to be enemy by our destroyers sighting them. In one case two of our light cruisers chased two of our torpedo boat destroyers at full speed to the west, each supposing the other to be the enemy. They blocked the air with wireless at the very time when *Arethusa* and her destroyers were being overwhelmed by superior forces.[8]
>
> Commander Reginald Drax, HMS *Lion*, 1st Battlecruiser Squadron

Running battles followed as the Germans retreated before unleashing their own trap as a strong force of light cruisers emerged from the mists. Then, just as all seemed lost, Beatty and the battlecruisers swept up and overwhelmed the outclassed German light forces, sinking three light cruisers and a destroyer. Although the *Arethusa* had been badly damaged the British only had 75 casualties in contrast to some 1,200 suffered by the Germans. Likely disaster had been transformed into a significant triumph which disguised both the sheer madness of the plans and the endemic ineptitude in both command and control of the operations.

It was to be the only good news for a while for the British. Even without risking the perils of maintaining a close blockade they still suffered a draining series of losses from German submarine and mine warfare. There is no doubt, however, that the German U-boat crews faced a considerable ordeal in their living conditions. One enlightening account was left by Lieutenant Johannes Speiss, who was an officer aboard the *U-9*, captained by Otto Weddigen.

> Far forward in the pressure hull, which was cylindrical, was the forward torpedo room containing two torpedo tubes and two reserve torpedoes. Further astern was the warrant officers' compartment, which contained only small bunks and was particularly wet and cold. Then came the commanding officer's cabin, fitted with only a small bunk and clothes closet, no desk being furnished. Whenever a torpedo had to be loaded forward or the tube prepared for a shot, both cabins had to be completely cleared out. Bunks and clothes cabinets then had to be moved into the adjacent officers' compartment, which was no light task owing to the lack of space in the latter compartment. In order to live at all in the officers' compartments a certain degree of finesse was required. The watch officer's bunk was too small to permit him to lie on his back. He was forced to lie on one side and then, being wedged between the bulkhead to the right and the clothes-press on the left, to hold fast against the movements of the boat in a seaway. On the port side of the officers' compartment was the berth of the Chief Engineer, while the centre of the compartment served as a passageway through the boat. On each side was a small upholstered transom between which a folding table could be inserted. Two folding camp-chairs completed the furniture. While the Commanding Officer, Watch Officer and Chief Engineer took their meals, men had to pass back and forth through the boat, and each time anyone passed the table had to be folded. Further aft, the crew space was separated from the officers' compartment by a watertight bulkhead with a round watertight door for passage. On one side of the crew space a small electric range was supposed to serve for cooking – but the electric heating coil and the bake-oven short-circuited every time an attempt was made to use them. Meals were always prepared on deck! For this purpose we had a small paraffin stove. This had the particular advantage of being serviceable even in a high wind. The crew space had bunks for only a few of the crew – the rest slept in hammocks, when not on watch or on board the submarine mother-ship while in port. The living spaces were not cased with wood.

Since the temperature inside the boat was considerably greater than the sea outside, moisture in the air condensed on the steel hull-plates; the condensation had a very disconcerting way of dropping on a sleeping face, with every movement of the vessel. It was in reality like a damp cellar. From a hygienic standpoint the sleeping arrangements left much to be desired; one awoke in the morning with considerable mucus in the nostrils and a so-called 'oil-head'.[9]

Lieutenant Johannes Speiss, *U-9*

The oceans were large and for the U-boats, restricted by their low speed, success at sea was often a matter of luck. It was crucial for a commander to make the most of rare opportunities. Captain Lieutenant Otto Weddigen, commanding the *U-9*, certainly made the most of his good fortune when, on 22 September 1914, he encountered three obsolescent British armoured cruisers, the *Aboukir*, *Cressy* and *Hogue*, patrolling in line off the Dutch coast.

I loosed one of my torpedoes at the middle ship. I was then about 12 feet under water, and got the shot off in good shape, my men handling the boat as if she had been a skiff. I climbed to the surface to get a sight through my tube of the effect, and discovered that the shot had gone straight and true, striking the ship, which I later learned was the *Aboukir*, under one of her magazines, which in exploding helped the torpedo's work of destruction. There was a fountain of water, a burst of smoke, a flash of fire, and part of the cruiser rose in the air. Then I heard a roar and felt reverberations sent through the water by the detonation. She had been broken apart, and sank in a few minutes. I submerged at once. But I had stayed on top long enough to see the other cruisers, which I learned were the *Cressy* and the *Hogue*, turn and steam full speed to their dying sister, whose plight they could not understand, unless it had been due to an accident. As I reached my torpedo depth I sent a second charge at the nearest of the oncoming vessels, which was the *Hogue*. The English were playing my game, for I had scarcely to move out of my position, which was a great aid, since it helped to keep me from detection. The attack on the *Hogue* went true. But this time I did not have the advantageous aid of having the torpedo detonate under the magazine, so for twenty minutes the *Hogue* lay wounded and helpless on the surface before she heaved, half turned over and sank. By this time, the third cruiser knew of course that the enemy was upon her, she steamed a zigzag course, and this made it necessary for me to get nearer to the *Cressy*. When I got within suitable range I sent away my third attack. This time I sent a second torpedo after the first to make the strike doubly certain. My crew were aiming like sharpshooters and both torpedoes went to their bull's-eye. My luck was with me again, for the enemy was made useless and at once began sinking by her head. Then she careened far over, but all the while her men stayed at the guns looking for their invisible foe. Then she eventually suffered a boiler explosion and completely turned turtle. With her keel uppermost she floated until the air got out from under her and then she sank with a loud sound, as if from a creature in pain.[10]

Captain Lieutenant Otto Weddigen, *U-9*

The sequence of events as, one by one, the *Aboukir*, *Hogue* and *Cressy* were despatched was slightly absurd, but although the obsolescent cruisers themselves were of little military value, the human cost was appalling, with 1,459 deaths.

A few days later, on 27 October, the dreadnought *Audacious* was sunk by a mine off the Irish coast. Luckily she sank slowly and casualties were minimal, but the loss of this modern dreadnought was a terrible blow; indeed, the Admiralty went to considerable lengths to conceal it from the Germans. A combination of other commitments and the necessity for refits left the Grand Fleet reduced to an advantage of just three dreadnoughts and inferior in numbers of both battlecruisers and destroyers available. If the High Seas Fleet had chosen that moment; if von Ingenohl had followed the bolder policies espoused by Tirpitz rather than the voice of caution, then he could well have met the Grand Fleet at sea on near-equal terms.

By this time Jellicoe had got a grip of his new responsibilities. Although the British populace had cheerfully expected a great naval battle within days of the declaration of war, Jellicoe was well aware that the Germans would merely wait until losses eroded the Grand Fleet to their level – and he had no intention of falling into such an obvious trap.

The experience gained of German methods since the commencement of the war makes it possible and very desirable to consider the manner in which these methods are likely to be made use of tactically in a fleet action. The Germans have shown that they rely to a very great extent on submarines, mines and torpedoes, and there can be no doubt whatever that they will endeavour to make the fullest use of these weapons in a fleet action, especially since they possess an actual superiority over us in these particular directions. It, therefore, becomes necessary to consider our own tactical methods in relation to these forms of attack. In the first place, it is evident that the Germans cannot rely with certainty upon having their full complement of submarines and minelayers present in a fleet action, unless the battle is fought in waters selected by them and in the southern area of the North Sea. Aircraft, also, could only be brought into action in this locality. My object will therefore be to fight the fleet action in the northern portion of the North Sea.[11]

Admiral Sir John Jellicoe, HMS *Iron Duke*, Grand Fleet

He also outlined the cautious tactical approach he would take in any battle. Jellicoe was not willing to risk casting away the British global naval advantage for the sake of personal glory in combat.

If, for instance, the enemy battle fleet were to turn away from an advancing fleet, I should assume that the intention was to lead us over mines and submarines, and should decline to be so drawn. I desire particularly to draw the attention of Their Lordships to this point, since it may be deemed a refusal of battle, and, indeed, might possibly result in failure to bring the enemy to action as soon as is expected and hoped. Such a result would be absolutely repugnant to the feelings of all British naval officers and men, but with new and untried methods of warfare new tactics must be devised to meet them. I feel that such tactics, if not understood, may bring odium upon me, but so long as I have the confidence of their Lordships I intend to pursue what is, in my considered opinion, the proper course to defeat and annihilate the enemy's battle fleet, without regard to uninstructed opinion or criticism. The situation is a difficult one. It is quite within the bounds of possibility that half our battle fleet might be disabled by underwater attack before the guns opened fire at all, if a false move is made, and I feel that I must constantly bear in mind the great probability of such attack and be prepared tactically to prevent its success.[12]

Admiral Sir John Jellicoe, HMS *Iron Duke*, Grand Fleet

This cautious approach was fully endorsed by the Admiralty on 7 November 1914. Jellicoe's caution reveals that Tirpitz was entirely right in his frustration at the inactivity of the High Seas Fleet: the British did indeed fear the consequences of a pitched battle unless it was fought to their advantage within strictly and controlled circumstances. Meanwhile, the British utilised a potent combination of minefields, destroyers and the pre-dreadnoughts of the Channel Fleet based in the Medway, which effectively blocked off the English Channel. The German High Seas Fleet would be confined to the North Sea; that in consequence would be an area of contested waters, with neither side truly holding sway. But the rest of the oceans of the world would be relatively secure for British commerce and military expeditions – save only for the depredations of any German commerce-raiders. In view of this, many British officers were surprised by what they saw as the passive approach of the German Navy.

> When your adversary is very quiet one is always inclined to think they are up to some very deep laid scheme and it is the same with us now. One never imagined that the German Battle Fleet would come out until they had endeavoured to reduce some of our superiority but we did imagine they would drive home attacks with destroyers, submarines and mines with all their might and that they would make a very determined attack on our commerce during the first few days of the war, but their attempts in all directions seem to have been very poor ones. For instance, one would have thought that they would have sent their battlecruisers out into the Atlantic because until we had discovered it they could have created a pretty kettle of fish as none of the cruisers we have on trade protection could either fight them or run from them. Even after they had been discovered it would have taken some time for our battlecruisers to have hunted them down.[13]
>
> Commander Dudley Pound, HMS *St Vincent*, Grand Fleet

Although they did briefly consider such an operation, the Germans were not willing to sacrifice their battlecruisers and their crews on such a speculative venture. They would bide their time and hope the British would do something stupid.

In the absence of any great fleet actions, and with a constant drip of losses, the mood in the Royal Navy was somewhat despondent at this stage of the war. This was exacerbated by the difficulties encountered in dealing with the German commerce-raiders, the light cruisers *Dresden*, *Karlsruhe* and *Leipzig*, and the threatening German East Asiatic

Squadron, commanded by the resourceful Vice Admiral Maximilian von Spee, consisting of the two armoured cruisers *Scharnhorst* and *Gneisenau* accompanied by the light cruisers *Nürnberg*, *Emden*, *Leipzig* and *Dresden*. Assisted by a collection of colliers and supply ships, these ships would create havoc across the whole of the Pacific Ocean for several months, preying on the sea lanes and even threatening the troop convoys despatched from Australia and New Zealand. The detached exploits of the *Emden*, in particular, became the stuff of legend before she was sunk by the *Sydney* at the Cocos Islands on 9 November 1914. But von Spee's greatest triumph came when he engaged the British South American Squadron (the armoured cruisers *Good Hope* and *Monmouth*, the light cruiser *Glasgow* and the auxiliary cruiser *Otranto*), commanded by Rear Admiral Sir Christopher Cradock, at the Battle of Coronel, off Chile, on 1 November 1914. Cradock had been pushed by Admiralty signals into a series of rash decisions, seeking action with a German squadron which was clearly stronger and able, once contact had been made, to use its superior speed and armament. The encounter was to prove short-lived. Cradock impotently tried to close the range to allow his out-gunned ships some chance to inflict damage, but to no avail as Lieutenant Knoop observed from the *Scharnhorst*.

> In most cases hits by high explosive shells were immediately followed by outbreaks of fire. Twice I observed what I believed to be an explosion of ammunition. The flames shot up immediately after hits by high explosive shells and were distinguishable from the other fires by their dimensions and outline. Some hits, probably on the decks, sent up showers of sparks over a wide area. When armour was hit thick black clouds with sharp outlines were observed. Hits were so frequent that it was impossible to note them in chronological order. The *Good Hope* received serious hits in the fore part of the ship, on the upper bridge, on the mast about 30 feet above the deck, on the after side of the foretop, also hit repeatedly amidships, most of these causing fires. The after battery was hit several times and fires broke out. The flames in the interior of the ship could be seen through the portholes. Two shells struck the ship near the after turret. The *Monmouth* was hit on her fore 6-inch turret. The high explosive shell blew off the roof. A terrific explosion of charges must then have blown the whole turret off the forecastle for it disappeared completely. I observed that many shells

struck the ship amidships. A huge column of fire, almost as high as the mast and 60 to 90 feet across, suddenly shot up on the starboard side. Between thirty and forty hits were counted in all. At times three or four fires were burning simultaneously.[14]

Lieutenant Ernst Knoop, SMS *Scharnhorst*, East Asiatic Squadron

It was a cruel battle in which both the *Good Hope* and the *Monmouth* were sunk with the loss of all hands. The *Otranto* had early on been told to make a run for it, while the *Glasgow* bore a charmed life, escaping with only minor damage. The Battle of Coronel demonstrated the brutal consequences of a one-sided naval battle. Yet von Spee was doomed, too. Knowing that he had little chance of ever getting back to Germany, he saw it as his duty to maximise the damage he could inflict before the inevitable British retaliation burst upon him. It would not take long.

At the Admiralty the First Sea Lord Prince Louis of Battenberg had been under increasing populist press attack over his German ancestry and had been replaced by Sir John Fisher, the fiery old controversialist and progenitor of the *Dreadnought*. He would prove a disastrous choice – a muddled mixture of irrationality, rashness and an increasing inability, at the age of seventy-three, to maintain a coherent line of thought that meant he was unable to resist the misguided enthusiasms of his combative First Lord Sir Winston Churchill. Ultimately both would fall together, mired in the disaster of the Gallipoli campaigns of 1915. But Fisher was seen to his best advantage in this early crisis: action was his watchword as he over-ruled Jellicoe's protests and despatched not one, not two, but three battlecruisers to hunt down von Spee. The *Princess Royal* was sent from the Grand Fleet to guard the West Indies, while the *Invincible* and *Inflexible* were sent from the Mediterranean to the South Atlantic under the command of Vice Admiral Doveton Sturdee. Here, in company with a further three armoured cruisers (*Carnarvon*, *Cornwall* and *Kent*) and two light cruisers (*Glasgow* and *Bristol*), they made their way to join the old pre-dreadnought *Canopus* at Port Stanley on the Falkland Islands which they reached early on the morning of 8 December 1914. And there they were busy coaling when von Spee arrived intent on destroying the harbour installations and any ships within it. For a moment, there may have been the theoretical opportunity for the *Scharnhorst* and the *Gneisenau* to rake the near-helpless British ships in harbour, but the beached *Canopus* fired a long-range salvo of 12-inch shells which, not unnaturally, panicked the Germans who could already see the distinctive tripod masts of the battlecruisers. Once they had sorted themselves out the British ships emerged to begin a long stern chase. The disparity of speed was such that it was only a matter of time before the Germans were reeled in one by one and destroyed.

> This was a very bitter pill to swallow. We choked a little at the neck, the throat contracted and stiffened, for that meant a life and death grapple, or rather a fight ending in honourable death. The old law of naval warfare, which ordains that the less powerful and the less swift ships should be vanquished in free waters and in fine weather, was again to be exemplified in our case. It would have been vain to harbour the slightest illusion in this respect, for the sky remained clear; there was not the slightest cloud presaging bad weather to be seen, nor any wisp of fog to throw over us its friendly mantle and hide us from the enemy's sight.[15]
>
> Commander Hans Pochhammer, SMS *Gneisenau*, East Asiatic Squadron

During the battle that followed, von Spee played his poor hand as best he could. He freed his faster light cruisers to try and escape independently. Meanwhile, like Craddock before him, he struggled to close the range to enable his 8.2-inch guns to damage the mighty battlecruisers. But it was all for nothing and both his ships were steadily smashed to pieces.

> As we passed the *Scharnhorst* we noticed that she lay deeper than usual heeled slightly to the larboard. There was a large hole in the fore end and a similar one in the quarter deck. Smoke was rising from the ship and flames were visible in the interior through shell holes and portholes. But her gun thundered incessantly; the starboard batteries now came into action and brought fresh force into the fray. But it looked as if her fate was sealed. She moved more slowly in the water and suffered considerably under the hail of enemy shells. The Admiral must have felt that his ship was nearing her end. Just as he had previously sacrificed his armoured cruisers to save his light cruisers, so he proposed to sacrifice the *Scharnhorst* to save the *Gneisenau*. Determined to get the last ounce out of his resources and to fight as long as he could float, and in this way facilitate the escape of our ship, he swung round to the enemy on the starboard in the hope of

damaging him by firing torpedoes! The water had now risen to the fore upper deck. Fires were raging fore and aft, but the Admiral's flag floated proudly from the foremast, as also did the battle flags from the after mast and the gaff. The *Scharnhorst* gradually heeled over to larboard, and her bows became more and more submerged. Her fore turret was about six and a half feet above the water when it fired its last shot, then – the screws revolved in the air and the ship swiftly slid head first into the abyss.[16]

Commander Hans Pochhammer, SMS *Gneisenau*, East Asiatic Squadron

The *Scharnhorst* went down with the gallant admiral and all hands. Then it was the turn of the *Gneisenau*.

I felt the ship giving way under me. I heard the roaring and surging of the water come nearer and nearer, and was filled with the idea that I should be very cold. When the upper deck was submerged the speed at which the ship was capsizing somewhat diminished, owing to the resistance set up, and then the ship continued to turn on her axis. The sea invaded a corner of the bridge, caught me and those who were with me and tossed us away, a movement which I involuntarily accelerated by a vigorous push off. I was caught up by a whirlpool and dragged into an abyss. The water eddied and murmured around me and droned in my ears. But even before suffering from loss of breath I felt as if I were being drawn upwards by invisible hands. I opened my eyes and noticed it was brighter, 'Keep cool!' I thought to myself and then began to strike out. I came to the surface. The sea was heaving. The swell was due partly to the wind, which must have sprung up in the late afternoon, and partly to the displacement of water produced by the capsizing of our ship. The latter I saw a hundred or so yards away, her keel in the air. The red paint on her bottom glistened in the sunset.[17]

Commander Hans Pochhammer, SMS *Gneisenau*, East Asiatic Squadron

In the end Pochhammer and some 200 of his men were saved from the *Gneisenau*. The light cruisers *Nürnberg* and *Leipzig* were also overhauled and sank, although the *Dresden* escaped, to be eventually sunk by the vengeful *Glasgow* on 14 March 1915. The Battle of the Falklands was of little significance other than in restoring the damage to its reputation suffered by the Royal Navy at the Battle of Coronel a month earlier. In a sense, Admiral von Spee and his men were already doomed from the moment they commenced their mission: far from home, with finite resources, sailing the seas with their enemies all around them. Their conduct was a tribute to the spirit that had been engendered within the German Navy.

MEANWHILE, VON INGENOHL was tempted by the evident absence of British battlecruisers in the hunt for von Spee to launch a series of raids on the east coast of Britain. These raids were intended to provoke an unconsidered response from the British that might allow the chance of isolating and destroying elements of the Grand Fleet. Since October, Beatty's 1st Battlecruiser Squadron had been based at Cromarty in northern Scotland and so was the most promising candidate for a German ambush. Yet the British did have one huge theoretical advantage in this game of cat and mouse. Unknown to the Germans, their secret naval ciphers had been passed to the Admiralty by the Russians after they had been recovered from the wreck of the *Magdeburg* on 26 August 1914. A special department was set up to decode the German signals and to follow the constant permutations and changes of codes adopted by the Germans over the years that followed. Known as Room 40, it was augmented by the use of wireless directional stations dotted along the east coast that could identify the location of German units by taking cross-bearings on any wireless traffic.

The first German tip and run raid on Yarmouth, made on 3 November, came too early for Room 40. For the next raid, on 16 December, von Ingenohl planned a bombardment of British east coast towns by the battlecruisers of the 1st Scouting Force commanded by Admiral Franz von Hipper, with the further intention of trying to draw Jellicoe into a freshly laid minefield. Two days before it happened, the Admiralty were notified by Room 40 of the imminent raid, but the intelligence proved more of a hazard than a boon to Jellicoe. The Admiralty did not realise that Hipper would be supported by the whole of the High Seas Fleet and interfered in Jellicoe's dispositions to insist that he deploy just Beatty's four battlecruisers and the six dreadnoughts of the 2nd Battle Squadron with accompanying light forces. Both sides were attempting to trap the other, but in the circumstances of bad weather and poor visibility the operations were inconclusive – except for the people of Scarborough, Hartlepool and Whitby, who found the German shells crashing down on them. In the end von Ingenohl lacked the nerve to close the trap. At the first reports of fighting between the respective destroyer screens he reversed his course towards Germany, thereby abandoning Hipper to his fate. However, Beatty missed any chance to come to grips with Hipper's battlecruisers, in circumstances of deep confusion exacerbated by unclear signals from Beatty aboard his flagship *Lion* that allowed Hipper to escape unscathed. It had been a mutually unsatisfying non-event and yet both Hipper and Beatty had come close to disaster. How close was not necessarily appreciated at the time.

The immediate consequence was an outcry in the British popular press over the Navy's apparent inability to prevent these raids on British coastal towns. Although, in truth, there was little the Admiralty could do. The North Sea was not controlled by the Royal Navy – this was the penalty for the distant blockade – and so all that could be done was to move Beatty to a new base at Rosyth in the Firth of Forth to allow a slightly quicker response should Room 40 give warning of another raid.

He did not have long to wait. On 23 January 1915, Room 40 divined that Hipper and the 1st Scouting Group (*Seydlitz, Moltke, Derfflinger* and *Blücher*) would be emerging at 17.45 that very day. The intercepted signals did not make it clear what the Germans were about to do, so it was assumed that they were intent on another coastal raid. In fact Hipper was planning to entrap and destroy the British light forces operating in the Dogger Bank region but, as prior intelligence goes, it was still pure gold. Once again the Admiralty acted with an unwarranted degree of over-confidence. Beatty and Tyrwhitt's Harwich Force was despatched to inter-cept Hipper, but without the close support of Jellicoe's fleet. Thus Beatty sailed with the 1st Battlecruiser Squadron (the *Lion, Tiger, Princess Royal*), the 2nd Battlecruiser Squadron (the older *New Zealand* and *Indomitable*), the dubious support of the pre-dreadnoughts of the 3rd Battle Squad-ron, the 1st Light Cruiser Squadron and the usual screening destroyers. He intended to rendezvous with the Harwich Force near Dogger Bank at 07.00 on 24 January. Soon after, the light screens of both forces clashed and Hipper, astutely recognising what was happening, bolted for home. Beatty and his battlecruisers began a grim stern chase, seeking to over-haul and destroy their adversaries. Gradually the faster *Lion, Tiger* and *Princess Royal* began to get within range, until the *Lion* opened fire, at about 20,000 yards, concentrating initially on the rear ship, the hybrid battlecruiser *Blücher,* which was slightly lagging behind. From this promising position everything began to go wrong for Beatty. Insufficiently clear signals from his flagship led to confusion in the distribution of the fire from his battlecruisers. This was further exacerbated by appalling standards of gunnery which to some extent meant that the British superiority in numbers was discounted.

Yet, despite it all, one 13.5-inch shell from the *Lion,* fired at 09.50, did crash down on her opposite number, the *Seydlitz.* It tore through the quarter deck and partially penetrated the barbette armour of the aft turret. The burst ignited the cordite charges in the working chamber and triggered a flash that spread in an instant into the magazine handling room and up into the turret above. As desperate men tried to escape they opened the door connecting with the adjoining superimposed turret, thereby inadvertently allowing the flames to rip through both to deadly effect. For a few moments a magazine detonation which would have doomed the ship seemed likely, but was narrowly averted by the timely flooding of the after magazines. Nevertheless, 159 men were killed in the conflagration.

In response, the German fire was concentrated on the *Lion* at the head of the British line, hitting her fifteen times and causing serious damage. Listing to port, she began to fall out of line at around 10.50. Despite this Hipper and his ships were still in dire straits; the *Blücher* was by this time on fire and slowing down. But then fate intervened as Beatty sighted what he thought was a periscope and feared he had led his precious battlecruisers into a deadly submarine trap. He ordered an immediate turn to port, which had the effect of rapidly opening the range from his quarry and this coupled with the signalling blunder thereby allowed Hipper the precious breathing space to try to escape away to the south-east, abandoning the *Blücher* to her fate. Her crew fought to the end, but for the British the dramatic photos of her turning turtle as she sank were small compensation for the escape without further interference of the rest of the German battlecruisers. Yet the Germans were chastened by their experiences and shortly afterwards Admiral von Ingenohl was dismissed. It was considered he had been remiss in not sailing with his fleet in support of the Dogger Bank operations and had taken unnecessary risks without the chance of any significant gain. He was replaced on 2 February 1915 by Admiral Hugo von Pohl, a man who was to prove equally uninspired and hamstrung by the overall caution urged on the High Seas Fleet.

The Battle of Dogger Bank was a partial victory for the British, but its real importance arises from the lessons learnt, or ignored, by the two protagonists. The Germans were horrified by the near destruction of the *Seydlitz*, which had nearly exploded after the cordite fire. After a careful investigation, considerable precautionary measures were introduced to try and prevent such a flash travelling anywhere between the turret gunhouse, the handling chamber and the magazine. By contrast, the British appeared to have learnt little and there were no corresponding improvements in working practices in the chain from magazines to turret. Indeed, in an effort to improve their rate of fire, the British gunners began to take suicidal short cuts in the magazines and working chambers. The magazine doors were propped open and cordite charge linen bags piled up outside the doors ready to be hoisted up to the turret gunhouses. Such slack safety measures would have a considerable effect on the outcomes of future battles, especially as the armour protecting the British battlecruisers was much less extensive than that on their German counterparts. Once these thin skins were pierced the seeds of their destruction lay within them.

The British also failed to learn much from the demonstrable fallibilities in their command and control systems, in particular the weakness revealed aboard Beatty's flagship *Lion* in the process of generating and signalling orders without incorporating ambiguities which fatally confused his subordinates in the stress of battle. Furthermore, the overall standard of gunnery demonstrated by the British battlecruisers was simply dreadful; while they could hit the *Blücher* well enough when she was a crippled standing target, they scored only a handful of hits on the other German ships. While excuses could be made – lack of experience under battle conditions, the poor visibility caused by palls of smoke and spray from German shells – the fact remained that they were poor in the extreme, with the bulk of their shells sailing thousands of yards over their targets. Jellicoe was aware of the problem but it was difficult to secure increased opportunities for long-range practice for the battlecruisers in the relatively cramped and narrow confines of the Forth. In contrast, the Grand Fleet could practise with impunity in the far reaches of its huge Scapa Flow anchorage.

The blockade of Germany

The opening stages of the naval war saw the Grand Fleet exercise a brooding distant presence while cruisers guarded the northern exits to the North Sea enforcing the blockade which sought to prevent raw materials and supplies from reaching Germany. When it became apparent that the land war would not be over quickly, this became a key part of the Allied global strategy; this was after all why Britain was such a coveted ally. The 10th Cruiser Squadron assigned to the task consisted of eight protected cruisers of the *Edgar* class. These were old ships dating back to 1891. The North Sea was a hostile environment for such elderly matrons and the winter storms proved almost too much for them.

> It was blowing a full gale and it looked doubtful if the ship would weather it. My cabin was on the upper deck, in the after superstructure, and I lay down on my bunk in my clothes and being very tired I dozed off. I was awakened by a terrific crash and my cabin door was burst open and water poured in. All I could see outside was a swirling mass of foam on the upper deck. I thought the ship must be sinking. I swung myself out of my bunk and, up to my knees in water, waded up the slope through the doorway. The ship seemed on her beam ends and it looked as if nothing could save her. As I watched she slowly – miraculously – righted herself. A minute later another great wave swept her from stem to stern. It was then that a Midshipman was carried overboard from the foremost gun and on over the nettings aft and laid almost at my feet. After that there was a lull and I could take in the scene. The gun crews were clinging to the guns or whatever they could hold on to, while live ammunition rolled across the deck.[18]

> Lieutenant Harold Bowen, HMS *Edgar*, 10th Cruiser Squadron

Several of the other ships were caught in this terrible storm and it was decided to replace them with twenty-four armed liners.

It was the role of the 10th Cruiser Squadron to intercept merchantmen that were suspected of carrying contraband goods to Germany. Originally there was a narrow definition of prohibited goods, but this gradually broadened to include almost anything of value bound for Germany, or indeed for a neutral port from which it could then be re-exported. By rationing the amount of supplies they let through to that which a neutral country needed internally, Britain sought to prevent any significant re-export trade. Protests from neutral Scandinavian countries were inevitable, but Britain applied commercial pressures on them and also defined the North Sea as a military area, requiring all neutral traffic to be inspected before proceeding. This was an endless chore.

> I sighted and closed a steamer and found her to be the Norwegian steamer *Henrik* from New York to Bergen or Christiania, boarded her with some difficulty and found she had a general cargo of very considerable value, mainly copper ingots and wire, aluminium, flour, petroleum, motor-car parts, castings, etc., in fact most things which Germany is believed to want. It was more or less of a chance that I sighted this ship as I happened to be a good bit north of my line, and I do not think that there is much doubt that this ship was trying to get through unseen, for when I first saw her and stood towards her she altered course and was apparently inclined to run, but finally decided not to. Her captain was somewhat indignant at being boarded at all, and he produced the inevitable British Consular Certificate which he seemed to think cleared him of any further trouble. The mere fact that this ship was bound for Bergen or Christiania with such a cargo seems to me to be in itself gravely suspicious, and from what I gathered from my boarding officer as to the demeanour of the captain and mate I do not think there is much doubt that they were quite aware that they were running a very doubtful cargo, and their indignation was doubtless mainly due to the prospective loss of their bonus for getting safely through. This ship's cargo was some 5,000 tons or more. I had not time to make a careful examination of the manifest as the weather was threatening and I was anxious to get a prize crew on board before the sea got up.[19]

Captain Gerald Vivian, HMS *Patia*, 10th Cruiser Squadron

The British restrictions were not popular and indeed probably caused more disruption to neutral shipping lines than did their occasional losses to German submarines. There was the enduring risk of a clash with the United States and it would appear that American ships received special treatment with only the most perfunctory of inspections to avoid triggering too much American angst. The blockade would endure throughout the whole war.

German submarine blockade

When the war began submarines were regarded as a tactical adjunct to conventional surface ships. They would clearly be useful in both the defensive and offensive naval operations conducted by both sides, as had been proved in the early exchanges in the North Sea. Yet a true commerce destroying role was considered largely impractical due to the limited range of many of the early submarines and the difficulties of following the dictates of international law when sinking merchantmen. Civilian shipping – even from a hostile country – must not be sunk without proper warning and nor could crews be abandoned in lifeboats on the open seas. Neutral shipping was almost untouchable and could not be sunk, even if a search revealed the presence aboard of contraband goods intended for the British Isles. It is strange but this perception continued to exist on all sides for several months before gradually the penny (or pfennig) dropped that the more modern classes of submarines were capable of a great deal more. The first merchant ship was not sunk by a U-boat until 20 October 1914, when, still sticking to the rules, the *U-17* sank the small British steamer *Glitra* by boarding her and opening her sea cocks off the coast of Norway. It was a first, but only nine more British merchantmen had been sunk by the end of January 1915. Yet endemic dissatisfaction with the progress of the naval war, coupled with an unwillingness to risk the fleet in action left the Germans casting round for alternative plans in their efforts to inconvenience their naval adversaries.

The solution set upon was to make a bonfire of international law and the code of conduct hitherto assiduously followed. Instead of surfacing to stop, search and sink a ship, the U-boats would if necessary sink them by torpedo with no warning of any kind. On 4 February 1915, the Germans declared a war zone of the seas surrounding Great Britain and that any ship, Allied or neutral, caught inside its boundaries could be sunk at once. Justification for this action was based on the assertion that the British had already broken international law by changing the definition of contraband goods for the Royal Navy blockade of Germany. But the real reason was to allow the U-boats to attack while still preserving their invisibility. Freed from their shackles, the relatively small number of modern U-boats capable of reaching the western approaches to British ports were soon taking a cruel toll on shipping. The British seemed to have forgotten the value of convoys: the time-honoured method of warding off predators by gathering merchantmen together under the protection of armed vessels when passing through dangerous waters. Instead, destroyers and armed merchantmen roamed the seas randomly looking here, there and everywhere for the elusive U-boats in the vast emptiness of the seas. In the end the Germans were the victims of their own success when there was a series of high-profile scandals provoked by the sinking of civilian liners with a terrible loss of life – including American passengers.

A large outcry followed the sinking of the *Lusitania* by the *U-20* on 7 May 1915. It was some ten miles off the Old Head of Kinsale, near Queenstown, Ireland, when it was struck by a torpedo fired by Lieutenant Walther Schwieger at 14.10.

> Torpedo hits starboard side right behind the bridge. An unusually heavy explosion takes place with a very strong explosion cloud (cloud reaches far beyond front funnel). The explosion of the torpedo must have been followed by a second one (boiler or coal or powder?). The superstructure right above the point of impact and the bridge are torn asunder, fire breaks out, and smoke envelops the high bridge. The ship stops immediately and heels over to starboard very quickly, immersing simultaneously at the bow. It appears as if the ship were going to capsize very shortly, Great confusion ensues on board; the boats are made clear and some of them are lowered to the water with either stem or stern first and founder immediately.[20]
>
> Lieutenant Walther Schwieger, *U-20*

The ship sank within twenty minutes amidst many scenes of terror.

> The sea was calm; if the water had not been like that, there would have been many more lost. The most vivid scene of all was when it first started, when the explosion came. We were in the dining room. Everybody was frightened then – they panicked. Had we not been by a door we would never have got out, because a stream of people came down the dining room, there were others following at the back, and people were being stepped on, walked on. That was the most terrible thing – they just couldn't help themselves, the crowd was too strong. And when we were going down the staircase towards the boats someone fell on top of me – I would never have survived if my husband hadn't got hold of me and had the strength to pull me out.[21]
>
> Jane Lewis, passenger, RMS *Lusitania*

In the end, of 1,959 passengers and crew 1,195 were killed, of which 128 were American civilians. The uproar was enormous but the Germans were defiant, claiming that the liner was carrying contraband munitions and that their detonation had contributed to the ship's speedy demise. But then on 19 August the *U-24* sank the liner *Arabic* off Ireland. This time fatalities amounted to forty-four, of which only three were American citizens. Yet it sparked another furious round of US protests.

However, Germany was not alone in bending to destruction the international rules of law at sea. One of the British answers to the U-boat menace was the 'Q' Ship. This was a deeply unsporting measure, reliant as it was on the U-boats obeying the rules of war and being lured into surfacing by seemingly unarmed merchantmen. In the immediate aftermath of the sinking of the *Arabic* feelings ran very high. This boiled over into the infamous *Baralong* incident, which occurred the same day. The *Baralong* had arrived as the *U-27*, commanded by Lieutenant Bernard Wegener, was engaged in sinking the British steamer the *Nicosian*. On board the ship was a cargo of mules bound for the Western Front. Wegener let the crew and American muleteers board their lifeboats, but just as he was about to sink the ship by gunfire, the 'Q' Ship *Baralong* arrived on the scene. Disguised and flying the US flag, she approached signalling that she intended to rescue the *Nicosian*'s crew. At the last minute the *Baralong* unmasked her concealed 12-pounder guns.

> We could see the submarine lying above the surface on the water. Our captain commanded the chief gunman to fire, whereupon three shots were fired by our boat at the German submarine. The first shot took off the periscope. The second shot hit about 15 feet in the water before it reached the submarine. The third shot hit the gas tank, which exploded, and the submarine sank. In the meantime, the crew on the submarine, after the second shot, began to jump into the water. There were about fifteen of them and they began to swim to the *Nicosian*. While they were in the water our gunman shelled them by orders from our commanding officer, with 15-lb shells and also fired rifles at them. From the best I could see several of the crew on the German submarine were killed by our shell and rifle firing while in the water. Others were killed while attempting to climb up the ropes which had been thrown to them from the *Nicosian*. I should judge that three or four or five were killed while on these ropes. Some of our shots hit the

side of the *Nicosian*. After our crew boarded the *Nicosian* we found the only one of the crew of the submarine who had escaped on the deck, and found him to be the commander of the submarine. Our captain and others of our crew asked him for information concerning other German submarines. He refused to give such information. He was also asked if his submarine had sunk the *Arabic*. I do not remember certainly his reply. He was commanded to stand back and hold up his hands. He asked, as he stepped back and held up his hands, 'What for you shoot?' One of our marines, known as our engineer, fired one shot from his pistol into the body of the German Commander. He fell upon the deck on his face. Our crew, after ascertaining that he was dead, picked him up and threw him overboard.[22]

Ordinary Seaman Larimore Holland, HMS *Baralong*

Holland was a US citizen who had enlisted into the Royal Navy under the guise of being Canadian. There is considerable confusion as to what really happened aboard the *Nicosian* – lurid stories even circulated of a German sailor being disposed of in the furnace. There is little doubt, however, that it was a brutal and unnecessary exercise in vengeance.

Yet the intense storm of American protest over the *Lusitania* and the *Arabic* dwarfed the relatively small-scale uproar over the manifest criminality of the *Baralong* incident. Germany was forced to institute a moratorium on attacks on any liners without prior warnings. In addition, her U-boats were redeployed to operations centred in the North Sea and Mediterranean where there was far less chance of annoying the Americans. This had the effect of releasing the pressure on Britain. During 1915 some 748,000 tons of merchant shipping had been sunk by U-boats. This was a serious loss, but not enough to bring the British to their knees. The overall pattern of the naval war was unbroken and the stranglehold held by the Royal Navy over Germany would endure into 1916.

5

THE WESTERN FRONT, 1915

'Never do what the enemy wants for the very reason that he wants it; avoid a battleground that he has reconnoitred and studied; and with even more reason ground that he has fortified and where he is entrenched.'[1]

Napoleon I

WESTERN FRONT WARFARE would prove to be one of the most complex military conundrums of the modern age. Napoleon could rail against it from the past, but what alternative was there for the Allies other than to attack the German fortified positions when the trenches stretched from the English Channel to Switzerland? The soldiers on both sides were well dug in, although they only had simple defensive systems early in 1915. The trenches were over six feet deep, with the firing bays separated by solid earth traverses, a parapet in front and a parados behind, a fire step for men to stand on in action, wire or wood revetments holding up the sides, duckboards underfoot and simple drainage systems to hold back the water. Zigzagging communication trenches ran back to a support line which was generally a sketchy notational line rather than real trenches. In front there was a barbed wire defence of one or two 'double aprons'. Although by no means safe, the trenches enabled the troops to avoid the worst effects of artillery, machine gun and rifle fire. Only high explosives and shells from high-angle weapons dropped directly into the trenches posed a pressing danger. One thing was certain: a defending garrison tucked below ground level behind a tangle of barbed wire could deploy bolt-action rifles and enfilading heavy machine guns to deadly effect against troops attempting to cross No Man's Land. Anyone caught in the open was horribly vulnerable to artillery fire, so any attack was an intimidating prospect.

For the Germans, 1915 was a year of war that should not have been: their whole strategy had been based on a quick war. Now they found themselves embroiled in a two-front war, with two enemies – France and Russia – fully mobilised and another – Britain – slowly amassing her strength and relatively invulnerable behind her navy. The Chief of General Staff, General Erich von Falkenhayn, faced a grim situation.

> As a result of the unfortunately widespread catchword 'the war must be won in the East' even people in high leading circles inclined to the opinion that it would be possible for the Central Powers actually 'to force Russia to her knees' by force of arms, and by this success to induce the Western Powers to change their mind. This argument paid no heed either to the true character of the struggle for existence, in the most exact sense of the word, in which our enemies were engaged no less than we, nor to their strength of will. It was a grave mistake to believe that our Western enemies would give way, if and because Russia was beaten. No decision in the East, even though it were as thorough as was possible to imagine, could spare us from fighting to a conclusion in the West. For this Germany had to be prepared at all costs.[2]
>
> General Erich von Falkenhayn, General Headquarters, German Army

His personal preference was for a negotiated peace with one of Germany's adversaries – preferably Russia – allowing Germany to concentrate on beating first France and then Britain – whom he had come to see as the ultimate enemy. There was a great deal of dissent in the German High Command, with an opposing school of thought rapidly coalescing around Hindenburg and Ludendorff, the victors of Tannenberg, who were far more confident that outright victory could be achieved over Russia in 1915. Falkenhayn lacked the authority to enforce his will; indeed, there were widespread conspiracies against him across the German military and political hierarchy, involving the Chancellor Bethmann-Hollweg, Hindenburg (who sought the position of Chief of General Staff for himself) and the somewhat resentful Moltke. With the firm support of the Kaiser,

Falkenhayn remained in post, but he was somewhat weakened in the process and was forced to send part of his reserves to the Eastern Front: this was a victory without power. Perversely, events forced his hand when Austria-Hungary appealed for help after a series of terrible reverses against the Russians and Serbs left her teetering on the brink of military collapse. There were also rumbling noises emanating from Italy and Rumania; it seemed that, rather than join the Central Powers as had been hoped, they were far more likely to join the Allies. This could only add to the pressure on Austria-Hungary. This combination of circumstances left Falkenhayn with no choice: he may have been 'Westerner', but it was evident that the war was being lost in the east. He began to send his precious reserves to the Eastern Front, intent at first on stabilising Germany's faltering ally, then on making her secure from any future attack.

In contrast, the French and British had little option but to attack on the Western Front. The partial success of the Germans' offensive in August 1914 had left them able to dominate nearly all of Belgium and great swathes of northern France, with its wealth of coal and iron reserves. The Germans were also poised only some sixty or so miles from Paris. Joffre was determined not to adopt a passive approach, which would hand the initiative to the Germans, allowing them to make their own unfettered plans for a devastating offensive on the Western Front, or to transfer troops *en masse* to the Eastern Front in order to seek a victory over Russia. There was also a political dimension: Joffre was under intense pressure to remove the invaders from the sacred soil of France. Passively maintaining the *status quo* was not an option; the French wanted the invaders out of their country as soon as possible. The question was how?

The challenge facing British and French generals in early 1915 was immense. How could they get enough troops across No Man's Land to over-run the German front line? What about support trenches? How to consolidate gains from counter-attacks? How best to exploit any developing gap in the line? In the first engagements the problem was largely seen as how to take the German front line; after which, the presumption was, things would just sort themselves out and all would be well. But there was far more to it than that.

The French had a winter of heavy fighting as they sought to test the limitations of trench warfare with a series of major offensives that started in December 1914 and stretched deep into 1915. The first attack was on 17

December by the Tenth Army in the Artois region, with the objective of gaining control of the heights of the Vimy Ridge that dominated the Lens–Douai plain. Many of the techniques associated with the siege warfare of a bygone age found new applications as they painstakingly sapped trenches forward across No Man's Land, then connected them up to form jumping-off trenches as close as possible to the German lines. When the infantry attacked they fondly supposed there had been a devastating artillery prepa-ration; they were very soon be disabused of that notion. They had made only trivial gains by the time the offensive ended in mid-January 1915. One improvement for the men was the gradual issue of new horizon blue uni-forms gradually through the course of 1915. This was of course a massive undertaking and for a while the French soldiers presented an unprepossess-ing appearance in a bizarre mixture of old and new, although at least the light blue uniforms were less visible where it counted – on the battlefield.

Further south, an offensive in the Champagne area opened up on 20 December 1914. The Fourth Army, commanded by General Fernand de Langle de Cary, was attacking along a 25-mile stretch from Auberive to Massiges in an attempt to break through to the vital Mézières rail junc-tion, for which purpose some 258,000 troops had been amassed backed up by over 700 guns. A preliminary bombardment to cut the German barbed wire was followed by a brisk bombardment of the trenches and then the infantry assault moving forward in waves. They made minor gains but failed to break through: the artillery concentration may have seemed adequate but it was insufficient to break through well-established trench lines. After a pause, on 16 February the French launched the second phase of their offensive. By this time they had amassed even more guns, with a slightly higher proportion of heavier pieces. Their tactics involved a heavy emphasis on trying to maintain control in the chaos of battle: thus the artillery fired to a schedule and the infantry went over the top in accor-dance to an exact timetable. But when things did not go according to plan – and they hardly ever did – then the guns and infantry found themselves completely out of synchronisation.

The Champagne fighting was starkly attritional, as tactically signifi-cant positions were taken, lost, taken, and lost again. The French attacks segued into German counter-attacks of equal weight, with a particularly vicious battle being fought for the hitherto insignificant village of Perthes. Gradually the battlefield mutated into a sort of outdoor charnel house littered with human remains. There may not have been enough guns to create a breakthrough, but soldiers on both sides were horrified by the terrible destruction wrought by artillery on the human body.

> As we forced our way through the deep narrow trench, what a horrible sight met our eyes! In a place where a trench mortar shell had burst, there lay, torn to pieces, about eight of the Alpine Chasseurs – some of the finest French troops in a great bloody heap of mangled human bodies; dead and wounded. On the top a corpse without a head or torso and underneath some who were still alive, though with limbs torn off or horribly mutilated. They looked at us with bleeding, mournful eyes. The crying and moaning of these poor, doomed enemy soldiers went to our hearts. We couldn't get out of the trench to avoid this pile of bodies. However much our hearts shrank from trampling over them with our hob-nailed boots, we were forced to do it![3]
>
> Lieutenant Walter Ambroselli, 3rd Battalion, 12th Grenadier Regiment

The French had one advantage in their famous 75 mm guns that, notwithstanding their flat trajectory, could generate a reasonable bombardment through their sheer rapidity of fire. Ensign August Hopp would experience the awful reality of being caught at the centre of a French bombardment on the Heights of Combres on 21 February 1915. There was no romance in this mechanistic warfare in which human bodies were pitted against exploding shells.

> It started at 3 o'clock, and at the same time they poured in a terrific flanking fire on our left. One after another my brave men met his fate, either from artillery or infantry fire. It was ghastly; I had to keep urging the men to stick it out, not to lose courage, knowing all the time that I might be hit myself at any moment. I crawled out to the flank position, where there was no cover at all and encouraged the men lying there – Corporal Seckinger and Privates Platzr and Plemmer – to keep a good look out, so that the enemy should not suddenly fall upon our flank. I had to shout in their ears, such a thunder was going on all around. Then, just as I had crawled down again into the trench I was thrown over by a fearful concussion. Up above, there the three were lying, a soft gurgling sound was heard; the legs of the one nearest me jerked convulsively once; then all was deathly still. And so came the turn of one after another.[4]
>
> Ensign August Hopp, German Army

The French casualties on the Champagne Front in February and March totalled over 40,000.

Joffre ordered another spring offensive on the St Mihiel Salient commencing on 30 March. Heavy fighting produced only minor gains at great loss; indeed, it merely succeeded in triggering the first of a series of effective counter-attacks by the Germans which began on 23 April and soon stripped away the meagre French gains. Of course the French retaliated and there was a further welter of bitter fighting. Constant vigilance was required, as Lieutenant Maurice Genevoix discovered on the Les Éparges Ridge on 25 April.

> 'Take cover!' Too late: I fell on one knee on the ground. A sudden shock went through my left arm. It's behind me, bleeding profusely. I want to straighten it: I cannot. I want to get up: I cannot. I look at my arm as it shudders with the shock of a second bullet, and the blood pours from a second hole. My knees are stuck to the ground as if my body was made out of lead, my head bowed. Before my eyes a scrap of material jerks, the dull thud of a third bullet. Dully, I see the deep furrow of red flesh on my left breast near the armpit. I had to get up, drag myself out of sight. I didn't lose consciousness; my breathing sounded strange, gasping, quick and shallow. The treetops swirl across a dizzying sky.[5]
>
> Lieutenant Maurice Genevoix, 106th Infantry Regiment

He was one of some 65,000 French casualties in the St Mihiel Salient.

It was evident that the French artillery was still not equipped with enough heavy guns or shells to smash the German defences. As a result it was increasingly forced to rely on long preliminary bombardments by the field artillery to try and wear down the German trenches before the *poilus* went over the top. However, this put even more strain on French ammunition supplies and when replacement stocks proved to be of poor quality due to the sudden expansion in production, there were frequent cases of misfires and premature detonations. Such secondary considerations typified the nature of modern warfare in which the solution of one problem merely uncovered, or created, additional difficulties to be overcome. Analysis of the fighting threw up more difficulties: thus, while de Langle de Cary at one point emphasised the difficulties of achieving a breakthrough and advised concentrating on carefully chosen points of tactical significance, Joffre, by contrast, pointed to the necessity for adequate artillery support and warned against narrow front attacks against which the Germans could concentrate their artillery and machine gun response from neighbouring unaffected sectors. Neither was right; neither was wrong. This was clearly going to be a long and complex war.

The Battle of Neuve Chapelle, 10 March 1915

The French had gained a poor opinion of the BEF during the 1914 campaign, only alleviated by its late-flowering demonstration of determination during the First Battle of Ypres. Still doubtful of British capacity to undertake an offensive, Joffre's initial priority for the BEF in 1915 was to get his British allies to accept a greater share of the front line, stretching from the Ypres Salient down to the La Bassée area. This would allow the French to release more troops for their own offensives. Although the BEF was grossly tardy in taking over more of the line, Sir John French proved surprisingly willing to launch a supporting attack in what would ultimately be the Battle of Neuve Chapelle.

It is well worth examining the stages in which the different components of the BEF were added to the plans of the generals in their early attempts to crack the problem of a successful offensive. The first part was obvious: infantry were ever-present. The tactics were essentially those of fire and movement, an approach frequently decried as old-fashioned, with scornful reference to 'Boer War tactics'. Yet what else could it have been based on? It was far too soon to digest properly the lessons of 1914. The second traditional element was the use of cavalry. The role of cavalry had been deeply controversial before the war, with a strange dispute arising between those promulgating pure cavalry reliant on shock and awe and those in favour of mounted infantry. Although the cavalry had been invaluable in 1914 both for reconnaissance in open warfare and to plug gaps in an emergency, afterwards they became very much an afterthought – a force to be used when the battle was all but done to try to maximise the spoils of victory. In the absence of any other fast-moving strike force, it was the cavalry or nothing when it came to rapid exploitation.

The third primary grouping was the artillery. The Royal Artillery had gone to war with little grasp of its role in combat. It was thought the gunners' task was to shower the opposing infantry with shrapnel shells spraying out deadly steel balls. When batteries were deployed in a defensive role in support of the infantry it was not yet understood that this did not mean that the actual guns had to be sited close to the infantry their shells were defending. Positioned within a few hundred yards of the infantry, many gunners were soon despatched by the German artillery or infantry. When the guns were covering an attack there was also no concept of suppressing the ability of the German infantry and artillery to fire on British troops while they were vulnerable in No Man's Land; early in the war it was destruction or nothing – yet there was a shortage of the high-explosive shells that would make destruction feasible. There was a predominance of field guns, firing on a flat trajectory, with insufficient howitzers capable of dropping shells into the German trenches. And of course the Royal Artillery was simply too small: it lacked the thousands of guns, the trained gunners, the techniques, the tactical sophistication and the almost unlimited supplies of munitions necessary to dominate the modern battlefield. It would take years to remedy these stark deficiencies

The Battle of Neuve Chapelle, the first major BEF attack on German entrenched positions, would be conducted by the First Army (the IV Corps and Indian Corps) under the command of General Sir Douglas Haig. The Germans' situation on the Western Front had worsened after their strategic decision to send substantial forces to join the operations on the Eastern Front against the Russians. Consequently there were only two German divisions left to face the six divisions of the First Army between the La Bassée Canal and Bois Grenier; indeed, neither side had much in the way of reserves. The attack was originally envisaged as a joint offensive with the French, but they dropped out after finding themselves already over-committed. Sir John French decided that the BEF would carry on regardless. The British Commander in Chief was determined to dispel the prevailing view among his French allies that the BEF was incapable of launching an effective offensive action.

The German front line formed a salient around Neuve Chapelle. Haig's overall plans called for converging attacks by IV Corps, commanded by Lieutenant General Sir Henry Rawlinson, and the Indian Corps, commanded by Lieutenant General Sir James Willcocks, supported by massed artillery on a frontage of 2,000 yards, to seize the village before taking up defensive positions. Success would trigger further attacks on either side of the breakthrough intended to widen the gap and then push towards the Aubers Ridge which offered the possibility of disrupting German communications to Lille. As the artillery had only sufficient ammunition for three or four days of serious operations, contingency plans were also prepared to take up defensive positions depending on the degree of success of the whole operation. Throughout the planning process Haig adopted a broadly collegiate approach, consulting experts and holding conferences with the commanders and senior staff charged with carrying out the attack. His subordinates and their staff officers were expected to work out the elaborate details, but there is no doubt that Haig provided insightful guidance.

> I asked Corps Commanders to give me a written statement by Saturday, showing how they proposed to carry out the orders I had given them. On Monday next I would hold another meeting with Corps Commanders and discuss their proposals. Meantime the following points should be considered:
> 1. Arrangements for bringing up the attacking troops in position of readiness near front line.
> 2. How to get over our own wire obstacles. All wire should now be put down with this object in view.
> 3. Study ground. Officers on the spot should correct maps daily. The enemy's wire to be marked on map, etc.
> 4. Guns to practise destroying enemy's wire.
> 5. Guns should be gradually and secretly placed in position to suit the scheme of attack. Targets to be registered gradually, so as not to attract attention.
> 6. Most important. Officers should observe the enemy's line *daily* most closely. We want to locate his Maxims.
> 7. Mountain artillery and machine guns should follow the assaulting parties, so as to get into action quickly in new position.
> 8. Mines. What can we do to defeat the enemy's mines?
> 9. Make saps with the object of supporting the attack.
> 10. Can we bring trench mortars into position secretly, so that a large number of them can be massed against points which we mean to take?[6]
>
> General Sir Douglas Haig, Headquarters, First Army

The significance of these directions cannot be denied. Haig had clearly taken note of the French experience in the Champagne battles and was already grappling with many of the fundamental problems of making an assault against entrenched positions. In his notes we see the surreptitious registering of artillery, interest in the surprise deployment of massed mortars, recognition of the problems posed by barbed wire, the care taken over arrangements for bringing up attacking troops, the primary importance given to locating German machine gun positions and an eye to the possibilities of rapidly deploying forward support weapons to assist in consolidation.

Collectively his staff would devote much of their time to details of the artillery bombardment which lay at the heart of Haig's plans. The emphasis was placed on destroying the shallow German trenches which, due to the raised water-table in the area, had to be augmented by sandbag barricades. The idea was to smash them down, killing the defending garrison and destroying any machine guns; after which a defensive curtain of shells would crash down to prevent any German reinforcements moving forward. To meet these demands, most of the British batteries on the Western Front would have to be concentrated at Neuve Chapelle. Once in place they were carefully registered by firing just the occasional shot in a manner that would not attract German attention to the new arrivals. A fire programme was drawn up for every gun, denoting targets, the timings of switches in target and the number of rounds to be fired. It seemed complex at the time, but this was merely the start of a process that would grow out of all recognition. This was the future.

One specific problem becoming evident was that the guns would have to deal with the German barbed wire defences or the attacking infantry would not be able to get across No Man's Land under fire. Wire cutters and the like were simply too slow; their wielders too vulnerable. The guns would have to do it before they attacked. But how? This had never been seriously considered before the war. Tests were carried out behind the line to try to determine the best type of shell and the length of bombardment that would be required to clear the wire. Shrapnel shells proved best able to cut it into small scraps no longer connected to the stakes; in contrast, high-explosive shells blew the wire up into the air, which, when it fell back to earth, still posed a serious obstacle.

A tremendous debate ensued as to how long the preliminary bombardment should be before the troops attacked. Should it be a short, 'hurricane' bombardment or a more lengthy affair to ensure the destruction of the targets? Although Haig and his artillery specialists were not to know it, this choice would come to delineate the dichotomy between destruction and suppression. In February 1915, however, practical considerations held sway, not theory. Initial estimates required a bombardment of two and a half hours but, after considerable discussion and a series of tests, it was decided that a hurricane bombardment of thirty-five minutes would suffice for the 18-pounder field guns to clear the wire, by which time the 4.5-inch howitzers and heavy artillery would have destroyed the breastwork trenches. This was considered sufficient for such thin German defences as existed in March 1915; the calculations would change later in the war. In all, the First Army managed to amass surreptitiously 282 field guns and howitzers with an additional thirty-six heavier pieces. This amounted to one gun per six yards of front, which would rarely be equalled throughout the war. A special effort was made to secure a reasonable supply of ammunition, although this severely depleted the overall stocks available to the BEF on the Western Front. As the Germans had only twenty-four field guns and thirty-six heavy guns, the British now had a marked superiority of artillery. Of the British guns only a few were charged with tackling the German guns located back on Aubers Ridge. At this stage the German barbed wire and machine guns were considered greater threats to progress.

The Battle of Neuve Chapelle marked the first effective addition of aircraft by the British to the existing mix of infantry, cavalry and artillery. Aerial photographic reconnaissance had advanced apace since the beginning of the war and the images produced allowed a photographic map to be produced detailing the German trenches at a scale of 1:8000. There had also been huge advances in artillery observation from the air. Indirect fire was all very well, but there had to be someone who knew where the target was in order to correct the range and direction as necessary. Shooting 'from the map' required far more accurate maps and survey techniques than were available in 1915. Long gun ranges and terrain meant that even front line observers telephoning corrections back to the guns could not help if the target was concealed from view behind some trees or, even worse, a ridge. Guessing was useless and nothing more than a waste of shells. The great innovation was to use aircraft carrying wireless transmitters which allowed correcting messages to be sent directly to the gun batteries using specially lettered and numbered squared maps with a simple clock code to indicate the relative position of the shells as they fell around the target. Very early on in the planning process for Neuve Chapelle Haig brought in Lieutenant Colonel Hugh Trenchard, commander of First Wing, Royal Flying Corps (RFC) for a briefing meeting on 16 February 1915. There is no doubt that Trenchard was flattered to be granted such an audience.

> This was the first time I had ever seen Haig. I was very nervous beforehand as I had always heard that he was very reserved, austere, severe and that he did not believe in a great deal in air. He ordered me to go round to his HQ about five o'clock in the evening and asked me about the use of aircraft in battle. I tried to explain what I thought they would do in future besides reconnaissance work, how our machines would have to fight in the air against German machines and how we should have to develop machine guns and bombs. He was interested. Then he said he was going to tell me something that only three or four people in the world yet knew; in March, somewhere in the vicinity of Merville and Neuve Chapelle, we were to launch an attack on the Germans. I was not to tell anybody. He asked: 'What will you be able to do?' I explained rather badly about artillery observation, reporting to gun batteries by Morse and signal lamps, and of our early efforts to get wireless going. On the map I showed him the position of my squadrons and said what their several tasks could be. When I'd finished he said: 'Well, Trenchard, I shall expect you to tell me before the attack whether you can fly, because on your being able to observe for the artillery, and carry out reconnaissance, the battle will partly depend. If you can't fly because of the weather, I shall probably put off the attack.'[7]
>
> Lieutenant Colonel Hugh Trenchard, Headquarters, First Wing, RFC

Haig's account of the meeting is rather more prosaic: 'I told him the plan and asked for his proposals as to disposal of aeroplanes for reconnaissance and also for artillery observation.' But Haig's later actions showed that he had been paying close attention. On 22 February he noted:

> At 10 am I motored to Merville and held conference there regarding plans for offensive. I went into the plans sent in at some length, and insisted on the necessity of methodical preparation, and that every individual man should know exactly what his task was. Thanks to the

wonderful map of Enemy's trenches which we now had as the result
of airplane reconnaissance it was now possible to make our plans very
carefully beforehand.[8]

General Sir Douglas Haig, Headquarters, First Army

These first steps established a close association between Haig and Trenchard
that would endure for the whole war, and indeed defined the relationship
between the BEF and the RFC as a whole. From this moment onwards air
operations would be fundamental to every major offensive. Reconnaissance and artillery observation became the prime purpose of RFC operations and soon there were hundreds of the corps aircraft engaged on these
unglamorous but crucial missions. Ideas of bombers engaging in interdiction attacks to wreck German communications pinch points were nothing
but pipedream fantasies. Aircraft in 1915 could not carry a sufficient bomb
payload to do significant damage and, as their bomb-aimers were still relatively inaccurate, they rarely hit their targets anyway. In essence, the RFC
was the handmaiden of the Royal Artillery.

Haig also paid much consideration to the planning of the infantry
assault. Officers were carefully briefed with both aerial photographs and
sketch maps so that they would know where they were and what lay
ahead of them once they had broken into the German lines. Painstaking
preparations were also undertaken to improve the existing communication trenches and dig specially constructed assembly trenches where the
troops could form up under cover. When the moment of attack came at
08.05 Haig required his men to advance as quickly as possible to secure
maximum benefit to the chaos and panic engendered in the German ranks
by the bombardment. Arrangements were also in place to rapidly push
forward both machine guns and mountain guns to help support the infantry as they consolidated their anticipated gains. Attention was also paid to
improving telephone lines to allow the generals to follow what was going
on. Once they had secured the German front line a further assault would
be made on the village itself at 08.35 and through to occupy the trenches
previously occupied by the British in 1914, when they were known as the
Smith-Dorrien Line. Not all of these attempted innovations worked, but
there is no doubt that they prefigured many future developments.

The barrage blazed out at 07.30 on 10 March 1915. While half the
18-pounders thrashed the German barbed wire with shrapnel fire, the rest

combined with the heavier guns to flay the German trenches. After ten minutes the field artillery switched to creating a barrage line to the east of Neuve Chapelle to prevent either the escape or reinforcement of the German garrison troops. The waiting infantry watched on stunned.

> The noise almost split our numbed wits. As the shells went over our heads we grew more and more excited. We could not hear each other. Shots from the 18-pounders were screaming not far over our heads, and much higher up, higher than the highest mountain of Europe, high explosives from the 15-inch howitzers were rushing like express trains. After a while we could trace the different sounds. There was no difficulty in making out the German trenches. They had become long clouds of smoke and dust, flashing continuously with shell bursts, and with enormous masses of trench material and bodies sailing high above the smoke cloud. The purely physical effect on us was one of extreme exhilaration. We could have laughed and cried with excitement. We thought that bombardment was winning the war before our eyes. Incredible that the men in the German front line could have escaped. We felt sure we were going to pour through the gap.[9]
>
> Lance Corporal William Andrews, 4th Black Watch

In reality, the shrapnel shells had to be very well judged to have any effect on the wire, while to hit a relatively narrow trench line enough times to guarantee its destruction demanded careful registration and a plethora of HE shells. Given the grim consequences for infantry caught in the open under machine gun or artillery fire, failure meant that the term 'hanging on the old barbed wire' soon came to have a terrible resonance.

> Almost before I had time to realise it, I found myself up against the German wire. It was bared and twisted and almost unbroken, for the bombardment had proved ineffective at that particular point. Of how we got through that wire I have no clear idea. I have a vague recollection of tearing at it with my naked hands and, with the help of one of my corporals, dragging away the remains of a cheval-de-frise, while a German fired at us at a range of only 4 or 5 yards and missed us both. After that the fellow must have bolted, as I remember throwing myself through the remaining strands of wire.[10]
>
> Lieutenant Malcolm Kennedy, 2nd Cameronians (Scottish Rifles)

It is tempting to dwell on the dramatic stories of failure rather than the rather more mundane accounts of success, and this can skew our vision of the real progress that was made. Five of the eight assault battalions took their objectives advancing some 1,200 yards with minimal losses to take Neuve Chapelle and the flooded remnants of the Smith-Dorrien Line by 09.00. Many battalions went almost unscathed. It had also been demonstrated that, following these new tactics, the British tactics could break into the German lines. The question was, could they break through to the uplands of the Aubers Ridge and beyond? Haig gained permission from Sir John French to move forward a cavalry brigade in case it was needed for reconnaissance.

Yet just as everything seemed to be going so well the offensive began to fall apart. Winkling out the pockets of German resistance proved both difficult to organise and very costly in practice. Many of the troops were in a state of absolute confusion. Unused as they were to the headlong stresses of combat it was inevitable that many were incapable of thinking clearly. Although the junior officers had been well briefed, severe casualties meant that in many instances NCOs were left in command with little clue as to what they were meant to be doing. Delays multiplied as the communications fell apart under German shellfire, despite the best efforts to bury the telephone lines. The passing minutes turned into hours as Willcocks and Rawlinson, in charge of the Indian Corps amd IV Corps respectively, struggled to a get a grip on the situation. They were hesitant to order the next advance towards Aubers Ridge until all the original objectives had been secured. But every minute that passed was exploited by the Germans to reorganise and move up their reserves. As the breach torn in their lines measured only 2,000 yards across, they were soon able to plug the gap. Renewed British attacks were made over the next three days but resulted only in severe losses and no significant advances. By the time the battle was over the First Army had suffered 11,652 casualties.

Neuve Chapelle was a failure in attaining the declared objectives of Aubers Ridge: the capture of the battered remnants of the village of Neuve Chapelle and the straightening out of a minor salient were surely not worth such a cost. But real success was never likely given the greenness of almost everyone involved in offensive operations. And there were considerable benefits to the BEF from the experience. The innovations overseen by Haig would establish many of the basic features of British offensives for the rest of the war. That is not to say that the arrangements were perfect;

1. Archduke Franz Ferdinand and his wife Sophie photographed shortly before their assassination in Sarajevo, 28 June 1914.

2. Gavrilo Princip, the Bosnian Serb whose pistol shots triggered the start of the Great War. He himself would die in prison of tuberculosis, 28 April 1918.

3. A rear guard of Belgian infantry take aim with their rifles from a railway bridge that engineers are about to destroy in order to slow the German advance in Termonde, 18 September 1914.

4. British, Belgian and French troops fraternising happily in a French village, 15 October 1914.

5. The 16th Lancers on the march, September 1914. Cavalry still had a valuable role to play in warfare, providing valuable reconnaissance and acting as the only truly mobile troops.

6. Soldiers from the 1st Middlesex Regiment under shrapnel fire from German artillery on the Signy-Signets road during the Battle of the Marne, 8 September 1914.

7. The French Commander-in-Chief General Joseph Joffre with President Poincare, King George V, General Ferdinand Foch and Sir Douglas Haig on the terrace of Haig's headquarters at Beauquesne. Joffre was the key figure from 1914–16.

8. Field Marshal Sir John French, Earl of Ypres, Commander of the BEF, 1914–15. He was soon out of his depth, unable to deal with the complexities of modern warfare or the niceties of dealing with his French allies.

9. General Helmuth Von Moltke (the younger). Fearing the increasing strength of France and Russia he was willing to seize on the July 1914 crisis to provoke war.

10. German 5.9-inch howitzer battery on the Western Front, 14 November 1914. These superb guns gave the Germans a very real advantage in the Battle of the Frontiers, easily out-ranging the British and French field artillery.

11. German soldier looking out from an observation post in 1914. Trench warfare soon took hold and it was fatal to appear above ground.

12. French troops manning a ditch in the Argonne, 1914. Ditches like this soon became full-scale trenches, after which second lines and communications lines were added as trench warfare developed.

13. British troops move off into the attack through a cloud of poison gas on the opening day of the Battle of Loos, 25 September 1915. This photo was taken from the trench they had just left by a soldier of the London Rifle Brigade.

14. British artillery bombarding the German trenches prior to the attack on La Boisselle, 1 July 1916. It looked impressive at the time but the German garrison were safe underground in deep dugouts ready to slaughter the British when they attacked

15. Australian Battery of 9.2-inch howitzers in action at Fricourt, August 1916. Bigger calibre guns, with longer ranges, firing heavier shells brought devastation to the battlefields.

16. German dead in their front line trench during Battle of Flers-Courcelette, 15 September 1916.

17. Mark I Tank D17 which was ditched at Flers on 15 September 1916. This was the tank that advanced up the High Street of Flers, with the British Army 'walking behind' in the exaggerated reports of the British newspapers.

18. French soldiers of 68th Infantry Regiment in their dugout at Artois. The French had to endure a terrible ordeal as they attacked the German lines time and time again in an effort to break through.

19. French soldiers of the 3rd Infantry Regiment resting by the roadside near Houthem on their way to the front, 10 September 1917.

20. 8-inch Mark V howitzer in action at Monchy, near Arras, 31st May 1917. The power of the guns now dominated the battlefield.

21. Men of the 16th Canadian Machine Gun Company holding the line in the Ypres Salient, November 1917. This picture reveals the awful conditions in the morass of the Ypres Salient.

22. A tank of 'G' Battalion, Tank Corps, passing captured German field guns at Graincourt on its way to take part in the attack on Bourlon Wood, 23 November 1917. At Cambrai tanks began to show their potential as weapons of war.

23. Two New Zealanders leaving a badly damaged ammunition dugout in the captured German lines at Achiet-le-Petit, 21 August 1918.

24. German infantry preparing to advance in extended order across open country during the assault on Fismes, 28 May 1918.

25. German infantry storming the French village of Embermesnil.

26. Five of the top German aces of Jasta 11 including from left to right: Sebastian Festner, Karl-Emil Schäffer, Manfred von Richthofen, his brother Lothar von Richthofen and Kurt Wolff. The 'Red Baron' (Manfred von Richthofen) welded these men into a deadly force.

27. Manfred von Richthofen lands his Fokker DR 1 Triplane after a patrol. He would be killed in such a Triplane on 21 April 1918.

28. American machine gunners of the 77th American Division under training from the British 39th Battalion, Machine Gun Corps near Moulle, 22 May 1918. The Americans were keen but needed the accumulated expertise of their British and French Allies.

29. American troops of the 305th Machine Gun Battalion, the 77th Division on a route march near Watten, 19 May 1918. The sheer numbers of American troops meant that Germany had no hope of winning the war after June 1918.

30. Field Marshal Sir Douglas Haig (centre front) with his Army Commanders at Cambrai, 11 November 1918. Left to right behind him: General Sir Herbert Plumer (Second Army), General Sir Julian Byng (Third Army), General Sir William Birdwood (Fifth Army) and General Sir Henry Horne (Sixth Army), with various other senior officers. For all the sneers of 'lions led by donkeys' these are the men that won the war.

31. Canadian troops marching through the streets of Mons on the morning of 11 November 1918. For the BEF the war ended where it had all begun on 23 August 1914.

perfection at the first attempt would be remarkable indeed. But Neuve Chapelle represented a remarkable start. Haig welded a willingness to use innovatory techniques to a firm grasp of the practicalities of warfare in 1915 to oversee the creation of tactics that were fit for purpose in tackling a weak German front line backed only by a weak support trench with negligible artillery support. With more experience in maintaining command and control much more could be achieved.

As with the French there was a debate as to what the lessons actually meant. Rawlinson was of the same opinion as de Langle de Cary.

> What we want to do now is what I call 'bite and hold'. Bite off a piece of the enemy's line, like Neuve Chapelle, and hold it against counter-attack. The bite can be made without much loss, and, if we choose the right place and make every preparation to put it quickly in a state of defence, there ought to be no difficulty in holding it against the enemy's counter-attacks and inflicting on him at least twice the loss that we have suffered in making the bite.[11]
>
> Lieutenant General Sir Henry Rawlinson, Headquarters, IV Corps

The problem was that in 1915 the BEF had neither the artillery nor the shells to make 'bite and hold' a feasible operational methodology. As a tactic it was also far too slow to meet the political requirements imposed on Sir John French and Joffre. After the battle it was evident that the frontage attacked at Neuve Chapelle had been too narrow, and the gap it created far too easily plugged by the Germans. The rest of 1915 would see the British generals trying to expand the length of front attacked, but without the artillery and shells needed to have much chance of success.

Second Battle of Ypres, 22 April 1915

Having bowed to a combination of pressure and circumstance in diverting resources to the Eastern Front, Falkenhayn now attempted to maintain some degree of strategic surprise by covering the departure of his divisions from the Western Front. As he did not have the men or ammunition to launch a more conventional offensive, he sought to test the stalemate at Ypres by using the new German secret weapon of poisonous gas. At 17.00 on 22 April 1915, his Fourth Army launched an attack at Ypres employing some 168 tons of chlorine released from thousands of steel bottles in cloud form. The Germans and French had both tested the lethal potential of gas before to little effect, but this would be markedly different. The German troops were equipped with simple respirators but, despite a fair degree of accurate warning intelligence, the Allies had failed to take notice, preferring to believe that the Germans would not stoop so low. (The use of gas had been expressly forbidden by the Hague Convention of 1907.) In consequence, the men of the French 45th (Algerian) and 87th (Territorial) Divisions holding the northern sector of the salient were caught completely unawares with no protective masks. The chlorine invaded their bodies, burning and choking them and destroying their lungs. Colonel Henri Mordacq, a staff officer with the 45th Division, would witness the chaos at first hand.

> The scene was more than sad; it was tragic. Everywhere were fugitives: Territorials, *joyeux*,[12] tirailleurs, Zouaves, artillerymen – without weapons, haggard, greatcoats thrown away or wide open, running around like madmen, begging for water in loud cries, spitting blood, some even rolling on the ground making desperate efforts to breathe. I shall see for a long time, in particular, a staggering *joyeux* who with loud cries demanded water and noticing me, called, 'Colonel, those bastards have poisoned us!' No effort was made to stop the bewildered fugitives. We soon gave that up. It was no longer soldiers who were escaping but poor souls who had become suddenly insane. All along the canal was the same scene: without noticing bullets or shells, a crowd of unfortunate sufferers on both banks had come to beg for water to relieve their horrible sufferings.[13]
>
> Colonel Henri Mordacq, Headquarters, 45th Division

As the French broke and ran, the 1st Canadian Division of the recently arrived Canadian Expeditionary Force (CEF) was next in line to the south. They immediately bent back and shuffled across to try to block the gap that threatened the security of the whole salient. Lieutenant Colonel Arthur Currie was caught up in the drama.

> We had stayed a trifle too long in the village of St Julien while the streets were filled with this deadly gas. Some of our orderlies could hardly escape and several of the headquarters staff had to be sent to the hospital. I had taken on a pretty stiff cargo of it myself. When it is first breathed it is not unpleasant, smelling not unlike chloroform, but

very soon it stings the mucous membrane of the mouth, the eyes, and the nose. The lungs feel as if they were filled with rheumatism. The tissues of the lungs are scalded and broken down, and it takes a man a long time to recover, if he ever does fully recover after having some of the 'upholstering' of his lungs destroyed. We did not then quite realise the horror of this new form of cowardly and inhuman warfare, but we should have known that the Germans consider war a game without an umpire or a referee.[14]

Lieutenant Colonel Arthur Currie, 3rd Brigade, 1st Canadian Division, CEF

This was the prevailing reaction to the German use of gas: that it was unsporting and inhuman. The Canadian front line troops largely escaped the worst of the gas, but reserve units moving forward suffered a great deal. In the end they held on by dint of their own courage, coupled with a paucity of German reserves near the Ypres front to take advantage of their success. The very secrecy demanded by the presence of so many vulnerable gas cylinders in the front line, coupled with a lack of confidence in their own crude respirators, militated against any forceful follow-up by the German Fourth Army. Attacks would not properly resume until 24 April, by which time the Canadians had to some extent sorted themselves out and would fight brilliantly to stem the tide. The British moved up reserves to bolster Smith-Dorrien's Second Army, which had overall responsibility for most of the Ypres Salient. Among these reserves were a significant number of battalions of the Territorial Army. These units were part of a long-standing British tradition of part-time soldiers, originally in various forms of militia, but reorganised in 1908 to create volunteer battalions within the county regiments, training on a drill night, on weekends and at an annual camp. Originally intended for home service, but soon offered the chance to serve overseas, the best regarded units had begun to reach the Western Front in 1914. Nicknamed the 'Saturday night soldiers', these men's training fell below the old 'regular' standards, but they were often remarkably keen to learn. By 1915, the process of reinforcement was accelerating but there were still questions as to whether they were adequately prepared for action. For the 50th Division, a Northumbrian formation, Ypres would be a harsh induction to war for raw troops with inexperienced officers.

We found that the only way to advance was for a few men, under
an officer or an NCO, to make a short rush forward, and then to lie
down flat and regain their breath. It was a case of every man using his
own intelligence with courage. We made a good deal of progress, and
took up a strong line with a hedge in front of it, which afforded some
shelter. In front of this position was a large open field, and at the other
end of it, a few hundred yards distant, lay the village of St Julien and
the Germans. To cross this field, without adequate artillery support,
was impossible, and yet we had been ordered to advance. Our present
position by the farm, however, was being shelled to such an extent that,
as far as our safety went, it did not much matter where we were. We
began our last advance, and made two or three short rushes. I had just
finished the last of these, and was going to lie down, when I received a
staggering blow on the back, and fell forward. I suffered an agonising
pain, and soon felt another blow on the back, also extremely violent. I
began to find difficulty in breathing and wondered if I would ever leave
this spot.[15]

Captain William Watson-Armstrong, 1/7th Northumberland Fusiliers

Many of the British counter-attacks ordered by Sir John French had little
chance of success and the resulting casualties were heavy. But when the
Germans resumed the offensive they found that the British lines generally held firm. At what cost can be indicated by this account from Private
William Quinton, who was in the support line on Hill 60 when his battalion fell victim to a gas attack on the evening of 1 May.

Suddenly over the top of our front line we saw what looked like clouds
of thin grey smoke, rolling slowly along with the slight wind. It hung
to the ground reaching to the height of 8 or 9 feet, and approached
so slowly that a man walking could have kept ahead of it. 'GAS!' The
word quickly passed round. Even now it held no terror for us, for we
had not yet tasted it. From our haversacks we hastily drew the flannel
belts, soaked them in water and tied them round our mouths and
noses. Suddenly, through the communication trench came rushing a
few khaki-clad figures. Their eyes glaring out of their heads, their hands
tearing at their throats, they came on. Some stumbled and fell, and
lay writhing in the bottom of the trench, choking and gasping, whilst
those following trampled over them. If ever men were raving mad with
terror, these men were. What was left of our section still crouched at the

support end of the communication trench. Our front line, judging from the number of men who had just come from it, had been abandoned, and we now waited for the first rush of the Germans. But they did not come. Our biggest enemy was now within a few yards of us, in the form of clouds of gas. We caught our first whiff of it: no words of mine can ever describe my feelings as we inhaled the first mouthful. We choked, spit, and coughed, my lungs felt as though they were being burnt out, and were going to burst. Red-hot needles were being thrust into my eyes. The first impulse was to run. We had just seen men running to certain death, and knew it, rather than stay and be choked into a slow and agonising death. It was one of those occasions when you do not know what you are doing. The man who stayed was no braver than the man who ran away. We crouched there, terrified, stupefied. A large shell burst on the parapet just where we were sheltered. We were almost buried beneath the falling earth. Young Addington, a chap about my own age, was screaming at the top of his voice and trying to free his buried legs. He got free and before we could stop him he rushed off – God knows where! We then saw the reason for his screams. His left arm was blown off above the elbow. He left a trail of blood over my tunic as he climbed over me in his mad rush to get away.[16]

Private William Quinton, 1st Bedfordshire Regiment

Later Quinton's battalion moved forward to take over the front line, where they found the men who had been unable to run from the gas cloud.

Black in the face, their tunics and shirt fronts torn open at the necks in their last desperate fight for breath, many of them lay quite still, while others were still wriggling and kicking in the agonies of the most awful death I have ever seen. Some were wounded in the bargain and their gaping wounds lay open, blood still oozing from them. One poor devil was tearing at his throat with his hands, I doubt if he knew, or felt, that he had only one hand, and that the other was just a stump where the hand should have been. This stump he worked around his throat as if the hand were still there, and the blood from it was streaming over his bluish-black face and neck. A few minutes later and he was still except for occasional shudders as he breathed his last.[17]

Private William Quinton, 1st Bedfordshire Regiment

Gradually the British troops received gas masks which at first were all but useless, but later far more effective. And gas became just another weapon in the huge arsenal of war. The British, for all their initial moral objections, would be using gas themselves before the year was out.

The fighting stirred up at Ypres did not die down for months – officially the battle lasted from 22 April to 31 May, during which time British casualties were 60,000 (their ill-considered counter-attacks swelling the numbers), while the Germans were estimated to have lost 35,000 dead, wounded and missing. There was some bitterness at British High Command that the French did not send in reinforcements to replace their two shattered divisions, but this sidesteps the British prior not-yet-honoured commitment to take over the defence of the Ypres Salient. In the end the British had no choice but to withdraw from the extremities of the salient exposed by the initial German breakthrough on 22 April. At great cost a new line was carved out which, although tested time and time again by the Germans, did hold. Perhaps the BEF should have abandoned the dangerous Ypres Salient entirely and fallen back to a straighter, more easily defensible line. Yet there was very little room for manoeuvre and the emotional investment in holding the last corner of Belgium not under German control was difficult to ignore. So the Ypres Salient became a place of dread for British troops.

The Spring Offensives, May 1915

Joffre was determined to launch another great offensive. He was confident that France had learnt the lessons of the Artois, Champagne and St Mihiel offensives and he sought to take advantage of the German reduction in strength on the Western Front while at the same time alleviating pressure on the Russians and the Serbs. Joffre was intent on another attack on Vimy Ridge in the Artois. The great question was, who had learnt most from the earlier battles of 1915? Joffre conceived of a massive continuous unrelenting offensive: 'Attackers at all echelons will be imbued with the idea of breaking through, of going beyond the first trenches seized, of continuing to attack without stopping until the final result.'[18] Had the French and British finally devised a method of breaking through the German lines? Or had the Germans discovered a more effective way of keeping them out? For the Germans had certainly been busy putting into effect their own conclusions as to how best to resist attack. Although it remained a mantra that the front line was to be defended to the death, and that every inch of ground must be regained through immediate counter-attacks, there was also a widespread acceptance of the need for multiple defensive lines connected by communication trenches, with deep dugouts to protect the troops under artillery bombardment. Trenches were also being strengthened to resist artillery bombardments, with special well-protected machine gun posts carefully sited to attain the best possible enfilading fire across No Man's Land, while ever more, ever thicker belts of barbed wire were built for attackers to contend with. These needs, however, were tempered by the shortage of the labour required for such a programme of defence works. This was not a single learning curve; no simplistic story here of unremitting progress as one side mastered the problems of trench warfare and moved seamlessly towards victory. Rather, it is of two roller-coasters: one Allied and the other German, running side by side on their own separate tracks, with their relative position 'high' or 'low', 'rising' or 'falling', depending on a combination of their own latest tactical innovations, their success in assimilating the lessons of the fighting, the tactical advances of their enemies, and the restricting factor of the availability (or otherwise) of military resources. Thus a tactic that seemed to work well one month might result in disaster just a few weeks later.

The assault on Vimy Ridge would be made by the French Tenth Army, now commanded by General Victor d'Urbal, while the BEF launched a supporting attack in the Aubers Ridge sector. On the left the Tenth Army would attack along the hill of Notre Dame de Lorette while the main thrust on the right would push for Vimy Ridge itself. This was an ambitious plan as the Germans had made considerable headway in creating a strong defensive system. The French preparations were extensive, with aerial photographic reconnaissance used to pinpoint targets for what was then considered a heavy artillery bombardment by over 1,000 guns, which opened on 4 May. When the infantry went over the top at 10.00 on 9 May, only the XXXIII Corps, commanded by General Philippe Pétain, made any real progress in the centre, smashing their way up on to Vimy Ridge. This triggered a strong German counter-attack which hurled them back before nightfall. The problem was becoming increasingly evident: the methodology employed to seize a tactical feature could also be used by the other side to reclaim it. The fighting degenerated into a murderous slog as the French battered their way slowly across the Notre Dame de Lorette Spur. This was a true slaughterhouse.

Meanwhile the British contribution had been the Battle of Aubers Ridge, in which Haig's First Army launched two attacks converging on the ridge. His infantry attacked at 05.40 on 9 May after a 40-minute bombardment by 636 guns. This proved inadequate to deal with the German defensive preparations which nullified the British tactical advances tested at Neuve Chapelle just two months before. The infantry were for the most part slaughtered in No Man's Land. At the same time it was evident the war was gaining in depth. Now, not only were the Germans digging more lines but their artillery was gaining the expertise to pound the front line or splatter communication trenches with shells. The reinforcing troops were in danger long before they arrived at the front.

> High explosive shrapnel and common shrapnel was sweeping the 500 yards of communication rampart leading up to the front line. A solid wall of shells seemed to be everywhere. The enemy's ramparts and all the country for further than 800 yards was in a fog of yellow smoke, through which flashes appeared. These fumes literally darkened the sun. All around were crashing branches and trees being felled. Occasionally a huge shell would land in a ruined house and the brick dust would form a London fog in itself. Every now and then a huge black smoke shell would blow up in our rampart killing and maiming people. Campbell, Merrilees's servant, was unrecognisable minus two arms, head and one leg. Carson in my platoon was worse off as his remains could have been buried in a cigarette case. Meanwhile heavy German rifle fire was sweeping overhead so I kept under the parapet. It seemed impossible to me that we could ever reach the first line. At last we marched off. We rushed along the communication [trench] at awful speed. The wounded were crawling about in the passage and dead there were innumerable. At last we reached the front line.[19]
>
> Second Lieutenant Lionel Sotheby, 2nd Black Watch

Haig's First Army was soon in dire trouble: not enough guns, not enough ammunition, defective shells, but worst of all the German trenches were improving and their artillery were beginning to act in concert, with the capability to generate impenetrable barrages which could seal off the front, rendering the British assaulting infantry even more likely to be overwhelmed by German counter-attacks. The combination of the exploding shells and the bodies of the dead, the dying and the wounded littering the trenches made it almost impossible for reinforcements to get forward. When the 2nd Black Watch finally charged over the top they suffered some 500 casualties in a few hours – and that pattern was being repeated up and down. It had a severe psychological effect on the troops.

> I feel a changed person at present and unable to laugh, or smile, or anything, feeling almost in a dream. Next time the Germans will get it. Given a chance with wire down and at close quarters, they will be slaughtered, and I feel quite mad at it, and long for a decent smash at them. I shall get the chance yet with any luck.[20]
>
> Second Lieutenant Lionel Sotheby, 2nd Black Watch

Haig called off the attack after the failure of a second attempt. The British had failed to make a telling contribution to the main Artois battle still raging to the south. Pressure from the French forced another attempt at the Battle of Festubert, launched on 15 May. It was a disaster. The relatively inexperienced British had still not mastered the complexities of artillery support, the detailed command and control arrangements or the multi-layered briefings and special training required to carry them out.

In the Arras area, step by miserable step the French tried to grind their way forward, seeking to capture valuable tactical vantage points before launching the next big phase of the Artois Offensive on 16 June. The barrage opened some six days before, a wide-ranging affair, which attempted to conceal what was going on by switching between targets. Every barrage seemed to dwarf its predecessor, but there never seemed to be enough. It was already becoming evident that, although a long barrage might guarantee the destruction of the German defences, it also alerted the Germans to where and when the next blow was going to fall, allowing them to make their own preparations. When the assault finally went in, the gains were derisory for another swathe of terrible casualty figures. The offensive was formally suspended on 25 June. France was bleeding herself dry.

The failure of his spring offensives did not alter Joffre's overall perspective of the war. In his view the situation had not changed: the French and British still had to bear their burden on the Western Front in order to help Russia on the Eastern Front. He saw the British fixation with the Gallipoli Campaign, which had begun in 1915, as a costly distraction which contributed nothing to the fight against the real prime enemy, Germany.

Russia was different: she was deploying hundreds of thousands of troops against the Germans and must be supported, as the French Minister of War made clear in a letter of 14 August.

> The Russian Army has now been retreating for 3 months, during which the daily battle losses have been stupendous. All the officers returning from the front state that it is impossible to picture the horrors of this continual struggle, in which the artillery is without ammunition and the infantry without rifles. Our offensive is, therefore, awaited with utmost impatience. I am assured that the same question is being asked everywhere: what are the French doing?[22]
>
> Minister of War Alexandre Millerand

This was one of the exigencies of alliance warfare, and Joffre was determined that France could not – and would not – let Russia down. The British were dragged along on the coat-tails of the French, their contribution generally unenthusiastic in tenor, distracted, still largely symbolic and of peripheral importance.

The Autumn Offensives, 25 September 1915

In planning for his autumn offensives Joffre tweaked his operational ideas to reflect what had been learnt in the earlier campaigns. The lessons were by no means clear and there was wide disagreement within the French High Command as to the best way to proceed. Joffre now sought, not an easily plugged breakthrough on a narrow front, but a wide-ranging series of mutually supporting major offensives to promote confusion in the German High Command, prevent the concentrated deployment of German reserves and precipitate a wholesale rupture of the lines at the decisive point. Foch, however, favoured more restrained processes of methodical attack, somewhat similar in concept to 'bite and hold', consisting of a series of carefully planned and prepared steps, delineated by the range of the field artillery batteries. The far less senior, but increasingly highly respected Pétain saw the war in terms of attrition. To him victory would belong to the last man standing, and so he advocated a largely defensive strategy designed to conserve manpower with only limited well-prepared attacks to avoid excessive losses. The French tragedy would be that while none of these approaches was wrong *per se*, nor did they offer a coherent solution to the problems of waging a successful offensive in the conditions on the Western Front in 1915. Week by week, month by month, the German lines became stronger: more trenches and barbed wire; the advent of deeper dugouts, concrete fortifications and self-contained redoubts. A whole second trench system was established, a couple of miles behind the first, out of field artillery range and, where possible, sited on a reverse slope to avoid direct observation. The German artillery had also begun to refine its tactics, preparing different types of barrages to counter the different stages of the French attacks. Thus there was a barrage ready to fall on the forming-up trenches, the whirlwind bombardment of the French front line and finally a curtain barrage across No Man's Land to break up the attack and isolate any troops fortunate enough to break into the German front line.

The German numbers may have fallen on the Western Front, thanks to the despatch of units to bolster the Eastern Front offensives, but those that remained were increasingly well dug in. Joffre had his own answer to the augmented German defences: to blast them from the face of the earth. He demanded ever more heavy artillery, with the intention of achieving a rough parity of numbers with his field artillery. As a result, by the summer of 1915 the French had 4,646 field guns and 3,538 heavy guns. These were intended to act like an old-fashioned battering ram in the new version of siege warfare.

After a root and branch analysis of the options by his staff, Joffre decided to launch the autumn offensives in the Artois and Champagne on 25 September. The lure of the Vimy Ridge in Artois and the railway junctions tucked just behind the German lines at Mézières in the Champagne region was as strong as ever. This time the main attack would be carried out by the Fourth Army in Champagne, with significant 'secondary' attacks to be launched on the same day by the Tenth Army in the Artois and by the British First Army at Loos. These, it was fondly hoped, would suck in German reserves away from the main attack. Ultimately, Joffre had his eye on the Artois and Champagne offensives squeezing out the so-called Noyon Salient pointing towards Paris. In July 1915, at a conference held at Chantilly with the intention of establishing a common Allied policy, Joffre expressed his strategic preferences and the British, while refusing on principle to accept his direct command, none the less eventually fell into line. The British Secretary of State for War, Field Marshal Lord Kitchener, and

Sir John French would have preferred to have waited until 1916 when they believed all the Allies would be ready to attack at full strength, but such prevarications were overwhelmed by the continuing deterioration of the Russian position. For the British the Loos Offensive would be characterised as the 'Big Push', the moment when their 'New' Armies would at last begin to play a major role in the war; for the French it was just more of the same.

The German defences facing the French Tenth Army in the Vimy Ridge area were exceptionally strong and the attacks launched at 12.25 on 25 September had little success. It was an excruciating business for the advancing French infantry, coming to terms with their own mortality in a matter of moments.

> *'En avant!'* The command was passed rapidly as if transmitted by an electric current. Without hesitation we leapt over the parapet. Immediately men were hit and fell back heavily into the trench. Straining every sinew, the survivors threw themselves towards the enemy, screaming. The firing redoubled in intensity; a roaring fire of rifle and machine guns. The bullets come from everywhere. I hear the rattle in my ears, an endless banging. One bullet cuts the 'Zero' from my tunic collar, others pierce my greatcoat and shred the handkerchief in my trousers. The barrage of artillery shells fall close around us. The noise was indescribable, terrifying explosions erupt everywhere, and acrid smoke rises up. All around me, our assaulting wave is crumbling, falling apart; men tumbling on top of each other. The Adjutant ran behind me, he was wounded in the forehead and blood trickled down his cheek. He shouted, 'The bastards! They've punctured my brandy flask! *En avant! En avant!'* brandishing his revolver, apparently indifferent to his wound, but another bullet finishes him off. For a few appalling seconds, I run on, with fixed bayonet. How far have I got: 50 metres, 100 metres? I don't know. Suddenly, I am brutally brought up short and fall full length to the ground without letting go of my rifle, A bullet or shrapnel ball has hit me, but at the time, I don't know what it was, or where I have been hit. I got up immediately and went forward looking for a hole in which to hide. At the same time I did not let go of my rifle. How could I go on? I un-sling all my kit, my belt, my bandolier and threw myself into a shell hole. This will save me. Barely hidden behind in this shallow hole, I can draw breath and reflect. I can feel that I have been wounded in the left buttock; blood flows but it doesn't bother me – I want to save my skin and completely forget the pain. The

bullets continue to hiss past, the shells fall and the last remnants still standing are soon killed.[22]

Sergeant Émile Morin, 60th Infantry Regiment

While some gains were made on the Lorette Spur towards Souchez, further south the tale was one of unrelieved slaughter with nothing gained. Further thrusts over the next day brought the capture of Souchez and significant gains on Vimy Ridge, but Joffre was losing faith in the operations and came to consider them as more of a demonstration to encourage the British attacking further north at Loos before the operations were suspended on 30 September.

The focal point of Joffre's plans was the assault by the Second and Fourth Armies in the Champagne area on a front once again stretching from Auberive to Massiges and with supporting attacks with the centre facing the grim killing ground of the hills of the Bois de Perthes. At 09.15 on 25 September an enormous force of eighteen divisions attacked the German positions. Wave upon wave of troops advanced across No Man's Land. In places they broke through, employing specially trained soldiers to mop up German resistance, while the assault troops pushed on to the next trenches. In places three German lines were over-run and there were genuine hopes of a real breakthrough. But lurking a further one and a half to two miles behind this front line system was the second set of German trenches, inviolate on reverse hill slopes, providing an obstacle to further advances. Over the next few days the French would try to break through, but found it difficult to move sufficient artillery forward, while the Germans brought up their reserves to allow them to launch stinging counter-attacks whenever, and wherever, lodgements were made. Further attacks brought sharply diminishing returns and vastly increased casualties until Joffre was again forced to suspend the offensive, on 30 September.

Thus the great Artois and Champagne Offensives were both ignominiously closed down, with brief reprises in October achieving nothing but more casualties. The battlefields of Champagne had become places of dread to the French troops, as its desolate landscape bleached of hope sucked them in and surrounded them.

The Champagne battlefields had a strange appearance! Moist soil, chalky, white and grey. A little vegetation at the camp exit – some clumps of meagre trees – followed by the great sad and desolate plain, like a vast cemetery for the living. After an hour's march in the open, we advanced in single file through communication trenches filled with water and white mud, freezing cold and glutinous. Ever since we set off it rained non-stop, like melted snow. After marching for 3 long hours we at last reached the trenches, but what a pitiable state of utter filth! The rain never stopped falling. We occupied the front line trench and found the Germans were about 100 metres from us. Apart from surprise attacks, it was no longer a war of bombs and grenades; the artillery was the real threat. The sector, for the moment, was pretty quiet. The temperature was totally freezing, the rain had stopped, but what mud! We were covered from head to foot! That evening, my half-section was not on duty. When night fell, we divided into ten two-man dugouts about 2 metres deep underneath the parapet. We were obliged to bail out the water that flooded our shelters, to a depth of about 50 centimetres: water seeping down the chalk walls. We used a canvas bucket and made a chain, passing it back to throw the water behind the parapet. After half an hour of this toil, we wrapped ourselves in our soaking wet blankets, heads resting against the walls – luckily our helmets protected us from some of the damp. We tried to get some sleep, but the cold made it impossible. Moreover, the water seeped in and soon forced us to repeat the operation. A few shells bursting from time to time reminding us of the reality of our position.[23]

Corporal Henri Laporte, 2nd Battalion, 151st Infantry Regiment

The French had fired nearly 5 million shells in pursuit of the elusive break-through, with their combined losses in the Artois and Champagne offensives totalling a vast 191,795. Yet all for nothing, when confronted with the vastly improved German defence works and tactics.

The Battle of Loos

As part of the French autumn offensive, the British were required to launch a full-scale attack on the widest possible front at Loos on 25 September 1915. The late summer months had featured a good deal of attempted backsliding by the British, using a variety of excuses, but Sir John French was kept to the mark by the obdurate Joffre, who was resolute that the BEF would attack alongside the Tenth Army in the Artois. Yet there were plentiful causes for concern. The attack would be carried out by the IV

Corps, led by Rawlinson, and the I Corps, led by Lieutenant General Sir Hubert Gough, of Haig's First Army. But the BEF lacked the guns and shells for a bombardment on such a wide front, with only 533 guns to carry out a 11,200-yard frontage of two strongly fortified German trench lines. In desperation, it was decided to use a release of cloud gas for the first time to cover the gaping chasm between ambition and reality. There could be no hurricane bombardment as at Neuve Chapelle; that was simply impossible. Instead, a four-day preliminary bombardment to grind down the German defences would precede the release of gas and the infantry assault across No Man's Land. Soon preparations were underway for the gas attack.

> On the 19th the gas cylinders were brought up: no vocabulary could express the men's thoughts of those cylinders as they struggled and sweated up the narrow trenches, festooned with detached telephone wires that gripped sometimes the throat, sometimes the feet. The men were then instructed in the method of working the gas cylinders, in what to do in case they became casualties, or in the case of a direct hit on one of the cylinders both prior to and during that attack. By the 20th everything was ready. The cylinders were all in position. The long, double, rectangular nozzles that were to discharge the gas clear of the parapet were ready to be joined up. With the approach of Zero Hour on the 25th September we were ready. The nozzles had been screwed on to the cylinders, and we were standing by in our gas masks. At 5.30 am the gas was released. On the front of our division the wind was in the right direction and the right strength – the gas went over well. When the cylinders were exhausted, a smoke screen was put down, the trenches were bridged over with duckboards, and the infantry, wearing their gas masks, went over at 6.30 am.[25]
>
> Lieutenant H. G. Picton Davies, 4th Royal Welsh Fusiliers

The British infantry, wearing their 'P' gas helmets to protect them from their own gas, were generally inexperienced and their accounts of going over the top often betray a certain casualness borne of naivety.

> I remember having difficulty in breathing and was stumbling along. After a few minutes of this I thought I would sniff the air, it didn't seem too bad to me so I took my helmet off. I thought I was completely alone in No Man's Land but then I started to stumble on wounded men –

three of them. From them I collected a shovel, a pick and an artillery disc. So, weighed down with all this extra kit I carried on towards the German lines, then when I got to within about 20 yards of their wire, I realised there may still be some Germans there and I wouldn't be able to fight with all this extra kit so I threw it aside. I got to the German front line and it seemed much deeper than our trenches and I thought it was unoccupied, although very quickly other members of 'D' Company appeared and we started work in consolidating the position. There was soon a shortage of sandbags so a working party was organised to scrounge these from men in the old No Man's Land. Then one of my soldiers said to me, 'Corporal, there's some Germans in this dugout!' So I said, 'Well, get them out!' The reply came back, 'Corporal, they won't come out!' So I then said, 'Well, we'll see about that!' It seemed that there were two entrances/exits to this particular dugout so I posted two men at one of them and I went down the other with one other man. I led with my bayonet fixed and he had a grenade ready. I shouted down, 'Anybody there?' A reply came in reasonable English, 'Yes!' I said, 'How many?' The response to this question was 'Two!' So I ordered them to come out one at a time and we retired to the dugout entrance. Eventually nine Germans appeared and we took possession of their very fine helmets.[26]

Lance Corporal Reginald Thorpe-Tracey, 1/6th London Regiment

Although the British had some early success, capturing the town of Loos, they could not break through the German second line. Also, the deployment of the reserve divisions was disrupted by problems in command and control, as Sir John French had held them too far back to be deployed when needed, causing a loss of momentum. The fighting lasted several days, but even as fresh British troops were brought into battle, so the Germans moved in their own reserves and the battle degenerated into the usual round of attacks and counter-attacks. Final British casualties at Loos approached 50,500, while Germans losses stood at around, 20,000. Continental warfare was finally beckoning for the BEF.

IT WAS EVIDENT AS 1915 DREW TO A CLOSE that, although the Allies had made considerable advances in their tactical thinking, the Germans had made substantive defensive developments which trumped that progress. Relatively speaking, the German tactical rollercoaster was in the ascendant: multiple lines of well-constructed trenches; the introduction of deep dugouts; the depth and complexity of barbed wire entanglements; the deployment of more machine guns with deadly interlocking fields of fire; the use of villages and farms to form strongpoints; the massed artillery batteries waiting to destroy anything and everything that showed itself above ground. In France, whisperings had begun about the command of Joffre. After all, by the end of 1915 the French had suffered over 2 million casualties, of which 730,000 were dead. Joffre's failure to gain success despite the sacrifice of so many French lives had done his reputation serious damage, although his status as the victor of the Marne protected him for the moment.

His British counterpart was not so lucky. It may not have been fair, but the failure of the British 1915 offensives – and in particular the debacle at Loos – demanded a scapegoat and Field Marshal Sir John French was the obvious candidate. In truth French, although an able cavalry leader in the Boer War, had never been up to the demands of his role in this frightening new military landscape. He had floundered tactically, failed to establish the necessary rapport with his French counterparts, lacked the administrative grip required in such a nightmarish logistical situation, and had no underlying vision of the war to guide him through the horrendous challenges his troops faced on a daily basis. Above all, Sir John French had lost the confidence of his political masters and, after some unsavoury manoeuvring, he was replaced as Commander in Chief by General Sir Douglas Haig on 19 December 1915. As the BEF moved forward into 1916, it was clear that the Battles of Neuve Chapelle, Aubers Ridge, Festubert and Loos in which it was involved were mere skirmishes when compared with the battles fought by the French Army in 1915. The French had continued to bear the brunt of the strain of facing the German Army on the Western Front and their casualties had been excruciatingly high. It was only their blood sacrifice that had given the BEF the time to gather its resources and train its men in the basic language of war.

Great strides in expanding the BEF had been instituted back in 1914 by Kitchener, widely acclaimed as the greatest British soldier of his generation. Right from the start, he had been convinced that the war would be a long, hard-fought endeavour, to be measured in years and certainly not 'all over by Christmas'. An independent figure, he was not enamoured of the idea of expanding the Territorial Army, which he rather distrusted as 'amateur soldiers', but instead sought to start anew, raising hundreds of thousands of men with a new improvised structure of volunteer 'Service Battalions' linked to the county regiments. He launched a successful recruiting campaign in which by far the most long-standing image proved to be a poster of Kitchener himself with the caption 'Your Country Needs You!' The response from the British public was unparalleled and soon the new legions of 'Kitchener's Army' offered the chance to expand the BEF into a truly continental army. But these masses of new young soldiers were terrifyingly inexperienced. Would the Germans allow them the chance to attain full maturity as fighting units?

6

THE EASTERN FRONT, 1915

'As regards Russia it seemed of less consequence than usual merely to gain ground. The essential thing was to smash the enemy's fighting machine.'[1]

General Erich von Falkenhayn, General Headquarters, German Army

THE EASTERN FRONT would move to centre stage in 1915. Although the German Chief of Staff General Erich von Falkenhayn was convinced of the primacy of the Western Front, he had been pressured by forces within the German military and political hierarchy to amend his plans and send reinforcements to the east where the twin stars of Hindenburg and Ludendorff were firmly in the ascendant. The Eastern Front had been frozen during the depths of winter and, although the fighting had slowed in pace, the minds of the staff officers were racing as they planned their next moves. Ludendorff, working in co-operation with the Austrian Chief of Staff General Franz Conrad von Hötzendorf, agreed a programme for offensives by the Austrians in Galicia and the Germans in East Prussia, near-simultaneous in order to maximise the impact and with the ambitious overall intention of forcing the Russians to evacuate central Poland or run the risk of being cut off. The Germans had reorganised their forces and managed to construct a new Tenth Army in East Prussia, capitalising on the divisions so grudgingly extracted from Falkenhayn.

The Russians were also still engaged in an increasingly vituperative debate between those who considered they should concentrate on the Germans in East Prussia or Silesia and those who advocated a renewed offensive in Galicia and the Carpathians in an attempt to knock the struggling Austrio-Hungarians right out of the war. It was no coincidence that one of the main advocates of the former approach should be General Nikolai Ruzsky, commanding the North-West Front, while the other faction was led by General Nikolai Ivanov, who commanded the South-West Front. This tension led to a failure to co-operate or concentrate resources for a joint course of action as each of the two front commanders clung to his own plans. In the event, Ruzsky decided to launch a new offensive in East Prussia in mid-February, in anticipation of which he slowly built up his new Twelfth Army around the Narew River sector on the southern frontier of East Prussia. However, the Russian plans would be rendered redundant when the Germans struck first.

On 7 February 1915, Ludendorff launched the Second Battle of the Masurian Lakes with a two-pronged attack by the Tenth Army in the north and the Eighth Army in the south, both driving in on the flanks of the Russian Tenth Army which was occupying defensive lines in East Prussia, wedged neatly between the sea and the Masurian Lakes. As on the Western Front, at this stage of the war the Russian trench defences were hardly sophisticated, often amounting to little more than deep ditches, usually with no support lines or communication trenches. The Tenth Army was also in poor shape, suffering from low morale, with many units considered to be of only second line status. Shortages of rifles and ammunition meant reinforcements often arrived at the front unarmed, reliant on pillaging the bodies of the dead for weapons. The weather was dreadful, with howling blizzards reducing visibility almost to nothing. Initially the Russians were taken by surprise. The German forces massed on both flanks, then drove forward seeking to choke off escape routes and achieve another battle of annihilation. They were at least partially successful, but the Russians soon began to fall back and it was difficult for the Germans to maintain their momentum in such awful conditions. Both sides suffered problems of command and control, but the bulk of the Russian Tenth Army managed to evade the net as it retreated back into Russia, although the fate of the XX Corps – cut off and captured in the dark depths of the Augustów Forest – showed what might have been. Following an unsuccessful siege of the Osowiec Fortress, the German attacks pressed east into Russia to try to create a buffer zone. However, in March the Germans withdrew to their own borders under heavy pressure from the Russian Tenth and Twelfth Armies. Afterwards Hindenburg and Ludendorff claimed a great victory, pointing out that they had liberated the last slice of occupied German mainland territory. Falkenhayn was less sanguine, considering it a meaningless success which had cost the lives of far too many highly trained reinforcements while it had cost the Russians only manpower, of which they had a near-endless supply.

The Austrian contribution to the winter offensives had actually begun earlier, on 23 January 1915, when Conrad ordered forward his troops, assisted by a joint Austrian–German Südarmee group. It was a bold, some might say suicidal scheme, launching a series of attacks to secure control of the passes of the western and central Carpathian Mountains in the freezing cold of January. It was also intended to push deep into Galicia and relieve the besieged fortress town of Przemyśl. A further flanking attack was to be made to the east into Bukovina. The conditions in the Carpathians made military operations almost impossible. The soldiers found that their rifle bolts froze solid and could not be fired; the advance through the passes slowed to a crawl. Frozen corpses littered the ground, for burial was impossible. Some progress was made but only at a terrible cost. Soon it became evident that nothing of substance could be achieved, while relieving Przemyśl was out of the question. Then the Russians counter-attacked and for the Austrians the situation deteriorated still further, although the Russians would be stymied too by the horrendous conditions, with the casualty figures on both sides ballooning through the multiplier effects of exposure and rampant frostbite. By early March, the fate of Przemyśl was beginning to dominate Austrian thoughts. The garrison had launched occasional attempts to break out, which had been fended off easily by the Russians. Equally the Russians were unable to batter down the fortress due to their continuing problems in deploying the super-heavy artillery required to smash the fortifications. But at last the stores began to run out and, with no hope of relief, the garrison finally surrendered on 22 March.

These were desperate times for the Austrians, with a multi-national army which, when placed under this kind of pressure, began to fray at the edges. Throughout the war there had been speculation that various nationalities – Czechs, Ukrainians, Hungarians and various Slav groupings – were surrendering far too easily or, worse still, were going over voluntarily to the other side. These rumours had a corrosive effect on morale and would do much to undermine the Austrian Army's performance for the rest of the war.

With the fall of Przemyśl, Ivanov was finally allowed to launch a major offensive on the South-West Front designed to capture the Carpathian passes and finally defeat the Austrians. To facilitate this plan the North-West Front was put on a defensive basis, which promptly triggered the resignation of the 'exhausted' Ruzsky. His replacement would be General Mikhail Alekseyev, who had been Ivanov's Chief of Staff, and whom the Stavka expected to form a more harmonious liaison with his old chief. They would be sadly disappointed, for as soon as Alekseyev arrived at the North-West Front headquarters he immediately adopted all the old Ruzsky arguments as his own with the passion of a convert. This led to a continuing failure to release sufficient troops to allow Ivanov to capitalise on his initial successes against the Austro-Hungarian Army. A further problem was the spring thaw, which brought flooding rendering many of the mountain passes impassable. The Russian Carpathian Offensive was eventually suspended on 10 April. By this time it has been estimated that the Austrians had suffered some 750,000 casualties already in 1915. As Ivanov amassed such forces as he could for the next stage of the fighting it appeared that Austria-Hungary was finished, especially as her old adversary, Italy, was considering joining the war on the side of the Allies in an attempt to make territorial gains at Austria's expense. However, strong forces were moving against Ivanov's command.

The imminent collapse of Austria-Hungary left Falkenhayn with no choice but to accede to the piteous demands for reinforcements emanating from the Eastern Front. This was entirely against his own inclinations to concentrate on the Western Front. However, he was determined to retain some strategic control of what was going on, resisting the idea of simply passing the divisions to Hindenburg. Instead, Falkenhayn adopted a plan that originated, at least in part, with Conrad to send eight divisions from the Western Front to form a new Eleventh Army, which would be combined with the Austrian Third and Fourth Armies as an army group under the overall independent command of General August von Mackensen and deployed in the Cracow area for an offensive on the Russian Third Army in the Gorlice–Tarnów sector, with the intention of achieving a local superiority of numbers. This had the additional advantage of placing Austrian troops under German command, making a force of some 300,000. Mackensen also had the inestimable advantage of having a huge concentration of artillery – some 1,700 guns, of which over 500 were heavy artillery, all served with plentiful ammunition supplies. For Falkenhayn there was the additional political consideration that Mackensen was not operating under the aegis of the Hindenburg-Ludendorff team. The stresses that had fractured German High Command over the question of an East versus West grand strategy were beginning to take effect.

There was an extensive amount of diversionary activity undertaken prior to Mackensen's offensive, with attacks made by the Germans in the north and by the Austrians in the south in order to deflect Russian attention from the crucial sector. In any case the Russians ignored a series of intelligence reports drawing attention to the German build-up in the Cracow area, distracted as they were by their own plans for a Carpathian Offensive. The Russians were also hampered by the continuing failure of the commanders of the South-West Front and the North-West Front to co-operate in any meaningful way. The result was that the Third Army, commanded by General Radko Dimitriev, was left facing vastly superior forces. Yet through over-confidence Dimitriev had failed to ensure that his men had dug themselves in properly on a front which stretched from the Vistula, all along the Dunajec and Biala Rivers and across into the Carpathians. Mackensen planned to use his guns to blast aside the thin defences between Gorlice and Tarnow, allowing his three armies then to burst through the Russian lines, with the German Twelfth Army driving onwards at the front, while the Austrian Third and Fourth Armies advanced in echelon on either side, protecting the flanks.

When the guns blazed out on 1 May 1915, everything went according to plan as the heavy German and Austrian shells smashed through the Russians' simple linear trench lines, killing and burying many. Those who ran for their lives were massacred by the shrapnel fire of the German field guns. By the time the infantry attacked on 2 May it was a procession, as they smashed through the Dunajec and Biala line. The minimal Russian reserves were thrown into the bonfire and merely added to the flames. The Third Army – or what was left of it – tumbled back in confusion all the way to the San River, the armies on either side of it being forced to conform or themselves be destroyed. Then the San River line was also breached, with the Germans pouring through, and it looked like Przemyśl would fall. Even the news that the Italians had finally decided to join the Allies on 23 May 1915 could do nothing to save the Russians. The Germans and Austrians emphatically did have the heavy – and super-heavy – artillery that the Russians had so conspicuously lacked in their siege of the fortress. Discretion was the better part of valour and Przemyśl fell without a struggle on 4 June, while the city of Lemberg was also recaptured on 22 June. All the Russian gains of 1914 had been swept away.

By mid-June the situation was desperate for the Russians. The German-led assault had destabilised their whole line and Russian Poland was looking particularly vulnerable to being pinched out by the German forces running rampant in East Prussia and Galicia. In the end the Grand Duke Nicholas and the Stavka sanctioned the Russian withdrawal from Galicia, while resolving to cling on to Warsaw and their Polish possessions. For the Germans, with the Austrians acting firmly under their directions, there seemed to be only opportunities: attacks were being prepared in Galicia, Poland and in Lithuania to the north with all three timed to start in mid-July. Falkenhayn was still in overall control and he put aside Ludendorff's plans for a gigantic battle of encirclement, preferring instead to chew up the Russian forces in tightly controlled battles using his artillery as a battering ram. Most of all he was determined not to repeat Napoleon's mistake and venture too far into the Russian interior. It was summer then; but in Russia winter never seems far away.

As part of the series of offensives, huge forces were concentrated on both the north and south frontiers of Russian Poland, with the intent of smashing through to take Warsaw. If the Russians sought to retain the city then they would risk another disaster like Tannenberg. In the end they had little choice but to fall back, finally surrendering control of Warsaw to the Germans on 5 August. By the end of August the Russians had lost all of Russian Poland but as they fell back they relied on a scorched earth policy, destroying and burning everything of possible value to the Germans. The Russians were losing ground elsewhere, too, falling back in the area of the Baltic provinces to a German thrust that threatened the important port of Riga. For Falkenhayn it was a strange time: while rejoicing at the successes achieved, his underlying conviction remained that ultimate victory over Russia was impossible. Even during these glorious triumphs, the Germans and Austro-Hungarians were still suffering casualties at an unacceptable rate. The two bugbears of fighting the Russians: the immense distances and their inexhaustible manpower remained to haunt them. Falkenhayn was determined to control the more ambitious activities of Hindenburg and Ludendorff; indeed, having already created the Mackensen army group to operate independently with the Austrians, he now created a new central German army group under the independent command of Prince Leopold of Bavaria, thus further diluting Hindenburg's power. What Falkenhayn still really wanted was a separate peace with Russia, but his compatriots were blinded by their successes and could not envisage making the kind of territorial surrenders that might tempt Russia to desert her allies. Worse still, feelers put out to the Russians were brusquely rejected. Falkenhayn would have to settle for the long-term military damage to Russia that would shore up the position of Austria-Hungary. That, by his judgement, had been achieved by the late summer of 1915. At the end of September, a combination of increasing Russian resistance and Falkenhayn's insistence that troops would have to be diverted back to the Western Front forced the Germans to come to a halt. As they dug in it was evident that the war was not yet over in the east.

For the Russians had not given up. They had lost a depth of up to 300 miles of territory, and had suffered over 2 million casualties, but if anything their army was still growing. Indeed, tactically the new defence line had considerable merits in that it was safer than the ungainly Polish Salient. The new line ran from close to Riga in the north all the way down to the Dniester River and the border with Rumania, which had the effect of shortening its overall length from 1,100 miles to 650 miles, a saving which allowed the creation of reserves behind the new defensive positions. A further advantage lay in the superior defensive terrain they were now occupying. A combination of lakes, rivers, forests and the vast expanses of the Pripyat Marshes helped to buttress the line, making it less vulnerable to sudden breakthroughs. In essence the Russian position had been strengthened.

The Russians now engaged in a thorough reorganisation of their High Command. At the top Grand Duke Nicholas was dismissed and replaced as titular head by Tsar Nicholas on 1 September 1915. As Chief of Staff of the Stavka he appointed General Mikhail Alekseyev, who would be the man actually responsible for the direction of the Russian armies. They were now to be divided up into three fronts: the North Front, with General Nikolai Ruzsky restored to its command (although he would be replaced by General

Alexei Kuropatkin in February 1916); the West Front, commanded by General Alexei Evert; and the South-West Front, commanded by General Nikolai Ivanov, although he too was replaced, in March 1916, by General Alexei Brusilov. Born in 1853, Brusilov had served as a young officer in the Russo-Turkish War of 1870 and afterwards become an acclaimed cavalry expert eventually being promoted to lieutenant general. During the war he had excelled, demonstrating a rare combination of aggression and tactical acumen. By 1916 he was confident that he had the measure of the Austrians – if only he could get at them without German interference.

Buoyed up by such positive thoughts, the new Russian High Command began to turn its collective mind to the possibilities for 1916. Indeed at another Allied conference held at Chantilly in December 1915, they were enthusiastic about co-ordinating their offensives to hit the Germans on both main fronts simultaneously so that the Germans were unable to switch divisions from one front to the other. Thus, while the British and French attacked on the Somme, the Russians would launch a major new offensive on the Eastern Front in June 1916. They also agreed that, should one of them be attacked, they would all act in concert to try to alleviate the situation by launching their own attacks.

Yet, before the year ended there was one enemy that Falkenhayn accepted could be dealt with permanently in the period of grace granted by the string of defeats suffered by Russia in 1915: Serbia. He allocated the German Eleventh Army to the task of joining with Conrad's Austrian armies in an assault on Serbia under the overall command of Mackensen. They were also to be helped by a new ally: the Bulgarians, who had been greatly impressed by the triumph at the Battle of Gorlice-Tarnow and had begun serious negotiations with a view to joining the war on the side of the Central Powers. Germany astutely played on the Bulgarian resentments stemming from the chastening treatment meted out to Bulgaria in the second stage of the Balkan War of 1912, and offered them substantial territorial gains at the expense of Serbia or indeed any other Balkan countries that had the temerity to join the Allies. These diplomatic moves were co-ordinated to coincide with the Mackensen Offensive, timed to commence in early October 1915, with the express intention not only of knocking Serbia out of the war but also of opening up a land route via Serbia and Bulgaria to Turkey to allow guns and munitions to get through to assist the Turks in the Gallipoli Campaign. Allied counter-diplomacy, even a last-ditch ultimatum from Russia, failed to have any impact: the Bulgarians under Tsar Ferdinand I were determined to join the Central Powers.

On 6 October Mackensen launched his assault with a heavy bombardment pounding the Serbian positions all along the Sava and Danube Rivers. The German Eleventh Army and Austrian Third Army managed to establish significant bridgeheads and, once the integrity of the Serbian river lines was broken, their weight of numbers soon hurled back the Serbians and Belgrade fell again on 9 October. Then, on 14 October, the Bulgarian First and Second Armies invaded Serbia from the east. The campaign that ensued was brutal. But the Central Powers had underestimated both the sheer bloody-mindedness of the Serbs and the impact of the winter weather in the mountainous areas of the central Balkans. With their totemic but still ailing leader, Field Marshal Radomir Putnik, travelling in a sedan car, the Serbians eluded attempts to cut them off and fell back through the mountain passes into Montenegro and Albania. Ravaged by disease, freezing to death in the bitter winter, lacking food or transport, harassed all the while by unsympathetic Albanian guerrillas, left with little or no hope to sustain them, the survivors managed somehow to stagger to the Albanian coast from where they could hope to be evacuated to safety by the Royal Navy. The Central Powers had captured Serbia, but the Serbian Army would fight on regardless. It was a potent example of the difficulties attached to fighting a war against nation states that will not accept defeat.

THE END OF 1915 HAD NOT BROUGHT DECISIVE VICTORY to the Central Powers on the Eastern Front. Falkenhayn had never thought it would; for him it would always be a sideshow. He could not envisage any circumstances under which the Russians had enough of their men destroyed to force surrender; and nor could he imagine which tactical objectives or cities would have to be captured to make the Russians give up. His troops had captured Warsaw without a flicker of defeatism from the Russians. As a student of military history the German Chief of General Staff knew enough not to push on towards Moscow; that way lay only madness and defeat. Falkenhayn had only ever turned to the Eastern Front in order to bolster the Austrians. With the Russians momentarily cowed, the Bulgarians on the side of the Central Powers and the Serbs seemingly defeated, his mind turned to the Western Front. Once again the troop trains began to move the German divisions, this time from east to west.

7

GALLIPOLI, 1915

'This is one of the great campaigns of history. Think what Constantinople is to the East. It is more than London, Paris and Berlin all rolled into one are to the West. Think how it has dominated the East. Think what its fall will mean.'[1]

First Lord of the Admiralty Sir Winston Churchill

THE CONSEQUENCES OF EVEN A MOMENTARY LOSS of naval control by the Royal Navy could not have been more starkly illustrated than by the escape of the German battlecruiser *Goeben* and the accompanying light cruiser *Breslau* from the Mediterranean at the outbreak of the war. Since 1912 these two ships, under the command of Rear Admiral Wilhelm Souchon, had been acting as symbols of the German state during their regular visits to Constantinople where their presence made a considerable impact on Turkish popular opinion, creating the perception that German military power had a strong naval dimension. The Germans already maintained a Military Mission providing advice to the Turkish Army, while the Royal Navy had a Naval Mission performing a similar role for the Turkish Navy. However, even before hostilities began, the First Lord of the Admiralty Winston Churchill had undermined Britain's position in Turkey by unilaterally confiscating the two Turkish dreadnoughts nearing completion in British naval yards. This decision, although not taken lightly, resounded across Turkey. The ships had been financed by popular subscription and embodied a considerable degree of national pride. To have them wrenched away was intolerable.

On 4 August, the day after Franco-German hostilities began, Souchon attempted to interfere with the French convoy operations transporting the XIX Corps from North Africa to Marseilles and what was to become the Western Front. Despite the attentions of the French and British Mediterranean Fleet, the *Goeben* and *Breslau* managed to escape in circumstances of considerable confusion not helped by a plethora of Admiralty signals attempting to control affairs from London. Souchon arrived at the Dardanelles on 10 August, whereupon his ships were promptly 'sold' to Turkey to 'replace' the two dreadnoughts confiscated by the British. This proved a great step in Turkey's journey to war which, after a considerable period of politicking and intrigue, finally triggered a raid by the Turkish fleet led by Souchon aboard the *Goeben* on the Russian Black Sea ports. This in turn provoked the Russia declaration of war on Turkey on 2 November 1914. The focus of attention was on the Dardanelles, the narrow strip of water between Europe and Asia, one of the great maritime sea lanes, acting as the gateway to Constantinople, the Black Sea and Russia. Shortly afterwards, the Turkish Sultan Mehmed V, as the titular head of the Muslim Caliphate, declared a Holy War with a clarion call to all Muslim subjects in British, French or Russian domains to rise up against their infidel masters. This would have a minimal impact but it was nevertheless worrying, in particular to the British, who were concerned as to the possible impact on the large Muslim population within the Empire.

The Allies were ordered into immediate action and bombarded the forts at the entrance of the Dardanelles on 4 November 1914, thereby drawing attention to the paucity of the existing Turkish defences covering that vital waterway. While the Turks subsequently put much effort into improving their fortifications the Royal Navy bided its time. This remained the situation until Kitchener received a request for help from the Russians hard-pressed by a Turkish offensive in the Carpathian Mountains in December 1914. The British response was to despatch a joint Anglo-French fleet under the command of Vice Admiral Sackville Carden to force the Dardanelles. Early bombardments of the Turkish forts achieved little, not helped by the restrictive flat trajectory of the naval guns coupled with difficulties in observation. The British operation was further hamstrung by the entirely legitimate opposition of both the First Sea Lord Sir John Fisher and the Commander in Chief of the Grand Fleet Sir John Jellicoe who were jealous of any naval resources denied the Grand Fleet as it faced the High Seas Fleet across the North Sea.

Finally, on 18 March, the Allied fleet made a major effort to force open the Dardanelles. Carden had folded under the pressure and had been replaced in command by Vice Admiral John de Robeck when at 10.30 in the bright sunshine of a lovely spring day the fleet sailed into the Straits. The naval guns blazed out, pounding the forts, but the effects were minimal. When under fire the forts fell silent, but the moment the ships moved closer the Turkish guns burst back into life. More dangerous still, on the night of 8 March the Turkish minelayer *Nusrat* had laid a line of mines right where the ships were accustomed to manoeuvre. These had not been detected and the consequences were devastating. At 14.00 the French pre-dreadnought *Bouvet* ran on to a mine. There was a dreadful internal explosion and she sank within minutes. Some 639 French lives were lost in this tragedy. Still the battle raged on. Things began to get desperate for the Allies when the battlecruiser *Inflexible*, already battered by shells, also ran on to a mine, followed by the pre-dreadnoughts *Ocean* and *Irresistible*. Although the *Inflexible* managed to withdraw and run herself aground, the other two sank. Fortunately, the crews were for the most part saved. Bowing to the inevitable and with his minesweepers making no progress, at 17.50 de Robeck ordered the fleet to retreat. He had lost nearly a third of his ships and had achieved nothing. Subsequently siren voices claimed that the fleet had fallen back at the point of victory, that the Turks had been ready to give way. Nothing could have been further from the truth. The Turks still had plenty of shells left for both forts and howitzer batteries; the minefields and torpedo tubes were still intact. From this total defeat would be born the Gallipoli land campaign.

The Allies had already wavered from the original intention of a purely naval assault. The strategic confusion at the heart of the British government was indicative of the inability of politicians to grasp the implications of their involvement in a continental war based firmly on Europe, rather than the traditional random maritime interventions of yore. Troops had begun to gather in the Mediterranean area almost by default, with no real attention paid to their readiness for war. The bedrock was the 29th Division, hastily patched together from regular garrison troops gathered from around the Empire, while the French 1st Division of the Corps Expéditionnaire d'Orient (CEO) was a well-trained formation with a full artillery complement. Sadly, the Australian and New Zealand Army Corps (ANZAC) and Royal Naval Division (RND) were filled with promising material, but had little experience as soldiers. These gathering forces were placed under the command of General Sir Ian Hamilton, who had arrived the day before the abortive naval attempt. In reserve Hamilton had access to the 42nd Division of Lancashire Territorials and an Indian Brigade. Failure on 18 March triggered the decision to attempt a landing on the Gallipoli Peninsula with the aim of seizing the Kilid Bahr Plateau which dominated the narrows of the Dardanelles.

The challenge ahead of Hamilton should not be underestimated. This would be the first opposed landing in the era of modern weapons; not only that, but it would have to be conducted on a narrow peninsula in terrain that greatly favoured the defenders. Furthermore, there was an inevitable delay while the Mediterranean Expeditionary Force (MEF) gathered and prepared for action, a delay which allowed the Turks to improve their defences. All chance of a strategic surprise had been lost by the previous naval bombardments; now all Hamilton could hope to strive for was an element of tactical subtlety to try and wrong-foot the Turks. His complex plans, designed to confuse the Turks, were predicated on the Turks posing minimum resistance. No less than five separate landings were to be made by the 29th Division around the Helles tip of the Peninsula. The ANZAC Corps was to land on the beaches just north of Gaba Tepe further up the Peninsula and opposite Kilid Bahr, while the French would land at Kum Kale on the Asiatic coast in order to protect the rear of the 29th Division. Just to complicate matters further, diversionary operations would be launched by the French at Besika Bay and the RND at the Bulair neck of the Peninsula. In trying to confuse the Turks, Hamilton divided his forces, failing to concentrate them at any one point and opening up the possibility of failure everywhere. The Turkish Fifth Army charged with defending Gallipoli was under the command of General Otto Liman von Sanders. His plans revolved around light coastal screens charged with causing the maximum possible delay while the reserves would march to the point of danger and launch counter-attacks designed to sweep the invaders into the sea. As such, by accident or design, he happened on the perfect counter to Hamilton's scattergun approach.

The ANZAC Corps would be landed at night at 04.30 on 25 April, the men being towed in strings of naval cutters behind steam boats. As they approached the shore stealthily there was a tremendous amount of confusion with the end result being that the boats landed bunched together around the Ari Burnu promontory at the northern end of a small sheltered beach which would soon become known as Anzac Cove.

> Boats ground in 4 or 5 feet of water owing to the human weight contained in them. We scramble out, struggle to the shore and, rushing across the beach, take cover under a low sandbank. 'Here, take off my pack and I'll take off yours!' We help one another to lift the heavy water-soaked packs off. 'Hurry up, there!' says our Sergeant. 'Fix bayonets!' Click! And the bayonets are fixed. 'Forward!' And away we scramble up the hills in our front. Up, up we go, stumbling in holes and ruts. With a ringing cheer we charge the steep hill, pulling ourselves up by roots and branches of trees; at times digging our bayonets into the ground and pushing ourselves up to a foothold, until, topping the hill, we find the enemy have made themselves very scarce.[2]
>
> Private Alfred Perry, 10th (South Australia) Battalion, AIF

The initial landing was all but unopposed – just one company of the 2/27th Regiment faced the invaders – but a combination of the tortuous terrain and cautious leadership restricted the Australian advance to about quarter of a mile inland. The arrival of the rest of the 27th Regiment prevented any further progress.

> We guessed that the enemy was advancing slowly and cautiously in order to capture the ridge where we were which dominated all sides – namely Chunuk Bair to Gaba Tepe. We set about our task of throwing the enemy and we felt a moral force in ourselves for performing this task. All the signs indicated that opposing our 2,000 armed men was a force of at least four or five times that size – or even bigger. We had to prevent the enemy from reaching and occupying the dominating line of Chunuk Bair–Gaba Tepe and had to gain time until the 19th Division arrived.[3]
>
> Lieutenant Colonel Mehmet Sefik, Headquarters, Fifth Turkish Army

The arrival of the 19th Turkish Division under the command of Lieutenant Colonel Mustafa Kemal on the dominating bulk of Chunuk Bair changed the situation radically. Soon it was the Turks, not the Anzacs, who were attacking.

> To my mind there was a more important factor than this tactical situation – that was, everybody hurled himself on the enemy to kill and to die. This was no ordinary attack. Everybody was eager to succeed or go forward with the determination to die. Here is the order which I gave verbally to the commanders: 'I don't order you to attack – I order you to die. In the time which passes until we die, other troops and commanders can take our places.'[4]
>
> Lieutenant Colonel Mustafa Kemal, Headquarters, Fifth Turkish Army

Kemal's words perfectly encapsulate the spirit of grim determination that motivated the Turkish troops. The Anzacs were pinned back and, after the failure of the Turkish attempt to push them finally into the sea on 19 May, here they would remain, relatively quiescent, but defending a minute bridgehead that defied all military sense.

At Helles the British landed after dawn on 25 April, confident that once they got their troops ashore the Turks would cut and run. The main landings were to be made by the 86th Brigade at V and W Beaches at the tip of the Peninsula, with subsidiary landings at S, X and Y Beaches to try and threaten the Turks' flanks, with the French landing at Kum Kale on the other side of the Straits in order to cover their backs from the fire of the Asiatic forts. It was intended that the British troops would reach the hill of Achi Baba which dominated Helles by the end of the day before moving up the Peninsula to attack the Kilid Bahr Plateau in conjunction with the ANZAC Corps.

The troops came ashore almost unopposed at S, X and Y Beaches, but then failed to advance in a purposeful manner, indeed, the Y Beach force soon found itself battling to survive as Turkish reinforcements forced a somewhat panicked evacuation on the morning of 26 April. The story of the assaults of W and V Beach are a mixture of horror, heroism and gross British exaggeration of the odds they faced. The Turks had just two companies of the 3/26th Regiment defending these two beaches, although they were well dug in with barbed wire defences. At W Beach the Lancashire Fusiliers were initially held up, but the Turks were soon outflanked and swept away. Yet at V Beach it was a different matter. Here the Turks fought brilliantly, pouring concentrated rifle fire on to the tows of rowing boats carrying the 1st Dublin Fusiliers and the 1st Munster Fusiliers emerging on to the exit ramps of a specially adapted tramp steamer, the *River Clyde*, which had been deliberately run ashore.

> I had to run about 100–150 yards in the water and being the first away from the cutter escaped the fire a bit to start with. But as soon as a few followed me, the water around seemed to be alive, the bullets striking the sea all around us. Heaven alone knows how I got thro' a perfect hail of bullets. The beach sloped very gently – fortunately! When I was about 50 yards from the water's edge I felt one bullet go thro' the pack on my back and then thought I had got through safely when they put one through my left arm. The fellows in the regiment had told me I was getting too fat to run, but those who saw me go through that bit of water changed their opinions later – I ran like hell!!!!!⁵
>
> Captain David French, 1st Royal Dublin Fusiliers

The survivors were pinned down until the fall of night allowed the bulk of the troops to come ashore, exposing the numerical weakness of the Turkish garrison. The British troops had over-run the Turkish positions by the early afternoon of 26 April. But by this time the timetable had been thrown completely out of kilter. Communications had broken down and staff procedures collapsed as inexperienced officers lost control over the situation. There was no sense of a combined purpose; each beach landing was fought as a separate operation, with no effective co-operation to assist each other when things went wrong. This was not unique to the 29th Division; exactly the same problems had been encountered after the initial breakthrough at Neuve Chapelle on 10 March.

The next couple of days were not marked by a bold thrust for Achi Baba. Instead, there was a period of reorganisation and consolidation. The French were brought back from their covering landing at Kum Kale and given the position on the right of Helles adjoining the Dardanelles, ironically rendering themselves cruelly vulnerable to fire into their rear by Turkish batteries across the Straits. Once they were finally sorted out, the Allies began to press forward on Achi Baba during the First Battle of Krithia of 28 April, only to find progress first stalled and then utter defeat staring them in the face, during Turkish night counter-attacks launched by fresh reserves on 1 and 3 May. These attacks were crude: rushing forward in massed hordes, the Turks were attacking in the dark primarily to avoid being flayed by the guns of the fleet. Nevertheless they almost broke through, although the casualties they suffered reduced them to a defensive posture. At this point the Turks were still not properly dug in across the Peninsula, having just a string of outposts and defensive positions.

Desperate to get his stalled campaign moving, Hamilton brought in his reserves and sanctioned a series of attacks for 6, 7 and 8 May which together are known as the Second Battle of Krithia. There was nothing of tactical subtlety here. Every time the Allied troops felt their way forward they came under scything fire. At last, at 19.00 on 8 May, Hamilton and the commander of the 29th Division, Lieutenant General Sir Aylmer Hunter-Weston, accepted the inevitable. Over the three days they had suffered some 6,500 casualties for the gain of at most 600 yards. It was a disaster. Hamilton was forced to appeal, cap in hand, to Kitchener for more troops; this would prove the pattern for the campaign. Every time Allied reserves arrived they were soon matched by Turkish reinforcements and swiftly frittered away in attacks that had little or no military justification.

By the start of June 1915 there was a fully fledged trench system criss-crossing the Helles Peninsula. The British response was to use some of the new assault tactics already being employed on the Western Front in their next attack, the Third Battle of Krithia on 4 June. Essentially this was intended as a 'bite and hold' to break the deadlock by seizing the three defensive lines held by the Turks, which would then allow the next assault to be made on Achi Baba direct.

> We scramble up and over the top into a withering machine gun and rifle fire with shrapnel bursting overhead. Many fell back into the trench before they got properly over, we spread out as we went and charged with fixed bayonets through No Man's Land which is all shell holes and deep crevices. F. Royle[6] on my left was killed by my side, also the next man on my right. I felt as though I was alone for the moment until I saw a Turk about to throw a bomb at a bunch of chaps on my left. Kneeling, I took a steady aim and fired twice rapid, he ducked down sharp, but whether I hit him or not I do not know. I ran on soaked in sweat and white with dust. We dashed on and on over barbed wire and shell holes, jumping gullies, through thick gorse or wild thyme, knee deep; this was on fire in many places and we were choked by smoke and dust. The Turks were keeping up a rapid rifle and machine gun fire, and as we got nearer threw bombs amongst us, also

shrapnel bursting overhead, we were being mown down like corn. We kept on and on with our artillery lengthening their range as we went and helping us all they could. Suddenly we let out a wild yell all along the line, then we were on their parapet. It was now all hell let loose and then we were down amongst them in their trench. It was a shambles and the slaughter was terrible on each side, and here we were at a disadvantage as the enemy were using bombs with deadly effect and we were being blown to pieces. This drove us into a frenzy of rage and we went at them like madmen. They nearly drove us out as they were three to one, but we rallied and at last we drove them out and had captured the trench and many prisoners.[7]

Private Jack Gatley, 1/7th Manchester Regiment

The 42nd Division had done exceptionally well, but on the right the French CEO was charging towards disaster, baulked by the redoubts clustered on the Kereves Spur and around the head of the deep ravine of Kereves Dere. This failure opened the flanks of the RND and the 42nd Division. The Turkish reserves launched counter-attacks over the next couple of days, swarming down the gullies and at one point appearing to be about to break through themselves. For all the slaughter, only a meagre few hundred yards of British gains were retained. It was evident that, as on the Western Front, neither side could break through at Helles.

By now Hamilton and Hunter-Weston had lost sight of the real objective – to break through to seize the Kilid Bahr Plateau which overlooked the Narrows. They were fixated on Achi Baba, which in reality was just a stepping stone. It had tactical significance at Helles, dominating the skyline and allowing the Turks to see everything above ground across the whole Allied sector, but it had no view over the Narrows. Also, the ground that lay between it and the imposing bulk of Kilid Bahr was perfectly configured for defence. At Helles fantasy had overcome reason.

Their failure at the Third Battle of Krithia caused Hunter-Weston and the French CEO commander, General Henri Gouraud, to introduce a more refined version of 'bite and hold' by attacking on a very small frontage to allow the maximum concentration of guns. The French attacked first, at the head of Kereves Dere on 21 June, while the British followed up on 28 June with an attack on Gully Ravine. They were encouraged by their partial success, but hampered by the dreadful shortage of guns and shells. This was not a temporary problem. The British munitions industry could not keep up with demand and priority was being given to the BEF on the Western Front. At Gallipoli, the Allies were indeed making small advances, but they were using a disproportionate amount of their ammunition stocks to do so. When they tried to launch a two-staged attack by the recently arrived 52nd Division on 12 and 13 July, some limited progress was made but it did not justify the casualties incurred. Helles was becoming a hopeless nightmare. The embittered commander of 52nd Division summed it up perfectly.

> It seems to me that the fighting of this battle was premature and at the actual moment worse than unnecessary – I submit that it was cruel and wasteful. The troops on the Peninsula were tired and worn out; there were only two Infantry Brigades, the 155th and the 157th, that had not been seriously engaged. It was well known to the higher command that large reinforcements were arriving from England and a grand attack was to be made at Suvla. Was it not therefore obvious that the exhausted garrison at Helles should be given a fortnight's respite and that the fresh attacks from that position should synchronise with those at Suvla and Anzac? I contend that the Battle of July 12–13th was due to a complete want of a true appreciation of the situation. If the conception of the battle was wrong the tactics of the action were far worse. The division of the attack of two Brigades on a narrow front into two phases, no less than 9 hours apart, was positively wicked.[8]
>
> Major General Granville Egerton, Headquarters, 52nd Division

Egerton laid bare the stupidity of these attacks. Hamilton had indeed been promised massive reinforcements but had decided to deploy them away from the layered Turkish trenches of Helles.

THE SECOND CHAPTER OF THE GALLIPOLI CAMPAIGN began with all the strategic indecision and lack of realistic planning that had been the hallmark of the first fumbling stumble to disaster on 25 April. Hamilton had requested substantial reinforcements back on 17 May, but the advent of the Coalition Government and the subsequent reconstitution of the War Council as the Dardanelles Committee caused a considerable delay in the decision-making process. When the committee finally met on 7 June the decisive voice proved to be that of Winston Churchill, who, although deposed as First Lord of the Admiralty, was still an influential member of the committee. In a superb example of political sophistry, he urged a major new investment of troops and resources in bringing the Gallipoli campaign to a successful conclusion, after which the entire resources of the Entente would be directed against the Germans on the Western Front. In consequence it was agreed that three more divisions should be sent to the Peninsula: the 10th, 11th and 13th Divisions from Kitchener's 'New Army'. When it was realised that Hamilton's force had already degraded to such an extent that these would merely restore the balance it was subsequently agreed to send the 53rd and 54th Territorial Divisions. In allocating these troops to Gallipoli no proper consideration was taken of the poor state of their training and leadership, the continuing crippling lack of artillery and shells or, indeed, the situation on the Western Front.

Hamilton had many options before him in deciding where to deploy his new forces. After due consideration he decided to use one division in bolstering an ANZAC Corps plan to launch a left hook from that diminutive bridgehead. First there would be a diversionary attack on 6 August on the Turkish Lone Pine trenches on the Anzac right flank. Then, when it was dark, assaulting columns would march north. After all identified Turkish outposts had been swept away, the New Zealand Brigade would climb up Rhododendron Ridge on to Chunuk Bair behind the Turkish lines. They would then drive down into the rear of the Turkish trenches in conjunction with a frontal attack by the Australian Light Horse Brigade across The Nek timed for 04.30 on 7 August. The second assaulting column would move further along the coast before the 4th Australian Brigade would move inland and ascend on to Hill 971, the highest point of the Sari Bair Ridge. This plan for a night attack across some of the most tortuous terrain in the Peninsula by a combination of exhausted veterans and untried new troops was spectacularly optimistic. Hamilton and Birdwood were relying on wish-fulfilment rather than a realistic assessment of what was – and wasn't – possible.

At the same time Hamilton had fixed upon a new landing in the Suvla Bay area. The 11th Division, supported by the 10th Division, would land on the beaches on the night of 6 August and rapidly deploy inland to seize first the foothills and then the commanding heights of Kiretch Tepe and Tekke Tepe that overlooked and dominated the whole of the Suvla Plain. Then, if possible, they were to assist in the ANZAC Corps operations up on Sari Bair Ridge. Hamilton made the worst possible start when he resolved to deprive Lieutenant General Sir Bryan Mahon (already present and leading the 10th Division) of the chance to take command of the IX Corps that would be created to carry out the Suvla operations. Hamilton had got it into his head that Mahon was not up to the task, but the only available general of sufficient seniority to outrank Mahon was Lieutenant General Sir Frederick Stopford, a man in poor health, semi-retired and acting as Governor of the Tower of London. He would prove a disastrous choice. The intentions of the original Hamilton plan were soon watered down by Stopford, who feared the consequences of advancing inland without proper artillery support. The plans lost all focus and became over-complicated as he obsessed over Turkish defences that barely existed. Soon, any idea of a rapid rush for the hills disappeared and the primary concern became establishing a safe base. Yet nothing was done by Hamilton to hammer home the real priorities. Stopford was allowed to drift along unchecked. To Hamilton the ANZAC Corps thrust was at the very heart of his plans; on that would depend success or failure. What they would do next had barely been considered: once again the Turks were presumed to be teetering on the edge of the abyss and success would trigger abject surrender.

The great adventure – it could hardly be called a campaign – would begin on 6 August. Symbolically, it would start with one more sacrifice made by the men of the VIII Corps at Helles, who were required to throw themselves against the Turkish trenches to 'pin down' the garrison and prevent the Turks from marching to Anzac. The initial plans were remarkably similar to the earlier disastrous July attacks: they were to attempt two highly localised attacks to concentrate their artillery resources for maximum effect. The results were similar, too. Any temporary successes were soon negated as the Turkish counter-attacks threw the British back across No Man's Land at a cost of nearly 3,500 casualties. The Turks not only held them back with ease but were able to deploy forces to assist at Anzac. All told this was a disaster.

Then it was the turn of the Australian 1st Division which launched a heroic assault across the bare No Man's Land between the trenches at Lone Pine. The fighting took on a raw savagery as both sides fought to the death in covered trenches.

I was trying to get my breath when from the right end of the traverse a big fellow of a Turk came bolting along the trench. He took no notice of me because close at his heels were two Aussies and as he passed me I raised my rifle and let him have it fair in the middle of the back, almost at the same time as the other two. He went down like a pole-axed bull and the three of us then followed on down the trench to be met by some Turks who came at us suddenly and savagely. I lunged at the nearest, but my bayonet stuck in his leather equipment and for the moment I was helpless. Instantly he raised his rifle to shoot me, but before he could there was an awful bang alongside my ear and he crumpled up at my feet. My mate behind had put his rifle over my shoulder and had shot him but that discharge nearly blew my head off. A dark head appeared round the traverse. I immediately let fly with my rifle from my hip and missed. In reply came two cricket ball bombs. One was kicked by one of my mates round a corner, but the other was behind us. I had a moment or two of uncontrollable paralysing fear – to be utterly helpless with that thing sizzling within a few feet of me. I flattened myself in the side of the trench, clawing at it with my fingers and certainly thought my last moment had come. By some miracle none of us was seriously hurt.[9]

Private Charles Duke, 4th (New South Wales) Battalion, AIF

Over the three days of the fighting seven VCs were awarded. In the end the Turkish front line trenches were safely incorporated into the Australian lines. But the ground gained was negligible and as a diversion the attack had been only partially successful.

The main assault forces began to creep out of Anzac at 21.00 that night. At first everything went well as the Turkish outposts were easily over-run. Then everything went wrong: the 4th Australian Brigade and 29th Indian Brigade became lost, stumbling around harassed by Turkish snipers, following blind alleys and unable to locate the designated route. Dawn found them still in the foothills, and nowhere near Hill 971; they never would be. The New Zealand Brigade was also soon lost in the tortuous valleys and complex ridges on the approach to Rhododendron Ridge. They fell hopelessly behind schedule, failing to reach Chunuk Bair in time to launch the attack in concert with the Australian Light Horse Brigade. So it was that at 04.30 the Light Horse went over the top into legend on The Nek. They had to go just sixty yards across a narrow col about the size of a tennis court. It might as well have been miles.

> There was the din of rifles, machine guns and bombs. On mounting
> the parapet just in front of us was a double row of Turks with bayonets
> fixed, firing at us. Most of the first wave were down: either killed,
> wounded, or had taken cover. I was soon laid out with a couple of bullet
> wounds in my body and a graze on my head. I could not move and was
> eventually dragged back into our trenches, while the Turks seemed to
> pause for a few minutes, realising that they had stopped the attack.[10]
>
> Lieutenant Andrew Crawford, 8th (Victoria) Light Horse, AIF

Up on Rhododendron Ridge the tired New Zealanders were finally
approaching Chunuk Bair, but it was too late. The Turks were already
there; not in great numbers, but enough to stop the New Zealanders in
their tracks. By 08.00 it was evident that they would get no further that
day. The ambitious plans had fallen to pieces under the combined pressure of impossible terrain, tired troops, timid commanders and a robust
Turkish defence.

For the next few days the fighting raged on. Much is made of the
temporary occupation of Chunuk Bair and Hill Q but these positions were
isolated, the troops outnumbered, in cruelly exposed positions facing
superior Turkish forces and living on borrowed time. Colonel Mustafa
Kemal led a dawn attack at 04.45 on 10 August which swept them away. At
the end of the day the British were back in the foothills, or perched below
the Turkish positions on the dominating heights. The Anzac offensive had
been an abject failure.

The Suvla landings started well on 6 August. The 32nd and 33rd Brigades of the 11th Division got ashore unopposed from their new armoured
lighters on B and C Beaches south of Nibrunesi Point. Amidst some confusion, the 6th Yorkshire Regiment over-ran the Turkish positions at Lala
Baba – an attack significant because it was the first made by troops of
Kitchener's Army.

> On arriving at the base of Lala Baba I ordered a charge and we ran up
> the hill. About three-quarters of the way up we came upon a Turkish
> trench, very narrow and flush with the ground. We ran over this and
> the enemy fired into our rear, firing going on at this time from several
> directions. I shouted out that the Yorkshire Regiment was coming, in
> order to avoid running into our own people. We ran on and about

twelve paces further on, as far as I can judge, came to another trench; this we also crossed and again were fired into from the rear. I ordered the company to jump back into the second trench, and we got into this, which was so narrow that it was quite impossible for one man to pass another, or even to walk up it unless he moved sideways; another difficulty was that if there were any wounded or dead men in the bottom of the trench it was impossible to avoid treading on them in passing. There was a little communication trench running from right to left behind me, and whenever I shouted an order a Turk, who appeared to be in the trench, fired at me from a distance of apparently 5 or 10 yards. I had some difficulty in getting anybody to fire down the communication trench in order to quiet the enterprising Turk, who was endeavouring to pot me with great regularity, but I eventually got him shot.[11]

Major William Boyd Shannon, 6th Yorkshire Regiment

Although they suffered considerable casualties Lala Baba was soon cleared.

At A Beach, which was actually inside the horns of Suvla Bay, the situation was very different. Here the invading troops would have been better off in the old rowing boats, as the deeper draught of the lighters soon caused them to run aground in the rapidly shoaling waters – leaving the men trapped up to 200 yards offshore. Eventually, by hook or by crook, they all got ashore, but a great deal of time had been lost and the units were disrupted. With the exception of the 11th Manchesters, who resolutely set off along the Karakol Dagh and on to Kiretch Tepe, the rest of 34th Brigade milled about on the plain – a pointless pursuit in which they were soon joined by the 32nd Brigade. At no senior level of command, from lieutenant general to major, was anyone able to wrest control of the situation. A mish-mash of orders, counter-orders and disorder hamstrung progress; they all feared responsibility, everyone was scared of making a mistake and hence made the greatest mistake of all by doing little or nothing. So time trickled away and soon the day had all but gone. Instead of capturing the commanding heights of Tekke Tepe, it was only with a last-ditch effort that they managed to capture the lowest of the foothills, Chocolate Hill, before nightfall. The callow troops had not excelled themselves but there were many reasons: negligible leadership and non-existent communications; their own lack of experience and ingrained military skills; the dreadful shortage of water. But the most important reason for the British lack of success was the vibrant and skilful defence of the Turks. Under the command of a Bavarian cavalry officer, Major Wilhelm Willmer, just three battalions of infantry and a few field guns had managed to thwart the progress of a whole division. A controlled defence had allowed the Turks to cull the slowly advancing British, firing until the last moment and then melting into the scrub ready to fight again. Even as they did so, their reserves were on the march up from the Bulair Isthmus, where their 7th and 12th Divisions had been bivouacked. The British were in a race, but they didn't seem to know or care.

On 8 August, the IX Corps remained stagnant, unable to gather the impetus to get themselves up on to the dominating ridges. Instead they fiddled about, reorganising and preparing to advance – but not actually advancing. The senior officers were bereft of command skills, the troops were exhausted. Instead of driving on his subordinates, Stopford accepted their excuses, while Major General Frederick Hammersley, in charge of the 11th Division at Suvla Bay, planned an advance only at daybreak on 9 August. At last Hamilton lifted his eyes from the Anzac debacle to realise that his subsidiary operations were also collapsing into oblivion. A desperate Hamilton resolved to intervene directly and went to Suvla to meet Stopford and Hammersley. Taking command of the situation, he ordered an immediate attack by the only troops immediately to hand. So an utterly hopeless attempt to take Tekke Tepe was launched. The staff work was non-existent, no one knew where anybody else was and in the confusion just one battalion – the 6th East Yorkshires – was sent off in time. They had been holding a recently captured foothill, Scimitar Hill, but were recalled and despatched on their way without a passing thought. As they advanced up the hill they were overwhelmed by a furious Turkish counter-attack sweeping down around them.

The Suvla operations were effectively over: the Turks would control the hills. But Hamilton kept on raising the stakes. The 53rd Division was thrown into action piecemeal with the objective of recapturing the self-same Scimitar Hill that had been so precipitously abandoned the night before. After two days of chaos the division was emasculated as a fighting force. Next to arrive was the 54th Division. It was decided to employ them in trying to clear the main Suvla Plain of Turkish snipers by the kind of 'beating' operation familiar to gamekeepers. The 163rd Brigade would advance stretched thinly right across the plain and flush out the snipers. It didn't quite work like that. The Turks simply fell back and indeed in some places enveloped the advancing British – most famously, a party from the 1/5th Norfolks who passed into legend and unmarked graves. This forestalled any more attempts to improve the IX Corps position until the 10th and 54th Divisions were ordered to advance along Kiretch Tepe and Kidney Hill on the afternoon of 15 August. Another disaster. The Turks just shot them down as the troops stumbled through rough scrub towards well-concealed positions. By now the writing was on the wall for Stopford and Hamilton was busy exculpating himself from all blame. His neat aphorism has gone down in legend: 'No man putteth new wine into old bottles so the combination between new troops and old generals seems to be proving unsuitable.'[12] Kitchener wielded the axe as Stopford and his divisional generals and brigadiers were savagely culled, while Major General Sir Henry de Beauvoir de Lisle was temporarily moved from the 29th Division to command the IX Corps.

Despite the evidence of defeat all around him, de Lisle managed to convince himself that reinforcements from his old 29th Division, coupled with the arrival of the dismounted Yeomanry of the perversely named 2nd Mounted Division, gave him enough leeway to consider a major attack. By now the horizons had shrunk to a futile squabble over the foothills that guarded the way to the hills in front of Tekke Tepe, but the battle of 21 August was to be the largest engagement in the whole campaign. After an inadequate bombardment the infantry went over the top.

> At 3 pm the Battalion shoved off 700 strong. The furthest any got was 500 yards and none came back from there. They all got mown down by machine gun fire. We lost nine officers and nearly 400 men. The Turks shelled us very heavily and the whole country, which is covered with gorse, caught fire. This split up the attack and parties got cut up. Many of our wounded were burnt alive and it was as nasty a sight as I ever want to see. Our Headquarters was very heavily shelled and then the fire surrounded the place and we all thought we were going to be burnt alive. Where the telephone was, the heat was appalling. The roar of the flames drowned the noise of the shrapnel, and we had to lie flat at the bottom of the trench while the flames swept over the top. Luckily both sides didn't catch simultaneously, or I don't know what would have happened. After the gorse was all burnt, the smoke nearly asphyxiated us! All this time our battalion was being cut up in the open and it really

was very unpleasant trying to send down calm messages to the brigade headquarters, while you were lying at the bottom of the trench like an oven, expecting to be burnt every minute, and knowing your battalion was getting hell a hundred yards away. The telephone wires finally fused from the heat.[13]

Captain Guy Nightingale, 1st Royal Munster Fusiliers

The 29th Division was slaughtered. Alongside them the 11th Division fared no better. Then the last throw of the dice. The dismounted Yeomanry of the 2nd Mounted Division began their long march – in full view of the Turkish gunners – across the Salt Lake. Casualties were inevitable and on reaching Chocolate Hill they stumbled into action, disorientated, and the pace of killing redoubled. That night was a miserable frenzy of death and heroism on both sides. But the conclusion was certain: the British achieved nothing for the loss of 5,300 casualties.

THE GALLIPOLI CAMPAIGN was now all but over, although its death throes would take another four months. The French began to drift away, scenting defeat and preferring to devote their resources to the campaign building in Salonika. The Bulgarians had mobilised ready to enter the war on the side of the Central Powers in September 1915 and it was soon apparent that without Allied intervention the Serbs were doomed, so a force had been despatched to the Macedonian town of Salonika. The nearest source of troops was Gallipoli and thus Hamilton lost both the French 2nd Division, CEO and the 10th Division.

The Turks sat on the hills above the Allied lines at Helles, Anzac and Suvla, from where they could look down in total control of the situation. But still Hamilton refused to accept defeat. An unscrupulous Australian journalist, Keith Murdoch, sent a sharply critical unofficial letter to the Australian and British Prime Ministers, which caused a considerable degree of concern as to the handling of the campaign, which was then exacerbated by the whispering campaign led by Stopford on his return to London. When Hamilton refused to even consider evacuation he was summarily dismissed on 14 October and replaced by Lieutenant General Sir Charles Monro. This veteran of the Western Front visited the Gallipoli bridgeheads and was frankly appalled by what he saw. The tactical state of affairs was farcically bad, the logistical situation impossible. Monro recommended a swift evacuation but Kitchener demurred: he was afraid of triggering a reaction within Muslim parts of the Empire to such a humiliating defeat by the Turks. The old warrior decided to take a look for himself and in November came out to tour the battlefields. What he saw shocked him and he too recommended evacuation. The British government hesitated, fearing the casualties that a botched evacuation could cause, but in the end they had to acquiesce.

Ironically, the final evacuation was conducted brilliantly. The staff planned with a marked attention to detail, exemplary innovation and a realistic approach to what was and wasn't possible. It was late in the day but at least staff functions were belatedly beginning to improve as they learnt their job. First Anzac and Suvla were evacuated on 19–20 December, then the much more dangerous task of evacuating Helles was carried out under the very noses of the Turks on the night of 8–9 January 1916.

Apologists for the Gallipoli Campaign have long tried to boast of what could have been, with a heavy emphasis on 'if only'. This fails to recognise that the Allies fought the campaign with levels of naval and military support that were considered acceptable until the Turks defeated them. Time and time again Hamilton promised success; again and again he failed. Gallipoli was one of a series of military 'Easterner' adventures launched without proper analysis of the global strategic situation, without consideration of the local tactical situation, ignoring logistical realities, underestimating the strength of the opposition and predicated on a hugely optimistic assessment of the military capabilities of their own troops. Not for nothing is hubris regarded as the 'English disease'. But the Gallipoli Campaign was a serious matter: vital resources had been drawn away from where it really mattered. The Turks were all but helpless if left on their own. They had tried to launch an ambitious attack across the Sinai Desert on the Suez Canal but had been easily thwarted. Gallipoli achieved nothing but to provide the Turks with the opportunity to slaughter British and French troops in copious numbers in a situation in which everything was in the defenders' favour. Meanwhile, back on the Western Front, was the real enemy: the German Empire. Men, guns and munitions were in the process of being deployed to Gallipoli during the first British offensive at Neuve Chapelle; they were still there when the Germans launched their deadly gas attack at Ypres in April, during the debacles of Aubers Ridge and

Festubert, and during the first 'great push' at the Battle of Loos in September 1915. At sea Jellicoe was facing the High Seas Fleet which could pick its moment to contest the ultimate control of the seas. This was the real war – Gallipoli was nothing but a foolish sideshow.

8

SALONIKA, 1915–18

'These men of our Eastern Armies have had the dust and toil, without the laurel, of the race to victory.'[1]

Bishop of London Arthur Winnington-Ingram

THE SALONIKA CAMPAIGN HAD ITS GENESIS in the bold strategic action taken by the Germans to shore up the Austro-Hungarian position in the Balkans in 1915. This was bad news for the Serbians, who had hitherto been waging war with relative success against the Austro-Hungarian Army since the outbreak of war in 1914. By September it had become apparent to the Allies that only a show of force could prevent the Bulgarians from taking advantage of the situation by attacking Serbia. The question was, could such a demonstration be arranged? With the Austrian Navy a threat in the Adriatic and the absence of harbours capable of supporting any serious expeditionary force on the Albanian coast, this left only the Greek port of Salonika as a feasible base for the launch of such a campaign. Greece was both torn from within and fearful of being drawn actively into the war. Although technically victorious in the Balkan Wars, the Greeks had still suffered a painful experience which they would rather not repeat quite so soon. So, at the outbreak of the Great War, Greece remained neutral, although this did not prevent bitter internal political battles ensuing over which side it should favour. King Constantine naturally favoured the Central Powers, having been educated and carried out his military service in Germany; indeed, he was married to the Kaiser's sister, Sophia. But the Greek Prime Minister, Eleutherios Venizelos had long favoured the Allies and saw their intervention as a means of expanding Greek influence in the Balkans. As the threat to Serbia became more acute and a Bulgarian intervention appeared more likely, the Allies attempted to bully Greece using Venizelos as the 'inside man' who made the initial offer to allow an Anglo-French force to land at Salonika. If the justification was the greater good, it was certainly not the interests of Greece that motivated the Allies.

For the Allies, to generate a suitable Salonika Expeditionary Force (SEF) to intervene in the Balkans was no easy matter. It was only the acceptance of the total failure of the Gallipoli operations that allowed the French to contribute their 156th Division, previously known as the 2nd Division (CEO), while the British sent the 10th Division commanded by Lieutenant General Sir Bryan Mahon. In overall command was the French General Maurice Sarrail. He was an interesting character, a politically left-leaning general who had done well during the opening campaigns in France in 1914, but who had then fallen foul of Joffre and had been dismissed in July 1915. Sarrail had some powerful friends, but also some equally powerful enemies, so the French military authorities considered that the command of the SEF would be an ideal compromise posting for him: it was a serious appointment, but a long way from the Western Front.

The first Allied troops began to disembark at Salonika port on 5 October 1915. Bulgaria had still not joined the war, but there was a more immediate complication in a violent disagreement between King Constantine and Venizelos over what in effect was a flagrant breech of Greek neutrality. The Greek prime minister was forced to resign and a prolonged period of political instability ensued. But in the end the Greeks offered no resistance to the Allies' presence at Salonika. Yet what exactly were they there to do? When, on 6 October, Mackensen launched his offensive against Serbia, joined shortly afterwards by the Bulgarians, it was evident that whatever the SEF had been meant to achieve had been rendered redundant. Mahon had been given cautious orders from London, requiring him to stay close to Salonika pending the final decision of the Greek government as to whether to abandon neutrality, but Sarrail was determined to push inland anyway. He crossed the Serbian border on 15 October and advanced into the Vardar Valley with the intention of supporting the Serb forces. The most he could hope to achieve was to hold open a line of retreat for the Serbs. When the

British finally moved forward, in early November, it was all far too little, too late, and, with hindsight, probably best not at all. The Serbian Army was already defeated, its remnants falling back towards the Adriatic coast. As they congregated in the small ports up and down the Albanian coast they were eventually to be rescued by the Royal Navy. Some 250,000 Serbian troops were evacuated to the Greek island of Corfu. It was a massive undertaking and must have appeared of little real military value as the emaciated Serbian scarecrows boarded the ships. Yet, given the chance to recover, new men would rise from what appeared like worthless dregs – some six Serbian divisions would eventually return to serve on the Salonika Front.

As the British and French fell back, they formed a line just inside the Greek border to try and hold back the Bulgarians. The British wanted to evacuate, but the French would not consider it. This attitude may seem inexplicable, given that a vital part of France was occupied by the German Army, but significant sections of the French political and military establishment considered the war there to be a hopeless stalemate and that another avenue must be taken to achieve victory. In this they were enthusiastically supported by the arch 'Easterner', the British Chancellor of the Exchequer David Lloyd George, who was quite obsessed with dreams of a breakthrough in the Balkans. In the end the French had their way and once again the British would ignore their better instincts in the cause of alliance warfare. The Salonika Front became a permanent fixture for the rest of the war: fighting the Bulgarians for reasons that seem opaque to this day. Clearly if they were to stay the Allies needed reinforcements, so the British 22nd, 26th, 27th, 28th and (temporarily) 60th Divisions were despatched, while the French allotted more and more reserves to the campaign until they had nine divisions serving in Salonika. The reconstituted Serbian divisions began to arrive from Corfu from April 1916. The Italians sent a division and even the Russians contributed a brigade. Sarrail was confirmed as commander of this Armée d'Orient. The truth of Clausewitz's dictum 'always direct [our] principal operation against the main body of the enemy army' was to be demonstrated by the failure of the Allies to observe it.[7] Despite all their efforts, the Allies still only had enough forces to defend themselves, and not enough to attack with much hope of success. As the Bulgarians were forbidden to press into Greece by the Germans, fearful of triggering direct Greek involvement in the war, there they would stay in a static oblivion that made a mockery of the fantasies of the 'Easterners'.

Sarrail had his work cut out just building up the logistical framework within which his polyglot army could exist. Salonika itself was almost swamped as it was required to act simultaneously as a port, the main supply base depot and as a huge entrenched camp. Communications with the front lines were not good, with a paucity of roads and a long march beckoning for most of the newly arrived troops. The weather was also not conducive to the soldiers' health: too hot in summer and far too bitterly cold in winter, especially in the mountain regions. There were also severe problems in controlling the endemic malaria which plagued the area. There was a plethora of pools, ponds and lakes, all of which provided the perfect habitat for the mosquitoes and any stagnant water soon became infested with their larvae. This was a concern that would endure throughout the campaign. Anti-malaria measures were vital, necessitating a constant vigilance in eradicating unnecessary standing water and regular issues of quinine to every man.

> Any stranger seeing a soldier dressed up in anti-mosquito garb would for the first time imagine himself face to face with a scarecrow. The face and arms are thoroughly smeared with an anti-mosquito preparation called 'parakit', an excellent thing whilst it lasts; but its tendency is, of course, to get absorbed into the skin after an hour or two, and one often had to smear on a second coating. The mosquitoes didn't like it, though, and always kept very clear of a 'parakit' face. I can recommend it to any young lady worried by an over-zealous admirer! After this, shorts were turned down and tucked up into the top of the puttees, thus safeguarding the knee. Thick gloves were worn, attached by a piece of tape running through the arms and under the tunic over the back. Over the tin hat was worn a mosquito net veil, which, like that apparatus worn by a bee-keeper, rendered the face and neck immune from danger.[3]
>
> Second Lieutenant Richard Skilbeck-Smith, 1st Leinster Regiment

Despite all these preventative measures the British would suffer over 162,000 cases of malaria during the campaign. Outbreaks of dysentery also weakened the troops, especially those who had already suffered at Gallipoli. Morale was a problem throughout the entire army, indeed many of the units were not of the highest quality and the overall situation in Salonika did little to inspire any great élan.

Sarrail was also forced to grapple with a complex political situation as Constantine maintained what might be called unfriendly neutrality after the fall of the Venizelos government. This was not unnatural as the French were very high-handed, first bringing the whole Salonika region under military control and then instituting a naval blockade to force the Greek government to adopt a less pro-German aspect. The position of the Allies was undoubtedly morally suspect in their treatment of a supposedly independent neutral country.

There was a further complication in that the success of the Russian offensive directed against Austria-Hungary in June 1916 had triggered the ambitions of Rumania to share in any spoils of war. This was very welcome to the Allies, for the Rumanian Army was some 400,000 strong and so obviously a valuable addition to the Allied forces. But one condition of Rumanian participation was a Salonikan offensive to pin down the Bulgarian Army. As the British, under the sway of the Westerner CIGS General Sir William Robertson, were still markedly unenthusiastic, Sarrail planned an attack mainly by Serbian and French troops on the left and centre, which entailed the British taking over the front line covering the Serbian border between the Vardar River and Lake Doiran. Despite the complication of a Bulgarian offensive which had to be countered in August, the French and Serbian assault began in mid-September. Although some gains were made – including a tiny symbolic corner of Serbia at Monastir – the onset of the Balkan winter brought the offensive to an inconclusive end in December. Meanwhile the chimera of a pan-Balkan alliance to sweep away Austria-Hungary was exposed by the humiliating defeat of the Rumanian forces by a combined German, Austro-Hungarian and Bulgarian army. And so once again the Allied Salonika forces were left busy doing nothing.

In early 1917, Sarrail was given the role of 'fixing' as many Central Powers resources as possible while Nivelle won the war with his much-vaunted offensive on the Western Front in April. But Sarrail, perhaps recognising that his forces were achieving little of substance, resolved to launch his own major offensive that April. In this ambitious attack, the British Salonika Force, now commanded by Lieutenant General Sir George Milne, would for the first time play a major role, by attacking in the Struma Valley. Milne demurred, fearing that the low-lying valley, which was riddled with mosquitoes, was not a suitable arena for a major battle and instead suggested an attack on Bulgarian positions in the hill country west of Lake

Doiran, thereby threatening the tactically significant Kosturino Pass. The terrain was tortuous, with deep ravines, steep-sided ridges and hills rising to 2,000 feet. The hills had been converted into a fortress by a series of trench lines carved out of the rock creating a defensive barrier some two miles deep. Although the aim of the British attack was initially only to take the Bulgarian first line, this was still an extremely tough proposition. After a sadly inadequate three-day barrage, the 22nd and 26th Divisions made a night attack with Zero Hour at 21.45 on 24 April. When the attack came it was certainly no surprise to the Bulgarian artillery, who laid down an effective barrage on the British front lines before shrapnel fizzed across the torn ground of No Man's Land. The experiences of the men of the 10th Devonshire Regiment, given the thankless task of assaulting the imposing mass of the Petit Couronné, were not untypical.

> Our guns had been blasting away all day blowing up the barbed wire and the front line trenches. As soon as it got dark we moved out of our trenches and down one side of the hill to get in the lower end of Jumeaux Ravine, 'Johnny' knew we were on the move and our route – they gave us a right pasting. We soon had many casualties. They seemed to know our every move. We got so far in the ravine and then it was hell let loose. Our lads were being knocked over like ninepins. We that were able, got about halfway, the noise of the explosions was terrific. Suddenly I found myself alone. We had to walk behind each other as it was not very wide. My mates behind and in front were knocked out, one poor chap was calling out for his mother, I was nearly choked with cordite fumes, but I was unhurt, not even blown over and my bag of bombs was untouched. I had to go on. I picked my way over the bodies, I could only see by the flash of the explosions.[4]
>
> Private Francis Mullins, 10th Devonshire Regiment

Despite it all, the Devons managed to over-run some Bulgarian trenches on the lower slopes of Petit Couronné. While the British tried to get forward reinforcements across the precipitous wasteland, the Bulgarians launched a series of increasingly furious counter-attacks. The Petit Couronné was the key to their positions and they were determined to eject the interlopers.

> They came up blowing their bugles and shouting, I suppose they thought they were going to frighten us. It was the biggest mistake they

made as we knew they were there, if they had crept up quietly in the dark they would have got us quite easy, as there was not many of us left. Well, they came up, I had used up all my bombs bar one, and this one saved my life: it seems unbelievable, the pin of this bomb would not come out – if it had I would have been blown up by my own bomb – as at that moment they pitched one of their bombs in with us and knocked us all out. When I came round I knew I had to get out. I then found that I couldn't use my right leg very well, it seemed paralysed. However, there was another chap there who was hit in the fingers and he helped to drag me up over the trench as it was every man for himself. We left about three lying in the trench, we could do nothing to help them as the Bulgars were right on top of us. I do not think that I should have got back if it had not been for this lad sticking to me, and I haven't seen him from that day to this. I have thought many a time how I would like to thank him. Going back over Petit Couronné was no joke, we fell into the barbed wire as it was not quite daylight. There were bodies everywhere.[5]

Private Francis Mullins, 10th Devonshire Regiment

He would find that the bomb fragments had cut his sciatic nerve as well as inflicted some twenty minor wounds to his buttocks and legs. The attack was a dismal failure, with over 3,100 casualties in sharp contrast to just 835 lost by the successful defenders. A repeat attack ordered for a fortnight later, at 21.50 on 8 May, in a further attempt to pin the Bulgarians while the French and Serbs attacked to the west, met with no more success and the loss of over 1,800 casualties. The Serbian and French forces did no better, with any insignificant gains soon abandoned in the face of trenchant Bulgarian counter-attacks.

The failure of these offensives provoked a final crisis with the resolutely neutral Greek government. In June 1917 the Allies forced the abdication of Constantine and replaced him with his son, Alexander, who was far more malleable to their point of view. Almost immediately Venizelos, who had been running a pro-Allied government in exile on Crete, was reinstated as Prime Minister. He promptly declared war on the Central Powers on 27 June 1917. Most of the Balkans were now embroiled in the Great War. But still nothing much seemed to change. Certainly, the Greek Army seemed to lack any enthusiasm for the fray. As the Salonika campaign staggered. on, Sarrail himself would be replaced after a change in government in France brought in the distinctly unsympathetic Georges Clemenceau as premier in November 1917. Sarrail's replacement was first General Marie-Louis Guillaumat and then, on his recall to France in June 1918, the highly regarded General Louis Franchet d'Espèrey.

In d'Espèrey the Armée d'Orient had a commander committed to an 'Easterner' strategy; indeed, he had proposed a Balkan offensive as long ago as 1914. Now he managed to gain permission to launch an offensive as long as he did not require extra troops. The main attack was to be made by the Serbs and French through mountainous terrain to the west of the Vardar Valley. This was even more treacherous than the Doiran sector, but d'Espèrey had managed to assemble covertly superior forces that outnumbered the Bulgarians by some three to one. He had also amassed sufficient guns to deliver a bombardment that was extremely heavy by the standards of the campaign when the offensive opened on 14 September. This time the French were successful and, after hard fighting, managed to take the mountain peaks. In front of them lay the valleys which would channel behind the Bulgarian lines. On 18 September Milne was required to launch a pinning attack alongside the Greeks to prevent the Bulgarians rushing troops to the threatened sector. The result was disaster and the Second Battle of Doiran would cost some 7,100 British and Greek casualties. But this time the French broke through and, on 20 September, fearing encirclement, the Bulgarians finally abandoned their mountain fastness and began to retreat all along the line. There was considerable elation among the British once they realised that the Bulgarians had gone.

> We really are on the move after the Bulgar who stole away in the night. Our patrols were in their line by 9 last night and now we have followed them up and infantry and guns are well inside. It was a very hurried flitting as two deserters told us they got the order to move at 8 at 7.30. I visited a bit of their line this afternoon. They have blown up a lot, but there are still some wonderful dugouts. The wire is tremendous everywhere.[6]
>
> Captain Robert Townsend, 10th Devonshire Regiment

Soon they were in hot pursuit.

> It has been a tremendous day. We started off on sudden orders about 9 and have marched hard over two tremendous passes and down to

a village called Strumnica which is at the head of the Struma Valley and we are well into Bulgaria at last. It is a pretty country, but the dust on the road has been simply awful. The Bulgar has gone quickly but it has been a fearfully hard march and I didn't get in until 10 o'clock absolutely beat. However it is all part of a day's work and we are finishing off the Bulgar in great style.[7]

Captain Robert Townsend, 10th Devonshire Regiment

As the Allied aircraft and cavalry tore into the retreating Bulgarian columns, they soon became a rabble. Their morale was not helped by the unavoidable realisation that they had been following the wrong lodestar: the news from the Western Front made it clear that Germany was defeated and the Central Powers were doomed.

On 29 September the Bulgarian forces occupying Skopje, the Serbian capital, surrendered and a day later Bulgaria formally surrendered. It was a bitter-sweet moment for the British Salonika Force. It had been on the winning team; but the excitement of victory had belonged to its allies. It had battled for the best part of three years but then had to be content with nothing more than a secondary role in the ultimate dénouement. Salonika proved a truly forgettable campaign – and with good reason. Little was achieved here that victory on the Western Front would not have secured in good time. And the cost, for the British, had been horrendous, for although they lost only 23,787 casualties in the actual fighting they suffered far more casualties from the pernicious effects of disease. At the height of the British deployment over 182,500 British troops were kicking their heels, left vulnerable to the depradations of the mosquito and malaria. There could be few more depressing fronts than Salonika.

9

THE WESTERN FRONT, 1916

'There is some very strong leaning at home towards easy victories in unimportant theatres, with small casualties and no real results. How on earth one can hope to beat Germany by killing Turks or Bulgars passes comprehension. It is like a prize-fighter leaving the ring to trounce his opponent's seconds.'[1]

Brigadier General John Charteris, General Headquarters, BEF

THE NEW YEAR SAW A NEW TEAM at the heart of the British military effort. In London, General Sir William Robertson had been appointed as Chief of Imperial General Staff on 23 December 1915. Just a few days earlier, on 19 December, General Sir Douglas Haig had been promoted to command the BEF. The two would work in harmony, united in their belief that the prevailing strategic situation meant that the bulk of British resources should be devoted to fighting the main enemy – Germany – in the deciding theatre of war – the Western Front. The balance of power on the Western Front was changing, for although the Germans had strengthened their forces in the west after their successful campaigns on the Eastern Front, the BEF too was expanding. It now had around a million men under arms – a total of thirty-eight infantry divisions and still growing. Nevertheless the French remained the dominant ally, with some ninety-six divisions under the command of General Joseph Joffre in January 1916. There was no denying that the French had borne the brunt of the war on the Western Front since August 1914. By comparison, the British contribution had been negligible: those battles in which they had been involved, such as Neuve Chapelle or Loos, barely registered as skirmishes when compared to the titanic clashes in the Artois and Champagne.

The French had been waiting impatiently for some time for their maritime ally to pull its weight on land as well. In 1916 that time had come. At the Allied co-ordinating conference held at Chantilly in December 1915 it had been decided that there would be a huge Anglo-French offensive on the Western Front to coincide with simultaneous offensives by the Russians and the Italians. Joffre had selected the Somme area where the British and French would fight side by side and he could exert control to ensure that the British did not slacken their efforts. This was alliance warfare and Haig was left with no option but to comply if the union was to survive and prosper. Yet neither Joffre nor Haig would have the chance to dictate what was about to happen on the Western Front. For the first half of 1916, it was another general, the German Chief of General Staff, General Erich von Falkenhayn, who would control the agenda.

Falkenhayn had been encouraged by the series of successes on the Eastern Front in 1915 and believed that, although total defeat of Russia was an unlikely prospect, his armies had achieved enough to render her at least quiescent during 1916. Serbia, too, had been reduced to a shadow, while the position of Austria-Hungary had undoubtedly improved. Yet for all that, the overall strategic situation remained the same: Russia obstinately refused to make a separate peace and hence Germany was still doomed to fight on two fronts. In these circumstances Falkenhayn was convinced that the war would have to be ended before 1916 drew to a close, or Germany – but even more likely Austria-Hungary and Turkey – would simply collapse under the weight of the immense burdens of war. And so, the Central Powers were forced on to the offensive. If they stood back and waited, the Allies would only get stronger, mobilising ever more of their industrial and military strength behind the wheel of war. Indeed, in some ways Falkenhayn had been fortunate that the French and British had largely failed to gain any concrete advantage on the Western Front in 1915, making only trivial gains without taking any really important objectives.

With Russia apparently tamed, Falkenhayn was intent on seeking a decision in the west, while Austria-Hungary turned on the Italians. But who to attack: the French or the British? In making his decision Falkenhayn weighed up many factors. He still considered Britain the main enemy, but how to seriously harm the British war effort remained problematical. Eventually, he resolved to attack the French, reasoning that they would knock 'England's best sword out of its hand – France!'[2] The French had already been drained by the combination of horrendous losses in the Battle of the Frontiers in 1914 and the failed offensives of 1915. French manpower was not a bottomless well and she could not afford that rate of loss for long. In the assessment of their military opponents German intelligence suggested that Britain's new 'Kitchener Armies' were not militarily competent, although they seem to have respected both the reconstituted Regular divisions and the Territorial divisions. They were also aware of the generally good morale still prevailing in the British units. In contrast, the Germans looked down on the French divisions, considering them both unskilled in the military arts and low in morale. This view may have been wrong, but it was widespread in the German High Command, which did not lack in self-confidence, assessing their own troops as both highly skilled and well motivated in action. Finally Falkenhayn and his staff believed that the French nation and her democratically elected politicians were not strong enough to withstand the terrible rigours of war for much longer. They would put the matter to the test in 1916.

The Battle of Verdun

During the long-drawn-out planning process for what would be the Battle of Verdun, Falkenhayn developed a new concept of warfare. In the final version he would launch an assault on the salient that protruded around the fortress town of Verdun on both banks of the River Meuse, where a potent mixture of tactical necessity and national pride would force the French to launch counter-attacks that would in effect bleed their army to death, grinding down reserves division by division through the 'mincing machine' of the strong German artillery – in all, 1,220 guns would be moved up, of which a large number were either heavy or super-heavy. Whether the French counter-attacked at Verdun or attempted to relieve the pressure with a major attack elsewhere, the Germans believed that the effect would be the same – huge losses unsustainable for the French nation in the third year of the war. A British intervention was not particularly feared, as Falkenhayn doubted that the BEF was ready for serious fighting on a continental scale. When the Allies had worn themselves out, a final German offensive would sweep the remnants of the French Army from the field of battle. With France knocked out of the war, the BEF could be dealt with unceremoniously.

The German Fifth Army, commanded by Crown Prince Wilhelm, would launch the attack on the east bank of the Meuse to seize swiftly the commanding heights using relatively small numbers of infantry in open order, accompanied by flamethrowers and backed by overwhelming artillery fire on the French front line until the actual moment of assault, at which the guns would switch to the Second Line positions. Amidst all the mayhem and destruction, the sophistication of the bombardment had also taken a step forward with the widespread use of gas shells on the battery positions to suppress the ability of the French guns to fire during the German attack across No Man's Land. Above all, it was intended that German casualties should be kept to a minimum. As Falkenhayn succinctly put it: 'Our object ... was to inflict upon the enemy the utmost possible injury with the least possible expenditure of lives on our part.'³ Once in control of the heights above the Meuse, the massed German heavy artillery could dominate the whole battlefield and Verdun itself. Special arrangements had been made to ensure that throughout the next phase of the offensive the German guns would be able to maintain a constant heavy bombardment, with shells continually lashing down on the French front lines and harassing their communications: this, then, would be the ever-turning screw of the 'mincing machine'.

Falkenhayn wanted the attack to be restricted to just the east bank of the Meuse, at least in the initial stages, as he doubted he had sufficient troops for such a large-scale effort on both banks. There was a clear divergence of view here with that of the Fifth Army staff, who not only preferred the idea of a simultaneous assault on both banks, but also seemed more intent on swiftly capturing the Verdun fortress than on 'bleeding white' the body of the French Army. Obsessed with secrecy, Falkenhayn denied access to the overall plans to his subordinates, with the result that many in the German High Command on the Western Front did not either understand or endorse his overall strategic approach. But Falkenhayn was determined to minimise intelligence leaks and secure strategic surprise, to which end he also allowed preparations to be made for several other offensives up and down the Western Front, thereby muddying the water for the Allies, who guessed an offensive was coming, but could not pin-point where the blow would fall.

At the start of 1916 the French position at Verdun was not healthy. A generally quiet sector since 1914, the great fortress had been denuded of most of its guns during the desperate combing out of heavy artillery for the autumn offensives of 1915. The whole sector was only defended by four divisions and two brigades of Territorial troops and there had been a definite complacency at Joffre's headquarters despite warnings as to the inadequacy of the French defences. But the advent of a period of heavy snow and rain on 12 February 1916, the date of the originally intended attack, militated against the effective deployment of the German artillery that was essential to the success of the attack and forced a 9-day postpone-ment. These precious few days allowed the French the chance to realise what was about to happen and belatedly to concentrate their forces. By the time the Germans attacked, the French had eight divisions and over 600 guns on the east and west banks of the Meuse.

When the German bombardment began at 04.00 on 21 February it was far more concentrated than that which the French had employed in their wide-front autumn offensives the year before. Supporting barrages on either side of Verdun gave an apparent breadth to the attack, but the real meat was in an 8-mile sector east of the Meuse. Gradually, the shell-ing built up to a crescendo, but what followed was to some extent an anti-climax as the German patrols felt their way forward, investigating the situation, not committing masses of troops that first night. Verdun marked one of the first appearances of the German stormtroopers, a spe-cially trained elite intended to feel the way forward, infiltrating centres of resistance and employing the flamethrowers premiered at Ypres in the summer of 1915. On the left the Germans over-ran the Bois d'Haumont, but stalled in the neighbouring Bois des Caures, where the defence was led by Colonel Émile Driant, who had been campaigning vigorously for improved defences in the Verdun area in late 1915. A second terrible bombardment lashed Driant's positions on the morning of the 22 Febru-ary and this time the German assault was pressed home in earnest. Driant was an inspirational figure as he co-ordinated the resistance but was killed as he tried to evacuate the last French survivors from the wood at about 16.30.

> I had just fallen in a shell hole, when a Sergeant who was accompanying Colonel Driant and was walking a pace or two in front of him, fell in the same hole. I distinctly saw Colonel Driant throw out his arms exclaiming, 'Oh my God!' then he made a half-turn and collapsed behind the hole, facing the wood. His body being stretched out flat, we could not see it from inside the hole, owing to the amount of earth that had been thrown up all around. We wanted to get him down into the shell hole with us without leaving the hole ourselves. When we had cleared enough earth to be able to look out, we could see the colonel. He gave no sign of life, blood was flowing from a wound in his head and also from his mouth. He had the colour of a dead man and his eyes were half closed.[4]
>
> Sergeant Jules Hacquin, 56th Light Infantry

Driant's unit was not alone in its defiance and several others performed exceptionally well in holding back, or at least delaying, the German advance, thereby buying time for their comrades to reorganise.

The German advance was very gradual – just 1–2 miles in the first three days. Then there was a terrible shock for the French born of the sheer confusion of battle. Fort Douaumont was tactically the most significant of the forts, its glowering presence dominating the northern approaches to Verdun. It had only been completed in 1913 and was armed with a 155 mm gun, 75 mm guns and machine guns, all housed in steel turrets. The original brick construction had been covered with a thick layer of concrete which proved at least partially resistant to the huge shells that crashed down on its structure. Sadly for the French, the company of infantry attached to the fort had been despatched to help stiffen their front line and by some mischance had not been replaced, leaving the fort empty but for a few gunners. On 25 February, patrols from the 24th Brandenburg Regiment penetrated the outer defences of the fort and broke in to discover the building all but deserted. The great imagined bastion of Douaumont had fallen without a shot being fired. Although its guns were all but irrelevant, the psychological effect on both sides was considerable, while the military value of the fort lay in its position as an all-seeing observation point from which the German artillery could now be directed. The French fell back and the German advance continued until exhaustion and terrible weather brought it to a shuddering stop on the last ridge of hills only two miles from Verdun itself.

At this point it seemed that the French were going to abandon the east bank of the Meuse to the Germans. However, Joffre's Chief of Staff, General Édouard de Castelnau, was aware of what did, and did not, make military sense. Taking into consideration the likely impact of the loss of Verdun on French national morale, he persuaded Joffre that it must be held. This meant not only holding the last positions on the east bank but also ordering a policy of no retreat on the west bank, should the Germans attack there. It was resolved to place General Phillipe Pétain, in command of the Second Army, in charge of holding Verdun. A well organised, tenacious commander, Pétain had not had his career affected by his failure in the Champagne autumn offensives, and, more to the point, he had a reputation as a master of defence – clearly a useful attribute at Verdun. In deciding to stand at Verdun the French were unknowingly falling for Falkenhayn's snare, but they had little choice. Indeed, Pétain ordered his men to 'Beat off at all costs the attacks of the enemy, and retake immediately any piece of land taken by him.'[5] Falkenhayn could have written this for him! Yet the Germans were also falling into their own trap created by the ambivalence of the Crown Prince Wilhelm and the staff of the Fifth Army to the original intention of the offensive. They began to press harder and harder, tempted by the success at Douaumont, with the result that their losses began to rise. By the end of February the German and French casualties had achieved a rough parity. This was not the German plan.

Pétain applied his methodical talents to sorting out the defences at Verdun. Massive reinforcements were moved up and Pétain ensured that they concentrated not only on front-line positions but also on creating a coherent system of defence in depth. His staff were ordered to ensure that the troops were constantly rotated so that no unit spent too long at the front. This meant that most of the French Army would gradually be introduced to the hell of Verdun, but not for long enough to break their morale or grind them to nothing. Pétain also deployed his vastly augmented heavy artillery on the west bank, tucked away in the hills, where they could fire *en masse* into the exposed flank of the German advance.

The French flat-trajectory 75 mm guns were of little use against trenches, but Pétain reorganised them so that they could respond whenever the German infantry exposed themselves crossing No Man's Land – then the 75 mms were as deadly as ever. So, just as the German guns were struggling with the enormous practical difficulties of moving forward across the shell-cratered battlefield in dreadful weather, the French artillery began to exert an equal and opposite force. Pétain also reorganised the frail supply route into Verdun: the railway had been cut and all that was left was one arterial road – soon to be tritely christened the *Voie Sacrée* – along which countless lorries passed carrying the supplies and munitions needed to keep Pétain's army in the battle.

After a lull the Germans attacked again, on 6 March, this time including the west bank of the Meuse, reaching for the French artillery in the hills. Here the focus of the assault would be the ridge of Mort Homme and the rather more prosaically named Côte 304. The soon-to-be-denuded woods and hills would become another slaughterhouse. Sometimes the French would fall back, deterred by a particularly vicious bombardment that tore at their spirits, but they always seemed to have another battalion to launch a desperate counter-attack, catching the Germans before they could consolidate. And all the while the French artillery was taking its own heavy toll on the German infantry. As days turned into weeks and months, the front line was never static, but nor did it move much. Meanwhile, a similar month-long battle raged on the east bank as the Germans tried to prise Fort Vaux from the grip of the French. On, on the fighting raged, deep into April, with German assaults, French counter-attacks, segueing into yet more German attacks. And still the rain poured down.

Pétain did not last long, for all his virtues. He demanded more, ever more, reinforcements from Joffre, who was desperate to conserve his reserves in case the Germans attacked elsewhere, but also for the huge joint offensive with the British planned in the Somme area. Joffre was a man who did not brook continual demands, no matter how they were phrased. At the end of April he had had enough, but as Pétain was by then a national hero, he promoted him to command the Central Group of Armies. General Robert Nivelle took over the Second Army at Verdun. Nothing much changed, Pétain had set in train the necessary reorganisation to, as far as possible, secure the defence of Verdun. Nivelle had a more offensive-minded approach and sought to make major counter-attacks to reverse the totality of German gains. This would have been playing into their hands were it not for the fact that the Germans themselves had lost the focus of their own operations: they had become intent in pressing on when a suspension of the offensive, or switching it to another area, might have been more logical. But the fighting had gained its own momentum: some progress forward was necessary to maintain the morale of front line troops undergoing absolute torture. In essence the Germans had fallen into their own 'mincing machine'.

Soon the wet spring was replaced by a long hot summer – and still the fighting raged. Soldiers arriving at Verdun for the first time were daunted by the grim reputation of the sector.

> We set off in clouds of white dust. So began our ascent to Verdun, an ascent to Mount Calvary which was to last ten days, ten days in which we had the feeling that we were being carried along on that gigantic supply chain which kept the battle regularly fed, like those bucket pumps in Mediterranean countries which bring the water up to the parched earth; ten days of piercing agony, which for me were more painful than the nine days that we were to spend in the heart of the battle. The worst mental suffering during wartime occurs when one's thoughts run ahead of one's actions, when the imagination has full rein to contemplate the dangers in advance – and multiplies them a hundredfold. It is well known that the fear of danger is more nerve-racking than the danger itself, just as the desire is more intoxicating than the fulfilment of it.[6]
>
> Second Lieutenant René Arnaud, 337th Infantry Regiment

Finally, on 2 June, the Germans managed to encircle Fort Vaux, holding the ring of the Meuse Heights. The officer in charge of the fort was Commander Sylvain Eugène Reynal, who had already been badly wounded in September 1914 but whose idea of recuperation was active service commanding a vital lynchpin in the Verdun defences. Having run out of water, his garrison had few prospects of survival.

> Towards 23.00 our artillery ceased abruptly, and the night passed away in a silence, more nerve-racking for me than the storm of battle. Not a sound, not a sign of movement. Had I the right to prolong resistance beyond human strength and to jeopardise unnecessarily the lives

of these brave men who had so heroically done their duty? I took a tour of the corridors. What I saw was awful. Men were overcome with vomiting, for so wretched were they that they had reached the point of drinking their own urine. Some lost consciousness. In the main gallery a man was licking a small wet streak on the wall. 7th June! Day broke, and we barely noticed it. For us it was still night, a night in which all hope was extinguished. Aid from outside, if it came, would come too late. I sent my last message, the last salute of the fort and its defenders to their country. Then I returned to my men, 'It is all over, my friends. You have done your duty, all of your duty. Thank you!'[7]

Commander Sylvain Eugène Reynal, Fort Vaux Garrison

The final surrender came at 06.00 on 7 June.

As was so often the case, the capture of one vital feature merely brought to prominence the next string of objectives, one more last line of defence stretching from the Ouvrage de Thiaumont strongpoint, through the desiccated remnants of Fleury village to Fort Souville. Both sides expended reserves with the recklessness of gamblers believing success must come with one last throw of the dice. Equally, neither side could achieve victory. The Germans also knew that Joffre's long-planned major offensive on the Somme was about to commence. A last desperate German thrust captured Thiaumont and Fleury on 23 June, utilising to deadly effect the new weapon of phosgene gas shells – each shell marked with a distinctive green cross – falling all around the French batteries to stem much of their fire. The German infantry reached the ramparts of Fort Souville, but were ultimately forced back.

On 24 June 1916, the British and French bombardment had opened on the Somme. Slowly, the German reserves that remained – severely depleted already by the intensity of the Verdun fighting – were deployed to counter the new Allied thrust. Battery by battery, the German guns began to move north. One last gasp effort was made to take Fort Souville, on 11 July, but the French gunners had by this time been issued with more effective gas masks and the phosgene was less of a deadly threat to them and more of a nuisance. The Germans were held back and Fort Souville remained in French hands. The German Fifth Army adopted a posture of 'aggressive defence' and the threat to Verdun was ended.

Yet the Battle of Verdun was by no means over.

Now it was the turn of the French to hit back. The French Army was learning all the time. New weapons were being issued to the infantry. The 1907 Berthier 8 mm bolt-action, firing 3-round clips, marked a considerable improvement on the obsolete Lebel rifle, while there were increasing numbers of the Chauchat light machine gun and the excellent Hotchkiss machine gun to help bolster firepower. Rifle grenades, mortars and 37 mm mini versions of the 75 mm gun were made available to act as close-support weapons. The infantry attack tactics had also developed, with less emphasis on a single wave of attack and more on specialist functions, with bombers, men with rifle grenades and 'mopper uppers' to eradicate any pockets of resistance and to ensure there were no Germans left concealed in captured dugouts ready to emerge behind the advancing lines.

Time and time again the French attacked the Germans, who responded with characteristic aggression: the village of Fleury would change hands fifteen times in some of the worst fighting of the whole war before the French finally took it for good on 18 August. By now the French artillery was dominant as much of the German artillery had departed for the Somme. The next major thrust was the scheme of General Charles Mangin, a truly determined officer who would let nothing stop him once he had his enemy in his sights. His plan was cunning. A dummy attack, preceded by a major bombardment, would cause the hidden German batteries to open fire and thereby reveal their positions to the watching French reconnaissance aircraft. By the time the real attack was launched on 24 October most of those German guns had been silenced. Verdun was hell on earth for the German infantry. Private William Hermanns of the 67th Infantry Regiment was based in the battered structure of the Thiaumont strongpoint.

> The entrance was a mere hole in the scarred battlefield, and the silhouettes of cowering men constantly crawling in or out looked like huge ants in the dark. I descended an iron ladder some forty feet into the concrete cavern. It was an enormous place crowded with many hundreds of soldiers. Some lay on bunks sleeping, snoring and moaning. Some cluttered the passages between the bunks, chatting or writing letters. Others sat or knelt in corners, packing or unpacking their belongings. Here a flashlight, there a candle, match or cigarette dotted the dark with flickering islands of light, continually shifting

in brightness. From this subterranean stronghold, a small patch of
sky could be seen when one stood close to the iron ladder or looked
through the shaft which contained the ventilator fans. A current
of warm, stale air from 40 feet beneath brought to my nostrils the
sickening smell of first aid medications. Every one of the chicken-wire
berths was filled with mutilated, muddy, torn and befouled uniforms.
A dismal sight. There was a man with closed eyes, a blood-soaked
bandage around his head. Another beside him lay twisting in pain. I
saw some lice-ridden men who had scratched their bandages off to ease
the itching. The passages between the bunks were crowded. There must
have been a thousand men there. Some had been relieved, but could
not withdraw to the rear, and some who had come to relieve the others
could not proceed to the front line. All were imprisoned deep within
the concrete and rock entrails.[8]

Private William Hermanns, Machine Gun Company, 67th Infantry Regiment

As the French drove forward behind a wall of shells, Hermanns' account
gives a vivid impression of the terror afflicting these exhausted German
soldiers in the dank tomb of Thiaumont.

I heard the cry, 'Poison gas!' I saw people around me putting on their
gas masks. I adjusted mine, which still hung over my shoulder. There
it was – a yellowish gas glimmering near the iron ladder. A gas bomb
must have been thrown into the entrance shaft. The cry 'Gas masks
on!' electrified the whole shelter. Soldiers ran to get their masks,
which they had hung on the walls and in the corners or laid on their
packs. Many who had lost theirs on the battlefield began to cough.
The wounded in the bunks tried to climb into the upper berths, while
beneath the gas crept forward along its way, extinguishing one candle
after another. Soon many were dying and the bunks and floors were
filled with bodies over which the living stepped and stumbled in search
of air. The alarm surged like a wave from bunk to bunk. Before long it
had reached the farthest man, a hundred yards away. The panic was so
great that I saw badly wounded men throw themselves onto the floor
as though they wanted to drink in the gas, while others tore the masks
from their neighbors' faces. Some had a reddish foam oozing from their
mouths.[9]

Private William Hermanns, Machine Gun Company, 67th Infantry Regiment

When the survivors of the gas attack scrambled out they found themselves trapped behind the attacking French infantry who had already swept on. Thiaumont fell without a fight.

> The terrain, no longer anything but shell holes, rose gradually to the hilltop of Fort Douaumont, which stood before us a mile away. Dark objects, large and small, protruded from the ground everywhere, but nothing moved except us. Corporal Schulze, with his long legs, was about 60 feet ahead of me. Now and then, I could just see his dark contour as he crept and walked through the thick veil of night. Suddenly a shot rang out. I threw myself into a shell hole. I heard the voice of Schulze, 'I'm hit!' I left the machine gun and jumped up to run towards him, but he called, 'Hermanns, run! The French!' Before me several men grew out of the darkness. I ran in the opposite direction. They ran after me for a short distance, then stopped and fired several volleys of bullets. I ran, falling, leaping, and falling again, from crater to crater, not knowing where – just away from them. Suddenly I fell into a huge pit, the walls of which were nearly vertical. While I lay there in the pitch dark catching my breath, I saw something white move in the far end of the crater. Something else moved with it, creeping forward like an enormous cat. The whole crater now became alive. It looked as if big chunks of loam had detached themselves from the walls of the murky hole. Eight or ten huge men rose before me, one with a rifle pointed at my head. I was still in a half-kneeling position. I cried, *'Pardon, je suis votre prisonnier!'* Somebody drew back the hand of the man with the gun, saying, *'Tiens, il parle Français!'* I stammered in French, 'I don't hate you. I don't hate anyone!' And then I collapsed.[10]
>
> Private William Hermanns, Machine Gun Company, 67th Infantry Regiment

Fort Douaumont was blasted by huge French railway guns, their gigantic shells smashing home with a terrible devastating impact. In the end flesh and blood could withstand the onslaught no more than concrete and the shell-shocked garrison evacuated the fort, which thus fell to the French. Even then it was still not all over. The French nibbled away at the German lines step by step. Fort Vaux was recaptured on 2 November and, in a final flourish, the French charged forward nearly two miles on 15 December. It had been a long year: the Germans had lost some 330,000 casualties at Verdun, the French around 377,000. For both sides Verdun had proved an almost unbearable trial.

The Battle of the Somme

The sheer size of the commitment demanded by the Battle of Verdun soon derailed any thoughts of the French Army making the major contribution to the planned offensive on the Somme in the summer of 1916. Instead, Joffre exerted increasing pressure on Haig to launch a British-led offensive as early as possible. Haig was dubious and preferred to delay as he recognised that many of his new divisions were little more than a collection of half-trained units which would need time to evolve into a powerful attacking force. Yet Joffre was desperate and Haig, again bound by the collective dictates of alliance warfare, had little option but to accept a start date of – at the very latest – 1 July 1916. Much nonsense has been written as to what Haig was trying to achieve on the Somme, but his intentions seem clear enough.

> My policy is briefly to: 1. Train my divisions, and to collect as much ammunition and as many guns as possible. 2. To make arrangements to support the French ... attacking in order to draw off pressure from Verdun, when the French consider the military situation demands it. 3. But while attacking to help our Allies, not to think that we can for a certainty destroy the power of Germany this year. So in our attacks we must also aim at improving our positions with a view to making sure of the result of the campaign next year.[11]
>
> General Sir Douglas Haig, General Headquarters, BEF

There were no major strategic objectives. The Somme battlefield had been chosen by Joffre simply because it was adjacent to his forces rather than for any more cogent reasons.

By this time Haig had settled his General Headquarters in the small château of Montreuil. There has been much ill-informed criticism speculating on the life of luxury supposedly led by the 'château generals', but the GHQ was in itself a large organisation of staff officers which required space and an excellent communications system if it was to function properly. Haig and his staff certainly had a stern and unwavering work ethic.

> Punctually at 8.25 each morning Haig's bedroom door opened and he walked downstairs. He then went for a short 4 minutes' walk in the garden. At 8.30 precisely he came into the mess for breakfast. If he had a guest present, he always insisted on serving the guest before he helped

himself. He talked very little, and generally confined himself to asking his personal staff what their plans were for the day. At nine o'clock he went into his study and worked until eleven or half past. At half-past eleven he saw army commanders, the heads of departments at General Headquarters, and others whom he might desire to see. At 1 o'clock he had lunch, which only lasted half an hour, and then he either motored or rode to the headquarters of some army or corps or division. Generally when returning from these visits he would arrange for his horse to meet the car so that he could travel the last 3 or 4 miles on horseback. When not motoring he always rode in the afternoon, accompanied by an aide de camp and his escort of 17th Lancers, without which he never went out for a ride. Always on the return journey from his ride he would stop about 3 miles from home and hand his horse over to a groom and walk back to headquarters. On arrival there he would go straight up to his room, have a bath, do his physical exercises and then change into slacks. From then until dinner time at 8 o'clock he would sit at his desk and work, but he was always available if any of his staff or guests wished to see him. He never objected to interruptions at this hour. At 8 o'clock he dined. After dinner, which lasted about an hour, he returned to his room and worked until a quarter to 11.[12]

Brigadier General John Charteris, General Headquarters, BEF

Haig's routine rarely changed. He and his staff had an overwhelming amount of work to get through.

The Fourth Army, commanded by General Sir Henry Rawlinson, was charged with carrying out the Somme Offensive, while the Reserve Army, commanded by General Sir Hubert Gough, would exploit any break-through. Rawlinson had a daunting task ahead of him and he naturally gravitated to a cautious two-stage approach – he aimed to over-run the German First Line system in the first assault and then pause for reorgan-isation before making a separate attack on the Second Line system. He would have preferred a hurricane bombardment but there were still not enough guns so he opted for a prolonged bombardment of several days to achieve his ends. These plans were not well received by Haig, who insisted that Rawlinson include in the initial objectives an attack on the German Second Line system – fearing that early opportunities might be missed and then positions would have to be attacked when German reinforcements had arrived and were well set. Haig was employing a system of scenario planning although he would not have recognised the term. He wanted to ensure that the Fourth and Reserve Armies were prepared for different degrees of success – or failure. He insisted that they plan for a possible breakthrough, but he also allowed for a slower rate of progress. As part of this process cavalry were to be held ready to exploit any breakthrough. In 1916 there was no alternative to cavalry.

The Somme operation demanded logistical preparations which dwarfed anything previously attempted by the BEF. Hundreds of thousands of men and horses had to be moved up to the front; millions of shells brought forward; millions upon millions of tons of food and stores provided; road and rail links greatly improved; concealed gun positions prepared; assembly trenches dug, tunnels carved out and huge explosive mines laid ready for detonation under the German strongpoints. Here was a learning curve based in practical skills that took time to master: it was no simple matter to achieve logistical coherence while maintaining a degree of secrecy, and all the while under harassing fire from the Germans.

The British believed that they had digested the various lessons of the Allied 1915 offensives and taken due note of the methods employed in the German offensive at Verdun. However, they were still unable to resolve two incompatible requirements: the tactical necessity of attacking on a wide front was demonstrable, but there was a shortage of guns and ammunition to allow a Neuve Chapelle-style hurricane bombardment over such a length of frontage. And there was a further complication: they were learning but so were the Germans. The German trenches on the ridges of the Somme bore little resemblance to the single trench line at Neuve Chapelle, or even the series of lines and strongpoints at Loos. By the summer of 1916 the British were faced by a number of separate trench systems under various stages of completion. Behind belts of barbed wire up to thirty yards thick the German Front Line System consisted of three trench lines, complete with deep dugouts and a system of linking communication trenches. After a careful review of best practice in the line, the Germans had decided that at least 6–7 yards of depth underground was needed to protect the dugouts' occupants from the heavier British shells – any deeper and the men would run the risk of being trapped when the eventual assault came. It was also evident that more than one exit was needed to avoid their being buried alive. By this time the Germans had also recognised the potential of concrete to give dugouts, command headquarters and observation posts a massively increased resistance to bursting shells. Rural villages were incorporated wholesale into the front line, with ordinary buildings and cellars reinforced with concrete that converted cottages into shellproof fortresses. In addition there were intermediate positions of strong earthwork redoubts such as the Schwaben Redoubt lying behind the Front Line System at Thiepval. These usually performed a specific tactical function – in this case dominating the high ground between Thiepval and St Pierre Divion. A similar Second Line System was being dug some 2,000–5,000 yards further back, while a Third Line System was also under construction. All this took a huge military investment by the German Army: the prior identification of possible points of weakness based on past experience; the intuition and skill necessary to devise the appropriate solutions; the allotment of scarce resources; and finally the hard grafting construction work required to carry out all the improvements. Tactically the Germans depended heavily on the vigilance of their sentries to alert the garrison to give them enough time to man the parapets and bring up their machine guns from the dugouts. They intended to hold their first line trenches if possible and their positions were carefully placed to allow concentrations of flanking machine gun fire to break up assaulting infantry in No Man's Land. The second line troops would not only hold the line, but had well-trained bombing parties ready to countermand immediately any breaches in the front line. Local sector reserves would be moved up into the third line and launched as soon as possible into counter-attacks to capitalise on the inevitable confusion as the British strove to consolidate their new positions. Meanwhile the German artillery batteries had well-protected concealed gun emplacements, dugouts for the gun detachments and ammunition stores, concrete observations posts and deep-laid telephone lines. The gunners had practised their gun drill and fire control to perfection, while a simple squared-map system allowed the rapid identification of targets for a near-instant response. British gun batteries and other observable targets were carefully registered one by one. The overall combination of the strong physical defences and well-rehearsed defensive tactics was a considerable step beyond anything the British had hitherto encountered.

The British response to these challenges was to some extent simple:

they would rely on the power of their massed guns. In all, they had 1,010 field artillery guns and howitzers, 182 medium and heavy guns and 245 medium and heavy howitzers, with an additional 100 French guns ready to assist them on the right flank. This sounds a lot but it worked out at just one field gun to every twenty yards of front and one heavy gun to every fifty-eight yards of front, in contrast to the one gun per six yards of trench at Neuve Chapelle. Yet the guns were required to clear the (much deeper) barbed wire, destroy several lines of well-constructed trenches and strongpoints and eradicate the threat of far more numerous German gun batteries.

One tactical innovation employed by some divisions was the 'creeping barrage'. A line of shells dropping in No Man's Land and then moving slowly forward ahead of the attacking British infantry towards the German front line, thereby severely restricting the garrison's ability to fire at the key moment as the British infantry drew near. This marked the beginning of a policy of suppression rather than destruction as an alternative role for the artillery. But there were still many practical difficulties to be overcome. Such barrages demanded a high degree of theoretical and practical gunnery skills, which many senior Royal Artillery officers doubted their newly trained batteries could achieve. Also, some of the more conservative divisional commanders were unable to grasp the whole concept of why the barrage should commence in No Man's Land before rolling forward, preferring the simplicity of a direct trench barrage which would then lift according to a pre-determined timetable to alternative targets as the British infantry attacked. The default plan for the infantry issued by the Fourth Army was fairly simple, involving the troops advancing at walking pace in a series of waves that would build up to finally storm any obstruction to progress. Yet at the same time considerable latitude was granted to commanding officers in how they should approach the problem of the advance across No Man's Land.

Another crucial British tactical advance was the integration of aircraft into the battle plans. Since August 1915, Brigadier General Hugh Trenchard had been in command of the RFC on the Western Front and he was in no doubt as to what was required of his men. He was in regular personal touch with Commandant Paul du Peuty of the French Air Service which was unquestionably at the forefront of aerial experimentation. The advice Trenchard received was entirely in accordance with his own aggressive instincts: to fight an air war well over the German side of the lines, pushing forward his RFC scouts to harry the German aircraft to destruction. This would prevent, or obstruct, German reconnaissance and artillery observation flights while leaving the front line sectors open for the operations of their British equivalents. Of course German scouts would break through to cause havoc at times, but these would be the exception rather than the rule. Casualties would simply have to be endured to ensure that the full requirements of the Army were properly fulfilled.

For the RFC the Battle of the Somme began months before the first shells of the preliminary bombardment. Ever since the British Army had taken over the Somme sector from the French back in 1915 the RFC had as a matter of routine been engaged in photographing every inch of the ground. But this process was given an added impetus by the imminent offensive. Thousands of photographs had to be taken mapping every German trench and experts then pored over blown-up prints to tease out hidden details behind the German veil, identifying machine gun posts, dugouts, headquarters, minenwerfers and gun batteries. Photographic interpretation may have been in its infancy but the results were still invaluable to the Royal Artillery. One method of artillery observation employed large kite balloons with specially trained observers dangling in the baskets below, communicating directly with the gun batteries on the ground via a telephone link. Although the balloons were far more inflexible than aircraft by dint of being tethered to one spot they had the great advantage of being able to remain aloft for hours. Yet aircraft remained the key to success, especially in identifying targets set back from the lines. They allowed a far greater range of vision and used the clock code to guide shells right down on to their targets. This may sound simple but there were still serious problems. In particular, many battery commanders were not accustomed to allowing their guns being controlled by relatively junior officers.

> The real crux of the matter is that the artillery have a profound distrust and contempt for the Flying Corps, and have a terror of 'allowing their guns to be run by the Flying Corps'. This is the phrase which is always produced in such controversies. As a matter of fact there are many cases when the Flying Corps are the only people who can run the artillery,

and if they are not even allowed to have priority in the use of one gun they are practically wasted. The artillery are apt to exaggerate their accuracy when firing without aerial observation I think. Both sides lost their tempers.[13]

Lieutenant Thomas Hughes, 1st Squadron, RFC

This difference of opinion highlights the natural friction that arises between new thinking and the conservative 'common sense' approach that had served so well in the past. It would die down over time, but it was a drag on progress. The process of education would continue throughout 1916. The war in the air formed an integral part not only of military planning, but of the practical execution of the bombardments which was the determining factor of success or failure in any offensive.

As the reconnaissance and artillery observation aircraft of both sides became increasingly effective in fulfilling their functions, it became ever more important to thwart them. The most simple expedient was to shoot them down and both sides developed the use of anti-aircraft guns. They too were at a fairly primitive stage of evolution and best practice consisted of little more than guessing the altitude and firing a shrapnel shell timed to burst where the aircraft would be by the time the shell got there. But as anti-aircraft gunners gained experience they became more accurate and the pilots had to take evasive action. Scout aircraft were also developed to shoot down enemy aeroplanes. The first really effective scout was the German Fokker E III monoplane. Fitted with a synchronised machine gun firing through the span of the propeller, it began to play an important role: not just in shooting down or protecting reconnaissance or artillery observation aircraft, but also in shooting down opposing Allied scouts. The Fokker scourge may have been largely a fixation of newspaper headlines, but the imminent Somme Offensive made it essential that the RFC shake off any residual fears; in this it was greatly assisted by a new generation of aircraft that could compete on equal terms with the Fokker. The first was the FE2 B, a two-seater 'pusher' aircraft in which the gunner perched precariously in a front nacelle seat armed with Lewis guns. It proved a sturdy and combative aircraft which, by flying in formation and acting in concert, could keep at bay the marginally superior Fokker. The FE2 B pilots found that the best method of defence was to circle round to protect each other's vulnerable tail from the lurking Fokkers. The second new British aircraft was the DH2, a single-seater 'pusher' fighter armed with just one Lewis gun fixed in front of the pilot. The DH2 became an effective scout, preying on German reconnaissance aircraft and meeting the Fokkers head on. A further valuable multi-purpose aircraft was the Sopwith 1½ Strutter, a two-seater tractor biplane with a synchronised Vickers machine gun firing through the propeller. The final piece in the jigsaw was the single-seater Nieuport 16 Scout provided by the French, which, with a speed of up to 110 miles per hour, was both more manoeuvrable and faster than the Fokker, although it was only armed with a Lewis gun fixed on the top wing and firing over the propeller. With these new types to counter the Fokker scourge, the threat gradually evaporated leaving the British corps aircraft – largely variants of the BE2 C – to carry out their vital role. In all the RFC amassed 185 aircraft (76 scouts) in the Somme area, plus other aircraft flying on bombing missions. The German Air Force had only 129 aircraft (19 scouts). The Germans were soon struggling. Their first great ace, Max Immelmann, was killed in combat with FE2 Bs, and the other best known German Fokker ace, Oswald Boelcke, was promptly removed from the line. Soon the Germans were near helpless in the air, which therefore left them vulnerable on the ground.

All this effort was in aid of the guns: the photographic reconnaissance enabled them to identify targets; the artillery observation helped them to destroy them. The preliminary barrage intended to harvest all the grafting work of the RFC commenced with the roar of hundreds of guns on 24 June 1916. The bombardment was intended to last for five days, but overcast weather hampered the crucial work of the RFC and there was a two-day postponement. The final date of the assault was 1 July 1916. From the British perspective the barrage seemed devastating.

> Armageddon started today and we are right in the thick of it. There is such a row going on I absolutely can't hear myself think! Day and night and all day and all night, guns and nothing but guns – and the shattering clang of bursting high explosives. This is the great offensive, the long looked for 'Big Push', and the whole course of the war will be settled in the next ten days – some time to be living in. I get a wonderful view from my observing station and in front of me and right and left, as far as I can see, there is nothing but bursting shells. It's a weird sight, not a living soul or beast, but countless puffs of

smoke, from the white fleecy ball of the field gun shrapnel to the dense greasy pall of the heavy howitzer HE. It's quite funny to think that in London life is going on just as usual and no one even knows this show has started – while out here at least seven different kinds of Hell are rampant.[14]

Captain Cuthbert Lawson, 369th Battery 15th Brigade, Royal Horse Artillery

At first some of the German garrison looked upon the barrage as little more than a minor inconvenience.

A storm of artillery broke with a crash along the entire line. As far as the eye could see clouds of shrapnel filled the sky, like dust blown on the wind. The bursts were constantly renewed and, toil as it might, the morning breeze could not sweep the sky clear. All around there was howling, snarling and hissing. With a sharp ringing sound, the death-dealing shells burst, spewing their leaden fragments against our line. The balls fell like hail on the roofs of the half-destroyed villages, whistled through the branches of the still green trees and beat down hard on the parched ground, whipping up small clouds of smoke and dust from the earth. Large calibre shells droned through the air like giant bumblebees, crashing, smashing and boring down into the earth. Occasionally small calibre high explosive shells broke the pattern. What was it? The men of the trench garrison pricked up their ears in collective astonishment. Had the Tommies gone off their heads? Did they believe that they could wear us down with shrapnel? We, who had dug ourselves deep into the earth? The very thought made the infantry smile.[15]

Lieutenant M. Gerster, 119th Reserve Infantry Regiment

Any such insouciant attitudes did not survive long as the constant barrage wore away at their defences, slowly eroding their numbers and severely testing their morale. Although the shrapnel shells had little effect on the front line trenches, the ever-increasing deluge of trench mortar shells caused severe damage and tested the resilience of the defenders.

Of course seven days of drum fire had not left the defenders untouched. The feeling of powerlessness against this storm of steel depressed even the strongest. Despite all efforts, the rations were inadequate. The uninterrupted high state of readiness, which had to be maintained because of the entire situation, as well as the frequent gas attacks,

hindered the troops from getting the sleep that they needed because of
the nerve-shattering artillery fire. Tired and indifferent to everything,
the troops sat it out on wooden benches or lay on the hard metal beds,
staring into the darkness when the tallow lights were extinguished by
the overpressure of the explosions. Nobody had washed for days. Black
stubble stood out on the pale haggard faces, whilst the eyes of some
flashed strangely as though they had looked beyond the portals of the
other side. Some trembled when the sound of death roared around
the underground protected places. Whose heart was not in his mouth
at times during this appalling storm of steel? All longed for an end
to it one way or the other. All were seized by a deep bitterness at the
inhuman machine of destruction which hammered endlessly. A searing
rage against the enemy burned in their minds.[16]

Lieutenant M. Gerster, 119th Reserve Infantry Regiment

Gerster and his men would get their chance for revenge at 07.30 on 1 July
1916.

The final reports from the front that filtered back to the British High
Command were generally positive in tone. Overall the visual impression
of the barrage proved far more devastating than the truth on the ground.
British progress had been more than discounted by German improvements in their defences. But that was not known at the time on the British
side of the wire. In any case, they had no choice; the offensive had to go
ahead as the future of the alliance with France depended on it. In the last
few hours as Haig's men prepared for the ordeal, many wrote their sad
last letters home. One was so beautifully expressed that it exemplifies the
feelings of men trapped and tormented by the conflicting calls of country
and family.

I must not allow myself to dwell on the personal – there is no room
for it here. Also it is demoralising. But I do not want to die. Not that I
mind for myself. If it be that I am to go, I am ready. But the thought
that I may never see you or our darling baby again turns my bowels
to water. I cannot think of it with even the semblance of equanimity.
My one consolation is the happiness that has been ours. Also my
conscience is clear that I have always tried to make life a joy to you.
I know at least that if I go you will not want. That is something. But
it is the thought that we may be cut off from one another which is so
terrible and that our babe may grow up without my knowing her and

without her knowing me. It is difficult to face. And I know your life without me would be a dull blank. Yet you must never let it become wholly so. For to you will be left the greatest charge in all the world: the upbringing of our baby. God bless that child, she is the hope of life to me. My darling, *au revoir*. It may well be that you will only have to read these lines as ones of passing interest. On the other hand, they may well be my last message to you. If they are, know through all your life that I loved you and baby with all my heart and soul, that you two sweet things were just all the world to me. I pray God I may do my duty, for I know, whatever that may entail, you would not have it otherwise.[17]

Captain Charles May, 22nd Manchester Regiment

Charles May, the loving husband of Bessie May and father to his baby Pauline, would indeed be killed the next day. He is buried in the Danzig Alley British Cemetery. Small-scale tragedies litter the history of war: sad reminders that the necessities of war ruin the lives of millions.

ON 1 JULY 1916 the barrage swelled up to a crescendo at 06.30 and the men got ready to advance across No Man's Land. This is the moment that has come to symbolise the whole of the Great War. The 'lions led by donkeys' school see it as a savage indictment of the stupidity of British generals; the long lines of overburdened men stumbling towards the German machine guns are painted as victims, dying for no reason. However, it is crucial to dispel this myth. The British generals' tactics were the best that could have been conceived at the time given a vibrant German defence that incorporated all the lessons from the fighting of 1915. This would only become truly apparent when the British troops emerged from their trenches at 07.30.

The attack was a disaster. On the left and in the centre of the Allied advance the artillery had not achieved its objectives. The wire was not always cut. The German trenches, although battered, were still functioning as defence works; their machine gun posts and artillery batteries had survived; their systems of command and control, although disrupted, were not shattered. It was a fully functioning German defence system that awaited the British assault. The experience of Lieutenant William Colyer and the 2nd Royal Dublin Fusiliers was not untypical.

Here goes. I clamber out of the front of the deep trench by the scaling ladder, and face my platoon. I am smoking a cigarette and superficially am serene and cheerful – at least, I hope I appear so. As I give the order to advance a sudden thought occurs to me: will they all obey? This is instantly answered in the affirmative, for they all climb out of the trench, and the advance begins. We are on top of the ridge and under direct fire. I am trying not to mind it, but it is impossible. I am wondering unpleasantly whether I shall be killed outright or whether I shall be wounded; and if the latter, which part of me will be hit. A traversing machine gun rips up the ground just in front of us. That's enough for me; we can't remain in this formation. 'Extend by sections!' I shout. The men carry out the movement well. The Bosche artillery and machine guns are terrific. The anticipation of being hit has become so agonising that I can scarcely bear it; I almost wish to God I could be hit and have done with it. I have lost some of my men. I feel an overwhelming desire to swear, to blaspheme, to shout out the wickedest oaths I can think of, but I am much too inarticulate to do anything of the kind. A shell bursts near and I feel the hot blast. It seems to me this is a ghastly failure already. A trench runs diagonally across our path. Half of my remaining men are already in it. My whole being cries out in protest against this ordeal. I am streaming with perspiration. I think I shall go mad. I am in the trench, trying to collect the rest of the men together. Where the devil have they all got to?[18]

Lieutenant William Colyer, 2nd Royal Dublin Fusiliers

All along the line the moment of decision had come for the German front line garrison troops. Rushing headlong from their dugouts they began to avenge their last few days in hell. Corporal Otto Lais of the 169th Infantry Regiment was facing the 'Pals' Battalions of the 31st Division as they made their ill-fated attack on the village of Serre.

Wild firing slammed into the masses of the enemy. All around us was the rushing, whistling and roaring of a storm a hurricane, as the destructive British shells rushed towards our artillery which was firing courageously, our reserves and our rear areas. Throughout all this racket, this rumbling, growling, bursting, cracking and wild banging and crashing of small arms, could be heard the heavy, hard and regular 'Tack! Tack!' of the machine guns. That one tiring slower, this other with a faster rhythm – it was the precision work of fine material and skill and both were playing a gruesome tune to the enemy.[19]

Corporal Otto Lais, 169th Infantry Regiment

It became an utter slaughter. His men had to change the worn-out machine gun barrels again and again. They also ran out of cooling water and had to resort to urine to refill the water jacket. But the guns were kept firing and he noted that one gun fired some 20,000 rounds in the course of that awful day.

In a sense the story of 1 July has been inverted. This was not a tale of incompetence by the British, but rather a reflection on the strength of the German defences, coupled with the malleable resilience of their soldiers. Where the British over-ran their front line system, the Germans just moved smoothly into the next phase of their defensive plans: robust counter-attacks pressed home diligently, covered by a barrage that cut off the attacking British troops from reinforcements and then gradually eradicated these enclaves in the German lines. Even when the British tried something different, harvesting the incredible sustained effort of their Tunnelling Companies in laying deep mines under the German front, success was not guaranteed. This was best illustrated in the attack on the La Boisselle Salient. A pincer attack had been planned based on the Y Sap containing 40,000 pounds of explosives on the north flank and to the south the Lochnagar containing 60,000 pounds of explosives under the Schwaben Redoubt. It had seemed a good plan – the mines tore gaping craters in the ground – but the effect was far too localised. The surrounding barrages had not removed the threat of the German machine guns and artillery. When the Tynesiders of the 34th Division attacked, they were ravaged.

> Silently our machine guns and the infantrymen waited until our opponents came closer. Then, when they were only a few metres from the trenches, the serried ranks of the enemy were sprayed with a hurricane of defensive fire from the machine guns and the aimed fire of the individual riflemen. Standing exposed on the parapet, some individuals hurled hand grenades at the enemy who had taken cover to the front. Within moments it seemed as though the battle had died away completely. But then, initially in small groups, but later in huge masses, the enemy began to pull back, until finally it seemed as

though every man in the entire field was attempting to flee back to his jumping-off point.[20]

Senior Lieutenant Kienitz, Machine Gun Company, 110th Reserve Infantry Regiment

This was a true massacre of the innocents.

Further south, the situation was more mixed as British troops attacked the fortress villages of Fricourt and Mametz on two of the spurs running down from the higher ground of the Pozières Plateau. Here the German artillery had been better targeted and, to some extent, silenced. The attacking troops were supported by a series of small mines being detonated and also covered by a creeping barrage with the wall of shells edging forward at a rate of fifty yards per minute. However, the barrage was too thin to have the required suppressing effect. Only in the far south of the British line was there any real success. Here the configuration of the line was such that the Maricourt Ridge behind the British lines provided good observation over the German lines and at the same time shelter for the massed guns of the Royal Artillery augmented by a deadly fire from the more experienced neighbouring French batteries. Acting in concert they achieved an artillery domination that eradicated the German batteries. Not only was the German artillery silenced, but the wire was cut, their trenches badly battered and the German garrison was caught sheltering for too long inside its dugout, leaving little or nothing that could seriously threaten the British troops as they crossed No Man's Land. Here, too, mines and another early version of the creeping barrage were employed. As a result, the troops soon captured the village of Montauban. When the Germans tried to counter-attack the British guns came into their own again, pouring down an effective defensive barrage of shells to bar their way.

South of the British, the French attack was launched on both sides of the River Somme by their Sixth Army under the command of General Émile Fayolle. The Germans were not expecting an assault here and had thinned out their troops, but the French also had the inestimable advantage of copious experience of offensive action over the last eighteen months, in contrast to the callow British troops. In particular the French artillery was a truly lethal beast which ruthlessly targeted and then silenced the German batteries. In the last hours before the attack the

German gun positions were deluged by a combination of gas and high explosive shells designed to suppress their ability to return fire when the moment arrived – another inkling of a future when suppression would become much more important than destruction.

The French were able to deploy a far greater proportion of heavy guns than the British, which meant that the destructive force of their shells was magnified accordingly. The German guns were soon put out of action or rendered incapable of firing, leaving their infantry to resist as best they could from their smashed trenches and dugouts. Many of the dreaded machine guns were out of action well before the French infantry emerged. The French had also delayed their start time of 09.30, which had confused the defenders, who were well aware that the assault north of the river had already begun. The French infantry were by this time possessed of a collective experience that greatly advantaged them in comparison to the British.

> Our artillery preparation was wonderful. It completely destroyed the German defences and our assault waves managed to cross the lines without much resistance. Only an enemy counter-barrage claimed a few victims. As soon as the first wave had set off, we advanced over the heavily cratered ground, ready to help out those in front. The enemy continued to send over a heavy barrage so we dug in when we reached the outskirts of Fay to avoid taking too many casualties. The shells fell very close by, but we were right at the bottom of our trench and they didn't touch us.[21]
>
> Joseph Foy, 265th Infantry Regiment

The French infantry smashed through the German front lines and soon over-ran the villages of Frise, Dompierre, Becquincourt and Fay, before pushing on to Herbécourt and Assevillers by the late afternoon. Here they were hit by vicious counter-attacks which for the moment stemmed the tide. Aware that the British were falling behind, the French paused. By the time they were ready to resume the offensive the Germans had reinforced their positions and the Somme had become as hard a slog for the French as it was for the British.

The pattern of the fighting on 1 July appears clear enough from our perspective, but the breakdown in communications on the day was such that few of the senior British generals had much idea of what was happening to their troops. Certainly, the briefings forwarded on to Haig lacked both detail and accuracy – yet he had to make an almost immediate decision as to what do next. In essence he had two choices: reinforce success in the south where, for all their achievement, the Germans' Second Line System on Bazentin Ridge still lay ahead, or make a second attempt to storm up on to the more significant tactical objective on Pozières Plateau, Thiepval Spur and Redan Ridge in the north. What Haig did not know was the scale of the disaster that had befallen the Fourth Army, which had suffered 57,470 casualties, of which 19,240 were dead. It is this inconceivable loss that can cloud our judgement in assessing the fighting on 1 July.

The British tactics were not ill-considered, but they proved inadequate to cope with the augmented strength of the German defences. The millions of shells expended in the bombardment might have been sufficient to deal with the German defences at Neuve Chapelle, or even Loos in 1915, but that was last year. The new German concrete reinforced deep dugouts proved resistant to all but the very heaviest shells – and heavy artillery was still in short supply. Also, many of the shells failed to explode. This was not surprising given the rapid expansion of British munitions factories in order to meet demand, with a commensurate reduction in quality control standards. But most of all the bombardment was fatally diluted in the attempt to attack on a wide front while at the same time reaching back to cover the German Second Line System as well as the series of lines and redoubts that made up the Front Line System. The risk, as at Aubers Ridge, Festubert and Loos, was that in being ambitious one risked catastrophe.

Yet there was no question of abandoning the offensive. To abandon that was to abandon France. The French likely reaction to any backsliding can be judged from the strongly expressed views of Joffre when he met Haig on 3 July. Joffre considered that the value of the high ground in the north far outweighed the likelihood of further savage casualty lists. In this he may well have been right: the Germans themselves certainly knew the importance of the Schwaben Redoubt behind the Thiepral front lines.

> The Scbwaben Redoubt was a point of decisive importance. If the enemy succeeded in establishing himself here on a long term basis, not only would the whole position of the 26th Reserve Division on the southern bank of the Ancre have been extraordinarily endangered, but

also the entire operational viability of the divisional artillery on the northern bank would have been called into question, because from the Redoubt all the batteries there would have been in full view.[22]

Captain Herbert von Wurmb, 8th Bavarian Reserve Infantry Regiment

Without the benefit of hindsight, rightly or wrongly, Haig was determined to resist tactical interference from Joffre and decided to reinforce the relative degree of success attained in the south. To this end he reorganised his forces, directing the Fourth Army under Rawlinson to push on in the southern sector, while Gough's Reserve Army (later recast as the Fifth Army) was given the northern sector.

The Germans, meanwhile, had their own tactical issues to consider. Falkenhayn had a clear and simple dictat: that any lost ground should be recaptured immediately, no matter the cost. In consequence, on 3 July an order was issued by the Second Army commander.

The outcome of the war depends on the Second Army being victorious on the Somme. Despite the current enemy superiority in artillery and infantry we have got to win this battle. The large areas of ground that we have lost in certain places will be attacked and wrested back from the enemy, just as soon as the reinforcements which are on the way arrive. For the time being, we must hold our current positions without fail and improve on them by means of minor counter-attacks. I forbid the voluntary relinquishment of positions. Every commander is responsible for making each man in the Army aware about this determination to fight it out. The enemy must be made to pick his way forward over corpses.[23]

General Fritz von Below, Headquarters, Second Army

This intransigence would cost the Germans dear.

The next few days saw a series of piecemeal British attacks intended to improve the tactical position prior to the next 'Big Push' by the Fourth Army against the German Second Line System on Bazentin Ridge. Many of these attacks were hopeless affairs, characterised by a lack of artillery co-ordination, and with foolishly staggered start times which allowed the Germans to destroy the attacks in sequence. The corps and divisional commanders were fighting each small battle in isolation and no one was fusing their efforts to positive effect. The losses in some fifty or more of these attacks came to 25,000 casualties. What the British had been working towards was the Battle of Bazentin Ridge, which began on the night of 14 July. This marked an overdue lurch forward for the British tactical roller coaster. The instigator of the new plans was Rawlinson, who was determined to concentrate sufficient artillery tailored to the basic requirements to cut the German wire, smash the trench lines and disable their batteries by means of a three-day preliminary barrage followed by a massive hurricane bombardment of just five minutes. It was also proposed that the attack should be made at night, with the attacking troops creeping out under cover of darkness into No Man's Land to take up positions closer to the German lines. At first this was seen as overly bold by Haig, who insisted that Rawlinson redouble his efforts in order to secure effective counter-battery fire to suppress the German artillery should this surreptitious move be detected.

When the barrage began it was far more concentrated than that before 1 July. This time there were 1,000 guns, of which 311 were the all-important heavy artillery. It was also concentrated on a frontage of just 6,000 yards and against trenches which were far less developed than the original German front line. Without sufficient cover, the German garrison was vulnerable to the shells that crashed all around when the barrage proper opened up at 03.20. Meanwhile, behind the bursting shells the British infantry moved forward ready to close with the Germans a few seconds after the barrage lifted. When they reached the Germans trenches there were varying degrees of resistance but they managed to breach the German Second Line System and capture the villages of Longueval, Bazentin-le-Petit and Bazentin-le-Grand.

> I shouted at the gunner of a heavy machine gun of the 6th Company that he should bring down fire on the British soldiers who were heading for Longueval, but he did not respond. So I dashed from the trench to the gun – my men meanwhile kept the heads down of the British in front of the obstacle with heavy small arms fire. I threw myself down by the gunner and saw that he was dead, shot through the temples. Hardly had I prised his cramped grip off the handles of the gun, pushed him to one side and tried to fire at the British platoon in the hollow road, than the weapon jammed. It had been hit in the breech by a rifle bullet. I yanked the belt out of the gun, grabbed another from the ammunition box, wrapped them around me and

raced back to the trench through the fire of the British infantrymen, who were only 25 to 30 metres away. Meanwhile the British were firing at us from windows and holes in the roofs of Longueval. Then things got very serious. I was standing behind a parapet when simultaneously British grenades landed on the parapet and the edge of the trench and fell down into the trench next to me. I only escaped from this hopeless position by instinctively grabbing the grenades which had fallen in the trench and hurling them out. They were still in the air when they exploded.[24]

Lieutenant E. Gerhardinger, 16th Bavarian Infantry Regiment

In most places the German resistance was fairly short-lived as they found themselves outflanked or even surrounded. Yet British attempts to exploit partial breakthrough proved stillborn. The cavalry, the only available rapid exploitation force, were stymied by a combination of broken ground and stiffening German resistance. When the German counter-attacks developed later in the day it was clear that the British had succeeded in breaking *in* to the German system but not in breaking *through* it.

During this first phase on the Somme the cumulative developments and experimentation that pushed forward the boundaries of air warfare severely disadvantaged the Germans, whose air force was found wanting at this crucial moment. This did not go unnoticed by elements of the German High Command, who were appalled at the consequences of this inability to contest for dominance of the skies on behalf of their troops on the ground.

The beginning and the first weeks of the Somme battle were marked by a complete inferiority of our own air forces. The enemy's aeroplanes enjoyed complete freedom in carrying out distant reconnaissances. With the aid of aeroplane observation, the hostile artillery neutralised our guns and was able to range with the most extreme accuracy on the trenches occupied by our infantry; the required data for this was provided by undisturbed trench reconnaissance and photography. By means of bombing and machine-gun attacks from a low height against infantry, battery positions and marching columns, the enemy's aircraft inspired our troops with a feeling of defencelessness against the enemy's mastery of the air. On the other hand, our own aeroplanes only succeeded in quite exceptional cases in breaking through the hostile patrol barrage and carrying out distant reconnaissances; our artillery machines were driven off whenever they attempted to carry out registration for their own batteries. Photographic reconnaissance could not fulfil the demands made upon it. Thus, at decisive moments, the infantry frequently lacked the support of the German artillery either in counter-battery work or in barrage on the enemy's infantry massing for attack.[25]

General Fritz von Below, Headquarters, First Army

But the Germans were already moving fast to correct the aerial imbalance with a new generation of fighter scouts. Soon the RFC would face a sterner challenge in the skies above the Somme.

THE SUCCESS OF THE NEW TACTICS unveiled on 14 July did not set the pattern for subsequent British attacks. Instead, there was a failure to concentrate sufficient artillery during a plethora of narrow front attacks which provoked thousands more casualties and only minor gains. Haig railed from the sidelines, but he seemed unable to get a grip on his subordinates too immersed in the day-to-day complexities of fighting the battle to look at the bigger picture. There was a fear that spending time organising and concentrating British forces would allow the Germans time to do the same. The Germans were indeed sending reinforcements to the Somme area, including many batteries from the Verdun Front. They were also mutating their defensive tactics as they began to occupy improvised defensive positions with machine gun teams lurking in shell holes away from the actual trenches which were being deluged with shells. This massively increased the area of ground that had to be thoroughly covered by the British barrage. Creeping barrages became a necessity not a luxury and they had to be thickened to form a true wall of bursting shells edging forward across the battlefield. The fighting became more and more attritional as the British ground their way forward. Intensive fighting flared first of all around the village of Longueval and Delville Wood. Then High Wood dominated the skyline, while on the right of the line Ginchy and Guillemont became key objectives. The power of the massed guns allowed the British infantry to capture a local objective; but the German guns allowed them to counter-attack successfully. The attack was expanded to the north, where Gough's Reserve Army began a series of operations designed to capture the German Second Line System on the Pozières Ridge and thereby weaken the German grip on Thiepval Spur. The 1st Australian Division, newly arrived from Gallipoli, was flung into the fight. They would find it a brutal awakening to the grim realities of industrialised warfare.

> Down came our barrage on to the enemy lines and Pozières village, the Germans replying with artillery and machine-gun fire. As we lay out among the poppies in No Man's Land we could see the bullets cutting off the poppies almost against our heads. The flashes of the guns, the bursting of the shells and the Very lights made the night like day and, as I lay as flat to the ground as possible, I was expecting to stop one any time. Jamming my tin helmet down on my head I brought the body of my rifle across my face to stop anything that might happen to drop low. In the tumult it was impossible to hear orders. My ears were ringing with the cracking of bullets. A man alongside me was crying like a baby, and although I tried to reassure him he kept on saying that we would never get out of it. Suddenly, I saw men scrambling to their feet. Taking this to be the signal for the charge I jumped up and dashed across.[26]

Sergeant Harold Preston, 9th (Queensland) Battalion, AIF

After Pozières, the next objective that lay ahead of them was Mouquet Farm, hitherto an insignificant name on the map that was to become the graveyard of thousands of young Australians. One British artillery officer summed up the prevailing mood.

> I am afraid we are settling down to siege warfare in earnest and of a most sanguinary kind, very far from our hopes in July. But it's always the same: Festubert, Loos, and now this. Both sides are too strong for a finish yet. God knows how long it will be at this rate. None of us will ever see its end and children still at school will have to take over.[27]

Captain Philip Pilditch, 'C' Battery, 235th Brigade, Royal Field Artillery

Pilditch was quite right. This was the wearing-out phase of the battle. Both sides would come to realise that the Somme – when added to the equivalent attritional blood-letting of Verdun – was a crucial battle in the grim process of grinding down the Germany reserves. But it was an inhuman business all the same: this was the pity of war. The German soldiers at the front were suffering just as much as their Allied opponents, with the prevailing mood one of despair.

> Because there were no dugouts, we sheltered in shell holes. With the help of a mate, I dug mine down a bit deeper. Lying flat out, we carefully lifted thistles and other shrubby weeds, which we planted around the rim of our shell hole to give us cover from view. We lay in this hole for three and a half hours, unable, because of the heavy fire, to move or be relieved. Frequently we also sheltered in foxholes with our legs drawn up, or we would scrabble our way from shell hole to shell hole, linking them together. The water was green and full of muddy clay but we had to use it to brew coffee, because the ration parties could not get through to us. We were always short of bread. On one occasion the section was able to share a bottle of wine. Once came the shout, 'Tommy is attacking!' We waited in painful impatience and looked forward to giving him a warm reception, but not a single Tommy appeared! What a shame, what a bloody shame![28]
>
> Private Rabe, 15th Reserve Infantry Regiment

The message is clear: Rabe and his comrades were suffering, but as long as they survived and still had ammunition they were dangerous opponents. As such, he symbolised the whole German Army during the long agony of the Somme.

Yet at the level of High Command the Germans were showing the signs of the incredible strain not only of operating on two fronts, but of fighting two major attritional battles at the same time. When the Brusilov Offensive burst upon the Austro-Hungarians on the Eastern Front on 4 June 1916, Falkenhayn's overall strategy was already unravelling. Although his reasons for launching the Verdun Offensive had been cogent, he had underestimated the French will to resist and they showed no signs of collapse or of being brought to the peace table by their suffering; indeed, they seemed even more determined to carry on the fight. Falkenhayn had also anticipated that the French infantry would be minced by the collective power of the German guns. But here too he had been disappointed. The French had deployed their own massed guns and the attritional fighting had affected both sides equally. These failures had not gone unnoticed among the military and political establishment, so Hindenburg and Ludendorff, sensing their chance, resumed their campaigning for Falkenhayn's dismissal. When Falkenhayn made the mistake of errone-ously assuring the Kaiser that Rumania would not join the Allies – which it promptly did on 27 August 1916 – it proved his undoing. Hindenburg, the victor of Tannenberg, the most popular general in the country, a man widely seen as a hero of Germany, was his obvious replacement. On 29 August, Falkenhayn was called upon to resign and Hindenburg was appointed Chief of General Staff, with Ludendorff appointed to the new position of Quartermaster General.

THE NEXT GREAT OFFENSIVE on the Somme would be the Battle of Flers-Courcelette, which began on 15 September 1916. This was the battle intended to reap the rewards from all the hard graft that had pre-ceded it. Success here might foreshorten the war; failure would certainly prolong it. Over ten divisions of the Fourth and Reserve Armies would advance together on the German lines. This was a battle the scale of which would have been unthinkable for the BEF just a year before. It also marked a significant step forward in the British tactical approach to the offensive with the first use of the tank. The gestation of the tank has been much debated, but it originated in the clear necessity for some kind of armoured vehicle that could cross No Man's Land, brush through barbed wire and use its onboard armaments to assault German strongpoints. There was much experimentation before the emergence of the lozenge-shaped Mark I 'tank', an armoured tracked vehicle based on the Holt tractor which came in two variants: the 'male', armed with two 6-pounder guns and four machine guns, and the 'female', with just six machine guns. No one knew their capabilities or drawbacks: this could only be discovered in battle. What better time to test them out than at the crucial Battle of Flers-Courcelette, the climax of the main Allied offensive of 1916?

In September 1916 the British were still faced by three defensive trench systems on the Somme, but these – at least superficially – were far less fearsome than those of 1 July. The press of events meant that the Germans did not have the time to dig a sophisticated interconnected system of trenches and switch lines, nor to build the mass of concrete reinforced fortifications and deep dugouts to stiffen the line. But they still presented a formidable series of trenches, with the added threat of the hidden shell hole machine gunners. Among the British High Command there was a considerable debate as to tactics, with Rawlinson preferring a step-by-step approach while Haig pressed for a greater return for the huge investment of resources devoted to the offensive. In the end the attack was to be carried out on a wide front, but with the main thrust centred on the village of Flers-Courcelette. The powerful barrage was based on a concentration of one field gun per ten yards of front, with a further medium or heavy gun every twenty-nine yards. By now the concept of using a creeping barrage as the troops attacked was fully accepted, but the importance of counter-battery fire to silence the German guns was still not properly grasped and the fifty-six guns assigned to the task were nowhere near sufficient. The guns were still, as at Neuve Chapelle, Loos and on 1 July, at the very centre of the plans, with the tank just a promising addition. Indeed, integrating tanks into the existing tactical mix posed a complex series of problems to which there were no obvious solutions. Should they be concentrated together? Was it best if they moved in front of, alongside or behind the infantry? In the end the tanks were spread out in small groups, sent ahead of the infantry to breech the German front line and tackle machine gun posts. To facilitate this, 100-yard gaps were left in the creeping barrage tracking the planned route of each tank as far as the front line, after which the infantry and tanks would advance together behind another creeping barrage. Once they were beyond the range of the supporting field artillery the tanks would be used to flatten the German barbed wire while their guns would attempt to provide close support for the infantry. This was an ambitious programme for untested weapons. In the event, the sheer unreliability of the tanks proved greater than expected. Of the forty-nine tanks intended to be used in the attack only thirty-six reached the starting lines by the time the final barrage burst out at 06.20 on 15 September. When they went into action they often broke down or lost their way, which left the infantry in the 'lanes' left by the creeping barrage advancing into uncurbed fire. For the Germans it was the new British barrage techniques, not the tanks, that had the biggest impact.

> A forest of guns opened up in a ceaseless rolling thunder of fire throughout the High Wood–Flers–Martinpuich–Courcelette sector. A sea of iron crashed down on all the front and support lines of the area.

The noise was terrible. Impact after impact. The whole of No Man's Land was a seething cauldron. The work of destruction grew and grew. Chaos! It was impossible to imagine that anyone could live through it. Square metre after square metre was ploughed up. An unparalleled hurricane of fire blew over from the front. It was like a crashing machine, mechanical, without feelings; snuffing out the last resistance with a thousand hammers. It is totally inappropriate to play such a game with fellow men. We are all human beings, made in the image of the Lord God. But what account does the Devil take of mankind, or God, when he feels himself to be Lord of the Elements; when chaos celebrates his omnipotence? From the direction of High Wood we can hear the sound of voices and confused shouting, which persists until the few remaining survivors, wakened from mental confusion, find themselves shocked back into the reality of the moment and fight on, until the British flood overwhelms them, consumes them and passes on. Wave upon wave. An extraordinary number of men and there, between them, spewing death, unearthly monsters: the first British tanks.[29]

Second Lieutenant Hermann Kohl, 17th Bavarian Infantry Regiment

Communication was almost non-existent between the tanks and the infantry. Often the tanks were left behind by the infantry desperate to keep up with the more certain protection offered by the creeping barrage. The much-advertised tank proceeding along the main street of Flers was a journalist's dream in the days following, but the tank concerned did nothing more than trundle up and down the road before breaking down. Meanwhile, the Germans may have been stunned by the appearance of tanks on the battlefield but they could fight back hard. The C-22 'female' tank was commanded by Second Lieutenant Basil Henriques which for unknown reasons advanced before Zero Hour towards German positions at the Quadrilateral. At first the German trenches remained quiet but as he crossed the front line and opened fire the Germans retaliated with small arms using armour-piercing ammunition normally employed against the loop-holed steel plates used by British snipers.

All the time I had the front flaps open, for visibility was far too restricted if they were shut; but after a hail of machine gun fire, I closed them tightly for the first time. Then the periscope got hit away; then the small prisms got broken one after another; then armour piercing bullets began to penetrate, in spite of the fact that tanks were said to be completely proof against them. Then my driver got hit; then one of my gunners; then I got splinters in the face and legs. Meanwhile the gunners claim to have killed or hit twenty or thirty of the enemy. I could see absolutely nothing. The only thing to do was to open the front flap slightly and peep through. Eventually this got hit so that it was hanging only by a thread, and the enemy could fire in at us at close range.[30]

Second Lieutenant Basil Henriques, C Company, Heavy Branch, Motor Machine Gun Company

Another weakness of the tanks was becoming apparent – they were susceptible to well-directed artillery fire. All told the tanks achieved little that would not have been gained by more conventional means – yet at times they did also give an inkling of what might be. They certainly made an impression on the Germans.

A man came running in from the left, shouting, 'There is a crocodile crawling into our lines!' The poor wretch was off his head. He had seen a tank for the first time and had imagined this giant of a machine, rearing up and dipping down as it came, to be a monster. It presented a fantastic picture, this Colossus in the dawn light. One moment its front section would disappear into a crater, with the rear section still protruding, the next its yawning mouth would rear up out of the crater, to roll slowly forward with terrifying assurance.[31]

Sergeant Weinert, 211th Infantry Regiment

Haig was sufficiently encouraged by the development of the tank, though, to order a thousand shortly after the battle. He was also consoled by the success of the latest version of British offensive tactics. Many of the German First Line positions had been over-run all along the 9,000-yard front, while in the Flers sector the Second Line had been breached to such an extent that a couple of days later the Germans retreated to Le Transloy Ridge. The Germans were in deep trouble, but the British had still not broken through.

Within ten days the British had assimilated some of the lessons learnt. In their plans for the Battle of Morval launched at 12.35 on 25 September they reined in their ambitions to a more 'bite and hold' format aiming for an advance of about 1,500 yards to take the latest German front line. This allowed for a more concentrated artillery bombardment with no gaps in the coverage, a much greater attention to counter-battery work and a return to the concept of a standing barrage dropping in front of newly captured ground to break up any attempted German counter-attacks. The tanks were also used in a more focussed way, following the infantry in order to assist in the destruction of troublesome strongpoints – in other words, as a useful but secondary weapon. The result was a dramatic success and indeed in most places the tanks could not keep up with the infantry as they advanced across the ground razed by the barrage. Similar tactics brought equal success the following day when Gough attacked Thiepval Spur and Schwaben Redoubt at 12.35 on 26 September. This triggered an intensive period of vicious fighting, but slowly the British were inching forward and loosening the German grip on the high ground that had remained inviolate since 1 July. Yet there was a price to pay: whenever they captured a German position there always seemed to be more lines ahead of them. In the time it took to organise and execute a 'bite and hold' attack the Germans could dig new trench lines; and so the process rumbled on *ad infinitum*. A new development in German tactics was the placing of concealed machine gun posts well behind their lines, beyond the range of British field artillery, but still able to cover open ground near or just behind their own front line. As the tactical rollercoaster ride hurtled on, each side adapted their methods to counter the other, every step forward only seemed to preface a step back. Captain Pilditch's grim prophecy of an eternal torment of trench warfare appeared all too feasible. Yet Haig, aware that his embattled armies were creeping closer to tactically significant battlefield features, concluded that the Germans were ready for the taking.

> We had already broken through all the enemy's prepared lines and now only extemporised defences stood between us and the Bapaume ridge: moreover the enemy had suffered much in men, in material, and in morale. If we rested even for a month, the enemy would be able to strengthen his defences, to recover his equilibrium, to make good deficiencies, and, worse still, would regain the initiative! The longer we rested, the more difficult would our problem again become, so in my opinion we must continue to press the enemy to the utmost of our power.[32]
>
> General Sir Douglas Haig, General Headquarters, BEF

Haig was determined to press on, trusting that the twin hammer blows of the Somme and Verdun would undermine German resolve. This time his plan was fairly simple: keep attacking in order to exert all possible pressure. But the Germans responded to the challenge by moving up more gun batteries and sending in fresh divisions. Once again the campaign degenerated into a series of small-scale assaults launched to ever-diminishing effect throughout October. Failure again became the norm for the British attacks.

As they edged forwards the British were suffering from the diminishing effectiveness of their main weapon, the massed guns of the Royal Artillery. The over-worked gunners were becoming physically exhausted; their guns too were wearing out and losing accuracy. The increasingly wet autumnal weather amplified the logistical problems of moving millions of shells across the devastated wasteland behind the British lines. The guns themselves sank deep into the mud, creating unstable platforms which made a nonsense of precise adjustments of angle and range. The all-pervading mud even smothered the explosive effects of the shells as they burst.

There was a new challenge in the air, too. By this time the Royal Artillery was relying heavily on the RFC to photograph and chart the exact locations of German trenches and gun batteries before using the aircraft artillery observation to eliminate them. But flying was often impossible due to the inclement weather. Also, the German Air Service was starting to offer more vigorous opposition. The first step was a deadly new aircraft, the Albatros DI. This was the first scout to be armed with twin Spandau machine guns firing through the propeller; it also had a powerful 160 horse power Mercedes engine which gave it a top speed of nearly 110mph. Just as deadly was the codified version of aerial tactics prepared by Captain Oswald Boelcke, who was placed in command of the newly formed Jasta 2 based at Bertincourt on 27 August. He inculcated his pilots with the simple principles of combat fighting in the air which included the importance of taking an opponent by surprise, preferably from behind coming out of the sun, and only shooting at close range. The first inkling the British had of this new force on the Western Front came when Boelcke led his ingénues into action against a group of BE2 Cs and FE2 Bs engaged in a raid on the railway junction at Marcoing. One of his young pilots, Lieutenant Manfred von Richthofen, was desperate to shoot down his first victim. Despite his inexperience, the tremendous superiority of his Albatros allowed him to get behind an FE2 B flown by veterans Lieutenant Lionel Morris and Lieutenant Tom Rees.

> A struggle began and the great point for me was to get to the rear of the fellow. Apparently he was no beginner, for he knew exactly that his last hour had arrived at the moment I got at the back of him. My Englishman twisted and turned, flying in zig-zags. At last a favourable moment arrived. My opponent had apparently lost sight of me. Instead of twisting and turning, he flew straight along. In a fraction of a second, I was at his back with my excellent machine. I gave a short burst of shots with my machine gun. I had gone so close that I was afraid I might crash into the Englishman. Suddenly I nearly yelled with joy, for the propeller of the enemy machine had stopped turning. Hurrah! I had shot his engine to pieces; the enemy was compelled to land, for it was impossible for him to reach his own lines. The English machine was swinging curiously to and fro. Probably something had happened to the pilot. The observer was no longer visible.[33]
>
> Second Lieutenant Manfred von Richthofen, Jasta 2, German Air Service

Both Morris and Rees were killed; all their experience could not save them. Von Richthofen's Albatros more than compensated for his lack of combat skills. It allowed the fledgling German pilots to take their kills almost at will. But Boelcke did not stint in his training, constantly going through the minutiae of every aerial encounter with his young charges. As for Richthofen, he would rise to be the greatest German ace of the war. It was becoming apparent that the RFC would have to suffer severe casualties if they were to continue carrying out their functions in the face of this new scourge. Brigadier General Hugh Trenchard was well aware of the problem, but he was determined that the RFC would continue to carry out its duty to the men on the ground, come what may. He decided to rely on numerical supremacy and to accept casualties as best they could.

Below the leaden skies the conditions on the Somme in the late autumn and winter of 1916 began to match the horrors of Verdun. By the end of October the Somme had become a place of utter horror beyond all normal human comprehension.

> I will never forget that trench – it was simply packed with German corpses in the stage where face and hands were inky black with a

greenish tinge from decomposition and whites of the eyes and teeth gave them a horrible appearance. How so many came to be in one trench I cannot tell, unless one of our tanks caught them there. Fritz had tried to get rid of some, for they were laid in rows on the parapets at the level of one's head, stuck into walls, buried in the floor and felt like an air cushion to walk on, and one was continually rubbing against heads, legs, arms etc., sticking out of the walls at all heights. The floor one walked on was in a fearful state, in some parts covered several deep with bodies or a face with grinning teeth looked up at you from the soft mud, and one often saw an arm or a leg by itself and occasionally a head cut off. Everywhere are Prussian helmets with their eagle badge, belts and equipment, many bodies had wristwatches etc. We did not collect many souvenirs, for our own skin was the best souvenir we could think of that day.[34]

Signaller Ron Buckell, 1st Canadian Artillery Brigade, CEF

Morale was declining among the British soldiers called to endure these impossible conditions of service. As the months wore on, divisions, brigades and battalions who had already fought on the Somme were returned to the front, rarely having had time for deep wounds to heal, for the memories of recent sacrifices to fade. And in front of them the Germans seemed as implacable as ever.

By November it was apparent that there was no longer time for the BEF to finish their grim business that year. With the depths of winter looming, it was evident that the German Army was simply too strong – the war would continue deep into 1917. The priorities of the British High Command changed: now they sought to gain the best possible tactical positions for the winter, ready for the resumption of fighting in the new year. And so there was to be one final attack, with the Battle of the Ancre commencing at 05.45 on 13 November. This time they bit the bullet and attacked north towards St Pierre Divion to finally clear the south bank of the Ancre River, while at the same time an assault was made along the line from Serre to Beaucourt on the north bank of the river. In some ways this was a thorough exploration of the effectiveness of the new British tactics, for this was the very blood-soaked ground on which the attack of 1 July had failed.

The preparations were commendably thorough: the troops sapped forward to narrow No Man's Land, while underneath the surface the tunnellers once again laid their mines deep under the German lines. This time when the mines exploded under Hawthorn Ridge a powerful creeping barrage chaperoned the troops of the 51st Division as they swept forward to capture Beaumont Hamel. During the fighting that followed Beaucourt fell and the British also made ground on Redan Ridge. The German tactical position was rapidly deteriorating but it was too late in the year for the British to exploit this. By the time their last attack was made on 18 November it was on a freezing ice-bound battlefield and little was achieved as both sides had fought themselves to a standstill. Haig accepted that no further progress was possible and the offensive was formally closed down, although for the men on the ground the aftershocks reverberated on with 'line straightening' operations still draining away lives on both sides.

FOR MANY PEOPLE THE Somme and the equally ugly Verdun have come to symbolise the Great War: futile battles fought with other people's lives by incompetent and uncaring generals. In particular, for the British, the disaster of 1 July, on the Somme, has become the sole prism through which the conduct of the whole of the Great War has been viewed. There is no light and shade here; just a dark despair at the numbing horror of the teeming casualties. Explanations of what went wrong and why are thrust aside; indeed in the past, subdued references to a 'learning curve' for the generals have been seen as an insult to the dead. There remains a widespread belief that 'there must have been a better way'; something else could, or should, have been done; someone must be blamed. Much of this opprobrium has fallen on the head of Douglas Haig, who has at times been reviled as a mass murderer. Yet this was the inevitable price of engaging in continental warfare on the main field of battle against the primary enemy. France was well accustomed to the pain of continental warfare, but for Britain it was a new experience. Germany had no exposed flanks, just the imposing fortifications of the Western Front defending their 1914 gains wrested from France and Belgium. Unfortunately, for all their tactical improvements and technical innovations, the British were simply not yet able to breach those defences or kill sufficient Germans, even in concert with the French at Verdun, to bring Germany to its knees. British losses on the Somme totalled 419,654 (131,000 dead), while the

French lost 204,253. The German figures have been endlessly debated, but they probably totalled between 450,000 and 600,000. Ludendorff was all too aware of the implications of the situation.

> GHQ had to bear in mind that the enemy's great superiority in men and material would be even more painfully felt in 1917 than in 1916. They had to face the danger that 'Somme fighting' would soon break out at various points on our fronts, and that even our troops would not be able to withstand such attacks indefinitely, especially if the enemy gave us no time for rest and for the accumulation of material. Our position was uncommonly difficult and a way out hard to find. We could not contemplate an offensive ourselves, having to keep our reserves available for defence. There was no hope of a collapse of any of the Entente Powers. If the war lasted our defeat seemed inevitable. Economically we were in a highly unfavourable position for a war of exhaustion. At home our strength was badly shaken. Questions of the supply of foodstuffs caused great anxiety, and so, too, did questions of morale. We were not undermining the spirits of the enemy populations with starvation blockades and propaganda. The future looked dark.[35]
>
> General Erich Ludendorff, General Headquarters

By the end of 1916 it was the very nature of war that had changed. Success in battle was not necessarily measured in terms of ground gained, unless it included objectives of supreme tactical significance or threatened a genuine breakthrough of prepared fortifications. Perversely, such success only provoked a wild intensification of counter-attacks. By the end of 1916 combatant states had strained every sinew to mobilise all their resources to the cause. Young men had become a national resource to be measured in millions. But millions at arms meant millions of casualties. Germany was a mighty industrial state, its army second to none, and it was not done yet. Verdun and the Somme had raised the threshold of horror but there was far worse to come. For the men caught up in Armegeddon there was little to look forward to.

> I do not think we are any nearer the finish than a year or so ago, except for the fact that many hundreds of thousands more are dead on both sides. I am convinced that the end can only come that way and that at the end there will be nothing but an enormous barrage of enormous shells on both sides and that whichever side has the last few infantry to

face it will win. That is if both sides don't get nerve shattered to death before and give in from pure exhaustion and hatred of it all.[36]

Captain Philip Pilditch, C Battery, 235th Brigade, Royal Field Artillery

This was the authentic voice of despair; Captain Pilditch was not alone.

10

THE EASTERN FRONT, 1916

'All we know is that, sometimes, in our battles with the Russians, we had to remove the mounds of enemy corpses from before our trenches, in order to get a clear field of fire against fresh assaulting waves.'[1]

Field Marshal Paul von Hindenburg, Headquarters, Eastern Front

IN 1916 THE RUSSIANS WOULD DEMONSTRATE their amazing powers of recovery. Yet the underlying problems faced by the Russian Empire had not gone away. The fact that the weak and indecisive Tsar Nicholas II was nominally Commander in Chief could have stood as a metaphor for the undeveloped and primitive state of the country, in thrall to an inefficient and despotic system of government. Yet at the same time the Tsar's symbolic accession to that position also underlined the continuing determination of the Russians to fight on regardless of losses. And the losses had indeed been grievous in 1915. The Russians had plenty more men; indeed, they still mobilised a far smaller percentage of their teeming population than many other nations – as the French did not fail to remind them. But how much longer would the morale of the ordinary Russian soldier hold steady?

Russian resolve would be tested at an early stage of 1916. When Falkenhayn launched his devastating attack at Verdun on the Western Front on 21 February 1916, the French were soon vehemently demanding that the Russians should launch an offensive on the Eastern Front in order to relieve some of the pressure. Nicholas II simply passed on the responsibility to his subordinates on the North and West Fronts. It was decided to attack the Germans in the Belarus area, in what would become known as the Battle of Lake Naroch, with an ambitious pincer movement deploying some 350,000 troops and over 1,000 guns. After a barrage which would commence on 18 March 1916, the Russian infantry would attack in massed waves, while there was also an attempt further north to clear the Germans back from the vital port of Riga. But, as the British were to discover on the Somme on 1 July, an effective barrage requires more than just a large number of guns; in particular, a detailed programme of specifically targeted – and accurately aimed – fire. But the Russian gunners had none of the skills required to draw up a complex gun programme, spot the fall of shot or communicate the necessary corrections to their batteries. Counter-battery work was also weak; they proved unable to target German strongpoints, machine guns or headquarters to any great effect. The result was that some 100,000 Russian casualties were suffered over the two attacks, for minimal gain, while inflicting only 20,000 German losses. All in all, the attacks failed in their primary aim to reduce the pressure on the French.

The Russians were still required to launch a June 1916 offensive, in accordance with promises made at the Chantilly conference of December 1915. But it soon became evident that, after the failure at Lake Naroch, there was a general unwillingness among the senior commanders to risk their reputations further. Indeed, the only general willing to step up to the mark was General Alexei Brusilov, who had recently been appointed commander of the South West Front. When he discovered that eight German divisions had been withdrawn by Falkenhayn and despatched to the Western Front – he was more than willing to use his four armies (the Eighth, Eleventh, Seventh and Ninth Armies) to attack the Austro-Hungarians south of the Pripyat Marshes, with the intention of pushing them back through Galicia. This was none the less an ambitious undertaking, as the Austrian lines by this time were generally well-constructed trench systems equipped with plentiful deep dugouts and covered by copious barbed wire entanglements. However, Brusilov had already established a reputation as by far the most competent and aggressive of the Russian generals. He had also demonstrated a mastery of the new techniques of warfare through a combination of practical experience and diligent study. By 1916 he had managed to produce a blueprint for success, some of which predated the tactical methodology being established on the Western Front. In this he was greatly assisted by his specially selected and highly trained staff officers, who were the men who would have to convert his intentions into action on the ground. He was also assisted by a better supply of shells and guns as the Russian munitions industry slowly improved. Even the supply of rifles had at long last began to approach the number of soldiers serving the Tsar.

Like Joffre and Haig, Brusilov had deduced that an offensive must be carried out on a broad front to reduce the possibility of deadly flanking fire and also to allow for multiple breakthroughs which could further confuse the opposition. He was also convinced that surprise was crucial to success and so he used an advanced deception campaign involving fake wireless messages, the diversionary movement of troops and guns, and the very late deployment of the guns intended to support the ultimate attack. There would be no long bombardment, which would reveal his intentions, but instead his infantry would attack after a relatively short, but tightly focussed, artillery barrage, launching their assault from trenches sapped as far forward as possible in order to reduce the amount of time they spent exposed in No Man's Land. One of Brusilov's important innovations was to hold his reserves close to the front, ready to add immediate weight to faltering attacks, or indeed to respond to any breakthrough opportunities, without the dreadful delays inherent in mass troop movements of any distance on the diabolical Russian railway system. These reserve troops were sheltered out of sight in a series of specially prepared earthworks and dugouts. Brusilov recognised the importance of diligently training his gunners in all aspects of gunnery and then to assign each battery to a specific task, while the Russian Air Service was properly harnessed to provide photographic reconnaissance. Finally, he also recognised the need to improve the training of his infantry prior to the attack; he wanted them to be more than massed cannon fodder. His men had to have a grasp of the basic soldierly skills and were given proper briefings in order to ensure that they knew what was required of them when the moment came. His staff even constructed scale models of the Austrian trenches to allow troops to rehearse their movements. This evinced a considerable degree of tactical innovation, with four distinct waves envisioned: the men in the first wave would carry large numbers of hand grenades and would capture the Austrian first line; the second wave, similarly armed, would push straight on for the second line, which Brusilov believed to be the centre of Austrian resistance; after which the third and fourth waves would drag forward the machine guns for consolidation, while at the same time looking for opportunities to expand the breakthrough. Altogether, Brusilov's innovations marked a new level of military best practice for 1916. As such they would be closely studied by the armies of all the major combatants.

The Austrians noticed some of the preparations in front of their lines, but refused to believe that the Russians were capable of launching anything other than crude mass attacks reliant on the press of numbers alone. Indeed, Conrad was considerably more preoccupied with supervising the offensive he had launched (against German advice) on the Italian front on 4 May than with what Brusilov might be planning on the South-West Front.

Brusilov finally launched his offensive at 04.00 on 4 June 1916. The bombardment worked spectacularly, with the field guns clearing the barbed wire while the heavier guns targeted the Austrian batteries, machine gun posts and command centres. After three hours the guns abruptly stopped, then just as mysteriously resumed again; a pattern that would be repeated several times, successfully confusing the Austrians as to what was happening. Over the next two days, at varying times, the Russian infantry emerged to charge across the narrow No Man's Land, often catching the Austrians unawares deep in their dugouts. In many places whole units surrendered to the Russians, especially those made up of men of minority nationalities, who were no longer willing to sacrifice their lives for the sake of an empire that seemed foreign to them, too. Overall, Austro-Hungarian desertions reached epidemic proportions. Under the coruscating pressure the front collapsed, while multiple breakthroughs triggered further forced withdrawals by the units on the flanks in order to avoid being cut off. Soon the Austrians were falling back all along a 250-mile front stretching from the Pripyat Marshes right down to the Carpathian Mountains. This left only one realistic option for Conrad: appeal for help from the Germans once more.

On 8 June Conrad travelled to Berlin, cap metaphorically in hand, for an audience with the unprepossessing figure of Falkenhayn. It did not go well. An incensed Falkenhayn not only brusquely rejected all thoughts of suspending his Verdun Offensive in order to divert large numbers of German divisions back to the Eastern Front, but he demanded the peremptory suspension of Conrad's precious Italian Offensive. Finally, Falkenhayn revealed his true price for sending German reinforcements: all Austrian units in Galicia would henceforth operate under direct German control. Conrad was furious, but had no choice but to accept this humiliation.

Just as the Germans were flexing their power over the Austrians, the Russians were demonstrating that there was a complete absence of unified direction within the Russian Army itself. While Brusilov had paused to rest his troops he had fully expected that in mid-June General Alexei Evert, in command of the neighbouring West Front, would launch the next phase of the attack designed to maintain the momentum and further stretch the Austrians. Instead, Evert produced a variety of excuses to justify delaying his attacks. So it was that the Brusilov Offensive stalled at the very moment when the man himself was no longer in command of its destiny. While Evert prevaricated, the Germans moved up their reserves, with three divisions grudgingly despatched from the Western Front, where by this time the imminent Anglo-French assault on the Somme was further adding to Falkenhayn's woes. More divisions and numerous artillery batteries were also sent from the accumulated German reserves held on the Eastern Front, while Conrad himself was forced to despatch several divisions from the Italian front. It was the combination of the arrival of these massed reserves and Evert's obtuse inactivity that gave the Central Powers the chance to stabilise the line.

By the time Evert was ready to attack, on 2 July, Brusilov's armies had already returned to the fray, although any visions he might have had of knocking Austria-Hungary out of the war were fast fading. The relative lack of tactical sophistication of Evert's West Front armies when they did belatedly attack was also starkly apparent and their casualties were correspondingly high. Still, Brusilov's South-West Front armies continued to make progress, hurling back the Austrian Fourth, First and Second Armies. Now, though, the Austrians' resolve began to stiffen as German divisions filtered into the line, forming solid blocks to further Russian advances. There was also a deliberate programme of Germanification of the Austrian armies, whereby German officers would take control right down to battalion and even company level.

The late summer of 1916 saw a concerted move by Hindenburg to re-establish his pre-eminent position. He had been nominally in charge of the German Army in the east, but had hitherto been adroitly sidestepped by Falkenhayn, who had appointed first General August von Mackensen and then Prince Leopold of Bavaria to command independent groups of armies in both the central and southern sectors of the front, leaving Hindenburg with direct control only of the northern armies. However, Falkenhayn's position was fast deteriorating, due to the perceived failure of his Western Front strategy. Hindenburg saw his chance and demanded the appointment of a unified Commander in Chief on the Eastern Front. Naturally, he had only one person in mind for the task – himself. By this time all Falkenhayn's political capital had been expended and he was obliged, at least theoretically, to accept the need for a unified command. Conrad had even more reason to object, but he was just a pauper at the German table and could be safely ignored. Thus it was that at the end of July 1916, Hindenburg was confirmed as Commander in Chief of all the armies of the Central Powers on the Eastern Front. Falkenhayn's fall was imminent and he was finally replaced as the German Chief of General Staff by his old adversary Hindenburg on 29 August 1916.

The Russian troops now surged across Galicia, advancing towards the foothills of the Carpathians, although they were still nowhere near as far advanced as they had been in 1915. The offensive would continue deep into September, but the rate of Russian casualties was rising steeply. Perhaps even more disturbing, the incidence of desertions from the Russian armies began to escalate under the twin impacts of war weariness and excessive casualties suffered to little or no avail. Even to Brusilov it had become apparent that ultimate victory was dependent on defeating Germany, which seemed as unlikely as ever. Failing to capitalise on their numerical advantage, the Russian attacks were either incompetently handled or, where successful, unsupported through the chaos endemic in the Russian High Command.

One consequence of the relative success of the Brusilov Offensive was to convince Rumania that now was the time to join the Entente Allies. Bordered by Russia, Austria-Hungary, Serbia and Bulgaria, she had the misfortune to be weaker than any of them. The Rumanian Army had not yet recovered from the drubbing it had received in the debacle of the Balkan Wars; nor had it undergone a programme of much-needed modernisation. Many members of the Rumanian royal family and politicians were overtly pro-German, but the country's best opportunities for profitable national expansion all seemed to involve the break-up of the Austro-Hungarian Empire. The British had already promised Rumania the acquisition of Transylvania if it joined the Allies and the Russian successes in the summer of 1916 meant that it was now or never. The Rumanians were well aware that once the Russians occupied the provinces of Bukovina and Transylvania they would never voluntarily relinquish them; these provinces were therefore the price demanded by the Rumanians for joining the war on the side of the Allies. The Russians were naturally dubious, doubting the worth of the Rumanian Army, but the political advantages of another ally seemed to outweigh the disadvantages. Thus it was that Rumania declared war on Austria-Hungary on 27 August 1916 and promptly invaded Transylvania via the passes through the Carpathians and Transylvanian Alps. It would prove a momentous decision, but not quite in the way that the Rumanians had hoped.

Newly installed as the German Chief of Staff, Hindenburg reacted immediately. He used the unified command established in the Eastern Front (now handed over to Field Marshal Prince Leopold of Bavaria) to good effect. Two armies were swiftly established from disparate elements of German, Austrian, Bulgarian and Turkish units: one, the Army of the Danube, was to be commanded by the ubiquitous Mackensen and would invade Rumania from their Bulgarian frontier in the south in early September; the other, the German Ninth Army, would first rebuff the Rumanian invasion of Transylvania, then invade Rumania from the west. This would be led by none other than Falkenhayn himself, eager to repair his reputation on the field of battle. It soon became clear that the Rumanian armies would be incapable of prolonged resistance. Even the wide waters of the Danube could not stop Mackensen, while Falkenhayn eventually burst through the deep passes of the Transylvanian Alps in mid-November. By now the hapless Rumanians were in a state of collapse and there was nothing their new allies could do to help them. On 6 December, Mackensen entered Bucharest in triumph and the Rumanians were forced to acknowledge defeat. The Ploiesti oil fields, thirty-five miles north of the capital, were also over-run and, despite the Allies' dramatic attempts at sabotage by firing the wells, they would prove an invaluable prize to the oil-starved Central Powers. Over the next year the Germans would ravage Rumania for much-needed supplies of oil, grain, farm animals and wood, succeeding to an extent in defraying the inconveniences of the British blockade in the North Sea. All told, the Rumanian interlude had been a disaster for the Allies and a morale-boosting victory with very tangible rewards for the Central Powers.

11

THE SEA WAR, 1916

'This time perhaps, "Der Tag" as we also called it had dawned at last. That evening the thrill was immensely multiplied, for everybody seemed to have a premonition that the day had really arrived. There was an almost electric atmosphere of expectation and suppressed excitement as officers and men went about the work of preparing for sea.'[1]

Midshipman John Croome, HMS *Indomitable*, 3rd Battlecruiser Squadron

IN JANUARY 1916 THE COMPLEXION OF THE NAVAL WAR changed with the replacement of the ineffectual Admiral Hugo von der Pohl as commander of the German High Seas Fleet by the far more dynamic Admiral Reinhard Scheer. The fleet had spent most of 1915 in harbour maintaining its status as a 'fleet in being' not to be risked in action, while the U-boats had been withdrawn from the Atlantic and English Channel. This had allowed the Royal Navy to exert an almost unchallenged domination of the oceans. On taking over, Scheer was determined to find a fit and proper role for the High Seas Fleet. But he faced a considerable distraction early on when, in February 1916, it was decided to resume the U-boat campaign in the war zone around Britain. This meant that attacks were allowed without warning within the zone, but not of unarmed merchant ships outside of the zone, and no attacks on passenger liners anywhere at all. This was far too complicated for U-boat commanders to follow under circumstances of great stress and confusion. Errors of judgement were pre-dictable and, on 24 March 1916, the French ferry steamer *Sussex* was mis-taken for a minelayer and torpedoed by the *UB-29* coastal submarine in the English Channel. Although she did not sink, several of the passengers injured in the attack were American and once again there was a storm of protest from across the Atlantic. In April American President Woodrow Wilson fired his own shot across the bows of the U-boats.

> I have deemed it my duty, therefore, to say to the Imperial German Government that if it is still its purpose to prosecute relentless and indiscriminate warfare against vessels of commerce by the use of submarines, notwithstanding the now demonstrated impossibility of conducting that warfare in accordance with what the Government of the United States must consider the sacred and indisputable rules of international law and the universally recognized dictates of humanity, the Government of the United States is at last forced to the conclusion that there is but one course it can pursue; and that unless the Imperial German Government should now immediately declare and effect an abandonment of its present methods of warfare against passenger and freight carrying vessels this Government can have no choice but to sever diplomatic relations with the Government of the German Empire altogether.[2]
>
> President Woodrow Wilson

Unwilling to risk war with America, the German government gave way without demur and the U-boats were meekly ordered to follow all the stipulations of international law. But this rendered the U-boats themselves far too vulnerable and they were withdrawn to port.

This setback nevertheless provided Scheer with the opportunity to use his otherwise idle submarines as an integral part in his plans to rein-vigorate the naval war against Britain. He was no longer prepared to allow the Grand Fleet to exercise all the benefits of naval supremacy without ever having that put to the test.

> England's purpose of strangling Germany economically without seriously exposing her own fleet to the German guns had to be defeated. This offensive effort on our part was intensified by the fact that the prohibition of the U-Boat trade war made it impossible for us to aim a direct blow at England's vital nerve. We were therefore bound

to try and prove by all possible means that Germany's High Seas Fleet
was able and willing to wage war with England at sea.[3]

Admiral Reinhard Scheer, SMS *Friedrich der Grosse*

His methods of achieving this demanded the deployment of every possible German naval resource in leading the Grand Fleet into a trap in
which a significant element of the fleet could be destroyed, thereby allowing a serious challenge by the High Seas Fleet on more equal terms. In
practice this meant drawing the main fleet into a submarine or mine trap
and/or cutting off and defeating in detail the Battlecruiser Force under
the command of Admiral Sir David Beatty. Scheer raised the tempo by
resuming sweeps into the North Sea and bombarding both Lowestoft and
Yarmouth on 25 April. This increased activity did not escape the attention of Jellicoe, who was none the less determined to maintain his unro-
mantic, but effective, domination of the seas. While his ships successfully
effected an economic blockade on Germany, British trade was continuing
relatively unhampered, the lines of communication of British land forces
were not being seriously threatened and there was no chance of a successful German invasion of Britain. Jellicoe kept the bulk of the Grand Fleet
safely tucked away at Scapa Flow, although he had begun to think of ways
of provoking a clash with the High Seas Fleet on favourable terms.

By mid-1916 Jellicoe had received a very welcome reinforcement in
the Fifth Battle Squadron, composed of the *Queen Elizabeth* class super-
dreadnoughts. These behemoths were a portent of the future, the gradual
fusion of the dreadnought and battlecruiser concepts to create mighty
battleships that boasted a displacement of 27,500 tons, with eight 15-inch
guns that could fire a 1,920-pound shell accurately up to about 24,000
yards, protected by armour up to 13 inches thick and propelled by huge
oil-fired turbine engines that gave them a speed of nearly 24 knots. When
it was decided to address the proven inadequacies in the gunnery standards achieved by the Battlecruiser Force by sending squadrons one at a
time to practise in the open spaces of Scapa Flow, the Fifth Battle Squadron was the obvious temporary replacement.

The Battle of Jutland

By May 1916 both sides were planning aggressive operations: Jellicoe was intent on entrapping the High Seas Fleet, while Scheer was trying to force a mistake from his cautious opponent. In the end it would be Scheer who triggered the Battle of Jutland by launching a sweep into the Skagerrak, south-east of Norway, to prey on any British light forces there, with the aim of entrapping Beatty and pulling Jellicoe out into a submarine ambush. But, helped by the remarkable work of the intelligence specialists of Room 40 in decoding German wireless signals, Jellicoe was forewarned that Scheer was about to sail; indeed, the Grand Fleet left Scapa Flow late on 30 May before the High Seas Fleet had even put to sea. It was an amazing sight as the mighty dreadnoughts emerged, their very names embodying an enduring naval tradition that stretched back across three centuries. Young Midshipman John Croome watched in awe from the *Indomitable*, which with the rest of 3rd Battlecruiser Squadron had been practising its gunnery at Scapa Flow.

> The grey monsters wheeled in succession and silent majesty which marks the departure to sea of a perfectly trained fleet. Finally as the last of the long line passed us, we in turn began to swing, weighed the last few links of cable and stole stealthily away in the wake of the Grand Fleet. A more powerful exhibition of majestic strength and efficiency devised solely for the utter destruction of the enemy it would be hard to imagine and the impression upon my youthful mind can never be erased. Moreover, I was proudly conscious that I was part of this huge machine and firmly convinced that the machine was invincible, if not even invulnerable.[4]
>
> Midshipman **John Croome**, HMS *Indomitable*, 3rd Battlecruiser Squadron

They were steaming into a trap. The Germans had eighteen U-boats waiting outside their bases. Yet Scheer would suffer an early disappointment when his submarine ambush and the associated newly laid minefields failed to have any impact whatsoever. The oceans were large and the compact formation of the Grand Fleet passed by unobserved and unscathed.

Jellicoe had arranged a rendezvous with Beatty and the Battlecruiser Force some ninety miles from the Skagerrak at 14.00 on 31 May. The whole situation was then confused when the intelligence from Room 40 was misinterpreted by Admiralty staff and both Jellicoe and Beatty were erroneously informed at 12.30 that the High Seas Fleet was not at sea after all. This would have considerable repercussions. The result was that the two fleets were drawing ever closer to each other, but neither had any idea that their opponents were at sea. In fact the light forces made only accidental contact when both sides went to investigate a harmless merchant ship that happened to be sailing between the fleets. Once cleared for action, firing between the cruisers began at 14.28 on 31 May 1916. The Battle of Jutland had begun.

Hipper's battlecruisers fell back to the south, intending to draw Beatty on to Scheer's unseen High Seas Fleet. However, as Beatty ordered the pursuit, he utterly failed to concentrate his forces, allowing a 10-mile gap to open between the 1st and 2nd Battlecruiser Squadrons and the Fifth Battle Squadron This was a two-stage process: first, his original dispositions had placed the super-dreadnoughts some five miles behind his flagship the *Lion*, but then this was exacerbated by a further confusion over signalling protocol. Not for the first time, Beatty and his staff would betray their poor understanding of modern communication methods and the necessity for tight command and control in battle.

As the range closed between the opposing battlecruisers there was considerable tension before fire was finally opened between the battlecruisers at 15.48. Right from the start, the German gunnery was disconcertingly accurate and it was not long before it drew blood. The *Lion* was badly hit when at 16.00 a 12-inch shell crashed on to the 'Q' turret, causing a fire that, had the magazine not eventually been flooded, would surely have doomed the ship. At the back of the line the *Indefatigable* was not so lucky when 11-inch shells from the *Von der Tann* crashed home triggering a vast explosion that killed all but two of the ship's company of 1,019 men. Then, at about 16.21, there was a huge explosion as the *Queen Mary* was hit by shells from the *Seydlitz* and *Derfflinger*.

> Everything in the ship went as quiet as a church, the floor of the turret was bulged up and the guns were absolutely useless. I must mention here that there was not a sign of excitement. One man turned to me and said, 'What do you think has happened?' I said, 'Steady, everyone, I will speak to Mr Ewart.' I went back to the cabinet and said, 'What do you think has happened, Sir?' He said, 'God only knows!' 'Well, Sir,' I said, 'it's no use keeping them all down here, why not send them up

round the 4" guns and give them a chance to fight it out.' I put my head through the hole in the roof of the turret and I nearly fell through again. The after 4" Battery was smashed right out of all recognition and then I noticed that the ship had an awful list to port. I dropped back inside and told Lieutenant Ewart the state of affairs. He said, 'Francis, we can do no more than give them a chance, clear the turret.' 'Clear the turret!' I called out and out they went. Lieutenant Ewart was following me; suddenly he stopped and went back into the turret. I believe he went back because he thought there was someone left inside. When I got to the ship's side there seemed to be a fair crowd and they did not appear to be very anxious to take to the water. I called out to them, 'Come on, you chaps, who's coming for a swim?' Someone answered, 'She will float for a long time yet!' But something, I don't pretend to understand what it was, seemed to be urging me to get away, so I clambered up over the slimy bilge keel and fell off into the water, followed I should think by about five more men.[5]

Petty Officer Ernest Francis, HMS *Queen Mary*, 1st Battlecruiser Squadron

A few seconds later the *Queen Mary* was blown to pieces, killing 1,266 of her crew. Beatty, however, was unmoved, as witnessed by his Flag Captain, Alfred Chatfield.

I was standing beside Sir David Beatty and we both turned round in time to see the unpleasant spectacle. The thought of my friends in her flashed through my mind; I thought also how lucky we had evidently been in the *Lion*. Beatty turned to me and said, 'There seems to be something wrong with our bloody ships today!' A remark that needed neither comment nor answer. There *was* something wrong.[6]

Flag Captain Alfred Chatfield, HMS *Lion*, 1st Battlecruiser Squadron

It was simple: the armour of the British battlecruisers was not thick enough to withstand the shells of their German equivalents. And, once a shell had penetrated their armour, the inadequate anti-flash precautions coupled with dangerous working practices intended to improve the rate of fire meant that a flash could rip from the working chambers down into the magazine below, with disastrous consequences. No ship could survive such an explosion. This second disaster left Beatty badly outnumbered, although the Fifth Battle Squadron had at last, by cutting corners, begun to catch up and was beginning to engage the rear ships of the German line.

Meanwhile Beatty had sent his destroyers into the attack at 16.09. As the German light forces responded, the No Man's Land between the opposing lines of battlecruisers was filled with destroyers.

> In a matter of minutes we were caught up in a maelstrom of whirling ships as we swerved and jockeyed for a breakthrough position. We were under helm most of the time, the ship heeling as she spun. Events moved far too quickly for stereotyped gun control procedure and we let fire at anything hostile that came within our arc of fire. It became a personal affair and I have a vivid recollection of the sweating Trainer cursing as he strove to change his point of aim from ship to ship as I tried to seize fleeting opportunities. Quite apart from the difficulty in making split second decisions on friend or foe our legitimate enemies swept past at aggregate speeds of up to 60 knots and there was scant time to make a wild guess at range and deflection and get the gun pointed and fired before the chance passed and we were frantically trying to focus on a new target. It was quite impossible to pick out one's own fall of shot in a sea pocked with shell splashes, nor was there time to correct the range had we been able to do so. We fired many rounds at more or less point blank range but had no idea if any found their mark though several bright flashes gave hope that we had inflicted punishment. In the heat of swift action senses become keyed up by the high tempo and feeling for time is lost. I would have been at a loss to say if we had been engaged for minutes or hours. Crowding incidents made it seem an eternity and yet the period of action passed in a flash.[7]
>
> Sub-Lieutenant Henry Oram, HMS *Obdurate*, 13th Flotilla

The two forces cancelled each other and little of note was achieved. Even though the *Seydlitz* was hit by one torpedo, the resulting damage barely impeded her progress. The German battlecruisers were indeed proving tough opponents.

By this time Hipper had succeeded in leading Beatty almost into the very jaws of Scheer and his High Seas Fleet. Scouting ahead of Beatty, the 2nd Light Cruiser Squadron sighted the long line of approaching German dreadnoughts. It was a chilling moment: exciting, but at the same time threatening. On board the *Lion* Beatty reacted with exemplary speed and decisiveness. After checking the sighting, he reversed course and headed straight back towards the Grand Fleet, seeking to reverse the situation and lead the High Seas Fleet into the grip of the Grand Fleet. Sadly, a further signalling blunder needlessly endangered the Fifth Battle Squadron when it was allowed to continue sailing south after the battlecruisers had turned, before conforming belatedly. The chance to cut off and destroy the Fifth Battle Squadron represented a great opportunity for Scheer and during the run to the north German shells crashed around and about the mighty super-dreadnoughts. But their thick armour prevented anything but superficial damage. Meanwhile, their own 15-inch shells were crashing down on the German battlecruisers and the leading dreadnoughts of the High Seas Fleet.

> We suffered bad hits, two or three heavy shells striking us during this phase. When a heavy shell hit the armour of our ship, the terrific crash of the explosion was followed by a vibration of the whole ship, affecting even the conning tower. The shells which exploded in the interior of the ship caused rather a dull roar, which was transmitted all over by the countless voice-pipes and telephones. This part of the action, fought against a numerically inferior but more powerfully armed enemy, who kept us under fire at ranges at which we were helpless, was highly depressing, nerve-wracking, and exasperating. Our only means of defence was to leave the line for a short time when we saw that the enemy had our range. As this manoeuvre was imperceptible to the enemy, we extricated ourselves at regular intervals from the hail of fire.[8]
>
> Commander Georg von Hase, SMS *Derfflinger*, 1st Scouting Group

Although the thicker armour of the German battlecruisers prevented any catastrophic damage, their fighting ability was being rapidly eroded. All in all, this phase of the battle would prove a deep disappointment for the Germans.

Worse still, unbeknownst to Scheer, every minute he steamed north brought the High Seas Fleet ever closer to Jellicoe's massed guns. The Grand Fleet was sailing in six tight-knit columns each of four ships, with the 3rd Battlecruiser Squadron forging ahead and the whole ensemble surrounded by screens of light cruisers and destroyers. Jellicoe was naturally desperate for accurate information on the whereabouts of Scheer's High Seas Fleet, but unfortunately Beatty failed to send any useful reports during this crucial period. As the main fleets closed, the British and German screens clashed in a series of skirmishes which proved disastrous for ships suddenly caught unawares. Jellicoe would soon have to make the final decision on how to deploy his fleet. Tension ratcheted up on the bridge of his flagship the *Iron Duke* and even when Beatty finally hove into view Jellicoe still did not know exactly where the German dreadnoughts were. Finally, at 18.01, he signalled in desperation, 'Where is the enemy fleet?' Beatty replied: 'Enemy's battlecruisers bearing South East.'[9] This did not answer the question. Where was Scheer and the High Seas Fleet?

> Before it is possible for anyone to realise the difficulties which confronted me as Commander in Chief of the Grand Fleet at the Battle of Jutland it is essential for a clear idea to be formed and clearly kept in view of the two main factors to which those difficulties were entirely due. These two factors were: 1) The absence of even approximately correct information from the Battlecruiser Fleet and its attendant light cruisers regarding the position, formation and strength of the High Seas Fleet. 2) The lack of visibility when the Battle Fleet came in sight of a portion of the High Seas Fleet, due largely to mist, and partly to smoke from our own battlecruisers and other vessels.[10]
>
> Admiral Sir John Jellicoe, HMS *Iron Duke*, Fourth Battle Squadron

In these circumstances Jellicoe's priority was to make sure that the Grand Fleet did not lose control of the seas. He was not willing to risk everything for the sake of a short-term victory. At last the news came and he sprang into action at 18.16. He could not deploy on the starboard column as the ships were already too close to the German fleet, so he formed up on the port column, creating a huge line ahead, with all guns bearing on the head of the German line: or 'crossing the T', as it was called. This supremely pragmatic decision would set the tone for the next phase of the battle.

Ahead of the Grand Fleet the 1st Cruiser Squadron, commanded by Rear Admiral Sir Robert Arbuthnot aboard the *Defence*, was suddenly caught under the very guns of the onrushing German fleet. In a few seconds the *Defence* was sent to the bottom while, behind her, the *Warrior* was pelted with shells. Below decks Engineer Commander Henry Kitching was going about his duties.

> I heard a tremendous explosion at the after end, a heavy jar went through the whole fabric and most of the lights went out. Immediately afterwards there was a heavy roar of water and steam and my impression was that we had been torpedoed. Several men came running

forward from that end, one of them with blood streaming down his face. In that moment I realised fully what cold drawn funk is like. But I had to make a decision and, advancing towards the after end, I tried to gauge the extent of the damage. The engines still went on running, which seemed to show that the cylinders had not been hit, but in the dim uncertain light I perceived what appeared to be Niagara at the after end of the engine room though whether the sheet of water was rising up from below or pouring down from above I couldn't be sure at the time. Anyhow, a blast of steam on my face warned me that I hadn't long to think about it and I soon made up my mind that no pumps could deal with the quantity of water that was coming in, and that the only thing to do was to get the men out as quickly as possible.[11]

Engineer Commander Henry Kitching, HMS *Warrior*, 1st Cruiser Squadron

Trapped below decks they had to find their way out from a ship that seemed to be sinking beneath their very feet.

At first the men didn't know what to do, as the ladders at the after end were inaccessible, but I shouted to them to go up the midships ladder and hustled all towards it in front of me. As soon as it appeared that they had all gone up, I followed them myself, but by that time all the lights had gone out and it was pitch dark. When I got to the top, knowing it was hopeless to go aft, I turned forward and felt my way by the handrails along the platform at the tops of the cylinders towards the door at the fore end, which communicated with the port engine room and with the mess deck. When I got there, however, a stoker told me that we could not get through there, as the mess deck was on fire, and when I tried to do so I was met with a rush of thick smoke and blinding fumes that drove me back. At this moment with this in front and the roar of steam behind me I felt like a trapped rat, for there seemed to be no possibility of lifting the heavy armoured hatches overhead, and a spasm of sheer terror came over me; but just then I realised that the man was calling my attention to a glimmer of light above, and the next minute I found myself climbing out though a torn rent in the deck.[12]

Engineer Commander Henry Kitching, HMS *Warrior*, 1st Cruiser Squadron

While the crew of the *Warrior* awaited the German shells that would surely send them to the bottom, the Germans were distracted by the arrival of the Fifth Battle Squadron manoeuvring to join the main battle line of the

Grand Fleet. As they did so the *Warspite* was hit by numerous shells, suffered damage to her steering and began circling randomly between the fleets. An obvious target, only her magnificent armour protected her from terminal damage and, once control was regained, she was able to make it back to port without undue drama. But she had distracted the German gunners from their hounding of the hapless *Warrior*, which was also able to limp away.

Amidst Jellicoe's deployment, the ships of the 3rd Battlecruiser Squadron had taken station at the head of the line. As their guns blazed out, they deluged Hipper's battlecruisers with shells. The changing light conditions meant that the Germans could not see their tormentors and their response was ineffectual. Then, just for a few moments, the mists parted and the German shells crashed down in retaliation on the *Invincible*. Fisher's dictum that 'speed would be her armour' was tested to destruction and swiftly found wanting when she blew up with shocking violence at 18.34. Marine Bryan Gasson was acting as a rangefinder inside the 'Q' starboard midships turret.

> Suddenly our turret manned was struck between the two 12″ guns and appeared to me to lift off the top of the turret and another of the same salvo followed. The flashes passed down to both midship magazines containing 50 tons of cordite. The explosion broke the ship in half. I owe my survival, I think, to the fact that I was in a separate compartment at the back of the turret with my head through a hole cut in the top. Some of the initial flash must have got through to my compartment as I was burnt on the hands, arms and head – luckily my eyes escaped, I must have instinctively covered them with my hands. The rangefinder and myself had only a light armour covering. I think this came off and, as the ship sunk, I floated to the surface.[13]
>
> Marine Bryan Gasson, HMS *Invincible*, 3rd Battlecruiser Squadron

Just six survived of the crew of 1,032 men. The ship split in the middle, its two halves resting upright on the seabed in a haunting scene that was etched on the minds of everyone who saw it.

The sinking of the *Invincible* was a triumph, but it did not change the difficult tactical situation facing the High Seas Fleet. Jellicoe's dreadnoughts were now arraigned in one long line so that their shells rained down on the exposed vanguard of the German fleet, causing serious damage and threatening annihilation. Scheer had to act quickly.

I could see nothing of our cruisers, which were still farther forward. Owing to the turning aside that was inevitable in drawing nearer, they found themselves between the fire of both lines. For this reason I decided to turn our line and bring it on to an opposite course. Otherwise an awkward situation would have arisen round the pivot which the enemy line by degrees was passing, as long-distance shots from the enemy would certainly have hit our rear ships. As regards the effectiveness of the artillery, the enemy was more favourably situated, as our ships stood out against the clear western horizon, whereas his own ships were hidden by the smoke and mist of the battle. A running artillery fight on a southerly course would therefore not have been advantageous to us.[14]

Admiral Reinhard Scheer, SMS *Friedrich der Grosse*, Third Battle Squadron

Scheer ordered a specially developed battle turn to starboard, a manoeuvre whereby the ship at the rear of the line would put her helm over first, followed by each successive ship in sequence, rippling along the line towards the front. As the German ships disappeared from his vision, Jellicoe had to decide whether to follow them into the mist and hazard everything to complete the victory, or to settle for a more cautious approach. Rather than follow in the German tracks, risking, for all he knew, mines, submarines and destroyers, Jellicoe decided to hold on a little further to the east and then turned south to place himself between the High Seas Fleet and its base at Wilhelmshaven. His manoeuvre was soon justified when, at 18.55, Scheer ordered a second battle turn to bring his ships on to an easterly course. This meant Scheer's dreadnoughts were heading directly towards the British line. From 19.10 they came under an increasingly devastating fire. Scheer took near-instant action and, at 19.13, he ordered a further battle turn away while the battered battlecruisers and destroyers were ordered forward to cover the retreat. As the shells rained down they suffered terrible damage. No British battlecruiser could have survived this kind of assault, but Scheer's ships had better armour, superior gunnery safety procedures and were better subdivided below decks into watertight compartments. Meanwhile, the German destroyers were churning their way towards the British line, launching torpedoes, thereby giving the wounded German battlecruisers time to slink back into the mists. Now Jellicoe had to decide whether he would turn towards the Germans, turn away or simply hold course and face the consequences.

The alternatives to a turn away were a turn towards, or holding the course and dodging the torpedoes. A turn towards would have led to great danger if the first attack had been followed by a second and a third, and no one could say that this would not be the case. To hold on and dodge might meet with success if the tracks could be seen. Information had reached me that the Germans had succeeded in making the tracks of their torpedoes more or less invisible. Therefore there was danger in this alternative.[15]

Admiral Sir John Jellicoe, HMS *Iron Duke*, Fourth Battle Squadron

His caution has been condemned by populist commentators who believe he should have turned towards the High Seas Fleet, thereby triggering a final decisive action. But Jellicoe's innate caution was grounded on a realistic assessment of what could and could not be risked to achieve the destruction of the High Seas Fleet. For the moment contact was lost, but his Grand Fleet still remained between Scheer and the sanctuary of the German home ports. Over the next hour brief flurries of action blew up as various detachments of the fleets encountered each other in the rapidly fading light. Unsurprisingly, little of importance was achieved by either side. By 21.00, when the light had completely faded away, it remained to be seen whether Scheer could evade the Grand Fleet during the night and return to port or would he be fended off and forced to fight a decisive fleet action come the dawn.

To Jellicoe the Germans appeared to have several options: to sail back north-east and pass through the Skagerrak into the Baltic; to go via Horns Reef north of the British minefields filling the Heligoland Bight; to take the navigationally tricky passage that went right through the minefields; or try and sail south of the minefields to pass along the north Friesian coast to safety. As several of his battlecruisers were close to sinking, Scheer had little choice but to take the shortest feasible route, which was via Horns Reef. But Jellicoe was in ignorance of this and, given the last reported German position, he decided that the route via the north Friesian coast was the most likely option. He therefore set his battle fleet on a steady southerly course at a speed of 17 knots. His destroyer flotillas would follow some five miles behind the fleet, to cover the Horns Reef channel and the minefield gap options, while at the same time removing them from the possibility of being involved in accidental clashes with the Grand Fleet in the pitch dark. The High Seas Fleet was now sailing on a directly converging course, with Jellicoe's destroyers at the rear of the line.

A series of confused actions followed as the High Seas Fleet crashed into the destroyer flotillas. Unlike the Germans, the British lacked properly shuttered searchlights, had no star shells and scant knowledge of the techniques required in making night-identification signals. Wary of the black shapes moving towards them, yet terrified of opening fire in error on their own dreadnoughts, the British light forces proved easy meat for the Germans who, by contrast, had been well drilled in night fighting. The clashes began about 21.40. There could be no co-ordinated action. But, worst of all, nobody told Jellicoe some five miles ahead what was happening.

One typical incident occurred when the 4th Flotilla encountered a line of German dreadnoughts led by the *Westfalen* at about 23.15. In the darkness the British challenged, at which point the dazzling German searchlights blazed on and the 11-inch turrets and secondary 5.9-inch batteries crashed out.

> They were so close that I remember the guns seemed to be firing from some appreciable height above us. At about the same instant the *Tipperary* shook violently from the impact of being hit by shells. I was told afterwards that the first salvo hit the bridge and it must have killed the Captain and everyone there. I opened fire with the after guns as soon as the enemy opened on us. Proper spotting was out of the question, but crouching behind the canvas screen of my control position – I felt much safer with this thin weather screen between me and the enemy guns, though it wouldn't have kept out a spent rifle bullet – I yelled at the guns to fire. I don't think they heard me, but they opened fire all right. During this time both our starboard torpedo tubes were fired, but the enemy was so close that I think that the initial dive that torpedoes usually take as they enter the water made them go under the enemy ships. The enemy's second salvo hit and burst one of our main steam pipes, and the after part of the ship was enveloped in a cloud of steam through which I could see nothing.[16]
>
> Sub-Lieutenant Newton William-Powlett, HMS *Tipperary*, 4th Flotilla

From another ship in the flotilla, the *Spitfire*, it was a terrible sight.

We closed the *Tipperary*, now a mass of burning wreckage and looking a very sad sight indeed. At a distance her bridge, wheelhouse and charthouse appeared to be one sheet of flame, giving one the impression of a burning house and so bright was the light from this part that it seemed to obliterate one's vision of the remainder of the ship and of the sea round about, except that part close to her which was all lit up, reflecting the flames.[17]

Lieutenant Athelstan Bush, HMS *Spitfire*, 4th Flotilla

Again and again the British officers saw their enemies and had a brief opportunity to launch deadly concentrated torpedo attacks, but they lacked the courage of their convictions to take sufficiently bold action as they sought more confirmation that the blackened shapes slipping by were indeed German dreadnoughts. As they waited, so their chances slipped away. In one last attack the 12th Flotilla managed a direct hit and sank the pre-dreadnought *Pommern,* exploding her magazine and killing all 844 of her crew. Yet the bulk of the High Seas Fleet swept past without further damage.

At the same time the crippled German battlecruisers were limping their way through the British columns of dreadnoughts. They were sighted at various times by British officers, but in the inspiring words of Captain James Fergusson of the *Thunderer*, 'It was considered inadvisable to show up battle fleet unless obvious attack was intended.'[18] And so the battered *Moltke*, which he had had squarely in his sights, escaped to fight another day. The *Seydlitz* was another beneficiary of this incredible laxness.

In this situation, the aft look-out reported: 'Several large ships, darkened, approaching from astern.' Our night glasses showed four huge ships, British, no more than 2,000 yards away. Blast! They must have seen us and would therefore open fire at any moment. Should we try to ram? But their guns were still trained fore and aft! Our ship was too heavily damaged to attack, and I gave the orders: 'Hard a-starboard, full speed ahead, engine room make as much smoke as possible – give British recognition signal.' A yeoman flashed the latter, 'J', the leading ship promptly answered, 'O'. That was the only light they showed for they had an excellently darkened ship. In a minute we got up so much smoke that they disappeared from view.[19]

Captain Moritz von Egidy, SMS *Seydlitz*, 1st Scouting Group

None of the British dreadnoughts, belying their proud names, dared open fire. Only the *Lutzow* went down and, even then, she was vanquished as much by the sea as by her opponents. She had been so badly damaged that she had no hope of getting home and was eventually scuttled at about 01.45 on 1 June. At about roughly the same time the severely battered light cruiser the *Wiesbaden* also finally sank beneath the waves.

> A terrible gargling came from inside the ship, and we noticed we had slipped a little further to starboard. We realised that we would die a sailor's death. Now everything went as quick as a flash. The ship lay further over to starboard, sinking deeper. I ran to the quarterdeck, undid the mooring of a rescue raft and climbed onboard and pushed off the starboard side. Lying on my knees I paddled with my hands desperately to the rear, to escape the suction when the ship sank. Everything was quite quiet. The companions who stood on deck jumped off towards aft and swam to my raft. We saw our wounded companions, who were lying on deck and who had previously in part fallen asleep from exhaustion, slide from the ship into the water. Now our ship *Wiesbaden* sank before our eyes. Until the last her masts towered from the water and our battle flag, which blew from the spanker gaff, slowly sank into the waves. We looked around ourselves. We floated between dead companions, dead fishes, hammocks and life jackets. Where this trip would take us nobody could say. We had to leave ourselves to our destiny. I asked my God not to let it last too long. All the feelings of confidence had disappeared from me. As long as one has a ship below oneself one hopes; but when one hangs in the water on a raft, the cold slowly rises from the toes and then slowly the limbs go stiff.[20]
>
> Stoker Hugo Zenne, SMS *Wiesbaden*, 2nd Scouting Group

One by one his comrades lost their battle with the freezing cold and slipped away. Zenne was picked up by a Norwegian steamer some thirty-eight hours later, the only survivor from the gallant *Wiesbaden* crew.

So, why did Jellicoe not react to the signs of battle behind him? It would appear that, in the complete absence of wireless reports to the contrary, he considered these to be just clashes between the British and German light forces. In this Jellicoe was certainly guilty of an error of judgement, and he should have been more pro-active in trying to determine what was occurring. But at the same time this is to ignore the draining exhaustion of battle and the enormous stress that he was under – and profits from the simple certainties of hindsight. A further subplot was the interception by Room 40 back in London of several of Scheer's wireless messages. These were sent in summary form to Jellicoe: 'German battle fleet ordered home at 9.14 pm. Battlecruisers to the rear. Course south-south-east ¾ east. Speed 16 knots.' This clearly indicated Scheer was intent on taking the Horns Reef route, but when it was passed to Jellicoe at 23.15 he did not believe it – after all, had he not been told the High Seas Fleet was not at sea? The Admiralty had also, by combining the signals into one outline briefing, inadvertently concealed crucial information from Jellicoe, such as Scheer's signal ordering an airship reconnaissance cover at Horns Reef. So it was that the Grand Fleet sailed on, preparing for a renewed battle at dawn; a battle that would never be.

Come the dawn Scheer was safely on his way back to Wilhelmshaven, which he reached in the early afternoon of 1 June. For the disappointed men of the Grand Fleet, dawn brought only the miserable realisation that the High Seas Fleet had escaped retribution. There was little they could do but bury their dead.

> The ship had slowed down and there was a burial going on of the poor unrecognisable scraps of humanity from the explosion. I had been asked previously to try and identify Young and Cotton, but it was impossible. It was a gloomy scene, the grey sky, the grey sea, the stitched-up hammocks, the padre with his gown blowing in the breeze. The 'Last Post' was sounded by the Marine buglers and our shipmates plunged into the sullen waters.[21]
>
> Surgeon Lieutenant Duncan Lorimer, HMS *Malaya*, Fifth Battle Squadron

The British ships made their way dolorously back to their home ports.

But who had won the battle? The Germans were back in port first and staked their claim with considerable vigour, exaggerating the numbers of ships they had sunk and concealing some of their own losses. Indeed, they had sunk 3 British battlecruisers, 3 armoured cruisers and 8 destroyers, while the British had accounted for just 1 German battlecruiser, 1 pre-dreadnought, 4 light cruisers and 5 destroyers. In the Grand Fleet the prevailing mood was one of deep disappointment that it had not managed to destroy the High Seas Fleet. But on 2 June 1916 it still had twenty-four dreadnoughts and battlecruisers ready for action, as opposed to just ten available to Scheer. Furthermore the Germans failed in their ambition to destroy a significant portion of the Grand Fleet, whether by submarine trap or in battle. The British losses, although costing the lives of 6,094 sailors, were easily replaced from ships undergoing refitting, while new and more powerful ships were also approaching completion. Jellicoe had not managed to annihilate the High Seas Fleet, but that had always been a secondary consideration to this most practical of men. His priority had been to maintain the maritime supremacy of the Royal Navy across the globe; that he could never risk, not even for the chance of glory. Jellicoe was above all a pragmatist: his success at Jutland was made in that image – the *status quo* would continue and for Germany that marked a strategic defeat.

12

MESOPOTAMIA, 1914–18

'It was believed to be a sideshow and "no man's child".'[1]
Lieutenant General George Gorringe, Headquarters, Tigris Corps

THE ORIGINS OF THE MESOPOTAMIAN CAMPAIGN lay at sea with the adoption by the Royal Navy of oil-fired turbines for the new generations of warships that were rolling off the stocks. Much of Britain's oil supply was sourced from the recently developed oil fields at Ahwaz in the Arabistan province of Persia. The oil pipeline ran alongside the Karun River to the Shatt al-Arab and the refineries on Abadan Island. Turkish-controlled Mesopotamia itself was the alluvial plain formed by the mighty Euphrates and Tigris Rivers as they meandered their way to the Persian Gulf, joining together before passing by the town of Basra which lies at the head of the Shatt al-Arab estuary about seventy miles from the sea. The importance of an uninterrupted oil supply to the British meant that it was essential that Abadan be secured from disruption as the likelihood of Turkey joining the war grew ever greater in the autumn of 1914. Indeed, in August, Turkish troops had already been mobilised and moved forward into the Basra region, occupying an area right down to the entrance of the Shatt al-Arab. The Royal Navy had despatched the sloop *Espiegle*, accompanied by an armed merchantman the *Dalhousie*, to lie off Abadan as a tangible representation of Britain's concern. Furthermore, the Indian government was ordered to raise and despatch a land force in case military operations were required. Yet right from the start there was confusion over the chain of command.

A 1912 agreement had laid out the support required from India in the event of war and this included taking responsibility for any possible campaigns within the area of the Persian Gulf and Mesopotamia. Officially, therefore, the Indian Expeditionary Force (IEF) 'D' was to be raised by, and under the control of, the British-run Indian government based at Delhi.[2] However, there is no doubt but that the British government in London still retained not just a paternalistic interest but a desire to interfere directly in the conduct of operations. This may not have mattered but, right from the start, the two governments had markedly different strategic visions: London was engaged in a continental war in Europe and had its eye on the Turkish threat to the Suez Canal and Egypt. Hence it looked to mount an essentially defensive campaign in Mesopotamia tailored to securing the oil fields and not much else. In contrast, although initially reluctant to do anything due to commitments elsewhere and the continuing threat on the North-West Frontier, Delhi soon came to envisage a full-scale campaign, intended to bring not just Abadan, not just the town of Basra, but the whole of Mesopotamia right up to Baghdad under British control. The Indian Army had been undergoing a prolonged period of economy due to the perceived reduction of the threat emanating from Russia, and the prevailing expectation was that it would only be deployed internally on the North-West Frontier. Therefore, little attention had been paid to its new external Imperial obligations, which meant it was not well equipped with artillery, transport, medical facilities or any of the other requirements of modern warfare.

The first troops to be despatched to Mesopotamia were the augmented 16th Indian Brigade, made up of regular British and Indian battalions. This force left India on 16 October 1914 and took up a watching brief off the island of Bahrain in the Gulf, pending events. The day after the Turkish declaration of war on 5 November, the 16th Indian Brigade fought its first action, capturing the Fao Fort and Turkish cable station located close to the entrance of the Shatt. On 7 November the troops sailed on up the Shatt beyond Abadan and landed at Sanniyat, where they established camp to await the arrival of Lieutenant General Sir Arthur Barrett and the rest of IEF 'D', made up largely of elements of the 6th Indian Division. A weak counter-attack by the Turkish 38th Division was repulsed and afterwards a series of minor actions were fought, culminating in the capture of Basra on 21 November 1914. The campaign could have been over; the campaign *should* have been over. The primary objectives of securing the oil fields and the pipelines from Persia had been achieved.

Basra proved not to be an ideal base for, although it was a minor port, it lacked many of the basic modern amenities. The water supply came from the river, sanitary arrangements were primitive and it was dominated by the tidal river and a maze of creeks that stretched inland across a flood plain that was actually swamped on a daily basis. Worse still, the entire area flooded between March and October, leaving Basra effectively as an island. Whatever the season, movement by land was always extremely difficult, with few passable roads and no railways. As the Navy explored further up the river, it became apparent that the Turkish forces had fallen back the fifty miles to Qurna, which lay at the old confluence of the Euphrates and the Tigris. Barrett decided that in order to consolidate his position at Basra he must establish a defensive outpost at Qurna. It would prove a remarkable operation. His troops landed on the eastern bank, but then faced the monumental problem of crossing the swollen Tigris, as wide as the Thames in London. In the finest traditions of the *Boys' Own* comics, Royal Navy sloops forced their way past the town, from where they could provide a distracting artillery support, while two Indian battalions managed to cross higher up the river on 8 December. The Turks found themselves cut off and on 9 December they surrendered. Thus far the operations had been a triumph and Turkish resistance again was negligible. Now surely the IEF 'D' could rest on their well-earned laurels?

Yet Lord Hardinge, the Viceroy in Delhi, and the Indian Army Head-quarters based at Simla were becoming increasingly ambitious. With such weak opposition from the Turks, could not more be achieved, perhaps even the capture of Baghdad? It cannot be denied that this would have secured Abadan beyond question, but was it really necessary? Further-more, little consideration was being given to the means required for such a 'forward defence' policy. Did the Indian government really have enough troops spare to face whatever the Turks might throw at them in such grand operations? Also, how was an army supposed to move in an area devoid of communications – except on the great waterways of the Tigris and Euphrates?

Meanwhile the British and Indian troops were accustoming

themselves to the pleasures of service in Mesopotamia. Qurna was reputedly the site of the Garden of Eden, but conditions had deteriorated somewhat since those halcyon days. Hot during the day, often cold at night, with naggingly persistent winds which soon stirred up clouds of choking dust, when not actually immersed in water the flood plain was still chopped up by canals and deep waterways dotted around with marshes and brackish lakes. Digging trenches was difficult as below two feet they became flooded and breastwork trenches had to be built up to provide protection. The flies were everywhere and, in conjunction with the poor-quality water supplies and sanitation, soon led to a disturbing incidence of dysentery. All this against a backdrop of the constant attentions of the local Marsh Arabs who were hostile to anyone – Turkish or British – who trespassed for long on their domain. Their natural antipathy was increased by the potent combination of the 'Holy War' declared against the British by the Turks, coupled with well-placed bribes for the more venal. As a result, the British camp was disturbed every night by the persistent rattle of pot-shots from a conglomeration of archaic weapons that could have provided a brief history of firearms. They were not particularly effective, but they were irritating. It was also difficult to judge the strength of the opposing Turkish forces and the legitimacy of various rumoured threats against Qurna, Basra and the oil fields in Persia. All too soon the British began to appreciate the merits of the old Arab saying that 'God had created hell but it wasn't bad enough so he created Mesopotamia'.

The British themselves strengthened the IEF 'D' with the 12th Indian Division commanded by Major General Sir George Gorringe. When the long-anticipated Turkish blow fell it was beaten off – not without difficulty – at the Battle of Shaiba in a series of engagements fought between 11 and 14 April 1915 which prevented a large Turkish and Arab force from descending on to Basra via the Euphrates from the west.

At this time, Barrett had fallen sick and had been replaced as overall commander by Lieutenant General Sir John Nixon. Nixon had been briefed by General Sir Beauchamp Duff, the Indian Army Commander in Chief, who charged him not only with the responsibility of guarding the oil fields and occupying the Basra vilayet (province) which stretched as far almost as the town of Kut al Amara, but also – more dramatically – with planning an advance on Baghdad. Yet this expansionary thrust was unknown to the authorities in London, whose point of view was summarised by Lord Crewe in a telegram sent on 24 April 1915.

> Any advance beyond the present theatre of operations will not be sanctioned by Government at this moment, and I presume Nixon clearly understands this. During the summer we must confine ourselves to the defence of oil interests in Arabistan and of the Basra Vilayet. If an advance to Amara with a view to establishing an outpost for the purpose of controlling tribesmen between there and Karun, thus adding to the security of the pipeline, is possible after smashing the enemy in the direction of Karun, I should be prepared to sanction it. Any proposal involving possible demands for reinforcements or undue extension is to be deprecated however. Our present position is strategically a sound one and we cannot afford to take risks by extending it unduly. In Mesopotamia a safe game must be played.[3]
>
> Secretary of State for India Lord Crewe

Lord Crewe clearly did not appreciate the scope of Nixon's instructions. From this point in the campaign the Indian government effectively wrested the initiative from London.

On the ground the operations became divided in focus. Gorringe had been despatched on 22 April with his 12th Indian Division to clear the area around the Persian oil wells and along the Karun River of any Turkish or Arab threat in order to allow pumping (which had been interrupted) to resume. This was, after all, the original purpose of the campaign. Gorringe's operations were successful and the oil began to flow again, but meanwhile the operations of the 6th Indian Division, commanded by Major General Charles Townshend, were rather more dramatic in their nature. Nixon decided to order his new subordinate to advance along the Tigris some ninety miles to Amara, having obtained the grudging consent first of Lord Crewe and then of Austen Chamberlain, his replacement as Secretary of State for India after the formation of a Coalition Government on 25 May.

Townshend was widely considered a tactically brilliant commander – not least by himself. He had studied military history deeply and attempted to put into action the maxims of his hero Napoleon. During his career he had already attracted much attention for his determined and ultimately triumphant defence of the besieged fort of Chitral on the North-West

Frontier in 1895. Now he was facing a true test of his capabilities, for no advance from Qurna would be easy. The whole area was flooded, with the Turks ensconced on low hill positions that peeked above the marshes. Advance was only possible by boat. So the assaulting 17th Indian Brigade had to take to the waters. This was an incredible undertaking demanding enormous preparations.

> An average of sixty-five boats per battalion was necessary. Each bellum was to carry ten men, two to pole, eight to fight, with their equipment, reserve ammunition, water, two picks, two shovels, 30 feet of rope and caulking materials, two spare poles, and four paddles. In addition, boats had to be found for the Signal Company and for the field ambulance, and also for machine gun sections and a battery of mountain guns. These latter were mounted on rafts, made from two bellums decked together, the guns protected by steel plates and the whole roofed over with reeds to make them more inconspicuous. It was decided that the bellums should also be armoured by placing two long strips of boiler-plating across the boats, bow and stern, projecting about 3 feet on either side and only just clearing the water: the idea being that, if held up by frontal fire, the men could jump out and, wading behind the projecting wings of armour, push their boat forward. 'Expert' opinion was against the scheme.[4]
>
> Captain Henry Birch Reynardson, 1st Oxfordshire and Buckinghamshire Light Infantry

'Expert' opinion was right. The armour made the bellums top-heavy and caused them to snag in the reeds or run aground. To try to reduce the enormous risks, Townshend planned a staged advance, carefully preparing a co-ordinated naval and artillery bombardment on the Turkish outposts before launching his assault on 31 May 1915.

> We had never seen a bombardment in Mesopotamia before, and now that about forty guns, from 5-inch to 10-pounders, were hard at it, we were suitably impressed. Norfolk and Gun Hills disappeared in a cloud of smoke and dust, which drifted like a dirty smudge across the clear blue of the sky. The bombardment continued for half an hour, then lifted off Norfolk Hill and concentrated on Tower Hill and Gun Hill, while the mountain battery took on Norfolk Hill and sprinkled it with shrapnel, while the boats began their slow advance. After the bombardment that Norfolk Hill had suffered, it seemed that nothing

could have remained alive, but as the boats of the Oxfordshire Light
Infantry approached, it was clear that somehow or other a good many
of the garrison were still very much all there. A line of grey puffs
broke out all along the position, and the boats came under a sharp
rifle fire; at the same time the enemy guns opened fire – shooting very
erratically – on the sloops in the river. Norfolk Hill was carried with
the bayonet soon after seven o'clock, at the cost of one officer killed
and five men wounded – surprisingly light losses considering that the
company concerned was under rifle fire at a range of 100 yards while
they disembarked and waded up to the trenches. These, well-sited and
provided with overhead cover in places, were simply full of dead and
wounded.[5]

Captain Henry Birch Reynardson, 1st Oxfordshire and Buckinghamshire Light
Infantry

Stunned by the shell fire, the Turkish outposts were overwhelmed. Next
morning an aerial reconnaissance flight discovered that the Turks had cut
and run. What happened next was simply amazing. With one brigade
swiftly embarked aboard paddle steamers, Townshend and his staff aboard
the *Espiegle*, accompanied by the other sloops *Clio* and *Odin,* set off up the
Tigris in hot pursuit of the Turks. Mile after mile, the ramshackle convoy
sailed up the narrowing uncharted river, bypassing obstacles and risking
mines or deadly ambush. Perhaps the Turks could, or should, have done
more to punish his daring, but Townshend gave them no time to think. He
harried them mercilessly. Even when the sloops ran out of water beneath
their keels, he merely transferred his retinue to the shallow-draught gunboats and launches to continue the chase with a mere hundred or so men.
Only colossal chutzpah carried them through.

My first idea was to wait until my leading brigade should arrive in
ships, as the probability was that the Turkish troops at Amara would
defend the town. Indeed I felt certain that they would fight, and that
it would be ridiculous to attempt to take the place with the armed tug
Shaitan, with a 3-pounder gun and some ten hands as a crew, and the
Comet, a small paddle-wheel river steamer, armed with a 12-pounder
and a total crew of fifteen seamen and British soldiers doing work of
marines. Captain Nunn was anxious that I should go on and chance
it – as is the way with sailors. But I said emphatically, 'No, I won't do
anything foolish. I must unite some troops before attacking, for there is

sure to be a defence!' But, after waiting for about an hour, I told Nunn that after all I would go on and chance it. I told him to send the *Shaitan* about 2 miles ahead as an advanced guard; and we followed with the *Comet, Shaitan,* and *Lewis Pelly,* armed tug-boats, and three 4.7 guns towed in horse boats. At 1.30 pm I was alongside the customs house at Amara, where the Turkish commander in the Battle at Qurna, Halim Bey, the Governor of Amara, Aziz Bey, three or four colonels and some thirty or forty officers came on board to surrender. A whole battalion of the Turkish *pompiers* from Constantinople sent off word that they were ready to surrender at the barracks; so I told Nunn to send one of his naval officers. Accordingly he sent a lieutenant with the coxswain of the boat and a British soldier from the Dorsets, who, I think, was acting as a marine. These three received the surrender of the battalion and marched them down to the quay and on board one of the big iron lighters there, as I wanted them in the lighter and anchored in mid stream under our guns! It must be remembered that I had only about twenty-five British sailors and soldiers with me. To keep up appearances, I made a scene with the Governor, who said he had no supplies available. I spoke of the 15,000 troops close on my heels with a fleet of ships.[6]

Major General Sir Charles Townshend, Headquarters, 6th Indian Division

Before the Turks had a chance to realise what was happening, it was too late. The follow-up infantry arrived just in time to consolidate the gains, on the morning of 4 June.

In the next phase in these endlessly extended operations, Nixon des-patched Gorringe with the 12th Indian Division to fight their way along the convoluted channels of the Euphrates to secure the town of Nasiriyah. After some incredible logistical difficulties and some stiff fighting, they managed to eject the Turks from their positions on 24 July 1915. With both Amara on the Tigris and Nasiriyah on the Euphrates now taken, almost all the Basra vilayet was secure while, far behind the lines, the Ara-bistan oil fields were back in action and all was well. Yet Nixon was still not satisfied, this time pointing to the concentration of Turks gathering at the town of Kut al-Amara, some 120 miles beyond Amara at the confluence of the Tigris and the Shatt-al-Hai Canal, which led across to the Euphra-tes. The same old arguments were deployed: if only they could capture Kut all would be well, the Basra vilayet would be safe and the oil fields secured. This, however, was nonsense as an advance to Kut would achieve little more than elongate what was already a severely over-stretched line of communications. Kut only had any significance if it was to be used to launch an attack right up the Tigris to Baghdad: that, indeed, was Nixon's real objective, in sharp contrast to the far more pragmatic inclinations of Austen Chamberlain.

The Turks were digging defensive positions on both banks of the Tigris some eight miles south of Kut and Townshend was faced with a difficult task. The shortage of river transport was having a terrible effect on the whole supply and reinforcements chain stretching right back to Basra, which was itself still in chaos. The problems were obvious but intractable. The main problem was the Tigris. Plagued by strong currents and winding like a corkscrew, the river was only navigable through a narrow channel, even though it was up to 150 yards wide. Townshend asked for more troops, more munitions, more transport. Nixon's reply was terse: he was told to 'cut his coat according to his cloth'.[7]

Slowly the troops of the 6th Indian Division advanced up the Tigris, some taken in shuttles aboard river transports, but many having to march far more miles than was good for them across inhospitable terrain in the blazing sun. After concentrating at Sheikh Sa'ad, they made a feint attack on the main Turkish defences of the Es Sinn trench lines on the west bank, before assaulting on the east bank on 28 September 1915. This was carefully planned by Townshend in his trademark style, using the cover of night to switch his forces by pontoon bridge across the river and then launch a complex combination of fixing and flanking attacks. It did not go entirely according to plan but, after a hard-fought battle, the Turks fell back beyond Kut. This time the Turks retired in relatively good order as the British river boats could no longer charge ahead, given the worsening navigational conditions on the Tigris. In the event, Townshend entered Kut on 29 September 1915.

Nixon had no intention of stopping as thoughts of capturing Baghdad filled his mind. Townshend was ordered to pursue the Turks. He, however, had a very different perception, as he was to confide to his diary on 3 October.

> The Army Commander does not seem to realise the weakness and
> danger of his line of communications. We are now some 380 miles from

the sea and we have only two weak divisions, including my own, in the country. There is my division to do the fighting and Gorringe's to hold the line of communications from Kut to the sea. Thus there is no possible support to give me if I receive a check.[8]

Major General Sir Charles Townshend, Headquarters, 6th Indian Division

Chamberlain was also concerned about further advances to Baghdad, but Nixon simply brushed his objections aside. Confusion blossomed between London and Delhi. Worried by the dangerous situation at Gallipoli and desperate for success over the Turks, the War Office in London allowed itself to be reassured that there were indeed enough troops and means of river transport in Mesopotamia to make the capture of Baghdad perfectly feasible. On 23 October, permission was granted for a further advance. Townshend remained unconvinced.

I was determined to carry out the operation if it could possibly be done, and it was my plain and simple duty to carry out the orders of my superior to the best of my ability, although his orders were against my better judgement. Personally, I had no doubts in my mind as to the extreme gravity of the results of this advance – an offensive undertaken with insufficient forces, and not only that, but an offensive undertaken in a secondary theatre of the war, where our strategy should have been to have remained on the defensive with minimum forces sufficient for that purpose. All my study indicated disaster to me.[9]

Major General Sir Charles Townshend, Headquarters, 6th Indian Division

Townshend felt any further advance was unwise without at least two divisions to make the advance and a third to hold the lines of communication. He was also well aware of the increasing navigational difficulties for his flotillas in the shallows of the Tigris above Kut. But no one was listening and Townshend had little choice but to obey orders.

The next Turkish defensive positions were located close to the Ctesiphon Arch, the remnants of a huge palace from the heyday of Parthian civilisation. At the Battle of Ctesiphon, fought on 22 November, Townshend faced a roughly equal number of entrenched Turks well dug in on both sides of the Tigris. He again chose to attack on the east bank, trying to pin the Turks with a frontal attack while his flanking column manoeuvred around. But things did not go according to plan: the Turks stood firm;

even when their first line of trenches was over-run, they stuck fast in the second line. It was a real soldiers' battle, devoid of tactical sophistication, with both sides launching frontal attacks across the open flat desert and both suffering severe casualties. For two days the fighting continued, then suddenly the Turks withdrew. But this time there was no question of a British pursuit. Townshend's force had suffered some 4,600 casualties and his men could do no more. Ctesiphon was a truly Pyrrhic victory. Townshend had won the battle, but in doing so he had destroyed the fighting capability of the 6th Indian Division. He had no reserves; advance was impossible yet his men could not stay perched out in the open desert. Retreat was the only option.

Once it was confirmed that the Turks were not in headlong retreat and had not retired far, Townshend ordered the withdrawal to commence on the night of 25 November. The retreat was difficult in the extreme. The exhausted troops had a long way to march under the burning sun and their accompanying boats were constantly running aground. All the while the Arabs sniped around the columns. Not far behind them were the Turks; once they realised that the British were retreating, they soon launched a pursuit.

The total inadequacy of the transport facilities showed up in the evacuation of the wounded. From start to finish this was a disaster: everything that could go wrong did go wrong.

I was standing on the bridge in the evening when the *Medjidieh* arrived. She had two steel barges without any protection against the rain, as far as I remember. I saw that she was absolutely packed, and the barges, too, with men. The barges were slipped, and the *Medjidieh* was brought alongside the *Varela*. When she was about 300 or 400 yards off it looked as if she was festooned with ropes. The stench when she was close was quite definite, and I found that what I mistook for ropes were dried stalactites of human faeces. The patients were so huddled and crowded together on the ship that they could not perform the offices of nature clear of the edge of the ship. A certain number of men were standing and kneeling on the immediate perimeter of the ship. Then we found a mass of men huddled up anyhow – some with blankets, some without. They were lying in a pool of dysentery about 30 feet square. They were covered with dysentery and dejecta generally from head to foot. With regard to the first man I examined, I put my hand into his trousers and

I thought that he had a haemorrhage. His trousers were full almost to the waist with something warm and slimy. I took my hand out, and thought it was a blood clot. It was dysentery. The man had a fractured thigh, and his thigh was perforated in five or six places. He had apparently been writhing about the deck of the ship. Many cases were almost as bad.[10]

Major Robert Markham Carter, Indian Medical Service, SS *Varela*

The scandal triggered by this suffering was so great that a full-scale inquiry was later ordered into its circumstances by the British government.

Behind the wounded, Townshend's exhausted troops finally reached Kut on 3 December 1915. Nixon decided that Townshend should stand and fight. From 7 December the Turks besieged the British lines, which lay across the loop in the river that contained Kut. For the second time in his life the eyes of the Empire were on Townshend: would he succeed as he had at Chitral in 1895, or would Kut fall? In December the Turks launched a speculative series of attacks which were repulsed with heavy losses, after which they settled down to siege operations with the intention of starving the British out. On 28 December, the bulk of the Turkish forces began marching past Kut, leaving just enough behind to lock in Townshend, and moved down to occupy defensive lines in front of Sheikh Sa'ad.

Hitherto, Townshend had performed well during the Mesopotamian Campaign in 1915, but his conduct and judgement during the siege was poor.

Townshend is a hopeless incapable dreamer and ass – vain as a peacock and full of military history comparisons, but as a practical soldier one's grandmother would be as good. Sometimes one doesn't know whether to laugh or cry at his incapacity! He never goes near his men or rarely – never goes near the front line of trenches and sees things for himself. But he is not the only rotter – there are several in high places. I tell you honestly, although it sounds conceited for me to say it, but I can say it to you, I am the best man in this force of the senior Generals and what I suggest is accepted at once. It is not saying much though, but there are amongst the seniors an awful set of incompetents.[11]

Major General Charles Meliss, VC, Headquarters, 30th Indian Brigade

This wonderful quote calls to mind Arthur Conan Doyle's marvellous comic creation Brigadier Gerard and his firm conviction that he was the finest soldier, swordsman and horseman in the whole of Napoleon's Grande Armée. Yet the ebulliently confident Meliss was certainly not alone in criticising Townshend's conduct during the siege. His tactical position was dire, but he appeared to be in no doubt that – as at Chitral twenty years before – he would be relieved. All told, there were 14,500 British and Indian troops and dependants in Kut, with some 6,000 Arab civilian inhabitants who had been allowed to stay for humanitarian reasons and who also needed to be fed. Stupidly, no proper search had been undertaken by Tonwshend's staff at the commencement of the siege to determine the food stocks at Kut and thereby maximise the period they could resist. At first there was an abundance of confidence.

> Luckily there was lots of food. In addition to our full ration the men found in the village hundreds of chickens, lots of ghee and flour, and hundreds of tons of barley lying about. I have never seen men eat like it, but they had hardly had a decent meal since the 21st November and had had the devil of a time in addition. Leckie, our wonderful quartermaster, had found two cases of stout (ownerless?!) on the town front and put them in a safe place, i.e. our Mess! We had also some brown sherry and best of all [they] sent us four hams by mistake for bully beef: we ate them up and 'Regretted the error'! We were all very cheery and pleased with ourselves and put Christmas or early January as the outside by which time a big force would arrive from India, we should join up and drive the enemy back up the river again.[12]

Major Ernest Walker, Indian Medical Service, attached to 120th Rajputana Infantry

On 7 December Townshend claimed he had enough food to last for only sixty days, that is, until early February 1916. Somewhat perversely, he decided to adopt the contrary positions of both keeping his men on full rations and demanding immediate relief from Nixon.

With Townshend bottled up in Kut, the Indian and British governments were unified at last in their response to operations in Mesopotamia. Divisions were now despatched that, had they arrived earlier, would surely have allowed the advance to continue the last few miles from Ctesiphon to Baghdad. Still smarting from the final humiliating evacuation from Gallipoli in January 1916, the British were desperate to prevent another disaster at the hands of the Turks, with a consequent loss of prestige across the Muslim world. A new Tigris Corps began to form in Mesopotamia under the command of Lieutenant General Sir Fenton Aylmer, VC, although it was matched by the Turkish divisions arriving from Gallipoli.

The relief operations that followed had some similarities with the earlier phases of the campaign. The British were confident, but they still lacked sufficient river transport or a robust enough supply chain to maintain operations some 200 miles from their rudimentary base at Basra. They were also short of artillery suitable for trench warfare conditions. Above all, they were in a hurry this time, with the pressing necessity to relieve Kut. There was, however, one real difference: many of the Turkish troops that they faced had acquired an ominous proficiency in defensive operations on the battlefields of Gallipoli that would serve them well in the Tigris campaigns. They also had a competent leader in the German officer assigned to take command of them, Field Marshal Colmar von der Goltz, who may have been seventy-two but who would prove to have one last effective campaign in his old bones.

The British attacks of January and February 1916 had a depressing similarity. The underlying characteristic was urgency: Aylmer was aware of the dangers of attacking up the Tigris before he was ready, but he was being pressurised by both Townshend and Nixon to make haste. The result was disaster. The Turks had amassed equal and opposite forces along a series of strong defensive positions at Sheikh Sa'ad, Sanniyat and Es Sinn. These layers of concealed trenches left Aylmer very little room for manoeuvre as they were carefully sited to leave a gap of just a mile or so between the river and the flooded marshlands on either side. Frontal attacks across flat open ground with inadequate artillery preparation against experienced and determined opponents was a recipe for disaster. At the Battle of Sheikh Sa'ad on 7 January, the Battle of Wadi on 13 January and the climactic Battle of Hanna on 21 January, the British and Indian troops went through hell. Early on Aylmer realised that he was in deep trouble.

> I determined to continue the advance on Kut, but it is my distinct duty to point out that it is a most precarious undertaking, for which I, of course, accept full responsibility as I consider the situation demands a supreme effort to relieve Townshend.[13]
>
> Lieutenant General Sir Fenton Aylmer, Headquarters, Tigris Corps

It wasn't just the grimly efficient Turkish forces that were hindering Aylmer's progress. The weather broke, lashing his troops with freezing rain. Medical arrangements broke down again and Mesopotamia became a hell for the wounded.

In January Nixon was invalided back to India but his baleful influence on the campaign still remained. His replacement in charge of the IEF 'D' was General Sir Percy Lake, who had been Chief of General Staff in India and was deeply implicated in Nixon's ambitious plans. During all these heroic efforts the Kut garrison was able to contribute nothing; the Turks may not have been able to break in, but at the same time nor could Townshend's men break out. Given the imminence of the annual floods in March, which would greatly impede relief operations, Aylmer, prodded on by Lake, decided not to await the arrival of further reinforcements in the form of the 13th Division, which had been involved in the later stages of the Gallipoli Campaign. On 8 March he launched another frontal attack against the Dujaila Redoubt, a continuation of the Es Sinn positions on the west bank of the Tigris. This, too, was a total disaster. Aylmer had tried various diversionary and flanking tactics, but he was not a lucky general as Townshend had been. Even where he achieved tactical surprise it was often undermined by an insistence on sticking to the defined programme, which allowed the Turks to regroup. Moreover, the Turkish resistance was nowhere near as friable as it had been in 1915. Even when sections of the redoubt were breached the Turks launched successful counter-attacks and so it had to be done all over again. British efforts became more and more frantic, but the Turks held firm. There was nothing new, no tactical innovations, just hard slog for very little gain – and an awful lot of losses. A few days later Aylmer was sacked and command was handed over to the newly promoted Lieutenant General George Gorringe.

It is incongruous that even as these terrible sacrifices were being made to rescue the Kut garrison, Townshend discovered that there was a great deal more food than he had originally contended. This reflects badly on the original scaremongering estimates, which were belatedly revealed as the product of shoddy staff work.

> No accurate account was made of all food supplies available; nor were they seized. In our village there were, lying in the open and in huts, quite 400 tons of barley and wheat and not until March did Supply and Transport bestir themselves about this – by which time two floods had occurred and much had been stolen. Of course our people never

anticipated a siege of five months and were always expecting relief
in a week or two. Still if Arabs had all been expelled except, say, five
hundred coolies for digging, etc. – and if every pound of food had
been rigorously collected and the whole force put on half rations from
December 3rd, we could have lasted for 6 to 8 months, and would have
given time for an overwhelming force to collect.[14]

Major Ernest Walker, Indian Medical Service, attached to 120th Rajputana Infantry
Regiment

Even as more grain turned up, it was belatedly realised that the horses
could be killed for meat, allowing the garrison to last out until early April.
But by the time they had discovered this reassuring fact, the damage had
already been done by the unnecessary rushing of Aylmer's relief operations. Indeed, over the first month of the siege, the general health of the
men probably improved, such was their dreadful condition on arrival, and
the beneficial effect of full rations coupled with a period of relative ease.
But, inexorably, the rations declined in both quantity and quality, with
the meat portion being made up from bullocks, mules and horses. The
artillery officers kept their personal chargers till very last.

Poor Don Juan has taken his last hedge! I have hitherto managed
extend his reprieve, but today the order came. I gathered his last feed of
grass myself. His companions stood by him trembling as the quick shot
despatched one after another. Not so he! Now and then he stamped,
but otherwise stood perfectly still. I asked the NCO to be careful that his
first bullet was effective and to tell me when it was over. I kissed Don
on the cheek 'Goodbye!' He turned to watch me go. Shortly afterwards
they brought me his black tail, as I asked for a souvenir. Strange as it
may seem we ate his heart and kidneys for dinner, as they are now
reserved for owners. I am sure he would have preferred that I, rather
than another, should do so.[15]

Lieutenant Edward Mousley, 82nd Battery, Royal Field Artillery

Many Indian troops refused to eat horse meat for religious reasons and
suffered accordingly. But those who suffered worst of all were the Arab
occupants of Kut – these truly were nobody's children as far as all sides
were concerned.

The Arab children make their appearance in groups wailing piteously. Once the babes in their mothers' arms used to cry the whole day long, but the unfortunates are probably since gone. The Arab population has been dying by the hundreds and they look dreadfully shrunken and gaunt. Arabs continued to wait around the butchery for horse bladders on which to float downstream. They are shot at by the Turks, who want them to stay on here and eat our food, or else they are killed by hostile Arabs. Every night they go down and a little later one hears their cries from the darkness.[16]

Lieutenant Edward Mousley, 82nd Battery, Royal Field Artillery

As the weeks turned into months, the situation inside Kut grew increasingly serious and a terrible decline set in towards the end of March.

Up to this time the men were moderately cheerful and in fair spirits. One saw, however, how deeply they were disappointed each time the relief failed. From this time onwards there was a rapid lowering of stamina, vitality, physical condition and health generally to the end of the siege. When Kut capitulated the whole garrison was in an exceedingly low state of health. During the last month of the siege, men at fatigues, such as trench-digging, after ten minutes work had to rest a while, and go at it again; men on sentry-go would drop down, those carrying loads would rest every few hundred yards; men availed themselves of every opportunity of lolling about or lying down. There were instances of Indians returning from trench duty in the evening seemingly with nothing the matter, who laid down and were found dead in the morning – death due to starvation asthenia. Men in such a low state of vitality can stand little in the shape of illness – an attack of diarrhoea that they would have got rid of in a day or so at the beginning of the siege, often ended fatally – all recuperative power had gone. At the end of the siege I doubt whether there was a single person equal to a 5-mile march carrying his equipment.[17]

Colonel Patrick Hehir, Indian Medical Service

Trapped in an insanitary, disease-ridden enclave plagued by dysentery and diarrhoea, scurvy, malaria and pneumonia, and with few medical facilities, the troops had been rendered incapable of serious military action.

Having taken over operations, Gorringe found himself as hard-pressed for time as Aylmer had been. He was forced to try a frontal attack on the eastern bank of the Tigris, using the newly arrived 13th Division to smash through first the Hanna trenches, then the lines at Fallahiyeh, Sanniyat and finally Es Sinn. Gorringe laid his plans carefully, forgoing an artillery bombardment to secure early surprise in the attack made on 5 April. But the wily Turks had a bigger surprise for him. They fell back from the Hanna lines without resistance, willing to forgo a few miles of desert in order to make the carefully planned assault miss the target. At Fallahiyeh it was a different matter and, although the 13th Division took the Turkish trenches, the casualties were high. Gorringe then sent the 7th Indian Division forward to take over the attack on Sanniyat on 7 April, but a slaughter ensued, with lines of khaki bodies marking where the attacks had broken down. On the morning of 9 April, it was again the turn of the 13th Division, which tried a dawn attack to no avail but more heavy casualties. Amidst the carnage the flood waters were hemming the battling forces on to narrow strips of land and making a frontal assault the only feasible tactic. With little or no cover, this was little more than suicide.

> The Turks hold their line with a good many machine guns and are very well equipped with Very lights. We have superiority of guns and numbers and it's just these infernal machine guns that make one man as good as a battalion on this level coverless country. If it weren't for these damned machine guns we'd be in Kut now![18]
>
> Second Lieutenant Cuthbert Aston, 8th Welsh Regiment

In desperation the operations switched to the west side of the Tigris, with two more attempts, on 15 and 17 April, to strike at the Bait Asia trenches in front of the Es Sinn lines. But any progress was soon reversed by determined Turkish counter-attacks. So Gorringe returned to the east bank with a final assault by the 7th Indian Division on Sanniyat on 22 April. It was the last forlorn hope; everyone realised that the Kut garrison was on its last legs. But there was to be no fairy tale ending; just another deeply depressing disappointment for the relief force. The Tigris Corps could do no more; the Turks had fought them to a standstill. During the relief operations Aylmer's and Gorringe's forces had collectively suffered some 23,000 casualties – approaching twice the effective strength of those trapped in Kut.

In their anxiety the British had tried to drop stores by air – the first time resupply had been attempted in this way, as aircraft still had modest load-carrying capacities.

The first visit of aeroplanes took place bringing sacks of food which they dropped from a good height and we soon knew that this was the beginning of a new scheme for enabling us to hold out longer. At first thought it appeared ridiculous to think of feeding a starving garrison of our size with food dropped by a handful of aeroplanes, but short calculations of weight carried each trip, etc., soon revised ideas and the clamour was as to why it had not been started much earlier. It was only in the mornings and evenings that the aeroplanes could fly, owing to the heat which overheated their engines and the number of trips per day seemed fearfully disappointing. The Turks were not long in grasping what was up and forced the machines to fly high, but double-sacking was strong enough in most cases. One native had the ill luck to be hit by a falling sack and was so injured that he died. A few sacks fell in the river and some had to be marked down and recovered after dark but the quantity eventually proved enough to keep us going until 29th April.[19]

Major Alexander Anderson, Volunteer Artillery Battery, Indian Army

The amounts being dropped were derisory compared to the needs of the garrison; indeed, the air missions were more precursors of the future than of any real practical assistance to Townshend. A final desperate attempt on the night of 24 April to despatch 270 tons of supplies aboard the steamer *Julnar* ended in predictable failure and, with that, all hope was gone. There was no food left in Kut.

Townshend was forced to bow to the inevitable on 26 April. He requested a six-day armistice and commenced to parley over surrender terms. Some of the negotiations seem fanciful to the modern eye, with Townshend offering the Turks £1,000,000 and envisioning a scenario whereby his men give their parole and so are allowed to march out with colours and spend the rest of the war in India, having promised they would never fight on a Turkish front again. All his requests were rejected out of hand. What need did the Turks have for negotiations? They sought, and ultimately extracted, an unconditional surrender from Townshend on 29 April 1916.

Before daylight further orders came to destroy the guns and everything remaining of any military value. We had no desire that the Turks should get anything out of us and we set to with a will. With the help of the rest of the cartridges all the leather work, rifles (after being well-broken), saddles, tents, directors, telescopes, telephones, compasses, papers etc., were burnt in a trench. The Supply and Transport meantime were at work next door shooting the few remaining animals and burning the carts. Last of all we destroyed the guns – a slab of gun cotton in the breech which was tamped and closed and another slab in the muzzle – and there was precious little left of them to call guns. Having a spare slab for the last gun, it got a double charge and most of one side of it flew through the air and landed through the roof of an Arab house 2–300 yards away![20]

Major Alexander Anderson, Volunteer Artillery Battery, Indian Army

However defiant they were, when the white flag fluttered above Kut it marked the truly humiliating capitulation of around 12,500 British and Indian soldiers. While Townshend himself was treated well and most of his officers were treated reasonably, the other ranks faced a dreadful ordeal. Already weakened, their treament at the hand of the Turks was at best was uncaring and sometimes veered into downright brutality.

At Shumran we joined the rest of the garrison encircled by armed sentries on a desolate and completely bare strip of land close to the Tigris. We had been without food or drink since the previous day and like castaways were without protection from the elements – there being no provision whatsoever for even our most simple needs. When at last we were issued with sour and mildewed Turkish ration biscuits, devoured somewhat ravenously to ward off the pangs of hunger, our stomachs were in no fit condition for such treatment. Fortunately, for some like myself it resulted in violent sickness, but in not a few cases men died during the following night in frightful agony from gastro-enteritis. There were many such deaths during the next few days and it was unnerving having to watch their bodies taken away.[21]

Private Harold Wheeler, 1/4th Hampshire Regiment

Things would get worse during the long march to Baghdad and beyond.

A daily trek of not more than 10 or 12 miles along the featureless dusty desert track seemed never ending as with parched lips, burning brows and aching limbs we struggled to keep on the move. Even when it was absolutely necessary to fall out to satisfy the call of nature, the mounted Kurds would adopt a menacing attitude shouting, 'Yallah! Yallah! Imshee!' and what sounded like 'Bollocks!' making indiscriminate use of the whip to force us to our feet. Those suffering from dysentery or other ailments, obliged to drop out on the march, were shewn no compassion whatsoever by the escort and if unable to catch up with the column were left by the wayside to die, or worse still to be butchered by Arab brigands hovering around, who would strip them of their uniform and clothing. One day on the march I noticed the body of a British soldier, completely naked, by the side of the track and witnessed a Turkish officer placing a topee over his abdomen – possibly the only humane act known to have been performed on this terrible march.[22]

Private Harold Wheeler, 1/4th Hampshire Regiment

Thousands would die through what could best be described as 'aggravated neglect' by the Turks.

THE CONSEQUENCES OF HUBRIS could not have been clearer than the ashes of the Mesopotamian Campaign as viewed from the perspective of May 1916. It was fought with insufficient troops and inadequate logistical arrangements; a campaign which ignored the unique terrain characteristics of the region and was underpinned by the presumption that the Turks were not capable of serious opposition. Britain had to face up to a second shattering defeat by the Turkish Army: first at Gallipoli, now in Mesopotamia. The British Empire was left with no choice but to strike back. On the Western Front the Battle of Verdun was raging, the Battle of the Somme was about to start, the Battle of Jutland had been a disappointment, the Salonika Campaign was faltering, so the British already had plenty to worry about, but the future of the Empire in India and the Middle East demanded that the dire situation in Mesopotamia must be improved as soon as possible.

The British did what they should have done from the start if they had been serious about the capture of Baghdad – they reorganised their transport and supply system from top to bottom. This was a massive undertaking, extremely costly and demanded a huge allocation of scarce resources to the campaign. But they had no choice if British prestige was to be restored. The War Office took control of the campaign from the rather more financially hamstrung and incompetent Indian administration in Delhi. Meanwhile, in April 1916, Major General George MacMunn was appointed Inspector General of Communications. He was appalled by what he found on his arrival at Basra.

As we entered the anchorage, a melancholy sight appeared, twenty ocean steamers loaded with supplies and military stores lay awaiting unloading and had been so for weeks, so devoid was Basra of wharfage, port labour or port craft to handle all that was now pouring into the river. The staff in India in modern times had not studied modern movement and logistics, while even at the War Office the organisation of longshore and river service was only partially understood.[23]

Major General Sir George MacMunn, Headquarters, IEF 'D'

MacMunn brought out specialists to revitalise – or, more often, create – the requisite logistical necessities. Thus a prominent consulting engineer, Sir George Buchanan, was sent out to organise the port facilities Basra needed if it was to act as the base for such a major expedition. Land was reclaimed, navigational channels and harbours were deepened, jetties and warehouses were built. The Indian Labour Corps was brought in to do the manual work and release troops for the front. Huge reinforcement camps appeared and several military hospitals were established. A special class of steamer was designed and constructed at great expense specifically for conditions on the Tigris: shallow draught and capable of dealing with strong currents. The results of these endeavours, P-50 steamers, would begin to arrive in late 1916 and proved invaluable. As more and more barges and steamers were pressed into service the amount of tonnage carried forward increased massively while the evacuation of the sick and wounded improved in tandem. Meanwhile, a railway line was constructed to alleviate the river congestion in the narrows between Qurna and Amara, while further upriver a light railway helped move supplies from Sheikh Sa'ad to behind the front line area. Gradually a proper metalled road with bridges over the innumerable creeks was constructed, pushing forward from Basra right up to the front. A company of transport lorries was soon toiling back and forth. The situation was by no means perfect: the line of communications was still overly long and prone to disruption, but at least it was not the farce that had so badly hampered operations in 1915.

Military supplies of every kind poured into Mesopotamia. The munitions position had radically improved since the outbreak of war and by late 1916 batteries of guns and howitzers could be sent out, along with a munificence of ammunition supplies. They would supply one devastating response to the Turkish trenches. All the paraphernalia of modern war was flooding in, from machine guns to mortars, purpose-built bridging materials to reconnaissance and scout aircraft – everything the Tigris Corps could need. The four divisions that were already there were brought up to full strength of some 160,000 men and were now collectively known as the Mesopotamia Expeditionary Force (MEF). This time the British were serious.

There was also a change in the High Command, with the appointment of Lieutenant General Sir Stanley Maude to replace General Sir Percy Lake. Maude was determined to take a more 'hands on' command of his forces than his predecessor and so moved his headquarters up to the front. He had been given clear instructions by the Chief of Imperial General Staff, General Sir William Robertson, which restated the necessity of securing the oil fields, the pipelines and the Basra area. The prospect of taking Baghdad was raised but only with the stern warning that 'This further advance should not be undertaken unless and until sanction for it is given.'[24] Maude, however, while unwilling to move until he was certain of success, was intent on achieving total victory over the Turks in Mesopotamia.

During the summer of 1916 the Tigris Corps remained stuck in its trenches with the Turks still well entrenched in front of them. Both sides were in a relatively quiescent mood: the Turks resting while the British restocked their depleted divisions. By the autumn, Maude's forces had been split into two corps: Gorringe had been replaced by Lieutenant General Alexander Cobbe as commander of the I Indian Corps (3rd and 7th Indian Divisions), while the III Indian Corps (13th Division and 14th Indian Division) was commanded by Lieutenant General Sir William Marshall.

Maude made his first carefully planned move on 13 December 1916. His generalship was not so very different from that of Townshend, it was just that this time everything required for success was firmly in place, his advance was not hemmed in by the floods and he was not under the same pressing time constraints as Aylmer and Gorringe. Using a bombardment of the Sanniyat lines to deflect attention, and a night march, the cavalry and the 13th Division managed to cross the Shatt al Hai feeding into the Tigris on the western bank opposite Kut. The Turks were then thrown into further confusion when RFC bombing missions managed to harass the Turkish steamer responsible for their pontoon bridge into releasing its tows and thereby scattering vital pontoons all across the Tigris. This denied the Turks the means of rapidly crossing the river and, over the next few days, Maude attempted to further threaten their communications, thereby forcing them to withdraw.

Bad weather caused the suspension of operations but fighting recommenced in January 1917, with Maude's forces making considerable progress. Turkish morale began to crack as large numbers were taken prisoner. A vital factor in British successes was the increasing intensity of the artillery barrages which had the potential to overwhelm any Turkish response – modern mechanical war was coming to Mesopotamia. The Turks still held the formidable Sanniyat positions on the eastern bank of the Tigris, but as a whole the Turkish forces were starting to struggle. Their commander, General Khalil Pasha, had been overconfident in the ability of his forces to hold back the British on the Tigris and hence had detached several divisions to engage in abortive secondary operations in Persia, thereby leaving far too few troops to face the revitalised British. Hubris, it seemed, was not a solely British failing. Maude conceived of a plan to avoid more direct frontal assaults on the Sanniyat lines by making a crossing on to the east bank of the Tigris at the Shumran Bend upstream of Kut on 23 February. It was an exceptionally risky operation, but Maude tried to ensure that preparations were thorough: three pontoon bridges were prepared, all personnel were carefully trained and deceptions and a diversionary attack at Sanniyat were planned to pin the Turkish reserves, while overall there was a heightened sense of secrecy.

The boats were launched into the water at the Shumran Bend at 05.15 on 23 February. Once the Turks spotted them they opened up a rapid fire. However, the British held the bridgehead just long enough to allow a pontoon bridge to be created. When it became apparent what was happening, the Sanniyat positions were skilfully evacuated by the Turks as they fell back to avoid being cut off. For a moment it was like the old days under Townshend: the naval gunboats raced off up the river, harassing the retreating Turks and sinking most of their shipping. Kut fell on 25 February as the Turks retreated towards Baghdad. Some 7,000 Turks had been captured in the operations, while large quantities of artillery, machine guns, mortars, supplies, transport equipment, bridging equipment and riverboats were captured or destroyed. But should Maude should carry on to Baghdad? Could he with his four divisions deal with the Turkish reinforcements that would undoubtedly rush to the area? Was there really any point in a further advance? Had not the objectives as delineated by Robertson been achieved? There was much discussion of the correct course of action but, in the end, Maude's conviction that the Turks were well and truly beaten held considerable weight in view of his cautious performance to date. As such he was given permission to commence the advance to Baghdad.

Whatever the logic or otherwise of taking Baghdad, militarily it proved the right decision. The Turks failed to inundate the plains around Baghdad and, when defences on the line of the River Diyala were swept aside, they withdrew from the city, leaving Maude's troops to enter Baghdad on 11 March 1917. The fabled city proved a great disappointment to the first soldiers to arrive. They had enjoyed mental images of something grander than the reality of the filthy dirty streets of Baghdad.

In many ways the capture of Baghdad did not really change the overall situation, as had been pointed out in the wise words of warnings from the likes of Robertson, who counselled not to risk too much in capturing the city. For the capture of Baghdad was not an end in itself; it certainly did not mark outright victory. The Turks still had to be harried and pursued back to avoid them posing a future threat; it was still necessary to prevent them from uniting their forces and certain key points would have to be secured to stop them flooding the whole area by manipulating the river waters. Mesopotamia was like a vast sponge sucking in British military resources. Everything had to be done for the best of military reasons, but what really had been gained once the oil fields had been secured in 1914? Nothing. The whole Mesopotamia Campaign had become an object lesson in mission creep: the original goal had been achieved, but enormous risks had been undertaken to achieve a progression of ostensible objectives that had no real justification.

It had been presumed that with the capture of Baghdad and with the possibility of working in conjunction with the Russian forces now operating in the Caucasus and Persia, the Mesopotamian Campaign was all but over. But the Russians had been crippled in the aftermath of the March 1917 Revolution which caused an increasing deterioration in Russian military morale. So it was that Maude found there was still much hard fighting to be done. Battle followed battle, but the campaign never seemed to be quite over. Usually the British won and gained a few more miles of desert and the latest 'essential' tactical prize, but occasionally there were painful reverses. Operations were finally suspended during the long hot summer of 1917, lasting from May right through to September.

The resumption of fighting saw a slightly different situation as the Russian collapse freed up Turkish troops for offensive operations against Maude's forces. But the British too had been busy and had extended their supply lines forward to create an effective modern transport system that stretched from Basra to Baghdad. Flood control and irrigation measures had been instituted to manage the flow of the great rivers. The threat of marauding Arabs along the lines of communication had been reduced by a combination of pacification and slaughter. Maude's attitude had not changed over the summer break; he was still resolved on the destruction of all organised Turkish resistance. So the campaign continued: pushing ever higher up the Tigris, Euphrates and Diyala rivers. Then Maude himself died of typhoid on 18 November 1917 and General Sir William Marshall took overall command of the Mesopotamia Expeditionary Force. The guiding hand had been stilled, but operations continued unabated; Maude's final instruction is reputed to have been that they should 'carry on'.

Over the last year of the war the British pushed north towards the Mosul oilfields and across to the Caspian Sea. This was a world away from the original aims and objectives of the campaign; this was fighting for the sake of it, of localised priorities and tactical considerations rather than some rational analysis of where troops were best deployed on a global basis. Robertson, always the realist, in his instructions to Marshall called for consideration to be given to how the Mesopotamian army could be reduced. This pious hope attained greater urgency when the capture of Jerusalem by Allenby in December 1917 seemed to indicate that the Palestinian Campaign (being waged in tandem) offered a greater potential for successful operations against Turkey. In consequence, two divisions were redeployed to Palestine. Yet plenty of troops still remained in Mesopotamia.

Following the long lull during the hot season of 1918 the Turkish situation was desperate and Marshall was ordered to advance on Kirkuk with the intention of dominating the Mosul oil fields. The operations were successful and, following the signing of the Armistice on 30 October 1918, the whole Mosul area was successfully occupied and the four-year campaign was finally over. At the point of surrender there was an active strength of some 217,000 British and Indian soldiers serving in Mesopotamia (plus some 71,000 in the Labour Corps and 42,000 in the Inland Water Transport), but in all over 675,000 troops had been deployed over that period, of whom 92,500 had become casualties. All this for operations that had achieved their original declared objectives in the first few days of the campaign in November 1914; everything else had been vainglorious nonsense. Mesopotamia was a tragedy from start to finish, fought in circumstances of exceptional difficulty. For the first two years it had been starved of resources. It had also proved the graveyard for the reputations of many generals, even though the tactical skills they had demonstrated had by and large been adequate. But in the end the British had won: the Empire had gained its oil fields and one more sector of the globe was under British control.

13

EASTERN FRONT, 1917–18

'The Russian people are suffering from economic fatigue and from disillusionment with the Allies! The world thinks the Russian Revolution is at an end. Do not be mistaken. The Russian Revolution is just beginning.'[1]

Minister of War Alexander Kerensky

THE RUMANIAN FIASCO had done nothing to help the Russians. As the Rumanian armies collapsed the Russians were forced to extend their lines to the south, triggering a considerable degree of military reorganisation across the board, which became the responsibility of the new Chief of Staff at the Stavka, General Vasily Gurko, who had temporarily replaced General Mikhail Alekseyev who was on extended sick leave. To expand the number of divisions in the line, Gurko converted them from sixteen battalions per division to twelve, thereby bringing the Russian Army into line with the German system. This was a very ambitious programme, for although it promised to create another sixty divisions, the question was whether the Russians had the experienced senior officers and staff to bring them into action, or indeed the artillery batteries needed to give them the requisite firepower. The extra divisions were supposed to be of front line quality, but were soon allowed to deteriorate into second line formations, incapable of reaching the standards required. All told these reforms did little to improve military efficiency while proving a distraction from some far more pressing underlying problems.

Meanwhile, Allied efforts for 1917 were concentrated on General Robert Nivelle's ambitious plans for a war-winning French offensive in the Champagne area, supported by a diversionary attack by the British at Arras, both scheduled for April. Yet a prominent role was still envisaged for the Russians, who were expected to add further pressure on the Germans by launching a major new spring offensive on the Eastern Front. Gurko cautiously insisted that May 1917 would be the earliest that the Russians would be ready to attack. But by then everything would have changed.

The winter of 1916–17 was exceptionally severe, which exacerbated the transport and supply difficulties faced by the Russians already struggling to cover the new Rumanian sector of the front. Although the performance of the munitions industries had improved, it was apparent that the supply of many of the basics of life: food, winter uniforms and even essentials like boots was still lagging far behind demand. Ominously, this triggered several mutinous riots among the worst affected regiments, even though on the surface everything seemed to be proceeding as normal.

Discontent within the Army was, however, only a small part of the story. The Russian home front was gradually collapsing under the intolerable strain of war. The Tsarist government did not have the flexibility necessary to cope with the plague of economic, political and social problems that infected the land. The Tsar himself perceived any form of democracy as a threat to his regime and, rather than introducing an increased measure of liberalism, was more attracted to the idea of a total dissolution of even the tokenistic Duma. Appointments to positions of considerable authority were routinely assigned by the Tsar on the grounds of either naked favouritism or the authoritarian credentials of the candidate. Spy scares raged through society, with particular suspicion falling on any Russian general unfortunate enough to have a Germanic name. Meanwhile, incompetence and corruption blossomed unfettered, while at the centre the Tsar was publically embarrassed by the adherence of the Tsarina Alexandra to the ludicrous cult of Rasputin, an unhinged religious mystic with a penchant for irreligious pursuits. The whole despotic system of government was resting on just a few weak individuals. Russia was being hollowed out from within and the vacuum at the centre was creating dangerous instability.

The Russian armies may have been short of food rations, but they actually had priority in the allotment of the harvests; the result was increasing food shortages in the major cities. Production of agricultural food stuffs was generally in sharp decline, severely affected by the call-up of so many farm workers, shortages of essentials like fertilisers and the continuing distribution problems on the vastly overstretched railway system. As the population of the cities began to starve, popular discontent spread. Inflation was soaring, but wages remained static, so the poor were priced out of the market for whatever food was available. In a severe winter there were also shortages of fuel. The result was food riots, widespread industrial strikes and open political dissent, with most participants unanimous in blaming the Tsar and his government for their suffering.

The Tsar himself was oblivious to the threat; he ruled by divine right and was therefore above such mundane considerations. Meanwhile, all about him his regime was falling apart with amazing rapidity. Political demonstrations multiplied exponentially and there was ever-increasing vigour in the protestors' demands for food, political change and, increasingly, direct action. As more and more military units began to go over wholesale to the revolutionaries, the functionaries of Imperial government found themselves subverted on all sides. Many fled, while those who overtly resisted risked their lives. By the time General Mikhail Alekseyev had returned from sick leave to resume his position as Chief of General Staff, he could offer little support to the beleaguered Tsar. In 1906 the Russian Army had put down a revolution, but in 1917 it both lacked the enthusiasm and was far too occupied with the war to open fire on the people.

By March 1917, Russia was in a state of flux, racked by an incoherent revolution: not a rigorously planned affair, but rather a series of simultaneous uprisings against a corrupt and introspective regime. Two organisations emerged with ambitions to control events: the first was the liberal-minded Provisional Government, set up by prominent members of the Duma to try and control developments until democratic elections could be organised for later in the year; more threatening to the establishment was the Council of Workers' and Soldiers' Deputies (or Soviet), which adopted a socialist viewpoint. In the early stages of the revolution the competing bodies were able to adopt a *modus vivendi,* co-existing in a dual structure and, for the most part, putting aside their differences to protect their position from the prospect of a counter-revolution. The Tsar, however, could find support from nowhere. The Russian Army stood aloof, its senior generals bluntly recommending his abdication as the solution: this was hardly what Nicholas II wanted – or, indeed, expected – to hear, but as the situation spiralled out of control he was left with no choice. Finally, on 15 March 1917, he abdicated in favour of his brother, the Grand Duke Michael, who promptly rejected the poisoned chalice. The Allies, too, showed little concern for the Tsar's person, officially recognising the Provisional Government as his legitimate successor within a week of his abdication. In this they were encouraged mainly by the fact that the new regime seemed inclined to continue the Russian war effort. It also meant that they were better able to present the war as one of the democracies of the Entente fighting against the despotic regimes of the Central Powers – something they could hardly push with much conviction while Russia was still ruled by tsars. This would prove especially useful in trying to inveigle the United States of America into the war.

Yet there was trouble in the wings for the Russian generals, too. On 14 March the Petrograd Soviet had been induced by an incursion of armed soldiers to pass 'Order Number One', a manifesto for military personnel allowing political representation, much expanded individual freedoms and a degree of Soviet control, all of which ran entirely contrary to any concept of military discipline. Although originally only directed to the Petrograd area, the order spread rapidly throughout the services, including the Army at the front. Soon Soviet-style committees were thriving almost everywhere. To try and sort out the continuing shortages of food and basic supplies it was decided to reduce the size of the army by releasing all men over forty-three years old. Even so, desertions continued to rise and soon the Russian Army was a rapidly shrinking force. In these circumstances, Alexeyev admitted that he would have to delay the promised May offensive.

It might be thought that the Germans would launch an offensive on the Eastern Front in order to try and capitalise on the state of chaos within the Russian Army. However, they took a more subtle course of action. A direct military assault ran the risk of triggering the underlying patriotism of the Russian troops; far better to let them tear themselves apart from within. As a result it was decided to facilitate the passage of the Communist-inspired Bolshevik party leader, Vladimir Lenin, in a special sealed train travelling from Switzerland through Germany, Sweden and Finland to Russia where, the Germans hoped, this experienced political

1. General Allenby leaving Jerusalem by the Jaffa Gate on his official entry into the city, 11 December 1917. He had made sure that he entered the city on foot to avoid invidious comparisons.

2. Officers of the Surrey Yeomanry examining the wire road laid down across the desert to facilitate marching across the sand.

3. Bulgarian machine gunners in action in the hills near Monastir during the Salonika campaign, 1916.

4. Bulgarian infantry tentatively advancing under cover of an artillery barrage, 1916.

5. British troops taking their daily dose of quinine in July 1916. The British Salonika Force suffered huge numbers of malaria casualties during the campaign

6. Cavalry charging with drawn swords across a Macedonian plain following the retreat of Bulgarian forces in September 1918.

7. Indian troops in the trenches during the Turkish attack on Shaiba, Mesopotamia, April 1915. India made an enormous contribution of troops to the war effort of the British Empire.

8. An aerial view of the town of Kut el Amara on the banks of the River Tigris to which Major General Sir Charles Townsend retreated after the Battle of Ctesiphon in December 1915. The subsequent siege lasted 147 days before Townshend and the garrison surrendered on 29 April 1916.

9. A platoon of the 1/2 Rajputs passing a heavy artillery battery in action at Samarra, Mesopotamia.

10. A Lance Corporal of the Indian 112th Infantry, 34th Brigade (17th Division), kneeling in a trench during the Battle of Sharqat, Mesopotamia, October 1918. The Turks would seek an armistice within days.

11. A patrol of Austro-Hungarian mountain troops climbing in the Alps. The terrain should have been impossible, but the fighting raged for three long years.

12. An Austro-Hungarian infantry NCO captured by British troops on the Italian Front in 1918: the human face of war.

13. Italian troops taking up supplies through a snow-clad pass. The surreal logistical difficulties are evident.

14. An Austro-Hungarian soldier taking aim high in the mountains, a beautiful but deadly terrain.

15. The Canadian ace, Major William Barker of No. 28 Squadron, flying in his Sopwith Camel above the Italian front.

16. Austro-Hungarian soldiers of the 19th Infantry Regiment in trenches on the Italian Front. As on all fronts, trench life was characterised by long periods of boredom followed by sudden death and mayhem.

17. Admiral Reinhard Scheer, Commander-in-Chief of the German High Sea Fleet at the Battle of Jutland. A competent officer who managed to deny the British the great victory they craved.

18. Vice Admiral Franz von Hipper, Commander of the German battlecruisers 1st Scouting Force. The German battlecruisers were much more robust than their British counterparts.

19. Admiral Sir John Jellicoe, Commander-in-Chief of the Grand Fleet aboard his flagship HMS *Iron Duke*. The only man who could have lost the war in an afternoon. The British could not have survived the defeat of the Grand Fleet.

20. Admiral Sir David Beatty commanded the British Battlecruiser Force. He had not done well at Jutland but proved a safe enough pair of hands when he replaced Jellicoe in late 1916.

21. The German hybrid battlecruiser *Blucher* capsizing during the battle of Dogger Bank, 24 January 1915.

22. The dreadnoughts of the Grand Fleet cruising in line-abreast columns in the North Sea. British naval power exemplified.

23. The German Submarine U-35 cruising in the Mediterranean by moonlight, April 1917. The failure of the High Seas Fleet meant that the U-boats were the only chance to defeat Britain at sea.

24. An aerial photograph of British ships at anchor in the Firth of Forth, taken from the R.9 Airship, 1916.

25. View of the landing at V Beach taken from the *River Clyde* on 25 April 1915. The remnants of the Dublin Fusiliers are sheltering behind the low bank at the back of the beach and wounded Munster Fusiliers are lying onboard the lighter in the foreground.

26. Australians in a trench on Walker's Ridge at Anzac, Gallipoli, 1915. The inexperienced Australians would go on to be formidable troops when they reached the Western Front.

27. German cavalry on the Eastern Front, 1914. The cavalry had a very important reconnaissance role in the vast open spaces of the Eastern Front in the first few months of the war.

28. The victors of the Battle of Tannenberg. General Paul von Hindenburg with his staff, shortly after the battle in August 1914. To the left of Hindenburg is Major General Erich Ludendorff and to the right Lieutenant Colonel Max Hoffman.

29. German troops taking a welcome break during operations on the Eastern Front, winter 1914.

30. Tsar Nicholas II in military uniform in September 1915, around the time he became the titular commander of the Russian Army.

31. Russian sentry in a front line trench, 1915. The troops of all sides had to endure bitingly cold winters on the Eastern Front.

32. Group of Russian prisoners near Lodz, 1915. Enormous numbers of Russians were made POWs but they still had huge reservoirs of manpower.

33. The Russian Commander General Alexei Brusilov studying a map. Brusilov proved himself one of the truly great innovators of the war in his offensive in June 1916.

34. An Austro-Hungarian machine gun position in the front lines in Poland, 1917.

35. Russian troops in panicked retreat in Galicia, July 1917. By 1917 the Russian state was at the end of its tether. Revolution beckoned and the army crumbled.

agitator would act as a plague bacillus and destroy the host body. On his arrival in April 1917, Lenin duly called for an end to the war and a socialist redistribution of land.

The Provisional Government had continued on its more moderate course, calling for an expanded session of the Duma while reaffirming its intentions to continue the war. Among the most prominent delegates was Alexander Kerensky, an orator of considerable power who was appointed the new Minister of War on 16 May. Kerensky engaged in a well-publicised tour of the front, using all his presentational skills in proselytising for a new offensive, picturing the despotic German regime as the real enemy to long-term peace. A series of co-ordinated attacks on the North, West and South-West Fronts was planned, timed to commence in early July 1917. As Kerensky considered Alekseyev tainted by his former close links to the Tsar, he appointed General Alexei Brusilov as Commander in Chief with responsibility for carrying out the offensives. Wishing to seize the moment, Brusilov was obliged to forego some of the detailed preparations that had made his 1916 offensive so successful. He was at least facing a different opponent, as the death of the elderly Emperor Franz Josef in November 1916 had brought the far more liberal figure of Karl I to the throne of Austria-Hungary. Karl was not impressed with his Chief of General Staff Conrad's performance in the war so far and in March 1917 replaced him with General Arthur Arz von Straussenburg. By this time, however, the main power in the Central Powers lay with the Germans and von Straussenburg had little independence of action.

After a two-day bombardment, the Second Brusilov Offensive attack began with a flourish, with the attack of the Russian Seventh and Eleventh Armies on the South-West Front. When the infantry went over the top on 1 July, early results were promising, but then everything started to go wrong. The best and most loyal units had been chosen as the assault troops, while the follow-up and reserve formations were far less committed; indeed, when it came to moving forwards, many regiments simply refused. The attack petered out in ignominy and further planned attacks were either cancelled or abandoned. Then a vigorous Austro-Hungarian counter-offensive was launched at Tarnopol in Galicia on 19 July. The Russians broke and retreated in chaos. This disaster triggered the replacement of Brusilov as Commander in Chief by General Lavr Kornilov on 1 August. The Russian Army was falling apart and such attacks as had been carried out only served to cull the few remaining loyalist units still willing actively to prosecute the war. The vast majority of Russian soldiers were now content to be passive observers at best; indeed, by the autumn it was estimated that some two million had deserted.

Behind the front line the ties that bound the Provisional Government and the Soviet councils were beginning to fray. On 15 July a minor revolt by the Bolsheviks at Kronstadt had been relatively easily suppressed and one of the ringleaders, Leon Trotsky, had been arrested, while Lenin had gone into hiding, both men having been denounced as 'German agents'. Now Kerensky was sufficiently emboldened to try and seize more power, proclaiming himself Prime Minister and then declaring Russia a republic. But he would be hampered terribly in his attempts to gain control of Russia by his continued belief in the prosecution of the war, fearing as he did the abrupt withdrawal of British and French economic subsidies and support if he reneged on the Entente. The Bolsheviks, in sharp contrast, offered an outright opposition to the continuation of war. There was a further cause of tension when Kornilov determined to stamp out political influences within the Army and demanded the restoration of martial law, backed up by the death penalty for a multiplicity of offences including all forms of political agitation within the ranks. These moves triggered a political crisis in Petrograd, where the Soviets were already campaigning for the abolition of the death penalty altogether, while the more right-wing elements within the Provisional Government tended to support the hard-line Kornilov proposals.

It was at this very point that the Germans struck. The port of Riga in Latvia had long been a German objective situated as it was at the mouth of the Dvina River on the Baltic coast. The Russian defences ran along the eastern riverbank but with a substantial bridgehead on the western bank. The river at this point was about 450 yards in width, representing a formidable obstacle to the German Eighth Army, commanded by General Oskar von Hutier. Not only had the Germans amassed some 750 guns and a further 550 heavy mortars for the offensive, but von Hutier also intended to employ the sophisticated barrage techniques devised by his artillery adviser, Lieutenant Colonel Georg Bruchmüller. This brilliant officer had developed a system of short, intense bombardments which left the defending forces stunned and unable to respond when the main assault was launched. A heavy concentration of 75 per cent gas shells mixed with

25 per cent high explosive shells would be directed at the Russian batteries: the aim was not necessarily to destroy, but rather to saturate the area with gas, forcing the Russian gunners to don their gas masks, which vastly reduced their ability to carry out their tasks. Meanwhile, all the identified observation posts, command posts and communication centres would be pounded, with the intention of blinding the Russian commanders and preventing them from reacting as they became isolated from events.

The bombardment would move through distinct phases, like the movements of a musical symphony, culminating in ten minutes of mayhem as all batteries concentrated on pounding the Russian infantry positions, before finally a creeping barrage, the *feuerwalze*, would roll forward, preceding the infantry into attack. Under von Hutier's guidance, specialist assault squads had also been trained in stormtrooper tactics, building on the operational experience and experimentation already extant within the German Army, but also taking note of the increasingly sophisticated infantry tactics of the Allies. The stormtroopers were generally armed with light machine guns, flamethrowers and hand grenades, while their tactics emphasised the importance of bypassing centres of resistance to break through to the vital gun batteries and headquarters. Isolated strongpoints could then be dealt with by the heavier weapons brought up by the follow up troops.

At Riga everything would be complicated by the serious additional obstacle of the river, so the infantry assault units were carefully trained in amphibious operations, using boats to establish bridgeheads that would then allow for the rapid construction of pontoon bridges by specialist engineers. At 04.00 on 1 September the Bruchmüller bombardment began, to devastating effect, as hundreds of thousands of shells were fired in just a few hours. The Russian guns were silenced and the Russian infantry were pounded into submission, abandoning their posts in terror, so that the tricky river crossing which commenced at 08.30 encountered little serious opposition. As the German engineers completed the bridges behind the new bridgehead, the Russians fell back in disarray. The front line would only stabilise some twenty miles north-east of Riga after this, the fourth largest city in Russia, was over-run by the Germans with disturbing ease.

The loss of Riga was a huge blow for the Russians. Kornilov chose to present it not as a result of German military skill, but rather as the consequence of the undermining activities by the Bolshevik conspirators within the ranks. These trenchant and tactlessly expressed views brought him into conflict with Kerensky, who came to believe – with good reason – that Kornilov was about to launch a military counter-revolution. This belief seemed to be confirmed on 10 September, when Kornilov accused the Provisional Government and the Bolsheviks of being nothing more than the tools of the German High Command. This outlandish statement temporarily reunited the Provisional Government and the Soviets, who set up armed militias and prepared to repel a military intervention by Kornilov. In the end Kornilov could not generate sufficient support within the Army for his proposed counter-revolution and he was peremptorily dismissed by Kerensky, who took on the title of Commander in Chief himself and rehabilitated General Mikhail Alekseyev to act as his Chief of General Staff. But the dispute resulted in collateral damage to Kerensky's reputation as well: denounced by the Bolsheviks to the left and threatened by the conservatives to the right, whether fairly or not, many came to believe that Kerensky was little better than the Tsar he had replaced.

During that autumn, Kerensky's political position deteriorated still further in conjunction with the inexorable rise in popularity of the Bolsheviks, now seen as the only grouping that had consistently opposed the war, while their promises of the widespread redistribution of land had an obvious attraction to ordinary workers and soldiers. They were also well organised, with the recently released Trotsky engaged in creating a strong armed militia known as the Red Guard. A further problem was the hitherto buried nationalism within the Russian Empire which was beginning to express itself through popular independence movements in the Ukraine and Finland. Then came another sharp jab from the Germans: not enough to trigger a national tide of resistance but just enough to promote war-weariness and despair amidst the Russian ranks. On 12 October the Germans launched Operation Albion, a brilliantly conceived combined operation to seize the Estonian islands at the mouth of the Gulf of Riga, which they successfully completed by 21 October. The Germans were getting threateningly close to Petrograd.

It was then that Lenin and the Bolsheviks finally chose to make their move, breaking all their remaining links with the Provisional Government and launching the second Russian Revolution on 7 November 1917. The thin facade of Kerensky's government was soon cracked as armed Bolsheviks seized government buildings and grabbed control of communications and key commercial institutions. The Winter Palace, the seat of the Provisional Government, was stormed and most of the delegates were swiftly arrested, although Kerensky himself managed to escape. Kerensky tried to arouse resistance to the Bolsheviks in the Army, but the response was lukewarm at best and the few units that answered his call were unable to over-throw the well-armed and highly motivated Red Guards. By mid-November Moscow too had fallen to the Bolsheviks. Kerensky fled the country, never to return, although he would survive until 1970.

Unsurprisingly, the Allied governments refused to recognise the new Bolshevik government headed by the Soviet of Peoples' Commissars, fearing that it would make peace with the Germans. They were right to be concerned. The Germans, on the other hand, were delighted. Lenin had no choice but to deliver peace to his supporters, that was at the heart of his mass appeal. Immediate orders were issued encouraging elected representatives from front line units to undertake local negotiations with the Germans and Austro-Hungarians to secure early informal ceasefires, while more formal negotiations began at Brest-Litovsk on 2 December 1917. A provisional armistice was declared on 15 December and the Russian Army immediately began to demobilise *en masse*. The formal peace negotiations would drag on deep into 1918, dogged by the threat of independence movements and the sheer scale of planned German annexations. Attempts by the Soviet negotiating team led by Trotsky to break off negotiations were punished by a German resumption of military operations against the deserted Russian lines. As a result the Russians were forced to accept even more stringent German demands when peace was finally signed, under duress, on 3 March 1918. The vast expanses of the Ukraine became an independent state, as did Finland and Estonia. Lithuania and Poland were supposed to be independent, too, but in reality were still occupied by German forces. The economic consequences for Russia were exorbitant. At a stroke she lost most of her coal fields and industrial heartlands. There were also extensive concessions of foodstuffs, all of which had to be collected from an already starving populace. The Russians had no choice but to sign, although Lenin and Trotsky consoled themselves in their fervent belief that revolution was also nigh in Germany and that these humiliating concessions were therefore only temporary embarrassments. Shortly afterwards came the formal surrender of Rumania, now totally isolated, under the Treaty of Bucharest signed on 7 May 1918. For the Russians the war with the Central Powers was over, while the civil war between the Red Army and the conservative royalist factions of the White Army was only just beginning.

For the Central Powers the collapse of Russia was an absolute triumph. At a stroke the Austrians had spare divisions to transfer to the Italian Front, where they could hope to finally defeat the Italian Army. For the Germans, victory meant that the best of their battle-hardened Eastern Front divisions could be transferred to the Western Front, where they could make one final attempt to secure victory over the French and the British. Nevertheless, the widespread chaos caused by the punitive provisions of the Treaty of Brest-Litovsk, coupled with the need to occupy, protect and police their new gains, meant that there were still far more German divisions – almost a million men – retained in the east than had been the case back in 1914.

14

THE SEA WAR, 1917–18

'Our losses in merchant ships, combined with the losses in neutral merchant ships, may, by the early summer of 1917, have such a serious effect upon the import of food and other necessaries into the Allied countries as to force us into accepting peace terms which the military position on the Continent would not justify.'[1]

First Sea Lord Admiral Sir John Jellicoe

THEY MAY STILL HAVE RULED THE WAVES outside of the North Sea, but the British were deeply unhappy with the outcome of the Jutland fighting. They had dreamed of a glorious triumph but although they had gained a strategic victory it had been at high cost and there was a nagging feeling that a great opportunity had been missed. This air of depression was augmented by the sense of loss as Kitchener became a belated victim of the Scheer submarine and mine trap intended for the Grand Fleet, when the ship on which he was travelling, the *Hampshire*, was mined and sunk on the night of 5 June off the coast of Orkney. Kitchener may have lost some of his lustre after two years of war, but he was still a hero of the Empire and he had died while in the care of the Royal Navy. Much of the angst over the Battle of Jutland was caused by unrealistic expectations rather than any real likelihood of destroying the High Seas Fleet during a confused encounter in low visibility with night looming. Nevertheless, there were anguished discussions as to what had gone wrong at Jutland with an undercurrent of murmurings as to who was to blame, centred on a degree of ill-informed criticism of Jellicoe by the acolytes of Beatty. In the event, Jellicoe did not retain his command much longer, as he was required to leave his beloved Grand Fleet to become First Sea Lord at the Admiralty in November 1916. He was replaced as Commander in Chief by Beatty but, interestingly, for all his bravado, Beatty would institute only minor adjustments to the cautious tactics enshrined in Jellicoe's Grand Fleet Battle Orders.

After the first fleet action in the dreadnought age it is not surprising that there was a great number of technical and material considerations for the British to digest. One thing was evident: something had gone wrong with the battlecruisers and a full investigation into their explosive demise was begun, resulting in strict anti-flash precautions being implemented, plus additional armour protection for all those ships still under construction. But urgent improvements were also required in the design of British shells, which had shown a distinct tendency to break up on impact and hence not to cause the anticipated damage. Night fighting may still have been abhorred, but Jutland forced a belated recognition of the necessity for proper training and preparations. There was a general tightening of ship-to-ship identification procedures, coverable searchlights were fitted and night exercises were begun in earnest. The method of handling and disseminating naval intelligence was also improved to avoid the kind of errors which had dogged Jellicoe at Jutland. The British had certainly learnt some valuable lessons from their bitter disappointment.

Despite their protestations of victory the Germans were deeply chastened by some aspects of their Jutland experience. They knew they had done well, but they also knew how close they had come to annihilation. Whatever they would do next, it would not involve another fully fledged fleet confrontation. Scheer did seek to lure the Grand Fleet into a submarine trap again by using battlecruisers to bombard Sunderland on 19 August. The operations were inconclusive as although Jellicoe was once again forewarned of their arrival by Room 40, he adopted a cautious approach, fearing just such a trap as Scheer had laid. In the end there was no confrontation, and when Scheer realised that there had again been a theoretical chance of his being ambushed by the whole Grand Fleet, he lost all further enthusiasm for adventures in the North Sea. If the British would not take risks, then the High Seas Fleet had little to gain and a lot to lose by exposing itself to the possibility of defeat.

> In view of England's plan of campaign, there was no alternative but to inflict direct injury upon English commerce. We could not build a sufficiently great number of additional large ships to compensate for the inevitable losses which we were bound to suffer in the long run in a conflict with the numerically superior English fleet. We ought to have tried earlier what the result of a victory by our fleet would be. It was a mistake on the part of the naval leaders not to do so.[2]
>
> Admiral Reinhard Scheer, SMS *Friedrich der Grosse*, Third Battle Squadron

The German High Command could only bewail the pusillanimity that had held them back in 1914; for by late 1916 it was far too late. With a successful fleet action ruled out, there seemed to be only one option left that promised any concrete results against their implacable enemy: submarine warfare. In October 1916 the Germans took their first cautious steps when they announced a return to restricted submarine warfare with at least lip service being paid to the international rules. The U-boats took a rising toll of British shipping, but they were still hamstrung by international conventions and Scheer wanted a far more robust approach.

> A victorious end to the war at not too distant a date can only be looked for by the crushing of English economic life through U-Boat action against English commerce. Prompted by the convictions of duty, I earnestly advise Your Majesty to abstain from deciding on too lenient a form of procedure on the ground that it is opposed to military views, and that the risk of the boats would be out of all proportion to the expected gain, for, in spite of the greatest conscientiousness on the part of the Chiefs, it would not be possible in English waters, where American interests are so prevalent, to avoid occurrences which might force us to make humiliating concessions if we do not act with the greatest severity.[3]
>
> Admiral Reinhard Scheer, SMS *Friedrich der Grosse*, Third Battle Squadron

The seeds were set for unrestricted submarine warfare; yet this would be a gamble based on the lack of a realistic alternative rather than the inherent merits of the policy. German naval experts believed that they could knock Britain out of the war if they managed to sink some 600,000 tons of shipping a month for just five months. The British would simply run out of shipping while neutral shipping would be either frightened away or sunk as well. As to the likely bellicose American reaction, the German High Command believed that US goods and services were effectively already at Britain's beck and call; all that was missing was her armed forces. As the US Army was inconsequentially small, it would be more than a year before a mass army could be mobilised; by which time it would be far too late. The Germans decided to ignore the American protests and take their chance. After all, Jutland and their failure to gain victory on the Western Front had left them with no viable alternative.

Crisis of the Submarine War, 1917

On 1 February 1917, Germany announced a full resumption of unrestricted submarine warfare, not only in the war zone around the British Isles but also across the Mediterranean and shortly afterwards – and most controversially – off the eastern coast of the United States. By this time the German U-boat fleet had swollen to over 150 modern submarines with an ocean-going capability, although only around a third could be maintained out on patrol at the same time. But this proved enough to cause chaos to the essential sea lanes that fed and supplied Britain. The Allied merchant shipping losses to submarines grew rapidly: 464,599 tons in February; 507,001 in March; a stunning 834,549 tons sunk in April. This was a catastrophic level of loss that could not be endured for long. If it carried on at this rate it would threaten not only foodstuff provision and the importation of other essential goods to Britain, but also the huge quantities of war materials and munitions required for the war being waged on the Western Front. Then, of course, there was the additional need to supply all the far-flung 'Easterner' campaigns in Salonika, Palestine, Mesopotamia and Italy. Although the rate of U-boat sinkings had accelerated marginally it was still well below the rate at which the German shipyards were churning out new submarines.

The Americans were incensed at the resumption of unrestricted submarine warfare and almost immediately severed diplomatic relations with Imperial Germany. Britain then fanned the flames of heightened American emotions by releasing the text of an ill-judged telegram from the State Secretary for Foreign Affairs Arthur Zimmermann despatched in January 1917 to his Ambassador in Mexico.

We intend to begin on the first of February unrestricted submarine warfare. We shall endeavour in spite of this to keep the United States of America neutral. In the event of this not succeeding, we make Mexico a proposal of alliance on the following basis: make war together, make peace together, generous financial support and an understanding on our part that Mexico is to reconquer the lost territory in Texas, New Mexico and Arizona.[4]

State Secretary for Foreign Affairs Arthur Zimmermann

The message was intercepted and decoded by the cryptologists of Room 40, after which the British cheerfully passed on the contents to the Americans. Their reaction was predictable. In a speech to Congress on 2 April 1917 President Woodrow Wilson used the crass offer as a battering ram to subdue any remaining anti-war elements within the United States, while also claiming the moral high ground.

With a profound sense of the solemn and even tragical character of the step I am taking and of the grave responsibilities which it involves, but in unhesitating obedience to what I deem my constitutional duty, I advise that the Congress declare the recent course of the Imperial German Government to be in fact nothing less than war against the government and people of the United States; that it formally accept the status of belligerent which has thus been thrust upon it; and that it take immediate steps not only to put the country in a more thorough state of defense but also to exert all its power and employ all its resources to bring the Government of the German Empire to terms and end the war.[5]

President Woodrow Wilson

The United States declared war on Germany on 6 April 1917. The potential addition of several American dreadnoughts to the Grand Fleet merely emphasised the hopelessness of any ideas the High Seas Fleet might have to contest openly British naval supremacy. But the Americans also brought the promise of an increased number of destroyers to fight the submarine war, while their booming shipbuilding industry would ultimately help replace lost Allied merchant tonnage. German shipping that had been trapped in American harbours on the outbreak of war was immediately confiscated, thereby changing sides overnight. And of course the Royal Navy no longer had to deal with American susceptibilities in enforcing the blockade of Germany. It was true that on land the American troops would not be able to make their presence felt until deep into the summer of 1918, but it was at sea that the Germans were trying to win the war in 1917.

As First Sea Lord at the Admiralty, Jellicoe still found himself right at the heart of events. After all the nervous tension of facing down the High Seas Fleet across the North Sea from 1914 to 1916, he now became the man responsible for devising a solution to the U-boat menace in 1917. The on–off nature of the campaign had hitherto prevented the Admiralty from developing a coherent policy, so it was reliant on a fairly random combination of *ad hoc* measures, including endlessly patrolling warships, minefield barrage nets, the arming of more and more merchantmen and the unpleasant *ruse de guerre* of the Q-ship. There was even a nod to the future with the employment of airships, aircraft and seaplanes to hunt for submarines, although efforts to bomb them from the skies were singularly unsuccessful. The most effective anti-submarine weapon currently developed was the depth charge which could be detonated by a hydrostatic pistol at the estimated depth of the intended U-boat prey. They contained some 300 pounds of high explosives, but tests had shown the British that they could not destroy a submarine unless they went off within 14 feet of it, although within 28 feet would probably cause enough damage to force the submarine to surface, where she could be swiftly dealt with by ramming or gunfire. What was needed was a method of determining with a fair degree of accuracy both the location and depth of a submarine. Yet here technology lagged well behind need, as there was still no effective way of tracking a submarine's movements once it had submerged, except by honest guesswork. Hydrophones that could pick up the noise of the submarine propeller or engines were found to be almost useless, as all they did was indicate the likely presence of a U-boat without giving any idea of its direction or depth. Worse still, they required the ship employing them to stop still in the water, otherwise the hydrophone would merely pick up the sound of its own engines; yet stopping was clearly a risky stratagem in the presence of a U-boat.

In December 1916 the ever-methodical Jellicoe had established an Anti-Submarine Division at the Admiralty to examine and co-ordinate the British response to the threat. Unfortunately, that was as far as his inspiration seems to have taken him. Jellicoe had always been a details man, marked by an inability to delegate even mundane matters. He had coped well enough at the Grand Fleet, but at the Admiralty a combination of exhaustion and stress seem to have prevented him from discerning with sufficient speed what was, with hindsight, the obvious solution. For although Jellicoe was correct in his belief that there was no one answer to the U-boat problem, at the same time it should have been evident that a very important component of any solution would be the introduction of a convoy system as employed by Britain in times of war since time immemorial. Traditionally, vulnerable merchantmen were gathered into a convoy with an armed escort to protect them from the attentions of commerce raiders. If introduced, such a system would have at a stroke cleared the seas of helpless victims and even if a submarine had located a convoy, it would have been exposing itself to attack from the escort. But Jellicoe could see only problems. He blanched at the sheer complexity of the administrative arrangements required to organise thousands of ships into convoys, pointing to the shortage of suitable escort vessels. He also dreaded the carnage that would result should they run into a minefield; he fretted over the practical problems of maintaining convoy speed and of co-ordinating the zigzagging courses of ships of vastly different capabilities. Underneath it all he had the lurking fear that a convoy would merely gather together potential victims for an orgy of destruction should the U-boats get among them. Convoys had been successfully employed right from the start of the war for troop transports, but it was argued that they were effective because they were composed of the very finest merchantmen and liners with highly experienced crews capable of operating with military precision.

The pressure to introduce convoys continued to grow, receiving further impetus with a successful experiment for the Scandinavian trade which dramatically reduced losses. Still the arguments continued as this was just one of several major sea routes. Many at the Admiralty rejected the idea of organising all the sea routes into a comprehensive convoy system but, in the event, the losses suffered in April 1917 were such that by the end of the month it was belatedly decided to give convoys a proper trial. The US declaration of war had also eased slightly the shortage of appropriate naval escorts. The first experimental convoys began in May 1917 and proved a great success with none of the anticipated problems in station-keeping. But the introduction of a fully fledged convoy system was very slow and shipping losses remained high throughout the summer of 1917.

Jellicoe was still swamped by the real or imagined practical difficulties of the convoy system and so felt no urgency in addressing the implementation of the policy. A dull pessimism began to colour his whole outlook on the war. This showed itself most clearly in a controversy over the measures required to destroy or render useless the German destroyer and submarine bases established in the Belgian ports of Zeebrugge and Ostend. Jellicoe had correctly pointed out the impossibility of achieving anything worthwhile using long-range naval bombardments and he had become convinced that the Army must assist in clearing the north Belgian coast before the winter of 1917 brought an end to the campaigning season. This was not so controversial in itself, but Haig would become an aghast spectator when Jellicoe made an ill-judged intervention at a meeting of the War Policy Committee on 20 June 1917. He was speaking in support of Haig's planned Flanders offensive, but his line of reasoning went well beyond acceptable limits.

> A most serious and startling situation was disclosed today. At today's conference, Admiral Jellicoe, as First Sea Lord, stated that owing to the great shortage of shipping due to German submarines it would be impossible for Great Britain to continue the war in 1918. This was a bombshell for the Cabinet and all present. A full enquiry is to be made as to the real facts on which this opinion of the Naval Authorities is based. No one present shared Jellicoe's view, and all seemed satisfied that the food reserves in Great Britain are adequate. Jellicoe's words were, 'There is no use discussing plans for next spring – we cannot go on!'[6]
>
> Field Marshal Sir Douglas Haig, General Headquarters, BEF

Haig was characteristically blunt in his overall appraisal of Jellicoe: 'I am afraid he does not impress me – indeed, he strikes me as being an old woman!'[7] Haig was being a little unfair to a great naval commander who was hampered by the effects of chronic fatigue caused by his own devoted service to his country in positions of the highest responsibility throughout the war. But, in essence, Haig was right: the diminished power of Jellicoe's decision-making had made him a liability. Jellicoe still had the complete support of the First Lord of the Admiralty Lord Carson, but the new Prime

Minister, David Lloyd George, ever the consummate politician, 'promoted' Carson into the War Cabinet and appointed the vigorous former industrialist Sir Eric Geddes in his stead on 20 July. The amateur naval man Geddes would in fact bring a thoroughgoing professionalism to the Admiralty, reorganising the function of the Sea Lords and the Admiralty staff to increase performance at all levels of the administration. Jellicoe was left exposed and knew that he was next in the Prime Minister's sights.

The slow introduction of convoys was indeed a complex matter, demanding both a huge organisational effort and a steep learning curve for everyone concerned. The civilian crews of merchant navy vessels had to familiarise themselves with new working methods and accept the requirement for constant vigilance if they were not to be involved in a collision or lose touch with the convoy – especially when steaming without lights at night. Most coped better than the Admiralty had ever dreamed possible.

> Convoy has added many new duties to the sum of our activities when at sea. Signals have assumed an importance in the navigation. The flutter of a single flag may set us off on a new course at any minute of the day. Failure to read a hoist correctly may result in instant collision with a sister ship. We have need of all eyes on the bridge to keep apace with the orders of the commodore. In station-keeping we are brought to the practice of a branch of seamanship with which not many of us were familiar. Steaming independently, we had only one order for the engineer when we had dropped the pilot. 'Full speed ahead!' we said, and rang a triple jangle of the telegraph to let the engineer on watch know that there would be no more 'backing and filling' – and that he could now nip into the stokehold to see to the state of the fires. Gone – our easy ways! We have now to keep close watch on the guide-ship and fret the engineer to adjustments of the speed that keep him permanently at the levers. The fires may clag and grey down through unskillful stoking – the steam go 'back' without warning: ever and on, he has to jump to the gaping mouth of the voice-tube, 'Whit? Two revolutions? Ach! Ah cannae gi' her any mair!' but he does! Slowly perhaps, but surely, as he coaxes steam from the errant stokers, we draw ahead and regain our place in the line. No small measure of the success of convoy is built up in the engine-rooms of our mercantile fleets.[8]
>
> Captain David Bone, SS *Cameronia*

All the hard work proved a worthwhile investment. By the end of September some eighty-three inward convoys had arrived, totalling 1,306 merchantmen. Only eighteen ships had been sunk, eight of which had been lost after dropping out of their convoys. Similarly just two ships were sunk in the fifty-five outward-bound convoys. There was a further boon as the convoys also allowed a more effective use of the naval intelligence still pouring in from Room 40 and the wireless directional stations. This provided a wealth of information as to the approximate location of German submarines which seemed to have no concept of wireless silence. Although too geographically vague to be of much use for the multifarious patrols engaged in the generally fruitless task of tracking down and sinking U-boats, it did greatly assist convoys as they could be diverted round the dangerous waters where U-boats were known to be operating. The U-boats found the oceans bare and empty as a group of ships sailing in a tightly packed convoy were only marginally more visible to a submarine than a single ship. Even as early as August 1917, Lieutenant Commander Alfred Saalwächter commanding the *U-94*, realised the impact of the new system.

> The convoys, with their strong and efficient escorts making an attack extremely difficult, are in my view quite capable of drastically reducing shipping losses. The chances of sighting a convoy of seven ships is less than that of sighting seven independent ships. In the case of a convoy it is mostly possible to only fire on one ship. For any ship torpedoed in convoy, the chance of immediate help is a factor of considerable importance to morale.[9]
>
> Lieutenant Commander Alfred Saalwächter, *U-94*

When they did encounter a convoy, the submarine commanders were forced to take excessive risks to score their kills, all the while harried by armed escorts and liberally bespattered with depth charges. The log book kept by Lieutenant Commander Hans Adam of the *U-82* reveals the chances that had to be taken and difficulties surmounted to make a successful attack on a convoy in September 1917.

> I shot past the bows of this steamer towards Steamers 4 and 5. Steamer 4 I hit. Steamer 2 had hoisted a red flag, which was probably to announce the presence of the U-boat; for several torpedo boats make for

the steamer. As there was no chance of firing from the only remaining usable tube (stern tube), I dived. The destroyers dropped about ten depth charges; one burst pretty near the stern. The attack was rendered very difficult by the bad weather, swell, seaway and rain squalls. The success of the attack was due to the excellent steering under water. Made off noiselessly south-east under water. 4.45 pm rose to surface. I try to come up with the convoy again, as it is still to be seen. But a destroyer forces me under water again. 6.37 pm rose to surface. Two destroyers prevent me from steaming up. Owing to heavy seas from south-east it is impossible to proceed south so as to get ahead of them. Moreover, sea and swell make it impossible to fire a torpedo. Therefore gave up pursuit.[10]

Lieutenant Commander Hans Adam, *U-82*

Gradually the rate at which Allied shipping was being sunk began to fall in a direct proportion to the number of ships travelling in convoy; at the same time the numbers of U-boats sunk began to rise. Almost despite itself, the Admiralty had stumbled across the solution to the submarine crisis. Nevertheless, it was all too late for Jellicoe: exhausted by his efforts and dogged by the enmity – or worse, ill-disguised contempt – of both Lloyd George and Geddes, he would be finally dismissed by Geddes on 24 December 1917. The new First Sea Lord, Vice Admiral Sir Rosslyn Wemyss, had a far greater residual energy and was able to build on the sure foundations that Jellicoe had laid. Wemyss would continue Jellicoe's reforms within the Admiralty, building a logical staff structure that allowed the proper delegation of decisions and responsibility.

By the end of 1917 one of the great questions of the war had been answered: Britain would not after all be starved out. The failure of their submarines to achieve their ambitious targets resulted in a severe blow to German morale and the German High Command realised that the war would not be won by the U-boats. The Battle of Jutland had confirmed that the British blockade of Germany would endure. The 1917 defeat of the U-boats, however, would ultimately result in the 1918 Spring Offensives designed to knock Britain out of the war on land before the Americans could arrive in strength on the Western Front.

By 1918, the Americans were firmly welded into the Grand Fleet which would move south to Rosyth, in the Firth of Forth, at Beatty's instigation in April 1918. The Americans contributed the five fast dreadnoughts of the 6th Battle Squadron, under the command of Rear Admiral Hugh Rodman, which were soon integrated into the fleet. Rodman showed a refreshing willingness to conform to British methods of tactics, gunnery and signals, recognising the value of the long years of war experience possessed by the Royal Navy. This stood in sharp contrast to the attitude adopted by General John Pershing and the American Expeditionary Force on the Western Front, who blatantly ignored the advice of British and French commanders at every turn.

In the war against U-boats, the convoy system was now in full swing and operating with ever-increasing effectiveness. Submarines were hunted down with a remorseless savagery. For the U-boat crews it could be a terrible ordeal, as Captain Lieutenant Johannes Speiss, by this time in command of the *U-19*, experienced off the Scottish island of Oversay on 15 April.

At 8.25 pm, I cautiously ran out the periscope in order to make a general survey, since the *Foxglove* must have been passed according to my calculations. To my astonishment I saw him dead ahead of us about 1,000 metres distant and apparently stopped. 'Periscope in!' 'Submerge to 20 metres!' At the same moment BRUMMMS ... As a result of the shock I almost fell into the central station. The depth charge landed right near the conning tower, everything was shaking. 'Submerge deeper!' 'Full speed!' BRUMMMS ... Damn, that was some explosion, the lighting globes broke. 'Cut in emergency lighting system! Noiseless speed, course west!' The storage batteries are almost discharged. Twenty minutes pass and everything is quiet. Apparently the listening devices have lost us and there is no oil streak or propeller wash on the surface to betray the boat. I wanted to renew the attack and at first came up towards the surface very cautiously. Suddenly BRUMMMS ... right on top of us! BRUMMMS ... somewhat further away. He has lost us again. Deeper with the boat. 'All hands forward!' BRUMMMS ... BRUMMMS ... these damned charges. BRUMMMS ... another shock, everything was knocked – we had touched bottom. 'Stop the engines! Flood all tanks, stay on the bottom!' The depth indicator shows 50 metres. The boat has negative buoyancy and remains motionless on the bottom. BRUMMMS ... another depth charge, probably dropped on the water eddies we stirred up, the water must be very clear for him to see so plainly. BRUMMMS ... another one. 'Stop everything, in the boat, so that he cannot hear us!' The situation was more than critical.

Quite overcome by the severe explosions we sat, small and angry, on the bottom of the Atlantic Ocean where fortunately the water was somewhat shallow.[11]

Captain Lieutenant Johannes Speiss, *U-19*

In the end Speiss and his men were very lucky as the escort vessel moved off. Had it not done so, with his electrical batteries almost totally expended, Speiss would have had no choice but to blow the *U-19*'s tanks, surface and accept his fate.

One incident among hundreds of clashes between submarines and escort vessels occurred on 31 May 1918 when a convoy of some thirty merchantmen was being escorted past Flamborough Head on the east coast of Yorkshire by a conglomeration of armed whalers and trawlers led by Lieutenant Geoffrey Barnish aboard the destroyer *Fairy*. Suddenly, not far off Bridlington, Barnish heard a loud thump from the convoy and rushed to the bridge to find that the steamer *Blaydonian* had collided with a submarine. At first Barnish was in a quandary.

In the past we had all had one or two scares over our own submarines suddenly appearing on the surface after their patrol in the Bight, and wanting the bearing and distance of Middlesbrough or the Tyne. I couldn't understand a German submarine being in this position, so you can well imagine my extreme anxiety. We made challenge after challenge, while all the time we were rapidly approaching our friend or foe. Then I decided we must cripple her, so that, if she did turn out to be British, our own unfortunate fellows would have a chance to save their lives. With that object in view, I ordered the torpedo coxswain (William James Spinner) to steer for her stern, or what I thought to be her stern. We were very close to her by now, and I cannot express to you my relief when I heard a voice from her conning-tower calling, '*Kamerad! Kamerad!*' I knew exactly what to do now, and quickly ordered the coxswain to port the helm in order to hit her in a more vital spot. But we were too close for the helm to have any effect, and quickly passed over the stern of our enemy. I don't remember feeling any considerable force of impact at this time, and we probably damaged ourselves more than we did him. However, on passing over him, I determined to renew the attack by ram, and, sending the gunner aft to open fire with our after gun, proceeded to turn the *Fairy* round. The submarine fired her gun but we shelled her from point blank range with the after 6-pounder. In all, forty direct hits were made. The Germans on the submarine's bridge now jumped into the water as we came on again with our ram. I always remember wondering how far back our bows would be pushed in, and with these feelings I backed to the wheel and kept my hand on the coxswain, probably deriving a feeling of comfort, as well as knowing that the coxswain would do what I wanted him to do with my hand directing. The destroyer's bows struck the U-boat close beside the gun. We on the bridge found ourselves all mixed up on the deck. How far we pushed our stem in I don't really know, for the next thing I realised was that our fore-deck was under water and the submarine had disappeared, leaving two Germans calmly standing on our submerged forecastle with their hands held up. We picked up three more later.[12]

Lieutenant Geoffrey Barnish, HMS *Fairy*

They would soon be back in the water! Sadly, the *Fairy* was one of the very first destroyers, built back in 1897, and the damage she suffered was such that she too would soon join her erstwhile adversary beneath the waves.

The net and mine barrage was also being steadily extended to try to prevent U-boats from gaining access to the open seas. Much work was carried out on the barrage across the Dover Straits while a far more ambitious project created a new Northern Barrage stretching 240 miles from the Orkneys across to the Norwegian coast. This was never really effective due to practical problems with the mines, which were not only laid too deep to affect submarines on the surface but also had an disquieting tendency to self-detonate in chains of spectacular explosions. Yet the Northern Barrage, for all its faults, was still a stern test for the nerves of U-boat crews, who were forced to pass over or through it twice on every voyage.

The ships of the 10th Cruiser Squadron had been ploughing their lonely furrows across the northern waters since 1914. The squadron continued its low-key but important role in enforcing the naval blockade on Germany. The blockade had been steadily tightened by more patrolling cruisers augmented by the ever-useful armed trawlers. The careful monitoring and control of the passage of neutral cargoes by direct inspection, coupled with the merciless application of economic power vouchsafed through British control of steamer coal supplies, gradually brought the neutral countries to heel and they ceased to attempt blockade running.

As the war went on it had also become clear that neutral shipping companies could make far more money trading legitimately without recourse to blockade running and risking the wrath of the British. Finally, the combination of the entry of the United States into the war, coupled with an effective convoy system, removed the need for the northern patrol. Its armed merchant cruisers would gradually be reassigned to convoy escorts between June 1917 and January 1918. The patrol endured only in skeleton form with the trawlers and drifters that tended to the net and mine barrage across the North Sea.

One adventurous operation sanctioned by the Admiralty against the submarine menace was the Zeebrugge Raid of 23 April 1918. There had long been a variety of plans to try and block the Zeebrugge and Ostend entrances via canals to the Bruges lair of the Flanders U-boats. The final version of the plan was overseen by Vice Admiral Sir Roger Keyes. An aged – and hence expendable – cruiser, the *Vindictive*, was to lie alongside the long Zeebrugge harbour mole and launch an attack by a 900-strong landing party who were to overwhelm the German gun batteries covering the entrance to the harbour. To prevent reinforcements intervening the *C1* and *C2* submarines had each taken on board some five tons of high explosives to destroy the viaduct linking the mole with the shore. During the chaos created by these actions and amidst a smokescreen, three more old cruisers, the *Thetis*, the *Intrepid* and the *Iphigenia*, would be scuttled across the entrance to the Bruges Canal.

The *Vindictive* and the block ships were all crewed by volunteers. When Able Seaman Wilfred Wainwright first went aboard the *Vindictive* he was greatly impressed by the measures that had been taken to fit her out for her special – and extremely dangerous – role alongside the Zeebrugge Mole.

> She had been stripped bare of everything bar the essential parts, her mainmast having gone and her foremast cut short above the fighting top. Along her portside ran an immense wooden chafing band reinforced with huge hazelwood fenders and on the port quarter a part of the main mast had been cemented to the deck to enable her to lay alongside any wall without swinging out, head on stern. Covering her port battery ran a false deck lined with sandbags, and towering above this deck was an array of improvised gangways, sixteen in all, flanked by two huge metal huts housing the foremost and aftermost

flame throwers. At the break of the fo'c'sle and the quarter deck
were two grapnels fitted to wire pennants and leading respectively to
the foremost and after capstans. Here fore and after guns had been
replaced by 7.5 howitzers and midships abaft the after funnel was an
11-inch howitzer, the port battery had been replaced with 2-pound
pom-poms, with the exception of the foremost and after 6-inch gun,
whilst two pom-poms adorned the fighting top. There is no denying
it she was ugly, as she lay there, a veritable floating fortress, a death-
trap fitted with all the ingenious contrivances of war that the human
brain could think of, but we took unholy pride and a fiendish delight
in her.[13]

Ordinary Seaman Wilfred Wainwright, HMS *Vindictive*

Naturally, the atmosphere was extremely tense aboard the ships as they
sailed across the North Sea. The men could not but be aware of the terrible risks they were taking. The success of the raid demanded that almost
everything went off perfectly. There was no margin for error. But for the
most part they were young and ready for anything. As they approached
the mole, despite the smokescreen, they were soon detected and exposed
to close-range fire from the German batteries.

Night had turned into day by searchlights and star shells, and all the
venom and hatred of the shore batteries seemed concentrated on us,
salvo after salvo struck the ship, doing indescribable damage in the
packed starboard battery where all the storming party were awaiting to
land; the foremost howitzer's crew were wiped out with the exception
of the voice pipeman, who was a couple of yards away. The strangest
part of this was that the trench mortar battery, not more than 4 feet
away, did not receive injury at that time. Within the space of a few
seconds the leading seaman in charge of our battery had been hit in
the back of the head, whilst half a dozen of our battery had received
superficial scratches. We were now alongside the Mole and sheltered a
little from the murderous hail of shell from the forts, which continued
to keep up a burst of shrapnel around our funnels, which showed
up and made excellent targets. Every gun in the *Vindictive* that could
bear had now given tongue and the night was made hideous by the
nerve-racking shatter of the pom-poms, the deep bell-like boom of the
howitzers and trench mortars, and all-pervading rattle of musketry and

machine-gun fire; it was hell with a vengeance and it seemed well-nigh miraculous that human beings could live in such an inferno.[14]

Ordinary Seaman Wilfred Wainwright, HMS *Vindictive*

Just after midnight the *Vindictive* had crashed alongside the Mole some 300 yards further away from the German fortified area and gun batteries than had been intended. This added to the already intense difficulties facing the landing parties forced to clamber ashore under heavy fire.

Already a gaping hole had been torn in the side of our ship by a shell. As we swarmed down the landing boards we hurriedly bade our nearest comrade 'goodbye' and 'good luck'. Each section had its appointed task. Shells were raking backwards and forwards, terrific explosions followed, and groans and cries and shouts filled the air. Star shells shed their light on the scene, and all the time our lads were creeping steadily forwards in the darkness, pelting away at the black masses of the enemy, which loomed ahead.[15]

Able Seaman Cyril Widdison, HMS *Vindictive*

It proved impossible to reach the batteries so they did what damage they could. Private William Gough was encumbered with a flamethrower intended for use against the occupants of sheds located on the inner side of the mole.

The flamethrower was a heavy, unwieldy cylinder containing a mixture of fuel oil and petrol, squirted from a nozzle, and ignited by a electrically fired flare in front of the nozzle. The jet of flame extended for about 30 yards. Because of the awkwardness of this weapon, I lost much time reaching the sheds, having to negotiate several obstacles including a 15–20 foot wall, using ropes and ladders to scramble down it. As a result I lost touch with my little party of marines. On reaching my objective, and entering the shed, I realised I was not needed there. The building had been blown up leaving four wrecked walls, shattered rifles and two dead Germans. Pressing on, I found myself up against an iron handrail at the water's edge, and in front of me a German destroyer, with her guns firing and most of her crew on deck. I turned my flammenwerfer on them, sweeping the deck with flames. I must have killed a whole lot of them. I tried to reach the bridge, from which someone was potting at me with a revolver, but the range was too great, and my flamethrower ran out of fuel. As the bullets from a machine-gun further up the mole got too close for comfort, I left my now useless weapon and took cover behind a low wall.[16]

Private William Gough, 4th Battalion, Royal Marines, HMS *Vindictive*

Getting back on to the *Vindictive* was no easy matter.

Just after one o'clock the retreat was sounded, and all those of us who were left ran breathlessly back – ran for our lives amid a hail of shot and shell. Of 14 or 16 landing boards only two remained, and these creaked and bent ominously as 300 or 400 of us scrambled aboard. Some of us were helping wounded comrades along; and whilst other fellows had to be carried aboard, I found one poor lad lying helplessly on the shore, only a few yards from the gangway, and with a pal's assistance I managed to get him safely on board.[17]

Able Seaman Cyril Widdison, HMS *Vindictive*

From the *Vindictive* Captain Alfred Carpenter watched the block ships make their way into the harbour, sadly still under heavy fire from the mole batteries. They had all been filled to the gills with concrete in readiness for the detonation of explosive charges placed aboard their hulls to facilitate rapid scuttling.

We saw *Thetis* come steaming into the harbour in grand style. She made straight for the opening to the Canal, and you can imagine that she was a blaze of light and a target for every big thing they could bring to bear. She was going toppingly, all the same, when she had the rotten luck to catch her propeller in the defence nets. Even then, however, she did fine work. She signalled instructions to the *Intrepid* and *Iphigenia*, and so they managed to avoid the nets. It was a gorgeous piece of co-operation! In went *Intrepid*, and in after her went *Iphigenia*. They weren't content, you know, to sink themselves at the mouth of the Canal. That was not the idea at all. They had to go right in, with guns firing point-blank at them from both banks, sink their ships, and get back as best they could. And they did it. They blocked that Canal as neatly and effectively as we could have wished in our most optimistic moments, and then, thanks to the little motor-launches, which were handled with the finest skill and pluck, the commanders and men got back to safety. As soon as we saw that the block ships were sunk we knew that our job was done.[18]

Captain Alfred Carpenter, HMS *Vindictive*

As they withdrew it was time for the British to count the cost: they had lost a destroyer and two motor launches and suffered 170 dead, 400 wounded and 45 missing. But had Captain Carpenter been right? Had they really managed to block the Zeebrugge entrance to the Bruges Canal? Certainly, the simultaneous raid on Ostend had been an abject failure, but at least at first there seemed good reason to celebrate success at Zeebrugge and eight VCs were awarded. In the event, the Germans were merely inconvenienced in their navigation by the block ships before a new channel was dredged just three weeks later. All that the British had achieved was a short-lived propaganda coup which had no effect on the submarine war in contrast to the less glamorous hard graft of convoys escort details where the submarine war was being fought and won.

Coincidentally, the High Seas Fleet had made a sortie on 24 April 1918 into the North Sea to try and intercept one of the regular Scandinavian convoys. These large convoys were often escorted by heavy ships and posed a tempting – and isolated – target. This time the Germans concealed their intentions from the British by maintaining strict wireless silence and a great success looked likely. Yet, for all the planning, Scheer had omitted to check with the German embassy in Norway as to the sailing dates of the convoys. In fact, none was scheduled for 24 April. The problems mounted when the battlecruiser *Moltke* suffered a catastrophic engine breakdown which ultimately required her to be taken in tow. The wireless signals exchanged during this incident were intercepted by Room 40 with the result that Beatty and the Grand Fleet sailed from Rosyth, steaming across the North Sea on an intercepting course. In the end, they were too late and Scheer escaped back to harbour. Both sides had failed, but the British still held the ring around Germany. It would be the last outing for the High Seas Fleet.

In August Scheer was appointed Chief of the German Admiralty Staff, with Hipper succeeding him as Commander in Chief of the High Seas Fleet. The British considered Hipper more aggressive than Scheer and nurtured hopes that *'Der Tag'* might finally dawn. They were also well aware of evidence of unrest in the German fleet. Crews, cooped up in harbour for too long, had been increasingly influenced by socialist propaganda. British optimists hoped that the Germans might despatch the fleet off to sea – to allow the simmering crews to kill or be killed. In the event Hipper did plan one last great operation in the North Sea, but it was stillborn when the German crews mutinied on being ordered to leave Wilhelm-shaven on 29 October. Seaman Richard Stumpf watched events from the pre-dreadnought *Lothringen*.

> We all knew within our hearts – today is the last time we shall ever see many of our ships. My mind contemplated what would happen if we engaged and destroyed the enemy fleet. I toyed with the most grotesque possibilities. In the final analysis this might still result in our victory. Soon, however, an impregnable veil of fog descended upon the sea. The weather made any thought of sailing out impossible. In the sea of fog and fine rain one could no longer make out the stem of the vessel from amidship. Soon thereafter we heard that the stokers on three battlecruisers had deliberately allowed the fires to die down and had even extinguished them. At this time about a hundred men from *Von der Tann* were running loose about town; *Seydlitz* and *Derfflinger* were missing men. Thus the fleet could not have sailed even if there had been no fog. It is sad, tragic that it could go so far as this. But somehow even with the best of intentions I cannot suppress a certain sense of *Schadenfreude*. What has happened to the almighty power of the proud captains and staff engineers? Now at last, after many years, the suppressed stokers and sailors realise that nothing, no, nothing, can be accomplished without them. On the *Thüringen*, the former model ship of the fleet, the mutiny was at its worst. The crew simply locked up the petty officers and refused to weigh anchor. The men told the Captain that they would only fight against the English if their fleet appeared in German waters. They no longer wanted to risk their lives uselessly.[19]
>
> Seaman Richard Stumpf, SMS *Lothringen*

The High Seas Fleet was finished as a combative force. Hipper called off the operation and dispersed his fleet to try and dispel the mutiny. A sub-sequent investigation carried out by Hipper's Chief of Staff, Rear Admiral Adolf von Trotha, ranged wide and in its findings echoed earlier pre-war fears as to Germany's ability to withstand a prolonged conflict against the Triple Entente.

> There appears to be ample proof that our armed forces were unable to withstand such a long war, as soon as the moral boost of success was missing and particularly when want and deprivation were presenting the Home Front with such a prodigious struggle. The unceasing depletion in the front line ranks, of youthful enthusiasm and ability

in officers and men; their replacement by older age groups already burdened by home worries, or by the very young and inexperienced age-groups, already influenced by the eroding effects of the struggle on the Home Front – this endless and inevitable trend created an unsound foundation and provided the essential ingredients for discontent. In spite of its much lighter losses, this process wormed its way into the Navy, too.[20]

Rear Admiral Adolf von Trotha, Headquarters, High Seas Fleet

The German Navy had been defeated. Worse still, it had never really been put to the test in full-scale battle. No one would ever know what might have been had they sought out battle in 1914 when the Royal Navy was at its most stretched. The High Seas Fleet was a 'risk fleet' that in the end the Kaiser lacked the nerve. The Royal Navy was left frustrated not to have secured the destruction of the High Seas Fleet in battle; that indeed would rankle as long as the memoirs were written. Yet it had carried out its main duties in the Great War successfully. The safe passage of the British Army to the Western Front had been secured and guaranteed; the sea ways across the globe had been defended, even against the U-boat threat; and throughout the war Germany had been partially starved of raw materials by the blockade. These were the valuable rewards of the exercise of pure naval power. In the end the High Seas Fleet created by Tirpitz at such expense, the fleet that had guaranteed British enmity towards Germany, had not achieved much more than the harbour-locked Prussian fleet during the Franco-Prussian War back in 1870. It had all been for nothing.

15

THE WESTERN FRONT, 1917

'If our resources are concentrated in France to the fullest possible extent, the British Armies are capable and can be relied on to effect great results this summer – results which will make final victory more assured and which may even bring it within reach this year. To fail in concentrating our resources in the Western theatres, or to divert them from it, would be most dangerous. It might lead to the collapse of France. It would certainly encourage Germany.'[1]

Field Marshal Sir Douglas Haig, General Headquarters, BEF

THE BRITISH AND FRENCH APPROACHED 1917 with a considerable degree of confidence. Lacking the benefit of hindsight, the Allied leaders had no idea that revolution would first cripple and then remove their Russian ally from the war. All they knew was that the Somme and Verdun campaigns had been horrendous experiences for the German Army, while the Russian Brusilov Offensive had put it under additional pressure on the Eastern Front. There was a hope – a conviction, even – that the German Army must be approaching exhaustion. Ever since the war had begun the German Army had been outnumbered and the male population of military age was a finite resource. Although their superior military preparation and competence had brought the Germans success, there was a temptation among the Allies to believe that surely the pressure would tell in the end. Germany's accumulating military problems were matched by straitened economic conditions caused by a combination of the Royal Navy blockade and the exorbitant cost of war. Foodstuff and clothes both had to be rationed severely and for the German High Command the overall outlook was bleak: they had no option but to stand on the defensive. But this did not mean that they were passive; indeed, they had conducted a root and branch re-assessment of their defensive tactics in view of the increasing evidence that both the British on the Somme and the French at Verdun had begun to master the existing tactical configuration.

> The course of the Somme battle had also supplied important lessons with regard to the construction and plan of our lines. The very deep underground forts in the front line trenches had to be replaced by shallower constructions. Concrete pillboxes (which, however, unfortunately took a long time to build) had acquired an increasing value. The conspicuous lines of trenches, which appeared as sharp lines on every aerial photograph, supplied far too good a target for the enemy artillery. The whole system of defence had to be made broader, looser and better adapted to the ground.[2]
>
> General Erich Ludendorff, General Headquarters

Instead of a linear system the Germans began to look at the possibility of deeper defensive zones with different functions. The forward zone, which was bound to be lashed by the shells of the Allied field artillery, would in future be lightly held, but with the reduced garrisons protected in reinforced concrete pillboxes from which they would rely on the crossfire of their machine guns and great swathes of barbed wire to cover the gaps between them. Forward troops were no longer expected necessarily to fight to the last man, but were granted the freedom to fall back and carry on fighting from a less hopeless situation. The counter-attack divisions were to be kept further back, well out of reach of the field artillery, ready to attack just as the Allied assaulting troops were tiring and no longer supported by their own guns. Several officers were involved in the gestation of these techniques, but the key proponent was Colonel Fritz von Lossberg, who was despatched as a senior staff officer to many of the areas most threatened by imminent French or British offensives. The reorganisation of the German defences on these principles represented an enormous investment of time, manpower and materials.

The Allied plans for 1917 called for more sustained attacks on the

German lines. At another co-ordinating conference held at Chantilly in November 1916, Joffre, in his usual dominant role, was determined to maintain the pressure on the Germans over the winter before launching further great French and British Spring Offensives on either side of the Somme battlefields. The BEF was to launch a major offensive between Vimy Ridge and the Ancre River, while the French would attack first between the Somme and the Oise Rivers, and then switch to another great attack in the Aisne and Chemin des Dames area. There were also plans for a British Summer Offensive in Flanders in order to sustain the pressure on the Germans.

Yet Germany was not the only nation that was suffering in 1916. The French Army had suffered heavy casualties during the Battle of the Frontiers; it had fought a series of painful offensive battles in 1915; then it had endured not only the long agony of Verdun, but had also played a considerable part on the Somme. Joffre seemed in control but, within a month, he had fallen from power. His reputation, once so bright after the Battle of the Marne, had been diminished by his inability to achieve victory in his costly offensives. His political masters were not interested in excuses and took little account of the strength of the Germans or the terrible problems of trench warfare. All they saw was failure and, informed by hindsight, pointed to his denuding of the defences of Verdun. Throughout 1916 a malicious whispering campaign had done much to undermine Joffre's position. Then, on 13 December 1916, he was effectively dismissed and appointed as military adviser to the government, a meaningless sop to deflect criticism. His replacement was General Robert Nivelle, who had built a considerable reputation during the later stages of Verdun and who was confident that he could deliver victory on a larger stage.

The British, too, were under strain. The Asquith Coalition, never the most robust of governments, had fallen in December 1916. The new Prime Minster was the Liberal, David Lloyd George, who managed to form another coalition based, to a large extent, on support from the Conservative Party. Lloyd George gave a far greater drive and energy than his predecessor to prosecuting the war. His eloquence was allied to a formidable intellect and a proven aptitude for hard work. In order to win Conservative support he had promised not to interfere in the strategic direction of the war, but nevertheless remained a firm devotee of Easterner operations that left him well adrift of his professional advisers. His schemes were entirely devoid of military logic and, when he promulgated his vague ideas for an offensive in Italy at the Allied Conference in Rome in January 1917, they were soon crushed by a combination of the British and French High Commands. The Italians, especially, took a dim view of being thrust forward into such a prominent role. Yet, at the same time, Lloyd George was able to hold back Haig, who would have liked more consideration of his long-standing plans for a major offensive in the Ypres area. Given Lloyd George's aversion to the prospect of more British casualties in the mire of the Western Front this plan was also discarded.

So it was that the last plan standing was that put forward by Nivelle. His success in the later offensives at Verdun in 1916 had convinced him that his methods were infallible, that he had the key to success. As such he planned a stupendous offensive in April 1917 against the long-contested Chemin des Dames Ridge lying behind the River Aisne, while the British pinned the German reserves with a separate offensive at Arras. Nivelle had a considerable ability to sell his plans.

> Our goal is nothing less than the destruction of the major part of the enemy's forces on the Western Front. We will achieve this only as the result of a decisive battle which engages all his available forces, followed up by an intensive exploitation. In the first and second phases, this means that we will have to break through his front, then beyond that breach engage any of his forces we have not yet fixed in other regions, and finally turn the bulk of our attacking force against his main lines of communication, forcing him into speedily abandoning his current front lines or accepting further combat under the most adverse of conditions. We will achieve these results by using a portion of our forces to fix the enemy and breach his front, then by committing our reserves beyond the point selected by me for the breakthrough.[3]
>
> General Robert Nivelle, General Headquarters

The Nivelle methodology lacked a certain subtlety as it envisioned a huge accumulation of artillery to create an utterly crushing bombardment under the cover of which two French armies would smash their way through the German lines before a third army burst through the breach. This was indeed an ambitious plan and there was a cautious response from Haig, who had concerns over the requirement on the BEF to take over the section of line stretching south from the Somme to the Oise River. Yet he was more than willing to allow the French to resume the main burden of the Allied effort. When it came to dealing with the politicians, Nivelle was far more persuasive than most of the more reserved generals that they had hitherto encountered. His vision of swift, certain success entranced in particular Lloyd George, who saw this as a way to avoid a prolonged bloodbath such as the Somme. And so it was that Nivelle's plan was accepted as the centrepiece of Allied efforts in 1917.

A month later Lloyd George, always an accomplished conspirator, ambushed his own generals at the joint Anglo-French Conference held at Calais on 26 February 1917. By careful prior liaison with French generals and politicians he manoeuvred to place Haig directly under the command of Nivelle. The splenetic row that followed was only calmed by a compromise proposed by the War Cabinet Secretary, Maurice Hankey. This placed Haig under Nivelle only for the duration of the offensive and allowed him the right of appeal to the British government should he consider the BEF to be in danger. Haig and the British GHQ were, none the less, furious.

> If the big French attack is indecisive in its result, then inevitably, as the war goes on, our army will become the biggest on the Western Front (unless Lloyd George sends everybody off on side-shows), and there is bound to be interminable friction. If the French attack fails altogether, we shall have the whole weight of the German Army on the top of us, and the position will be even more difficult. If Joffre were still in command of the French and they were putting the British Army under him there might be some justification for it, for he has all the experience of the war behind him, but Nivelle is new to the game, with far less experience of actual fighting than Douglas Haig, and, according to what we are hearing from French officers, he does not seem to have the confidence even of his own generals.[4]
>
> Brigadier General John Charteris, General Headquarters, BEF

Increasingly, the British political and military establishments were finding themselves at loggerheads. This was a dangerous state of affairs.

British Arras Offensive, April 1917

The Battle of Arras, although a diversionary operation, was a huge undertaking in itself. The plan was that the First Army, commanded by General

Sir Henry Horne, would capture Vimy Ridge rising up three miles north-east of the city of Arras, while the Third Army, commanded by General Sir Edmund Allenby, would drive forward towards the hill of Monchy-le-Preux with the intent of breaking through the main German defensive lines across the River Scarpe and allowing a thrust southwards towards Croisilles and Bullecourt. Many lessons had been learnt from the Somme and artillery was at the heart of the plans. And the Royal Artillery had come a long way since 1915. The thousands upon thousands of new recruits had learnt their trades well: the gun detachments, the layers, the NCOs, the officers were all now welded into efficient batteries that were capable of increasingly sophisticated and complex bombardments. The guns themselves were now plentiful and there were vast numbers of medium and heavy artillery pieces joining the masses of ordinary 18-pounder and 4.5-inch howitzer field artillery. Advances in technology and science also combined to give a greater understanding of the mechanics of a shell in flight and the measurable adjustments caused by different meteorological conditions. Accuracy was improving and the advent of the 106 fuse meant that shells would burst instantaneously on the slightest contact, which made clearing barbed wire a great deal simpler. Smoke shells were also now routinely incorporated into the barrages to try and mask the attacking infantry from the German defenders. Gas shells were a key part of the barrages: they were less visually dramatic than the clouds of gas released from cylinders, but they were far easier to deploy and much more predictable in their effects. Progress in the linked tasks of photographic reconnaissance and artillery observation allowed targets to be identified and then destroyed by indirect fire. New techniques of flash spotting and sound ranging also assisted in locating the exact positions of the German batteries. The idea of suppressing the ability of the German infantry and artillery to return fire at vital moments was now central to operations.

The primacy of the guns meant that the Battle of Arras would prove a particular trial for the RFC, charged with photographing the battlefield to record every new development and flying endless artillery observation missions to direct the guns on which the operations depended. The problem for the RFC was that the battle had come too early in the year for them to upgrade their sadly ageing aircraft with new models better able to hold their own against the new German aircraft such as the Albatros scout. The basic BE2 C army co-operation aircraft had done sterling work since its inception back in 1914, but it was now hopelessly outclassed: too slow and unable to manoeuvre or defend itself. Its intended replacement, the RE8, had been delayed and was only just beginning to arrive on the Western Front in early 1917. This meant that the latest upgraded versions of the BE2 C would have to struggle on for a few more months before they could be replaced. Multi-purpose aircraft like the FE2 B and the Sopwith 1½ Stutter were also showing their age. The British scouts were also lagging behind their German counterparts. The DH2, the FE8 and the Sopwith Pup, were all inadequate and although the French supplied the excellent Nieuport 17 and Spad VII to help in the interval before the next generation of British scouts arrived, the gap still loomed large. Trenchard was livid.

> You are asking me to fight the battle this year with the same machines as I fought it last year. We shall be hopelessly outclassed, and something must be done. I am not panicking, but the Hun is getting more aggressive. I warned you fairly as far back as last September, and the Chief also warned you in November. And I warned the Air Board personally on 12th December. All I can say is that there will be an outcry from all the pilots out here if we do not have at least these few squadrons of fast machines, and what I have asked for is absolutely necessary.[5]
>
> Brigadier General Hugh Trenchard, Headquarters, RFC

Trenchard drove his men forward, accepting casualties in order to obtain the photographs needed in the run-up to the offensive. The Imperial German Air Service also had its problems. Vastly outnumbered by the British and French in the air, it had no choice but to fight on as best it could. In doing so one of the key figures would be Lieutenant Manfred von Richthofen, an acolyte of Oswald Boelcke – who had been killed in a mid-air collision in October 1916. Richthofen had taken command of Jasta 11 and soon whipped his men into shape. Through a combination of his practical demonstration of superb air-fighting skills, astute tactical leadership and his ability to disseminate the lessons of air warfare, he converted pilots previously of no particular distinction into flying aces preying on the British aircraft almost at will. But they could not stop all of them and the RFC continued to deliver the photographs required by the Army.

One complication to the Allied plans was the German decision to withdraw to the Hindenburg Line far behind the existing positions on the Somme front. Built in accordance with the principles of defence in depth it was a formidable construction, shortening the German front by twenty-five miles and so freeing up some fourteen divisions from defensive duties holding the line. The retreat started in earnest on 14 March as the Germans abandoned their tactically suspect positions stretching from Arras down to the Aisne in the French area, implementing a vigorous scorched earth policy as they went. The cavalry came into their own as the Allies cautiously advanced across the new wastelands, with small patrols feeling their way forward. There was good reason to be cautious, for the Germans had also scattered booby traps to catch the unwary, with concealed delayed-action bombs timed to go off days afterwards. Throughout the advance the sappers were kept busy clearing booby traps and trying to restore basic elements of the wrecked infrastructure.

As the moment approached for the Battle of Arras to commence, on 9 April 1917, the artillery concentration had been completed with some 2,817 British guns facing only 1,014 German guns. There had been an interesting debate over the format of the opening bombardment which throws light on the continuing developments in British tactical thought. General Sir Edmund Allenby and his artillery advisers had favoured a short 48-hour bombardment, but Haig had demurred, pointing out that although the new 106 fuses offered hope of efficiently clearing the German barbed wire in the near future, there were simply not enough of them available at that point in time to allow for a short bombardment – something had to clear the wire, and a long bombardment was the only method then available. Tanks were a possible solution, but production had not kept up with demand from the front. Only sixty were available for the attack and hence their role was confined to taking out troublesome nests of German strongpoints. The final plans featured a four-day bombardment that drenched the German trenches and supporting gun batteries with tens of thousands of shells. Then, as the British and Canadian infantry went over the top, the thunderous creeping barrages would create a wall of shells, mixing high explosive, shrapnel and smoke shells, to chaperone them safely over the German lines. One interesting innovation was the use of Livens projectors, which could hurl large barrels of gas some 1,200 yards to saturate a locality with gas. The planning and preparations were complex in the extreme. Just moving the guns was a herculean effort, but then huge mines had to be dug, charges laid and tunnels hacked out in order to move the troops safely to the front. And of course the infantry had to be trained in using all the most modern techniques. Everything that could be done had been done; but that had been the case on the Somme as well. Had the Allies got it right this time?

On 4 April the British barrage began: a naked demonstration of the power of the guns as the shells rained down on the German trenches, strongpoints, machine gun posts, command headquarters and artillery batteries. One relatively new development was the use of batteries of Vickers machine guns firing on indirect lines of fire at long range to hose bullets down on road junctions. The barrage also marked the beginning of the offensive in the air. Trenchard was determined to deliver on his obligations to the Army, which meant innumerable artillery observation flights to correct the gunnery and photographic missions to determine the damage inflicted. The RFC intended to dominate the air above the battle zone and for up to twenty miles behind it – or die trying. Many British air crew would indeed lose their lives as they encountered the deadly guns of Richthofen, popularly known as the Red Baron, and the other German aces – not for nothing would this become known as 'Bloody April' by the RFC. Lieutenant Peter Warren, accompanied by his observer Sergeant Reuel Dunn, discovered for himself the deadly effectiveness of Richthofen, when he pounced on their Sopwith 1½ Stutter while on a vital mission of photographing defence works to the east of Vimy Ridge.

> Another burst of lead from behind and the bullets spattered on the breech of my own machine gun, cutting the cartridge belt. At the same time, my engine stopped and I knew that the fuel tanks had been hit. There were more clouds below me. I dove for them and tried to pull up in them as soon as I reached them. No luck! My elevators didn't answer the stick. The control wires had been shot away. There was nothing to do but go down and hope to keep out of a spin as best as I could. I side-slipped and then went into a dive which fast became a spiral. I don't know how I got out of it. I was busy with the useless controls all the time, and going down at a frightful speed, but the red machine seemed to be able to keep itself poised just above and behind me all the time, and its machine guns were working every minute. I found later that bullets had gone through both of my sleeves and both of my boot

legs, but in all of the firing, not one of them touched me. I managed to flatten out somehow in the landing and piled up with an awful crash. As I hit the ground, the red machine swooped over me, but I don't remember him firing on me when I was on the ground.[6]

Lieutenant Peter Warren, 43rd Squadron, RFC

Both sides risked everything knowing that if they failed in the air the consequences could be disastrous for their comrades on the ground.

At 05.30 on Easter Monday, 9 April, the Battle of Arras began as the massed guns blazed out all along the line and two mines ripped open the ground under the German positions. At the same time every German battery identified by the RFC was deluged with high explosives and gas shells.

All of a sudden, as though at a single word of command, down came drum fire from thousands of large and small calibre muzzles. Shell fire rose to crazy heights. It was impossible to distinguish the firing signatures from the shell bursts. It was just one mass of fire amidst an extraordinary racket. It was like the final intake of breath before a race. Nerves were stretched to breaking point as we took in these scenes, which were like a painting of terrible beauty. Standing there for just a few seconds, a shell landed just to my left and a fragment hit my left side at chest height. My nerves took another knock. My heart was like lead, the gorge rose in my throat; blood ran into my mouth, taking my breath away. I was at the end of my strength, ready to faint.[7]

Second Lieutenant Bittkau, 263rd Reserve Infantry Regiment

After just three minutes the creeping barrages began to roll their way forward. On Vimy Ridge, close behind came the Canadian infantry, partially concealed by a smoke screen. The summit was far too narrow to allow any practical defence in depth; here the Germans had to hold their front lines or lose the ridge. The Canadians were on the Germans before they knew what was happening. Many, like Second Lieutenant Bittkau, were trapped in their dugouts.

Suddenly came a thin shout, seemingly from far off, 'The British! Get out! Get out!' They were coming from the left, through the hollow, heading directly for Bonval Wood. Battle was joined – rifle shots – shouts – hand grenades. Hans Voigt came running up carrying ammunition and information, whilst down below secret documents were being burned. 'They are coming from the left – here they are!' More bawling and shouting. 'They are right above us!' Then it was quieter – completely quiet – until a strange voice called down, 'Come out!' The light flickered. Thoughts ran through my numbed head: what were they going to do? Throw down hand grenades? Smash my skull? No, better to shoot myself. But the revolver was lying on the table and I could not move. Should I wait for a counter-attack? A Tommy came through the tunnel, looked carefully round the corner, a large revolver in his hand. 'Officer?' he asked, then left to fetch his comrades.[8]

Second Lieutenant Bittkau, 263rd Reserve Infantry Regiment

The Canadians pushed on, seeking to take the whole ridge before the Germans could reorganise themselves.

There were several bodies lying in its ruins, and there was no resistance until we had passed it, making for the second line. Then we came under fire from machine guns in pillboxes on the hillside. Still we went forward, losing only a very few men at this stage, until, as if from nowhere, there came a withering burst of fire from hidden machine guns well ahead of us. We were really into it now. We halted for a short time, to get our breath back and plan for the next move. Then a trench mortar group came along, sighted on the machine gun post and secured direct hits on it. We again went forward, slowly and deliberately. When we finally reached the point at which we were to halt and allow other units to continue over our heads, we were surprised to find that we had been in action for three hours. It had been hard slogging but we had reached our objective.[9]

Private Magnus McIntyre Hood, 24th Battalion (Victoria Rifles), CEF

The Canadians and the British 51st Division to their right had already consolidated their position on Vimy Ridge before the German counter-attack divisions had any chance of getting there.

This has often been the sole memory retained of that day's fighting, but in many ways the assault by the Third Army up the Scarpe Valley to the hills around Monchy-le-Preux is a more dramatic story. The counter-battery arrangements had worked perfectly and as the British troops crashed through the German defences the German counter-attacks were thwarted by the walls of shells of the standing barrages. There were hold ups of course but the new artillery 'Zone Call' technique could bring down an awesome concentration of shells on any worthwhile target. Surviving German batteries made for ideal targets.

> My job was to direct the artillery and let them know which enemy batteries were in action. This was done by sending down what was known as a 'Zone Call'; by this signal a certain number of Batteries would fire on the target indicated and go on firing till I told them to stop or they had expended their quota of ammunition. It was grand to see them answering and the Hun getting hell. I managed to send down fourteen calls on active batteries which was great fun. After ten minutes shells could be seen falling all round the located batteries, the gunners are bursting with joy. I should think that our casualties from German artillery must be small as every time a Battery opened fire it was immediately 'zone called' and shelled to hell.[10]
>
> Captain Eric Routh, 16th Squadron, RFC

As the first wave of the assault divisions began to slow to a halt so the next wave pushed on for a total of three and a half miles. But then the advance faltered as it moved beyond the range of the field artillery. Some batteries were rushed forward in support, but were given little chance to establish their communications and register their targets, which considerably reduced their effectiveness. Tanks were quite incapable of providing any desperately needed stimulus, so Allenby turned to his only available mobile force – his cavalry – in an attempt to break through. But by the time they had moved forward the Germans had plugged the gaps and reorganised. For all their technical and tactical improvements, the British still had neither the method nor the means to break through the German defence system.

The Battle of Arras then moved into the depressing secondary stage which seemed to blight so many British offensives. The snowy weather helped to slow down attempts to capitalise on the moment and by the time they made a fully fledged renewed assault on 11 April the Germans were ready for them. The fighting centred on the villages of Monchy-le-Preux, Wancourt and the old Roeux chemical works, but the Germans held firm. The first day had seen a carefully prepared plan; this was a purely *ad hoc* attack. It failed totally. Even worse was an attempt by General Sir Hubert Gough's Fifth Army, who had only just struggled through the wasteland left by the retreating Germans, to launch an attack on the new Hindenburg Line in the Bullecourt sector. By the time the aftershocks had died down it became clear that the British were not going to break through to achieve any more major tactical objectives. In any event, they had already performed their diversionary role for Nivelle's great offensive at Chemin des Dames scheduled to start on 16 April. Even then, Haig was expected to keep up the pressure, with the upshot that a huge nine division attack was thrown together with the bare minimum of planning and preparation for the Second Battle of the Scarpe along a 9-mile front at Arras on 23 April 1917. It may have been a major offensive but it was woefully underresourced in comparison to the original attacks. Worse still, the Germans had by this time learnt most of the lessons that could be gleaned from the earlier fighting. In particular, they realised that when acting in a purely defensive capacity their artillery batteries could be located further back. From there they could still slaughter troops crossing No Man's Land, but were themselves safely out of range of most of the British guns. This made generating sufficient counter-battery fire a nigh-on impossible task for the Royal Artillery. The Germans had also moved up fresh divisions and re-organised their defences. The fighting was bitter; in essence the British made a painful blood sacrifice in the cause of diverting attention from the French offensive further south.

The Nivelle Offensive, 16 April 1917

Nivelle was confident that the tactics he had used at Verdun would bring him success on a larger scale. There he had relied on narrow front attacks in which the artillery created a narrow corridor through which the infantry could push forward. Now, at last, he believed the French had enough heavy, long-range guns to attack on a wide front, allowing a single, crunching thrust to be made by the French Fifth and Sixth Armies. The heavy artillery would then be moved forward as quickly as possible to maintain the momentum, forcing a complete breakthrough by the Tenth Army. Throughout, the infantry would be required to move forward as quickly as possible, bypassing German strongpoints and leaving them isolated and helpless, to be dealt with by the follow-up troops. Nivelle had convinced the politicians, but it would not be these august gentlemen that would be climbing out of the trenches on 16 April. And there is no doubt that there was a fractious mood abroad among the French troops. This is evident in the memoirs of Private Louis Barthas, serving in one of the intended follow-up battalions. Even before the battle they were embittered, as demonstrated by their reaction to the supposedly inspiring 'order of the day'.

> They read out an order of the day from that mass-murderer of 16 April, General Nivelle, to inform his troops (that is to say, his victims!) saying amidst other nonsense that, 'The hour of sacrifice has arrived and we must not think about leave!' Reading this patriotic nonsense aroused no enthusiasm. On the contrary, it only demoralised the soldiers, who heard nothing but another terrible threat: new suffering, great dangers, the prospect of an awful death in a vain and useless sacrifice, because no one trusted the outcome of this new butchery. However, our commanders did not seem to doubt for a moment that the Germans would be routed.[11]
>
> Private Louis Barthas, 296th Infantry Regiment

The ordinary French soldiers were becoming war weary. In ordering them forward for yet another great new offensive, Nivelle was risking more than he realised.

One key feature of the offensive was to be surprise; but surprise proved impossible. Nivelle was himself less than discreet in discussing his plans in front of civilians and security was further compromised by an assortment of French deserters. All this provided General Max von Boehn, commander of the German Seventh Army, with a fairly clear picture of what was going on, which was confirmed when the preliminary bombardment opened on 9 April. The German defences were primed and ready when, at 06.00 on 16 April, nineteen divisions of French infantry attacked on a wide front supported by 5,350 guns all along the Chemin des Dames front stretching from Soissons to Rheims. To make matters worse for the French, the barrage was ineffective as their observation flights had been dogged by the severe wintry weather, while the Germans were protected from much of the shelling by their plethora of deep shelters, supplemented by deep quarries scattered around the sector. On top of the Chemin des Dames above the Aisne River the French at first made only trivial gains.

Both sides were using new weapons. Technology was on the march and the Germans had developed a lighter version of the original Maxim 1908 machine gun. Instead of the heavy-sled mounting that had rendered it almost unmoveable in battle conditions, the new MG08/15 had a bipod mounting, wooden stock and pistol grip for firing, all of which made it relatively lightweight. Although not a great weapon, it was present in increasing numbers and gave the Germans appreciably greater firepower than the French might have expected. The parameters of battle were changing all the time.

The French had also taken a step forward and were using tanks for the first time. Their Schneider CA (Char d'Assaut) tank was armed with a 75 mm gun and two Hotchkiss machine guns, had a crew of six and a theo-retical speed of 5 miles per hour. In all eight battalions consisting of 132 Schneider tanks were employed in the assault on Berry-au-Bac, but they suffered heavy losses from the German artillery. Although these imposing-looking machines raised the spirits of the long-suffering *poilus*, the tanks had not yet been properly integrated into French tactical doctrine and they had not been tested on the battlefield. This made it doubly unfortu-nate that the Schneider CA design had a fatal flaw: its petrol tanks were not only inadequately armoured but, worse still, they were positioned at the front of the vehicle. Any direct hit by a shell would cause a disastrous fire, spraying the crew members with burning petrol.

> The tank on the left suddenly becomes an inferno. In front of it is the still smouldering shell which set it alight. Two torches escape: two torches making a mad, frenzied dash towards the rear, two torches which twist, which roll on the ground. A tank blazing to the right; another one behind. And on our left, it looks as if someone is setting our line of steel tanks alight like a row of flares. Fires, explosions. All at once the tanks are enveloped in flames, and immediately, with a terrible crackling sound, everything is blown apart, thrown up into the sky. Sixty shells exploding and thousands of bullets![12]
>
> Lieutenant Charles-Maurice Chenu, 4th Battery, 5th Special Artillery

In all, fifty-seven French tanks were put out of action by the German guns and a further nineteen broke down. Modifications were set in train but the Schneider CA remained an ineffectual tank incapable of coping with the wide German trenches introduced after the British launched their tanks on the Somme in 1916.

As the Nivelle Offensive continued, some gains were made over the next few days. Such a huge concentration of armies, the mass deployment of artillery, the millions of shells and the sheer determined effort: all of this could not be held back everywhere. Indeed, on the left, the Sixth Army ultimately advanced up to four miles as the Germans retired from exposed positions. But such gains as were made still came at great cost. The aims of the operation had to be scaled down, with no more wild talk of ending the war, but rather of completing the far more localised objective of capturing the Chemin des Dames Ridge. Further progress was made and, by 10 May, the French had taken the Ridge, along with an impressive 28,500 prisoners and 187 guns. In many ways Nivelle's Offensive was not a disaster *per se*, but it seemed so because of the damaging hyperbole he had used to promote it. The 48-hour pledge in particular made him a hostage to fortune. The French politicians were, of course, horrified. This was not the outcome they had intended when they had dismissed Joffre. Waveringly, as an interim step, they appointed the cautious Pétain as Nivelle's Chief of General Staff on 29 April. There was immediately friction between Nivelle and Pétain. Pétain was intent on pursuing a far more defensive strategy than Nivelle, sensibly influenced by the collapse of the Russians on the Eastern Front and the desire to let Britain and the new ally, America, take their share of the burden. This in turn caused a degree of consternation in the British High Command, which feared the consequences of the French taking a back seat for up to a year. After a locking of horns at a conference of military leaders (Haig, Nivelle, Pétain and Robertson) on 4 May, it was agreed that, although the overall strategy remained offensive, the methodology of wearing down German resources would be best served by attacks that used artillery to the maximum degree while seeking only limited objectives to reduce the investment of their own men in the attack. Essentially this was a version of 'bite and hold'. It was also agreed that the British would carry forward the offensive role for the rest of 1917, while Haig was relieved of direct control by Nivelle. On 15 May Pétain was appointed Commander in Chief of the French Army, while the ebullient Foch was appointed as Chief of General Staff.

Nivelle's ultimate fall was probably inevitable. Under his tenure, the French Army had finally reached the end of its endurance. Too many Frenchmen had already died for their country and, if the war continued, many more would share their fate. In just over a week from 16 April another 30,000 had been killed, 100,000 wounded and 4,000 were missing. One of them was Second Lieutenant Jean-Louis Cros, who had the misfortune to be hit by shrapnel and was lying abandoned in a shell hole on 16 April 1917 when he painstakingly wrote a last card to his family. He had not been particularly lucky in life; two of his three daughters had died of tuberculosis and only one, Lucie, survived. His last note is a poignant document.

> My dear wife, my dear parents and all I love,
> I have been wounded. I hope it will be nothing. Care well for the children, my dear Lucie; Leopold will help you if I don't get out of this. I have a crushed thigh and am all alone in a shell hole. I hope they will soon come to fetch me. My last thought is of you.[13]
>
> Second Lieutenant Jean-Louis Cros, 201st Infantry Regiment

Very shortly afterwards he died, probably as a result of a haemorrhage. When his corpse was found, his stiffened fingers were still clutching the card. It was sent on to his grieving family. More than a million French families had been thrown into mourning by the war; millions more had to face the return of their badly wounded sons.

Even in the months leading up to the Nivelle Offensive, morale had not been good in several regiments, particularly in the infantry, who had borne the brunt of the carnage. Now many *poilus* looked abroad to the recent Russian Revolution for inspiration as to what could be done.

> These Slavic soldiers, until just yesterday enslaved by an iron discipline and going to their slaughter like lemmings, had broken their yoke, declared their freedom and imposed peace on their masters – their persecutors. The whole world was stunned, petrified of this revolution, the collapse of the vast ancient empire of the Tsars. These events had repercussion on the French front blowing a wind of revolt through almost every regiment. There were, besides, reasons for the unrest: the painful failure and frightful carnage of the Chemin des Dames offensive, the prospect of more long months of war with no guarantee of a decision and finally the long wait for leave – it was that I believe that most irritated the troops.[14]
>
> Private Louis Barthas, 296th Infantry Regiment

As the Nivelle Offensive fell apart, the French Army began to boil over. Discontented mutterings and vehement complaints led to incidents of indiscipline that contravened all military regulations. The level of desertions increased rapidly, with thousands of individuals absenting themselves from the line. In the 296th Infantry Regiment, in which Private Louis Barthas served, the mass disobedience, or mutiny, began in a fairly typical manner. At night the men had taken to giving enthusiastic renditions of revolutionary songs and shouting slogans. But then events took a more serious turn.

> At noon on May 30 there was even a meeting outside the village to form a Russian style 'Soviet' composed of three men from each company to take control of the regiment. To my amazement they offered me the presidency of the Soviet, that is to say to replace the Colonel, no less! Of course I refused, I did not want to know the power of the firing squad to ape the Russians. However, I resolved to give a veneer of legality to these revolutionary demonstrations. I drew up a manifesto to convey to our company leaders in protest against the delay in our leave. It began, 'The day before the offensive General Nivelle had an order read to the troops saying, "The time has come for the sacrifice!" We have offered our lives as a sacrifice for our country but we in turn say that the time has come for our vastly overdue leave!' The revolt was thus put into a context of law and justice. This manifesto was read by a *poilu* in a sonorous voice, perched astride an oak tree branch and wild applause greeted the last lines. This didn't flatter my vanity much, because we learned afterwards that whoever wrote this protest, moderate though it was, their fate would be clear: a certain court martial and very likely twelve Lebel bullets destined to dispatch me to another world before my destined time.[15]
>
> Private Louis Barthas, 296th Infantry Regiment

He was lucky that no one gave away who had written the 'manifesto'. Soon most of the French Army was affected. When the crackdown began in early June there were mass courts martial at which 23,385 men were convicted for various degrees of mutinous behaviour, of whom around 500 were given death sentences, although the vast majority of these were commuted. Pétain favoured a reasonably moderate approach as he sought to repair the morale of the long-suffering *poilus* by the twin means of ending large attacks – at least in the near future – and introducing regular, longer and more equitably distributed leave. A fair amount of tact was needed in handling the recalcitrant units.

> The powers that be deemed it prudent to isolate the three battalions of the 296th Regiment from each other and we were quartered in widely

separated locations. Our battalion was placed in barracks 4 kilometres from Sainte-Ménehould. It was only when we got there that we realised we were missing the other two battalions. The next evening at seven o'clock, we gathered to start off for the trenches. Noisy demonstrations took place: shouting, singing, screaming, whistling and, of course, the singing of 'The Internationale'. If the officers had made a gesture, or said a word against this noise, I sincerely believe that they would have been ruthlessly massacred, so high was the tension. They took the most sensible course, waiting patiently until calm was restored. You cannot shout, whistle and scream for ever and there was no leader among the rebels capable of making a decision, or of giving us direction. So we ended up heading off towards the trenches, although not without grumbling and griping. Soon, to our great surprise, a column of cavalry reached us and we walked alongside them. They accompanied us to the trenches like slaves being led off to hard labour! Greatly upset and suffocated by the dust raised by horses, it was not long before there were altercations between the infantry and cavalry. Fights soon broke out – there were even a few blows with rifle butt on the one hand and the flat of the sword on the other. To avoid a real battle, we had to get away from the cavalry – which probably did not displease them.[16]

Private Louis Barthas, 296th Infantry Regiment

Pétain saw the summer of 1917 as a period of healing and rebuilding; but the French Army was not yet broken and, under his careful stewardship, it would regain much of its martial ardour within a matter of months.

As part of this process Pétain sought to revitalise its operational efficiency. He adopted a system of defence in depth, ensuring that the main line of resistance was set back beyond the range of the German field artillery, while reserve divisions were held back ready to counter-attack any serious incursions. The developments in German tactics were being closely studied and, where necessary, mimicked; in war there is no disgrace in copying ideas no matter where they come from. The divisions holding the line would also be rotated more frequently to allow them time both to rest and train. Petain accepted that an entirely defensive posture would benefit only the Germans. But offensives in future would be strictly limited, relying heavily on artillery and designed to incur the minimum losses possible.

Development work also continued on the tank. The first tanks the French Army had introduced, the Schneider CA and the St-Chamond, had both proved disappointments, mechanically unreliable and incapable of dealing with the demands of trench warfare. But the French were also pushing ahead with the concept of a light two-man tank, armed with a machine gun or 37 mm cannon, which could be manufactured cheaply and quickly in large numbers. The design was revolutionary, with a central rotating turret which prefigured the 'classic' shape of the tank for much of the twentieth century. Relatively light, this new tank, the Renault FT, had a speed of just under 5 miles per hour and was capable of crossing a 6-foot trench. The idea was to have swarms of these tanks which collectively would provide a far more difficult target to the German gunners than their lumbering predecessors. A thousand were ordered in April 1917, eventually rising to nearly 8,000. More were manufactured in the United States, although the inevitable delays meant that it would be mid-1918 before large numbers reached the front. The French were edging towards a new method of waging war

Over to the British

The failure of the French offensive freed Haig from the formal shackles of Nivelle's leadership. Yet at the same time he was left with little option in his immediate course of action. Although he may have wished to conserve assets for his long-cherished offensive at Ypres, the sheer scope of the French defeat, coupled with the scale of the mutinies, forced his hand. Pétain had been less than forthright in his descriptions of the scale of the problem, but the British had their own intelligence sources and rumours filled the gaps. It was evident that the British must fight on at Arras in order to help give the French Army time to recuperate. The attacks continued and the casualty lists expanded dramatically as the fighting raged on for another fortnight. The difficulties of combining the theoretical necessities of good generalship with the draining, insistent pressure of events are neatly demonstrated by the planning process for the Third Battle of the Scarpe and Second Battle of Bullecourt, both launched on 3 May. The conference to discuss the plans was only held on 1 May – just two days before. The requirement for a long bombardment was now forgotten, there was no time for detailed operational planning. The larger strategic situation demanded an immediate offensive from the British at Arras; so, ready or not, over the top they went at 03.45 on 3 May on a 16-mile front from Vimy Ridge to Bullecourt. The collated experience of the Western Front hitherto would have left few doubts as to the likely outcomes of ill-prepared attacks on strong defensive positions.

> Our orders didn't get through until the last minute and then they were all garbled. No one, including our officers, seemed to know what we were supposed to be doing, or where we were going. Officers were supposed to have synchronised their watches in so far as it was possible at that time of day. At a certain time, our barrage was supposed to lift and we were to climb out of the trenches and go forward. Well, we did – but it wasn't all at the same time! We were given false information and told the artillery had smashed the enemy defences and we would get through the wire – did we hell! [17]
>
> Sergeant Jack Cousins, 7th Bedfordshire and Hertfordshire Regiment

Even where there were localised successes, the high casualty meant that such victories were pyrrhic indeed.

The Battle of Arras marked a midpoint in the development of British offensive tactics. They had learnt a great deal but they still had much to discover. Although the artillery was rapidly expanding with more of the crucial heavy batteries and promising advances in munitions, collectively it still had not perfected all the complex techniques that they would need. And there were still not enough guns to allow the smooth switching of offensives up and down the front; the batteries had to be laboriously moved into place. The time would come when each of the five armies of the BEF had enough artillery to launch a major offensive using its own artillery resources, but that time had not arrived in 1917. The infantry tactics also needed work, and much more had to be done to augment their firepower in the form of more Lewis guns, Stokes mortars and rifle grenades. Despite all the promises, the BEF remained desperately short of tanks, as production lagged behind requirements. In the sky, however, the lot of the RFC was beginning to improve with the advent of large numbers of the new corps machine, the RE8. It was still relatively slow and unmanoeuvrable, but it was a good deal better than the tottering BE2 C. The new generation of scouts that could match the German Albatros were also coming on stream; too late for the Battle of Arras, it was true, but the success of the Sopwith Camel and SE5 A boded well for the future.

And what of the cost? The Battle of Arras was an exceptionally painful experience for the BEF. It had begun so well but then the desperate flailing to distract attention from the French failure lead to terrible losses of around 150,000. In fact, the BEF's average daily casualties for the duration of the battle would prove to be the highest of the war – worse, even, than the Battle of the Somme. Nivelle's attempt to win the war at a stroke had failed and on 1 May Haig had restated his views on the underlying situation on the Western Front.

> The guiding principles are those which have proved successful in war from time immemorial, viz., that the first step must always be to wear down the enemy's power of resistance and to continue to do so until he is so weakened that he will be unable to withstand a decisive blow; then with all one's forces to deliver the decisive blow and finally reap the fruits of victory. The enemy has already been weakened appreciably, but time is required to wear down his great numbers of troops. The situation is not yet ripe for the decisive blow. We must therefore continue to wear down the enemy until his powers of resistance has been further reduced. The cause for General Nivelle's comparative failure appears primarily to have been a miscalculation in this respect, and the remedy now is to return to wearing down methods for a further period, the duration of which cannot be calculated.[18]
>
> Field Marshal Sir Douglas Haig, General Headquarters, BEF

Haig's view may have been depressing – indeed, distressing – to politicians and others seeking an easy way to victory, but the grim reality was that the German Army had not yet been eroded to the point whereby there was much chance of victory in the immediate future.

Battle of Messines

After the debacle of Arras, Allied attention turned to Haig's long-awaited Flanders offensive. The final splutterings of the Arras offensive had been diversionary in nature, fought to deflect attention from both the problems of the French and the burgeoning preparations already being started in Flanders. But now underpinning everything was the necessity to focus German attention on the BEF and thereby allow the French Army more recovery time. Before any operations to clear the Ypres Salient could begin it was necessary to push the Germans back from their positions on the 'heights' of the Messines Ridge to the immediate south. Preparations had long been underway, by General Sir Herbert Plumer's Second Army, and since 1915 an incredible series of deep-driven tunnels had been burrowed under the ridge and filled with explosives. Early in 1917, the process had been accelerated in anticipation of the attacks planned to capitalise on the promised success of the Nivelle offensive. The planning for the Flanders offensive was dogged throughout by the necessity of choosing between the 'bite and hold'-style approach with restricted objectives and the natural desire to maximise possible gains to capitalise on the enormous allocation of resources represented by such an offensive. Plumer in particular was inclined to restrict his horizons initially to just the Messines and Pilckem Ridges; this was not enough for Haig, who preferred a more ambitious agenda with built in contingency plans to maximise potential gains. Seeking a more aggressive approach than that offered by Plumer, Haig selected General Sir Hubert Gough to command the main Ypres offensive, while Plumer commanded the opening assault on Messines Ridge. There would, however, still be a delay of some weeks after Messines as the artillery were moved northwards to amass in front of Ypres. The original plan was that the BEF attack would be supported by a parallel French attack, but this had to be abandoned when the mutinies proliferated across the French Army. Haig would have to go it alone, which meant that the Germans too would be free to concentrate all their attentions on Flanders. This may have benefited the weakened French but it promised pain and suffering for the BEF.

The Messines plans produced by Plumer represented another high point in the development of the 'bite and hold' tactics. There would be a 4-day barrage followed by the intended detonation of twenty-one mines containing a million pounds of high explosive underneath key German defensive positions all along the length of the ridge. Plumer originally planned an advance of only 1,500 yards but Haig, not unnaturally in view of the almost incalculable expenditure of valuable military resources, wanted to attempt both the seizure of the German second line at the back of the ridge and the Oosttaverne Line on its rearward slopes. All together this would entail a total advance of some 3,000 yards. To achieve this Plumer had been given nine assault divisions, with three more as a reserve force. In all he had a total of 2,266 guns of which 1,510 were field artillery and the rest were the heavy artillery required to take on the German batteries and destroy reinforced concrete strongpoints. In the preliminary bombardment 3,561,530 shells were fired. The plans for the creeping barrage to protect the advancing troops were also gaining in complexity, for it was now mixed with barrages directed at a sequence of identified strongpoints further ahead of the troops. Once these objectives had been achieved the creeping barrage would then settle as a standing barrage just ahead of the new lines in order to protect them from the inevitable German counter-attacks. The infantry would be accompanied in their attack by some seventy-two tanks, while throughout the attack the massed Vickers machine guns of the Machine Gun Corps would be firing over their heads spraying millions of bullets over the target areas. But the eye-catching innovation was the sheer size of the mines. Captain Oliver Woodward of the 1st Australian Tunnelling Company was on tenterhooks as he waited to detonate his mine under Hill 60.

> I approached the task of final testing with a feeling of intense excitement. With the Wheatstone Bridge on an improvised table, I set out to check the leads and as each one in turn proved correct I felt greatly relieved. At 2.25 am I made the last resistance test and then made the final connections for firing the mines. This was a rather nerve-racking task as one began to feel the strain and wonder whether the leads were correctly joined up. Just before 3 am, General Lambart took up his position in the firing dugout. It was his responsibility to give the order, 'Fire!' Watch in hand, he stood there and in a silence that could almost be felt he said, 'Five minutes to go.' I again finally checked up the leads and Lieutenants Royle and Bowry stood with an exploder at their feet ready to fire should the dynamo fail. Then the General, in what seemed to be interminable periods, called out, 'Three minutes to go!' 'Two minutes to go!' 'One minute to go!' I grabbed the handle firmly and in throwing the switch over my hand came in contact with the terminals, so that I received a strong shock that threw me backward. For a fraction of a second I failed to realise what had happened, but there was soon joy in the knowledge that Hill 60 mines had done their work.[19]
>
> Captain Oliver Woodward, 1st Australian Tunnelling Company, AIF

The explosion was cataclysmic – and even before the ground had settled the massed British artillery had burst into life.

Never could I have imagined such a sight. First, there was a double shock that shook the earth here 15,000 yards away like a gigantic earthquake. I was nearly flung off my feet. Then an immense wall of fire that seemed to go halfway up to heaven. The whole country was lit with a red light like in a photographic darkroom. At the same moment all the guns spoke and the battle began on this part of the line. The noise surpasses even the Somme; it is terrific, magnificent, overwhelming. It makes one almost drunk with exhilaration and one simply does not care about the fact that we are under the concentrated fire of all the Hun batteries. Their shells are bursting round now as I write at 3.40am, but it makes one laugh to think of their little efforts compared to the 'Ausgezeichnete Ausstellung' that we are providing. We are getting our revenge for 1914 with a vengeance.[20]

Major Ralph Hamilton, Headquarters, 106th Brigade, Royal Field Artillery

For the Germans the impact of the massive explosions was incredible.

The earth roared, trembled, rocked – this was followed by an utterly amazing crash and there, before us in a huge arc, kilometres long, was raised a curtain of fire about one hundred metres high. The scene was quite extraordinary; almost beyond description. It was like a thunderstorm magnified one thousand times! This was followed by thousands of thunderclaps, as the guns opened up simultaneously, adding their contribution to the power just unleashed. The wall of fire hung in the air for several seconds, then subsided to be replaced by the flashes of the artillery muzzles, which were clearly visible in the half light. For an instant we just stood, mesmerised by the spectacle. There was no question of returning to the rear to have wounds dressed, because hardly had the wall of fire died away to nothing than the entire earth seemed to come to life. Scrabbling their way forward from hundreds of starting points came steel-helmeted men. Line upon line of infantrymen emerged and the enemy launched forward.[21]

Second Lieutenant Meinke, 176th Infantry Regiment

The infantry went over the top, sweeping over the utterly shattered German front line positions on the forward crest. After a short pause they moved on at 07.00, with the battalions leapfrogging to maintain the impetus of the assault. The Germans were unable to hold them and Haig was proved right as his men pushed through to take the fortified village of Wytschaete by 09.00. After a further break to re-organise, the infantry began to attack the reverse slope positions at 15.10. By this time they were beyond the range of the British field artillery and, without the massed support of the guns, casualties began to increase sharply. Even so, the Oosttaverne Line was safely in British hands before the end of the day. Subsequent painful tidying-up operations would finally succeed in attaining all the British objectives within the week, although they suffered a total of 24,562 casualties during the battle as a whole. None the less the Battle of Messines was a triumph for Plumer. His methodical tactics had overwhelmed a strong German fortress in a key location with the capture to boot of 7,354 prisoners, 48 guns, 218 machine guns and 60 mortars. With the Messines Ridge under British control the way was open for Gough's assault on the German lines that almost encircled Ypres.

The Third Battle of Ypres

Haig's motives in the great Flanders offensive of the Third Battle of Ypres have often been questioned, but he had several compelling reasons. He was required by the situation of the French to distract the Germans and prevent them from launching a devastating attack on the wavering *poilus* Haig believed that more attacks might bring the German Army to the point of collapse. He based this on the reports of his chief intelligence officer, Brigadier General John Charteris: 'It is a fair deduction that, given a continuance of the existing circumstances and of the effort of the Allies, Germany may well be forced to conclude a peace on our terms before the end of the year.'[22] This would prove an optimistic assertion, as the German armies on the Western Front would ultimately be refreshed and restocked by the divisions freed from the Eastern Front following the collapse of the Russians. Action was also necessary, according to Admiral Sir John Jellicoe, First Sea Lord, to clear the Belgian coast in order to eradicate the German submarine bases at Ostend and Zeebrugge. Tactical objectives included the Passchendaele Ridge overlooking Ypres, the German rail junction at Roulers, clearing the German threat to the Channel ports, and removing the necessity of maintaining the Ypres Salient, which was a constant drain on British manpower. This all added up to a strong case but Haig was exposed to a considerable amount of interference from Lloyd George. The

British Prime Minister marshalled his arguments against the offensive to considerable effect.

> The Cabinet must regard themselves as trustees for the fine fellows that constitute our army. They are willing to face any dangers, and they do so without complaint, but they trust to the leaders of the nation to see that their lives are not needlessly thrown away, and that they are not sacrificed on mere gambles which are resorted to merely because those who are directing the War can think of nothing better to do with the men under their command. It is therefore imperative that before we embark upon a gigantic attack which must necessarily entail the loss of scores of thousands of valuable lives, and produce that sense of discouragement which might very well rush nations into premature peace, that we should feel a fair confidence that such an attack has a reasonable chance of succeeding. A mere gamble would be both a folly and a crime.[23]
>
> Prime Minister David Lloyd George

Whatever the merits of this his credibility was then undermined when he followed up with an appeal for more resources for the Italian campaign. Here Haig and the Chief of Imperial General Staff, General Sir William Robertson, stood together on solid ground, able to demonstrate the crucial importance of concentrating on the main enemy – Germany – on the Western Front, rather than embarking on any Italian adventures. In the end Cabinet approval of the offensive was granted, although with the proviso that it should be abandoned if things went wrong.

Haig had originally intended swiftly to follow up the capture of Messines Ridge with his Ypres Offensive, but the delays multiplied, reflecting the logistical difficulties of waging a war which required thousands of guns and millions of shells to be amassed in the muddy ground of the Ypres Salient. The infantry, too, had to be moved up to the line. Training and planning had to be perfected. All this took time.

The German defences at Ypres were carefully laid out in accordance with the principles of defence in depth. A thinly held front line and forward zone ran along the low Pilckem Ridge, with a second line tucked away on the reverse slope. Behind this were a series of additional lines stretching back up on to the Passchendaele Ridge, while the whole area was dotted with concrete pillboxes and fortified farm buildings. These were carefully sited to catch advancing troops in deadly machine gun crossfire. The overall concept was to slow down and break up the British attacks, leaving the survivors vulnerable to German counter-attack divisions held back beyond the reach of the British artillery. One new weapon beginning to make its presence felt among the British troops was the German mustard gas contained in their Yellow Cross gas shells. Falling with an almost inaudible 'plop' and relatively odourless, this gas caused severe blisters, temporary blindness and dreadful internal damage if it was inhaled. As it lingered both in the air and on the ground, soldiers were forced to wear their gas masks for days.

The British plans featured the usual tensions over the question of advancing in stages or attempting to maximise initial gains by going for the Second and Third Lines. This argument could never be fully resolved, as it all depended on what happened. If the attack was a success then it would be irresponsible not to be ready to leap successive German lines – many senior British commanders felt that the opportunities to do so had been missed on the first day of the Battle of Arras a few months before. But then again, if the deeper lines were included in the original barrage then its impact might be diluted and total failure ensue. The depth of the German defensive system also meant that delays were inevitable as the field artillery was moved forward at each stage. In the end Haig resolved to maximise gains within the overall context of a staged advance – not, therefore, an attempt to secure an immediate breakthrough.

The plans emphasised the importance of artillery – this was the British way. The Fifth and Second Armies amassed 3,091 guns, which was twice as many as the Germans had in that sector. The bombardment would last for fifteen days, followed by a thunderous creeping barrage to accompany the attacking infantry across No Man's Land. They would also be accompanied by tanks, although these were restricted in what they could do by the difficult ground conditions.

The final stages of the barrage were beyond belief.

A flooded Amazon of steel flowed roaring, immensely fast, over our heads and the machine gun bullets made a pattern of sharper purpose and maniac language against that diluvian rush. Flaring lights, small ones, great ones, flew up and went spinning sideways in the cloud of night; one's eyes seemed not quick enough; one heard nothing from one's shouting neighbour.[24]

Lieutenant Edmund Blunden, 11th Royal Sussex Regiment

It was a desperate business for Germans gunners who were attempting to return fire.

> Darkness alternates with light as bright as day. The earth trembles and shakes like a jelly. Flares illumine the darkness with their white, yellow, green and red lights and cause the tall stumps of the poplars to throw weird shadows. And we crouch between mountains of ammunition (some of us up to our knees in water) and fire and fire, while all around us shells upon shells plunge into the mire, shatter our emplacement, root up trees, flatten the house behind us to the level of the ground, and scatter wet dirt all over us so that we look as if we had come out of a mud-bath. We sweat like stokers on a ship; the barrel is red-hot; the cases are still burning hot when we take them out of the breech; and still the one and only order is, 'Fire! Fire! Fire!'until one is quite dazed.[25]

Gerhard Gurtler, German Artillery

When the Allied infantry attacked at 03.50 that morning they did so with varying degrees of success. Two divisions of the French First Army on the left flank reached all their objectives and even pushed on to contest the streets of Bixschoote. On their right the British swept up on the low rise of the Pilckem Ridge and over into the shallow Steenbeek Valley that lay behind to capture St Julien. There they encountered a steadily increasing resistance centred around pillboxes and the Gheluvelt–Langemarck Line lying in front of the London Ridge promontory of the main Passchendaele–Gheluvelt Ridge. If one man's story tells the story of thousands, let it be that of Company Sergeant Major John Handley of the 1/6th King's Liverpool Regiment, who went over the top with his company headquarters in the third wave.

> Following the white tape, I was horrified to find myself tangled up in our own wire. Knowing from experience that the enemy would rain a deluge of blasting shells on our front line within three minutes – at the most – I frantically tore myself through the obstructing wire, hurrying forward out of the most dangerous area. When I felt clear I looked about me, but in the darkness could see no one. There was no sign of

those who should have been following me i.e. the acting captain, his servant, signallers, first aid men, stretcher bearers, and so forth. As far as I could make out I was alone. But I went forward, till suddenly I fell, tripped up by the German wire. As I plunged into the mud several rifle shots flashed and cracked from the enemy trench just in front of me. The bullets whizzed past my head and, incidentally, for weeks afterwards, I was partially deaf in the left ear. My rifle was useless, choked with mud. Pulling out a hand grenade, I released the lever and lobbed it as near as I could to the area from which the shots came. Bobbing up to see the explosion, I saw several heads silhouetted against the flash. I had aimed well. At that moment one of our Lewis gun teams came up and I led them into the German trench where, in the half light of dawn, we only found one badly wounded Hun.[26]

Company Sergeant Major John Handley, 1/6th King's Liverpool Regiment

As Handley pushed on across a near-featureless wilderness pounded by the constant shellfire he was soon lost.

I had to find Jasper Farm and set up the Company headquarters. On the map it was shown as halfway down a central communication trench. Going down the first connecting trench I failed to find it, so came back to the German front line and went down the next one. As trenches they were difficult to discern, for our bombardment had almost erased them. It was a case of plodding through shell holes and round small earth mounds. Skirting one mound I came into full view of Jasper Farm. It was a huge mound of bare concrete with gun slits – a pillbox. Stark and bare, it looked grotesque, our bombardments having blown away the earth which concealed it. I was surprised and even more so when I saw six Germans lined up in front of it. They immediately put their hands up in surrender. Pointing my useless rifle at them, I released an arm to wave them forward in the direction of the British lines. On reaching the old German front line I handed them over to one of my sergeants for escorting back to captivity.[27]

Company Sergeant Major John Handley, 1/6th King's Liverpool Regiment

The condition of these stunned German troops should not have been a surprise. Even the concrete walls and roof of a blockhouse could not protect them from the British bombardment.

The fire increased to an intensity that was simply beyond our power to comprehend. Our blockhouse and a nearby mortar battery received more than a thousand large calibre shells. The earth trembled, the air shimmered. My pillbox heaved and rocked as though it was going to collapse. Almost by a miracle it received no direct hits. Everyone who dared to go out was wounded. At 6.00 am there was a gas alarm. I went outside and watched as a cloud of gas 10 metres thick drifted slowly by. The entire pillbox stank of it. I had every tiny gap wedged up with wet cloths. At 7.00 am the firing reached a peak of intensity. It was simply ghastly. The men in the outer room were wounded or died of gas poisoning. The small reserve of gas masks was exhausted because many men needed replacements for masks which had been shot through. The enemy followed up behind the gas cloud.[28]

Lieutenant Colonel Freiherr von Forstner, 164th Infantry Regiment

The task ahead of the assaulting divisions got more and more difficult in the Gheluvelt Plateau sector, which stretched from the Westhoek Ridge to the Shrewsbury Forest. On Westhoek Ridge they had some considerable initial success and captured the village before being halted by German machine guns. But the troops facing Sanctuary Wood had an almost impossible task. In the dreadful ground conditions they soon lost touch with their creeping barrage and were thus exposed to the unsuppressed fire of the German garrison. In addition, the masses of German batteries concealed behind the Gheluvelt Plateau had not been dealt with and their shells tore the advancing battalions to shreds. The tanks which were meant to help overcome the opposition were not only vulnerable to the artillery but most were very soon bogged down in the glutinous mud, unable to liaise properly with the infantry around them. Of the forty-eight tanks in this sector, all but one either broke down or were destroyed. Clapham Junction, where seventeen tanks were wrecked, became known as the 'tank graveyard'. They had done little to help the infantry. Although the advance managed to over-run the German front line positions, it was brought up sharply by the German second line stretching across Gheluvelt Plateau.

At this stage, the overall advantage may have seemed to be with the French and British troops. But the German tactics were based on counter-attacks and they had fresh divisions ready for action safely positioned in the folds of ground behind the Gheluvelt Plateau and Passchendaele Ridge. The German barrage opened up in the early afternoon and soon their infantry were swarming forward across the ridges and pushing forward on the British gains at St Julien and in the Steenbeek Valley. Driving in at the flanks, the Germans forced back the increasingly exhausted British troops.

By nightfall the results were somewhat mixed. On the left the French and their neighbouring British divisions had succeeded in over-running two German defensive systems which included both the Pilckem and Bellewaarde Ridges. On the right, on the Gheluvelt Plateau, progress had been far more limited, although even here they had taken the German first line. But the cost had been very high, with the British and French suffering losses of about 33,500. German casualties seem to have been around 30,000, of which 6,000 were prisoners. Gough's willingness to try to maximise gains on the first day had, as some had warned before the battle, rendered his troops vulnerable to German counter-attacks through having over-stretched themselves and run beyond the cover that their artillery could provide. Haig may have practised a form of contingency planning, but it is also true that the outcome of the first day's fighting was at the lower end of the spectrum of what was acceptable. Furthermore, the heavy casualties, particularly in the Gheluvelt Plateau sector, meant that British options were significantly reduced. Certainly, it was now clear that any thoughts of swiftly breasting the main Passchendaele Ridge were fanciful. Indeed, the biggest obstacle to British progress was left largely unscathed – the Gheluvelt Plateau was still an inviolable fortress. It would be a long, hard slog; another battle of attrition.

Yet there was another serious unforeseen problem. On the first day of the battle it had begun to rain. This would not have been particularly untoward, but the rain poured down for most of August – indeed, there were only three dry days in the whole month. In an area where the drainage was already suspect, on a battlefield where millions of shells had ripped apart the drains and broken down the banks of streams to flood great swathes of the landscape, there now fell more than double the average monthly rainfall. In these circumstances, moving the guns and millions of shells forward became a horrendous task; finding suitable gun positions was near impossible; and, worst of all, the bad weather prevented the RFC from flying the photographic and artillery observation patrols essential to make the best use of the guns. The attack was supposed to continue on 2 August, but it proved impossible. The situation demanded a speedy exploitation before the Germans could bring forward their reserves and strengthen their defences, but there were other tactical considerations.

> We know from experience, however, that in these subsidiary operations, hurried preparations and the use of part-worn troops are generally the cause of failure, and that failure involves waste of valuable time and personnel. In this particular case we want to make absolutely certain of the artillery preparation, which will require very careful control and accurate shooting and one or two more days of good flying weather prior to the attack. To ensure success, which is all-important at this stage, the corps ought really to attack with three fresh divisions.[29]
>
> Brigadier General John Davidson, General Headquarters, BEF

Gough cancelled the planned assault. His hand may have been forced, but the delay gave the Germans more time to prepare their defences – and they did not waste it. There would be many similar situations in August 1917.

The Germans recognised the key importance of the Gheluvelt Plateau and concentrated the bulk of their batteries on its reverse slopes. In contrast, the British guns were spread more evenly along the whole front, thus allowing the Germans to establish an artillery superiority just where it most mattered. The Germans also used their massive experience of attritional battles to good effect. They opened a heavy continuous barrage on the British divisions in front of the Gheluvelt Plateau, with the effect of putting them through the 'mincing machine'. The British assault divisions were already weakened and the relentless barrage forced Gough to relieve them earlier than he would have wished with troops originally intended for the second stage of the offensive. But now these troops were exposed to endless shellfire and they, too, were gradually degraded as they waited for the weather to let up and give them the chance to attack. When the battle resumed, the fresh divisions were themselves battle-worn and the artillery barrage still inadequate. A pattern of desperate, unimaginative assaults, crushing German counter-attacks and an overwhelming sense of despair began to afflict the British campaign in Flanders. Like his men, Gough was floundering, hamstrung by factors beyond his control, but also by his own failure to concentrate his resources on the Gheluvelt Plateau. The gains were minimal, the casualties high, in near-futile assaults launched on 10 August, 16 August and 22 August.

The state of the ground was by this time frightful. The labour of
bringing up supplies and ammunition, of moving or firing the guns,
which often sunk up to their axles, was a fearful strain on the officers
and men, even during the daily task of maintaining the battle front.
When it came to the advance of infantry for an attack, across the
water-logged shell holes, movement was so slow and so fatiguing that
only the shortest advances could be contemplated. In consequence
I informed the Commander in Chief that tactical success was not
possible, or would be too costly, under such conditions, and advised
that the attack should be abandoned. I had many talks with Haig
during these days and repeated this opinion frequently, but he told me
that the attack must be continued.[30]

Lieutenant General Sir Hubert Gough, Headquarters, Fifth Army

Gough had failed to grasp that the offensive could not be just called off;
the real necessity was for him to concentrate his forces and overcome
these very considerable obstacles.

In the end Haig had to intervene. The failure of the attacks on 22
August caused a review of the campaign. One thing stood out: further
progress was almost impossible without the reduction of the series of
German lines and interlinked fortifications chained across the Gheluvelt Plateau. If the 'thruster' Gough and his Fifth Army were incapable of
doing this, then Haig was quite prepared to go back to Plumer, who had
so recently demonstrated his mastery of 'bite and hold' tactics at Messines. But Plumer needed time to prepare, so Gough and the Fifth Army
would have to struggle on into September. This led to a further series of
small-scale actions which achieved no worthwhile objective and repeated
many of the mistakes of the middle section of the Somme fighting. Yet
for all the British confusion the German Army was also suffering. For the
Germans the improvements in British offensive tactics were nothing short
of ominous.

In spite of all the concrete protection they seemed more or less
powerless under the enormous weight of the enemy's artillery. At some
points they no longer displayed the firmness which I, in common with
the local commanders, had hoped for. The enemy had managed to
adapt himself to our method of employing counter-attack divisions.
There were no more attacks with unlimited objectives, such as General
Nivelle had made in the Aisne–Champagne Battle. He was ready for

our counter-attacks and prepared for them by exercising restraint in exploitation of success. In other directions, of course, this suited us very well. I myself was being put to a terrible strain. The state of affairs in the West appeared to prevent the execution of our plans elsewhere. Our wastage had been so high as to cause grave misgivings, and had exceeded all expectation.[31]

General Erich Ludendorff, General Headquarters

Up until this point in the war the French had always been the real danger to the Germans. Now it was the British.

On 29 August Plumer presented his plans for the capture of the Gheluvelt Plateau to Haig. This was a strictly limited offensive; a 'bite and hold' *par excellence*. A massed artillery force was lined up of 1,295 guns, of which 575 were the vital medium or heavy artillery that could destroy the German pillboxes and blockhouses. It would require millions of shells, but here again progress was being made as Decauville light railways were installed to help carry the shells at least part of the way to the guns. But the Battle of Menin Road on 20 September was not just a mechanistic artillery battle; it would also reflect the considerable advances being made in infantry tactics. Rigid lines were all but useless against a pillbox based defence and a great deal more flexibility was inculcated into the troops. In a gradual accepting of the necessity for new tactics, they were following on from the French.

The waves of attack which have hitherto been used, do not give sufficient flexibility, nor are platoons and sections sufficiently under the control of their leaders to deal with sudden opposition likely to be encountered under the new conditions. The leading wave, in one or two lines should be extended to force the enemy to disclose his positions, the remainder in small groups or file ready to deal with unexpected machine guns or parties of the enemy. It must be impressed on all subordinate leaders that rapidity of action is of paramount importance, and that any delay in assaulting these points adds to the seriousness of the situation and increases the difficulties of dealing with it. Known machine gun emplacements and defended points are dealt with by parties previously told off for the duty. Careful study of the ground and aeroplane photographs will go a long way towards increasing the 'known' and giving all leaders a clear idea of the points from which opposition may be expected. The rear waves must keep closed up until across No Man's Land, and gradually gain the distance, after this officers must be trained to ensure this is done.[32]

Brigadier Charles Harrington, Headquarters, Second Army

The Second Army would advance in four bounds of about 1,500 yards, each followed by a six-day lull to allow for the preparation of the next step. Alongside it, the Fifth Army would use the same methodology to capture the protruding St Julien Spur and London Ridge. Then, and only then, would an attack be launched on the main Passchendaele Ridge. The overall plan was simple: each attack would aim to seize the German forward defensive zone, then swiftly consolidate, thereby effectively inviting German counter-attacks against well-prepared infantry backed up by massed machine guns and the full strength of the artillery. Plumer also proved to be a lucky general; September saw the onset of dry, sunny weather and the ground began to dry out. This was a great advantage to the Royal Artillery.

When the guns opened up at 05.40 on 20 September it seemed to dwarf all preceding barrages.

> Just look at our artillery. Just look at it, at those countless flashes. See how they stab at the darkness from their hiding places, not in dozens but in hundreds, and yet these are only the heavies, the lighter guns are well up and we cannot see them. See the red glares that light up the country for miles where a Hun shell has landed amongst some cordite. The whole place seems ablaze as far as the eye can see: flash after flash some singly, some in groups when a battery fires together, but isn't it all beyond description, beyond belief, even beyond imagination? Feel the terrific vibration and the jolting and hear the ear splitting, nerve-racking noise of it all. It is not a bit of use trying to talk, or even shout because bellow as you like no one can hear you.[33]

Lieutenant Cyril Lawrence, 1st Field Company, AIF

When the infantry advanced they were able to sweep forward exactly as planned, over-running the German forward zone to a depth of just under a mile. There were still painful rebuffs, strongpoints that did not fall, localised disasters, but overall the painstaking preparations paid off. Indeed, it was not the ground taken that made the Battle of Menin Road such a remarkable achievement; it was the successful final capture of objectives that had cost literally thousands of lives in futile assaults in the previous month. Then the British troops stopped, consolidated and awaited the German response. The infantry had done well, but in truth it was the massed fire of the British field artillery, all still well within range, that provided the most formidable opponent in destroying the German counter-attack divisions. Even so, the Germans knew what they were doing on a battlefield, they too could deploy massed artillery and casualties were heavy on both sides. Indeed, even in success the British casualties totalled 21,000.

Overall, Haig was delighted and looked forward to the incremental capture of the whole Passchendaele Ridge. He even began to consider a possible break through to the Belgian coast and the Roulers railhead. This optimism has been greeted with a considerable degree of derision in retrospect, but it was certainly Haig's responsibility to plan for any contingency including the possibility of amphibious combined landing operations or a cavalry exploitation. In truth, here was a case of 'damned if you do and damned if you don't'. The point is, surely, that Haig did not know what was going to happen next, but he had the duty to prepare for any eventuality.

After the requisite six days the next step was the Battle of Polygon Wood launched on 26 September. Although a spoiling attack by the Germans intended to disrupt preparations had some minor success, the British were still able to make an advance of some 1,000–1,250 yards on a front of 8,500 yards, although again the vicious fighting led to heavy casualties totalling some 15,500. By this time the German High Command had worked out what Plumer was doing. But how would they respond to these gradualist tactics?

> The depth of the penetration was limited so as to secure immunity from our counter-attacks, and the latter were then broken up by the massed fire of artillery. After each attack I discussed the tactical experiences with General von Kuhl and Colonel von Loszberg, sometimes at the front, sometimes on the telephone. This time I again went to the front in order to talk over the same questions with officers who had taken part in the fighting. Our defensive tactics had to be developed further, somehow or other. We were all agreed on that. The only thing was, it was so infinitely difficult to hit on the right remedy.[34]
>
> General Erich Ludendorff, General Headquarters

All the Germans could do in the short term was to strengthen the front line zone with more troops and machine guns and to delay their counter-attacks until they could organise them properly with the appropriate artillery support.

Meanwhile Plumer, encouraged by Haig, who hoped that the Germans might be about to crack, ordered the next Second Army assault on the Broodseinde Ridge, Zonnebeke Spur and Gravenstafel Spur, while the Fifth Army moved on Poelcappelle. Again he was aiming for just 1,500 yards, but the artillery arrangements were juggled. The preliminary bombardment would concentrate solely on the pillboxes and counter-battery work before a final hurricane bombardment crashed out at the Zero Hour of 06.00 on 4 October. The assault on Broodseinde Ridge was carried out in the main by the I and II Australian Corps. The German front line had been reinforced but no matter how many German troops were there it made little difference to their ability to defend themselves in this kind of earth-shattering bombardment. The Battle of Broodseinde Ridge proved another British triumph, despite a further 20,600 casualties.

Plumer's 'bite and hold' tactics had certainly achieved their aim of capturing the Gheluvelt Plateau; but the drawbacks of this attritional method of warfare were also becoming apparent. The limited scope of each advance meant that there was never a chance of over-running and capturing significant numbers of German guns. Therefore the threat posed by the German artillery remained relatively constant – every battle needed the same tremendous attention to detail and thorough counter-battery bombardment. The casualties suffered were also painful, even though the balance was in favour of the BEF. As a method of warfare it only had relevance in circumstances as at Ypres – where the Germans could not retreat without exposing important tactical and strategic objectives. But there was a further problem: time was running out for the BEF as they continued the offensive deep into October. Gradually the overall objectives shrivelled to reflect the changing situation. It was clear that Roulers and the ports of Zeebrugge and Ostend were out of reach. The only option left was to wear down the Germans, thereby also deflecting attention from Britain's faltering allies – for by late 1917 the French, Italian and Russian forces were all wilting under the intense strain of war. As a localised tactical objective Haig resolved to complete the capture of the Passchendaele Ridge which would allow his troops to winter in a strong defensive position. There is no doubt that the British sacrifice was to some extent effective.

> The wastage in the big actions of the Fourth Battle of Flanders was extraordinarily high. In the West we began to be short of troops. The two divisions that had been held in readiness in the East, and were already on the way to Italy, were diverted to Flanders.[35]
>
> General Erich Ludendorff, General Headquarters

The German experiment of strengthening the front zone had proved a disaster and Ludendorff ordered yet another rejig of defensive tactics to counter the massed British guns. This time they would simply expand the forward defensive zone, with the most advanced area only lightly held and relying on barbed wire and the artillery to prevent the attacking British infantry from getting through.

Yet even as the Germans reorganised their defences, it once again began to rain over Flanders – although there could be no real surprise at rain in October. But the effects, once again, were catastrophic: as the shallow valleys flooded, the morass spreading inexorably via the linked shell holes that covered almost the entire battlefield. The Royal Artillery once again found themselves crippled: they couldn't get their guns and ammunition forward, the gun platforms were unsteady, ruining accuracy, and the work of the RFC was stymied as the aircraft either could not get aloft or the visibility was so poor that they could not do their job. In contrast, the massed guns of the Germans were sited on higher, drier ground that had not been furrowed regularly by shells. As British counter-battery fire lost its accuracy the German guns regained their influence on the battle.

Ypres became a hell on earth for the men condemned to fight there and that dreadful experience has come to symbolise the whole of the war. All around them were the mangled corpses of their erstwhile comrades. Lieutenant Richard Dixon was a forward observation officer. He was incredulous at the horrors that surrounded him.

> All around us lay the dead, both friend and foe, half in, half out of the water-logged shell holes. Their hands and boots stuck out at us from the mud. Their rotting faces stared blindly at us from coverlets of mud; their decaying buttocks heaved themselves obscenely from the filth with which the shell bursts had smothered them. Skulls grinned at us; all around us stank unbelievably. These corpses were never buried, for it was impossible for us to retrieve them. They had lain, many of them,

for weeks and months; they would lie and rot and disintegrate foully into the muck until they were an inescapable part of it to manure the harvests of a future peace-time Belgium. Horror was everywhere.[36]

Lieutenant Richard Dixon, 14th Battery, Royal Garrison Artillery

The British were caught in a bind. Stuck in front of the Passchendaele Ridge, either they could go forward or they could go back to the Pilckem Ridge. Tactically they could not stay in the swamps down below the German lines.

The Germans too were suffering, but they still had the military resources and determination to cling on. Yet it is difficult to blame Haig for his determination to test the German resolve on the Passchendaele Ridge. He himself had commanded the I Corps as it struggled to hold back the Germans in 1914. The BEF had been staring defeat in the face when the German attacks had stopped in November 1914. Haig was resolved not to make the same mistake, but to press on, try to capitalise on German exhaustion and trigger a collapse in their resistance. Indeed, the next attack, the Battle of Poelcapelle, was actually brought forward a day to 9 October even as the rain teemed down. But the German Army proved to be nowhere near to accepting defeat: fresh divisions had moved forward, the artillery batteries had been replenished. The result was a terrible slaughter.

The approach to the ridge was a desolate swamp, over which brooded an evil menacing atmosphere that seemed to defy encroachment. Far more treacherous than the visible surface defences with which we were familiar, such as barbed wire; deep devouring mud spread deadly traps in all directions. We splashed and slithered, and dragged our feet from the pull of an invisible enemy determined to suck us into its depths. Every few steps someone would slide and stumble and, weighed down by rifle and equipment, rapidly sink into the squelching mess. Those nearest grabbed his arms, struggled against being themselves engulfed and, if humanly possible, dragged him out. When helpers floundered in as well and doubled the task, it became hopeless. All the straining efforts failed and the swamp swallowed its screaming victims, and we had to be ordered to plod on dejectedly and fight this relentless enemy as stubbornly as we did those we could see. It happened that one of those leading us was Lieutenant Chamberlain, and so distraught did he become at the spectacle of men drowning in mud, and the desperate attempts to rescue them that suddenly he began hysterically belabouring the shoulders of a sinking man with his swagger stick. We were horror-struck to see this most compassionate officer so unstrung as to resort to brutality, and our loud protests forced him to desist. The man was rescued, but some could not be and they sank shrieking with fear and agony. To be ordered to go ahead and leave a comrade to such a fate was the hardest experience one could be asked to endure, but the objective had to be reached, as we plunged on, bitter anger against the evil forces prevailing piled on to our exasperation. This was as near to Hell as I ever want to be.[37]

Private Norman Cliff, 1st Grenadier Guards

Some meagre advances were made towards the German fastness at Houthulst Forest, but overall the Battle of Poelcapelle was an utter failure.

Still the offensive ground on, but increasing desperation led Plumer, under pressure from Haig, to abandon many of the principles that had previously brought him success. With the weather outlook still grim, the British were running out of time if they were to secure the Passchendaele Ridge before winter arrived. Without the proper 'bite and hold' methodology, this was a recipe for disaster, which was accordingly delivered at the First Battle of Passchendaele on 12 October – at a cost of another 13,000 casualties. When Lieutenant Walde Fisher of the AIF moved back into the front line the next day he was greeted by a dreadful situation.

Our units sank to the lowest pitch of which I have ever been cognisant. It looked hopeless – the men were so utterly done. However, the attempt had to be made, and accordingly we moved up that night – a battalion ninety strong. I had 'A' Company with twenty-three men. We got up to our positions somehow or other – and the fellows were dropping out unconscious along the road – they have guts, my word! That's the way to express it. We found the line instead of being advanced, some 30 yards behind where we had left it – and the shell stricken and trodden ground thick with dead and wounded – some of the Manchesters were there yet, seven days wounded and not looked to. But men walked over them – no heed was paid to anything but the job. Our men gave all their food and water away, but that was all they could do. That night my two runners were killed as they sat beside me, and casualties were numerous again. He blew me out of my shell hole twice, so I shifted to an abandoned pillbox. There were twenty-four wounded men inside, two dead Huns on the floor and six outside, in various stages of decompositions. The stench was dreadful.[38]

Lieutenant Walde Fisher, 42nd Battalion, AIF

The dismal nature of the failure at least meant that it was decided to postpone further attacks until the weather had ameliorated sufficiently to allow proper artillery preparations. The exhausted I and II ANZAC Corps were withdrawn and the newly arrived Canadian Corps, under Lieutenant General Sir Arthur Currie, was given responsibility for one last attempt on Passchendaele. Currie took his time, planning staged attacks and reverting entirely to the methods of 'bite and hold'. On 26 October the Second Battle of Passchendaele began with a successful advance of just some 500 yards along the ridge. But elsewhere the attack by the Fifth Army on Houthulst Forest achieved nothing. The whole exercise was repeated after more careful preparations on 30 October, with similar results: a small but controlled advance by the Canadians after vicious fighting. By the beginning of November the great Third Ypres Offensive had shrunk down to the narrow frontage of the Canadian Corps' attempts to gain Passchendaele village on the tortured summit of that benighted ridge. The situation at this time was complicated by the collapse of the Italian Army in the face of the Caporetto Offensive launched by the Austrian Army on 24 October – indeed, Haig was forced to send two of his divisions to help the Italians on 28 October. Haig was also beginning to turn his mind to the planned raid using tanks at the Battle of Cambrai on 20 November 1917.

At 06.00 on 6 November the Canadian Corps resumed battle with the successful seizure of Passchendaele village. After one last attack on 10 November carried out in order to secure the position, the long agony was finally over. The British had achieved their minimal tactical objective, but had been denied any of their wider aims. Both sides knew that they had been in a tough fight.

On 26 and 30 October and 6 and 10 November the fighting was again of the severest description. The enemy charged like a wild bull against the iron wall which kept him from our submarine bases. He threw his weight against Houthulst Forest, Poelcapelle, Passchendaele, Becelaere, Gheluvelt and Zandvoorde. He dented it in many places, and it seemed as if he must knock it down, but it held, although a faint tremor ran through its foundations. The impressions I continuously received were very terrible. In a tactical sense, everything possible had been done. The advanced zone was good. The effectiveness of our artillery had considerably improved. Behind almost every division in the front line there was another in support; and we still had reserves in the third line. We knew that the enemy suffered heavily. But we also knew he was amazingly strong and, what was equally important, had an extraordinarily stubborn will.[39]

General Erich Ludendorff, General Headquarters

The Germans were suffering from the prolonged attritional warfare on the Western Front and the people at home were undoubtedly war-weary. But, as a nation, the Germans were not yet down and out.

So in the end Haig was wrong. The Germans did not collapse in the late autumn of 1917. But at the same time this was just one of the whole spectrum of possibilities that Haig had envisaged from the Flanders campaign. Haig's more ambitious strategical aims – to over-run the Roulers rail junction or liberate the Belgian ports of Antwerp and Ostend – were surely always near-impossible scenarios without the collapse of the German Army. But the BEF had certainly succeeded in attracting German resources that might otherwise have been expended to more deadly effect on Britain's tottering allies. The cost to the British was atrocious, with some 275,000 casualties, while the German losses numbered something like 200,000. But that was the price of alliance warfare. To abandon your allies was to lose everything. The risk can be illustrated by the collapse of Russia in November 1917 that allowed the Germans to concentrate their forces on the Western Front in 1918. The Third Battle of Ypres had seen the BEF develop a murderously efficient method of making small-scale gains, based on the raw power of the guns and subverting, at least in part, the German defence in depth. It was a method of fighting based on restricting all ambition to the achievement of small advances of less than a mile. Yet the war would not be won in this way; 'bite and hold' promised only a never-ending torment. A better way would have to be found.

The Battle of Cambrai

The underlying impetus for what became the Battle of Cambrai was provided by an artillery specialist called Brigadier General Hugh Tudor, who conceived a plan to capitalise on the vast improvements in artillery tactics and techniques, combined with the potential to use tanks, to reintroduce surprise attacks to the Western Front battlefields. Accurate surveying of the Western Front had been completed by 1917 and this enabled a battery position and its target to be pinpointed on the map. This was then combined with the careful calibration of every gun to enable the gunners to make the correct adjustments to allow for defined error. All this meant that the artillery could suddenly open fire with a reasonable degree of accuracy. This 'shooting off the map', or predicted fire, could be done without previously registering the targets – something which had previously alerted the Germans to an imminent attack. Tudor was unknowingly following a path of development similar to that of his German opposite number, Lieutenant Colonel Georg von Bruchmüller, who was engaged in similar experiments on the Eastern Front. This innovation was then combined with the proven ability of tanks to flatten barbed wire, thereby avoiding the need for prolonged barrages to cut the wire for the infantry with shrapnel or 106 fuse HE shells. This scheme and another idea for a 48-hour tank raid emanating from the staff of the Tank Corps were swiftly welded together by the staff of the Third Army holding the Cambrai front. Haig's support was easily secured, as he was not only in need of a morale boosting success after the Third Ypres Offensive, but he also recognised that the German forces would have been thinned out at Cambrai to reinforce the Ypres area. The ultimate scheme was ambitious, embracing the capture of both the German First and Second Line Systems, the crossing of the St Quentin Canal, all followed by a cavalry advance to take the railway junction at Cambrai and the tactically significant Bourlon Ridge which glowered down on the whole sector. Secrecy and speed would be all important for the assaulting force of six infantry divisions of the II, III and IV Corps, three tank brigades (476 tanks) and five cavalry divisions of the Cavalry Corps. After forty-eight hours the operations would be closed down if results were not satisfactory. There were no available reserves and this shortage of resources had been exacerbated, with the despatch of two British divisions and heavy artillery batteries to the Italian Front.

Although the 1,003 guns amassed for the barrage would be the key to success, another early focus of attention was inevitably the mass use of tanks. A workable system had to be hammered out to get the tanks across No Man's Land and the gaping trenches of the Hindenburg Line. One crucial advance was the reinvention of the fascine for the mechanical age – a huge roll of tightly bundled brushwood carried on the roof of the tank which could be dropped ahead of it to provide safe passage over a German trench. The infantry had to be trained to work in conjunction with the tanks and vice versa, communication still being a problem.

> A day came when we moved from our camp to a battle front in miniature – a series of trenches defended by rows of barbed wire. Several tanks were already there in attacking position. We lined up behind them and followed them to see, to our astonishment, these massive new and mysterious machines stride over the wire, crushing it into the ground as if it was so much waste paper. Then as we continued to follow, our amazement increasing, they surmounted the huge trenches, without effort, turning to bring their deadly quick firing guns and their Lewis guns to bear upon the defenders. Of course, there were no defenders, but the lesson was clear. No defences, however strong, no machine-gun fire or small arms fire, etc., would stop these thickly armoured monsters, driven forward by their powerful engines whose deep throbbing was music to our ears. Only a direct hit by shell fire would stop them as it would stop anything.[40]
>
> Private William Kirkby, 2/6th West Yorkshire Regiment

When the British opened up their barrage at 06.20 on 20 November, it crashed down on the German lines and artillery batteries, while the creeping barrages preceded the advance of the infantry and the rumbling tanks.

> A wounded man from 7th Company approached us from the right and gasped a few heavily charged words, 'The British have got tanks!' A cold shiver ran down my spine; the effect of this information on the morale of my men was plain to see. They, who had just been pouring scorn on the British, saying that they would all be tearing their trousers on our barbed wire, suddenly looked disconcerted. All of a sudden there was a muffled shout from a neighbouring sentry post. Everyone rushed to the parapet and then we saw, looming out of the swirling fog, a dreadful colossus heading straight for us. Every

single one of us could almost hear his heart beating in his chest! However, we were seized only momentarily by leaden indecision. With weapons tucked into our cheeks we fired shot after shot at the enemy. Unfortunately, this affected them not in the slightest. Slowly, but unstoppably, they drew closer. Firing also began left and right of us. As I pulled myself up to look over the parapet, I could see a whole chain of these steel monsters advancing towards our trenches. The tank to our front was barely a hundred metres away by now. The light machine gun had fired off its last belt of ammunition without visible effect. What was to be done?[41]

Second Lieutenant A. Saucke, 84th Infantry Regiment

The Germans fell back, hoping their wide trenches would thwart the tanks. It was here, though, that the fascines proved their worth, as a stunned Saucke watched on helplessly.

I watched one tank, which displayed a white flag as a special recognition mark and had some sort of attachment on its front. It approached the trench at right angles, then, when it reached the lip of the trench, the attachment suddenly fell vertically. I assumed that the tank had been hit or at least damaged and could scarcely believe my eyes when it continued onwards and its outline gradually became more clearly defined. There could be no doubt, it had crossed the trench and was pressing on towards us. What I had seen must have been a large wooden object or a great bundle of sticks which it had released at the appropriate moment in order to cross the trench. The following moments were difficult. We felt betrayed and sold out. Once more the most violent firing broke out as every barrel was brought to bear against these monstrous opponents. If only its infantry had put in an appearance! We could have dealt with men of flesh and blood like ourselves, but we were defenceless against these armoured machines.[42]

Second Lieutenant A. Saucke, 84th Infantry Regiment

Now the Germans were also harrassed from the air. The men of the RFC, who had become increasingly involved in ground-strafing operations, were flying ahead of the tanks. One of them was Second Lieutenant Arthur Gould Lee, who had been despatched to bomb a battery of 5.9-inch guns. The aircraft may not have carried a significant bombload, but the impact of swarms of busy-bee scouts was disruptive. And some of their little bombs struck home.

> Smoke shells burst ahead, a flash of red flame and masses of belching cloud, which we speed through – nauseous-smelling stuff that stings the eyes. In patches, where smoke merges with mist and cloud, we fly blind. Now we reach the rear of the Hindenburg defence system, two lots of trenches, with troops in field grey waiting in them, their forward view blocked by the pall of smoke. We skim just over their heads, I see them staring up at us in incredulous amazement. More smoke shells burst ahead, and suddenly, unexpectedly, we're at the wood. The 5.9s below are firing, producing more smoke. So there we are, the three of us, whirling blindly around at 50–100 feet, all but colliding, being shot at from below, and trying to place bombs accurately. In a sharp turn I saw a bunch of guns right in line for attack, so dived at 45 degrees and released all four bombs. As I swung aside I saw them burst, a group of white-grey puffs centred with red flames. One fell between two guns, the rest a few yards away. Splinters suddenly splash in my face – a bullet through a centre-section strut. This makes me go hot, and I dive at another group of guns, giving them 100 rounds, see a machine gun blazing at me, swing on to that, one short burst and he stops firing. As I climb up, a Camel whizzes past me out of the mist, missing me by a yard. It makes me sweat with fright. This is too dangerous.[43]
>
> Lieutenant Arthur Gould Lee, 46th Squadron, RFC

Inside the tanks the crews were achieving great things, but at the same time were enduring a tremendous physical and mental trial.

> I fired at anything I could see that looked like a target, any rise in the ground, trench, bush, anything that might shelter someone and I dropped most of the empty drums out of the flap in front. By now the inside of the tank was terribly hot, caused by the engine chiefly and the air was heavy and close, and caught your throat when you breathed; this, owing to the back-blast of the two guns and the ejector of the machine gun, and the noise was appalling.[44]
>
> Lieutenant Kenneth Wootton, 'Apollyon II', 'A' Battalion, Tank Corps

Tanks were superb weapons against demoralised infantry, but they were also large, slow-moving targets which were themselves vulnerable to artillery fire.

Soon after we came almost face to face with at least four more guns, also in the open. All pointing in our direction. They fired at me, just point-blank, and the shell struck us in front just where I was sitting and, bursting as it hit, blew a hole in the armour-plating by my left knee. The first thing that made me realise we had been hit was 'coming to' finding myself lying back over my seat with my head nearly on the floor and my left foot caught in something so that I couldn't move it. I felt no pain of any sort, being dazed and numb all over, with a tremendous sort of singing noise in both ears and some blood running into my left eye, which I wiped with my hand now and then. I slid back off the seat and sank to the floor having no use in my legs or arms, but still feeling nothing.[45]

Lieutenant Kenneth Wootton, 'Apollyon II', 'A' Battalion, Tank Corps

There was also a great problem getting the tanks across the St Quentin Canal. After a vigorous exchange of fire between tanks and German infantry in the cottages opposite, the Flying Fox II, festooned with infantry, tried to cross an already partially demolished bridge.

Swinging to the right again, we started across – going strong and no one hurt except odd splinters. We had almost got across, when 'Grruff Crash!' – the Bosche blew the far end of the span in, and we dropped smack into the canal. We thought the end of the world had come at least, but had the presence of mind to fling open all exits, and the water started to pour in from all directions. The air inside was thick with ammunition boxes and shells which had broken loose from their holders with the shock of landing, and flew about in all directions. Something outside hit the muzzle of my gun, and as the traversing arm was under my armpit, it lifted me up, bringing my head into violent contact with the steel plating of the roof. I was thankful that I was wearing a steel helmet at the time. Luckily, our tail had lodged on some masonry, and so held the rear end of the tank out of the water. I was delayed a few seconds by the tap I had received on the head, and in the meantime the others had 'shot' out of every exit, and jumped and scrambled until they gained the road, down which they 'beat it' in great style.[46]

Private Alfred Ballard, 'Flying Fox II', 'F' Battalion, Tank Corps

In the end the Front Line System of the Hindenburg Line was over-run to a depth of some 3–4 miles, a splendid achievement equal to the first day at Arras. On the other hand, the cavalry were unable to deploy forward to any effect, the German Second Line System between Masnières and Beaurevoir remained intact, the key bridge across the canal had been destroyed and the heights of Bourlon Ridge remained in German hands. The British had suffered some 4,000 casualties but had taken over 4,000 German prisoners. Significantly no less than 179 tanks had been put out of action or broken down.

Next day the offensive carried on, but by now both sides found themselves in a more familiar scenario played out countless times before. The Germans rushed forward reinforcements, while the British struggled to regain some momentum. There was no surprise now, the guns had been moved forward and their firing lost precision, the number of tanks was vastly depleted, the infantry were tiring and there were few reserves available. Vicious fighting took place in an effort to gain the Bourlon Ridge, but all the British had succeeded in doing was creating a vulnerable salient by the time operations staggered to a close on 27 November. But the Germans too had been learning some new tricks.

The German High Command were well aware of the opportunities presented by the newly created British salient. Some nine miles wide and four miles deep, it was vulnerable to attacks from both flanks to pinch it out, thereby cutting off the units holding the extremities. Soon preparations were underway for a major counter-attack by the Second Army led by General Georg von der Marwitz. The end result was a plan to fire a diversionary barrage at Bourlon Wood, before attacking the southern front of the salient, driving in towards the north. The German response typified the endurance of the German Empire. Despite all the trials of the year, they still managed to scrape together a formidable force of eighteen divisions, of which ten were still largely unaffected by the recent debilitating battles on the Western Front.

The German offensive tactical approach had been refined through the long years of war: their own experiences at Verdun and on the Eastern Front were melded with what they had observed in their British and French opponents. The German High Command still perceived no pressing need for tanks, relying on their massed artillery, now equalled by the British, but still a devastating weapon of war. There would be a short powerful bombardment of between thirty and sixty minutes, targeting in particular

batteries, headquarters, cutting communications routes and generally isolating the salient, while the ubiquitous high-angle mortars pummelled
the front lines to great effect. The infantry would then advance, once
again trialling the stormtrooper tactics that were still being refined. The
first wave would move forward in sections, using light machine guns,
grenades and flamethrowers, passing between strongpoints, feeling their
way through the cracks in the British defences, seeking out the vulnerable
artillery batteries and headquarters. Behind them would be mobile minenwerfers and even some 77 mm guns to provide close support in reducing
points of resistance. Above them would be swarms of low-flying aircraft
strafing the British wherever they were sighted.

The German barrage began at 06.00 on 30 November, quietly at first
but soon building up to a terrifying crescendo. The German gunners certainly enjoyed themselves in delivering the drumfire they had endured so
often from the British and French.

> Today is our day. Today it is we who are doing the drumming. 7.50
> am. The order to fire flies from the observation post to the guns. It
> passes along the chain of relays like a flat pebble skimming along the
> surface of a pond. The battery commander has lit a living time fuse.
> 'Rumm... rumm... rumm... rumm' and simultaneously angry streams
> of flame belch out from behind hedges and bushes, from hollows and
> the ruins of houses. 'Next target 3,000 metres! From the right, fire!'
> 'Rumm... rumm... rumm... ' That is revenge for the naval guns firing
> on the Lorette Spur, which ploughed up our cemeteries. '3,500 metres!
> Fire!' 'Rumm... rumm... rumm... rumm...' That is for the autumn
> battles in Champagne. Now the Tommies are picking up the bill for
> the French. '3,700!' 'Rumm... rumm... rumm... rumm...' Go on, crawl
> away into the earth, duck down low. Revenge for the whimpering of
> the helpless comrades buried alive on the Somme. '3,900!' 'Rumm...
> rumm... rumm... rumm...' Great fun, eh, Tommy? Swallow the gas and
> choke out your death rattles. That is for Verdun. 'Rolling Salvo! 4,000
> metres!' 'Rumm...' Revenge for Vermelles! '3,900!' 'Rumm...' Revenge
> for Givenchy! '3,800!' 'Rumm...' Revenge for St Hilaire! '3,700!' For
> Fontaine! '3,600!' '3,500!' Revenge for Wavrille and Herbebois! '3,000!
> Rapid fire!' What fun, Tommy! We are taking our revenge for the
> dismal years when we had to be patient. Long, long years of being on
> the receiving end of drum fire, helpless. 'Rumm... rumm... rumm...
> rumm... Today we are doing the drumming!'[47]

Second Lieutenant von der Goltz, 14th Field Artillery Regiment

As the infantry moved into No Man's Land, they cut through the British troops, many of whom were already exhausted.

> In no time at all we were in possession of the first enemy positions. Without pausing we assaulted the next hollow, where we came across numerous dugouts. We had soon cleared the enemy out of them. Up to this point, about 200 metres, we had doubled forward. I commanded the light machine guns, whose crews found the advance exceptionally strenuous because of their heavy loads. Despite the great effort involved, we stormed forward on to the hill to our front and, once again, we soon broke the tough defence of the enemy. We took numerous prisoners. We continued on unstoppably through the next dip, clearing the dugouts by the use of hand grenades.[48]
>
> Staff Sergeant Engesser, 40th Fusilier Regiment

In places they even broke through to the gun line. The Third Army awoke to near disaster: all available units were rushed forward to hold key tactical positions, Among them were the men of the Guards Division who launched a counter-attack.

> We felt 'We are the Guards. We'll show them', and we knew we had to keep cool, and maintain a disciplined line. Orders were passed along verbally. Over undulating down we went, and still no sign of Germans, but when we drew near Gouzeacourt Wood and, crossing a deserted trench, reached the crest of a hill, they met us with a blizzard of fire. Mates fell on all sides, and the order came to fall back to the trench. Many wounded were left behind, and I crept out and started to drag in a heavy fellow badly wounded in the legs. It wasn't easy going and, desperately, I appealed to him, 'Make an effort, chum!' 'Effort be damned!' he exclaimed, and it struck me as so comic a situation, with bullets spattering around, that I had to pause and chuckle before resuming the pull to the trench. Helping hands hauled him over the parapet to safety, and that was the last I saw or heard of him. He must have been swiftly carried to the rear.[49]
>
> Private Norman Cliff, 2nd Grenadier Guards

The British flung everything in to stem the tide: the disciplined troops of the Guards Division, low-flying strafing aircraft, the remnants of the tanks not yet withdrawn from the battlefield, dismounted cavalry, even charges by mounted Indian lancers. In the end it was just about enough. The fighting degenerated into a welter of attacks and counter-attacks. Eventually the British pulled back in relatively good order from the extremities of the salient, to a strong defensive line based on Flesquières – and there they stayed. The Third Army lost some 44,207 casualties, the Germans approximately 41,000. Neither side gained the objectives they craved; both did enough to deny their enemies success. The two tactical roller-coasters were rattling along side by side but for all their advances no one had yet solved the problem of breaking through their opponent's lines. The battle ended with the honours shared, but both sides had trialled the tactics that would come to centre stage in 1918. The advent of predicted fire and the mass use of tanks also left a lingering sword of Damocles: no longer could any German sector be considered truly quiet. An Allied offensive could burst out from anywhere at any time and the Germans were consequently forced to strengthen their defences and review their divisional dispositions all along the line.

16

ITALY, 1915–18

'If success was achieved on the Italian Front, I believed that victory in the War was assured. A separate peace with Austria would then be practicable, and having eliminated Austria from the War, Germany would be at our mercy.'[1]

Prime Minister David Lloyd George

ITALY HAD RENEGED ON ITS COMMITMENTS on the outbreak of war in August 1914, claiming that the aggressive nature of the actions taken by the Central Powers breached the defensive nature of the original treaty agreements. An alliance containing Austria-Hungary was never likely to sit well with an Italian population, who still harboured a grudge against the Austrians over disputed territories, particularly focussed on the Trentino and Trieste areas. There was a popular groundswell headed by a nationalist movement, Italia Irredenta (Unredeemed Italy), that these lands should be 'returned' to Italy thereby finally uniting the Italian population. This stance conveniently omitted consideration of the interests of the many Germans and Slavs who had also made their home in these lands. Once it became evident that Italy was not entering the war on the German side, there was a rush by British and French diplomats to secure the Italians to augment the ranks of the Entente. These efforts culminated in the secret Treaty of London, signed on 26 April 1915, under the provisions of which Italy would declare war on the Central Powers in return for promises of gains in the disputed provinces in the Tyrol and the Austrian Littoral which included the port of Trieste. Agreements were also hammered out over the division of the spoils with Serbia along the Dalmatian coastline of the Adriatic. In consequence, Italy declared war on Austria-Hungary on 23 May 1915, thereby opening up a new front stretching for some 400 miles along the border Italy shared with Austria-Hungary.

The frontier formed the shape of a huge 'S', with the Trentino Salient bulging into Italy and the Udine pushing into Austria. Most of the front was extremely mountainous in character and could be divided into three sectors: the Trent Front around the Trentino Salient; the Alpine Front; and finally the thirty miles of the Isonzo River sector running down to the Adriatic, although even here the ground was dominated be a series of hills and ridges. The configuration of the border bequeathed the Italians a significant strategic conundrum. If they were to attack on the Isonzo Front, where the terrain offered the best chance of progress, they would be vulnerable to a devastating Austrian attack emanating from the Trent Front, which was effectively behind the Italian lines, and would threaten to cut off both the Alpine and Isonzo Fronts.

The Italian Army was large, consisting of some 850,000 soldiers, and based on a conscription system, but there were severe problems with both equipment and training. The officers were still recruited from a fairly narrow regional base and there was an inherent lack of professionalism in their general approach. Although King Victor Emanuel was nominally Commander in Chief, the Italian Chief of General Staff and *de facto* commander was General Luigi Cadorna. Born in 1850, Cadorna had demonstrated considerable abilities as an administrative staff officer and was widely respected as a theoretical military strategist, although he had no relevant experience as a field commander. The lower ranks of his army were largely drawn from peasant stock and were dogged by high levels of illiteracy, which hampered the development of good NCOs. However, they would demonstrate a tough resilience to both harsh conditions and severe casualties on active service.

The standard infantry weapon was the magazine-charged 6.5 mm bolt-action Mannlicher-Carcano rifle which dated back to 1891. It proved hard-wearing and its lighter calibre made it eminently suited to the mountainous regions where much of the fighting would occur. They were also equipped with Fiat-Revelli machine guns, which proved perfectly sound weapons – the problem was the paucity of their numbers in service condition. Even worse was the shortage of modern artillery. The most common field guns were the 75 mm Krupp or Deport models, with a number of 65 mm mountain guns which could be broken down to be transported by mules in rough country. But again there were simply too few of them, while heavy artillery was also in scarce supply. The Italians had none of the high-trajectory mortars that were so essential in mountain warfare. Throughout the years that followed the Italians would be desperate for artillery support from their British and French allies. Nevertheless, the Italian Army deployed in the field in May 1915 thirty-six infantry divisions in fourteen corps, in contrast to the paltry six divisions of the BEF in 1914. And so, the Italian entry into the war was a considerable blow to the Central Powers.

The Austrio-Hungarian Army was already under relentless pressure in 1915. The addition of the Italians to its roster of enemies, which included the Russians and the Serbs, did not bode well. Indeed, the Austrian Chief of General Staff, General Franz Conrad von Hötzendorf, took the declaration of war by the Italians as a personal affront. Yet in another sense the Italian timing was dreadful as it coincided with the advent of a massively increased level of support from Germany for the ailing Austria-Hungary on the Eastern Front. This would greatly ease the situation for the Austrians and allow them to reinforce the Italian Front in a manner which otherwise would have been impossible.

The Austrians had carved out extremely strong defensive works on the mountainous Trent and Alpine fronts, carefully using the terrain to their best advantage. Trenches, dugouts and gunpits were often blasted from the solid rock and covered by barbed wire. Given the precipitous nature of the ground these positions would prove almost impregnable. Much work was also undertaken behind the lines to improve road and rail communications. The defences on the Isonzo sector was not so well progressed, although the Austrian line was still intimidatingly strong, tucked on to the hills and ridges just behind the Isonzo River. In the Upper Isonzo the river ran through a deep gorge surrounded by the Bainsizza Plateau and Julian Alps. The Isonzo then ran through the Gorizia area, named after the town on its west bank. Overlooking and dominating the sector were a series of mountains all heavily fortified: Monte Sabotino and Monte Podgora in an Austrian bridgehead to the west, and Monte Santo,

Monte San Gabriele and Monte San Daniele to the east. Finally, as the Isonzo flowed down to the Adriatic, it passed the dominant Carso Plateau on its east bank, running parallel to the sea and rising up to 1,000 feet, with one of the key positions being Monte San Michele.

Shortly after the declaration of war, the Italians began their advance across the border, pushing forward to the Isonzo, while the Austrians fell back across the flood plain to the higher ground east of the river. At first the Italians made some useful gains, including the town of Caporetto in the north, and some progress in the Julian Alps east of the Isonzo, but ultimately their offensive ground to a halt. The First Battle of the Isonzo followed shortly afterwards, with frontal attacks on the Austrian bridge-head opposite Gorizia and on the Carso Plateau commencing on 23 June. But these merely confirmed that any further advances would be extraordinarily difficult. Even where the Italians made small gains they were promptly hurled back by Austrian counter-attacks. The battle set a pattern for what would follow: the Italians used simplistic frontal tactics, relying on courage, élan and press of numbers to overwhelm the outnumbered Austrians, and in which hope they would be sadly disappointed. Cadorna showed himself to be an utterly inflexible leader, supremely self-confident, apparently learning nothing from the rebuffs; indeed, he considered that failure originated in a lack of determination from his officers and men.

In the Second (commencing on 18 July), Third (commencing on 18 October 1915) and Fourth Battles of the Isonzo (commencing 10 November 1915), the story was essentially the same as the Italians charged forward time and time again – a story retold as tragedy. Although he had scraped together every possible gun from forts and naval sources, Cadorna still had nothing like enough guns or shells, or indeed the gunners with the skills to target accurately Austrian strongpoints. The shortage of mortars was also clearly a severe disadvantage. In murderous fighting, the Italians managed briefly to capture the key tactical positions, like Monte San Michele overlooking Gorizia, only to be thrown off them again by determined Austrian counter-attacks. Eventually December brought mutual exhaustion and the fighting petered out as both sides tried to cope with the freezing cold of winter in the mountains. By this time the Italians had suffered up to 250,000 casualties and the Austrians over 128,000.

The next Italian assault, the Fifth Battle of the Isonzo, commenced on 11 March 1916 as part of the co-ordinated Allied response to the German

Verdun offensive, but nothing much had been achieved before the Austrians launched their own Tyrolean offensive, driving out of the mountains across the Asiago Plateau sector of the Trentino Salient with the intention of breaking through on to the coastal plain and severing the Italian communications running east to the Isonzo and Alpine fronts. This attack was conceived by Conrad, who was desperate to stamp down on the Italians, whom he still considered as traitors to the cause of the Central Powers. This planned offensive would cause a considerable amount of friction with Falkenhayn, who believed that it was a distraction from the main battle against Russia and France.

The Austrians attacked on 15 May. This was an amazing venue for modern warfare, the jagged ridges of the great mountains liberally slashed by yawning chasms, the splintering rock magnifying ten-fold the effect of bursting shells to produce a flensing spray of deadly splinters. The heavy Austrian guns took their terrible effect on the Italians, who were forced back across the Asiago Plateau. For a while it even looked as if the Austrians might break through to the Po River and the coastal plains. At this point a mixture of exhaustion and the knock-on effects of the successful Brusilov offensive on the Russian Front began to impact on the Austrian effort. Conrad was forced to divert divisions to help shore up the Eastern Front and the Austrians slowed to a halt. Taking advantage of this, the Italians managed to divert some troops from the Isonzo front and counter-attacked hard on 16 June, regaining much ground as the Austrians fell back to their prepared defensive positions. The Italians suffered some 147,000 casualties, the Austrians 81,000. Neither side could really afford this rate of attritional fighting.

Yet the Italians were determined to press on and, on 6 August 1916, they launched the Sixth Battle of the Isonzo. The Austrians had been weakened by the transfers to the Eastern Front and so, by dint of concentrating their forces, the Italians managed to at last to capture the town of Gorizia and make some gains on the Carso Plateau, although the fighting was as ferocious as ever. This victory, in conjunction with its relative success in holding the Trentino offensive, had a considerable beneficial effect on morale throughout the Italian Army. Indeed, the Italians were even emboldened enough to declare war finally on Germany on 28 August. Sadly, the Seventh, Eighth and Ninth Battles of the Isonzo (14 September–14 November 1916) soon dissipated any Italian optimism as they repeatedly attacked the Austrian lines seeking to expand their gains around Gorizia and the Carzo Plateau. Progress was almost non-existent, but casualties soared, with the Italians losing another 69,000 casualties and the Austrians 75,000. Throughout the long Isonzo campaigns, the Italians had failed to make any significant advances in their tactical thinking, still relying on courage and numbers to breach the Austrian lines, with the support of limited and largely unfocussed artillery barrages. Overall, Cadorna was driving his men on, setting a much higher tempo of offensive operations than had been established by the British, French or Russian generals. Units were being committed into battle on a far more regular basis, even during winter, which provided little respite due to the severity of the climatic conditions. Cadorna was a harsh disciplinarian and an enthusiastic devotee of using the threat of the death penalty to keep his men up to the required performance.

Operations resumed with the bombardment for the Tenth Battle of the Isonzo on 12 May 1917. By this time the British and French had at last been convinced by Italian appeals for additional artillery, with the British responding by deploying several batteries of 6-inch howitzers to the front, despite Haig's misgivings at moving such valuable resources from the Western Front. On their arrival, the British found the Italian soldier an enigma.

Of all armies I should say that it is most difficult to gauge the standard of the Italians. One is constantly confronted with surprises. The Italian is capable of doing everything, and is a master at doing nothing. As regards physique he is, I think, unsurpassed though of low stature, his strength is remarkable. He can carry more than a British or French soldier. Infantry may be seen straggling along a road, the reverse of our idea of 'smart', but he will walk all day and feed on little. He is practically never drunk and, though illiterate, extremely handy and ingenious. He has no idea of punctuality or time. 8 o'clock may mean 8.30 or 9.00. But when he works, he works extremely well. The morale of the Italian is easily affected. As an Italian officer said to me, 'Tell him he is a brave man, and he becomes one!' Hence the regiments with good traditions are excellent, those without traditions or with bad reputations are very bad, and the contrast is stronger than in other armies.[2]

Lieutenant Colonel Charles Buzzard, Headquarters, 144th Heavy Artillery Group, Royal Artillery

Despite these artillery reinforcements, little changed as the Italians sought to batter their way forward all along the Isonzo Front. At first things seemed to be going better, as Monte Kuk, north of Gorizia, was captured. There was also progress on the dreaded Carso Plateau, although in the end the Italians were thwarted by the heights of Monte Hermada which guarded the route through to Trieste. An Austrian counter-attack was fended away and in the end the Italians had more than 157,000 casualties, while the Austrians suffered some 75,000.

Undaunted, Cadorna readied himself for his next attempt, the Eleventh Battle of the Isonzo, which commenced on 18 August. The Italians attacked either side of Gorizia, this time making some progress on both the Bainsizza Plateau to the north and edging forwards towards Monte Hermada. Colonel Charles Buzzard, one of the senior British heavy artillery officers attached to the Italians, was quite astounded at the complete lack of sophistication in the artillery tactics employed by the Italians on the Carso Plateau. To him the following characteristics were painfully evident:

> 1. Almost entire lack of information supplied to the Heavy Artillery. We were never told which way the infantry would attack, the hours named were never adhered to. 2. Fire was lifted far too soon: infantry had no support in passing over four or five hundred yards of open and difficult ground. We could have kept on firing until the infantry was 200 yards from objectives. 3. Austrian prisoners say that during our bombardment all their men were in caverns, and they hardly lost any; the trenches were quite wrecked: no shells can touch their caverns. 4. The remarkable thing is that with such utter lack of co-operation between artillery and infantry, the Italian infantry ever take any of their objectives. The artillery preparation is good, a large number of the infantry are quite heroic; but to advance behind a proper creeping barrage is unheard of.[3]
>
> Lieutenant Colonel Charles Buzzard, Headquarters, 144th Heavy Artillery Group, Royal Artillery

The Italian successes, if such they can be called, were at crippling expense (166,000 Italian casualties against an estimated 85,000 Austrians) and were negligible in terms of real territorial gains, but at the same time had some tactical promise if only they could keep driving forward. But the Italians were fast tiring and unable to press home any advantage. Indeed,

Cadorna was forced to put his forces on to a defensive status, while they reorganised themselves, built up their reserves and rested ready to renew the attack in 1918. However, the Austrians were, if anything, in a worse state: exhausted from the long war with Russia, Serbia and now the Italians. On the Italian Front, as everywhere else, it was evident that the Austrians desperately needed support from the Germans; unfortunately for the Italians, they got it.

Ludendorff was only willing to supply German troops for offensive operations, not just to shore up the line, which he considered to be a waste of his valuable resources. The collapse of the Russians on the Eastern Front had given him a last chance to bring the war to a close. His plan was to knock Italy out of the war prior to the great assault he planned for the Western Front in 1918. He also had in mind another experiment with the assault tactics so effectively trialled by General Oskar von Hutier's Eighth Army at Riga on the Eastern Front in September 1917. This time he brought in General Otto von Below to command the composite German–Austro-Hungarian Fourteenth Army (consisting of seven German and a number of Austrian divisions). Inserted into the line in the Upper Isonzo sector facing the town of Caporetto, this formidably well-trained force was to spearhead the whole attack. Von Below made their priorities absolutely clear.

> The ruling principle for any offensive in the mountains is the conquest and holding of the crests, in order to get to the next objective by these land bridges. Even roundabout ways on the crests are to be preferred to the crossing of valleys and deep gorges, as the latter course takes longer and entails greater exertions. The valleys are to be used for the rapid bringing up of closed reserves, the field artillery and supply units. Every column on the heights must move forward without hesitation; by so doing opportunities will arise to help a neighbour who cannot get on, by swinging round in rear of the enemy opposing him.[4]
>
> General Otto von Below, Headquarters, Fourteenth Army

The bombardment opened at 02.00 on 24 October, a wave of gas, high explosive and smoke shells lashing the Italian batteries, command posts and strongpoints, splaying across the trenches.

It was a dark and rainy night and in no time a thousand gun muzzles were flashing on both sides of Tolmein. In the enemy territory an uninterrupted bursting and banging thundered and re-echoed from the mountains as powerfully as the severest thunderstorm. We saw and heard this tremendous activity with amazement. The Italian searchlights tried vainly to pierce the rain, and the expected enemy interdiction fire on the area around Tolmein did not materialise, for only a few hostile batteries answered the German fire. That was very reassuring and, half-asleep, we retired to our cover and listened to the lessening of our own artillery fire. At daybreak our fire increased in volume. Down by St Daniel heavy shells were smashing positions and obstacles and occasionally their smoke obscured the hostile installations. The fire activity of our artillery and mortars became more and more violent. The hostile counter-fire seemed to be rather weak.[5]

Lieutenant Erwin Rommel, Württemberg Mountain Battalion

The German and Austrian infantry had the good fortune to attack in misty conditions. Rommel and his detachment felt their way forward through the mountainous terrain, trying to avoid direct clashes with Italian strong-points, always seeking to circumnavigate them, take them from the rear and press on. His vivid account of mountain warfare shows the kind of tactics employed, but also how well he had assimilated von Below's instructions to concentrate on the peaks.

The ascent proved to be very difficult. Lieutenant Streicher and I followed 40 yards behind the new point. Close behind us came the crew of a heavy machine gun carrying their disassembled gun on their shoulders. At this moment a 100lb block of stone tumbled down on top of us. The draw was only 10 feet wide and dodging was difficult and escape impossible. In the fraction of a second it was clear that whoever was hit by the boulder would be pulverised. We all pressed against the left wall of the fold. The rock zigzagged between us and on downhill, without even scratching a single man. Happily, the supposition that the Italians were rolling stones down on us was false for the point had dislodged the stone. Finally the steep draw was behind us. In pouring rain, wet to the skin, we climbed the slope through dense undergrowth, looking and listening intently in all directions. The wood in front of us thinned out. If we moved rapidly then we might capture the hostile garrison without firing a shot. I singled out Lance Corporal Kiefner, a veritable giant, gave him eight men and told him to move down the path as if he and his men were Italians returning from up front, to penetrate into the hostile position and capture the garrison on both sides of the path. Again long, anxious minutes passed and we heard nothing but the steady rain on the trees. Then steps approached, and a soldier reported in a low voice, 'The Kiefner scout squad has captured a hostile dugout and taken seventeen Italians and a machine gun!' I then had to decide whether I should roll up the hostile position or break through in the direction of Hevnik Peak. I chose the latter. The elimination of the Italian positions was easy once we had possession of the peak. The farther we penetrated into the hostile zone of defence, the less prepared were the garrisons for our arrival, and the easier the fighting.[6]

Lieutenant Erwin Rommel, Württemberg Mountain Battalion

Nothing seemed to stop the Fourteenth Army and within just a day the Italians had fallen back up to fifteen miles, thereby uncovering the defences of first the Bainsizza Plateau, then Gorizia and finally the Carso Plateau. As the Italians began to fall apart small detachments like Rommel's had an entirely disproportionate effect.

We went downhill through the bushes with our machine guns and carbines at the ready and we soon saw the hostile position below us. It was heavily garrisoned. From above we looked down on the bottom of the trench. The enemy had no cover against our fire. The enemy did not suspect what threatened him. The assault squads made ready and we shouted down to the hostile garrison and told them to surrender. Frightened, the Italian soldiers stared up at us to the rear. Their rifles fell from their hands. They knew they were lost and gave the sign of surrender. My assault squads did not fire a single shot. Not only did the garrison of the positions between us and Jevszek, about three companies strong, surrender; but, to our great surprise, the hostile trench garrison as far north as the Matajur road also laid down its arms. An Italian regiment of thirty-seven officers and 1,000 men surrendered in the hollow 700 yards north of Jevszek. It marched up with full equipment and armament, and I had trouble finding enough men to carry out the disarmament.[7]

Lieutenant Erwin Rommel, Württemberg Mountain Battalion

All the gains that had cost so much in Italian blood had to be hastily abandoned as they were forced to pull right back to a new line established along the Tagliamento River. Soon there was chaos and only the fact that the German and Austrian communication lines had been overstretched prevented a real disaster. There was no chance of holding on to the Tagliamento Line, so back went the Italians all the way to the Piave River just in front of Venice, where they were able to form a more compact and easily defensible line that linked across to the Asiago Plateau and the Trent front sector.

Now the Allies reluctantly came to the help of the Italians. By the end of the year five British and six French divisions had been despatched to prop up the Italian Front, although by then the line had stabilised. It had been a stunning victory for the Central Powers and another demonstration of the potency of their new attack tactics which the Italians had been unable to counter. The Italian casualties were estimated at 305,000, of which the vast majority had become prisoners-of-war during their chaotic retreat. As a direct consequence, on 8 November General Cadorna was dismissed and replaced as Chief of General Staff by General Armando Diaz, who promptly began the arduous task of rebuilding confidence throughout his battered armies. A further consequence was an Allied conference that had been convened at the Italian town of Rapallo on 5 November. This assembly resolved to form an Allied Supreme War Council to establish some unity of command among the Allies, with a particular emphasis put on building up a collective reserve that could be employed in threatening situations such as had just been experienced in Italy. In some ways the worst was over for the Italians. On 10 November an attack by German and Austrian troops failed to break through. A further attempt on 4 December nearly did so, but in the end the Italian line again held. Shortly afterwards, the Germans withdrew their troops, intent on securing victory on the Western Front before the Americans arrived. They had run out of time to finish the job in Italy.

The Piave and Trent fronts were relatively quiet during the early part of 1918. Both sides had suffered too much to gather their resources easily for another offensive. The Italians had by now been thoroughly admitted to the inner circle of the Allies and much effort was expended on improving standards of training and inculcating a working knowledge of the new tactics. Thus Diaz reorganised his lines to secure defence in depth, preparing defence works not only on the Piave but also covering the Brenta,

Adige and Po rivers. In addition, a leaf was taken out of the Belgian book in that preparations were made to inundate the flood plains should disaster loom at the hands of the Austrians.

It was as well they were prepared, as the Germans demanded that the Austrians launch one last great attack. The Austrians had recently undergone a change in command, and the new Austrian Chief of Staff, General Arthur Arz von Straussenburg, was also keen to try to finish off the Italians. The offensive commenced on 15 June 1918, with a two-pronged assault, one into the main Piave defensive positions and the second thrusting down from the Trent front towards the Brenta. The Italians were augmented by the three British and two French divisions that still remained on the front – and perhaps even more importantly, by their 450 guns. Private Norman Gladden was occupying a defensive position up on the rocky peaks of the Asiago Plateau.

> Flashes lit up the hills on the far side of the plateau and a roar of artillery rolled along the entire front. A crescendo of sound, and then the storm burst upon us. Screaming shells rushed to earth amidst the wire, and behind us, or further over in the woods. Lumps of rock were hurled about by the explosions. The trench soon became swathed in a cloud of acrid smoke. Coloured lights went up out of the valley. The enemy's barrage continued unabated, but our own guns remained silent. The shells were dropping with awful regularity about the trench; only the hardness of the ground saved us from being buried. But this protective hardness had a terror of its own, as lumps of rock and stone hailed down into the trench. Over my shoulder, as I crouched, I could see the bursts of incendiary shells, and, as I watched, a tremendous flame rose up as some of the trees caught fire. The flames leapt up like gigantic red seas beating against a breakwater and glowed through the gaunt trees which banked up the hillside above us. It was a terrifying but magnificent sight.[8]
>
> Private Norman Gladden, 11th Northumberland Fusiliers

Until the very last moment, Gladden and his comrades were confident that this was just a demonstration by the Austrian artillery.

> Through the din, which had certainly lessened, we heard whistle blasts and were puzzled. Suddenly there was a shout from a watcher on the firestep to our right. 'Stand to! He is coming over!' A chill trickled down

my spine. My first impulse was to deny the possibility. The enemy to come all that way across the plateau to attack us: that was an absurd idea! We grasped our weapons and rushed pell-mell to the firestep. The barrage was lifting. More coloured lights went up – despairingly, it seemed – and the hollow crash of bombs punctuated the rattle of musketry. A stiff fight was being put up by our advance posts. Then I saw khaki figures running back, followed closely by grey lines of the enemy, moving more methodically, while reinforcements continued to stream across the plateau.[9]

Private Norman Gladden, 11th Northumberland Fusiliers

In the fighting that followed Gladden and his team had a close escape.

The attackers, appearing to enjoy charmed lives, then put something into the wire and ran back quickly. The bomb or torpedo exploded with considerable concussion, blowing a complete section of the wire into the air and clearing a passage through the belt. It was an amazing feat. A party of the enemy then rushed the gap under cover of the dense smoke from the explosion, and were in the trench in a matter of seconds. Almost simultaneously a stooping figure appeared above the brow about twenty-five yards in front of us, an enemy soldier bowed down with the weight of some infernal contrivance, a flame-thrower as we subsequently discovered. The trench belched fire from end to end and the poor brave devil fell forward on the skyline riddled by dozens of bullets. With one's knowledge of the possibilities of this fiery weapon, who can say how near to success this lone attacker had come?[10]

Private Norman Gladden, 11th Northumberland Fusiliers

It was a close-run thing all along the line, but the Austrian attacks could not break through. Even when they made small gains, the Italians counter-attacked vigorously and Austrian morale began to crumble as they were left utterly frustrated.

For a period all remained calm, but behind the lines Diaz was preparing for an offensive against the increasingly demoralised Austrians. As the Germans began to collapse on the Western Front this left the Austrians distraught, all their hopes for victory having been pinned on the Germans. Alone they were all but helpless by late 1918.

The final blow came on 24 October with the Battle of Vittorio Veneto, launched all along the Trent and Piave fronts. Although the Austrians resisted in places, their line soon began to crumble and the Italians and a British force both managed to establish bridgeheads across the Piave. Private Norman Gladden describes that crossing of the Piave late on 26 October.

> The bridge swayed. The dark waters swirled and foamed below between the boats. A shrapnel shell burst venomously above. Slowly, now, no panic! Tramp, tramp, tramp. The bridge swayed rhythmically. A shell screaming into the waters alongside threw up a column of water, which splashed across the planks. I wanted to run; but no, we kept our paces, proceeding as if by clockwork. And then I saw the opposite bank looming out of the darkness. A shell burst somewhere behind; the bridge trembled and there was a sound of rending woodwork. I ran and jumped clear, sinking to my knees on the welcoming shingle.[11]
>
> Private Norman Gladden, 11th Northumberland Fusiliers

They then had to wade across the final section of the river.

> In front of us swirled an ominous black current which, with the enemy barrage now well in the rear, we had the unmixed blessing of contemplating without other fears intervening. The guides started forward into the darkness; we linked together in continuous chains of four or five and scrambled after them. The cold waters swept up round my body. I gasped as my heart seemed to stand still and I felt my feet going from under me. I had to hold the gun well above the waters. We strove vigorously in the torrent, which now came up to our shoulders. Then the worst was past, and the bed sloped up to the shore, on to which I scrambled, frozen and breathless from the struggle. Drenched and bedraggled, we had little of the appearance of an assaulting force at that moment.[12]
>
> Private Norman Gladden, 11th Northumberland Fusiliers

At last they had broken through. But this was a new kind of warfare.

> We were already feeling very different in this open country warfare, which to us was a completely new experience. Despite our doubts as to where we ought to be, a new carefree attitude was taking control. We were no longer the frightened troops nailed to the earth by a storm of steel in many different forms. We were advancing into enemy-held

territory, victors at last, after all those months and years of fear and stultification. Death was still about, perhaps only just round the corner, but the dice were no longer weighted against each one of us. It felt good to be alive on that sunny autumn morning on the Plains of Lombardy.[13]

Private Norman Gladden, 11th Northumberland Fusiliers

For a while there was still some fighting to be done. The Italians and their allies commenced a drive on Vittorio Veneto in a successful attempt to separate the Austrian armies and cut the communications between them. Suddenly the brittle facade of the Austrian opposition crumbled apart as they commenced a withdrawal all along the line. The Trentino sector, that bastion of Austrian defence for three years, was over-run, and a general advance was commenced pushing north and east. As they fell back, over 300,000 Austrians became prisoners-of-war, mirroring the disaster of Caporetto the year before.

THE ITALIAN CAMPAIGN WAS FINALLY OVER. The formal armistice began on 3 November 1918. In the end the Italians had helped bring the Austro-Hungarians to their knees, already weakened as they were by their titanic battles with the Russians on the Eastern Front. The Italians had played a major role by distracting the bulk of the Austrian Army that might otherwise have been redeployed to other fronts after the Russian Revolution. Throughout the campaign had been a terrible carnage, fought in a hostile mountainous environment. Neither side had made any allowances for the appalling conditions as troops were ordered forward in circumstances in which they had minimal chances of success. The Italians had faltered when the Germans had briefly intervened during the Battle of Caporetto, but in the end they had re-established the defensive line along the Piave through their own efforts before moving forward with British and French assistance to achieve victory. The completeness of the Italian triumph can be seen in that the Austrians were forced to cede all the elements of the *Italia Irredenta* still under their control, including the South Tyrol, the Isonzo Valley, Trieste, Istria, Carniola and Dalmatia. The Italian gamble of 1915 may have paid off, but the cost had been excruciatingly high: some 651,000 killed during the three years of brutal war.

17

THE SINAI AND PALESTINIAN CAMPAIGNS, 1914–18

'The British Empire owes a great deal to sideshows. I have no doubt at all that, when the history of 1917 comes to be written, and comes to be read ages hence, these events in Mesopotamia and Palestine will hold a much more conspicuous place in the minds and the memories of people than many an event which looms much larger for the moment in our sight.'[1]

Prime Minister David Lloyd George

THE BRITISH HAD ESTABLISHED A STRANGLEHOLD on the Ottoman Empire suzerainty of Egypt in 1882 and, whatever the legal niceties of the situation, had been in effective control there ever since. The importance of Egypt lay in its location as the neck containing the jugular of the British Empire. The hundred miles of the Suez Canal stretching from Port Said on the Mediterranean through to Port Suez on the Red Sea provided a shortened sea route linking the British homeland with her dominions in India, Australia and New Zealand. This crucial waterway had to be defended at all costs, which entailed a considerable military commitment to prevent any hostile incursion or possible sabotage. After the outbreak of war with Turkey in November 1914, Egypt was formally declared a British Protectorate and a considerable army was built up under the command of General Sir John Maxwell. This was far from a homogeneous force, being made up of the Territorials of the British 42nd Division and the 10th and 11th

Indian Divisions, joined later by the ANZAC Corps, to complete its training with the original intention of then continuing on to the Western
Front. The Indian troops were deployed along the western bank of the
canal with strongposts on the eastern bank.

What was obvious to the British was also obvious to the Turks: by
taking Suez they could sever the life's blood of the Empire. A successful operation in Egypt would also add much weight to the 'Holy War'
declared by Sultan Mehmed and help his attempts at fermenting revolt
in Egypt. But equally the prime obstacle to a successful expedition was
obvious from a cursory glance at a map: the inhospitable wastes of the
Sinai Desert that separated Egypt from Palestine. The Turkish Suez Expeditionary Force (SEF) was placed under the command of a German staff
officer, Colonel Friedrich von Kressenstein, who was henceforth responsible for the meticulous logistical preparations that would have to be made
if the Turks were to have any chance of getting some 25,000 troops across
the wilderness. Thousands of camels were collected to carry stores, while
supply and water replenishing posts were established along the route to
be taken. But there still remained a 30-mile gap which would have to be
jumped as quickly as possible. The SEF finally started out on 14 January
1915, with three main columns and diversionary forces slogging their
way across the desert. The Turks were further hampered by the necessity
of dragging heavy steel bridging pontoons and bulky rafts to enable them
to cross the Canal.

At first the SEF movements were tracked by British aerial reconnaissance, but a deterioration in the weather brought swirling winds and a
blanking sandstorm which, in conjunction with a final bold night march,
concealed where the actual blow would fall. At 03.25 on 3 February, the
Turks were sighted massing on the eastern bank of the Canal, near Tussum
Post, where they launched their pontoons and rafts into the water and
boldly attempted to force a crossing. Two companies managed to get
across the Canal and dug in to establish a bridgehead supported by the
fire of Turkish batteries from the other side. It had been a courageous
attempt, bordering on foolhardy, but in the end it failed when an Indian
counter-attack eradicated the Turkish enclave on the east bank. There was
nothing left for the SEF to do but to retreat ignominiously; the Turks
could not maintain their position without any effective lines of communication. Had the British been a little more thoughtful they might have

noticed that, although the Turks had been beaten, they had fought with exemplary courage in near impossible circumstances.

The situation then settled down in Egypt as all eyes turned to the Gallipoli Campaign, with Egypt acting as a reservoir for troops. The Turks were also drawing on their troops in Palestine to bolster their defensive operations in both Gallipoli and Mesopotamia. Once Gallipoli was over, both sides would look again at the situation in Middle East.

The British priority remained to secure the defence of the Suez Canal, but until towards the end of 1915 it could fairly be said that the Canal was protecting the troops rather than the other way around. The inadequacies of the existing defence scheme had been brought to the attention of Maxwell by Kitchener in November. The response was the creation, in early 1916, of two full new defence lines out in the desert designed to fend back any aggressor from artillery range of the Canal itself. This demanded a huge investment of labour to dig the trenches and establish the water and supply arrangements necessary to allow men to exist out in the desert. In March 1916 General Sir Archibald Murray took formal command of the Egyptian Expeditionary Force (EEF) which was created from the remnants of the forces slinking back after the Gallipoli debacle. Many of the divisions were recycled through to France or Mesopotamia and by June 1916 the EEF consisted of four infantry divisions (all Territorial formations), a large force of cavalry and finally the Imperial Camel Corps.

There were considerable fears that the Turks would return to the offensive. Murray believed that an active defence would serve his men best. He conceived a plan for an advance right to the coastal town of El Arish close to the Egyptian border, from where his forces could threaten the flank of any renewed Turkish moves across the Sinai Desert. Water supplies were crucial, so Murray's first step in April 1916 was to secure the oasis area between Qatiya and Bir el Abd while at the same time sending smaller cavalry expeditions to destroy the Turkish water points that had been the basis for their attack in 1915, thereby severely restricting Turkish offensive options in the foreseeable future. The capture of the oasis was achieved, but not without difficulty as the Turks had recognised the importance of the brackish water supplies and launched spoiling attacks on the British outposts.

The British were intent on not repeating some of the mistakes made in Mesopotamia in 1915 and so were determined to secure a proper line of communications back to the Nile Delta. The Sinai Desert may not have resembled the muddy floodplains of the Tigris, but it nevertheless required a similar investment in resources to establish a viable transport infrastructure from scratch. One solution was startlingly simple: the wire road. Ordinary wire netting was unrolled and pegged out to form a 'road' which prevented soldiers from sinking into the sands as they marched. But the railway feeling its way out into the desert towards Romani (which lay some twenty-three miles from the Canal) was the only way that any large force could be maintained for long. Water was paramount and the amounts needed were huge; nothing could be done in the desert without securing water supplies. An impressive 12-inch-wide pipeline was laid to pump drinking water forward, with storage tanks established, from which the ubiquitous camels would carry the water to the forward positions in zinc containers. With temperatures spiralling, no shade and frequent sand storms, the desert environment was excessively harsh.

In August the Turks, still under the command of von Kressenstein, launched another daring attack on the Suez Canal, intent this time on the more limited objective of blocking or disrupting the Canal to traffic rather than securing a crossing and a revolt in Egypt. It was a bold but ultimately foolish attempt, for the EEF was well dug in, occupying a series of redoubts on the sand dunes and ridges stretching inland from the coastal region. In the event the Turks were hurled back at the Battle of Romani on 4 August 1916 with heavy losses and would never again manage to mount a credible threat to the Suez Canal. Yet this was only the beginning of what was to be two years of hard fighting involving hundreds of thousands of troops. As in Mesopotamia, any well-intentioned thoughts of restraint were overwhelmed by the perceived need for absolute security, driven by the legitimate desire to annihilate the local Turkish forces and sprinkled lightly with the personal ambitions of military commanders who would otherwise have found themselves confined to a backwater. Thus the advance would continue, its first objective being El Arish, a perfectly legitimate target in itself, but at the same time the start of a slippery slope down which would tumble hundreds of thousands of troops that could have been better employed in the battles that would decide the future of the war on the Western Front.

The advance to El Arish was a difficult logistical undertaking as the wire road, the railway, the supply dumps and water points all had to be painstakingly constructed. They were protected by the Royal Navy on their left flank abutting the sea, but their right flank was theoretically exposed, with miles of open desert. As Murray became more and more immersed in administration he delegated command in the field to Lieutenant General Sir Charles Dobell. In the end the long-awaited capture of El Arish on 22 December was something of an anti-climax as the wily von Kressenstein withdrew his troops before the actual blow fell, thus evading a near inevitable defeat. With El Arish in the hands of the British, their grip on the Suez Canal was finally secure: it offered copious water supplies for a garrison which could thwart any attempt by the Turks to march across the desert by striking at their open northern flank. Also, once the railway line and road had been completed, El Arish offered the ideal base for an assault on the Turkish bases over the Palestinian border. The Sinai Campaign was over; the Palestinian Campaign was about to begin. But something else was stirring in Arabia late in 1916.

The Arabian Campaign

The Arab Revolt was a minor distraction taking place alongside the Palestinian sideshow, but it would attract a great deal of attention and prove of considerable significance in the development of alternative methods of fighting a war. The key reason for this was Captain T. E. Lawrence, an academic and archaeologist who had been sequestered into British intelligence in Egypt and then employed as an adviser and liaison officer to the Arab rebel forces operating under the command of Emir Feisal, the son of Sherif Hussein of Mecca. Lawrence was not alone in this mission, but his energy and impact were such that he dominates most accounts of the two-year campaign fought in Arabia. His initial exploratory mission in October 1916 resulted in his building a strong relationship with local Arab leaders and an intuitive understanding of how to maximise the impact of the irregular Arab forces.

> As a mass they are not formidable, since they have no corporate spirit or discipline, or mutual confidence. Man by man they are good: I would suggest that the smaller the unit that is acting, the better will be its performance. A thousand of them in a mob would be ineffective against one fourth their number of trained troops: but three or four of

them, in their own alleys and hills, would account for a dozen Turkish soldiers. When they sit still they get nervous, and anxious to return home. Feisal himself goes rather to pieces in the same conditions. When, however, they have plenty to do, and are riding about in small parties tapping the Turks here and there, retiring always when the Turks advance, to appear in another direction immediately after, then they are in their element, and must cause the enemy not only anxiety, but bewilderment.[2]

Captain T. E. Lawrence, British Military Mission, Arabia

Lawrence sought not to attack the Turks where they were strong, avoiding frontal attacks, but instead to seek them out and harass them around the periphery, stretching out their forces and tormenting them with a myriad pinpricks rather than a single decisive blow. As other Arabs saw what the insurgents were capable of achieving, so they began to join the revolt against Turkish rule, creating a bandwagon effect.

The initial target was the Hedjaz railway which ran from Damascus to the main Turkish Arabian base at Medina. Lawrence used explosives to sabotage the line and bridges, attacking trains and driving the Turks mad with frustration as they sought to grasp this will o' the wisp. Later he captured the relatively lightly defended port of Aqaba in July 1917. This would subsequently act as a base for the Arab Revolt, funnelling through munitions and supplies from the British. Lawrence was promoted to Major and entrusted with the task of harrassing the relatively unprotected Turkish left flank in the Syrian and Trans-Jordan areas while the British pushed deep into Palestine. Lawrence's desert campaign would prove to be the stuff of legend, but his achievement was real enough: his 3,000 Arabian irregulars tied down up to 50,000 Turkish troops over the last two years of the war.

The Palestinian Campaign, 1917–18

Meanwhile Murray took stock, making administrative and logistical preparations ready for 1917. Although he had lost one division to the pressing demands of the Western Front, he still had four infantry divisions in his Eastern Force under Dobell made up of the 52nd, 53rd, 54th and 74th Divisions (the latter a scratch force made up from three brigades of

dismounted yeomanry). He also had Lieutenant General Sir Philip Chetwode in command of the Desert Column consisting of the Australian and
New Zealand Mounted Division and the Imperial Mounted Division. This
mobile force soon proved its worth in desert conditions with a series of
successful raids carried out by Major General Sir Harry Chauvel of the
A&NZ Mounted Division which cleared out isolated Turkish positions
perched just inside the Egyptian border.

When the main attack came, the British were confident it would be
more of a matter of bringing the Turks to battle and cutting off their
retreat than some grim battle. Yet despite all their planning and preparations they were once again rather over-optimistic. The Turks were not yet
present in great numbers around the town of Gaza, which commanded
the coastal region and hence the gateway to Palestine, but their units
had dug in on the hills and ridges above it, their trenches augmented by
thick cactus hedges which had considerable stopping power. The Turkish
reserves were further inland but could soon be deployed once they grasped
where exactly the British were making their thrust.

The British plan for the First Battle of Gaza on 26 March 1917 was
undoubtedly both bold and ambitious: Chetwode's cavalry would sweep
round the town to cut off the garrison which then would face a frontal
assault from the 53rd and 54th Divisions. At first everything went swim-
mingly as the cavalry penetrated right through to the sea to encircle Gaza,
while the night approach march of the infantry had gone unobserved.
However, inadequate guides, dense fog and poor staff work meant that
crippling delays crept in. When at last the 53rd Division attacked the
dominant Ali Muntar hill they met with a considerable resistance.

> Our great concern was a certain cactus hedge, from which machine
> guns might wipe us all out as soon as we got level with it. A small party
> was sent off to investigate, and all being reported well we got on a few
> yards further, leaving some behind – hit – at every rush forward. Worn
> out and heavily laden (besides their packs the men carried extra rations,
> a second water bottle and extra bandoliers of ammunition) the prospect
> of having to rush the entrenched and steep slopes was not a pleasant
> one, but with bayonets fixed and revolvers cocked, off we went with a
> cheer. The Turks vacated their trenches and ran. The top of the hill was
> reached and we rounded up many Turks, Those who ran were fired at
> and some bowled over. On looking round we found ourselves behind

Turks who were still firing on other oncoming troops and we got some fine firing at their backs, until they withdrew.[3]

Second Lieutenant Archibald Lee, 5th Welsh Regiment

The 53rd Division captured most of their objectives and even managed to establish tentative links with some of the cavalry, but it was fairly late in the day and they had not broken the Turkish opposition. Further attempts to advance were met with heavy fire, while ominous reports were coming in of Turkish reinforcements on the march from the south. The effective use of time is always important in warfare, but in Palestine it was particularly critical because unless they had secured water within a certain timeframe, the troops would have to be withdrawn. First Dobell pulled back his rather too exposed Desert Column cavalry forces, but then confusion caused a total collapse of command and control. In truth, the Turks too were confused: indeed, for a while both sides considered themselves to have lost the battle. But the Turks had the advantage, in that his pressing water situation meant that Dobell did not have the time to ponder his actions: an instant decision was required. So it was that he withdrew the 53rd and 54th Divisions and, on 27 March, the whole of Dobell's forces fell back, surrendering their hard won gains. It had been a close-run thing, but the upshot was a British defeat.

Murray, still in overall command, wrote up the battle in a despatch which was optimistic in the extreme, exaggerating three-fold the Turkish casualties. This would condemn Dobell and his men to a swift rematch, when a further period of consolidation might have been a better course of action. Taken in conjunction with reports of Maude's success in capturing Baghdad on 11 March, Murray's portrayal of the battle as a mere setback seemed to offer the continued opportunity for a significant success in Palestine. This was seized on by Lloyd George – ever the 'Easterner' – and sanction was given for a further advance on Palestine, with the capture of Jerusalem as Murray's ultimate goal. Murray was promised future reinforcements and a second attempt at Gaza was thus sanctioned. Murray had estimated in the past that he needed five infantry divisions to defend Egypt; but now he was attempting the invasion of Palestine with just four. Blind optimism – just as in Mesopotamia in 1915 – was replacing the sound application of common sense. The Turks were being under-estimated yet again; the British disease of hubris had not yet burned out.

The Second Battle of Gaza, fought on 19 April 1917, proved a disaster. Dobell, hamstrung by continuing water difficulties, decided not to pursue a flanking attack further south but instead ordered a head-on assault on Gaza. However, the Turks were not going to be caught by surprise again and had spent their time wisely, industriously digging a mutually support-ing system of strong redoubts and snaking concealed trenches across the broken ground. This was a tough nut to crack and, in an effort to help, Dobell was sent eight of the Mark I tanks which by this time were deemed obsolescent on the Western Front. Prone to mechanical breakdowns at the best of times and unbearably hot for their crews, the question was whether they would be of any use in harsh desert conditions. Although Dobell's men outnumbered the Turks by two to one in the Gaza Sector, the strength of the Turkish defences condemned his attack to failure. The tanks achieved little except to act as magnets for Turkish artillery fire. By the time Dobell accepted defeat the British had made negligible gains, failing in all their tactical objectives, and had suffered some 6,444 casualties.

Repercussions were swift. Dobell was relieved of his command to be replaced by Lieutenant General Sir Philip Chetwode, while Major General Sir Harry Chauvel took over command of the Desert Column. But the biggest change occurred when General Sir Edmund Allenby, the erstwhile commander of the Third Army recently engaged in the Battle of Arras on the Western Front, was despatched to replace Murray in June 1917; another sign that the British were not prepared to let the campaign drift. Murray had contributed much to the campaign through his mastery of its logistical and administrative demands, but Allenby would bring a greater vigour to field operations, albeit building on Murray's sound foundation. Allenby moved his headquarters forward to the Palestinian border and, after visiting his command, instituted a reorganisation to a more formal corps structure to create the Desert Mounted Corps under Chauvel, the XX Corps under Chetwode and the XXI Corps under Lieu-tenant General Edward Bulfin. He was further bolstered by the arrival of increasing numbers of equipment, troops, artillery and aircraft to mod-ernise his force.

Tactically, Allenby forswore another attack on the Gaza fortress, but instead resolved to assault Beersheba at the southern end of the Turkish lines. Here the defences were considerably less well developed, but Allenby had to counterbalance that advantage with evident problems in coping with a shortage of water during the long flanking march, coupled with the absolute necessity of immediately capturing the wells at Beersheba. There could be no margin for error. The assault force would require hundreds of thousands of gallons of water a day which could not be conjured up out of the arid wastes.

One interesting aspect of the operations was a cunning plan designed to convince the Turks that the offensive would be launched in November against the Gaza lines. The authorship of the plan and many of the details are mired in controversy, largely owing to the dubious character of one of the leading protagonists, intelligence officer Major Richard Meinertzhagen. Certainly there was a varied deception plan which had many strands woven together to dupe the Turkish commanders as to Allenby's real intentions. Fake preparations for an attack were embarked upon opposite Gaza, with an elaborate hoax involving a missing haversack filled with personal effects, fake intelligence reports and a set of notes for a British cipher that was no longer used for real messages but which could be used to feed false information to the Turks. This *ruse de guerre* backed up 'searches' for the 'missing' haversack in the area where it had been 'lost'. In the end, one way or another, the Turks seem to have been convinced that the attack would fall on Gaza. When a massed artillery barrage crashed down on to its defences the deception was complete.

The operations against Beersheba secured an enviable concentration of forces against the vastly outnumbered Turkish garrison. The XX Corps and Desert Mounted Corps both appeared out of the blue to fall upon the under-strength Turkish III Corps after sterling work by the RFC had prevented any aerial reconnaissance that might otherwise have revealed their movements. When the frontal blow fell from XX Corps at dawn on 31 October the Turks were swept aside, only to find that the Desert Mounted Corps had undertaken a flank march to appear behind them. Time was still of the essence; even hours mattered when it came to securing water supplies. In a spectacular incident the 4th Light Horse Brigade charged across an open plain to take Beersheba and prevent the Turks from sabotaging the vital wells. They were watched agog by Trooper Ion Idriess who, with the eye of a budding novelist, caught the drama of the occasion.

At a mile distant their thousand hooves were stuttering thunder, coming at a rate that frightened a man – they were an awe-inspiring sight, galloping through the red haze – knee to knee and horse to horse – the dying sun glinting on bayonet points. Machine guns and rifle fire just roared but the 4th Brigade galloped on. We heard shouts among the thundering hooves, saw balls of flame among those hooves – horse after horse crashed, but the massed squadrons thundered on. We laughed in delight when the shells began bursting behind them telling that the gunners could not keep their range, then suddenly the men ceased to fall and we knew instinctively that the Turkish infantry, wild with excitement and fear, had forgotten to lower their rifle sights and the bullets were flying overhead. The last half-mile was a berserk gallop with the squadrons in magnificent line, a heart-throbbing sight as they plunged up the slope, the horses leaping the redoubt trenches – my glasses showed me the Turkish bayonets thrusting up for the bellies of the horses – one regiment flung themselves from the saddle – we heard the mad shouts as the men jumped down into the trenches, a following regiment thundered over another redoubt, and to a triumphant roar of voices and hooves was galloping down the half-mile slope right into the town. Then came a whirlwind of movements from all over the field, galloping batteries – dense dust from mounting regiments – a rush as troops poured for the opening in the gathering dark – mad, mad excitement – terrific explosions from down in the town. Beersheba had fallen.[4]

Trooper Ion Idriess, 5th Light Horse Regiment,

The Turkish defence line was compromised and after two days of reorganisation operations were resumed. Again Allenby used deception to confuse the Turks as to his intentions. This time bombardments were augmented by serious seeming night attacks on the Gaza Sector, while the real blow fell on the centre of the Turkish lines at Tel es Sheria at dawn on 6 November. The Turks began to tumble back and Gaza fell the same day. Allenby set the tone for the pursuit in no uncertain terms.

In pursuit you must always stretch possibilities to the limit. Troops having beaten the enemy will want to rest. They must be given objectives, not those that you think they will reach, but the farthest that they could possibly reach.[5]

General Sir Edmund Allenby, Headquarters, EEF

One of the most interesting aspects of the campaign was the increasing use of the cavalry for their shock value in pell-mell charges culminating in hand-to-hand combat. One such incident occurred on 8 November, when the men of the Warwickshire and Worcestershire Yeomanry charged Turkish troops who were dug in and supported by both machine guns and artillery at Huj.

> Machine guns and rifles opened on us the moment we topped the rise behind which we had formed up. I remember thinking that the sound of the crackling bullets was just like a hailstorm on an iron-roofed building, so you may guess what the fusillade was. A whole heap of men and horses went down 20 or 30 yards from the muzzles of the guns. The squadron broke into a few scattered horsemen at the guns and then seemed to melt away completely. For a time I, at any rate, had the impression that I was the only man left alive. I was amazed to discover we were the victors.[6]
>
> Lieutenant Wilfred Mercer, Warwickshire Yeomanry

They had been concealed by a rise in the ground until they were just 800 yards away but it was still a remarkable achievement to run over the Turkish guns. What was certain was that cavalry could promote total panic once they broke through.

> Suddenly the terrific din of shrieking and exploding shells ceased, and we knew that the end had come. A wonderful and terrible sight met our view: in addition to the casualties which had already occurred, the ground was strewn with horses and fallen yeomen, many of whom were lying close to, and some beyond, the batteries. Twelve guns, three 5.9-inchers and nine field guns, were in various positions, surrounded by Austrian and German gunners, many of whom were dead or wounded. About 300 yards behind the rearmost battery a mass of enemy infantry were retreating, a few of whom were still firing occasional shots from various directions. Our squadrons had not fired a shot, and every single casualty we inflicted was caused by our sword thrusts. The German and Austrian gunners fought gamely round their guns when cornered, for a few moments, although the mass of the Turkish infantry had broken. Some enemy machine guns were seized and turned on the latter. We commenced to dress the wounded at once, and found them scattered in all directions. Wounded Turks came

crawling in, and one could not help contrasting their clean wounds, caused by our sword thrusts, with the ghastly wounds sustained by our men from shell fire and saw-bayonet.[7]

Captain Oscar Teichmann, Warwickshire Yeomanry

Despite such successes, the bulk of the Turks still managed to escape encirclement, pulling back to fight again. In the end Allenby had to rein back and reorganise his forces, aware of the need to counter the threat posed by the German inspired Yilderim commanded by the ubiquitous Falkenhayn. This force, composed of the Seventh and Eight Turkish Armies, was intended to revitalise operations in Mesopotamia but had been diverted towards the Palestine campaign. In the event even Falkenhayn proved unable to cope with the superior mobility, logistical resources and operational strength of Allenby's forces. The Turkish counter-attacks in late November were held at bay.

Allenby had pushed along the Palestinian coast to the port of Jaffa, then swung inland through the Judean Hills towards Jerusalem. There were still manifold difficulties with organising enough transport, supplies and water for the huge numbers of men involved in the pursuit. The situation became easier once the British had broken through into Palestine, where, though still not easy, there were plentiful water supplies and far better communications. The Turks were in some disarray but still capable of administering a painful rebuff. The fall of Jerusalem on 9 December 1917 was a significant moment with a huge propaganda value. Both sides had avoided fighting in the Holy City, but Allenby received some splendid advice from the gruff Robertson back in London based on memories of the pomp and ceremony surrounding the Kaiser's visit there back in 1898.

In the event of Jerusalem being occupied, it would be of considerable political importance if you, on officially entering the city, dismount at the city gate and enter on foot. German emperor rode in and the saying went round, 'A better man than he walked'. Advantage of contrast in conduct will be obvious.[8]

General Sir William Robertson, Imperial General Staff

In fact Jerusalem was surrendered by the city authorities under farcical conditions – a surrender that would pass into legend within the unit concerned.

Two of our London cooks, wanting water to brew drinks for the officers, picked up a couple of dixies and departed to seek a well, a pond or a stream. Unsuccessful in their search they plodded on and wandered about until they arrived at the outskirts of the City. Much to their surprise they were met, received and had a warm welcome from the Mayor and his little party, white flag and all. The Keys of Jerusalem were ceremoniously handed over for safe keeping to the grimy, travel-stained cooks in token of surrender. This was altogether too much for the poor chaps. They had not been taught how to conduct such diplomatic ceremonies, so they grabbed the keys, saluted and then retreated to try and find their cookhouse again. When they did eventually reach home the next day they were too scared to say anything about their amazing adventure to the officers. They thought they would 'catch a packet' for being away so long; might even be run for absent without leave. Wise counsel made them report to the officers and the keys were handed over for safe custody.[9]

Private Bernard Livermore, 2/20th London Regiment

Allenby would make his formal entrance into Jerusalem – on foot – at noon on 11 December. For the British, coming from what was still largely a Christian country, there were distinct echoes of a new Crusade. Of far greater importance, however, it was a solid victory that brightened up the scene after a year that had been a terrible disappointment.

A brief lull ensued before Allenby commenced operations moving towards Jericho, planning to push across to the Jordan River. The campaign was placed in context by the German offensives commencing on 21 March on the Somme which forced the recall of the 52nd and 74th Divisions. Suddenly it was brutally apparent that Palestine was only ever a sideshow; the real war was being fought against the Germans. Gradually Allenby rebuilt his stripped-down units with the addition of the 3rd and 7th Indian Divisions. A sensible commander, he devoted much time to training his raw troops and laying his plans.

Meanwhile the Turks had appointed General Otto Liman von Sanders, of Gallipoli renown, to command in Palestine from late February 1918. He pulled back his forces and had them dig in along a line stretching from the coast across to the Jordan Valley. This time Allenby resolved to drive north and attack along the coast, but he tried to deceive the Turks into thinking that he was going to attack far inland. It was ensured that the camps behind the front near the River Jordan were to all appearance expanding, while the camps on the coastal plain used pre-built spare capacity and carefully concealed locations where no daylight movement was allowed. All deployments from east to west were carried out at night, all movements in the opposite direction done visibly during the day. Some battalions found themselves marching east all day, only to be returned to their starting points by lorry at night, ready to repeat the journey next day. Countless patrols by the newly formed Royal Air Force fended off Turkish and German aerial reconnaissance machines, allowing them to see only what Allenby wanted them to see. Every possible subterfuge was used, from maintaining wireless traffic for units that had already moved to planting false evidence. The ruses worked and Allenby managed to amass a formidable 35,000 infantry, 9,000 cavalry and 383 guns to face just 8,000 Turkish infantry with 130 guns in the coastal strip. He had secured a decisive superiority where it mattered; along the rest of the front across to the Jordan the two sides were more equally matched. When Allenby attacked at 04.30 on 19 September the Turkish line crumbled before them in what became known as the Battle of Megiddo.

> The Turks are breaking, everywhere. I left here, at 4.30 am, and motored to Arsuf. There was General Shea, whose division attacked the Turkish right, on the coast. All was going well; and the head of the cavalry was just pushing along the beach, below the castle, making for the Nahr Falik. Two destroyers of ours were shelling the coast road. Then I motored to the Headquarters of the other Divisions; all doing well, too. Now my cavalry is many miles north of Arsuf, making for the Turks' communications in the Valley of Esdraelon. His infantry and artillery are falling back; hunted by my airmen, with machine gun fire and bombs. So far, many guns and 2,500 prisoners have been caught, but there will be many more. My losses are light. I bombed the Headquarters of Liman von Sanders and his two Army Commanders last night … Liman von Sanders has lost his only railway communication with the outer world. I really don't know what he can do, and I am beginning to think that we may have a very great success. The weather is perfect, not too hot, and very clear, just right for my artillery and my aeroplanes in pursuit. My horses are very fit, and there is plenty of water on the route which they will follow, and they are in sufficient strength to be irresistible.[10]

General Sir Edmund Allenby, Headquarters, EEF

The British infantry advanced some fourteen miles, while the cavalry surged through the gap to raise hell far and wide behind the lines. They seized the crucial rail junctions, threatened the Turkish command head-quarters and generally made a thorough nuisance of themselves. Mean-while, the modern 'cavalry', the aircraft of the RAF and Australian Flying Corps, tore into the retreating Turkish troops. It was a slaughter as Lieu-tenants Stan Nunan and Clive Conrick in their Bristol Fighter swooped down on the Turks threading their way through the Wadi Fara Pass which led to the only Jordan River crossing not already blocked to the Turks. The road was a teeming mass of transport, horses and hapless Turkish soldiers, pressing along an old Roman road hacked out of the precipitous hills and with a sheer drop to the other side.

> They had little chance of escape from my guns as we were so close to them. As I fired I saw chips of rock fly off the cliff face and red splotches suddenly appear on the Turks who would stop climbing and fall and their bodies were strewn along the base of the cliff like a lot of dirty rags. When Nunan was climbing again to renew his attack, I had a better opportunity to machine gun the troops and transports on the road. I saw my tracer bullets hit the lead horses pulling a gun-carriage. As they reared up, they turned away from the cliff side of the road and their heads were turned back towards me, so that I could see the terror in their faces as their forefeet came down and, missing the road altogether, they plunged over the cliff dragging the carriage with them. Their driver, realising what was happening, jumped back towards the road, but he was late, far too late. He seemed to float just above the gun-carriage, as it rolled over and over with the horses until the transport hit the cliff face, when he was thrown far out into the valley and his body disappeared in the haze far below.[11]
>
> Lieutenant Clive Conrick, 1st Australian Squadron, AFC

By 25 September the Turkish armies that had occupied the coastal lines had effectively ceased to exist. The British had taken over 50,000 prisoners and what remained of the Turkish forces were in no fit state to put up an organised resistance. Allenby set his men marching for Damascus, hard on the heels of the demoralised Turks. Linking up with Lawrence's Arab forces they took the city on 1 October. But even that was not the end. By now the Central Powers were collapsing and Allenby was required to push on to Aleppo a further 200 miles to the north. After a brief period of consolidation, his advance continued and Aleppo fell on 26 October. Four days later the Turks signed the Armistice on 30 October. The war with Turkey was over.

OVER FOUR YEARS THE CAMPAIGN IN PALESTINE had sucked in nearly 1,200,000 men from all over the British Empire. In all the British suffered 51,451 casualties in battle and lost a sobering further 550,000 through disease. It is difficult to weigh up what had been achieved, but such an enormous investment of military resources cannot be justified by specious sentimentality over the capture of Jerusalem. As in Gallipoli, this was another example of fighting the Turks simply because they were there. If the intention had been to knock Turkey out of the war then surely the Egyptian Expeditionary Force failed as Turkey only surrendered a month before the Germans. Was that month really worth such an effort? There were Imperial expansionist interests to be considered but first the war had to be won. As with Gallipoli, Mesopotamia and Salonika, Palestine proved to be a waste of resources. The strategic objectives – control of the Dardanelles at Gallipoli, oil in Mesopotamia, the survival of the Serbian Army at Salonika and the security of the Suez Canal in Egypt – could all have been secured with a far smaller investment of precious resources. The Easterners had believed that they had another way to win the war, one that could avoid the necessity of facing the German Army on the Western Front. But there was no easy way to victory and as a direct result of the proliferation of sideshows the BEF would be left starved of troops when it needed them on the Western Front during the great German offensives of 1918.

18

THE WESTERN FRONT, 1918

'There comes a time when war ceases to be an adventure and the young regard it cynically, disillusioned and disenchanted. I do not suppose any generation ever marched to war with the stars in their eyes as my generation did, but after the Somme and the even worse slaughter at Third Ypres there were no more stars. We continued to fight, and I think we fought well.'[1]

Lieutenant Richard Dixon, 251st Battery, 53rd Brigade, Royal Field Artillery

THE ALLIES WERE REELING at the start of 1918. The overall situation in the war had not really changed: Germany *was* still likely to lose, but the Bolshevik Revolution and collapse of Russia had given her just a small window of opportunity in which she might possibly wrest victory from the clutches of defeat. The Russians had fought hard, but now they were finished, torn apart internally by competing visions of society and about to enter a nightmare that would envelop the country for decades. The collapse of the Eastern Front freed the German High Command from the two-front conundrum that had racked it since the Kaiser had wrenched Bismarck's ageing hand from the tiller in 1890. By the spring of 1918 when the German divisions had transferred from the Eastern Front to the Western Front, they were able to deploy some 192 divisions opposing only 156 Allied divisions. Numerically the situation had never been more promising for the Germans, but the American forces were gathering and casting a long shadow across German plans.

When the United States of America entered the war in April 1917, her situation to some extent mirrored that of Britain in 1914. The American regular army was in the process of expanding from 25,000 to around 142,000 men as part of a programme triggered by the National Defence Act introduced by President Woodrow Wilson in 1916, which envisioned an army of 175,000 regulars backed up by a National Guard of 450,000 by 1921. The Americans would therefore face incredible problems in securing a rapid and massive increase in their Army, their only advantage over the BEF in 1914 being that they were not immediately embroiled in severe fighting, so at least they could draw on a solid core of trained regulars to help training masses of raw recruits. Wilson acted quickly, calling up the entire National Guard and introducing a system of conscription that would ultimately register some 24 million men for the draft, of which 2,800,000 were called up for service. In all, fifty-five divisions would be raised, of which forty-two would serve on the Western Front. However, there were immediate logistical problems. They lacked everything: uniforms, weapons, artillery, tanks, aircraft, transport, munitions, housing and rations. Some of these could be dealt with by the huge American industrial base, but when it came to sophisticated weapons systems such as artillery, aircraft and tanks the Americans were forced to rely on purchasing them off the shelf from their allies. They simply did not have the time to do otherwise. There were nowhere near enough officers or NCOs, not enough trained staff, gunners, signallers or machine gunners, or indeed any of the myriad specialist trades that make up an army. And of course they had no experienced generals qualified to take them into action in a continental war. The British and French suggested a solution, offering to take the American recruits into their own units and train and equip them ready for service. This may have had some logic, but it was not politically acceptable in the United States and was rejected out of hand. This was also the fate of a far more reasonable proposal by the British to include an American battalion in each British brigade, before creating American brigades which would serve in a British division, then an American division in a British corps and so on, until a fully fledged American Army was created. The American political and military establishment were determined to create their own American Expeditionary Force (AEF) fighting with a separate identity, under American leadership.

The leader they chose to command the AEF was a formidable character: General John Pershing. Born in 1860, after attending West Point he had participated in several campaigns against Native American tribes. He had also been involved in both the Spanish–American and Philippine–American Wars. He was promoted rapidly to Brigadier General, taking on various staff appointments. His most recent campaign had been on the Mexican border from 1916 to 1917. As a professional soldier Pershing had taken an interest in both the fighting and all the tactical ramifications thrown up on the Western Front, but had not grasped the severity of the problems imposed by trench warfare. He was critical of what he characterised as the defensive approach of the Allied generals, who accepted the restraints of attritional warfare and did not look to the 'offensive spirit' and bold manoeuvring to overcome the challenges. As such he had a naive confidence in the ability of the high morale and superior rifle skills of his men to overcome such factors as artillery barrages, machine guns and barbed wire. In harbouring these beliefs he was following a path trodden by many others with little success earlier in the war.

The AEF grew slowly. The 1st Division was sent to the Western Front almost immediately, in June 1917, but after that the programme stalled under the pressure of training the millions of recruits back home, and only four divisions had arrived by March 1918. They were organised on radically different lines to the Allied divisions and, with some 28,000 men, they were twice their size. Often, as their training and equipment had not yet reached acceptable levels, they required a prolonged acclimatisation and training period before they could be regarded as competent to take their place in the line of battle. In particular, they were taught trench warfare skills only after their arrival in France. Despite the initial intentions of the Americans, units had to be attached to British and French units in order to gain experience in the line, while a series of training schools was established to disseminate the disparate specialist skills required in a modern army. But in essence the AEF was still set on entering the line and making an impact as a separate entity. The Germans were certainly nervously awaiting their arrival.

> I felt obliged to count on the new American formations beginning
> to arrive in the spring of 1918. In what numbers they would appear
> could not be foreseen; but it might be taken as certain that they would

balance the loss of Russia; further, the relative strengths would be more in our favour in the spring than in the late summer and autumn, unless, indeed, we had by then gained a great victory.[2]

Quartermaster General Erich Ludendorff, General Headquarters

For the moment, as long as the ordinary soldiers could see the possibility of victory, German morale held good.

Our superiors and the newspapers assured us that big events were approaching. As far as we were told there were only 30,000 Americans in France, most of them inexperienced soldiers. There were more Americans to come, but then we had hundreds of submarines that controlled the seas. Now that the whole Eastern Army had been transferred to the West, a million men strong, it seemed to us that the next offensive would bring victory and peace.[3]

Corporal Frederick Meisel, 371st Infantry Regiment

For the Germans, time was of the essence: whatever they were going to do they would have to do it quickly. They had six months to change the course of the war. This would be the narrative that drove events in 1918. Nothing else would matter. All the specious dreams woven by the 'Easterners', the campaigns in Mesopotamia, Salonika, Palestine and East Africa were now being seen for what they were – a waste of military resources. The war would after all be decided on the Western Front.

The British High Command was well aware of the situation. In fact, the CIGS, General Sir William Robertson, had explicitly warned Lloyd George that the Central Powers would concentrate their resources on the Western Front and that they must match that concentration or risk defeat. Yet Lloyd George was blind to such warnings, convinced still that there was another way to victory through the soft underbelly of Italy and the Balkans, or indeed anywhere except the Western Front, where the British would have to face the might of the German Army. He had a horror of further offensives like the Somme or Third Ypres and had completely lost faith in his Commander in Chief Field Marshal Sir Douglas Haig. This was to prove a serious matter as Lloyd George, the consummate politician, was a formidable opponent for anyone. All that held him back from dismissing Haig outright was the necessity of working hand in glove with the Conservatives, who had been members of the Coalition Government since 1915. They were broadly in support of Haig and it was clear that an open move to dismiss him would probably trigger a political crisis that could bring down the whole administration.

To act directly, however, is not a necessity in the noble art of politics. To bring Haig to heel and to reduce his capacity to launch any great offensives Lloyd George sought to reduce the number of men made available to the BEF. In the first instance he backed the French demands that Haig take over more of the front line on the Western Front. This appeared to be fair, as the British had only 100 miles of front compared to the 350 miles held by the French. But a large part of the French sector was not active and could be held with minimal troops. This was in sharp contrast to the British line, with its concentration of hot spots at Ypres, Arras and the Somme. Through Lloyd George's intervention Haig was forced in January 1918 to take over another section of line south of the Somme River, with the consequence that half the German divisions on the Western Front were facing the British sector. This extra commitment had to be undertaken at a time when Lloyd George was also deliberately retaining huge numbers of troops in the British Isles, troops that Haig needed to restock his divisions eroded by the battles of 1917. He was left with the choice of either disbanding whole divisions or recasting them so that each brigade was reduced from four battalions to three, a reduction from twelve to nine battalions in each division. The spare battalions would then be broken up – cannibalised, if you like – to restock the depleted ranks of the others. This demanded an enormous shake-up of the entire BEF: relationships hammered out in the forge of war between regimental officers and brigade staff officers, established methods of working in a crisis, units with a proud battalion history – all were torn asunder. And all this while the Germans were preparing their great assault on the Western Front. In itself the reorganisation only brought the British into line with the system adopted by both the Germans and French, but its timing was unfortunate, promoting widespread anxiety and a great deal of avoidable stress. Meanwhile, hundreds of thousands of British soldiers were still engaged in the futile campaigns in Palestine, Mesopotamia and Salonika.

The 'Welsh wizard' had other strings to his political bow. He recognised an opportunity lurking within the proposals for a Supreme War Council to provide a unified direction for the Allies war effort which had been agreed at the Allied conference held in the aftermath of the disaster at the Battle of Caporetto. The membership was intended to include the national prime ministers and a senior military representative from each of the Allies. Early on, Lloyd George saw this as a chance to evade the Westerner influence of Haig and Robertson, his official professional advisers. He had already curried favour with the French government by adopting its point of view on numerous occasions against his own military. Now, in return he gained French support when he proposed that a permanent Allied General Staff should be formed without the involvement of the national Chiefs of General Staff. His selection for the British adviser would be the controversial figure of Lieutenant General Sir Henry Wilson, who was not a confidant of either Haig or Robertson. From the start, Lloyd George was intent on using the Supreme War Council to evade the unwelcome advice proffered by his own military advisers. This ultimately forced the resignation of an outraged Robertson, who was then promptly replaced as CIGS by Wilson.

The initial meetings of the Supreme War Council achieved little of note, for while everyone agreed on the necessity of establishing an Allied reserve force, no one was willing to contribute the troops that would make it a reality. But Lloyd George had removed a powerful ally of Haig with the departure of Robertson and he had certainly secured a more malleable source of professional advice in Wilson. Overall, he had ensured that Haig was forced to put his forces on to a defensive standing on the Western Front in 1918. In truth, the darkening strategic situation would have forced a more defensive approach in any event and all that Lloyd George achieved was to starve his field commander of the troops he needed to hold back the German offensive in one of the decisive battle of the war.

The Germans decided to launch their offensive against the British, whom they recognised as the driving force of the Allies on the Western Front in 1918. Ludendorff considered that a crushing victory against the British would be decisive as the French would then collapse in tandem. During the planning process a variety of schemes were drawn up by the German staff: Operation George, attacking in the Lys River sector in Flanders, then lunging straight for crucial rail junctions and the Channel ports; Operation Mars, an attack in the Arras area; and finally Operation Michael, in the southern Arras and Somme areas. In the end, put off by the problems of a spring offensive in the damp Flanders lowlands and slightly apprehensive of the strong Arras defences, Ludendorff opted for Operation Michael. The onslaught would be truly terrific, with three strong German armies crashing into the thin British lines. In the south the Eighteenth Army, commanded by General Oskar von Hutier, would attack either side of St Quentin and then advance to guard the southern flank of the whole offensive effort. In the centre the Second Army, commanded by General Georg von der Marwitz, would pinch out the southern sector of the Flesquières Salient and thrust on to Péronne, while in the north the Seventeenth Army, under General Otto von Below, would attack south of the River Scarpe, pinching out the north side of the Flesquières Salient and driving on towards Bapaume. Having broken right through, the intention then was to advance north and roll up the British line. However, strategic issues were not dominant in the mind of Ludendorff. His concentration was on securing a tactical victory on the battlefield rather than worrying exactly what might be achieved in the subsequent operations. If necessary, a few days later Operation Mars could be triggered attacking Arras directly, while finally Operation George was held in reserve should a further offensive be required in April to complete the destruction of the BEF.

The Germans would be unveiling their new offensive tactics, which had been developed over the last three years, partly on the Eastern Front, partly in the west, and which had been tested most recently in the counter-attack at Cambrai. They would use their artillery to give the defending British the opportunity to experience at first hand what the Germans had been enduring since 1916 – the awesome power of a mass hurricane barrage, concentrated to suppress or destroy all resistance. The Germans collected 6,608 guns and 3,534 heavy trench mortars and harnessed them to the principles espoused by their foremost artillery specialist, Lieutenant Colonel Georg Bruchmüller.

Haig was facing his most serious challenge yet, as he knew he did not have the troop numbers to be strong in defence everywhere, especially given the tremendous manpower implications of the switch to a defence in depth system, which sought to mimic many of the German measures of 1917. The Forward Zone was based on the old front line, but now with barbed wire and machine guns to cover the gaps between outposts and small redoubts. Behind this was the Battle Zone, constructed in lines but with strong redoubts to break up any German assaults. Finally, a further 4–8 miles further back was the Rear Zone, which was intended to be more of the same, but was mainly a theoretical construct with few trenches or strongpoints actually prepared on the ground.

Ignorant as he was of where Ludendorff intended to attack, Haig was brutally realistic in analysing his predicament: his priority was the north, where the key strategic targets of the Channel ports and the major rail junction at Hazebrouck lay only a few miles behind the lines. There was very little room for manoeuvre here for General Sir Herbert Plumer's Second Army – it had to hold. Further south, General Sir Henry Horne's First Army was responsible for the tactically significant heights of the Vimy and Lorette Ridges; next came General Sir Julian Byng's Third Army covering Arras; and finally General Sir Hubert Gough's Fifth Army held the Somme area. Here, in the most southern British sector, there were no really significant tactical or strategic objectives within forty miles of the front lines. Haig had to ignore Gough's pleas for reinforcements even when reports coming in from the RFC observers made it clear that the Somme would be the seat of Ludendorff's dreaded offensive. The Fifth Army would have to stand alone and, if attacked, fall back to a vaguely defined Emergency Line stretching along the Somme River.

The German attack began at 04.40 on 21 March 1918 with a devastating artillery bombardment.

> With a crash our barrage begins from thousands and thousands, it must be from tens of thousands, of gun barrels and mortars, a barrage that sounds as if the world were coming to an end. For the first hour we only strafe the enemy artillery with alternative shrapnel, Green Cross and Blue Cross. The booming is getting more and more dreadful, especially as we are in a town between the walls of houses. The gunners stand in their shirtsleeves, with the sweat running down and dripping off them. Shell after shell is fired.[4]
>
> Lieutenant Herbert Sulzbach, 63rd Field Artillery

The bombardment was in carefully planned phases building up to a veritable symphony of destruction. It is telling that some of the first targets were the guns of the Royal Artillery, which were splattered with a potent mixture of gas and high explosive shells. The gas shells held the less obvious, but more insidious, threat. There were three main types. The first were Blue Cross shells containing a non-lethal gas compound which promoted havoc in the human respiratory system, disrupting breathing and causing vomiting. This forced its victims to remove their masks, at which point they would succumb to the lethal phosgene gas contained in the Green Cross shells. Meanwhile, the Yellow Cross shells contained the mustard gas which not only forced the soldiers to wear their gas masks for long periods but could render an area almost uninhabitable. For the British gunners the sheer embuggerance of wearing gas masks had never been more obvious.

> I adjusted my box respirator over my face, groped my way up the dark steps, crept under the first gas curtain, adjusted it behind me, then under the second and so found myself outside in the sunken road. It was still almost dark and there was a thick mist. Shells were falling everywhere. It was a perfect hell – no other words can describe how utterly beastly it was. I felt my way up the sunken road towards the guns. The eyepieces of the respirator got fogged immediately and you could see nothing. I eventually found myself at the guns. The layers were experiencing the utmost difficulty in laying the guns, as they could not see owing to the mist. They had got their respirators off their faces in order to see better, retaining the nose clip and mouthpiece. I went to the map room and took the magnetic bearing of the target they were firing on, then, armed with a prismatic compass, I laid the guns as accurately as I could. I should not like to vouch for the accuracy of the fire, but the great thing was to get some shells over.[5]
>
> Lieutenant Edward Alfree, 111th Heavy Battery, Royal Garrison Artillery

The German fire plan also played havoc with command and control across the whole battlefield. Headquarters previously identified by aerial reconnaissance were lashed with shells and the telephone lines were soon cut. No one knew what was happening; there could be little or no co-ordinated response. The confusion was exacerbated by the Germans' secret weapon: fog. Not unexpected on an early spring morning, but the swirling mists that reduced visibility to just a few yards in the worst hit sectors proved a further severe handicap to the British. The survivors of the bombardment were left cut off in their battered outposts, peering into the fog, desperate to see what the Germans were doing. They would find out all too soon.

The main German attacks began at around 09.40. Often the British did not see the Germans crossing No Man's Land until it was too late and all their carefully planned interlocking fields of machine gun fire and artillery support fire were rendered almost useless as, in a matter of moments, they were upon them.

> The first attackers were into the trench long before the mist lifted. I was so occupied with the flanks that I barely saw them before they appeared out of the mist and leapt down into the trench. In a moment we were all mixed up in hand-to-hand fighting. I had two men coming at me with their bayonets, one of whom I think I shot with my revolver, while a sergeant standing just behind me shot the other at point-blank range with his rifle barrel over my shoulder. But almost at the same second a German stick bomb came whistling into the trench from the parapet right into the bunch of us, and killed or wounded practically the whole lot of us – English and German alike. Whether it was actually this bomb or a bayonet stab that gave me the wound in my neck I don't know – it might have been either. For a moment we were clear but there was a nasty little shambles round us – Sergeant Adcock, who had just saved my life, having his head blown off. I felt awfully weak and discovered that a river of blood was flowing from my neck. I tried to bandage it, but the bandage wouldn't hold. Before they attacked again they brought up some trench mortars and knocked seven bells out of us – then swarmed into the trench. By that time there were only a handful of us left on our feet and all I suppose wounded. I got another wound from a stick bomb, which put a bit of metal into my thigh. Before I collapsed I tried to give the surrender signal, and hope I succeeded thereby in saving a few lives. We had done our best.[6]
>
> Captain Charles Miller, 2nd Royal Inniskilling Fusiliers

All along the front the British Forward Zone was over-run by German stormtroopers, who pushed deep behind the lines, leaving any remaining centres of resistance to the follow-up troops.

> The infantry commander shouts, '*Drauf!*' and we rush forward. But where is the expected enemy fire? There is hardly any. His line is not so near as we thought and we had to run. I soon became out of breath and couldn't see out of the eye pieces of my gas mask so I tore it off. After all we thought this was going to be our last day; there isn't going to be any escape for us. There was a little machine gun fire and some of our chaps caught it. Lieutenant Wiese was hit and the man carrying the explosive

with me either fell over or was wounded. Then we reached the barbed
wire, our objective. But there was nothing for us to do. The wire was
completely destroyed. There wasn't really any trench left, just craters
and craters. Now I looked back the way we had come and there was a
swarm of men following, I couldn't stop a lump coming to my throat.
Only a few of the enemy had survived the storm; some were wounded.
They stood with their hands up.[7]

Private Paul Kretschmer, 28th Pioneer Battalion

Soon the Germans pressed forwards to attack the Battle Zone. This was
where the main defence works were supposed to be, but a shortage of
labour meant that they were not always ready for this kind of severe test.
In some places the sheer speed of the German advance caught the defenders by surprise.

There came an unholy 'BANG!' in the stairway, showering the dugout
with acrid smoke and dust. I guessed it was a hand grenade – and I
was right! Lucky for me the thing had exploded halfway down the
stairway otherwise I would have caught the full blast. Then there was a
commotion upstairs and a guttural voice screamed, 'Come up Tommy!
Raus! Raus!' Simultaneously a revolver cracked out, the bullet slapping
into a sandbag inches from my foot. We filed upstairs, our hands held
high above our heads, to be greeted by a group of youngsters looking
grim and threatening, bayonets fixed, rifles shoulder slung, each with
a hand grenade swinging from his right hand. Some had pistols. My
tongue felt like a dried frog.[8]

Private James Brady, 43rd Field Ambulance, Royal Army Medical Corps

The British resistance did, however, begin to stiffen in the Battle Zone,
although the British lacked the counter-attack divisions to recover lost
features of tactical significance as required in a well-organised defence
in depth. In consequence their defence was static and position-orien-
tated, lacking flexibility or fluency of response. This was the legacy of
Lloyd George's policy of starving the Western Front of the men needed
to restock the BEF. Yet the Germans also had increasing problems. Their
available artillery support was greatly diminished by the necessity of
moving forward their field guns. Furthermore, the fog gradually cleared
away and British batteries that had been held well back from the Forward
Zone could now take their toll on the advancing German troops. As the

British had found so many times before, the second phase of an offensive was fiendishly difficult to navigate. Sometimes the Germans were caught in the open; sometimes they found themselves engaging in vicious localised skirmishes to eliminate pockets of frenzied resistance, but always their casualty toll seemed to be rising as they strove to break through. Although the British suffered around 38,500 casualties (21,000 prisoners-of-war), with the loss of 500 guns, the Germans also lost between 35,000 to 40,000 casualties, of which up to 11,000 were dead.

By the end of the day the Germans had pushed their way deep into, or even through, the Battle Zone on both flanks of the Fifth Army. On the Third Army front the Germans were intent on pinching out the prominent Flesquières Salient left after the 1917 Cambrai fighting. They did not quite succeed in this, but the prospect of the entire garrison being cut off remained a distinct possibility.

British divisions from the First and Second Armies had been despatched to the threatened front once it became absolutely clear that this was the main attack, not some cunning diversionary ploy by the Germans. However, the French Commander-in-Chief, General Philippe Pétain, was concerned by powerful diversionary bombardments carried out on his front and still feared that the Germans might be intending a major thrust there. In consequence, he was wary of sending reinforcements. For the moment the Fifth and Third Armies would have to fight on alone. Gough sensibly planned a staged withdrawal rather than risk committing everything to holding a nominal line more evident on his maps than on the ground. Obviously, the German tactical position offered a great deal more potential, but Ludendorff's response to these opportunities illustrates his lack of clearly defined strategic priorities: the Eighteenth Army in the south had advanced furthest, so he decided to reinforce their success. The original intention of rolling up the British line to the north was gradually being forgotten.

Next day, 22 March, there was another thick fog and the Germans made further progress against the Fifth Army, breaching the line being set up along the Crozat Canal and battering away at the British troops as they fell back. The sketched out Green Line proved worse than useless. Back they went, this time retreating to the Emergency Line delineated for the most part by the Somme River. To the north the Third Army was also falling back, deeply concerned at the prospect of the Germans pinching out the V Corps which was dangerously close to being trapped in the Flesquières Salient. All along the line the British were being forced back, unable to gain the time to dig in and consolidate their positions. Soon chaos descended.

> The stream of traffic moved so slowly – at times coming to a standstill for minutes on end, to allow other traffic to come in from other roads. There were several streams of traffic converging on the village. First one stream was held up to let another come on, and then that one was allowed to go on while the other was held up. There were traffic controls doing their best to regulate the traffic in this way. It was a hell of a crush. There was just a block of traffic, miles in length. It seemed absolutely hopeless to expect ever to get on. And now, on the face of the ridge just behind us, appeared some of our tanks, creeping across country and occasionally firing at something. What I dreaded and every moment expected was to see the Hun cavalry swooping down on us. But this did not happen. I don't think the enemy could have had any cavalry, or he must have used it on an occasion such as this. What a haul he could have had! But he *had* got aeroplanes. Three of the beastly things appeared: swooping down low over the road and with machine guns rattling they flew up and down. They were also dropping bombs. I leapt lightly down a shell hole – a fairly deep one – and crouched against that side of the crater that afforded most protection. As the aeroplane passed over me, so I passed to the other side of the shell hole. I heard the bullets going 'Zipp! Zipp! Zipp!' into the ground. They were so low as to induce some officers to shoot at them with revolvers, but of course this was a futile thing to do.[9]
>
> Lieutenant Edward Alfree, 111th Heavy Battery, Royal Garrison Artillery

The German aircraft dived down, ripping into any tempting targets they encountered. There was surely plenty of choice. Even the greatest ace of all was ground-straffing.

> Richthofen continued to dive until he was close above the Roman road. Tearing along at a height of about 30 feet above the ground, he peppered the marching troops with his two guns. We followed close behind him and copied his example. The troops below us seemed to have been lamed with horror and, apart from the few men who took cover in the ditch at the roadside, hardly anyone returned our fire. On reaching the end of the road, the Captain turned and again fired at the

column. We could now observe the effect of our first assault: bolting horses and stranded guns blocked the road, bringing the column to a complete standstill. This time our fire was returned. Infantrymen stood, with rifles pressed against their cheeks, and fired as we passed over them. Machine guns posted in the roadside ditches fired viciously at us as we flew overhead. Yet, despite the fact that his wings were riddled with bullets, the Captain still continued to fly just as low as before. We followed in close formation behind him, firing burst after burst from our Spandaus. The whole flight was like a united body, obeying a single will. And that was how it should have been.[10]

Lieutenant Ernst Udet, Jasta 11, Jagdgeschwader 1

The fragile British line along the Somme was soon breached and the Germans began to flood across the river on 24 March. Gough had no reserves left and not enough reinforcements had yet arrived, although the French were beginning to stiffen the right of the British line. As the Fifth Army fell back the Third Army was forced to conform or allow a gap to open up for the Germans to exploit.

While his army commanders struggled to stem the tide, Haig was trying to secure the whole-hearted support of the French. This proved difficult as Pétain was more intent on defending Paris than providing a co-ordinated response in support of the BEF. He seemed to be willing to accept that the two great armies might be forced apart: Haig falling back to the Channel ports and the French to Paris. To Haig this was nothing short of madness, condemning the Allies to defeat. Desperate – and with good reason – he convened an emergency conference at Doullens on 26 March to be attended for the British by the Minister without Portfolio Lord Milner, the CIGS General Sir Henry Wilson and Haig himself, with the French represented by Premier Georges Clemenceau, President Raymond Poincaré, the Chief of General Staff Field Marshal Ferdinand Foch and Pétain. What exactly happened will always be a subject of debate, but Clemenceau seems to have used his bull-like force of personality to secure the French reinforcements and total commitment that Haig sought – but at a price.

It was decided that Amiens must be covered at all costs. French troops are being hurried up as rapidly as possible and Gough has been told to hold on with his left at Bray. It was proposed by Clemenceau that Foch should be appointed to co-ordinate the operations of an Allied force to cover Amiens and ensure that the French and British flanks remained united. This proposal seemed to me quite worthless, as Foch would be in a subordinate position to Pétain and myself. In my opinion it was essential to success that Foch should control Pétain, so I at once recommended that Foch should control the actions of all the Allied armies on the Western Front. Foch seemed sound and sensible, but Pétain had a terrible look. He had the appearance of a commander who was in a funk and had lost his nerve.[11]

Field Marshal Sir Douglas Haig, General Headquarters, BEF

Haig thus accepted the situation with good grace. In any event for the past two years he had fallen in with the requirements of first Joffre, then Nivelle and now Pétain, so this was not such a big step. After a further meeting it was formally agreed that Foch would now be the Supreme Commander responsible for the strategic direction of the French, British and American Armies on the Western Front.

Meanwhile on the ground the situation was deteriorating. Having crossed the Somme the Germans were pushing on vigorously to the west. Yet as they pressed forward they too were suffering reverses. Their losses were mounting. Their lines of communication were being increasingly stretched; their artillery was in a state of disorder, unable to cope with the sheer pace of the advance. Slowly the British reserves were beginning to arrive and the Royal Artillery were beginning to recover as new batteries were moved down from the north.

As the sky began to lighten in the dawn of 26th March we were as ready for them as if we had been preparing for a day's practice shooting on Salisbury Plain. What a day that was! I could watch the German columns approaching one of my registered targets, and time the salvos of my own, and other batteries too to arrive there with them. The smother of shell fire would disperse them: watching them reorganise, I could do the same to another column elsewhere, and then switch back to the first to break it up a second time. All day long they came on, and all day long we shifted our fire from one point to another across those valleys. They had plenty of other well-aimed opposition, too: in fact Bucquoy became a new bastion of the British line which was never lost.[12]

Major Richard Foot, 'D' Battery, 310th Brigade, Royal Field Artillery

On the Third Army front the situation was at last stabilising.

The Fifth Army was still in dire straits but was helped by the arrival of some French Army divisions, which were beginning to plug the gaps, allowing the line to solidify. The Germans had the vital rail junction of Amiens in their sights but, under the determined leadership of Foch, the French no longer entertained any idea of falling back and leaving the British to their fate. Soon the remnants of the Fifth Army were amalgamated with the French First and Third Armies to form the Group of Armies of Reserve under the unified command of General Émile Fayolle. Somewhat controversially, Gough was relieved of his command of the Fifth Army. This was widely perceived – especially by Gough – as unfair as there was little more he could have done in the circumstances. He was replaced by Sir Henry Rawlinson.

Between 21 March and 26 March the BEF suffered something like 75,000 casualties. Suddenly Lloyd George's objections to reinforcing the Western Front in accordance with the requirements of his generals were forgotten. Troops were released that had been held in Britain and divisions hitherto occupied by the plethora of minor campaigns in Italy, Palestine and elsewhere were suddenly made available. Hundreds of thousands of extra troops began to pour into France. The shallowness of the claims of the 'Easterners' was finally revealed by exposure to the reality of the Western Front.

Yet the Germans now unveiled a second string to their bow. On 28 March they launched another furious attack under Operation Mars by the Seventeenth Army on either side of the Scarpe River in front of Arras, with the intention of driving into the junction of the First and Third Armies. Here, however, they were not blessed by fog and the British defences were in far better shape. The stupefying bombardment opened at 03.00 and the German troops went over the top from 06.00. This time things did not go their way; the German batteries had failed to suppress the British artillery. Lieutenant John Capron was at the guns when the crucial moment came.

> But now a jabber of machine guns swept up and a thousand star shells, red–green–red, the British SOS. Rush up and hang in the upper darkness. The Germans are over the top. Now it is our turn to join in with the response barrage. Until now we have only been under a desultory

counter-battery fire but we are having to face a fiercer concentration – a determined blotting out. Faster and thicker whine down the shells, some well over, some short and some fearfully among us. The hideous energy, the dust and acrid reek, the blast and fury of each down rush makes us catch our breath – this is big stuff now! The ground heaves and seems to sway. It's a case of surviving – or not! How could the infantry have lived through a barrage such as now spouts around us? Yet, through the nearer tumult, fitfully comes and swells and fades, the sound of rifle fire. Heartened, we slip and stumble perilously to and fro between gunpits and ammunition recesses. 'Come on, 109s, the Londons are still there – give the bloody old Huns their rations!'[13]

Lieutenant John Capron, 109th Battery, 251st Brigade, Royal Field Artillery

The Londons were surviving sure enough and managed to deliver a severe rebuff to the advancing German infantry. Funnelled by barbed wire into machine gun traps, the Germans suffered heavy casualties.

Heavy machine gun fire unexpectedly appeared at the left flank from Fampoux, causing severe casualties especially among the officers. The attack slowed down a bit, causing the accompanying barrage of fire to lose connection with the attack and its purpose, covering the attacking infantry, was lost. In front of the Scots line, the English main position, the attack would be stopped, because the enemy infantry, protected by the cover of machine gun fire from their Fampoux positions, resisted fiercely, driving our infantry into the trenches for cover, halting further development. The repeated attack in the afternoon also didn't succeed. The strong English infantry defensive actions were backed by their regrouped artillery batteries that were firing at their own well known positions, now occupied and overfilled by us.[14]

Lieutenant Gerhard Dose, Headquarters, 187th Infantry Regiment

Although some small gains were made overall, Operation Mars was a failure and Ludendorff decided to close it down immediately.

In spite of employing extraordinary masses of artillery and ammunition, the attack of the Seventeenth Army on both banks of the Scarpe was a failure; it was fought under an unlucky star.[15]

Quartermaster General Erich Ludendorff, General Headquarters

The truth was it was nothing to do with luck: the Germans had been beaten by well-manned, well-prepared British defences, without the random factor of fog to cloud the issue or the British sights.

Back on the Somme, the Germans were also encountering stiff resistance. The French divisions were even beginning to launch counter-attacks to stabilise the front and secure tactically significant features. Many of the British troops were utterly exhausted, but now at last fresh troops were arriving.

> Our men are gaunt and weary, unwashed and with eight days' growth of beard, their lips raw and deeply chapped by the salted bully beef they have gnawed, and the coldness of the March winds. Most are limping painfully, for few have a change of socks with them or have had their boots off for eight days and nights. Over and over again we have been promised a relief which never comes, until a numbness of sensation has come over us all. They obey orders mechanically but sink fast asleep when opportunity offers.[16]
>
> Second Lieutenant Frank Warren, 17th King's Royal Rifle Corps

Yet their replacements managed to construct a solid front line, causing the German attacks to flounder, costing ever more men. Finally, on 30 March, Ludendorff called a pause to consider his options and allow his own exhausted troops to rest and reorganise. When the offensive burst back into life on 4 April with a concerted drive on the town of Villers-Bretonneux, in front of Amiens, the assault was checked with the assistance of the Australian Corps brought down from the north. The great German St Michael Spring Offensive was over.

The results had been a disappointment for the Germans, who needed outright victory here to give them any hope of winning the war before the Americans could deploy in strength on the Western Front. Their original intention to break through and roll up the British lines had been abandoned in an attempt to separate the British and French Armies by a powerful drive on the rail junction at Amiens. But this too had failed. However, some ground had been gained – about 1,200 square miles of French soil was once again under German control. But this was surely the whole point: much of that ground had been abandoned voluntarily during the retreat of March 1917 to secure a better tactical position. Now they were the proud possessors of an ugly 40-mile salient deep into the Allied lines that was far less secure than their previous Hindenburg Line fortress. They had achieved tactical successes, smashing the Fifth Army and inflicting some 178,000 British and 92,000 French casualties. Yet the Germans themselves suffered 239,000 casualties. And while the Allies lost a total of over 1,300 guns, 200 tanks, 2,000 machine guns and 400 aircraft, these losses were soon made good by their munitions industries. Almost as Helmuth Moltke the Elder had predicted so many years before, the Germans could not win in this kind of exchange. They had to win outright. But they had failed and, whatever the drama, whatever the trauma they were suffering, the Allies were still on course to win the war.

The Germans could not rest. How could they when the whole war was at stake? Ludendorff decided to attack the British again, but this time in Flanders, where they had little space to manoeuvre. The weather was by this time dry enough to permit the attack south of Ypres that had been at the centre of Operation George which was now reborn as Operation Georgette. The plan was to knock the British out of the war by crashing through the lines, surging forward to take the Hazebrouck rail centre some twenty miles east of Armentières, threatening the security of the Ypres Salient, and ultimately seeking to take Dunkirk and Calais. On the first day, the German Sixth Army would attack the Second and First Armies in the Lys Valley sector around Armentières and La Bassée Canal, while on the second day the German Fourth Army would assault all along the Messines Ridge, aiming for Mont Kemmel and threatening to encircle Ypres. This was the attack Haig had feared, and the reason why Gough had been forced to stand alone for so long while the safety of Flanders was ensured. But even so, of the fifty-six British divisions, forty-six had already been sucked into the fighting in repelling the German assaults on the Somme and at Arras.

The German barrage followed the usual pattern, beginning at 04.15 on 9 April 1918 before the infantry went forward at 08.45. Given the low-lying nature of the ground it is no surprise that the battlefield was swathed in a thick fog which concealed the movements of the German troops. The main thrust fell on to a weak Portuguese corps which was holding the Lys Valley sector. Portugal was a long-standing ally of Britain which had initially remained neutral, until tensions with Germany over U-boat warfare and a series of clashes with German forces around the Portuguese colonies in Africa had dragged her into the war in March 1916. Portuguese troops had begun to arrive on the Western Front where they were incorporated into the BEF. It would be fair to say, however, that the majority of the Portuguese troops were unenthusiastic participants in a global war for which they held little regard. After a long cold hard winter, they were overdue relief but, given the situation, it had not yet been achieved.

Dazed by the power of the German bombardment, many of the Portuguese units disintegrated and by 10.00 the Germans had burst through the Forward Zone. It is worth noticing, though, that the British 40th Division, next in line to the north, did little better as it too crumbled under the onslaught. Yet to the south the 55th Division not only repulsed the German attack but also managed to bend back to provide a defensive flank where the Portuguese had given way.

The German attack had achieved a considerable advance, advancing some five and a half miles and capturing around 100 guns. Yet they had still not broken through; the British reserves had managed to maintain a continuous line. Haig urgently demanded that the French take over more of the British line and send reserves, but Foch played a waiting game while he established whether this was just a diversion before another assault on the Somme.

On 10 April, the German Fourth Army made its attack stretching from Armentières all along the Messines Ridge manned by Plumer's Second Army. After a sustained barrage Corporal Frederick Meisel and the 371st Infantry Regiment pushed into the town, towards the railway station.

> From the station we were greeted with rifle and machine gun fire. Here and there some of the men were hit and fell. Cries and groans were heard, orders shouted, the war was on again, taking its toll of victims. Before we had time to form ourselves again and return the fire, the whining sound of heavy German shells passed over our heads. A second later they crashed into the station, caving it in with loud bursts of fire and steel, ripping up the platform and twisting the rails out of position. A few more shells hit around the station, uprooting telegraph poles and sending steel splinters and shrapnel flying through the air. The shell fire ceased and we attacked. But in the debris life still existed; desperate men defending a ruin. Bullets whistled from it and more familiar faces vanished. With fixed bayonets the station was stormed to be met by a handful of Scottish infantry. Our Lieutenant made gestures for them to surrender, but his good intentions were repulsed by a loud yell, 'Go to hell!' to be followed by several shots. Karl threw several

hand grenades into their barricades which exploded filling the ruins with smoke and dust, making the few shattered walls crack and fall, burying the defenders. Then we reached the station. Among piles of bricks and splintered planks lay bleeding and groaning men. Some lay stiff and cold, their bodies and faces covered with earth and blood. The place was littered with torn equipment, broken and twisted rifles and splintered furniture. On one of the cracked walls still hung the placard of the French railroad company, which ironically enough showed a beautiful seashore scene in the south of France.[17]

Corporal Frederick Meisel, 371st Infantry Regiment

The Second Army was forced to cede ground, falling back from the Messines Ridge, the prize gained in June 1917. Yet the Germans had still not broken through and the retreat all along the line was to a greater or lesser degree controlled in character. But the British had little room for manoeuvre, as the Germans were getting far too close to the Hazebrouck rail junction for comfort, behind which lay the Channel ports and the spectre of total defeat. On 11 April Haig tried to stiffen the morale of his men with a special order of the day.

Many amongst us now are tired. To those I would say that victory will belong to the side which holds out the longest. The French Army is moving rapidly and in great force to our support. There is no other course open to us but to fight it out. Every position must be held to the last man: there must be no retirement. With our backs to the wall and believing in the justice of our cause each one of us must fight on to the end. The safety of our homes and the freedom of mankind alike depend upon the conduct of each one of us at this critical moment.[18]

Field Marshal Sir Douglas Haig, General Headquarters, BEF

As British reserves began to reach the front the German advance was gradually stemmed: Merville, Nieppe and Bailleul fell in the days that followed, but fresh British divisions and the few French formations released by Foch managed to stop the German advance just short of Hazebrouck. The German plans to cut off the Ypres Salient garrison were also thwarted by a timely retreat right back to the Pilckem Ridge. The sacrificial ground for which they had suffered so much in the 1917 offensive had to be surrendered but the situation was stabilised. After a short pause to allow for some re-organisation, the Germans relaunched their offensive on 17 April 1918 all along the front, but suffered severe casualties for no gains. A further lull ended when, on 25 April, the Germans launched a mass attack on the French forces defending the heights of Mont Kemmel.

> Suddenly our artillery fire stopped. An awful silence followed the terrific noise. A whistle shrilled, bayonets were fixed. Another whistle signalled the descent into the valley. Not a sound, not a rifle shot could be heard from the opposite side. Crossing the valley we stopped to readjust ourselves and began to climb the hill before us. Now we discovered why it had been so quiet, for over this territory lay the silence of death. The shell holes were filled with ghastly and bloody messes; freshly built trenches had caved in burying the occupants. Stumbling over mutilated bodies we reached the summit.[19]
>
> Corporal Frederick Meisel, 371st Infantry Regiment

Although the French had been over-run, their artillery could still hit back hard.

> French shells began to hit to the right and left of us, leaving human forms writhing in agony. Our advance came to a stop and after hesitating a few minutes we drew back while the artillery fire followed us, ripping large gashes in our formation – soon the French drumfire engulfed us, the air was filled with gas and flying pieces of steel. We automatically mounted the machine gun for action. Then like animals we burrowed into the earth as if trying to find protection deep in its bosom. Something struck my back where I carried my gas mask, but I did not pay attention to it. A steel splinter broke the handle of my spade and another knocked the remains out of my hand. I kept digging with my bare hands, ducking my head every time a shell exploded nearby. A boy to my side was hit in the arm and cried out for help. I crawled over to him, ripped the sleeves of his coat and shirt open and started to bind the bleeding part. The gas was so thick now I could hardly discern what I was doing. My eyes began to water and I felt as if I would choke. I reached for my gas mask, pulled it out of its container – then noticed to my horror that a splinter had gone through it leaving a large hole. I had seen death thousands of times, stared it in the face, but never experienced the fear I felt then. Immediately I reverted to the primitive. I felt like an animal cornered by hunters. With the instinct of self-preservation uppermost, my eyes fell on the boy whose arm I had bandaged. Somehow he had managed to put the gas mask on his

face with his one good arm. I leapt at him and in the next moment had ripped the gas mask from his face. With a feeble gesture he tried to wrench it from my grasp; then fell back exhausted. The last thing I saw before putting on the mask were his pleading eyes.[20]

Corporal Frederick Meisel, 371st Infantry Regiment

The Germans and the French were locked in a death grip, neither seemingly able to let go. New units arrived and were fed into the maw of battle. There was little enthusiasm, that much is plain.

> We shall only be relieved after a 60 per cent loss of troops; the men are beginning to wish for, not death, but just to be wounded so that they can get out as soon as possible. This leads to endless suppositions; one man gives up his hand, another his arm, provided it's the left one; yet another goes as far as a leg, declaring that where he comes from men like this manage quite well. But what frightens them most, is being wounded in the stomach or some other vital organ. Then the conversation turns to the ambulance, the hospital, plans for convalescence, rest at home, and what to do so as not to return to the front. In every sort of sector like this, the conversation revolves around the same topic. There is no longer even any mention of the civilians and their cosy life. No, you are stuck there waiting, simply trying to snatch some part of yourself from death, you don't even ask to escape unharmed, it seems too impossible, your only wish is to leave as little as possible of yourself behind on the battlefield.[21]

Captain Henri Desagneux, 359th Infantry Regiment

Yet into battle went the French, soon inflicting their fears on their German counterparts. Now the Germans had to adapt to the horror of being counter-attacked in makeshift positions, deluged with shells while already exhausted by the accumulated traumas of trench fighting.

> Through the damp glasses of my mask I saw dim outlines of men appear and when they approached more closely I could distinguish French uniforms and dull blinking bayonets. Gruen threw himself behind the machine gun and I instinctively pointed the barrel of the machine gun into the mist towards the advancing enemy. His hands tightened themselves round the handles while his thumbs pressed on the triggers. Flames spurted from the barrel of the guns and I saw the Frenchmen plunge headlong into the grass.[22]

Corporal Frederick Meisel, 371st Infantry Regiment

In the end, despite their best efforts, the Germans failed to capture any significant objectives. They had gained ground, but they had not defeated their British and French opponents.

Meanwhile, Ludendorff had ordered another lunge at the tempting vista of Amiens in late April 1918. During the build-up to the attack one of the great German heroes of the war fought his last battles. Captain Manfred von Richthofen – the young ingénu of 1916, the merciless killer of 1917, the inspirational leader of 1918 – had recovered from the wounds he had received in the summer of 1917 and seemed to be back on top form. On 20 April, during a vicious dogfight with a group of Sopwith Camels, Richthofen had already shot down Major Richard Raymond-Barker in flames, but was soon on the tail of Second Lieutenant David Lewis.

> I had to turn round to save myself from bullets which I could see were ripping the fabric off my machine. I saw at once that my attacker was Richthofen himself, who had probably been waiting for some indiscreet pilot to get well below him. Then started a merry waltz; round and round, up and down to the staccato of the machine guns of the other fighters. Only once did I get my sights on his machine, but in a trice the positions were reversed, and I felt he was so much my master that he would get me sooner or later. Try as I would I simply could not shake him off my tail, and all the time the bullets from his hungry Spandau plastered my machine. His first burst shattered the compass in front of my face, the liquid there-from fogging my goggles, of which, however, I was relieved when a bullet severed the elastic from the frame, and they went over the side. My position was not improved, however, for my eyes filled with water caused by the rush of wind. Flying and landing wires struck by the bullets folded up before my eyes, and struts splintered before that withering fire. I do not think Richthofen was more than 50 feet from me all this time, for I could plainly see his begoggled and helmeted face, and his machine guns. Next I heard the sound of flames and the stream of bullets ceased. I turned round to find that my machine was on fire. My petrol tank was alight.[23]
>
> Second Lieutenant David Lewis, 3rd Squadron, RAF

But Lewis was incredibly lucky.

> I put my machine into a vertical nosedive and raced earthwards in an endeavour to drive the flames upwards and away from me, but every

now and then the flames overtook the speed of the machine and were blown back into my face. When about 500 feet from the ground the flames seemed to have subsided, so I pulled the control back to gain a horizontal position and was horrified to find the machine would not answer the elevators. I held the stick back instinctively, I suppose, and then noticed that the aircraft was slowly attaining the desired position, and I thought I should be able to land on an even keel. This was not to be, however. I hit the ground at terrific speed, but was hurled from the machine unhurt except for minor burns and bruises. I later saw that not a stitch of fabric was left between my seat and the tail, but noticed that a few strips of the material left on my elevators had saved me. The back of my Sidcot was in charred strips and my helmet crumpled when I took it off. I also had one bullet through my trouser leg and one through my sleeve.[24]

Second Lieutenant David Lewis, 3rd Squadron, RAF

It seemed that nothing could stop Richthofen. A combination of accurate intuitive pilot, brilliant tactician and patient teacher, he was the complete ace, an unbeatable force of nature. But the very next day, on 21 April, this potent symbol of German manhood would be shot down. His last moments were spent chasing a young Canadian pilot, Lieutenant Wilfred May.

The enemy aircraft were coming at me from all sides, I seemed to be missing some of them by inches, there seemed to be so many of them the best thing I thought to do was to go into a tight vertical turn, hold my guns open and spray as many as I could. The fight was at very close quarters; there seemed to be dozens of machines around me. Through lack of experience I held my guns open too long, one jammed and then the other. I could not clear them, so I spun out of the mess and headed west into the sun for home. After I levelled off I looked around but nobody was following me. I was patting myself on the back, feeling pretty good getting out of that scrape. This wasn't to last long, and the first thing I knew I was being fired on from the rear. I could not fight back unfortunately, so all I could do was to try to dodge my attacker. I noticed it was a red triplane, but if I had realised it was Richthofen I would have probably passed out on the spot. We came over the German lines, troops fired at us as we went over; this was also the case coming over the British lines. I got on the Somme River and started up the valley at a very low altitude. I kept on dodging and spinning, I imagine from about 12,000 feet until I ran out of sky and had to hedge-hop over the ground. Richthofen was firing at me continually, the only thing that saved me was my poor flying. I didn't know what I was doing myself and I do not suppose that Richthofen could figure out what I was going to do. Richthofen was very close on my tail. I went around a curve in the river just near Corbie. Richthofen beat me to it and came over the hill. At that point I was a sitting duck. I was too low down between the banks to make a turn away from him. I felt that he had me cold, and I was in such a state of mind at this time that I had to restrain myself from pushing my stick forward into the river as I knew that I had had it.[25]

Lieutenant Wilfred May, 209th Squadron, RAF

But Richthofen, the master of the skies, had made a series of dreadful mistakes. Perhaps tired, stressed, fixated by his latest target, or simply carried away by over-confidence, he was flying alone, well behind British lines. Failing to watch his tail, he came under a burst of fire from a Canadian ace, Captain Roy Brown; flying far too low, he was also vulnerable to several Vickers and Lewis machine guns firing from the ground; and of course he was a target for every strolling infantryman that fancied his chances. Who actually fired the fatal bullet matters little. The only important fact is that Richthofen's Fokker Triplane came down behind British lines with the great man dead in the cockpit. Richthofen had been one of the men who had defined aerial warfare, building on the pioneer work of Max Immelmann and Oswald Boelcke. Now he too was gone, but by this time the lessons had been disseminated throughout the whole German Air Service. His work was done.

The German attack commenced on the Somme Front on 24 April. It was noteworthy for featuring the first clash between opposing tanks as three lumbering German A7Vs encountered three British Mark IVs. The Germans had not considered tanks a particular priority, concentrating their efforts on artillery. They did, however, begin experimenting and eventually developed the A7V tank, which was a large high-sided tracked vehicle containing a crew of up to eighteen, armed with one 57 mm gun and six machine guns, and a claimed speed in active service conditions of about 3 miles per hour. The Germans had started too late and this, their first design was not entirely practical, being unable to cross trenches and prone to mechanical failure. There were also very few of them – a mere twenty in all – and the Germans supplemented them with about fifty captured British tanks. Lieutenant Frank Mitchell recalled his first view of the German tanks.

> Suddenly, out of the ground 10 yards away, an infantryman rose, waving his rifle furiously. We stopped. He ran forward and shouted through the flap, 'Look out! Jerry tanks about!' Swiftly he disappeared into the trench again. I informed the crew and a great thrill ran through us all. Opening a loophole, I looked out. There, some 300 yards away, a round, squat-looking monster was advancing. Behind it came waves of infantry, and further away to left and right crawled two more of these armed tortoises. The 6-pounder gunners crouching on the floor, their backs against the engine cover, loaded their guns expectantly. We still kept on a zig-zag course, threading the gaps between the lines of hastily dug trenches, and coming near the small protecting belt of wire, we turned left, and the right gunner, peering through his narrow slit, made a sighting shot. The shell burst some distance beyond the leading enemy tank. No reply came. A second shot boomed out, landing just to the right, but again there was no reply. More shots followed. Suddenly, a hurricane of hail pattered against our steel wall, filling the interior with myriads of sparks and flying splinters. Something rattled against the steel helmet of the driver sitting next to me and my face was stung with minute fragments of steel. The crew flung themselves flat on the floor. The driver ducked his head and drove straight on. Above the roar of our engine sounded the staccato rat-tat-tat-tat of machine guns and another furious jet of bullets sprayed our steel side, the splinters clanging viciously against the engine cover. The Jerry tank had treated us to a broadside of armour-piercing bullets![26]
>
> Lieutenant Frank Mitchell, 1st Battalion, Tank Corps

Their two female Mark IV tanks had been damaged by shells and were dropping back, so Mitchell decided that his tank must slow down to an absolute crawl if he was to have any chance of hitting his targets. He proved partially successful.

> The left gunner, registering carefully, began to hit the ground right in front of the Jerry tank. I took a risk and stopped the tank for a moment. The pause was justified; a well-aimed shot hit enemy's conning tower, bringing him to a standstill. Another roar and yet another white puff at

the front of the tank denoted a second hit! Peering with swollen eyes through his narrow slit, the gunner shouted words of triumph that were drowned by the roar of the engine. Then once more with great deliberation he aimed and hit for the third time. Through a loophole I saw the tank heel over to one side; then a door opened and out ran the crew. We had knocked the monster out! Quickly I signed to the machine gunner and he poured volley after volley into the retreating figure. I turned slowly at the other two, who were creeping forward relentlessly; if they both concentrated their fire on us at once we would be finished. We fired rapidly at the nearest tank and to my intense joy and amazement, I saw it slowly back away. Its companion did not appear to relish a fight, for it followed its mate and in a few minutes they had both disappeared, leaving our tank the sole possessor of the field.[27]

Lieutenant Frank Mitchell, 1st Battalion, Tank Corps

The knocked-out German A7V was the *Nixe*, commanded by Lieutenant Wilhelm Biltz, a professor of chemistry in his pre-war life. He was lucky to survive this sharp little action, a precursor of the future of armoured warfare.

The tanks' efforts were of little importance in the scheme of things and the German attack soon crashed through the badly weakened 8th Division. With the capture of Villers-Bretonneux the way to Amiens seemed wide open. It was left to the Australian Corps to launching a last-ditch night attack to regain the town.

There was a howling as of demons as the 57th, fighting mad, drove through the wire, through their enemy. The wild cry rose to a voluminous, vengeful roar. There was no quarter on either side. Bathed in spurting blood they killed and killed. Bayonets passed with ease through grey-clad bodies and were withdrawn with a sucking noise. Some found chances in the slaughter to light cigarettes, then continued the killing. Then, as they looked for more victims, there were cries of, 'There they go, there they go!' and over heaps of big, dead Germans they sprang in pursuit. One huge Australian advanced firing a Lewis gun from the shoulder, spraying the ground with lead. It is unlikely that any of the enemy escaped their swift, relentless pursuers. They were slaughtered against the lurid glare of the fire in the town. One saw running forms in the dark, and the flashes of rifles, then the evil pyre in the town flared and showed to their killers the white faces of Germans lurking in shell holes, or flinging away their arms and trying to escape, only to be stabbed or shot down as they ran. Machine gun positions were discovered burrowed under hay stacks, crammed with men, who on being found were smashed and mangled by bomb after bomb after bomb. It was impossible to take prisoners. Men could not be spared to take them to the rear.[28]

Sergeant William Downing, 57th Battalion, AIF

The Australian troops were beginning to carve out a formidable reputation on the Western Front. Villers-Bretonneux had been recaptured, but more importantly the gateway to Amiens had been firmly shut.

Ludendorff was becoming increasingly desperate. He had captured large swathes of despoiled ground, ruined villages, shattered copses and blasted roads, but he had failed to knock the British out of the war. Two large salients bulged into the British lines, but these were sources of weakness rather than strength. The British were still on their feet; the Americans were still on their way. This time Ludendorff resolved to launch an attack on the French using the contingency plans developed as Operation Blücher earlier in the year. The German Seventh and First Armies would attack the French Sixth Army stretched out along the Chemin des Dames Ridge. The idea was to suck in Allied reserves, thereby leaving the British vulnerable to a great new Flanders offensive, codenamed Operation Hagen, which was set to commence in July. It was ironic, then, that several British divisions were innocently holding a quiet sector of the French line that was about to be attacked. They had been sent there to recuperate, replacing some French divisions which were intended to allow Foch to create a mobile reserve.

When the Germans attacked, the battered British divisions were totally unable to hold the line. It was doubly unfortunate that General Denis August Duchêne, the commander of the French Sixth Army, was unable to grasp the concept of defence in depth, determined as he was to hold the ground along the ridge top that had been won at so much cost in previous years. As a result, far too high a proportion of his units were concentrated in the Forward Zone, which made them excessively vulnerable to the German bombardment that began with awesome force at 01.00 on 27 May 1918.

A thousand guns roared out their iron hurricane. The night was rent with sheets of flame. The earth shuddered under the avalanche of missiles, leapt skywards in dust and tumult. Even above the din screamed the fierce crescendo of approaching shells, ear-splitting crashes as they burst. All the time the dull thud, thud, thud of detonations and drum fire. Inferno raged and whirled round the Bois des Buttes. The dugouts rocked, filled with the acrid fumes of cordite, the sickly sweet tang of gas. Timbers started: earth showered from the roof. Men rushed for shelter, seizing kits, weapons, gas masks, message pads as they dived for safety. It was a descent into hell. Crowded with jostling, sweating humanity the dugouts reeked, and to make matters worse headquarters had no sooner got below than the gas began to filter down. Gas masks were hurriedly donned and anti-gas precautions taken – the entrances closed with saturated blankets, braziers lighted on the stairs. If gas could not enter, neither could the air. As a fact both did in small quantities and the long night was spent 40 foot underground, at the hottest time of the year, in stinking overcrowded holes, their entrances sealed up and charcoal burners alight drying up the atmosphere – suffocation rendered more complete by the gas masks with clip on nostrils and gag in the teeth.[29]

Captain Sydney Rogerson, Headquarters, 23rd Brigade

From 03.40 the German infantry tore through the French and British front lines. Soon the survivors were streaming back across the Aisne. There was much desperate fighting and many acts of heroism in what must have seemed a lost cause.

We each fall back in turn, pausing to fire when the black helmets appear from the pale fields. When a section gets up and moves off, the enemy mows it down from left, right and front. We can clearly see that Sirey is surrounded, struggling in the storm of grenades. If we can get two or three platoons to regroup, we can go forward to disengage a neighbouring company in trouble. Near the Saconin road, Lieutenant Chauveau defended himself for more than an hour. When the Germans got to him, he was lying wounded among his dead; he refused to surrender, went to his death firing on his attackers with his revolver.[30]

Private Georges Gaudy, 57th Infantry Regiment

The British divisions had been in a bad state to start, having been smashed up in both the Somme and Flanders. They were full of young recruits and veterans that had already been to the well too often. As they were pushed back from the Aisne they soon descended into deep disorder. At times there were very real echoes of the type of fighting in 1914.

> A German field gun battery galloped up to the top of the ridge, unlimbered and opened fire on us. Being fired at by guns over open sights was a new experience – and a shattering one! The shells arrived with such a vicious 'whizz' and each one seemed to be aimed at you personally. I was not the only one who found it unnerving. Everyone did and the whole lot of us just broke and ran. This was the only time I saw a real rout. It is true that we had been retreating the whole day, but not, most of the time, on the run and we had had in mind the finding of a position where we could make a stand. But now it was just panic flight; with each man, including me, thinking of nothing but saving his own skin.[31]
>
> Lieutenant John Nettleton, 2nd Rifle Brigade

As their units disintegrated, neither the British nor the French could stem the German advance. A hole some thirty-five miles wide and twelve miles deep was ripped into their lines. Over the next few days the French would try to plug the gap using their local reserves – but it is noticeable that Foch ignored pleas for access to the strategic reserve that he insisted on holding back until he knew exactly what the Germans intended. In contrast Ludendorff was swept away by the impressive tactical gains and began to abandon his original concept of a diversion before the last great Flanders offensive that would win the war. He could after all point to some 50,000 Allied prisoners and 800 guns captured during Operation Blücher – impressive by any standards. Ludendorff even had visions of an advance across the Marne River and all the way to Paris. He began to commit his own reserve divisions to the battle. Yet even as his troops pushed forwards, the age-old problems dogged their steps. The French reinforcements began to arrive in force while the German communications were stretched, their troops exhausted and their artillery disorganised. Most significantly of all, the American 2nd and 3rd Divisions helped shore up the French line at Château-Thierry on the Marne. Their attitude was summed up by Colonel Wendell C. Neville of the Marine Corps Brigade, when a local French officer suggested that tactical retreat might be in order, 'Retreat? Hell – we only just got here!' Having helped stem the tide of the German advance, on 6 June, the US Marine Brigade (part of 2nd Division) launched an attack to clear the Germans out of Belleau Woods.

> We started off in trench warfare formation, the only formation we knew, which consisted of four waves with the first wave and all waves holding their rifles at what is called 'high port,' not even aiming or firing or hip firing or anything like that. Now we got out of these woods and we moved towards Belleau Woods, nobody firing a shot. Bayonets fixed, moving at a low steady cadence that we had been taught. On our left, approximately 200 yards, was the redoubt of Belleau Woods. It's an eminence, a little raised place; the little hunting lodge was up there. It's a rocky place. It was teeming with machine guns; I mean it seemed that way. And nobody, literally nobody was firing a shot at these Germans. They had us enfiladed. They were to our left front; and as we got out far enough, we were perfectly enfiladed from them. So it was absolutely like a shooting gallery and not a single Marine of ours firing a shot. We weren't trained that way. We went on. Well, of course, as soon as we came out of this first band of woods in my platoon (there were approximately 52 men) there were only six people got across the first 75 yards. All the rest were killed, wounded and pinned down. I mean we were down into a ravine which was perfectly enfiladed and just 'Bloop!' a few machine guns – and that was it.[32]
>
> Sergeant Merwin Silverthorn, 5th Marines, AEF

Tactical naivety could be painful and a good deal of intense fighting ensued before the capture of the wood was completed on 26 June. So the learning process had begun for another army amidst the frenzy of the Western Front.

Falling into his own trap, Ludendorff triggered Operation Gneisenau to widen the salient from Noyon to Montdidier with an attack launched at 24.00 on 8 June. At first the Germans were successful, over-running the Forward Zone on 9 June and pushing forward some four miles. Then it was the same old story as the French managed to stabilise the front. But something new emerged on 11 June, when the French launched a counter-attack under General Charles Mangin driving into the western flank of the burgeoning salient. The French were using their own shock tactics as they attacked without a preliminary barrage to preserve surprise, utilised a deadly creeping barrage, with close support for the assaulting troops from large numbers of Renault FT tanks and ground-strafing aircraft. Stymied again, Ludendorff was forced to suspend the attacks. If the Germans ever had a real chance of winning the war on the Western Front in 1918, then now it had passed. The arrival of summer brought with it an accelerating stream of fresh American divisions on to the Western Front. Although unused to modern warfare, they represented the end of hope for the German Army.

Ludendorff was caught in a cleft stick. He could stand back on the defensive and prolong the war as long as possible; or he could make one last grab for outright victory. He decided to launch his *Friedensturm* – Peace Offensive – with an all-out attack on the French and the Americans with the Seventh, First and Third Armies from Servon to Château-Thierry in what would become known as the Second Battle of the Marne. Once the French were defeated Ludendorff resolved to turn for the final decisive battle with the British in Flanders. But the French easily detected the precursors of this huge offensive and were ready and waiting: the German methodology was now fully understood. Indeed, before the German bombardment opened up at 00.10 on 15 July, the French front lines were cleared to avoid casualties, while the massed French guns actually opened up their fire first, flaying the German gun batteries and crashing down on the infantry as they moved up for the assault planned to commence after 04.15. It was the start of a very bad day for the German Army. In the sector manned by Captain Jesse Woolridge the Germans attempted a crossing of the Marne on pontoons and a floating bridge.

> The general fire ceased and their creeping barrage started – behind which at 40 yards only, mind you, they came – with more machine guns than I thought the German Army owned. The enemy had to battle their way through the first platoon on the river bank – then they took on the second platoon on the forward edge of the railway where we had a thousand times the best of it – but the [Germans] gradually wiped it out. My third platoon [took] their place in desperate hand to hand fighting, in which some got through only to be picked up by the fourth platoon which was deployed simultaneously with the third. By the time they struck the fourth platoon they were all in and easy prey. It's God's truth that one company of American soldiers beat and routed a full regiment of picked shock troops of the German Army. At 10 o'clock, the Germans were carrying back wounded and dead [from] the river bank and we in our exhaustion let them do it – they carried back all but 600

which we counted later and fifty-two machine guns. We had started with 251 men and five lieutenants. I had left fifty-one men and two Second Lieutenants.[33]

Captain Jesse Woolridge, 38th Infantry Regiment, AEF

The Adjutant of the German 5th Grenadier Regiment certainly agreed as to the level of resistance offered by the Americans.

It was the severest defeat of the war! One only had to descend the northern slopes of the Marne: never have I seen so many dead, nor such frightful sights in battle. The Americans on the other shore had completely shot to pieces in a close combat two of our companies. They had lain in the grain, in semicircular formation, had let us approach, and then from 30 to 50 feet had shot almost all of us down. This foe had nerves, one must allow him this boast; but he also showed a bestial brutality. 'The Americans kill everything!' That was the cry of horror of 15 July, which long took hold of our men. A day like 15 July affects body and nerves for weeks. Our lines were thinned. Low spirits took hold of most of the men.[34]

Lieutenant Kurt Hesse, 5th Grenadier Regiment

Then came the main French riposte, commencing just three days later, on 18 July. Foch determined to strike hard at Soissons, augmenting his Sixth and Tenth Armies with four divisions from the AEF, thereby threatening the whole bloated Marne Salient carved out by Operation Blücher. This was a mighty assault led by Mangin's Tenth Army backed by over 1,500 guns and some 300 tanks. There would be no preliminary barrage, just a huge creeping barrage, a mixture of high explosive, shrapnel and smoke shells rolling along ahead of the attacking infantry, designed to blast, kill or blind the German machine gunners.

Absolute peace reigns! No roar of guns, not even a rifle shot! We are silent and a bit cast down just awaiting for the big moment. 04.35! A tremendous barrage roars out behind us with the sound of thunder; the creeping barrage that triggers our advance. The 75mm shells fly fast over our heads to explode in the valley at the edge of the forest. The heavier shells follow, flying higher in the sky to explode on our distant objectives: gun batteries, German reserves, etc. Without losing a moment we go down to the river, each section behind its leader.[35]

Lieutenant Émile Morin, 60th Infantry Regiment

As the barrage rolled forward the massed Renault, St Chamand and Schneider tanks crushed their way through the barbed wire. Of course, not everything went smoothly; in particular, the Americans found it difficult to fit in with the French plans and working methods, which led to a degree of confusion.

> The battle does not become coherent again until late afternoon. The reasons for this are evident; there was the haste and confusion incident to the last minute concentration for the attack – all made inevitable by the French Army and Corps instructions wherein order and deliberation were compromised to the end that a surprise might be achieved. Thus, no reconnaissance by the American officers was possible. Changes of direction in the course of action, especially on a terrain without prominent natural land marks, are difficult under the most favourable circumstances and to the best-trained troops. Finally, the Division orders enjoined rapidity of movement, and an advance without long halts on the successive objectives. The attack waves got off on time, they advanced, and continued to advance. They lost formation, but retained so much individual energy that the German formations on their front were destroyed or rendered incapable.[36]
>
> Second Lieutenant John Thomason, 5th Marines, AEF

Communications difficulties were particularly evident when French tanks, Senegalese infantry and American soldiers found themselves fighting in the same patch of ground.

> At 3:30 pm three small French tanks, supported by about sixty black Moroccans [Senegalese] in squad columns 50 yards behind the tanks, moved through us from the left rear and headed straight for Vierzy. There was some confusion as 'M' Company had some difficulty in keeping from being run down by the machines, lying, as we were, hidden in the wheat. The black men just followed along stoically – and too close. The machine guns in Vierzy opened up a terrific burst of fire and we were tight in the path of it. The Moroccans were simply mowed down but kept on until I did not see a single one left standing. This was literally the case. The tanks turned around and vanished to our left rear. 'M' Company had several casualties due to this foolish manoeuvre. How they happened to come there in the first place, I don't know. I got a bullet in the knee.[37]
>
> Lieutenant Ludislav Janda, 9th Infantry Regiment, AEF

But, for all the problems, the French and Americans drove back the Germans. The Renault tanks made a real difference, swarming over the battlefield, taking out German machine gun posts and generally assisting the infantry, with their fully rotating turret making them flexible in selecting targets. Although their small size precluded them crossing trenches, they were meant to work in tandem with sappers or specially trained infantry using picks and shovels to break down the trench walls and smooth out the way. As can be imagined, such arrangements did not often stand up to the test of battle. Like the British, the French would also find that the combination of high casualties, mechanical breakdowns and crew exhaustion meant that tank units melted away after a day or so in action.

Meanwhile, Lieutenant Émile Morin and his men were heading towards the Savière River. They managed to cross a bridge, but then found themselves trapped on a mid-stream island rather than on the far side as they had imagined.

> We sink knee-deep in sticky black mud, trudging through a thick covering of reeds. Suddenly, the ground disappears beneath my feet and I fall up to my waist in the mud stirred up by the explosion of a shell. I try to get out of this mess, but every move worsens my situation. I feel drawn into this bog and there is no one to rescue me. My whole section has disappeared into the reeds. I shout out, but will I be heard in the deafening din of the bombardment? The seconds tick by slowly and gradually I feel myself slipping limply to the bottom of this grave that will quietly close up over me! The slime already reached up to my armpits. A few more moments and I will disappear forever in a painless death. And when the attack has ended; when they call out, 'Lieutenant Morin?' a voice will answer, 'Missing 18 July!' Where exactly? Under what circumstances? Nobody will ever know and I will have joined the large cohort of soldiers without an official grave. Suddenly, the reeds part and the Sergeant Major of my section appears. In the blink of an eye he grasps the situation and reaches out to me with his rifle, which I grab with both hands and he manages to drag me out of the depths of my muddy grave.[38]
>
> Lieutenant Émile Morin, 60th Infantry Regiment

There were so many ways to die in service of the Republic. Shortly afterwards Morin was hit in the hand and thigh. His long war was over.

The Germans could not withstand the pressure and fell back towards the Aisne River. By 7 August all their gains from their 27 May offensive had been lost. Finally, Ludendorff was forced to face the fact that he no longer had the forces available to launch a viable offensive and would be on the defensive for the foreseeable future. His whole strategy for 1918 lay in ruins and defeat beckoned, no longer whispering softly, but shouting from the rooftops.

While the French took over the lead role, the British had been using the early summer interregnum to reorganise, giving valuable experience of Western Front conditions to the divisions sent from the sideshows and assimilating the copious drafts released from home service. On the newly constituted Fourth Army front on the Somme, General Sir Henry Rawlinson became aware that his German opponents were adopting a strangely placid role, failing to build up their defences in depth, indeed failing to build any proper defences at all. This was characteristic of a general decline in German military efficiency. Many of the better divisions had already been moved south, sucked into the great offensives against the French, while the best men from the divisions that remained had already been filtered out to restock the stormtrooper units. The remnants were in poor shape, unrecognisable from the German formations of earlier in the war. The failure to achieve a decisive victory coupled with the arrival of the American legions had undoubtedly dealt a severe blow to German morale.

> We were like animals, for we lived as such. At times we did not wash for days; our bodies were infested with vermin and most of us suffered from worms. Our clothes were torn and filthy, rags were used as socks. We ate anything that was barely edible and were content when they let us sleep without interruption. Our brains grew numb. Something had put new life into our enemies, who seemed more confident, more determined. Had they really been reinforced by two million Americans? The Allied forces hadn't struck yet, but we sensed that they were merely feeling out our weakened position. Their aircraft filled the air, raking us with machine gun fire and bombs from above, while artillery and trench mortars worked from every possible angle on the ground.[39]
>
> Corporal Frederick Meisel, 371st Infantry Regiment

The German Army was near to breaking poimt. Not only that but the situation on the home front was grim, with chronic food shortages, problems providing enough labour to cope with the demands of industry and problems with what labour force there was, as socialist views began to take a grip on many of the workers, causing an increasing number of strikes and protests.

Tempted by the apparently frail nature of the German defences he was presented with, Rawlinson asked Lieutenant General Sir John Monash, commanding the Australian Corps, to prepare an exploratory local attack. Monash and his staff planned a line-straightening operation for the village of Hamel, to be launched at 03.10 on 4 July 1918. The tactics employed reflected the shift from manpower to firepower, a shift that had been gradually forced upon the British Army, but which was now wholeheartedly embraced in the concept of the 'All Arms Battle'. The attack proved a stunning success achieving an advance of 2,000 yards.

> As we got to our objective we found two dugouts. I happened to be there first and I heard movement in one of these shelters. When I yelled out to the occupants, out came two hands with a loaf of black bread in each, and presently a pair of terrified eyes took a glimpse at me. They must have been reassured by my look, because the Huns came out at once, and, when I sized them up, all thoughts of revenge vanished. We could not kill children and these looked to be barely that. If any of us had been asked how old they were, most of us would have said between fourteen and fifteen, and that was giving them every day of their age. With a boot to help them along, they ran with their hands above their heads back to our lines.[40]
>
> Lieutenant Edgar Rule, 14th Battalion, AIF

The enfeebled German Army was in no fit state to withstand this kind of focussed onslaught.

Bolstered by this triumph, Rawlinson began to plan a much bigger battle to capitalise on the German weakness using a further development of the self-same tactics. But this was emphatically not the work of one man, or even of a small group of officers, but rather the synthesis of all that the British – aided by the French – had learnt over the previous three years, since the Battle of Neuve Chapelle. It was a collegiate effort, marked by the wholehearted involvement of experts at all levels of the BEF and fully integrating all the new weapons into one ferocious methodology of modern war. The guns of the Royal Artillery remained the backbone of the assault. A total of 1,386 carefully calibrated field guns and howitzers, with a further 684 heavy artillery pieces, were moved in secretly, their ammunition dumps stocked to the brim. The RAF, aided by flash spotters and sound rangers, had already managed to identify 504 of the 530 German guns. When the attack was launched, they would be neutralised by lashings of gas and high explosive shells to prevent them intervening as the infantry crossed No Man's Land. There was no longer any need to decide between counter-battery fire and a barrage: the BEF now had enough guns to allow for both with a comprehensive creeping barrage, forcing the Germans to keep their heads down as the British infantry approached. With them came the tanks: 324 heavy tanks to squash the barbed wire and help crush any surviving German strongpoints; then 96 light Whippet tanks to create havoc behind the German lines; while a further 120 supply tanks were loaded with munitions to resupply the infantry in case of German counter-attacks. This would be the biggest tank attack of the war. Above them flew the aircraft, strafing the battlefield and making contact reports to record progress, attacking airfields to neutralise their opposite numbers and launching interdiction bombing missions against rail junctions, arterial roads and key bridges. The infantry themselves were unrecognisable from the warriors of 1915. Fewer in number, perhaps, but covered by massed Vickers machine gun fire and carrying their own Lewis guns, Stokes mortars and rifle grenades for immediate powerful support. Furthermore, they no longer advanced in lines, but in 'short worms' of about eight men feeling their way in 'strings' across No Man's Land preceded by well-trained scouts.

Haig and Foch accepted Rawlinson's plans, indeed Foch intervened to expand the overall scale of the operations by including the neighbouring French First Army, commanded by General Marie-Eugène Debeney. Yet even as everything began to fall into place on the Western Front, back in London General Sir Henry Wilson, Lloyd George's choice to replace Robertson as Chief of Imperial General Staff, was expressing his cautious views as to what should be done.

> A period of preparation should ensue during which all the Allied resources should be husbanded, organised and trained for the culminating military effort at the decisive moment. This will not be a period of passive defence, far from it, but it will be a period during

which no final decision is attempted. The first question that arises is – when is this decisive effort to be made? That is to say, will it be possible to accomplish it in 1919, or must we wait until 1920?[41]

General Sir Henry Wilson, Imperial General Staff

Wilson felt the decisive thrust might be made on 1 July 1919. It is evident that the generals at the front had a far clearer sense of purpose in conceiving the Battle of Amiens. When the guns blazed out at Zero Hour of 04.20 on 8 August the battle plan began to work like clockwork.

> And suddenly, with a mighty roar, more than a thousand guns begin the symphony. A great illumination lights up the eastern horizon: and instantly the whole complex organisation, extending far back to areas almost beyond earshot of the guns, begins to move forward; every man, every unit, every vehicle and every tank on the appointed tasks and to their designated goals, sweeping on relentlessly and irresistibly. Viewed from a high vantage point and in the glimmer of the breaking day, a great artillery barrage surely surpasses in dynamic splendour any other manifestation of collective human effort.[42]
>
> Lieutenant General Sir John Monash, Headquarters, Australian Corps

As the infantry attacked, helped by the cover of fog, they were simply unstoppable.

> Then we were over the tape and away; me with my Lewis gun section. Off along with the tanks. But it was off in a fog as well, a fog that had been coming down all night, and was now so thick you could hardly see 20 yards in front of you. The tanks, unless one came very near to you, you could only place by sound. It was an eerie start. In no time Germans, ghost like in the mists, were showing up all over the place, most with their hands up above their heads in surrender. But here and there a machine gun still firing at random at us.[43]
>
> Corporal William Kerr, 5th (Western Cavalry) Battalion, 1st Canadian Division

Where possible the infantry kept close up to the tanks and the creeping barrage, seeking to catch the Germans by surprise.

> We knew that we had to follow our tanks so kept along after them. Every now and then 'Fritzes' would come running back with their hands up, well 'souvenired', watches and pocket books all gone. One

Hun came suddenly in sight of a tank that I was near. He was so scared that he bounded right at me and would have knocked me down, but I poked the old bayonet at him and he steadied up. Their main idea seemed to be to get taken prisoner and to get out of the line at the earliest.[44]

Private Geoffrey Rose, 30th Battalion, AIF

On most of the front, the Allies surged through the German lines, only to find the innermost workings of the German war machine exposed before them.

We passed the wood into a corn field; by this time I was in the driving seat again, and as we kept meeting machine gun fire, we had to resort to the old zigzag again. We passed hundreds of Germans with their hands up, these we left for the Canadians to deal with, and in the late afternoon we reached our objective on the top of the ridge. The infantry came up and started to dig in, and at last we were able to open the doors and get out, only to fall in a heap on the ground on top of each other, out to the world. Gradually we came round and out came the bottle of rum, and we came to. We could not believe our eyes – in the valley below we could see the enemy piling stuff on to trucks on a train, men pulling out guns to get them away, and they were hauling in the observation balloons and trying to put them on their trucks. Utter chaos.[45]

Private Charles Rowland, 14th Battalion, Tank Corps

Despite the faltering of the British III Corps on the left flank, where a difficult ground configuration hindered progress, the Canadian and Australian Corps both had stunning successes, advancing up to eight miles across a 10-mile-wide frontage. The Germans suffered 27,700 casualties, of which 15,000 were prisoners-of-war. They also lost over 400 guns and large quantities of mortars and machine guns. It was a disaster that Ludendorff could not deny: 'August 8 was the black day of the German Army in the history of this war.'[46] All this for the loss of 9,000 British casualties and commensurate French losses. With its 'All Arms Battle', the British tactical rollercoaster had reached a peak to which the Germans had no counter: the complex, inter-twined war of competing tactical developments was over at last.

Over the next few days, the British and French continued to move forward, although the law of diminishing returns stalked their steps. The artillery were dislocated, communications were soon disrupted result-ing in confusion in command and control, the infantry were becoming increasingly tired, the mechanically unreliable tanks broke down and the supply lines were stretched. Meanwhile, the Germans moved their reserves forward, stiffening the line and occupying the old trench lines that littered the whole Somme area. As resistance increased, it was beoming appar-ent that without efficient artillery and tank support British losses would rise astronomically. Rawlinson and his corps commanders realised that their attack was running out of momentum. But it was not their decision to suspend operations. That lay higher up the chain of command. Haig examined their case and decided his subordinates were right. But he still had to deal with Foch, who was determined to press on. A classic confron-tation ensued in which Foch tried to order the implacable Haig to bend to his will. He soon found that, Supreme Commander or not, he did not have the right to control British tactical deployments.

> Foch pressed me to attack the positions held by the enemy on the front Chaulnes–Roye. I declined to do so because they could only be taken after heavy casualties in men and tanks. I had ordered the First French and Fourth (British) Armies to postpone their attacks, but to keep up pressure on that front so as to make the enemy expect an attack on this front, while I transferred my reserves to Third Army. Foch now wanted to know what orders I had issued for attack: when I proposed to attack? Where? And with what troops? I think he really wanted a written statement to this effect from me for his records! I told Foch of my instructions to Byng and Horne; and that Rawlinson would also co-operate with his left between the Somme and the Ancre when Third Army had advanced and withdrawn some of the pressure which was still strong in that sector. I spoke to Foch quite straightly, and let him understand that I was responsible for the handling of the British forces. Foch's attitude at once changed and he said all he wanted was early information of my intentions, so that he might co-ordinate the operations of the other armies, and that he thought I was quite correct in my decision not to attack the enemy in his prepared position.[47]
>
> Field Marshal Sir Douglas Haig, General Headquarters, BEF

The result was that Haig ordered his Fourth Army to rest and recover its strength, while the neighbouring Third Army took over the attack. Thus the Battle of Amiens ended after just three days on 11 August 1918. A total advance of twelve miles had been achieved, but what really mattered was the severe body blow it had inflicted on the German Army. Although the Allies had lost some 46,000 casualties, estimates of the Germans losses range from 48,000 to 75,000, of which nearly 30,000 were prisoners of war. After the losses already suffered in the 1918 offensives the Germans could not sustain this level of sacrifice. Ludendorff could see the writing on the wall.

> Our war machine was no longer efficient. Our fighting power had suffered, even though the great majority of divisions still fought heroically. August 8 put the decline of that fighting power beyond all doubt, and in such a situation, as regards reserves, I had no hope of finding a strategic expedient whereby to turn the situation to our advantage. On the contrary, I became convinced that we were now without that safe foundation for the plans of General Headquarters, on which I had hitherto been able to build, at least so far as is possible in war. Leadership now assumed, as I then stated, the character of an irresponsible game of chance, a thing I have always considered fatal. The fate of the German people was to me too high a stake. The war must be ended.[48]
>
> Quartermaster General Erich Ludendorff, German Headquarters

Yet even so there was much hard fighting to go. The German Army was still a deadly enemy and open warfare, desired for so long, was a cruel mistress, as the French had discovered in 1914. This was the start of a 3-month campaign that was one of the hardest ever fought by the British Army, the only compensation lying in the fact that they were winning. The fighting ranged from full-on assaults on layered defensive positions to bloody ambushes and the resulting frantic skirmishes. There are few more stressful military operations than an advance to contact through unknown country against a concealed enemy. The war was in its last stages but the casualty lists were mushrooming fast. The war had never seemed more painful.

The Battle of Albert began on 21 August as the thirteen divisions of General Sir Julian Byng's Third Army hammered forward between the Ancre and Scarpe Rivers north of the Somme. Meanwhile, the French

Tenth Army had launched an attack south of the Fourth Army, starting on 20 August. Considerable progress was made as the German line began to fragment. Haig urged his generals to seize the moment.

> To turn the present situation to account, the most resolute offensive is everywhere desirable. Risks, which a month ago would have been criminal to incur, ought now to be incurred as a duty. It is no longer necessary to advance in regular lines and step by step. On the contrary, each division should be given a distant objective which must be reached independently of its neighbour, and even if one's flank is thereby exposed for the time being. Reinforcements must be directed on the points where our troops are gaining ground, not where they are checked. A vigorous offensive against the sectors where the enemy is weak will cause hostile strongpoints to fall, and in due course our whole army will be able to continue its advance. The situation is most favourable; let each one of us act energetically and without hesitation push forward to our objective.[49]
>
> Field Marshal Sir Douglas Haig, General Headquarters, BEF

For the rest of August the British and French ground their way forwards as the Germans, struggling to prevent them, threw in more reserves. Soon it was the turn of the First Army of General Sir Henry Horne, which attacked in the Arras sector on 26 August 1918, pushing the Germans back towards Monchy le Preux just as on 9 April 1917.

In the Somme area the German retreat became more general and Monash was determined to use the momentum gained for his Australian Corps to jump the Somme River, behind which the Germans were trying to stabilise their front. His men were exhausted, their numbers dwindling, as every day, every action took its toll. Soon brigades had shrunk to the size of not much more than a battalion. But they had the Germans on the run. The key battle took place at Mont St Quentin, a mile to the north of Peronne. The Australians crossed the river and tore into the German positions, taking the hill on 31 August, only to be ejected by a German counter-attack. Next day there was no mistake as the Australians swept over to a glorious victory which at a stroke broke the integrity of the German line along the Somme. But the Germans were now being thrown back everywhere.

On 2 September, the Canadian Corps attacked the Drocourt–Quéant

Switch Line, an extension of the Hindenburg Line. They too met with success as the patchy German resistance was overwhelmed.

> Our party of about twelve men took off under artillery and machine gun fire from the enemy. After a while we came to the right of the village and got onto a sunken road. Over to the right was a bunch of Heinies beating it from an old windmill. We potted at them with rifles and machine guns and caused some casualties. Advancing along the sunken road, we completely surprised and outflanked two machine gun posts simply swarming with men. After we fired a few shots we took the whole bunch of prisoners, about 100–150 of them. Proceeding up the sunken road to help with the prisoners, I happened to look over to my left. I saw there another thickly manned machine gun post of Heinies shooting over to the left from an embankment. I dropped down on the bank of this sunken road and fired at the man operating the machine gun. He fell over backwards and the machine gun with him. Some more of the boys arrived and joined in the firing. We got many others, but soon the remainder put up their hands to surrender.[50]
>
> Private Morley Timberlake, 46th (South Saskatchewan) Battalion, CEF

In the end the Germans were forced all the way back to the Canal du Nord and Hindenburg Line. In Flanders they were also forced to abandon their gains in the Lys area in order to shorten the line and conserve troops.

The fighting included a significant event: the launch, on 12 September, of the first fully fledged offensive by the Americans, on the St Mihiel Salient. It was the supreme learning experience for the inexperienced Americans, who had to master all the myriad disciplines of an offensive under the stressful conditions of modern warfare. The barrage was ferocious, although here the Americans had wisely leaned on French artillery expertise and support. There was a sense of exhilaration in the air.

> Leaping out of bed I put my head outside the tent. We had received orders to be over the lines at daybreak in large formations. It was an exciting moment in my life as I realized that the great American attack upon which so many hopes had been fastened was actually on. I suppose every American in the world wanted to be in that great attack. The very sound of the guns thrilled one and filled one with excitement. The good reputation of America seemed bound up in the outcome of that attack.[51]
>
> Captain Edward Rickenbacker, 94th Aero Squadron, AEF

At 05.00 the troops went over the top. Rickenbacker watched from the air.

> We found the Germans in full cry to the rear. One especially attractive target presented itself to us as we flew along this road. A whole battery of Bosche 3-inch guns was coming towards us on the double. They covered fully half a mile of the roadway. Dipping down at the head of the column I sprinkled a few bullets over the leading teams. Horses fell right and left. One driver leaped from his seat and started running for the ditch. Halfway across the road he threw up his arms and rolled over, upon his face. He had stepped full in front of my stream of machine-gun bullets! All down the line we continued our fire – now tilting our aeroplanes down for a short burst, then zooming back up for a little altitude in which to repeat the performance. The whole column was thrown into the wildest confusion. Horses plunged and broke away. Some were killed and fell in their tracks. Most of the drivers and gunners had taken to the trees before we reached them.[52]
>
> Captain Edward Rickenbacker, 94th Aero Squadron, AEF

The advance was a relatively easy triumph for the AEF as the Germans had been preparing in any event to evacuate the salient. But the Americans had achieved their objectives and gained experience that would stand them in good stead for greater trials.

Haig was determined to defeat the Germans in 1918. He had an all too painful familiarity with their ability to regenerate their forces and stabilise their defensive positions if given half a chance. Faced by the imposing fortifications of the Hindenburg Line he had the choice of attacking that autumn or suspending operations and attempting the same task in the spring of 1919. Fortunately, in Foch Haig had a superior who, after their initial confrontation, shared the same overall vision of the war; a man equally determined not to allow the Germans breathing space. Foch brilliantly co-ordinated the attacks up and down the Western Front: on the first day the French and Americans would strike hard in the Meuse–Argonne area, the very next day the British would launch their First and Third Armies at the Hindenburg Line attacking towards Cambrai. The day after the French, the Belgians and the British Second Army would attack in Flanders. Finally on the fourth day, a fourth offensive as the British Fourth Army would attack the Hindenburg Line in the Somme region. Blessed with a plentiful supply of guns and ammunition, Foch could attack anywhere he liked. Instead of persisting where the Germans were focussing their efforts and amassing reserves, he could switch away to where they were not so well prepared. In doing so Foch got within the German 'command loop' as Ludendorff was left floundering, always reacting to the last attack and never able to take control of a constantly fluctuating situation. This was an early form of manoeuvrist warfare in all but name – attempting to disrupt the German Army by applying constant pressure at the times and places where they were least able to respond.

This stupendous series of attacks, mirroring in scale the huge Battle of the Frontiers clashes of 1914, commenced at 05.30 on 26 September. The French Fourth Army and the American First Army attacked along a huge 44-mile front stretching between the Meuse and Reims. The French had done it all before. But the Americans were still raw and this time they found the Germans had no intention of retreating.

> Only five minutes more for a great many of the boys to live. Four minutes, three minutes, two, then one. 'Ready? Let's go!' The instant we started climbing out of the trench the artillery cut loose on the Germans. At the same instant the Germans cut loose with artillery and machine guns. Immediately men began to drop. Cries and moans, yells and screams rent the air, and could be heard even above the roaring of cannon and bursting shells of the enemy. Shells were bursting overhead and underfoot. The very air was exploding in our faces. The ground was moving, rolling under our feet. Enemy machine gun bullets were tearing through our soldiers like so much hail and taking a great toll. It was a roaring furnace, all fire, smoke, hot lead and shrapnel in which it seemed we were all trapped and must perish, but some of us went on and on. A large swamp lay between our lines and the Germans. In order to get us across this our engineers had built some walks under cover of the night. We soon found that crossing on these was much too slow and as we were losing troops heavily, Captain McCormack, our company commander, took the lead and plunged into the swamp. We all followed, holding our rifles over our heads. Breaking through the scum and water up to our armpits, we crossed the swamp. On the other side, the ground was marshy and would not hold our weight. Unless we could step on a bunch of water grass, we were continually pulling each other out of the mire. This condition of the ground probably saved a lot of men from getting hit by shrapnel. As the shells lit here, although their detonation was instantaneous, they would bury in the mud and

then explode. We got through the marsh, then came the German wire entanglement. We walked on top of the wires instead of trying to wade through it, but a lot of us broke through several times and got entangled. It was tough going. Soldiers everywhere were tearing their clothes in frantic efforts to extricate themselves and get to the trench and at the Germans.[53]

Private Charles Dermody, 132nd Infantry Regiment, AEF

The 'Doughboys', as they were nicknamed, fought well and managed to advance some seven miles before they bcame bogged down in the tangle of woods, ridges and valleys that make the Argonne Forest area ideal for defence. The fighting was an intensive, brutal experience for them against a German Army that may have been on its last legs but was still dangerous when cornered. All the same, the Americans endured, pushing on from ridge to ridge, grinding their way through the Argonne, their very presence and ever-growing strength a constant reminder to the Germans that there could be no escape from defeat. The fighting would continue with only short lulls throughout October and into November 1918.

We had reckoned without a German rear guard action. And no doubt they had heard us telling our men to get ready. They were soldiers who had trained 4 years at the front. They had left their lines checkerboarded with machine guns, had left their men in the rear to fight to the death, and had slowly moved out the heavy masses of troops. Most of us who were young American officers knew little of actual warfare – we had the daring but not the training of the old officer of the front. The Germans simply waited, and then laid a barrage of steel and fire. And the machine gunners poured it on us. Our company numbered two hundred men. Within a few minutes about half of them were either dead or wounded. Felbel was killed outright, and I did not even see his body. A runner came to me and told me he had been killed. I took command of the company. There was not a single sergeant. We literally lost each other. There were no bugles, no flags, no drums and, as far as we knew, no heroes. The great noise was like great stillness, everything seemed blotted out. We hardly knew where the Germans were. We were simply in a big black spot with streaks of screaming red and yellow, with roaring giants in the sky tearing and whirling and roaring. There is a great swishing scream, a smash-bang, and it seems to tear everything loose from you. The intensity of it simply enters your heart and brain and tears every nerve to pieces. Although so many men had been killed, there was nothing to do but keep on going. And in front were dense growths of trees and barbed wire to keep us from going farther.[54]

Lieutenant Maury Maverick, 28th Infantry Regiment, AEF

Despite it all he kept going, he managed to clamber through a gap in the wire, then:

A shell burst above my head. It tore out a piece of my shoulderblade and collarbone and knocked me down. It was a terrific blow, but I was not unconscious. I think it was the bursting of the shell, the air concussion, which knocked me down, and not the shell itself. It was not five seconds, it seemed, before a Medical Corps man was dressing my wounds. He cut my coat away from the wound and wrapped up my shoulder in such a way that it would not bleed too much. As he lifted me from the ground, I looked at my four runners, and I saw that the two in the middle had been cut down to a pile of horrid red guts and blood and meat, while the two men on the outside had been cut up somewhat less badly, but no less fatally. It reminded me of nothing I had ever seen before, except a Christmas hog butchering back on the Texas farm.[55]

Lieutenant Maury Maverick, 28th Infantry Regiment, AEF

Frequently, the Americans found that their lack of experience and poor tactical grasp cost them dearly, but they kept on going. Like the French in 1914 and the British in 1916, they were learning the hard way. And no one could doubt their courage. At times their losses were excruciating. In all the Americans would suffer some 117,000 casualties, the French fighting alongside them a further 70,000, while estimates of German losses range from 90,000 to 120,000.

Meanwhile, the second of the great Allied attacks was launched on 27 September by the British First and Third Armies. Here the greatest obstacle to progress lay in the partially constructed Canal du Nord. Although for the most part empty of water, it still presented a major obstacle in its own right and behind it lay three German defence systems stretching back some five miles. Lieutenant General Sir Arthur Currie tailored his artillery plans to the problem. A long slow barrage of the barbed wire had begun on 18 September, but there was no crescendo leading up to the assault, allowing some surprise to be achieved when the troops went over the top at

05.20 with a crushing creeping barrage. The Canadians captured all their objectives and, indeed, all along the front of the First and Third Armies they threw back the Germans.

Another day, another huge offensive as, on 28 September, Plumer's Second Army, accompanied by the French and the Belgians, sought finally to eradicate the Ypres Salient from the map. They were walking in the footsteps, indeed, treading over the graves of hundreds of thousands of their predecessors. But this time the German artillery were rendered silent by their counter-battery fire, the dreaded pillboxes blasted from the earth. The Allied forces' flexible offensive tactics were tailored to every situation, smoothly applying the required mix of weapons – artillery, gas shells, tanks, mortars, rifle grenades – to overcome any hold-ups. In just one day they swept across the whole of the Ypres battlefields to breast the Passchendaele Ridge.

Last but not least was the attack on the Hindenburg Line by Rawlinson's Fourth Army on 29 September. The American II Corps, placed for the occasion under the command of Monash, would attack where the St Quentin Canal ran underground between Bellicourt and Vendhuile. The Australian Corps would be ready to exploit any success. Most startling of all was the attempt by the 46th Division of the British IX Corps to leap across the still waters of the St Quentin Canal.

> An enormous barrage opened. It was tremendous. Everything possible was rained on the rear of the canal to prevent their reserves being brought up. The other side knew something was on by the intensity of our barrage, so, up went their flares, green and gold, and over came the counter-barrage. The racket was awe-inspiring, it was impossible to hear, even if orders were given. Over we went, slipping and sliding down the canal bank to the cold water below. The opposite bank was pitted with machine gun nests, in tunnels dug into the 30 feet high sloping bank. How any of us even reached the water beats me, but a surprising number did. The water was up to our armpits, and holding that gun above my head was bad enough without being machine gunned as well. Clawing our way on to the bank we were underneath some of the machine guns making it more difficult to hit us, so my team and many others flung Mills grenades into the various tunnels nearest to us, while clinging for dear life to any scrap of projection on the bank. After many years I still don't know how we got away with it.[56]
>
> Corporal George Parker, 1/8th Sherwood Foresters

But in the end they did it, and in the exploitation phase captured 4,200 prisoners, 70 guns and more than 1,000 machine guns. An ordinary British division with no great pedigree had achieved a dramatic feat of arms that would surely have been impossible earlier in the war. The Fourth Army had completely ruptured the Hindenburg Line and the advance on the German borders had begun. The deep-flowing Rhine might threaten to hold them up but the Allies had won the war, the only question was whether they could finish it in 1918.

In October the individual German soldiers could not help but know that they were beaten. At the front it was obvious; not only that but when they went home on leave they could see the dissolution of their economy and the cracks opening up in German society. Years of privation and suffering culminated in severe political unrest. On 3 October a new Chancellor, Prince Max von Baden, was appointed, but his cosmetic liberal reforms and the appointment of a few token socialist ministers did nothing to appease the raging left while still provoking the establishment right. The combination of defeat at the front, political division at home and no hope for the future was a potent brew that unsettled the troops in the line. One illustration can be found in the legend of Corporal Alvin York during the Ardennes fighting on 8 October. This enterprising American NCO, apparently acting for the most part on his own, had managed to force the surrender of a large number of prisoners. The Americans naturally hailed his achievements; the Germans were far more sceptical. One German officer, Lieutenant Schleicher, pondered on how such a state of affairs had come to pass.

> Anyone who knows the morale of our troops as it existed in those days must admit that it was comparatively easy for the Americans to perform heroic acts. I must confirm that the fighting value of the men in the trenches had sunk very low. A few days prior to this incident, we were unable to carry out a counter-attack because our men simply would no longer go over the top. Racing through the enemy barrage at the head of my company, I found myself in the front line with only one sergeant and four privates; the remainder of my company was 'unaccounted for'. When I ran back to the rear, I saw my men, together with other companies and even their commanding officers, lying at the edge of the woods. To apply force would have been useless. Yet this state of affairs was quite comprehensible. 1) Our unit had been in the firing

line since September 26, on which date the Allied forces launched their offensive. The protracted mental strain, inclement weather and soggy ground – we had to spend the nights in the open, without any kind of protection – had generally lowered the morale. 2) Many of our men were hardly fit for active service. The replacements that were sent to the front were poor in build and health as well as in training. These men were facing American troops who, so far as I know, were relieved every other day. Moreover, the Americans were strong and healthy-looking individuals; most of them were volunteers and, as I observed on my way to the prison camp, had at their disposal all kinds of auxiliaries. Provision dumps were located along the roads where everybody could help himself; and motor trucks were on hand in enormous numbers. I can readily see that these well-equipped troops found it easy to take our demoralised men by surprise.[57]

Lieutenant Schleicher, 212th Reserve Infantry

The Allied armies, British, French, American and Belgian, moved forward along most of the Western Front. They were winning all right, but casualties were still high – this was a truly murderous form of warfare. It is a sobering statistic that of the 1.2 million men serving in the BEF between August and November 1918, some 360,000 become casualties. This was unsustainable: the BEF was being consumed. The French and Americans were also suffering. This was Armageddon.

But Germany was finally beaten; more than that, the Central Powers were finished. The bad news was pouring in from everywhere. The Turks were in disarray in Palestine and Mesopotamia, while the Bulgarians were falling back in Salonika. The German High Command knew it was beaten, but at the same time sought an exit strategy looking to resume the battle in 1919.

The Armistice is militarily necessary to us. We shall soon be at the end of our strength. If the peace does not follow, then we have at least disengaged ourselves from the enemy, rested ourselves and won time. Then we shall be more fit to fight than now, if that is necessary.[58]

Field Marshal Paul von Hindenburg, German Headquarters

Both Hindenburg and Ludendorff clung to the idea that they could defend the German homeland and that their enemies were themselves tottering, at the end of their endurance.

> If the war should approach our own territory, if the feeling that he was
> protecting home and all that word meant entered into the heart of
> each man at the front, who knew full well the meaning of such terms
> as 'theatre of war', 'battlefield' and 'lines of communication', if the
> war with all its destruction threatened German soil, then I felt our 70
> million Germans would stand like one man, determined and ready to
> sacrifice for their country all the mighty strength that still remained to
> them.[59]
>
> Quartermaster General Erich Ludendorff, German Headquarters

Unsurprisingly, the Allies refused to fall into this obvious trap. They were collectively determined to impose conditions to any Armistice negotiations that would cripple the German war machine for the foreseeable future.

The German military and political leaders twisted and turned, with more than an eye on posterity, trying to avoid being held personally responsible for defeat. And as they did so, the war went on. But there was no chance of a last-minute redemption for Germany, its effort to overcome the existing European order was doomed to failure. By this time Ludendorff was suffering the after-effects of a partial mental breakdown and seemed unable to maintain a consistent approach from one day to the next. Finally he offered his resignation after a dispute with the Kaiser on 26 October. He was replaced as Hindenburg's Chief of Staff by General Wilhelm Groener, who was well aware that the game was up for Germany. With the capitulation of Bulgaria on 30 September, Turkey on 30 October, and the Austro-Hungarian acceptance of an armistice on the Italian Front on 3 November, Germany was left fighting alone and without hope.

The final Allied offensives began on 4 November. The British Fourth, Third and First Armies attacked on a wide front. The attacks were broadly successful, but blemished as ever by painful casualties. Among those killed on that miserable freezing day was a man who would have a long-lasting impact – certainly on the British understanding of the Great War. Lieutenant Wilfred Owen of the 2nd Manchester Regiment was a promising poet who had served on the Western Front in 1917 until he was diagnosed with shellshock and sent back to Britain to recuperate. Here he encountered the far better known writer Siegfried Sassoon, at the Craiglockhart War Hospital in Edinburgh. Under Sassoon's tutelage, Owen's poetry blossomed,

although it was not published until after his death. His war poems, such as
'*Dulce et Decorum Est*', 'Strange Meeting' and 'Anthem for Doomed Youth',
have come to epitomise the popular view of the futility and pity of war.
Tragically, he was killed as he led his men across the Sambre Canal under
heavy fire. He is buried at the Ors Communal Cemetery.

November was nearly always a miserable, desperate time for fighting,
but with the war teetering to its long-awaited close, it was a particular
trial in 1918. Wet weather hampered progress, but the Germans were still
trying their best to hold back their pursuers, blowing up bridges, felling
trees and blasting houses to block the roads. Booby traps and delayed-
action mines added to the delays inflicted on the advance. As the British
soldiers entered many of the towns and villages they encountered French
civilians now finally freed from years of German occupation.

> As we rode in people began to run out of their houses, regardless of the
> shelling. By the time we reached the *Grande Place* we were surrounded
> by a seething crowd of people simply delirious with joy. I had a little
> chocolate for the children, but it did not go very far. Luneau was
> dragged off his horse and smothered with kisses. I was almost dragged
> off but I managed to stick on. They kissed my boots and lifted up their
> babies to be kissed, all laughing, sobbing and shouting, '*Vive la France!
> Vive l'Angleterre!*' They fished out French flags from somewhere and
> hung them out of the window. They begged for French newspapers and
> any news we could give them. And all the time the Bosche was shelling
> the place and nobody cared a damn! As we dismounted at the house of
> the Mayor, a shell hit it and a splinter passed between Luneau and me –
> rotten luck if I get 'done in' with the end in view.[60]
>
> Major Thomas Westmacott, Headquarters, 24th Division

The same thought was at the back of every soldier's mind. Yet the advance
continued unabated. For the British there was a peculiar irony in the site
chosen by the German Seventeenth Army for a rearguard stand on 10
November: the Mons area where for the BEF it had all begun, thousands of
lifetimes ago. By 04.30 on 11 November the Canadians had cleared away
the last of the Germans and Mons was returned to British control. They
were truly back where they started.

THE SURRENDER NEGOTIATIONS were based on the framework of President Woodrow Wilson's Fourteen Points, which he had first put forward on 8 January 1918. These attempted to set out a vision as to how the Great Powers could co-exist after the war. Although in some ways a fairly naive document, it at least provided a starting point for the negotiations. Under its provisions Germany was invited to surrender all its gains in the east, allowing for the creation of a strong independent Polish state. In the west, Belgium was to be evacuated and Alsace-Lorraine returned to France. The Allied political leaders were united in their desire to make sure that the Germans were not only down, but stayed down for the foreseeable future. Hence crippling financial reparations were demanded to defray the exorbitant cost of the war damage suffered by the Allies. A minor hiccup arose over the American demand in the Fourteen Points for complete freedom of the seas, which worried the British as it would prohibit their habitual use of blockades as a legitimate weapon of war. This was, however, brushed under the carpet; no one wanted any lengthy hold-ups over this kind of complication. On 4 November, the Allied Supreme War Council offered Germany peace on the basis of the Fourteen Points, but also announced that it would be Foch who would negotiate the terms for an Armistice before a peace conference was convened.

In Germany itself there was a tremendous state of political flux. The High Seas Fleet was in open mutiny and there were crowds demonstrating on the streets of Berlin. Prince Max von Baden, the recently appointed Chancellor, realised the game was up and on 8 November he despatched a joint military and civilian negotiating team led by a relatively moderate politician, Matthias Erzberger, charged with the thankless task of sorting out the terms for an Armistice with the forbidding figure of Foch. At the same time he advised the Kaiser to resign in order to avoid the onrushing spectre of civil war. The Kaiser refused and the Prince himself resigned on 9 November, to be replaced as Chancellor by the socialist parliamentary leader, Friedrich Ebert. Meanwhile, at the Army Headquarters at Spa in Belgium the Kaiser was being given a stern lesson in reality by General Wilhelm Groener, who suggested that Wilhelm II go to the front and die at the head of his armies, an invitation politely declined by the Kaiser, who instead chose ignominious exile in the Netherlands, crossing the border on 10 November. His more formal abdication would occur on 28 November, but to all intents and purposes Germany was now a republic.

Foch, aided by Haig, Pétain and Pershing, had worked out exactly what was wanted from his negotiations with the German representatives: absolutely no chance that Germany would resume the war after a short armistice. The German armies would have just fourteen days to withdraw to Germany, and they would have to surrender 5,000 guns, 30,000 machine guns, 3,000 trench mortars and 2,000 aircraft. The German logistics system would also be effectively crippled by the surrender of 5,000 locomotives, 150,000 railway coaches and 5,000 lorries. At sea they had to give up 6 dreadnoughts, 160 U-boats and 8 light cruisers; while the rest of the High Seas Fleet would be interned in Allied waters – and even then the Royal Navy blockade would be maintained until the formal peace treaty was signed. Lastly, Allied armies would occupy the west bank of the Rhine, with fortified Allied bridgeheads at Mainz, Coblenz and Cologne standing out in an enforced demilitarised zone on the eastern bank. The German delegation finally met Foch in the inauspicious surroundings of a railway carriage in Compiègne Forest, where he gave them no real choice but to sign, which they duly did at 05.15 on the morning of 11 November, allowing just a few hours before the Armistice was promulgated to the world commencing at the eleventh hour of the eleventh day of the eleventh month.

Men carried on dying right up to the very end, but finally the rumble of the guns stopped at 11.00 on 11 November. The soldiers reacted in different ways. Maybe a few career soldiers or adventurers were disappointed, but most were delighted.

> Every man had a grin from ear to ear on his face. Nobody yelled or showed uncontained enthusiasm – everybody just grinned and I think the cause was that the men couldn't find words to express themselves. I think of the man who every day has his life in danger and who dreams of home more than heaven itself – suddenly finds that the danger is past and that his return is practically assumed – that he has won after personally risking his life – no wonder they couldn't say much – they simply grinned.[61]
>
> Captain Cecil Gray Frost, L Battery, 2nd Machine Gun Battalion, Canadian Machine Gun Corps, CEF

Many reflected on the blessed relief from the tensions and unremitting horrors of the fighting. The draining hopelessness of the war was not always apparent until it was suddenly lifted. Suddenly they were free.

'Dickie,' said Captain Brown, 'The bloody war's over! It's over!' And it was. No more slaughter, no more maiming, no more mud and blood, no more killing and disembowelling of horses and mules. No more of those hopeless dawns, with the rain chilling the spirits, no more crouching in inadequate dugouts scooped out of trench walls, no more dodging snipers' bullets, no more of that terrible shell fire. No more shovelling up of bits of men's bodies and dumping them into sandbags, no more cries of, 'Stretcher-bearers!' No more of those beastly gas masks and the odious smell of pear drops which was deadly to the lungs. And no more writing of those dreadfully difficult letters to the next-of-kin of the dead.[62]

Lieutenant Richard Dixon, 251st Battery, 53rd Brigade, Royal Artillery

The French soldiers had good reason to rejoice, but at the same time many good comrades to mourn. The French Army had fought with incredible determination, always – somehow – just about managing to keep going in the face of adversity.

Damn! A wave of joy swept over us. I don't know if I'd tears in my eyes. Like the others, I must have shouted, '*Vive la France!*' For a moment we were left breathless with happiness. Great sorrow is silent; so too is great joy. Then the shock passed; we recovered our power of speech and with it the reflex common to all Frenchmen, 'We'll have to drink a toast to that!' Yes, but with what? There was no red wine in this poor little place, just a bottle of lousy sparkling wine Bebert dug up in a shop where the bastard made us pay 15 francs. We split it sixteen ways, hardly enough to wet your whistle![63]

Private Ernest Brec, 77th Infantry Regiment

The Armistice was a glorious relief for the Germans, too, but even as they celebrated, they would have to face the bitter consequences of defeat.

I read the fateful sheet with bated breath and growing amazement. What were the terms? Evacuation of the left bank of the Rhine as well as the right to an extent of forty kilometres … 150,000 railroad cars … 10,000 automobiles … 5,000 heavy guns … the blockade to remain in effect … the navy to be surrendered! It can't be. This is ridiculous. It means a fight to the end. What a sudden change from the joy we had felt that morning! 'This is what you get for your God-damned brotherhood!' I shouted to the suddenly silent spectators. It was too

much for me to bear and I hurried off to grieve in a lonely corner. The
last of the rockets exploded; one siren after the other turned silent; but
within me the storm still raged as I was convulsed to the very core of
my soul by a deep and terrible anguish. It is sheer madness to subject
an industrious and undefeated nation such as ours to these shameful
terms.[64]

Seaman Richard Stumpf, SMS *Lothringen*

There was scant sympathy from the victorious Allies. During the Armistice
negotiations the humiliated Erzberger had read out a statement to Foch
protesting at the stringent terms demanded: 'A people of 70 million men
are suffering, but they are not dead.' In his reply Foch encapsulated the
Allied reaction to German anguish: '*Très bien!*' The war was over, but the
hatred would linger on.

19

A WORLD WITHOUT WAR?

'Sooner or later, Germany will be starved and beaten. Austria will be resolved into its component parts. England has always won in the end.'[1]

Minister for Munitions Winston Churchill

THE GREAT WAR WAS A HUMAN TRAGEDY. Over the four years and three months of war around 2 million German soldiers died for the Central Powers, along with 1,100,000 Austro-Hungarians, 770,000 Turks and 87,500 Bulgarians; and for the Allies, around 2 million Russians, 1,400,000 French, 1,115,000 from the British Empire, 650,000 Italians, 250,000 Rumanians and 116,000 Americans. Taking all the countries across the globe it is estimated that just under 9,722,000 soldiers died through military action in the war. In addition, roughly 21 million were injured: some recovered relatively unaffected, but many were scarred or maimed for life. Nor do these figures really take into account the mentally traumatised, ranging from shell-shocked men who would never be sane again to the millions suffering from what we would now recognise as post-traumatic stress disorder. These figures also fail to consider the civilians killed by the war – approximately 950,000 who died from direct military action, but also a shocking 5,893,000 civilians who died from the impact of war-related famine and disease. These figures are sobering indeed.

Germany had been at the very heart of the Great War. There had been many causes, many tensions, but in the end the German ambitions could not be restrained within the *status quo* of Europe in 1914. An unfortunate combination of bellicosity and inept diplomacy had left Germany facing war on two fronts. The military establishment, as represented by the Chief of General Staff, Helmuth von Moltke (the Younger), had staked everything on the gamble that in 1914 the superbly trained and disciplined German Army could swiftly defeat France and then use her central communications to move her armies over to smash the Russians in the east. Whether this was ever really feasible is a moot point, but it was certainly a high risk, driven by the fear of the increasing military strength of both Russia and France. In September 1914, the Battle of the Marne demonstrated that France would not be quickly defeated – the gamble had failed. With that failure, as Moltke the Elder and Schlieffen would both have recognised, Germany was almost certainly doomed to defeat. The addition of the British and Americans to the list of Germany's enemies only made matters more certain. If there was a futility in the Great War it was not the actions of the Entente Allies in countering German aggression, but rather the futility of Germany trying to provoke, fight and win a war in circumstances that always militated against success. This is not to say that the Allies were blameless. France and Russia had their own motives for going to war and did little to sidestep it, while all three members of the Triple Entente were aggressive imperialist colonial powers seeking to consolidate everything they held and make further gains wherever possible.

The French Army had been of paramount importance to the Allies, particularly in the first two years of the war. They had stood up to the brunt of the German assault in 1914, paying a phenomenal price in blood that should never be forgotten. In 1915, time and time again, they had smashed against the German lines on the Western Front, testing them to the utmost and exploring the strange new language of modern warfare. In 1916 they withstood the ultimate German challenge at Verdun, a battle that truly plumbed the depths of human misery. The French fought on, playing a significant part in the Battle of the Somme, before the failure of the Nivelle offensive in April 1917 triggered the widespread mutinies. Yet even this debacle did not mark the end: they made a solid contribution during the Third Battle of Ypres later in 1917 and helped prop up the British line during the German Spring offensives of 1918. Then they rebuffed the final German summer assaults before launching the first of the counter-attacks that ultimately would win the war. In 1918 they may not have taken the foremost lead, but were fighting hard, still crucial to Allied success – and after all in Foch they provided the Supreme Commander. Without a knowledge of what the French were doing – and suffering – the British role and actions are quite simply incomprehensible. The two armies were linked by a common front, a common enemy and had the same terrible challenges to be overcome. This was coalition warfare.

The Russian role is also sometime downplayed, masked by their ultimate defeat and the sullen acrimony of the post-war years. But from 1914 to 1917 the Russians had fought hard, rebounding time and time again from shocking defeats, along the way bludgeoning the Austro-Hungarians almost to the point of defeat and forcing the Germans to deploy ever more troops to the Eastern Front. The resilience of the Russians made the two front war an unshakeable reality for the Germans. The ultimate Russian collapse and defeat was a result of the inherent contradictions of the Russian state, but it came too late for the Germans to really capitalise on the opportunity.

The Italians had taken a gamble and joined the war with an eye to the possible territorial gains that victory would bring. Their motives may have been questionable, but they fought hard and, in the end, completed the demolition of the Austrians begun by Russia.

The Americans arrived late in the war but had an enormous impact. It left the Germans with little or no realistic hopes of victory, forcing the last gamble of the Spring offensives. Like the British the Americans were totally unprepared for a continental war and were unconscionably slow in deploying troops in significant numbers. But, by the summer of 1918, they were in situ, slowly learning the brutal art of modern war. After initial problems they proved adept pupils and the AEF would have been the dominant force had the war stretched into 1919.

We are left with the British role which was surely crucial: indeed Britain's very involvement in the war had been a sickening blow to German hopes of victory. At a stroke, the oceans of the globe became an Allied domain. For the first two years of the war the British military involvement on land was at largely symbolic, before the gradual mobilisation of the Empire brought millions of troops to the battlefield. By 1918 the BEF had attained a more pivotal role: still large enough to have a real impact, but also polished in the deadly tactics of the 'All Arms Battle' and driven on to act as the spear point of the Allied armies on the Western Front. Their time had come, but the victory nevertheless was a collective one, based on the struggle and sacrifice of all the Allies during more than four years of unremitting war.

It is has often been contended that Germany was not really defeated in the Great War, but that her heroic armed services were somehow stabbed in the back by revolutionary factors or other mysterious forces. This is utter nonsense. Rarely has a nation been so comprehensively defeated in the field as Germany was in 1918. Her armies were reeling back and were totally unable to defend the German frontier. Crossing the Rhine might have been a problem for the Allies, but their bombardment techniques coupled with the mass use of new and ever more deadly gases would have been the decisive factors, not appeals to national pride. Once across there would have been no way of holding them. And every month would have meant more American divisions arriving on the Western Front. At sea the Germans had been bottled up, their submarines overwhelmed by the convoy system and the High Seas Fleet had mutinied. In the air the German pilots were fighting bravely, but were severely outnumbered and fast running out of aviation fuel. Her allies, Austria-Hungary, Turkey and Bulgaria, had all been brought to their knees. There was no hope any-where for Germany: this was a total defeat writ large.

After the Armistice the German state fell apart. Nominally a republic, its Army had almost ceased to exist, the units fragmenting once they had crossed the German border as the men simply went home. This left a dangerous power vacuum. The political factions of the left soon fragmented and when the Communists took to the streets during the Spartacist Uprising of January 1919, they were countered with devastating brutality by unofficial Freikorps made up of ex-servicemen, bound together by their military past and an unswerving adherence to right-wing politics. Germany was in a desperate state, still ravaged by hunger, plagued by revolution, threatened by armed gangs and suffering the demoralising after-effects of the loss of some 2 million young men killed during the war. To survive, the fledgling government headed by Friedrich Ebert had had to compromise itself to gain the support of the Freikorps and the remnants of the regular Army. Against this background the economy, strained beyond reason by the war, continued to freefall, with most of the stringent provisions of the Allied blockade still in place. When the protracted Paris peace negotiations finally came to the crunch decisions, the Germans realised that they would be shown no leniency by the Allies intent on exacting their pound of flesh. The war reparations, the loss of Polish territory and Alsace-Lorraine, the humiliating occupation forces – all would be enforced when the Treaty of Versailles was finally signed on 28 June 1919. By the time the German Weimar Republic was formally founded in August 1919, it was already in dire trouble. Racked by raging inflation and economic turmoil, the Weimar Republic would spend the 1920s torn apart by competing visions of left and right-wing ideologues, all peddling their different visions of the future designed to have mass appeal. In the end it would be the right that won, with the advent of Hitler and the Nazi Party. And so the wheel of history turned again.

The Russians, too, had been set on a new and challenging course by the Great War. The tyranny of the Tsars had been usurped by the Bolsheviks and the advent of the Communist state. After the war several of the Allies intervened to assist the counter-revolutionary forces. The Soviets felt themselves attacked from all sides and became afflicted by a defensive and harshly repressive outlook which corrupted any lingering hopes of a more democratic future for the Russian people. The damage done would endure for the best part of the twentieth century. With Soviet Russia separated on ideological grounds from Britain and France, the Great War Allies were unable to act in collaboration to thwart the re-emergence of Germany as a great European power under the Nazi regime in the 1930s – a failure that would have terrible consequences.

The combined effect of the Treaties of Saint-Germain (10 September 1919), Neuilly (27 November 1919) and Trianon (4 June 1920) was the dissolution of the Austro-Hungarian Empire. However, this and the partial loss of territory by the Soviet Union did not resolve the complex nationalistic tensions festering in Eastern Europe and the Balkans. The emerging countries, such as Poland, Finland, Estonia, Latvia, Lithuania, Czechoslovakia, Yugoslavia; the defeated countries, such as Austria, Hungary and Bulgaria; and the newly triumphant Italy, Rumania and Greece – all found themselves in a state of flux surrounded by powerful enemies and often still containing aggrieved nationalistic minorities within their borders. The Balkans certainly remained a powder keg, but now Eastern Europe became equally unstable. The Bosnian Serb Gavrilo Princip, who fired the fatal first shots at Archduke Ferdinand, never lived to see this brave new world he had helped trigger. Too young to be executed, he was sentenced to twenty years in prison, where he contracted tuberculosis and died on 28 April 1918.

The prostrate remnants of the Ottoman Empire witnessed a feeding frenzy from the colonial empires. During the war the secret Sykes–Picot Agreement had been signed on 16 May 1916 between Britain, France and Russia, which envisioned dividing the spoils three ways: the British would get protectorates or control of parts of Palestine, Jordan and southern Iraq (Mesopotamia); the French would get Lebanon, Syria, south-east Turkey and northern Iraq; while Russia was promised – at last – Constantinople and control of the Bosphorus and the Dardanelles Straits, in addition to parts of western Armenia. It was a treaty that defined the ambitious war aims of the three powers, but it also oversimplified the political agreements being made with various other parties in the Middle East. In particular promises had been made to establish both an Arab state and a Zionist independent Jewish state in Palestine. The rise of the Soviets had resulted in the unilateral publication of the full clauses of the treaty in November 1917, which caused a substantial amount of suspicion between the various Arab and Jewish factions. With the advent of the more high-toned American influence, there was some back-tracking with the Anglo-French Agreement on 7 November 1918 promising the establishment of indigenous governments in Syria and Mesopotamia. This would prove to have been mainly for public consumption. After the war the web of conflicting agreements led to almost everyone being disappointed and many bitter – and vengeful – accusations of bad faith. In essence, the British and French cynically continued to pursue their own long-term colonial aims, freed from competition from Russia. The result was the birth of many of the Middle East problems that exist to this very day, not just over the question of Jewish or Arab control of Palestine/Israel, but also over the arbitrary nature of the borders drawn for Iraq, Syria and Turkey. This is all part of the grim legacy of the Great War.

The British and French finished the war in a seemingly impregnable position, whereby they appeared to have it all. Their main enemy, Germany, had been stamped down, while the old enemy, Russia, was in a state of turbulent flux.

So the old pirate state, England, has again succeeded in letting Europe tear herself to pieces, and by throwing in her own power and applying the most brutal methods, she has secured a victory which accords with her material interests. The liberty and independence of the people of the European continent has now vanished and the bloom of their civilization is perhaps destroyed forever. But England's day of judgment will have its birth in this very success.[2]

Grand Admiral Alfred von Tirpitz

It is true that the British and the French – both nakedly imperialist powers, now set free to expand their horizons by the removal of both the German and Russian threats – made considerable colonial gains in Africa, the Pacific and the Middle East.

Yet the war would prove the high tide for both the old empires. At first nothing much seemed to have changed: both were still energetic in pushing forward their imperial and colonial claims, and were aggressive in their dealings with smaller powers who got in their way. Yet behind the facade the imperial structures were crumbling away. Ground down by their losses, and suffering dire economic problems in consequence of the unbelievable sums expended during the war, they were soon losing their grip. And an old enemy would rise again under a new guise. Survival had been the Soviets' initial priority, but later the promulgation of Communist revolution around the world would prove an entirely different threat to the stumbling colonial empires. The Second World War confirmed and accelerated this process of decline.

And what of the performance of the generals in the Great War? They had tried their best, many of them quickly making complex tactical changes, incorporating huge technical developments into their plans and all the while training, deploying and maintaining the morale of millions of men in this most dreadful of wars. Some generals failed utterly, their reputations shattered by their own innate conservatism, personal flaws or sheer stupidity. But these were in the minority; most generals coped as well as could be expected. After all, the exercise of command in battle was a terrifyingly complex business, with the origins of victory – and defeat – buried in a myriad of factors all of which had knock-on effects, which made it almost impossible accurately to attribute cause and effect. Haig put it neatly: 'To direct attention to any single phase of that stupendous and incessant struggle and seek in it the explanation of our success, to the exclusion or neglect of other phases possibly less striking in their immediate or obvious consequences, is in my opinion to risk the formation of unsound doctrines regarding the character and requirements of modern war.'[3]

War was not a straightforward progression towards success for the British or anyone else. In truth, the Allies eventually won on the battlefields because of a massive superiority in numbers and resources. It cannot be denied that the performance of the German Army was incredible; indeed, its soldiers fought with a sustained heroism and a high degree of military skill right to the end. Some of the German generalship was also outstanding: ingenious and intuitive, aggressive and brutally simple, boldly heroic and sensibly cautious – there were many different ways to win a battle. Certainly Falkenhayn Ludendorff, Mackensen and many others all had sustained periods of brilliance in the field. In fact, all the Central Powers countries had competent and sometimes inspirational generals. But the British, French and Russians had great generals, too: the indomitable Haig, with his undying faith in the proper application of modern weapons yoked to his driving role in establishing the 'All Arms' battle; Joffre, the victor of the Marne; Brusilov, the outstanding innovator; and, of course, Foch – the man there at the beginning and the man still standing as Supreme Commander at the end.

In the miserable aftermath of the Great War there was a desperate search for scapegoats for all the suffering that had been endured. In Britain, the more devious politicians and their fawning commentators managed to transfer most of the responsibility on to the backs of their generals, culminating in the deeply offensive 'lions led by donkeys' construct. But such post-war shenanigans should not distract attention from the fact that in the end Britain and her Allies had emerged triumphant on the battlefields of the Great War: it was a painful victory, but a victory all the same. Whether it should be celebrated or mourned is for philosophers to decide. Unfortunately it was not – it never was – a war to end wars and the Great War proved an efficient catalyst in sowing the seeds for the numerous conflicts which have disfigured human history ever since. Within twenty-one short years the world would be at war again.

In many ways the Second World War set terrible new benchmarks for horror. Yet somehow a more potent folk memory of the Great War lingers still – even now all the last active participants have died. The sense of tragedy, of futility, of a slaughter of the innocents: these sentiments still pervade our popular culture. There is the widespread vision of humanity dragged down from the sunny uplands into the morass. But the war *did* have its causes and the Great Powers certainly had their deadly grievances that they felt unable to settle without recourse to arms. It was in truth a violent world – the prevalence of a rapacious colonialism, the brutal repression of minorities, the placid acceptance of inequalities and the overall belief that might was right – all these global traits tended towards the continued acceptance of war as a legitimate means of pursuing policy. When war came, it was truly devastating as the impact of new weapons systems created a Gordian knot of static trench lines, while the development of logistics allied to new methods of transport allowed armies of millions to be kept in the field almost indefinitely. Whatever happened it was always likely to be a long and terrible war – an unwaking nightmare for far too many.

And yet, and yet, and yet. Whatever the logical arguments, pointing to German culpability and the near-inevitability of this Armageddon, the fact that the Great War still has an enormous emotional impact cannot be denied. None of the warrior states may have been innocent, but the deaths and suffering imposed on their massed soldiery and citizenry cannot but evoke a human response. The carefully tended war memorials, the continuing acts of remembrance and commemoration, the growing interest in visiting the battlefields; these all illustrate the way the Great War still resonates deeply even today. The decimation of a generation is not forgotten; while the problems left unsolved or created by that terrible conflagration persist to threaten the peace of the world to this very day.

NOTES

1. The Road to War

1. O. von Bismarck, Speech, 1879, quoted in *The Riverside Dictionary of Biography* (Boston, MA: Houghton Mifflin, 2005), p. 87.
2. O. von Bismarck, quoted in E. Ludwig, *Wilhelm Hohenzollern: The Last of the Kaisers* (New York: G.P. Putnam's Sons, 1927), p. 73.
3. H. von Moltke, quoted in R. Foley, *German Strategy and the Path to Verdun: Erich von Falkenhayn and the Development of Attrition, 1870–1916* (Cambridge: Cambridge University Press, 2005), p. 23.
4. B. Jevtic quoted in R. Fox, We Were There: An Eyewitness History of the Twentieth Century (New York, Overlook, 2010), pp. 40–41.
5. See http://www.firstworldwar.com/source/harrachmemoir.htm.
6. H. von Moltke, quoted in A. Mombauer, *Helmuth von Moltke and the Origins of the First World War* (Cambridge: Cambridge University Press, 2001), p. 182.
7. H. Asquith, quoted in D. Fromkin, *Europe's Last Summer: Why the World Went to War in 1914* (London: William Heinemann, 2004), p. 188.
8. H. Asquith, quoted in Fromkin, *Europe's Last Summer*, p. 233.
9. E. Grey, quoted in *War Speeches by British Ministers, 1914–1916* (London: T. Fisher Unwin Ltd, 1917), p. 158.
10. E. Goschen, , http://www.firstworldwar.com/source/scrapofpaper1.htm
11. Viscount Grey of Fallodon, *Twenty-Five Years, 1892–1916* (New York: Frederick A. Stokes Company, 1925), p. 20.

2. The Western Front, 1914

1. H. von Moltke the Elder, quoted in D. J. Hughes (ed.), *Moltke on the Art of War: Selected Writings* (New York: Presidio Press, 1993), pp. 45–7.
2. E. von Ludendorff, *Ludendorff's Own Story* (New York: Harper & Bros, 1919), pp. 43–4.
3. G. Leman, http://www.firstworldwar.com/source/lemandiary.htm. Also C. F. Horne, ed., *Source Records of the Great War*, Vol. II (Indianapolis: National Alumni, 1923).

4. http://www.firstworldwar.com/source/joffre_alsace.htm.
5. Captain Ignard, quoted in J.-C. Delhez, *Le Jour de deuil de l'armée française* (Thonne-la-Long: Jean-Claude Delhez, 2011), p. 383.
6. P. Lebaud, quoted in J.-C. Delhez, *La bataille des Frontières racontée par les combattants* (Thonne-la-Long: Jean-Claude Delhez, 2007), p. 162.
7. A. Grasset, quoted in P. Young, 'Battle of the Frontiers: The Ardennes' in B. Pitt, ed., *Purnell's History of the First World War, Volume I* (London: Purnell and Sons Ltd, 1969–70), pp. 154–5.
8. P. Lintier, *My 75: Journal of a French Gunner* (New York: Grosset & Dunlap, 1917), pp. 91–3.
9. Lintier, *My 75*, pp. 94–5.
10. A. Joubaire, quoted in Delhez, *La bataille des Frontières*, p. 153.
11. D. E. Renault, quoted in J.-P. Guéno and Y. Laplume, *Paroles des Poilus 1914–1918* (Paris: Librio, 2003), p. 27.
12. M. Genevoix, *Ceux de 14* (Paris: Flammarion, 1950), pp. 93–4.
13. J. Cisterne, quoted in Delhez, *La bataille des Frontières*, pp. 34–5.
14. Lintier, *My 75*, pp. 119–20.
15. Lintier, *My 75*, pp. 119–20.
16. C. de Gaulle, quoted in P. M. de la Gorce, *De Gaulle entre deux mondes: une vie et une époque* (Paris: Fayard, 1964), p. 102.
17. W. Hermanns, *The Holocaust: From a Survivor of Verdun* (New York: Harper & Row, 1972), p. 74.
18. H. Smith-Dorrien, *Smith-Dorrien: Isandlwhana to the Great War* (Driffield: Leonaur, 2009), pp. 423–4.
19. G. Roupell, quoted in D. Ascoli, *The Mons Star: The British Expeditionary Force, 1914* (London: Harrap Ltd, 1981), p. 69.
20. T. Bradley, quoted in Ascoli, *The Mons Star*, p. 63.
21. W. Bloem, G. Wynne, trans., *The Advance from Mons, 1914* (London: Peter Davies Ltd, 1930), p. 56.
22. IWM DOCS: W. Morritt, manuscript letter, 3/9/1914–4/9/1914.
23. T. Zuber, *The Mons Myth: A Reassessment of the Battle* (Stroud: History Press, 2010). I am also indebted to the work of J. Sheldon.
24. Again see Zuber, *The Mons Myth*, p. 167.
25. IWM DOCS: H. Rees, transcript memoir, *A Personal Record of the First Three Months of the War*, p. 12.
26. IWM DOCS: B. T. St John, typescript account, part I, pp. 35–6 .
27. IWM DOCS: B. T. St John, typescript account, part I, p. 40.
28. J. Joffre, *The Memoirs of General Joffre, Vol. I* (London: Geoffrey Bles, 1932), pp. 137–8.
29. Joffre, *The Memoirs of General Joffre, Vol. I*, p. 185.
30. Joffre, *The Memoirs of General Joffre, Vol. I*, pp. 183–4.
31. Joffre, *The Memoirs of General Joffre, Vol. I*, p.190.
32. Joffre, *The Memoirs of General Joffre, Vol. I*, p. 197.
33. Joffre, *The Memoirs of General Joffre Vol. I*, p. 227.

34. A. von Kluck, *The March on Paris and the Battle of the Marne, 1914* (London: Edward Arnold, 1920), p. 69.
35. H. von Moltke order, quoted in von Kluck, *The March on Paris and the Battle of the Marne, 1914*, p. 94.
36. Von Kluck, *The March on Paris and the Battle of the Marne, 1914*, p. 99.
37. Joffre, *The Memoirs of General Joffre, Vol. I*, pp. 254–5.
38. Joffre, *The Memoirs of General Joffre, Vol. I*, p. 255.
39. J. French, *1914* (London: Constable & Co. Ltd, 1919), pp. 197–8.
40. F. Foch, quoted in M. S. Neiberg, *Foch* (Washington DC: Brasseys, 2003), p. 22.
41. E. von Falkenhayn, quoted in R. Foley, *German Strategy and the Path to Verdun: Erich von Falkenhayn and the Development of Attrition, 1870–1916* (Cambridge: Cambridge University Press, 2005), p. 102.
42. W. Kaht, quoted in J. Sheldon, *The German Army at Ypres, 1914* (Barnsley: Pen & Sword, 2010), pp. 105–6.
43. IWM DOCS: H. M. Dillon, letter, 25/10/1914.
44. IWM DOCS: W. A. Quinton, typescript account, p. 16.
45. IWM DOCS: W. A. Quinton, typescript account, p. 16.
46. IWM DOCS: W. A. Quinton, typescript account, p. 16.
47. J. Charteris, *Field Marshal Earl Haig* (London: Cassell & Co. Ltd, 1929), pp. 118–19.
48. F. Foch, quoted in J. Marshall-Cornwall, *Haig as Military Commander* (London: B. T. Batsford Ltd, 1973), p. 132.
49. IWM DOCS: B. T. St John typescript account, part 2, p. 44.
50. IWM DOCS: B. T. St John typescript account part 2, pp. 44–5.
51. P. Dupouey, quoted in *Ce Qui Demeure: Lettres de soldats tombés au champ d'honneur, 1914–1918* (Paris: Bartillat, 2009), p. 86.
52. IWM DOCS: W. A. Quinton, typescript account, pp. 23–4.
53. IWM DOCS: W. A. Quinton, typescript account, pp. 24–6.
54. G. Berthier, quoted in Guéno and Laplume, *Paroles des Poilus, 1914–18*, pp. 79–80.

3. The Eastern Front, 1914

1. E. von Ludendorff, *Ludendorff's Own Story* (New York: Harper & Bros., 1919), p. 68.

4. The Sea War, 1914–15

1. J. Jellicoe, quoted in *A. Temple Patterson (eds.), The Jellicoe Papers, Vol. I* (London: Naval Records Society, 1996), p. 252.
2. A. von Tirpitz, *My Memoirs, Vol. I* (New York: Dodd, Mead & Company, 1919), pp. 9–10.

3. Von Tirpitz, *My Memoirs, Vol. 1*, p. 77.
4. Quoted in O. Parkes, *British Battleships* (London: Seely Service & Co., 1957), p. 435.
5. J. Fisher, quoted in J. T. Sumida, *In Defence of Naval Supremacy: Finance, Technology and British Naval Policy, 1889–1914* (London: Routledge, 1993), p. 259.
6. Von Tirpitz, *My Memoirs, Vol. I*, pp. 170–72.
7. Von Tirpitz, *My Memoirs, Vol. II*, pp. 26–7 and 29–30.
8. R. Drax, quoted in R. Hough, *The Great War at Sea, 1914–18* (Oxford: Oxford Paperbacks, 1986), p. 132.
9. IWM Library: J. Speiss, *Six Years of Submarine Cruising*, Office of Naval Intelligence, 2/1926, pp. 2–3.
10. O. Weddigen, quoted in *The Times*, 12/10/1914, p. 3.
11. A. Temple Patterson (ed.), *The Jellicoe Papers, Vol. I*, (London: The Naval Records Society, 1966), pp. 75–9.
12. Temple Patterson (ed.), *The Jellicoe Papers, Vol. I*, pp. 75–9.
13. A. D. P. R. Pound diary entry for 16/8/1914, quoted in P. G. Halpern 'Dudley Pound in the Grand Fleet, 1914–15' in Michael Duffy (ed.), *The Naval Miscellany, Vol. VI* (Aldershot: Ashgate on behalf of the Naval Records Society, 2003), p. 398.
14. Knoop, quoted in G. Bennett, *Coronel and the Falklands* (London: Pan Books, 1967), p. 33.
15. H. Pochhammer, *Before Jutland: Admiral Spee's Last Voyage* (London: Jarrolds, 1931), pp. 202–3.
16. Pochhammer, *Before Jutland*, p. 212.
17. Pochhammer, *Before Jutland*, p. 217.
18. H. T. Bowen, quoted in J. D. Grainger (ed.), *The Maritime Blockade of Germany in the Great War: The Northern Patrol* (Aldershot: Ashgate on behalf of the Navy Records Society, 2003), p. 61.
19. G. W. Vivian, quoted in Grainger (ed.), *The Maritime Blockade of Germany in the Great War*, pp. 120–21.
20. W. Schwieger, quoted in D. Schmidt, *The Folly of War: American Foreign Policy, 1898–2004* (New York: Algora Publishing, 2005), p. 70.
21. IWM Sound Archive, J. Lewis, AC 7361.
22. L. Holland, quoted in *Memorandum of the German Government in Regard to Incidents Alleged to have Attended the Destruction of a German Submarine and Its Crew by His Majesty's Auxiliary Cruiser* Baralong *on August 19, 1915 and Reply of His Majesty's Government Thereto* (London: HMSO, 1916), annex 5.

5. The Western Front, 1915

1. Bonaparte, quoted in A. F. Becke, *Napoleon and Waterloo* (London: Kegan et al, 1914), p. 9.

2. E. von Falkenhayn, *General Headquarters, 1914–1916 and Its Critical Decisions* (Uckfield: Naval & Military Press, 2004), p. 56.
3. W. Ambroselli, quoted in P. Witkop, *German Students' War Letters* (Philadelphia: Pine Street Books, 2002), pp. 189–90.
4. A. Hopp, quoted in Witkop, *German Students' War Letters*, pp. 56–7. Hopp was killed on the Heights of Combres on 18 March 1915.
5. M. Genevoix, *Ceux de 14* (Paris: Flammarion, 1950), pp. 774–5.
6. D. Haig, quoted in Duff Cooper, *Haig, Vol. I* (London: Faber & Faber, 1935), pp. 223–4.
7. H. M. Trenchard, quoted in A. Boyle, *Trenchard: Man of Vision* (London: Collins, 1962) p. 128.
8. D. Haig diary entry 22/2/1915, quoted in G. Sheffield and J. Bourne (eds.), *Douglas Haig: War Diaries and Letters 1914–18* (London: Weidenfeld & Nicolson, 2005), p. 102.
9. W. L. Andrews, *Haunting Years: The Commentaries of a War Territorial* (London: Hutchinson & Co., 1930), pp. 48–9.
10. M. Kennedy, quoted in G. Bridger, *The Battle of Neuve Chapelle* (Barnsley: Pen & Sword, 2009), pp. 48–9.
11. H. Rawlinson, quoted in R. Prior and T. Wilson, *Command on the Western Front: The Military Career of Sir Henry Rawlinson, 1914–18* (Oxford: Blackwell, 1992), p. 78.
12. The French nickname for their African soldiers, loosely translated as 'the happy ones'.
13. H. Mordacq, *Le drame de l'Yser: la surprise des gaz (avril 1915)* (Paris: Editions des Portiques, 1933).
14. J. A. Currie, *The Red Watch: With the First Division in Flanders* (London: Constable & Co. Ltd, 1916), pp. 216–17.
15. W. Watson-Armstrong, *My First Week in Flanders* (London: Smith, Elder & Co., 1916), pp. 24–7.
16. IWM DOCS: W. A. Quinton, typescript account, pp. 50–51.
17. IWM DOCS: W. A. Quinton, typescript account, pp. 50–51.
18. J. Joffre, quoted in R. A. Doughty, *Pyrrhic Victory: French Strategy and Operations in the Great War* (Cambridge, MA: Harvard University Press, 2005), p. 156.
19. L. F. Sotheby, quoted in D. C. Richter, *Lionel Sotheby's Great War: Diaries and Letters from the Western Front* (Athens, OH: Ohio University Press, 1990), pp. 98–9.
20. L. F. Sotheby, quoted in Richter, *Lionel Sotheby's Great War*, p. 102.
21. A. Millerand, quoted in J. Joffre, *The Memoirs of General Joffre, Vol. II* (London: Geoffrey Bles, 1932), pp. 357–8.
22. E. Morin, *Lieutenant Morin: Combatant de la guerre, 1914–1918* (Besançon: Cêtre, 2002), p. 93.
23. H. Laporte, *Journal d'un poilu* (Paris: Editions Mille et Une Nuits, 1998), pp. 64–5.

24. H. G. Picton Davies, quoted in C. H. Dudley Ward, *Regimental Records of the Royal Welch Fusiliers, Vol. III* (London: Forster Groom & Co. Ltd, 1920), pp. 141–44.
25. IWM Sound Archive: R. Thorpe-Tracey, AC 00036.

6. The Eastern Front, 1915

1. E. von Falkenhayn, *General Headquarters, 1914–1916 and Its Critical Decisions* (Uckfield: Naval & Military Press, 2004), p. 88.

7. Gallipoli, 1915

1. W. Churchill, quoted by G. Riddell in M. Gilbert, *Winston S. Churchill, Vol. III, 1914–1916* (London: William Heinemann Ltd, 1971), p. 411.
2. A. R. Perry, quoted in S. Chambers, *Anzac: The Landing* (Barnsley: Pen & Sword, 2008), p. 44.
3. IWM DOCS: S. Aker, 'The Dardanelles: The Ari Burnu Battles and 27th Regiment' in the Rayfield Papers Collection.
4. IWM PRINTED BOOKS: Atatürk Memoirs, K03/1686, pp. 8–9.
5. National Army Museum: D. French, manuscript letter, 4/1915.
6. Frederick Royle, 1/7th Manchester Regiment, killed 4 June 1915. No known grave but commemorated on Helles Memorial.
7. IWM DOCS: J. S. Gatley, typescript diary account, pp. 30–31.
8. IWM DOCS: G. G. A. Egerton, typescript account, pp. 2–3.
9. Brotherton Special Collections Library, Leeds University, Liddle Collection, C. R. Duke, typescript account, pp. 99–100.
10. A. Crawford, '3rd Light Horse Brigade on Gallipoli', *Reveille*, 1/8/1932, p. 38.
11. W. B. Shannon, quoted by S. Chambers, Suvla: August Offensive (Barnsley: Pen & Sword, 2011), p. 38.
12. C. F. Aspinall-Oglander, *History of the Great War Based on Official Documents: Gallipoli Vol. II Military Operations: May 1915 to the Evacuation* (London: William Heinemann & Co., 1932), p. 325.
13. IWM DOCS: G. Nightingale, letter 25/8/1915.

8. Salonika, 1915–18

1. A. Winnington-Ingram, quoted in *Balkan News,* December 1918.
2. C. von Clausewitz, *Principles of War* (New York: Dover Publications, 2003), p. 45.
3. R. Skilbeck-Smith, *A Subaltern in Macedonia and Judaea* (London: Mitre Press, 1930), p. 98.
4. IWM Documents, F. T. Mullins, transcript account, p. 6.

5. IWM Documents: F. T. Mullins, transcript account, p. 7.

6. IWM Documents: R. W. Townsend, Letters, 9/1918.

7. IWM Documents: R. W. Townsend, Letters, 9/1918.

9. The Western Front, 1916

1. J. Charteris, *At G.H.Q.* (London: Cassell & Co., 1931), p. 134.

2. E. von Falkenhayn, quoted in R. Foley, *German Strategy and the Path to Verdun: Erich von Falkenhayn and the Development of Attrition, 1870–1916* (Cambridge: Cambridge University Press, 2005), p. 187.

3. E. von Falkenhayn, *General Headquarters, 1914–1916 and Its Critical Decisions* (Uckfield: Naval & Military Press, 2004), p. 224.

4. J. Hacquin, quoted in M. Brown, *Verdun, 1916* (Stroud: Tempus, 2000), p. 48.

5. H. Pétain, quoted in Foley, *German Strategy and the Path to Verdun*, p. 221.

6. R. Arnaud (translated by J. B. Donne), *Tragédie Bouffe* (London: Sidgwick & Jackson, 1966), p. 54.

7. S. E. Reynel, Le Drame du Fort de Vaux (Verdun: Editions Lorraines, 1949), pp. 171–2.

8. W. Hermanns, *The Holocaust: From a Survivor of Verdun* (New York: Harper & Row, 1972), pp. 79 and 104–5.

9. Hermanns, *The Holocaust*, p. 112.

10. Hermanns, *The Holocaust*, pp. 116–18.

11. D. Haig, letter to Viscount Bertie of Thame, 5/6/1916, quoted in G. Sheffield and J. Bourne (eds.), *Douglas Haig: War Diaries and Letters 1914–18* (London: Weidenfeld & Nicolson, 2005), p. 189.

12. J. Charteris, *Field Marshal Earl Haig* (London: Cassell & Co., 1929), pp. 205–6.

13. IWM DOCS: T. Hughes, transcript diary, 1/5/1916.

14. IWM DOCS: C. G. Lawson, typescript letter, 24/6/1916.

15. M. Gerster, quoted in J. Sheldon, *The German Army on the Somme* (Barnsley: Pen & Sword, 2005), pp. 121–2.

16. M. Gerster, quoted in Sheldon, *The German Army on the Somme*, pp. 133–4.

17. IWM DOCS: C. C. May, typescript diary and letter, 17/6/1916.

18. IWM DOCS: W. T. Colyer, manuscript account, 'War Impressions'.

19. O. Lais, quoted in Sheldon, *The German Army on the Somme*, p. 142.

20. Lieutenant Kienitz, quoted in Sheldon, *The German Army on the Somme*, pp. 159

21. J. Foy, quoted in I. Sumner, *They Shall Not Pass: The French Army on the Western Front, 1914–1918* (Barnsley: Pen & Sword, 2012), p. 135.

22. H. von Wurmb, quoted in Sheldon, *The German Army on the Somme*, p. 111.

23. F. von Below, quoted in Sheldon, *The German Army on the Somme*, p. 179.

24. E. Gerhardinger, quoted in Sheldon, *The German Army on the Somme*, pp. 197–8.

25. F. von Below, quoted in H. A. Jones, *History of the Great War Based on Official Documents: The War in the Air, Being the Story of the Part Played in*

the Great War by the Royal Air Force, Vol. II (Oxford: Clarendon Press, 1928), pp. 270–71.

26. H. Preston, *Reveille*, vol. 8, no. 12, p. 30.
27. IWM DOCS: P. H. Pilditch, typescript memoir, p. 315.
28. Pvt. Rabe, quoted in Sheldon, *The German Army on the Somme*, p. 201.
29. H. Kohl, quoted in Sheldon, *The German Army on the Somme, 1914–1916*, p. 292.
30. B. Henriques, *Indiscretions of a Warden* (London: Methuen & Co., 1937), pp. 118–19.
31. Sgt. Weinert quoted in T. Pidgeon, *The Tanks at Flers Vol. I* (Cobham: Fairmile Books, 1995), p. 132.
32. D. Haig, quoted in Sheffield and Bourne, *Douglas Haig*, p. 237
33. M. von Richthofen, *The Red Airfighter* (London: Greenhill Books, 1990), pp. 93–4.
34. National Army Museum: E. R. Buckell, typescript account, 'The Somme', p. 6.
35. E. Ludendorff, *My War Memories* (London: Hutchinson & Co., 1920), p. 307.
36. IWM DOCS: P. H. Pilditch, typescript memoir, p. 331.

10. The Eastern Front, 1916

1. P. von Hindenburg, *Out of My Life* (London: Cassel), p. 273.

11. The Sea War, 1916

1. IWM DOCS: J. C. Croome, typescript account.
2. http://wwi.lib.byu.edu/index.php/Wilson_on_the_Sussex_Case
3. R. Scheer, *Germany's High Seas Fleet in the World War* (London: Cassell & Co., 1920), p. 176.
4. IWM DOCS: J. C. Croome, typescript account.
5. IWM DOCS: T. M. Field Collection: E. Francis: 'Impressions of a Gunner's Mate at Jutland'.
6. A. E. M. Chatfield, *The Navy and Defence: The Autobiography of Admiral of the Fleet, Lord Chatfield* (London: William Heinemann Ltd, 1942), p. 143.
7. H. P. K. Oram, *Ready for Sea* (London: Seeley Service & Co. Ltd, 1974), pp. 155–6.
8. G. von Hase, *Kiel and Jutland* (London: Skeffington & Sons, 1921), pp. 171–4.
9. J. S. Corbett, *History of the Great War: Naval Operations, Vol. III.* (London: Longmans Green & Co., 1923), p. 355.
10. J. Jellicoe, statement quoted in David Beatty, *The Beatty Papers* (Aldershot: Scolar Press for the Navy Records Society, 1989), p. 470.
11. H. Kitching, quoted in H. W. Fawcett and G. W. W. Hooper, *The Fighting at Jutland: The Personal Experiences of Sixty Officers and Men of the British Fleet* (London: Maclure, Macdonald & Co., 1921), pp. 433–4.

12. H. Kitching, quoted in Fawcett and Hooper, *The Fighting at Jutland*, p. 434.

13. IWM DOCS: Misc. 1010, R. Church Collection: B. W. Gasson, manuscript answer to questionnaire, c. 1970–74.

14. Scheer, *German High Seas Fleet in the Great War*, p. 153.

15. J. Jellicoe, 'Errors in the Jutland Battle', quoted in F. C. Dreyer, *The Sea Heritage: A Study of Maritime Warfare* (London: Museum Press, 1955) p. 167.

16. N. J. W. Powlett, quoted in Fawcett and Hooper, *The Fighting at Jutland*, p. 190.

17. A. P. Bush, quoted in Fawcett and Hooper, *The Fighting at Jutland*, pp. 177–8.

18. J. A. Fergusson quoted in A. J. Marder, *From the Dreadnought to Scapa Flow: Jutland and After (May 1916–October 1916), Vol. III* (Oxford: Oxford University Press, 1966), p. 158.

19. M. von Egidy, 'Jutland: A German View', Purnell Partworks, *History of the First World War*, vol. 4, no. 3, p. 1418.

20. H. Zenne, typescript of newspaper report supplied by L. W. Burr.

21. IWM DOCS: D. Lorimer, typescript account, pp. 120–21.

12. Mesopotamia, 1914–18

1. G. Gorringe, quoted in A. J. Barker, *The First Iraq War, 1914–1918* (New York: Enigma Books, 2009), p. 17.

2. IEF 'A' was the force intended for the Western Front and Egypt, while IEF 'B' and 'C' were both East African expeditions.

3. Lord Crewe, quoted in *Mesopotamia Commission Report* (London: HMSO, 1917), p. 17.

4. H. B. Reynardson, *Mesopotamia, 1914–1915: Extracts from a Regimental Officer's Diary* (London: Andrew Melrose Ltd, 1919), pp.143–4.

5. Reynardson, *Mesopotamia, 1914–1915*, pp. 148–9.

6. C. V. F. Townshend, *My Campaign in Mesopotamia* (London: Thornton Butterworth Ltd, 1920), pp. 70–71.

7. J. Nixon, quoted in Townshend, *My Campaign in Mesopotamia*, p. 99.

8. Townshend, *My Campaign in Mesopotamia*, p. 124.

9. Townshend, *My Campaign in Mesopotamia, 1914–1915*, p. 161.

10. R. B. Carter, quoted in *Mesopotamia Commission Report*, pp. 76–7.

11. C. J. Meliss, quoted in M. Carver, *The National Army Museum Book of the Turkish Front, 1914–18* (London: Pan Books, second edition, 2004), p. 132.

12. IWM DOCS: E. Walker, typescript diary, 5/12/1915, p. 21.

13. F. Aylmer, quoted in F. J. Moberly, *History of the Great War Based on Official Documents: The Campaign in Mesopotamia, 1914–1918, Vol. II* (London: HMSO, 1924), p. 240.

14. IWM DOCS: E. Walker, typescript diary, 5/12/1915, p. 41.

15. E. O. Mousley, *The Secrets of a Kuttite* (London: John Lane Company, 1921), p. 131.

16. Mousley, *The Secrets of a Kuttite*, pp. 139 and 147.

17. P. Hehir, quoted in *Mesopotamia Commission Report*, p. 170.

18. IWM DOCS: C. C. Aston, letter, 11/4/1916.

19. IWM DOCS: A. J. Anderson, typescript account, pp. 88–9.

20. IWM DOCS: A. J. Anderson, typescript account, pp. 96–7.

21. IWM DOCS: H. V. Wheeler, typescript memoir/letter, 10/1/1974, p. 1.

22. IWM DOCS: H. V. Wheeler, typescript memoir/letter, 10/1/1974, pp. 2–3.

23. G. F. MacMunn, *Behind the Scenes in Many Wars* (London: John Murray, 1930), pp. 207–8.

24. W. Robertson, quoted in A. J. Barker, *The First Iraq War, 1914–1918* (New York: Enigma Books, 2009), p. 263.

13. The Eastern Front, 1917–18

1. A. Kerensky, quoted in J. Reed, *Ten Days That Shook the World* (London: Penguin Books, 2007), p. 60.

14. The Sea War, 1917–18

1. D. Lloyd George, *War Memoirs of David Lloyd George Vol. I* (London: Odhams Press, 1938), p. 673.

2. R. Scheer, *German High Seas Fleet in the Great War* (London: Cassell & Co., 1920), p. 360.

3. Scheer, *German High Seas Fleet in the Great War*, p. 169.

4. http://wwi.lib.byu.edu/index.php/1917_Documents

5. W. Wilson, speech to US Congress, 2/4/1917, in Charles F. Horne (ed), *Source Records of the Great War, Vol. V* (Indianapolis: National Alumni, 1923).

6. D. Haig, quoted in R. Blake, *The Private Papers of Douglas Haig, 1914–1919* (London: Eyre & Spottiswoode, 1952), pp. 240–41.

7. National Library of Scotland: D. Haig letter to Lady Haig, 7/5/1917, NLS Acc. 3155 147.

8. D. W. Bone, *Merchantmen-at-Arms: The British Merchants' Service in the War* (London: Chatto & Windus, 1919), p. 182. It would seem that one of the refraining lines of dialogue in *Star Trek* was indeed based on a sound nautical tradition.

9. A. Saalwächter, quoted in A. Marder, *From the Dreadnought to Scapa Flow, Vol. IV* (London: Oxford University Press, 1969), p. 285.

10. H. Adam, quoted in R. Scheer, *German High Seas Fleet in the Great War* (London, Cassell & Co., 1920), pp. 273–4.

11. J. Speiss, 'Six Years of Submarine Cruising', US Office of Naval Intelligence, February 1926, pp. 2–3.

12. G. H. Barnish, quoted in T. Dorling, *Endless Story* (London: Hodder & Stoughton, 1932), pp. 277–8, edited with extra material from R. Young and

P. Armstrong, *Silent Warriors: Submarine Wrecks of the British Isles – England's East Coast to Kent* (Stroud: The History Press, 2006).

13. W. Wainwright quoted by C. B. Purdon (editor), *Everyman at War* (London: J. M. Dent & Sons, 1930), pp. 399–400.
14. W. Wainwright quoted by C. B. Purdon (editor), *Everyman at War* (London: J. M. Dent & Sons, 1930), p. 403.
15. C. Widdison, *Nottinghamshire Weekly Express*, 3/5/1918.
16. IWM DOCS: W. H. Gough, typescript account.
17. C. Widdison, *Nottinghamshire Weekly Express*, 3/5/1918.
18. A. Carpenter http://www.firstworldwar.com/diaries/zeebrugge_carpenter.htm.
19. R. Stumpf, *The Private War of Seaman Stumpf* (London: Leslie Frewin, 1969), pp. 417–19.
20. A. von Trotha quoted in A. J. Marder, *From the Dreadnought to Scapa Flow, Vol V* (London: Oxford University Press, 1970), p. 174.

15. The Western Front, 1917

1. D. Haig, quoted in J. E. Edmonds, *Military Operations in France and Belgium, 1917, Vol. II* (London: HMSO, 1948), p. 426.
2. Erich von Ludendorff, *My War Memories Vol. I* (London: Hutchinson & Co. Ltd, 1919), p. 273.
3. R. Nivelle, quoted in I. Sumner, *They Shall Not Pass: The French Army on the Western Front, 1914–1918* (Barnsley: Pen & Sword, 2012), p. 145.
4. J. Charteris, *At G.H.Q.* (London: Cassell & Co., 1931), p. 200.
5. H. Trenchard, quoted in A. Boyle, *Trenchard: Man of Vision* (London: Collins, 1962), p. 209.
6. P. Warren, quoted in F. Gibbons, *The Red Knight of Germany* (New York: Garden City Publishing Co. Inc., 1927), pp. 170–71.
7. 2nd Lt. Bittkau, quoted in J. Sheldon, *The German Army on Vimy Ridge, 1914–1917* (Barnsley: Pen & Sword, 2008), p. 286.
8. 2nd Lt. Bittkau, quoted in Sheldon, *The German Army on Vimy Ridge, 1914–1917*, pp. 286–7.
9. IWM DOCS: M. I. Hood, typescript memoir.
10. IWM DOCS: E. J. D. Routh, typescript account and manuscript diary, 9/4/1917.
11. L. Barthas, *Les Carnets de guerre de Louis Barthas, tonnerlier, 1914–1918* (Paris: Éditions La Découverte, 1987), p. 449.
12. M. C. Chenu, quoted in I. Sumner, *They Shall Not Pass*, pp. 233–4.
13. J.-L. Cros, quoted in J. P. Guéno and Y. Laplume, *Paroles des Poilus* (Paris: Librio, 2003), p. 166.
14. Barthas, *Les Carnets de guerre de Louis Barthas, tonnerlier, 1914–1918*, p. 471.
15. Barthas, *Les Carnets de guerre de Louis Barthas, tonnerlier, 1914–1918*, pp. 472–3.

16. Barthas, *Les Carnets de guerre de Louis Barthas, tonnerlier, 1914–1918,* pp. 472–3.
17. J. Cousins, quoted in J. Nicholls, *Cheerful Sacrifice: The Battle of Arras, 1917* (London: Leo Cooper, 1995), p. 197.
18. D. Haig, diary, 1 May 1917, quoted in R. Blake, *The Private Papers of Douglas Haig, 1914–1919* (London: Eyre & Spottiswoode, 1952), p. 223.
19. O. H. Woodward, *The War Story of Oliver Holmes Woodward* (Adelaide: O. H. Woodward, 1932), pp. 96–7.
20. R. Hamilton, *The War Diary of the Master of Belhaven, 1914–1918* (Barnsley: Wharncliffe, 1990), pp. 303–4.
21. 2nd Lt. Meinke, quoted in J. Sheldon, *The German Army at Passchendaele* (Barnsley: Pen & Sword, 2007), p. 19.
22. J. Charteris, quoted in J. E. Edmonds, *Military Operations, France and Belgium, 1917, Vol. II* (London: HMSO, 1948), p. 97.
23. D. Lloyd George, *War Memoirs of David Lloyd George Vol. II* (London: Odhams Press, 1938), p. 280.
24. E. Blunden, *Undertones of War* (London: Cobden-Sanderson, 1930), pp. 219–20.
25. G. Gurtler, quoted in P. Witkop, *German Students' War Letters* (Philadelphia: Pine Street Books, 2002), p. 361. It has not been possible to trace details of Gurter's rank or unit.
26. IWM DOCS: J. S. Handley, typescript memoir, pp. 7–10.
27. IWM DOCS: J. S. Handley, typescript memoir, pp. 7–10.
28. F. von Forstner, quoted in J. Sheldon, *The German Army at Passchendaele,* pp. 52–3.
29. Operational memorandum, 1 August 1917, quoted in Edmonds, *Military Operations, France and Belgium, 1917, Vol. II,* p. 448.
30. H. Gough, *The Fifth Army* (London: Hodder & Stoughton, 1931), p. 205.
31. E. Ludendorff, *My War Memories, 1914–1918* (London: Hutchinson & Co, 1919), p. 480.
32. C. H. Harrington, quoted in Edmonds, *Military Operations, France and Belgium, 1917, Vol. II,* p. 460.
33. C. Lawrence, *Sergeant Lawrence Goes to France* (Melbourne: Melbourne University Press, 1987), pp. 124–5.
34. Ludendorff, *My War Memories, 1914–1918,* p. 489.
35. Ludendorff, *My War Memories, 1914–1918,* p. 490.
36. IWM DOCS: R. G. Dixon, typescript memoir, p. 32.
37. Norman Cliff, *To Hell and Back with the Guards* (Braunton: Merlin Books, 1988), p. 83.
38. W. G. Fisher, quoted in C. E. W. Bean (ed),*The Official History of Australia in the War of 1914–1918, Vol. IV* (Queensland: University of Queensland Press, 1982), p. 927.
39. Ludendorff, *My War Memories, 1914–1918, Vol. II,* p. 106.
40. IWM DOCS: W. R. Kirkby, typescript.

41. A. Saucke, quoted in J. Sheldon, *The German Army at Cambrai* (Barnsley: Pen & Sword, 2009), pp. 49–50.

42. A. Saucke quoted in Sheldon, *The German Army at Cambrai*, p. 51.

43. Arthur Gould Lee, *No Parachute: A Fighter Pilot in World War I* (London: The Adventurers Club, 1968), p. 163.

44. IWM DOCS: K. Wootton account in N. M. Dillon papers.

45. IWM DOCS: K. Wootton account in N. M. Dillon papers.

46. A. Ballard, quoted in B. Hammond, Cambrai, 1917 (London: Weidenfeld & Nicholson, 2008), p.169.

47. 2nd Lt. von der Goltz, quoted in Sheldon, *The German Army at Cambrai*, pp. 227–8.

48. S. Sgt. Engesser quoted in Sheldon, *The German Army at Cambrai*, pp. 238–9.

49. Cliff, *To Hell and Back with the Guards*, pp. 85–6.

16. Italy, 1915–18

1. D. Lloyd George, *War Memoirs Vol. II* (London: Odhams Press Ltd, 1936), p. 1302.

2. National Archives: CAB 25/22, C. N. Buzzard, *Italian Army: Impressions of Lt Col. Buzzard, RN*, p. 4.

3. C. N. Buzzard, quoted in J. E. Edmonds, *Military Operations, Italy, 1915–1919* (Nashville: Battery Press, 1991), p. 36.

4. O. von Below, quoted in Edmonds, *Military Operations, Italy, 1915–1919*, p. 51.

5. E. Rommel, *Infantry Attacks* (Washington: The Infantry Journal, 1944), p. 170.

6. Rommel, *Infantry Attacks*, pp. 174–7 (edited).

7. Rommel, *Infantry Attacks*, pp. 174–7 (edited).

8. N. Gladden, *Across the Piave* (London: HMSO, 1971), pp. 118–19.

9. Gladden, *Across the Piave*, pp. 121 and 122.

10. Gladden, *Across the Piave*, p. 124.

11. Gladden, *Across the Piave*, pp. 166–8.

12. Gladden, *Across the Piave*, pp. 166–8.

13. Gladden, *Across the Piave*, pp. 177–8.

17. Palestine, 1915–18

1. D. Lloyd George, *Hansard*, 20 December 1917.

2. T. E. Lawrence, quoted in M. Brown, *T. E Lawrence in War and Peace* (London: Greenhill Books, 2005), p. 99.

3. A. H. Lee, quoted in C. H. Dudley Ward, *History of the 53rd (Welsh) Division* (Cardiff: Western Mail, 1927), pp. 88–9.

4. I. L. Idriess, *The Desert Column* (Sydney: Angus & Robertson Ltd, 1935), p. 325.
5. E. Allenby, quoted in A. Wavell, *Allenby: A Study in Greatness* (London: George G. Harrap, 1940), p. 183.
6. W. B. Mercer, quoted in the Marquess of Anglesey, *A History of the British Cavalry, 1816–1919 Vol. VI* (London: Leo Cooper, 1995), p. 173.
7. O. Teichmann, *The Diary of a Yeoman* (London: Fisher & Unwin Ltd, 1921), pp. 184–5.
8. W. Robertson, quoted in M. Hughes, *Allenby in Palestine: The Middle East Correspondence of Field Marshal Viscount Allenby* (Stroud: Sutton Publishing Ltd, 2004), pp. 92–3.
9. B. Livermore, *Long 'un – A Damn Bad Soldier* (Batley: Harry Hayes, 1974), p. 128.
10. E. Allenby, quoted in Hughes, *Allenby in Palestine*, p. 178.
11. F. C. Conrick, quoted in M. Molkentin, *Fire in the Sky: The Australian Flying Corps in the First World War* (Crows Nest, NSW: Allen & Unwin, 2010), p. 162.

18. The Western Front, 1918

1. IWM DOCS: R. G. Dixon, typescript account, 'The Wheels of Darkness', p. 133.
2. E. Ludendorff, *Ludendorff's Own Story: August 1914–November 1918* (New York and London: Harper & Bros., 1919), pp. 160–61.
3. IWM DOCS: F. Meisel, typescript account, p. 19.
4. H. Sulzbach, *With the German Guns* (London: Frederick Warne, 1981), p. 150.
5. IWM DOCS: E. C. Alfree, typescript account, pp. 319–20.
6. IWM DOCS: C. C. Miller, typescript account, 'A Letter from India to My Daughters in England', pp. 33–4.
7. P. Kretschmer, quoted in S. Bull, *German Assault Troops of the First World War: The First Stormtroopers* (Stroud: Spellmount, 2007), p. vii.
8. IWM DOCS: J. Brady, typescript account, pp. 133–4.
9. IWM DOCS: E. C. Alfree, typescript account, pp. 347–9.
10. E. Udet, *Ace of the Black Cross* (London: Newnes, 1937), pp. 95–6.
11. D. Haig, quoted in G. Sheffield and J. Bourne, *Douglas Haig: War Diaries and Letters, 1914–1918* (London: Weidenfeld & Nicolson, 2005), pp. 393–4.
12. IWM DOCS: R. Foot, typescript account, 'Once a Gunner', p. 87.
13. IWM DOCS: J. T. Capron, typescript account, pp. 30–31.
14. http://wwi.lib.byu.edu/index.php/Diaries,_Memorials,_Personal_ Reminiscences) G. F. Dose, 'German 187th Infantry Regiment in Flanders, at Arras and Cambrai, 1917–18.
15. Ludendorff, *Ludendorff's Own Story: August 1914–November 1918*, pp. 237–8.
16. IWM DOCS: F. Warren, diary, 28/3/1918.
17. IWM DOCS: F. Meisel, typescript account, pp. 22–3.

18. D. Haig, quoted in J. E. Edmonds, *History of the Great War: Military Operations France and Belgium, 1918, Vol. II* (London: Macmillan & Co. Ltd, 1937), p. 512.
19. IWM DOCS: F. Meisel, typescript account, p. 30.
20. IWM DOCS: F. Meisel, typescript account, pp. 31–2.
21. H. Desagneux, *A French Soldier's War Diary, 1914–1918* (Morley: Elmfield Press, 1975), pp. 60–61.
22. IWM DOCS: F. Meisel, typescript account, p. 32.
23. D. G. Lewis, 'My Most Thrilling Flight: An Encounter with Richthofen', *Popular Flying*, May 1938, p. 75.
24. Lewis, 'My Most Thrilling Flight', p. 76.
25. W. May, 'Lieutenant Wilfred "Wop" May's Account', *Cross & Cockade*, vol. 23, no. 2, p. 112.
26. F. Mitchell, *Tank Warfare: The Story of the Tanks in the Great War* (London: Thomas Nelson & Sons, 1933), pp. 189–90.
27. Mitchell, *Tank Warfare*, pp. 191–2.
28. Edited from W. H. Downing, *To the Last Ridge* (London: Grub Street, 2005), pp. 118–19.
29. S. Rogerson, quoted in J. H. Boraston and C. E. O. Bax, *The Eighth Division at War, 1914–1918* (London: Medici Society, 1926), pp. 222–3.
30. G. Gaudy, quoted in I. Sumner, *They Shall Not Pass: The French Army on the Western Front, 1914–1918* (Barnsley: Pen & Sword, 2012), p. 193.
31. IWM DOCS: J. Nettleton, typescript account, pp. 148–9.
32. M. H. Silverthorn, quoted in J. H. Hallas, *Doughboy War: The American Expeditionary Force in WWI* (Mechanicsburg, PA: Stackpole Books, 2009), pp. 89–90.
33. Doughboy Center, http://www.worldwar1.com/dbc/2marne.htm
34. http://www.firstworldwar.com/diaries/secondmarne.htm Originally from C. F. Horne, *Source Records of the Great War, Vol. VI* (Indianapolis: US National Alumni, 1923).
35. E. Morin, *Lieutenant Morin: Combatant de la guerre, 1914–1918* (Besançon: Cêtre, 2002), p. 287.
36. J. W. Thomason, quoted in D. V. Johnson and R. L. Hillman, *Soissons, 1918* (Texas: Texas A & M University Press, 1999), p. 64.
37. L. T. Janda, quoted in Johnson and Hillman, *Soissons 1918*, p. 79.
38. Morin, *Lieutenant Morin*, p. 287.
39. IWM DOCS: F. Meisel, typescript account, pp. 51 and 60–61.
40. E. J. Rule, *Jacka's Mob: A Narrative of the Great War by Edgar John Rule* (Melbourne: Military Melbourne, 1999), p. 133.
41. H. Wilson, quoted in J. E. Edmonds, *History of the Great War: Military Operations France and Belgium, 1918, Vol. IV* (Nashville: Battery Press, 1993), p. 532.
42. J. Monash, quoted in N. Browning, *The Blue and White Diamond: The History of the 29th Battalion, 1915–1919* (Bassendean, WA: Advance Press), p. 412.

43. IWM DOCS: W. Kerr, typescript account, pp. 106–7.
44. IWM DOCS: G. V. Rose, typescript account, 'Three Years and a Day', p. 119.
45. Tank Museum, Bovington: C. Rowland, typescript account.
46. Ludendorff, *Ludendorff's Own Story*, p. 326.
47. D. Haig, quoted in Sheffield and Bourne, *Douglas Haig*, pp. 445–6.
48. Ludendorff, *Ludendorff's Own Story*, p. 332.
49. D. Haig, quoted in Edmonds, *Military Operations France and Belgium, 1918 Vol. IV*, appendix XX, p. 588.
50. M. Timberlake, quoted in J. L. McWilliams and R. James Steel, *The Suicide Battalion* (Stevenage: Spa Books, 1990), p. 163.
51. E. Rickenbacker, *Fighting the Flying Circus* (New York: Frederich Stokes Co., 1919), p. 232.
52. Rickenbacker, *Fighting the Flying Circus*, pp. 233–4.
53. http://www.htc.net/~dermody/yankww1.htm C. Dermody, 'A Yank in the First World War' (transcribed by L. McCauley).
54. M. Maverick, quoted in Hallas, *Doughboy War*, pp. 266–7.
55. M. Maverick, quoted in Hallas, *Doughboy War*, pp. 266–7.
56. IWM DOCS: G. K. Parker, typescript account, p. 29.
57. US National Archives: Schleicher quoted in translation by F. W. Norton, *Testimony of German Officers and Men, the Origins of War Legends: An Investigation of the Alleged Feat of Sgt York, October 8, 1918*, pp. 12–13.
58. P. von Hindenburg, quoted in J. Lee, *The Warlords* (London: Weidenfeld & Nicolson, 1919), pp. 375–6.
59. Ludendorff, *Ludendorff's Own Story*, pp. 375–6.
60. IWM DOCS: T. H. Westmacott, typescript letter, 7/11/1918.
61. http://freepages.genealogy.rootsweb.com/~brett/cmgc/cmgc_cgf_letters.html Trent University Archives: C. G. Frost, Letter, 17/11/1918.
62. IWM DOCS: R. G. Dixon, typescript account, 'The Wheels of Darkness', pp. 138–9.
63. E. Brec, quoted in Sumner, *They Shall Not Pass*, p. 211.
64. R. Stumpf, *The Private War of Seaman Stumpf* (London: Leslie Frewin, 1969), pp. 427–8.

19. A World Without War?

1. W. Churchill, quoted in M. Gilbert, *Winston S. Churchill, Vol. III, 1914–1916* (London: William Heinemann Ltd, 1971), p. 201.
2. A. von Tirpitz, *My Memoirs, Vol. I* (New York: Dodd, Mead & Co., 1919), p. 377.
3. Field Marshal Sir Douglas Haig on the 'Features of the War', *London Gazette*, 8 April 1919.

ACKNOWLEDGEMENTS

I AM A FIRM BELIEVER that no one human can master the Great War in its totality and several historians have been crucial in guiding me through some of the areas where I have not had the good fortune (or ability) to carry out original research. For me the series of British Official Histories of the War are always a firm starting point. Not perfect by any means, but certainly a solid grounding. I recommend for the Eastern Front a small coterie of authors including Nik Cornish, *The Russian Army and the First World War* (Stroud: Spellmount, 2006), G. Irving Root, *Battles East: A History of the Eastern Front of the First World War* (Baltimore: Publish America, 2007), John Lee, *The War Lords: Hindenburg and Ludendorff* (London: Weidenfeld & Nicolson, 2005) and Norman Stone, *The Eastern Front, 1914–1917* (London: Penguin Books; 2nd revised edition, 1998). The German side of events is brilliantly exposed by Robert T. Foley in his *German Strategy and the Path to Verdun: Erich von Falkenhayn and the Development of Attrition, 1870–1916* (Cambridge: Cambridge University Press, 2005). Jack Sheldon has written a wonderful series of books all of which I recommend without hesitation, including *The German Army at Ypres 1914* (Barnsley: Pen & Sword, 2010), *The German Army on Vimy Ridge, 1914–1917* (Barnsley: Pen & Sword, 2008), *The German Army on the Western Front 1915* (Barnsley: Pen & Sword, 2012), *The German Army on the Somme 1914–1916* (Barnsley: Pen & Sword, 2007), *The German Army at Passchendaele* (Barnsley: Pen & Sword, 2007) and *The German Army at Cambrai* (Barnsley: Pen & Sword, 2009). These are the sources of many of the German accounts which give us the feel of the other side of the wire. I would like to give special thanks to Jack who has been unstintingly helpful throughout. Although I do not share all his views, the works of Terence Zuber are very thought-provoking. In writing this book I have become convinced by the immensity of the French contribution to the war and am grateful to several authors. English sources are distressingly few, but I have made good use of Anthony Clayton, *Paths of Glory* (London: Cassell, 2005), Robert Doughty, *Pyrrhic Victory: French Strategy and Operations in the Great War* (Cambridge, MA: Harvard University Press, 2005) and Ian Sumner, *They Shall Not Pass: The French Army on the Western Front, 1914–1918* (Barnsley: Pen & Sword, 2012). But as my French reading skills have been slowly improving I found the books of Jean-Claude Delhez absolutely invaluable. It behoves all British students of Great War history to read *La Bataille des Frontières : racontée par les combattants* (Thonne-la-Long: J.-C. Delhez, 2007) and *Le jour de deuil de l'armée française* (Thonne-la-Long: J. C. Delhez, 2011). It really is worth the effort and once you've managed it, one thing is certain: the Battle of Mons will never seem quite as important again after exposure to the knowledge of the devastating slaughter suffered by the French. For American sources I am grateful for the work of James Hallas, *Doughboy War: The American Expeditionary Force in WWI* (Mechanicsburg, PA: Stackpole Books, 2009) and Douglas Johnson and Rolfe Hillman, *Soissons, 1918* (Texas: Texas A&M University Press, 1999).

It is always difficult to get the tone right with personal thanks, as it is so easy to annoy with faint praise or perhaps an ill-chosen pleasantry. I would like therefore to start by thanking Bryn Hammond and George Webster for their mild encouragement. I am also indebted to my chum John Paylor who, once again, proof-read an early version of the text. Unfortunately, this means I now hold him entirely responsible for all remaining errors. My old university chum Rob Massey was kind enough to check my French translations, demonstrating the enduring superiority of medieval historians over their less gifted military-minded brethren. Thanks also to my agent Ian Drury, whose sterling efforts keep me in work as an author. My colleagues at the Imperial War Museum have been wonderful and I would particularly mention Tony Richards, Richard McDonough, Richard Hughes and Simon Offord. At Profile, Daniel Crewe and Penny Daniel have been great to work with, while Sally Holloway is a marvel at translating my mangled prose into English. Thanks too, to Martin Lubikowski for the maps.

Lastly, I would thank my lovely wife, Polly Napper (apparently known to almost everybody as 'Long-suffering Polly'), and our two adorable children, Lily and Ruby Hart, both of whom seem to take after her in both temperament and looks! Collectively they have had a lot to put up with while I have been writing this book.

Peter Hart
East Finchley, January 2013

Picture Credits

All the photos in this book come from the Imperial War Museums huge collections which cover all aspects of conflict involving Britain and the Commonwealth since the start of the 20th century. These rich resources are available online to search, browse and buy at www.iwmcollections.org.uk. In addition to Collections Online, you can visit the Visitor Rooms where you can explore over eleven million photographs, thousands of hours of moving images, the largest sound archive of its kind in the world, thousands of diaries and letters written by people in wartime, and a huge reference library. To make an appointment, call (020) 7416 5320, or e-mail mail@iwm.org.uk. Imperial War Museum www.iwm.org.uk

INDEX